CHRYSLER OMNI/HORIZON/RAMPAGE
1978-89 REPAIR MANUAL

D1217460

CEO	Rick Van Dalen
President	Dean F. Morgantini, S.A.E.
Vice President–Finance	Barry L. Beck
Vice President–Sales	Glenn D. Potere
Executive Editor	Kevin M. G. Maher, A.S.E.
Manager–Consumer Automotive	Richard Schwartz, A.S.E.
Manager–Professional Automotive	Richard J. Rivele
Manager–Marine/Recreation	James R. Marotta, A.S.E.
Production Specialists	Brian Hollingsworth, Melinda Possinger
Project Managers	Thomas A. Mellon, A.S.E., S.A.E., Eric Michael Mihalyi, A.S.E., S.T.S., S.A.E., Christine L. Sheeky, S.A.E., Richard T. Smith, Ron Webb
Schematics Editors	Christopher G. Ritchie, A.S.E., S.A.E., S.T.S., Stephanie A. Spunt
Editor	Dawn M. Hoch, S.A.E.

PUBLISHED BY **W. G. NICHOLS, INC.**

Manufactured in USA
© 1996 W. G. Nichols, Inc.
1025 Andrew Drive
West Chester, PA 19380
ISBN 0-8019-8787-3
Library of Congress Catalog Card No. 96-83033
3456789012 9876543210

Chilton is a registered trademark of Cahners Business Information, a division of Reed Elsevier, Inc., and has been licensed to W. G. Nichols, Inc.

www.chiltononline.com

Bruton Memorial Library
Plant City, Florida 33563

Contents

Contents

SAFETY NOTICE

Proper service and repair procedures are vital to the safe, reliable operation of all motor vehicles, as well as the personal safety of those performing repairs. This manual outlines procedures for servicing and repairing vehicles using safe, effective methods. The procedures contain many NOTES, CAUTIONS and WARNINGS which should be followed, along with standard procedures to eliminate the possibility of personal injury or improper service which could damage the vehicle or compromise its safety.

It is important to note that repair procedures and techniques, tools and parts for servicing motor vehicles, as well as the skill and experience of the individual performing the work vary widely. It is not possible to anticipate all of the conceivable ways or conditions under which vehicles may be serviced, or to provide cautions as to all possible hazards that may result. Standard and accepted safety precautions and equipment should be used when handling toxic or flammable fluids, and safety goggles or other protection should be used during cutting, grinding, chiseling, prying, or any other process that can cause material removal or projectiles.

Some procedures require the use of tools specially designed for a specific purpose. Before substituting another tool or procedure, you must be completely satisfied that neither your personal safety, nor the performance of the vehicle will be endangered.

Although information in this manual is based on industry sources and is complete as possible at the time of publication, the possibility exists that some car manufacturers made later changes which could not be included here. While striving for total accuracy, Nichols Publishing cannot assume responsibility for any errors, changes or omissions that may occur in the compilation of this data.

PART NUMBERS

Part numbers listed in this reference are not recommendations by Nichols Publishing for any product brand name. They are references that can be used with interchange manuals and aftermarket supplier catalogs to locate each brand supplier's discrete part number.

SPECIAL TOOLS

Special tools are recommended by the vehicle manufacturer to perform their specific job. Use has been kept to a minimum, but where absolutely necessary, they are referred to in the text by the part number of the tool manufacturer. These tools can be purchased, under the appropriate part number, from your local dealer or regional distributor, or an equivalent tool can be purchased locally from a tool supplier or parts outlet. Before substituting any tool for the one recommended, read the SAFETY NOTICE at the top of this page.

ACKNOWLEDGMENTS

Nichols Publishing expresses appreciation to Chrysler Corporation for their generous assistance.

Nichols Publishing would like to express thanks to all of the fine companies who participate in the production of our books:
- Hand tools supplied by Craftsman are used during all phases of our vehicle teardown and photography.
- Many of the fine specialty tools used in our procedures were provided courtesy of Lisle Corporation.
- Lincoln Automotive Products (1 Lincoln Way, St. Louis, MO 63120) has provided their industrial shop equipment, including jacks (engine, transmission and floor), engine stands, fluid and lubrication tools, as well as shop presses.
- Rotary Lifts (1-800-640-5438 or www.Rotary-Lift.com), the largest automobile lift manufacturer in the world, offering the biggest variety of surface and in-ground lifts available, has fulfilled our shop's lift needs.
- Much of our shop's electronic testing equipment was supplied by Universal Enterprises Inc. (UEI).
- Safety-Kleen Systems Inc. has provided parts cleaning stations and assistance with environmentally sound disposal of residual wastes.
- United Gilsonite Laboratories (UGL), manufacturer of Drylok® concrete floor paint, has provided materials and expertise for the coating and protection of our shop floor.

No part of this publication may be reproduced, transmitted or stored in any form or by any means, electronic or mechanical, including photocopy, recording, or by information storage or retrieval system, without prior written permission from the publisher.

1

GENERAL INFORMATION AND MAINTENANCE

HOW TO USE THIS BOOK

Chilton's Total Car Care Manual for the Dodge Omni/Charger/Rampage and Plymouth Horizon/Turismo/Scamp is intended to help you learn more about the inner workings of your vehicle and save you money on its upkeep and operation.

The first two sections will be the most used, since they contain maintenance and tune-up information and procedures. Studies have shown that a properly tuned and maintained car can get at least 10% better gas mileage than an out-of-tune car. The other sections deal with the more complex systems of your car. Operating systems from engine through brakes are covered to the extent that the average do-it-yourselfer becomes mechanically involved. This book will not explain such things as rebuilding the differential for the simple reason that the expertise required and the investment in special tools make this task uneconomical. It will give you detailed instructions to help you change your own brake pads and shoes, replace points and plugs, and do many more jobs that will save you money, give you personal satisfaction, and help you avoid expensive problems.

A secondary purpose of this book is a reference for owners who want to understand their car and/or their mechanics better. In this case, no tools at all are required.

Before removing any bolts, read through the entire procedure. This will give you the overall view of what tools and supplies will be required. There is nothing more frustrating than having to walk to the bus stop on Monday morning because you were short one bolt on Sunday afternoon. So read ahead and plan ahead. Each operation should be approached logically and all procedures thoroughly understood before attempting any work.

All sections contain adjustments, maintenance, removal and installation procedures, and repair or overhaul procedures. When repair is not considered practical, we tell you how to remove the part and then how to install the new or rebuilt replacement. In this way, you at least save the labor costs.

Backyard repair of such components as the alternator is just not practical.

Two basic mechanic's rules should be mentioned here. One, whenever the left side of the car or engine is referred to, it is meant to specify the driver's side of the car. Conversely, the right side of the car means the passenger's side. Secondly, most screws and bolts are removed by turning counterclockwise, and tightened by turning clockwise.

Safety is always the most important rule. Constantly be aware of the dangers involved in working on an automobile and taking the proper precautions. (See "Servicing Your Vehicle Safely" and the SAFETY NOTICE on the acknowledgment page.)

Pay attention to the instructions provided. There are 3 common mistakes in mechanical work:

• Incorrect order of assembly, disassembly or adjustment. When taking something apart or putting it together, doing things in the wrong order usually just costs you extra time; however, it CAN break something. Read the entire procedure before beginning disassembly. Do everything in the order in which the instructions say you should do it, even if you can't immediately see a reason for it. When you're taking apart something that is very intricate (for example, a carburetor), you might want to draw a picture of how it looks when assembled at one point in order to make sure you get everything back in its proper position. (We will supply exploded views whenever possible.) When making adjustments, especially tune-up adjustments, do them in order; often, one adjustment affects another, and you cannot expect even satisfactory results unless each adjustment is made only when it cannot be changed by any other.

• Overtightening (or undertightening). While it is more common for overtorquing to cause damage, undertorquing can cause a fastener to vibrate loose causing serious damage. Especially when dealing with aluminum parts, pay attention to torque specifications and utilize a torque wrench in assembly. If a torque figure is not available, remember that if you are using the right tool to do the job, you will probably not have to strain yourself to get a fasten tight enough. The pitch of most threads is so slight that the tension you put on the wrench will be multiplied many, many times in actual force on what you are tightening. A good example of how critical tightness is, can be seen in the case of spark plug installation. Especially where you are putting the plug into an aluminum cylinder head. Too little torque can fail to crush the gasket, causing leakage of combustion gases and consequent overheating of the plug and engine parts. Too much torque can damage the threads, or distort the plug, which changes the spark gap. There are many commercial products available for ensuring that fasteners won't come loose, even if they are not tightened just right (a very common brand is Loctite®). If you're worried about getting something together tight enough to hold, but loose enough to avoid mechanical damage during assembly, one of these products might offer substantial insurance. Read the label on the package and make sure the product is compatible with the materials, fluids, etc. involved before choosing one.

• Crossthreading. This occurs when a part such as a bolt is screwed into a nut or casting at the wrong angle and forced. Crossthreading is more likely to occur if access is difficult. It helps to clean and lubricate fasteners, and to start threading with the part to be installed going straight in. Then, start the bolt, spark plug, etc. with your fingers. If you encounter resistance, unscrew the part and start over again at a different angle until it can be inserted and turned several turns without much effort. Keep in mind that many parts, especially spark plugs, use tapered threads so that gentle turning will automatically bring the part you're threading to the proper angle if you don't force it or resist a change in angle. Don't put a wrench on the part until it's been turned a couple of turns by hand. If you suddenly encounter resistance, and the part has not seated fully, don't force it. Pull it back out and make sure it's clean and threading properly.

Always take your time and be patient, once you have some experience, working on your car will become an enjoyable hobby.

TOOLS AND EQUIPMENT

▶ **See Figures 1, 2, 3, 4, 5, 6, 7, 8, 9, 10, 11, 12 and 13**

Naturally, without the proper tools and equipment it is impossible to properly service your vehicle. It would be impossible to catalog each tool that you would need to perform each or any operation in this book. It would also be unwise for the amateur to rush out and buy an expensive set of tools on the theory that he may need one or more of them at sometime.

The best approach is to proceed slowly, gathering together a good quality set of those tools that are used most frequently. Don't be misled by the low cost of bargain tools. It is far better to spend a little more for better quality. Forged wrenches, 6 or 12 point sockets and fine tooth ratchets are by far preferable to their less expensive counterparts. As any good mechanic can tell you, there are few worse experiences than trying to work on a car with bad tools. Your monetary savings will be far outweighed by frustration and mangled knuckles.

Begin accumulating those tools that are used most frequently; those associated with routine maintenance and tune-up.

In addition to the normal assortment of screwdrivers and pliers you should have the following tools for routine maintenance jobs. These models use both SAE and metric fasteners:

• SAE/Metric wrenches: sockets and combination open end/box end wrenches in sizes from 1/8 in. (3mm) to 3/4 in. (19mm); and a 13/16 in. (21mm) spark plug socket

• If possible, buy various length socket drive extensions. One break in this department is that the metric sockets available in the US will all fit the ratchet handles and extensions you may already have 1/4 in. (6mm), 3/4 in. (19mm), and 1/2 in. (13mm) drive

- Jackstands for support
- Oil filter wrench
- Oil filler spout for pouring oil
- Grease gun for chassis lubrication
- Hydrometer for checking the battery
- A container for draining oil
- Many rags for wiping up the inevitable mess

In addition to the above items there are several others that are not absolutely necessary, but handy to have around. These include oil dry, a transaxle funnel and the usual supply of lubricants, antifreeze and fluids, although these can be purchased as needed. This is a basic list for routine maintenance, but only your personal needs and desire can accurately determine your list of tools.

The second list of tools is for tune-ups. While the tools involved here are slightly more sophisticated, they need not be outrageously expensive. There are several inexpensive tach/dwell meters on the market that are every bit as good for the average mechanic as a professional model. Just be sure that it goes to at least 1200-1500 rpm on the tach scale and that it works on 4, 6 and 8 cylinder engines. A basic list of tune-up equipment could include:

- Tach/dwell meter
- Spark plug wrench
- Timing light (a DC light that works from the car's battery is best, although an AC light that plugs into 110V house current will suffice at some sacrifice in brightness)
- Wire spark plug gauge/adjusting tools
- Set of feeler blades

In addition to these basic tools, there are several other tools and gauges you may find useful. These include:

• A compression gauge. The screw-in type is slower to use, but eliminates the possibility of a faulty reading due to escaping pressure.

- A manifold vacuum gauge.
- A test light.

• An induction meter. This is used for determining whether or not there is current in a wire. These are handy for use if a wire is broken somewhere in a wiring harness.

As a final note, you will probably find a torque wrench necessary for all but the most basic work. The beam type models are perfectly adequate, although the newer click type are more precise.

Special Tools

Normally, the use of special factory tools is avoided for repair procedures, since these are not readily available for the do-it-yourself mechanic. When it is possible to perform the job with more commonly available tools, it will be pointed out, but occasionally, a special tool was designed to perform a specific function and should be used. Before substituting another tool, you should be convinced that neither your safety nor the performance of the vehicle will be compromised.

Some special tools are available commercially from major tool manufacturers. Others can be purchased from:

Utica Tool Company
32615 Park Lane
Garden City, Michigan 48135
Kent-Moore Tools
28635 Mound Rd.
Warren, MI 48092
1-800-345-2233

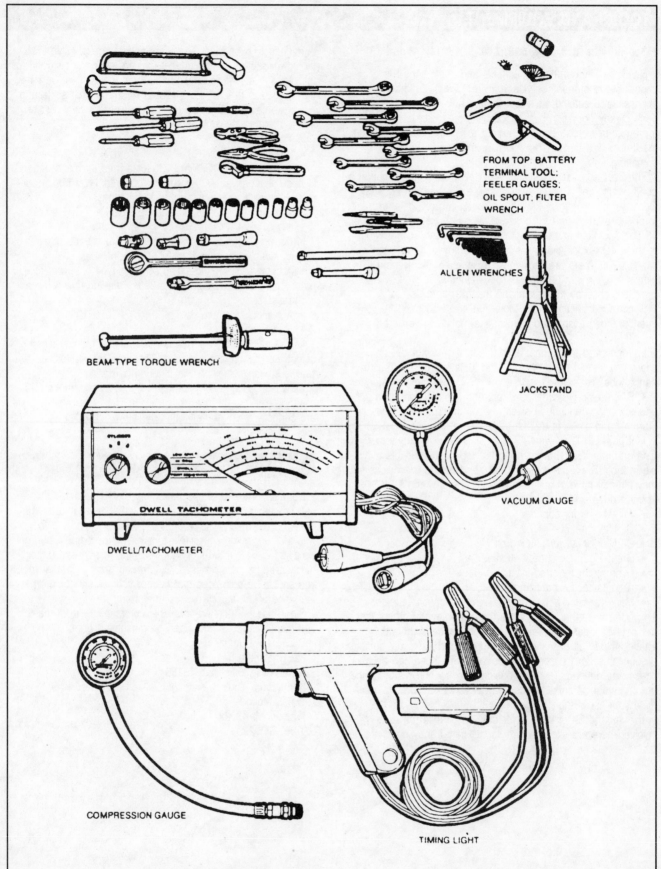

FROM TOP: BATTERY
TERMINAL TOOL;
FEELER GAUGES;
OIL SPOUT, FILTER
WRENCH

ALLEN WRENCHES

JACKSTAND

BEAM-TYPE TORQUE WRENCH

DWELL TACHOMETER

DWELL/TACHOMETER

VACUUM GAUGE

COMPRESSION GAUGE

TIMING LIGHT

TCCS1004

Fig. 1 A basic collection of tools and test instruments is all your need for most vehicle maintenance

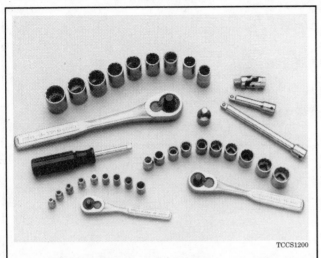

Fig. 2 All but the most basic procedure will require an assortment of ratchets and sockets

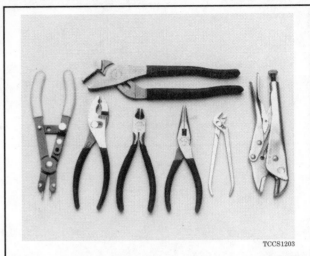

Fig. 5 An assortment of pliers will be handy, especially for old rusted parts and stripped bolt heads

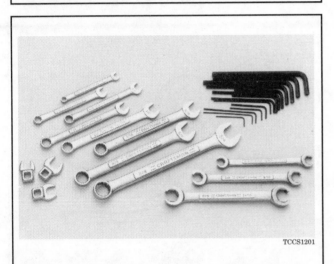

Fig. 3 In addition to ratchets, a good set of wrenches and hex keys will be necessary

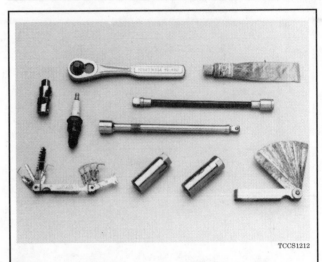

Fig. 6 A variety of tools and gauges are needed for spark plug service

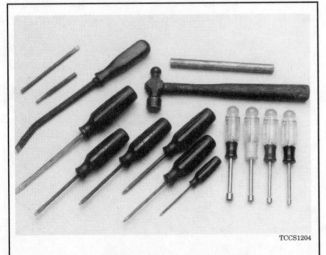

Fig. 4 Various screwdrivers, a hammer, chisels and prybars are necessary to have in your toolbox

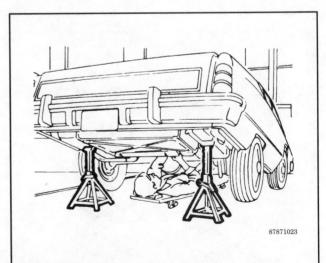

Fig. 7 Jackstands are a handy tool to have around when working under your vehicle

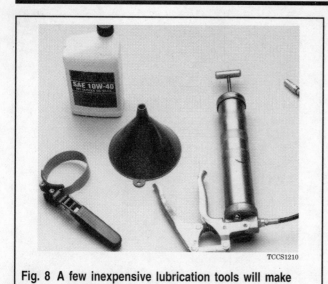

Fig. 8 A few inexpensive lubrication tools will make regular service easier

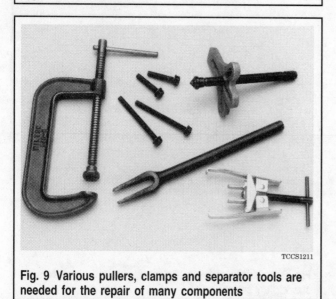

Fig. 9 Various pullers, clamps and separator tools are needed for the repair of many components

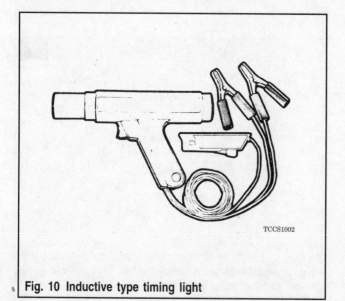

Fig. 10 Inductive type timing light

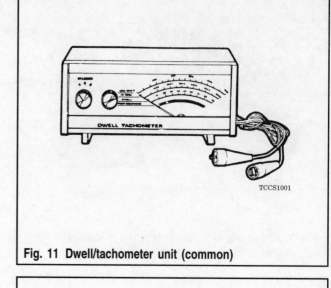

Fig. 11 Dwell/tachometer unit (common)

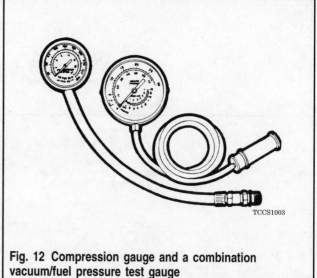

Fig. 12 Compression gauge and a combination vacuum/fuel pressure test gauge

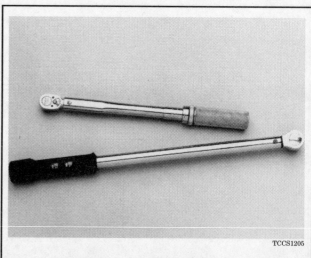

Fig. 13 Many repairs will require the use of a torque wrench to assure the components are properly fastened

SERVICING YOUR VEHICLE SAFELY

It is virtually impossible to anticipate all of the hazards involved with automotive maintenance and service but care and common sense will prevent most accidents.

The rules of safety for mechanics range from "don't smoke around gasoline," to "use the proper tool for the job." The trick to avoiding injuries is to develop safe work habits and take every possible precaution.

Do's

▶ **See Figures 14, 15 and 16**

• Do keep a fire extinguisher and first aid kit within easy reach.

• Do wear safety glasses or goggles when cutting, drilling, grinding or prying, even if you have 20/20 vision. If you wear glasses for the sake of vision, then they should be made of hardened glass that can serve also as safety glasses, or wear safety goggles over your regular glasses.

• Do shield your eyes whenever you work around the battery. Batteries contain sulfuric acid; in case of contact with the eyes or skin, flush the area with water or a mixture of water and baking soda and get medical attention immediately.

• Do use safety stands for any undercar service. Jacks are for raising vehicles; safety stands are for making sure the vehicle stays raised until you want it to come down. Whenever the vehicle is raised, block the wheels remaining on the ground and set the parking brake.

• Do use adequate ventilation when working with any chemicals. Like carbon monoxide, the asbestos dust resulting from brake lining wear can be poisonous in sufficient quantities.

• Do disconnect the negative battery cable when working on the electrical system. The primary ignition system can contain up to extremely high voltage.

• Do follow manufacturer's directions whenever working with potentially hazardous materials. Both brake fluid and antifreeze are poisonous if taken internally.

• Do properly maintain your tools. Loose hammerheads, mushroomed punches and chisels, frayed or poorly grounded electrical cords, excessively worn screwdrivers, spread wrenches (open end), cracked sockets, slipping ratchets, or faulty droplight sockets can cause accidents.

• Do use the proper size and type of tool for the job being done.

• Do when possible, pull on a wrench handle rather than push on it, and adjust your stance to prevent a fall.

• Do be sure that adjustable wrenches are tightly adjusted on the nut or bolt and pulled so that the face is on the side of the fixed jaw.

• Do select a wrench or socket that fits the nut or bolt. The wrench or socket should sit straight, not cocked.

• Do strike squarely with a hammer; avoid glancing blows.

• Do set the parking brake and block the drive wheels if the work requires that the engine be running.

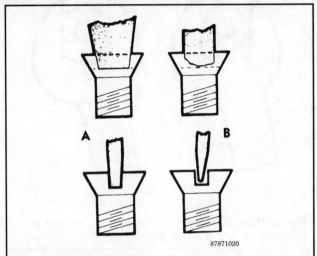

Fig. 14 Screwdrivers should be kept in good condition to prevent personal injury

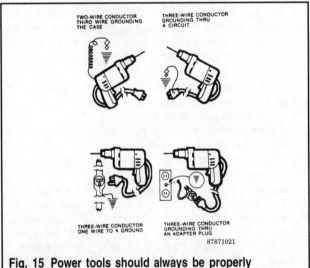

Fig. 15 Power tools should always be properly grounded

Don'ts

• Don't run an engine in a garage or anywhere else without proper ventilation; EVER! Carbon monoxide is poisonous, it takes a long time to leave the human body and you can build up a deadly supply of it in your system by simply breathing in a little every day. You may not realize you are slowly poisoning yourself. Always use power vents, windows, fans or open the garage doors.

• Don't work around moving parts while wearing a necktie or other loose clothing. Short sleeves are much safer than long, loose sleeves and hard-toed shoes with neoprene soles protect your toes and give a better grip on slippery surfaces. Jewelry such as watches, fancy belt buckles, beads or body adornment of any kind is not safe working around a car. Long hair should be hidden under a hat or cap.

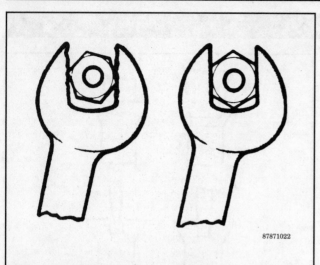

Fig. 16 Using the correct size wrench will prevent the rounding off of a nut or the tool itself

- Don't use pockets for toolboxes. A fall or bump can drive a screwdriver deep into your body. Even a wiping cloth hanging from the back pocket can wrap around a spinning shaft or fan.
- Don't smoke when working around gasoline, cleaning solvent or other flammable material.
- Don't smoke when working around the battery. When the battery is being charged, it gives off explosive hydrogen gas.
- Don't use gasoline to wash your hands; there are excellent soaps available. Gasoline removes all the natural oils from the skin so that bone dry hands will suck up oil and grease, and also contains additives.
- Don't service the air conditioning system unless you are equipped with the necessary tools and training. The refrigerant, R-12, is extremely cold and when exposed to the air, will instantly freeze any surface it comes in contact with, including your eyes. Although the refrigerant is normally non-toxic, R-12 becomes a deadly poisonous gas in the presence of an open flame. One good whiff of the vapors from burning refrigerant can be fatal.

HISTORY

In designing the these models, Chrysler didn't replace a car as much as design a brand new, efficiency sized car for the US market. The goal was to design a car with outstanding roominess, good handling characteristics, good fuel economy and flexibility of use.

According to chassis and body development studies the new car would be based on these criteria:
- A fuel efficient 4-cylinder engine
- Base weight less than 2100 pounds
- Overall length less than 165 inches
- Overall width less than 66 inches
- Front wheel drive

The starting point was a fuel efficient, 4-cylinder engine, the first 4-cylinder engine to power a domestic Chrysler Corporation passenger car in 45 years. The last 4-cylinder powered Chrysler Corporation passenger car was the 1932 Plymouth.

The base engine is a 1.7 liter powerplant purchased from Volkswagen in the form of an assembled cylinder block and cylinder head. The unit is shipped in special containers to the Trenton engine plant, where samples of each shipment are tested on a dynamometer and completely torn down during a complete quality control inspection. The other components; intake and exhaust manifolds, fuel pump, carburetor and controls, emission controls, alternator, power steering pump, clutch, air cleaner, ignition system, are all obtained from US suppliers and installed at the engine plant. Since the Omni and Horizon models are Chrysler's first metrically designed models built in the US, the cylinder block, head and crankshaft are built to metric measurements. Other components, mostly those obtained from domestic suppliers, such as the power steering pump or alternator retain inch-size dimensions.

In 1981, a new 2.2L (135 cu. in.) 4-cylinder engine was introduced as an option on all models except the fuel efficient Miser.

Early in the design stages, Chrysler engineers realized that even with their design parameters, the luggage carrying needs of people hadn't changed that much. Front wheel drive offered the dimensional advantages to obtain the desired front and rear legroom with a superior luggage carrying capacity, and still stay within the design criteria. The lower floor, made possible by front wheel drive eliminating the driveshaft tunnel, resulted in extra inches that could be devoted to a luggage area.

Front wheel drive also gave advantages in handling. The car was more stable and didn't drift during cornering; directional stability was increased and traction was improved due to more weight over the driving wheels. The front wheel drive transaxle allowed the car to be bigger on the inside and smaller on the outside to achieve the overall length and width parameters.

Emphasis was also put on minimal weight coupled with a solid, substantial look, to appeal to those who were used to larger cars. The solid, stable look was achieved through the use of a wider stance, and careful choice of line and form, the proper degree of curvature to the door and the proportion of body panels. Extensive use of strong, but lightweight, components allowed the final product to weigh in at slightly over 2000 pounds, just under the 2100 pound goal.

A strut type front suspension was chosen to keep weight to a minimum yet provide the best possible handling and ride qualities. The objective was to eliminate the harsh, choppy ride often associated with small cars, through the use of anti-sway bar, soft oval rubber pivot bushings, non-concentric coil springs and well balanced front and rear systems.

The actual design of the cars began in April of 1975, after preliminary planning had settled the issues of length, width, wheel base and configuration. More than 16 different exterior concepts were wind tunnel tested to determine their aerodynamic behavior. The results refined the 4-door hatchback configuration to obtain the minimum aerodynamic drag. Design improvements were translated in half scale, plastic models before producing a total of 84 prototypes that would log over 6,000,000 test miles. The final result, "Job Number One," rolled off the Belvidere assembly line on November 21, 1977.

Popularity of the Dodge Omni and Plymouth Horizon in their first full year in the marketplace, achieved a new production record for Chrysler Corporation's Belvidere assembly plant. In calender year 1978, 288,236 cars were built and sold. Demand was so great that the plant capacity was increased from the initial 960 cars per day to the present rate of almost 1200 per day.

In 1979 the Plymouth Horizon TC3 and Dodge Omni 024 were introduced. The sporty, 2-door hatchback design had all the basic ingredients that made the 4-door version a success, in addition to a low profile, 2+2 sport look. The aerodynamically styled 024 and TC3 are about 8 inches longer and almost 2½ inches lower than their sedan counterparts.

In 1982 the 024 Charger and the TC3 Turismo performance version were introduced. The Charger and Turismo body styles were refined versions of the original 024 and TC3 models, with added features such as mellow tuned exhaust, simulated hood scoop and fender exhaust vents. Also included on these models are bold nameplate graphics, rear spoiler and raised white letter tires.

Probably the most radical model introduced in this body style in 1982 was the Dodge Rampage pickup truck which was the first front wheel drive pickup to be built by a member of Detroit's "Big Three". Introduced in both the Sport and High-Line trim packages they share many of the same components with the other models. The major difference is in the rear suspension, where the other models have rear coil over strut type shocks and independent trailing arms the pickup model has conventional rear shocks, leaf springs and a tubular rear axle in order to support the additional rear weight capacity required in a pickup.

For the 1983 model year, Plymouth added a pickup to their model line called the Scamp. This model shared comparable features to the Dodge Rampage pickup introduced the previous year.

Introduced in mid-1983 was the aggressive styled Dodge Shelby Charger. Built to be a high performance "image car" with its high output 2.2 liter engine and 5-speed transaxle. Its designer, Carol Shelby, that's right, the same man who brought us the 0-100 and back to zero in ten seconds AC Cobra, and the famous Shelby Mustang once again proved that he could come up with a high performance car that would be popular in the 80's.

SERIAL NUMBER IDENTIFICATION

Vehicle

▶ **See Figures 17, 18, 19 and 20**

The vehicle identification number (VIN) is located on a plate attached to the upper lefthand corner of the instrument panel visible through the windshield. The complete VIN is also on the Safety Certification label located on the rear facing of the driver's door. An abbreviated form of the VIN is also stamped on a pad on the engine and on the transaxle housing.

All 1978-80 VIN's contain 13 digits coded to reveal the following information:
- 1st digit: Car line
- 2nd digit: Series
- 3rd and 4th digit: Body type
- 5th digit: Engine displacement
- 6th digit: Model year
- 7th digit: Assembly plant
- Last 6 digits: Sequential vehicle serial number

All 1981 and later VIN's contain 17 digits coded to reveal the following information:
- 1st digit: Country of Origin
- 2nd digit: Make
- 3rd digit: Type of Vehicle
- 4th digit: Pass Safety System
- 5th digit: Model Type
- 6th digit: Series
- 7th digit: Body Style

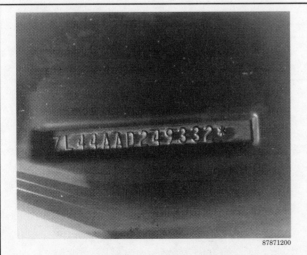

Fig. 17 The VIN plate is located on the left front dash panel and is visible through the windshield

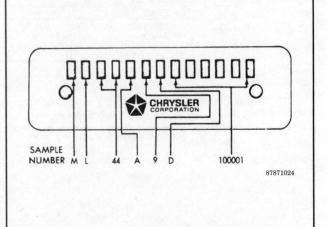

Fig. 18 Models from 1978-80 have a 13 digit serial number

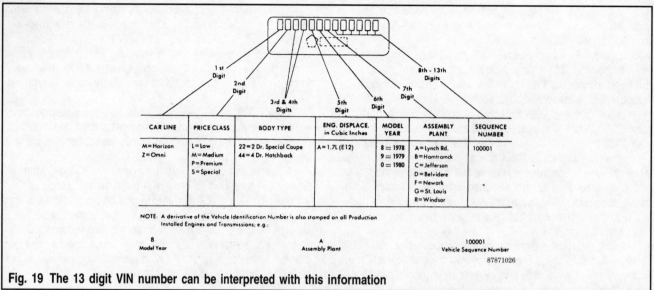

CAR LINE	PRICE CLASS	BODY TYPE	ENG. DISPLACE. in Cubic Inches	MODEL YEAR	ASSEMBLY PLANT	SEQUENCE NUMBER
M = Horizon Z = Omni	L = Low M = Medium P = Premium S = Special	22 = 2 Dr. Special Coupe 44 = 4 Dr. Hatchback	A = 1.7L (E12)	8 = 1978 9 = 1979 0 = 1980	A = Lynch Rd. B = Hamtramck C = Jefferson D = Belvidere F = Newark G = St. Louis R = Windsor	100001

NOTE: A derivative of the Vehicle Identification Number is also stamped on all Production Installed Engines and Transmissions; e.g.:

8   A   100001
Model Year   Assembly Plant   Vehicle Sequence Number

87871026

Fig. 19 The 13 digit VIN number can be interpreted with this information

POSITION	CODE OPTIONS			INTERPRETATION
1	1 = U.S. 2 = Canada	3 = Mexico J = Japan		Country of Origin
2	B = Dodge C = Chrysler	P = Plymouth		Make
3	3 = Passenger Car 7 = Truck			Type of Vehicle
4	B = Manual Seat Belts D = 1-3000 Lbs. GVW			Passenger Safety System
5	C = LeBaron D = Aries E = 600 T = New Yorker D = Lancer	L = Caravelle (Canada) M = Horizon P = Reliant J = Caravelle (U.S.)	V = 600 Z = Omni A = V Daytona A = C Laser C = LeBaron GTS	Line
6	1 = Economy 2 = Low	4 = High 5 = Premium	6 = Special	Series
7	1 = 2 Dr. Sedan 2 = 2 Dr. Specialty Hardtop 3 = 2 Dr. Hardtop 4 = 2 Dr. Hatchback	5 = 2 Dr. Convertible 6 = 4 Dr. Sedan 8 = 4 Dr. Hatchback 9 = 4 Dr. Wagon		Body Style
8	A = 1.6L C = 2.2L	D = 2.2L EFI E = 2.2L Turbo	G = 2.6L	Engine
9*	(1 thru 9, 0 or X)			Check Digit
10	F = 1985			Model Year
11	C = Jefferson D = Belvidere F = Newark G = St. Louis 1	K = Pillette Rd. N = Sterling R = Windsor	T = Toluca W = Clairpointe X = St. Louis 2	Assembly Plant
2 thru 17	(6 Digits)			Sequence Number

*Digit in position 9 is used for VIN verification

87871027

Fig. 20 On 1981-89 models, the 17 digit code can be interpreted with this information

- 8th digit: Engine
- 9th digit: Check Digit
- 10th digit: Model Year
- 11th digit: Assembly Plant
- 12th through 17th digit: Sequence Number

Engine

▶ See Figures 21, 22, 23 and 24

The engine identification numbers on the 1.6 and 1.7 liter engines are stamped on a pad on the engine block just above the fuel pump. The 2.2 liter engine has its number stamped on a pad just above the bellhousing.

Transaxle

▶ See Figures 25 and 26

The manual transaxle serial number is stamped on a metal pad or tag on top of the transaxle, just above the timing window. Four types of manual transaxle are used, the A412 VW design 4-spd., the A460 4-spd., the A465 5-spd., and the A525 close ratio 5-spd., used in the high performance models.

The automatic transaxle serial number is stamped on a metal pad located just above the oil pan at the rear of the transaxle.

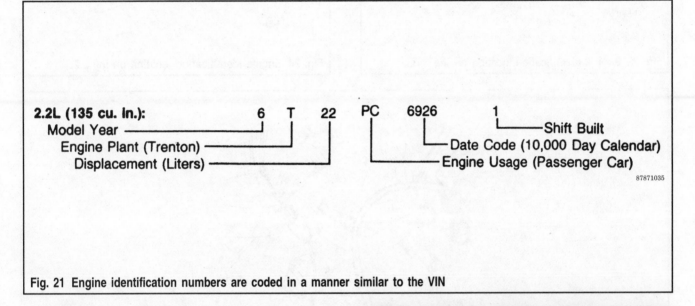

2.2L (135 cu. In.):   6   T   22   PC   6926   1
    Model Year ——————————— ┘ | | | | └— Shift Built
    Engine Plant (Trenton) ——————— ┘ | | └———— Date Code (10,000 Day Calendar)
    Displacement (Liters) ————————— ┘   └————————— Engine Usage (Passenger Car)

87871035

Fig. 21 Engine identification numbers are coded in a manner similar to the VIN

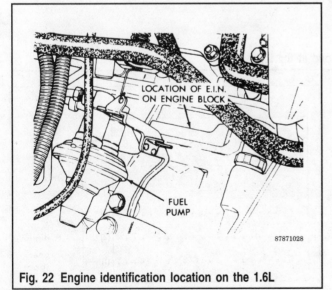

LOCATION OF E.I.N.
ON ENGINE BLOCK

FUEL
PUMP

87871028

Fig. 22 Engine identification location on the 1.6L

Body Code Plate

▶ See Figures 27 and 28

The body code plate contains important information about your particular car which is usually needed for any correspondence with the factory. The plate is located on the left front fender side shield, on the left side of the upper radiator support or on the wheel housing.

The information on the plate is coded in 6 rows of digits and is read from left to right. The information can be interpreted using the information shown in the illustration.

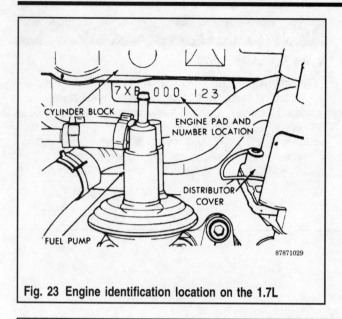

Fig. 23 Engine identification location on the 1.7L

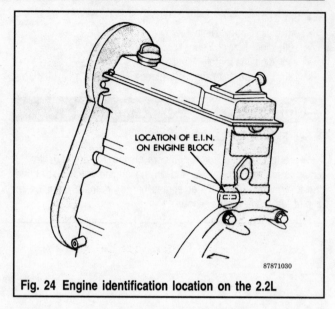

Fig. 24 Engine identification location on the 2.2L

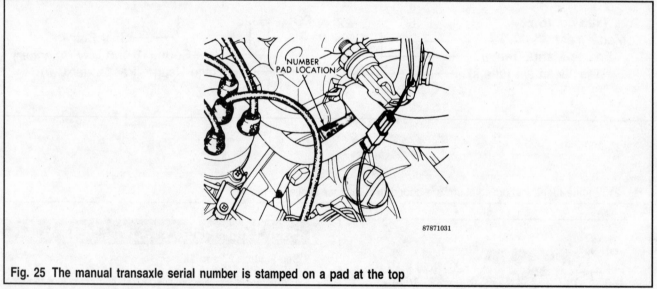

Fig. 25 The manual transaxle serial number is stamped on a pad at the top

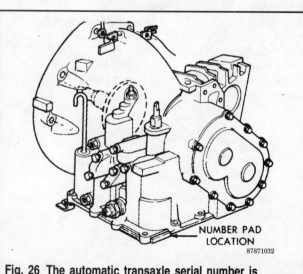

Fig. 26 The automatic transaxle serial number is stamped on a pad on the bottom side of the transaxle

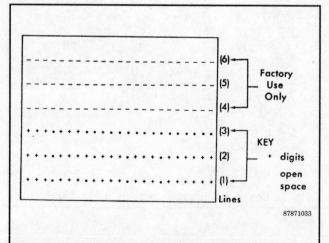

Fig. 27 The body plate may be found on the left front fender side shield, on the left side of the upper radiator support or on the wheel housing

LINE #1—1st 3 digits .... engine code
4th .... open space
5th thru 7th ...... transmission code
8th .... open space
remaining digits .. Vehicle Identification Number (VIN)

LINE #2—1st 3 digits .... lower body paint color code or fleet or special order paint codes
4th .... open space
5th thru 8th ...... trim code
9th .... open space
10th thru 12th .... interior paint colors and build code
13th .... open space
14th thru 23rd .... vehicle sales order number
14th digit .... month code
15th & 16th ...... day of month
17th .... open space
18th thru 23rd .... vehicle order number

LINE #3—1st 3 digits .... upper body color code or two tone color code
4th .... open space
5th thru 7th ...... vinyl roof code
8th & 9th .... open space
10th .... order code: U=U.S.
C=Canada
I=International
remaining digits .. open spaces

LINES #4 thru #6 .... For factory use only

87871034

Fig. 28 The body code plate can be interpreted using this information

ROUTINE MAINTENANCE

Air Cleaner

REMOVAL & INSTALLATION

1.7L Engine

▸ **See Figures 29, 30, 31, 32, 33 and 34**

The carburetor air cleaner should be replaced every 30,000 miles (50,790 km) under normal use. If the car is driven continuously in extremely dirty, dusty or sandy areas, the interval should be cut in half.

1. Disconnect the hoses to the air cleaner. Tag them if needed for installation.
2. Remove the 2 wing nuts and unclamp the retaining clips.

Fig. 31 Remove any wing nuts . . .

3. Remove the air cleaner cover with the filter attached.
4. Unscrew the wing nut on the bottom of the filter element and remove the filter.
5. If needed, replace the PCV filter located in the air cleaner housing.

To install:

6. Install a new filter and replace the wing nut.
7. Reinstall the cover and hand-tighten the wing nuts.
8. Snap the retaining clips into place.

1.6 and 2.2L Engines

▸ **See Figures 35 and 36**

1. Remove the three wing nuts that retain the air cleaner cover.
2. Remove the cover and lift out the element.

To install:

3. Install the new element.

Fig. 29 If applicable, disconnect the large hose connection at the air cleaner

Fig. 30 Also, disconnect any vacuum hoses attached to the air cleaner housing

Fig. 32 . . . and clamps securing the housing cover

Fig. 33 Remove the lower wing nut to access the filter

Fig. 34 Check the condition of the PCV filter in the air cleaner housing as well

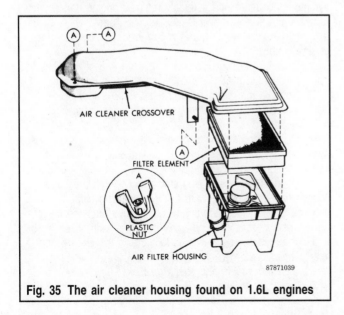

Fig. 35 The air cleaner housing found on 1.6L engines

4. Position the cover while aligning the three hold-down clips and allowing the two carburetor and one support bracket studs to protrude through each stud hole in the cover.

5. Install a wing nut on each of the carburetor studs first, and tighten them to 14 inch lbs. (2 Nm).

6. Install the third wing nut on the support bracket stud and tighten it to 14 inch lbs. (2 Nm).

➡It is important to follow this sequence to avoid air leaks due to air cleaner body distortion.

Fuel Filter

✳✳CAUTION

Never smoke when working around gasoline! Avoid all sources of sparks or ignition. Gasoline vapors are EXTREMELY volatile!

REMOVAL & INSTALLATION

Carbureted Engines

1978-79 MODELS

▸ See Figures 37 and 38

The fuel filter on the 1978-79 models is located behind the fuel inlet of the carburetor. Under normal operating conditions the filter should be replaced every 15,000 miles (24,139 km).

1. Remove the clamp from the rubber hose.

2. Spread some dry rags under the fuel filter to absorb the inevitable gasoline spillage.

3. Unscrew the fitting and remove the filter.

To install:

4. Install a new filter.

5. Install and tighten the fitting.

6. Connect the fuel line. You may want to use a new screw type clamp that will make future filter replacement easier.

7. Run the engine and check for leaks.

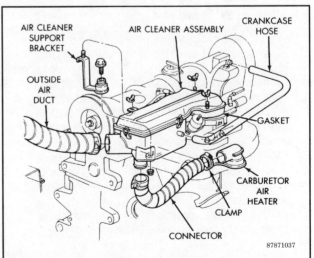

Fig. 36 Air cleaner housing commonly found on 2.2L engines

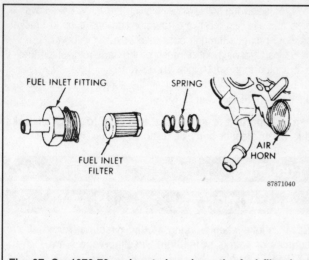

Fig. 37 On 1978-79 carbureted engines, the fuel filter is located behind this fitting

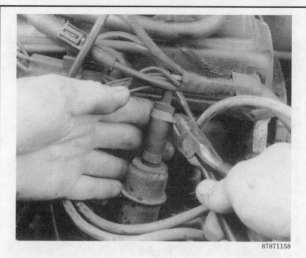

Fig. 39 Remove the hose clamps at both ends of the filter

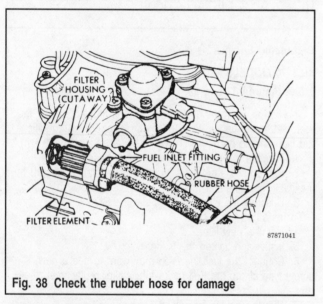

Fig. 38 Check the rubber hose for damage

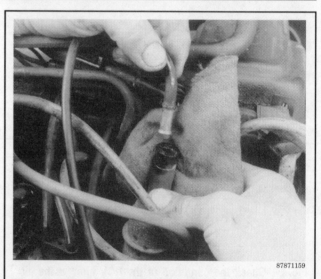

Fig. 40 Separate the hose ends from the fuel pipe lines

1980 AND LATER

▶ See Figures 39, 40 and 41

There are two fuel filters in this system. One is part of the gauge unit assembly located inside the fuel tank on the suction end of the tube. This filter normally does not need servicing, but may be replaced or cleaned if a very large amount of extremely coarse material gets into the tank and clogs it.

The 2.2 liter engine usually uses a disposable filter-vapor separator that is located on the front side of the engine block between the fuel pump and carburetor. On some applications, this filter has not only inlet and outlet connections, but a third connection designed to permit fuel to return to the tank so that vapor that accumulates in hot weather will not interfere with carburetion.

A plugged fuel filter can limit the speed at which a vehicle can be driven and may cause hard starting. The most critical symptom will usually be suddenly reduced engine performance at maximum engine power levels, as when passing.

1. Have a rag ready to catch spilled fuel. Make sure the engine is cool.

2. Remove the hose clamps from each end of the filter. Then, disconnect the hoses, collecting the fuel in the rag.

3. Remove the old filter and hoses. On the reservoir type filter, remove the two mounting nuts inside the air cleaner.

To install:

4. Put the new filter into position. If it has mounting studs, pass them through the mounting bracket and then install the attaching nuts snugly.

5. Connect the hoses, and install and tighten the hose clamps (if the hoses are hard to force onto the nipples, you can wet them inside just very slightly). Make sure the clamps are located a short distance away from the ends of the hoses and on the inside of the nipples located on the ends of the filter connections.

6. Start the engine and check for leaks.

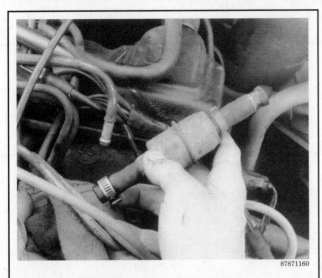

Fig. 41 Fuel will spill out, have a rag handy

Fuel Injected Engines

▶ See Figure 42

※※CAUTION

Fuel injected engines use high pressure in their operation. This pressure is maintained through the action of check valves even when the engine is off. Therefore, you must be sure to work on the fuel carrying parts of injected cars only when the engine has cooled off and only after you have properly bled the pressurized fuel from the system. Failure to do this could readily cause a fire!

1. Relieve fuel system pressure as follows:

a. Loosen the fuel tank cap to release any accumulated air pressure that may be there. Then, disconnect the electrical connector at the single fuel injector on the throttle body on cars with throttle body injection. On cars with multi-point injection, disconnect the electrical connector on the injector closest to the battery.

b. Use a jumper wire to ground one of the injector terminals for whichever injector you've disconnected.

c. Connect one end of a jumper wire to the other injector terminal. Then, just touch the other end of the second jumper to the battery positive post for nearly 10 seconds.

d. Make sure you do not maintain this connection for more than the maximum of 10 seconds or the injector could be damaged.

2. Remove the retaining screw that mounts the filter to its retaining bracket so you can reach the hose clamps.

3. Then, loosen the clamps for both the inlet and outlet lines. Quickly wrap a shop towel around these connections to collect escaping fuel safely. Then, dispose of this towel in such a way as to protect it from heat the the chance of fire.

4. Note the routing of the hoses. The high pressure hose from the tank and pump goes to the inlet connection, which is always located toward the outer edge of the filter. The outlet hose to the engine is labeled on some filters and is always at the center. Pull the hoses off the connections on the filter. Replace the filter, draining fuel into a metal container and disposing of it safely. Inspect the hoses and clamps and replace defective parts as necessary.

※※WARNING

Chrysler uses and recommends hoses that meet their specifications and are labeled EFM/EFI 18519. Make sure you use either this type of hose or an equivalent, high pressure (up to 55 psi) type of fuel hose available in the automotive aftermarket. Be sure not to use ordinary rubber fuel hose, as this is not tough enough for high pressure use and may not be able to resist the destruction caused by certain types of contamination. Also, if hose clamps require replacement, note that the original equipment clamps have rolled edges to keep the edge of the band from cutting into this hose, due to the necessary use of high clamping forces with a high pressure fuel system. Make sure that you use either an original equipment clamp or a similar type of clamp available in the aftermarket.

To install:

5. Reconnect the hoses, using the proper routing noted as you disconnected them. You may want to very slightly wet the inside diameter of the hoses to make it easier to install them onto the filter connections. Install them as far as possible, until they are well over the bulges at the ends of the connectors. Install the clamps so they are a short distance away from the ends of the hoses but well over the bulged areas at the ends of the filter connections. Tighten both clamps securely tighten to 10 inch lbs. (1 Nm).

6. Remount the filter on the bracket snugly with the screw. Start the engine and check for leaks, tightening the hose clamps, replacing parts, or forcing the hoses farther onto the connectors, if necessary.

PCV Valve

These models are equipped with a closed crankcase ventilation system. The PCV valve is located in a line running between the cylinder head cover and the air cleaner.

This valve must be kept clean for optimum engine performance and fuel economy. The PCV valve should be inspected

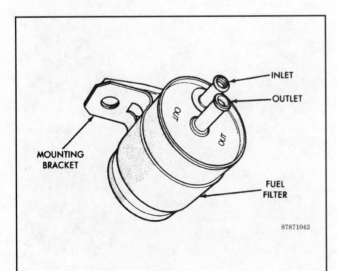

Fig. 42 Fuel injected engines use a canister type filter

every 15,000 miles (24,139 km) and replaced every 30,000 miles (48,279 km). In extremely dusty conditions or if the car is subjected to extensive idling or short trip operation, the interval should be halved.

TESTING

Refer to Section 4 for testing procedures.

REMOVAL & INSTALLATION

▶ **See Figures 43, 44, 45, 46 and 47**

1. Unfasten the PCV hose from the valve.
2. Remove the PCV valve from the rubber grommet in the cylinder head cover.
3. Clean the mounting area. If needed, replace the grommet.
4. Check the hose connected to the valve for any deterioration.
   To install:
5. Place a new valve into the grommet, then attach the hose.

Evaporative Canister

SERVICING

▶ **See Figures 48 and 49**

The charcoal canister is a feature on all models to store fuel vapors that evaporate from the fuel tank and, if equipped the carburetor bowl. Note that on some fuel bowls, the vent to the evaporative canister is capped since the fuel bowl is vented internally.

The only service is to replace the canister filter every 30,000 miles (50,700 km), if the car is driven in particularly dusty areas. Otherwise, no service is necessary.

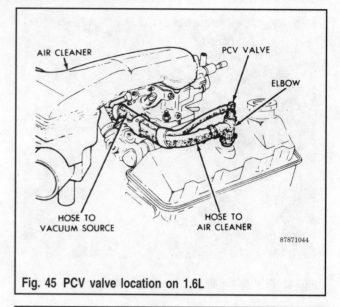

Fig. 45 PCV valve location on 1.6L

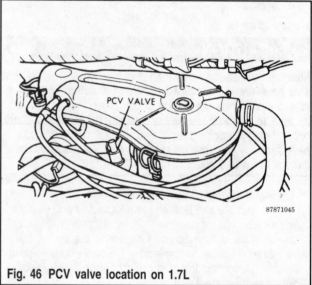

Fig. 46 PCV valve location on 1.7L

Fig. 43 Unfasten the hose from the PCV valve

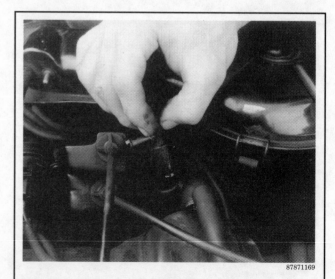

Fig. 44 Remove the PCV valve from the grommet

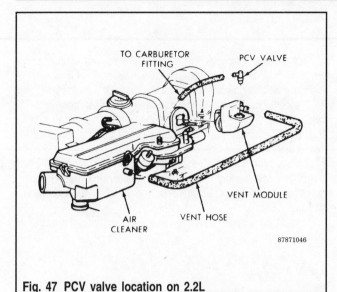

Fig. 47 PCV valve location on 2.2L

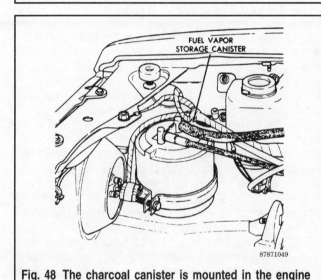

Fig. 48 The charcoal canister is mounted in the engine compartment

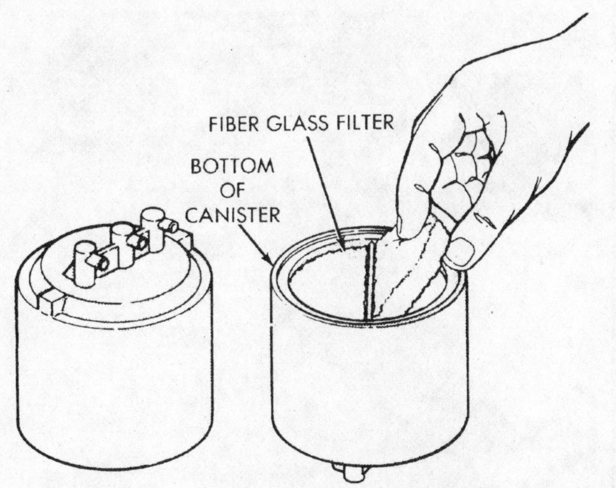

Fig. 49 The filter is in the bottom of the canister

All hoses used with this system should be inspected periodically and replaced if cracked or leaking. These hoses are of special fuel resistant material and must be replaced with the same type and quality. The OEM (Original Equipment Manufactured) clamps are "Keystone" type and will be destroyed when they are removed. Replacement types should be aircraft type screw clamps if the original equipment is not available (spring type clamps are not recommended). Position the clamps so that no sharp edges contact adjacent hoses.

Battery

GENERAL MAINTENANCE

◆ **See Figures 50, 51, 52 and 53**

Loose, dirty, or corroded battery terminals are a major cause of "no-start." Every 3 months or so, remove the battery terminals and clean them, giving them a light coating of petroleum jelly when you are finished. This will help to retard corrosion.

Check the battery cables for signs of wear or chafing and replace any cable or terminal that looks marginal. Battery terminals can be easily cleaned and inexpensive terminal cleaning tools are an excellent investment that will pay for themselves many times over. They can usually be purchased from any well-equipped auto store or parts department. The accumulated white power and corrosion can be cleaned from the top of the battery with an old toothbrush and a solution of baking soda and water.

Unless you have a maintenance-free battery, check the electrolyte level (see Battery under Fluid Level Checks in this section) and check the specific gravity of each cell. Be sure that the vent holes in each cell cap are not blocked by grease or dirt. The vent holes allow hydrogen gas, formed by the chemical reaction in the battery, to escape safely.

Fig. 50 Battery maintenance may be accomplished with household items (such as baking soda to neutralize spilled acid) or with special tools such as this post and terminal cleaner

TCCS1207

Fig. 51 The underside of this special battery tool has a wire brush to clean post terminals

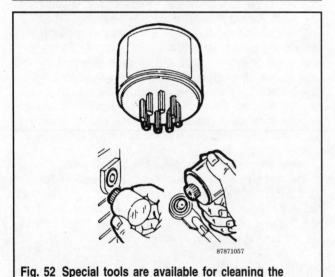

87871057

Fig. 52 Special tools are available for cleaning the terminals and cable clamps on side terminal batteries

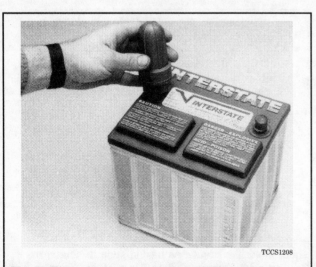

TCCS1208

Fig. 53 Place the tool over the terminals and twist to clean the post

FLUID LEVEL

Two types of batteries are used: Standard and Maintenance-Free. Both types are equipped with a Charge-Test Indicator, which is actually a miniature hydrometer built into the filler cap of the cell. The indicator will show green if the battery is above 75-80% charged, or dark if the battery needs recharging. Light yellow indicates the battery may be in need of water or replacement.

For standard batteries, check the level of the electrolyte every 2 months; more often on long trips or in extremely hot weather. If necessary add mineral free water to the bottom of the filler well.

At least once a year, check the specific gravity of a standard battery.

CABLES AND CLAMPS

▶ **See Figures 54, 55 and 56**

Once a year, the battery terminals and the cable clamps should be cleaned. Loosen the clamps and remove the cables, negative cable first. On batteries with posts on top, the use of a puller specially made for the purpose is recommended. These are inexpensive, and often available in auto parts stores. Side terminal battery cables are secured with a bolt.

Clean the cable clamps and the battery terminals with a wire brush until all corrosion, grease, etc..., is removed and the metal is shiny, It is especially important to clean the inside of the clamp thoroughly, since a small deposit of foreign material or oxidation will prevent a sound electrical connection and inhibit either starting or charging. Special tools are available for cleaning these parts, one type for conventional batteries and another type for side terminal batteries.

Before installing the cables, loosen the battery hold-down clamp or strap, remove the battery and check the battery tray. Clear it of any debris, and check it for soundness. Rust should be wire brushed away, and the metal should be given a coat of anti-rust paint. Install the battery and tighten the hold-down

87871161

Fig. 54 Loosen the clamps and disconnect the cables

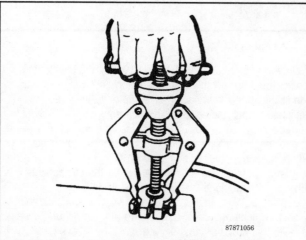

Fig. 55 If the cable cannot be disconnected easily, a terminal puller should be used to prevent possible damage to the battery case

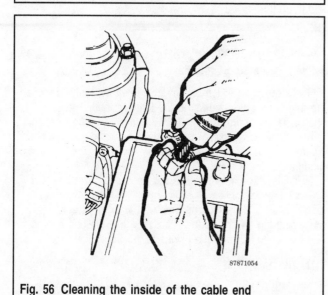

Fig. 56 Cleaning the inside of the cable end

clamp or strap securely, but be careful not to overtighten, which will crack the battery case.

After the clamps and terminals are clean, reinstall the cables, negative cable last; do not hammer on the clamps to install. Tighten the clamps securely, but do not distort them. Give the clamps and terminals a thin external coat of grease after installation, to retard corrosion.

Check the cables at the same time that the terminals are cleaned. If the insulation is cracked or broken, or if the ends are frayed, the cable should be replaced with a new cable of the same length and gauge.

❊❊CAUTION

Keep flame or sparks away from the battery; it gives off explosive hydrogen gas. Battery electrolyte contains sulfuric acid. If you should splash any on your skin or in your eyes, flush the affected area with plenty of clear water. NO MATTER WHAT! If it gets in your eyes, get medical help IMMEDIATELY.

TESTING SPECIFIC GRAVITY

Except Maintenance-Free Batteries
▶ See Figure 57

At least once a year, check the specific gravity of the battery. It should be between 1.20-1.26 at room temperature. The specific gravity can be checked with the use of a hydrometer, an inexpensive instrument available from many sources, including auto parts stores. The automotive battery hydrometer has a squeeze bulb at one end and a nozzle at the other. Battery electrolyte is sucked into the the hydrometer until the float is lifted from its seat. The specific gravity is read by noting the position of the float. Generally, if after charging, the specific gravity between any two cells varies more than 50 points (.50), the battery is bad and should be replaced.

Maintenance-Free Batteries
▶ See Figure 58

Most maintenance-free batteries are sealed, therefore it is not possible to check the specific gravity using a typical automotive hydrometer. Instead, the indicator built into the top of the case must be relied on to display any signs of battery deterioration. If the indicator is dark, the battery can be assumed to be OK. If the indicator is light, the specific gravity is low, and the battery should be charged or replaced. The indicator on some aftermarket batteries may vary, so be sure to check the instructions included with your battery if in doubt.

LOAD TEST

A true test of a battery's condition is the load test. It requires the use of a special carbon pile to simulate an electrical load on the battery. Normally, a battery is tested at half it's cold cranking amps rating or at three times the amp-hour rating for 15 seconds.

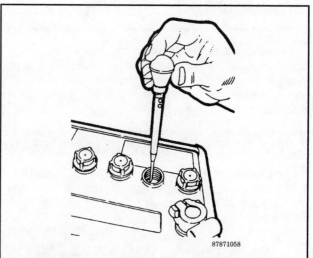

Fig. 57 Specific gravity can be checked with a simple float type hydrometer on non-sealed batteries

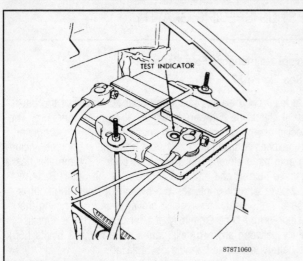

Fig. 58 Maintenance-free batteries are usually equipped with a test indicator

Generally, if after 15 seconds the battery voltage is not at 9.6 volts or more, the battery either needs to be recharged or replaced.

✳✳CAUTION

Never load test a battery unless the electrolyte level is sufficiently full, otherwise it may explode causing personal injury.

CHARGING

A battery should be charged at a slow rate to keep the plates inside from getting too hot. However if some maintenance-free batteries are allowed to discharge until they are almost "dead", they may have to be charged at a high rate to bring them back to "life". Always follow the battery charger manufacturer's instructions.

REPLACEMENT

The cold power rating of a battery measures battery starting performance and provides an approximate relationship between battery size and engine size. The cold power rating of a replacement battery should match or exceed your engine size in cubic inches.

Belts

Your particular car may have as few as one or as many as 4 drive belts for the following accessories: alternator, A/C compressor, power steering pump, water pump, or air pump (California models only).

INSPECTION

▶ **See Figure 59**

Once a year or at 12,000 mile (19,000 km) intervals, the tension (and condition) of the alternator, power steering, air conditioning, and Thermactor air pump drive belts (as equipped) should be checked. If necessary, the belts should be replaced or adjusted. Loose accessory drive belts can lead to poor engine cooling and diminish alternator, power steering pump, air conditioning compressor or air pump output. A belt that is too tight places a severe strain on the components it is driving which will lead to early component failure.

Replace any belt that is so glazed, worn or stretched that it cannot be tightened sufficiently. There are two different types of belts that may be found on your vehicle, V-belts (single ribbed) and serpentine type (multi-ribbed). Both of these types may drive one or more accessories.

ADJUSTING

Excluding 1.7L Alternator Belt
▶ **See Figures 60, 61 and 62**

Check the belt tension on any given belt by applying moderate thumb pressure midway in the longest span. The belt should deflect approximately ½ in. (13mm). If the longest span is not easily accessible, you can also check the shortest span, where the belt should deflect no more than ¼ in. (6mm) under moderate thumb pressure.

To adjust the tension, loosen the accessory pivot bolt. On A/C compressor loosen all bolts shown on the compressor decal. Insert a ½ in. (13mm) breaker bar in the accessory tensioning lug and move the accessory until the belt is properly tensioned. Tighten the pivot bolt.

1.7L Alternator Belt
▶ **See Figure 63**

Proper belt tension on the alternator belt is critical to proper alternator operation. For ease of adjusting alternator belt tension, a special tool has been developed that is easily fabricated or available from the tool company at a reasonable price. The tool, when used with a torque wrench, assures proper belt tension with greater accessibility. Do not use the thumb pressure method on these belts. It is essential that belt adjustment be performed from below the vehicle. The splash shield must be removed and on California models with an air pump, removing the horn will ease access to the adjustment bolt.

1. From underneath the vehicle, install a ½ in. (13mm) drive torque wrench in the adjusting tool. Position the adjusting tool.

2. Loosen the alternator pivot bolt. If you don't do this, you'll break the alternator housing.

3. Adjust the belt tension to 70 ft. lbs. (95 Nm) on a new belt, or 50 ft. lbs. (68 Nm) on a used belt.

➡**A belt is considered used after 15 minutes of running.**

4. Hold the alternator at the required torque. Tighten the adjusting bolt.

BATTERY DIAGNOSTICS CHART

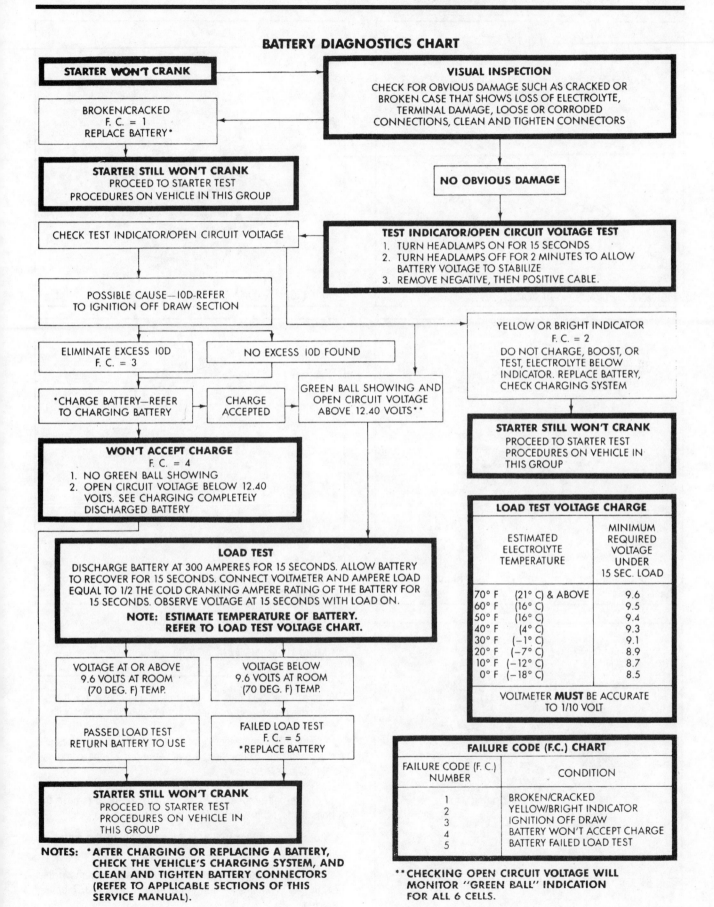

STARTER WON'T CRANK

VISUAL INSPECTION
CHECK FOR OBVIOUS DAMAGE SUCH AS CRACKED OR BROKEN CASE THAT SHOWS LOSS OF ELECTROLYTE, TERMINAL DAMAGE, LOOSE OR CORRODED CONNECTIONS, CLEAN AND TIGHTEN CONNECTORS

BROKEN/CRACKED
F. C. = 1
REPLACE BATTERY*

NO OBVIOUS DAMAGE

STARTER STILL WON'T CRANK
PROCEED TO STARTER TEST PROCEDURES ON VEHICLE IN THIS GROUP

TEST INDICATOR/OPEN CIRCUIT VOLTAGE TEST
1. TURN HEADLAMPS ON FOR 15 SECONDS
2. TURN HEADLAMPS OFF FOR 2 MINUTES TO ALLOW BATTERY VOLTAGE TO STABILIZE
3. REMOVE NEGATIVE, THEN POSITIVE CABLE.

CHECK TEST INDICATOR/OPEN CIRCUIT VOLTAGE

POSSIBLE CAUSE—IOD-REFER TO IGNITION OFF DRAW SECTION

ELIMINATE EXCESS IOD
F. C. = 3

NO EXCESS IOD FOUND

YELLOW OR BRIGHT INDICATOR
F. C. = 2
DO NOT CHARGE, BOOST, OR TEST, ELECTROLYTE BELOW INDICATOR. REPLACE BATTERY, CHECK CHARGING SYSTEM

*CHARGE BATTERY—REFER TO CHARGING BATTERY

CHARGE ACCEPTED

GREEN BALL SHOWING AND OPEN CIRCUIT VOLTAGE ABOVE 12.40 VOLTS**

STARTER STILL WON'T CRANK
PROCEED TO STARTER TEST PROCEDURES ON VEHICLE IN THIS GROUP

WON'T ACCEPT CHARGE
F. C. = 4
1. NO GREEN BALL SHOWING
2. OPEN CIRCUIT VOLTAGE BELOW 12.40 VOLTS. SEE CHARGING COMPLETELY DISCHARGED BATTERY

LOAD TEST VOLTAGE CHARGE	
ESTIMATED ELECTROLYTE TEMPERATURE	MINIMUM REQUIRED VOLTAGE UNDER 15 SEC. LOAD
70° F (21° C) & ABOVE	9.6
60° F (16° C)	9.5
50° F (16° C)	9.4
40° F (4° C)	9.3
30° F (−1° C)	9.1
20° F (−7° C)	8.9
10° F (−12° C)	8.7
0° F (−18° C)	8.5
VOLTMETER **MUST** BE ACCURATE TO 1/10 VOLT	

LOAD TEST
DISCHARGE BATTERY AT 300 AMPERES FOR 15 SECONDS. ALLOW BATTERY TO RECOVER FOR 15 SECONDS. CONNECT VOLTMETER AND AMPERE LOAD EQUAL TO 1/2 THE COLD CRANKING AMPERE RATING OF THE BATTERY FOR 15 SECONDS. OBSERVE VOLTAGE AT 15 SECONDS WITH LOAD ON.
NOTE: ESTIMATE TEMPERATURE OF BATTERY. REFER TO LOAD TEST VOLTAGE CHART.

VOLTAGE AT OR ABOVE 9.6 VOLTS AT ROOM (70 DEG. F) TEMP.

VOLTAGE BELOW 9.6 VOLTS AT ROOM (70 DEG. F) TEMP.

PASSED LOAD TEST RETURN BATTERY TO USE

FAILED LOAD TEST
F. C. = 5
*REPLACE BATTERY

FAILURE CODE (F.C.) CHART	
FAILURE CODE (F. C.) NUMBER	CONDITION
1	BROKEN/CRACKED
2	YELLOW/BRIGHT INDICATOR
3	IGNITION OFF DRAW
4	BATTERY WON'T ACCEPT CHARGE
5	BATTERY FAILED LOAD TEST

STARTER STILL WON'T CRANK
PROCEED TO STARTER TEST PROCEDURES ON VEHICLE IN THIS GROUP

NOTES: *AFTER CHARGING OR REPLACING A BATTERY, CHECK THE VEHICLE'S CHARGING SYSTEM, AND CLEAN AND TIGHTEN BATTERY CONNECTORS (REFER TO APPLICABLE SECTIONS OF THIS SERVICE MANUAL).

** CHECKING OPEN CIRCUIT VOLTAGE WILL MONITOR "GREEN BALL" INDICATION FOR ALL 6 CELLS.

87871400

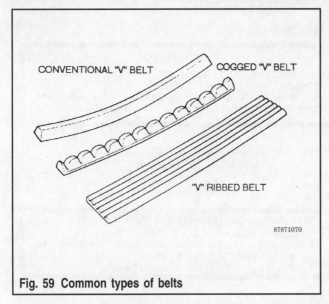

Fig. 59 Common types of belts

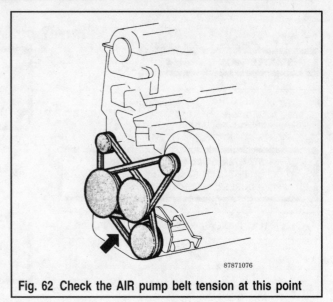

Fig. 62 Check the AIR pump belt tension at this point

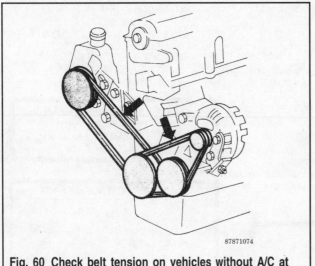
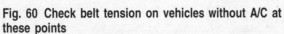

Fig. 60 Check belt tension on vehicles without A/C at these points

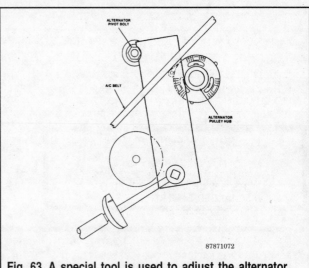

Fig. 63 A special tool is used to adjust the alternator belt tension on 1.7L engines

5. Reinstall the horn and splash shield.

REMOVAL & INSTALLATION

In most cases the car must be raised and supported, the splash shield removed and the horn removed from cars with air pumps.

1. The A/C compressor drive belt is removed first. Loosen the adjusting nut at the slotted bracket and push the compressor to its lowest position.

2. The alternator belt is removed second. Loosen the tension on the belt and use a ½ in. (13mm) socket to remove the 3 bolts holding the water pump pulley. Remove the pulley.

➡The air pump idler pulley is located behind the water pump pulley.

3. The air pump drive belt is removed next. To remove this belt, the A/C compressor and the alternator belts MUST be removed.

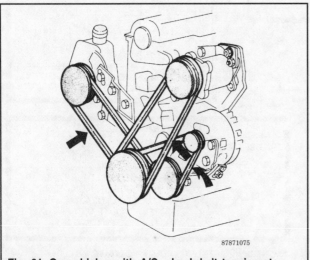

Fig. 61 On vehicles with A/C, check belt tension at these points

4. The power steering pump drive belt is removed last. It is necessary to remove all other belts, loosen the pump pivot bolt in the slotted bracket and move the pump to its lowest position.

5. New belts are installed in the reverse order. Tension all belts as outlined previously. New belts will usually stretch, so they should be checked after an hour's use.

Hoses

✳✳CAUTION

On models equipped with an electric cooling fan, disconnect the negative battery cable, or fan motor wiring harness connector before replacing any radiator/heater hose. The fan may come on, under certain circumstances, even though the ignition is OFF.

REMOVAL & INSTALLATION

▶ **See Figure 64**

Hoses can be removed or installed with pliers or a screwdriver. Some cars use spring type clamps while others use screw type clamps. If spring type clamps are used, it is recommended to remove these with hose clamp pliers to avoid pinching your fingers.

1. Drain the radiator.

✳✳CAUTION

When draining the coolant, keep in mind that cats and dogs are attracted by ethylene glycol antifreeze, and are quite likely to drink any that is left in an uncovered container or in puddles on the ground. This will prove fatal in sufficient quantity. Always drain the coolant into a sealable container. Coolant should be reused unless it is contaminated or several years old.

2. Remove the hose clamps.

3. Pull the hose off the fittings on the radiator and engine.
To install:
4. Install a new hose. A small amount of soapy water on the inside of the hose end will ease installation.

➡**Radiator hoses should be routed with no kinks and routed as the original. Use of molded hoses is not recommended.**

5. Refill the cooling system and check the level.

Cooling System

▶ **See Figures 65 and 66**

✳✳CAUTION

Never remove the radiator cap under any conditions while the engine is running! Failure to follow these instructions could result in damage to the cooling system or engine and/or in personal injury. To avoid having scalding hot coolant or steam blow out of the radiator, DO NOT remove the cap from a hot radiator. Wait until the engine has cooled sufficiently, then wrap a thick cloth around the radiator cap and turn it SLOWLY to the first stop. Step back while the pressure is released from the cooling system. When you are sure the pressure has been released, press down on the radiator cap (still have the cloth in position) turn and remove the radiator cap.

INSPECTION

At least once every 2 years, the engine cooling system should be inspected, flushed, and refilled with fresh coolant. If the coolant is left in the system too long, it loses its ability to prevent rust and corrosion. If the coolant has been diluted with too much water, it won't protect against freezing.

The radiator cap should be examined for signs of age or deterioration. Fan belts should be inspected and, if necessary, adjusted to the proper tension (please refer to Belt Adjustment in this section).

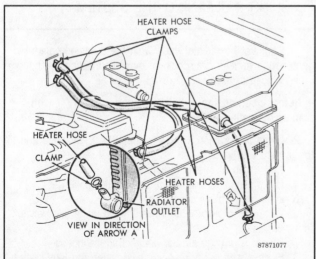

Fig. 64 Heater hose routing for 1978-83 vehicles. Other models are similar

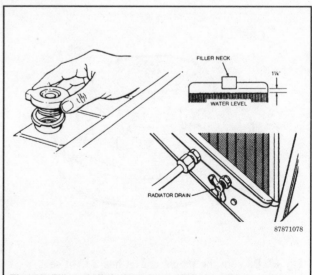

Fig. 65 Fill and drain locations of the cooling system

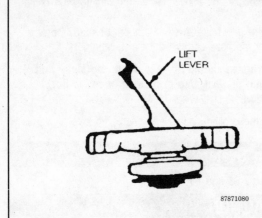

Fig. 66 On radiator caps equipped with a top lever, lift the lever to release pressure

Hose clamps should be tightened, and soft or cracked hoses replaced. Damp spots, or accumulations of rust or dye near hoses, the water pump or other areas, indicate possible leakage. This must be corrected before filling the system with fresh coolant.

Checking The Radiator Cap

◆ See Figure 67

While you are checking the coolant level, check the radiator cap for a worn or cracked gasket. If the cap doesn't seal properly, fluid will be lost in the form of steam and the engine will overheat. If necessary, replace the cap with a new one.

Radiator Debris

◆ See Figure 68

Periodically clean any debris (leaves, paper, insects, etc.) from the radiator fins. Pick the large pieces off by hand. The smaller pieces can be washed away with water pressure from a hose.

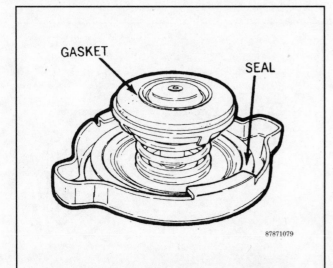

Fig. 67 Be sure the rubber gasket has a tight seal

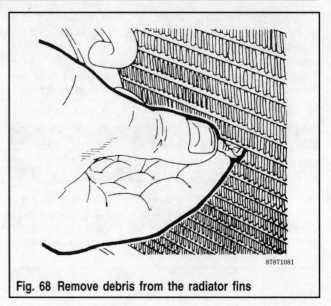

Fig. 68 Remove debris from the radiator fins

Carefully straighten any bent radiator fins with a pair of needle nose pliers. Be careful; the fins are very soft! Don't wiggle the fins back and forth too much. Straighten them once and try not to move them again.

FLUID RECOMMENDATIONS

Coolant used is normally a 50/50 mixture of ethylene glycol and water which can be used year round. Always use a good quality antifreeze with water pump lubricants, rust and other corrosion inhibitors, and acid neutralizers. Also available is another type of antifreeze, propylene glycol, which is non-toxic. Keep in mind that should you decide to use a propylene glycol antifreeze, you should follow the antifreeze manufacturer's instructions closely. Do not mix ethylene and propylene glycol together, as the benefits of the non-toxic propylene glycol would be lost. In the event you decide to change to propylene glycol, make sure to completely flush the cooling system of all ethylene glycol traces.

FLUSHING & CLEANING THE SYSTEM

1. Remove the radiator cap. Drain the existing coolant by opening the radiator draincock, or by disconnecting the bottom radiator hose at the radiator outlet.

➡Before opening the radiator draincock, spray it with some penetrating lubricant.

2. Close the draincock or re-connect the lower hose and fill the system with water.
3. Add a can of quality radiator flush.
4. Idle the engine until the upper radiator hose gets hot.
5. Drain the system again.
6. Repeat this process until the drained water is clear and free of scale.
7. Close all draincocks and connect all the hoses.
8. Flush the recovery reservoir with water and leave empty.

9. Determine the capacity of your cooling system, then add a 50/50 mix of quality antifreeze and water to provide the desired protection.

10. Run the engine to operating temperature.

11. Stop the engine and check the coolant level.

12. Check the level of protection with an antifreeze tester, replace the cap and check for leaks.

Air Conditioning

SAFETY WARNINGS

❄❄CAUTION

Because of the inherent dangers involved with working on air conditioning systems and R-12 refrigerant, NO-ONE should attempt to service their system unless they have the proper training and certification as well access to the necessary tools. When servicing an air conditioning system, all safety precautions must be strictly followed.

1. Avoid contact with a charged refrigeration system, even when working on another part of the air conditioning system or vehicle. If a heavy tool comes into contact with a section of tubing or a heat exchanger, it can easily cause the relatively soft material to rupture.

2. When it is necessary to apply force to a fitting which contains refrigerant, as when checking that all system couplings are securely tightened, use a wrench on both parts of the fitting involved, if possible. This will avoid putting torque on refrigerant tubing. (It is advisable, when possible, to use tube or line wrenches when tightening these flare nut fittings.)

➡**R-12 refrigerant is a chlorofluorocarbon which, when released into the atmosphere, can contribute to the depletion of the ozone layer in the upper atmosphere. Ozone filters out harmful radiation from the sun.**

3. Do not attempt to discharge the system by merely loosening a fitting, or removing the service valve caps and cracking these valves. Precise control is possible only when using the service gauges and a proper A/C refrigerant recovery station. Wear protective gloves when connecting or disconnecting service gauge hoses.

➡**Be sure to consult the laws in your area before servicing the air conditioning system. In many areas, it is illegal to perform repairs involving refrigerant unless the work is performed by a certified technician. Also, laws often restrict the sale of R-12 refrigerant only to people with proper certification.**

4. Work on the system only in a well ventilated area, should high concentrations of the gas accidentally escape it could exclude oxygen and act as an anesthetic. When leak testing or soldering, this is particularly important, as toxic gas is formed when R-12 contacts any flame.

5. Never start a system without first verifying that both service valves are properly installed, and that all fittings throughout the system are snugly connected.

6. Avoid applying heat to any refrigerant line or storage vessel. Charging may be aided by using water heated to less than 125°F (50°C) to warm the refrigerant container. Never allow a refrigerant storage container to sit out in the sun, or near any other source of heat, such as a radiator.

7. Always wear goggles to protect your eyes when working on a system. If refrigerant contacts the eyes, it is advisable in all cases to see a physician as soon as possible.

8. Frostbite from liquid refrigerant should be treated by first gradually warming the area with cool water, and then gently applying petroleum jelly. A physician should be consulted.

9. Always keep refrigerant drum fittings capped when not in use. If the container is equipped with a safety cap to protect the valve, make sure the cap is in place when the can is not being used. Avoid sudden shock to the drum, which might occur from dropping it, or from banging a heavy tool against it. Never carry a drum in the passenger compartment of a car.

10. Always completely discharge the system into a suitable recovery unit before painting the vehicle (if the paint is to be baked on), or before welding anywhere near refrigerant lines.

11. When servicing the system, minimize the time that any refrigerant line or fitting is open to the air in order to prevent moisture or dirt from entering the system. Contaminants such as moisture or dirt can damage internal system components. Always replace O-rings on lines or fittings which are disconnected. Prior to installation coat, but do not soak, replacement O-rings with suitable compressor oil.

GENERAL SERVICING PROCEDURES

The most important aspect of air conditioning service is the maintenance of a pure and adequate charge of refrigerant in the system. A refrigeration system cannot function properly if a significant percentage of the charge is lost. Leaks are common because the severe vibration encountered underhood in an automobile can easily cause cracking or loosening of the air conditioning fittings; allowing, the extreme operating pressures of the system to force refrigerant out.

The problem can be understood by considering what happens to the system as it is operated with a continuous leak. Because the expansion valve regulates the flow of refrigerant to the evaporator, the level of refrigerant there is fairly constant. The receiver/drier stores any excess of refrigerant, and so a loss will first appear there as a reduction in the level of liquid. As this level nears the bottom of the vessel, some refrigerant vapor bubbles will begin to appear in the stream of liquid supplied to the expansion valve. This vapor decreases the capacity of the expansion valve very little as the valve opens to compensate for its presence. As the quantity of liquid in the condenser decreases, the operating pressure will drop there and throughout the high side of the system. As the R-12 continues to be expelled, the pressure available to force the liquid through the expansion valve will continue to decrease, and, eventually, the valve's orifice will prove to be too much of a restriction for adequate flow even with the needle fully withdrawn.

At this point, low side pressure will start to drop, and a severe reduction in cooling capacity, marked by freeze-up of the evaporator coil, will result. Eventually, the operating pressure of the evaporator will be lower than the pressure of the atmosphere surrounding it, and air will be drawn into the system wherever there are leaks in the low side.

Because all atmospheric air contains at least some moisture, water will enter the system mixing with the R-12 and the oil. Trace amounts of moisture will cause slugging of the oil, and corrosion of the system. Saturation and clogging of the filter/drier, and freezing of the expansion valve orifice will eventually result. As air fills the system to a greater and greater extent, it will interfere more and more with the normal flows of refrigerant and heat.

From this description, it should be obvious how essential it is to find leaks, repair them, and then restore the purity and quantity of the refrigerant charge. A list of general rules should be followed in addition to all safety precautions:

1. Keep all tools as clean and dry as possible.

2. Thoroughly purge the service gauges and hoses of air and moisture before connecting them to the system. Keep them capped when not in use.

3. Thoroughly clean any refrigerant fitting before disconnecting it, in order to minimize the entrance of dirt into the system.

4. Plan any operation that requires opening the system beforehand, in order to minimize the length of time it will be exposed to open air. Cap or seal the open ends to minimize the entrance of foreign material.

5. When adding oil, pour it through an extremely clean and dry tube or funnel. Keep the oil capped whenever possible. Do not use oil that has not been kept tightly sealed.

6. Use only R-12 refrigerant. Purchase refrigerant intended for use only in automatic air conditioning systems.

7. Completely evacuate any system that has been opened to replace a component, or that has leaked sufficiently to draw in moisture and air. This requires evacuating air and moisture with a good vacuum pump for at least one hour. If a system has been open for a considerable length of time it may be advisable to evacuate the system for up to 12 hours (overnight).

8. Whenever possible, use a wrench on both halves of a fitting that is to be connected/disconnected, so as to avoid placing torque on any of the refrigerant lines.

9. When overhauling a compressor, pour some of the oil into a clean glass and inspect it. If there is evidence of dirt or metal particles, or both, flush all refrigerant components with clean refrigerant before evacuating and recharging the system. In addition, if metal particles are present, the compressor should be replaced.

10. Schrader valves may leak only when under full operating pressure. Therefore, if leakage is suspected but cannot be located, operate the system with a full charge of refrigerant and look for leaks from all Schrader valves. Replace any faulty valves.

SYSTEM INSPECTION

➡**R-12 refrigerant is a chlorofluorocarbon which, when released into the atmosphere, can contribute to the depletion of the ozone layer in the upper atmosphere. Ozone filters out harmful radiation from the sun.**

The easiest and often most important check for the air conditioning system consists of a visual inspection of the system components. Visually inspect the air conditioning system for refrigerant leaks, damaged compressor clutch, compressor drive belt tension and condition, plugged evaporator drain tube, blocked condenser fins, disconnected or broken wires, blown fuses, corroded connections and poor insulation.

A refrigerant leak will usually appear as an oily residue at the leakage point in the system. The oily residue soon picks up dust or dirt particles from the surrounding air and appears greasy. Through time, this will build up and appear to be a heavy dirt impregnated grease. Most leaks are caused by damaged or missing O-ring seals at the component connections, damaged charging valve cores or missing service gauge port caps.

For a thorough visual and operational inspection, check the following:

1. Check the surface of the radiator and condenser for dirt, leaves or other material which might block air flow.

2. Check for kinks in hoses and lines. Check the system for leaks.

3. Make sure the drive belt is under the proper tension. When the air conditioning is operating, make sure the drive belt is free of noise or slippage.

4. Make sure the blower motor operates at all appropriate positions, then check for distribution of the air from all outlets with the blower on HIGH.

➡**Keep in mind that under conditions of high humidity, air discharged from the A/C vents may not feel as cold as expected, even if the system is working properly. This is because the vaporized moisture in humid air retains heat more effectively than does dry air, making the humid air more difficult to cool.**

5. Start the engine and warm it to normal operating temperature, then make sure the hot/cold selection lever is operating correctly.

Checking for Oil Leaks

Refrigerant leaks show up as oily areas on the various components because the compressor oil is transported around the entire system along with the refrigerant. Look for oily spots on all the hoses and lines, and especially on the hose and tubing connections. If there are oily deposits, the system may have a leak, and you should have it checked by a qualified repairman.

➡**A small area of oil on the front of the compressor is normal and no cause for alarm.**

Keep the Condenser Clear

Periodically inspect the front of the condenser for bent fins or foreign material (dirt, bugs, leaves, etc.) If any cooling fins are bent, straighten them carefully with needle nosed pliers. You can remove any debris with a stiff bristle brush or hose.

Operate the A/C System Periodically

A lot of A/C problems can be avoided by simply running the air conditioner at least once a week, regardless of the season. Simply let the system run for at least 5 minutes a week (even in the winter), and you'll keep the internal parts lubricated as well as preventing the hoses from hardening.

REFRIGERANT LEVEL CHECK

▶ See Figure 69

The first order of business when checking the sight glass is to find it. It will be in the head of the receiver/drier. In some cases, it may be covered by a small rubber plug designed to keep it clean. Once you've found it, remove the cover, if necessary, wipe it clean and proceed as follows:

1. With the engine and the air conditioning system running, look for the flow of refrigerant through the sight glass. If the air conditioner is working properly, you'll be able to see a continuous flow of clear refrigerant through the sight glass, with perhaps an occasional bubble at very high outside temperatures.

2. Cycle the air conditioner on and off to make sure what you are seeing is a pure stream of liquid refrigerant. Since the refrigerant is clear, it is possible to mistake a completely discharged system for one that is fully charged. Turn the system off and watch the sight glass. If there is refrigerant in the system, you'll see bubbles during the off cycle. Also, the lines going into and out of the compressor will be at radically different temperatures (be careful about touching the line going forward to the condenser, which is in front of the radiator, as it will be very hot). If the bubbles disappear just after you start the compressor, there are no bubbles when the system is running, and the air flow from the unit in the car is cold, everything is O.K.

3. If you observe bubbles in the sight glass while the system is operating, the system is low on refrigerant. You may want to charge it yourself, as described later. Otherwise, have it checked by a professional.

4. If all you can see in the sight glass is oil streaks, this is an indication of trouble. This is true because there is no liquid refrigerant in the system (otherwise, the oil would mix with the refrigerant and would be invisible). Most of the time, if you see oil in the sight glass, it will appear as a series of streaks, although occasionally it may be a solid stream of oil. In either case, it means that part of the charge of refrigerant has been lost.

✳✳WARNING

Refrigerant work is usually performed by highly trained technicians. Improper use of the gauges can result in a leakage of refrigerant liquid, damage to the compressor, or even explosion of a system part. The do-it-yourselfer must be very careful to insure that he proceeds with extreme care and understands what he is doing before proceeding. The best insurance for safety is a complete understanding of the system and proper techniques for servicing it. Keep in mind that in many states it's illegal to service these systems if you're not certified.

GAUGE SETS

▶ See Figure 70

Generally described, this tool is a set of two gauges, a manifold and three hoses. By connecting the proper hoses to the car's system, the gauges can be used to "see" the air conditioning system at work.

DISCHARGING, EVACUATING AND CHARGING

Discharging, evacuating and charging the air conditioning system must be performed by properly trained and certified mechanic in a facility equipped with refrigerant recovery/recycling equipment that meets SAE standards for the type of system to be serviced.

If you don't have access to the necessary equipment, we recommend that you take your vehicle to a reputable service station to have the work done. If you still wish to perform repairs on the vehicle, have them discharge the system, then take your car home and perform the necessary work. When you are finished, return the vehicle to the station for evacuating and charging. Just be sure to cap ALL A/C system fittings

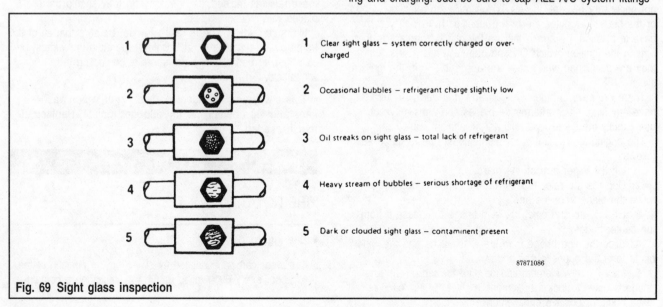

1 Clear sight glass — system correctly charged or over-charged

2 Occasional bubbles — refrigerant charge slightly low

3 Oil streaks on sight glass — total lack of refrigerant

4 Heavy stream of bubbles — serious shortage of refrigerant

5 Dark or clouded sight glass — contaminant present

87871086

Fig. 69 Sight glass inspection

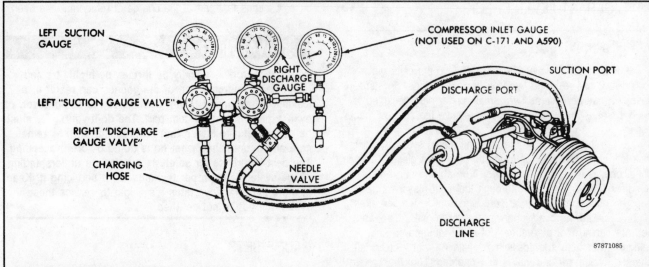

Fig. 70 The manifold gauge set can be used to "see" inside the air conditioning system

immediately after opening them and keep them protected until the system is recharged.

Windshield Wipers

Intense heat from the sun, snow and ice, road oils and the chemicals used in windshield washer solvents combine to deteriorate the rubber wiper refills. The refills should be replaced about twice a year or whenever the blades begin to streak or chatter.

REMOVAL & INSTALLATION

Wiper Refill
▶ **See Figure 71**

Normally, if the wipers are not cleaning the windshield properly, only the refill has to be replaced. The blade and arm usually require replacement only in the vent of damage. It is not necessary (except on new Tridon refills) to remove the arm or the blade to replace the refill (rubber part), though you may have to position the arm higher on the glass. You can do this turning the ignition switch **ON** and operating the wipers. When they are positioned where they are accessible, turn the ignition switch **OFF**.

There are several types of refills and your vehicle could have any kind, since aftermarket blades and arms may not use exactly the same type refill as the original equipment.

The original equipment wiper elements can be replaced as follows:
1. Lift the wiper arm off the glass.
2. Depress the release lever on the center bridge and remove the blade from the arm.
3. Lift the tab and pinch the end bridge to release it from the center bridge.
4. Slide the end bridge from the wiper blade and the wiper blade form the opposite end bridge.
5. Install a new element and be sure the tab on the end bridge is down to lock the element in place. Check each release point for positive engagement.

Most Trico styles use a release button that is pushed down to allow the refill to slide out of the yoke jaws. The new refill slides in and locks in place. Some Trico refills are removed by locating where the metal backing strip or the refill is wider. Insert a small screwdriver blade between the frame and metal backing strip. Press down to release the refill from the retaining tab.

The Anco style is unlocked at one end by squeezing 2 metal tabs, and the refill is slid out of the frame jaws. When the new refill is installed, the tabs will click into place, locking the refill.

The polycarbonate type is held in place by a locking lever that is pushed downward out of the groove in the arm to free the refill. When the new refill is installed, it will lock in place automatically.

The Tridon refill has a plastic backing strip with a notch about an inch from the end. Hold the blade (frame) on a hard surface so that the frame is tightly bowed. Grip the tip of the backing strip and pull up while twisting counterclockwise. The backing strip will snap out of the retaining tab. Do this for the remaining tabs until the refill is free of the arm. The length of these refills is molded into the end and they should be replaced with identical types.

No matter which type of refill you use, be sure that all of the frame claws engage the refill. Before operating the wipers, be sure that no part of the metal frame is contacting the windshield.

➡ **It is always a good idea to check your wiper washer lines and tee opening for any clogged points. Replace either if needed.**

Tires

TIRE ROTATION

▶ **See Figure 72**

Tire wear can be equalized by switching the position of the tires about every 6000 miles (9654 km). Including a conven-

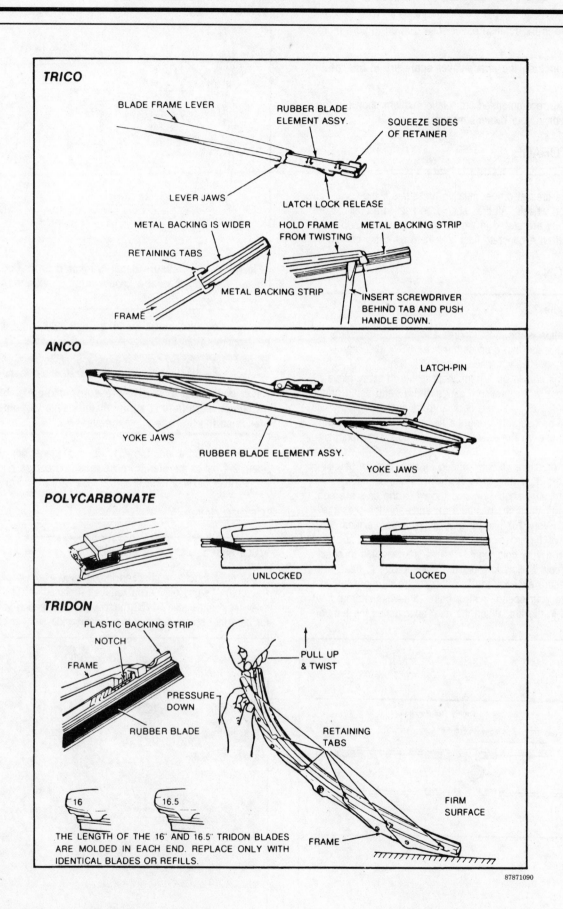

TRICO

BLADE FRAME LEVER

RUBBER BLADE ELEMENT ASSY.

SQUEEZE SIDES OF RETAINER

LEVER JAWS

LATCH LOCK RELEASE

METAL BACKING IS WIDER

RETAINING TABS

FRAME

METAL BACKING STRIP

HOLD FRAME FROM TWISTING

METAL BACKING STRIP

INSERT SCREWDRIVER BEHIND TAB AND PUSH HANDLE DOWN.

ANCO

LATCH-PIN

YOKE JAWS

RUBBER BLADE ELEMENT ASSY.

YOKE JAWS

POLYCARBONATE

UNLOCKED

LOCKED

TRIDON

PLASTIC BACKING STRIP

NOTCH

FRAME

PRESSURE DOWN

RUBBER BLADE

PULL UP & TWIST

RETAINING TABS

FIRM SURFACE

FRAME

16   16.5

THE LENGTH OF THE 16" AND 16.5" TRIDON BLADES ARE MOLDED IN EACH END. REPLACE ONLY WITH IDENTICAL BLADES OR REFILLS.

87871090

Fig. 71 Replacing the different styles of inserts

tional spare in the rotation pattern can give up to 20% more tire life.

➡**Do not include the space-saver spare tire in the rotation pattern.**

Follow the recommended tire rotation pattern shown in the illustration or in your owner's manual.

TIRE STORAGE

Store the tires at proper inflation pressures if they are mounted on wheels. All tires should be kept in a cool, dry place. If they are stored in the garage or basement, do not let them stand on a concrete floor; set them on strips of wood.

INFLATION

▸ **See Figure 73**

Tire inflation is the most ignored item of auto maintenance. Gasoline mileage can drop as much as 0.8% for every 1 pound per square inch (psi) of under inflation.

Two items should be a permanent fixture in every glove compartment; a tire pressure gauge and a tread depth gauge. Check the tire air pressure (including the spare) regularly with a pocket type gauge. Kicking the tires won't tell you a thing, and the gauge on the service station air hose is notoriously inaccurate.

The tire pressures recommended for your car are usually found on the door post or in the owner's manual. Ideally, inflation pressure should be checked when the tires are cool. When the air becomes heated it expands and the pressure increases. Every 10° rise (or drop) in temperature means a difference of 1 psi, which also explains why the tire appears to lose air on a very cold night. When it is impossible to check the tires "cold," allow for pressure build-up due to heat. If the "hot" pressure exceeds the "cold" pressure by more than 15 psi, reduce your speed, load or both. Otherwise internal heat is created in the tire. When the heat approaches the tempera-

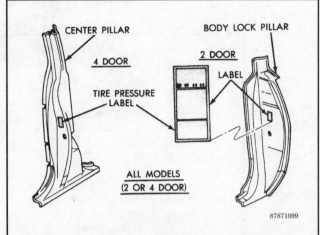

Fig. 73 A tire pressure decal is located on the door pillar. Keeping tires at a proper inflation extends their life

ture at which the tire was cured, during manufacture, the tread can separate from the body.

✳✳WARNING

Never counteract excessive pressure build-up by bleeding off air pressure (letting some air out). This will only further raise the tire operating temperature.

Before starting a long trip with lots of luggage, you can add about 2-4 psi to the tires to make them run cooler, but never exceed the maximum inflation pressure on the side of the tire.

INSPECTION

▸ **See Figures 74, 75, 76 and 77**

The tires should be checked for damage at every oil change. Any cuts or signs of bulging requires replacement of the tire.

All tires made since 1968, have 8 built-in tread wear indicator bars that show up as ½ in. (13mm) wide smooth bands

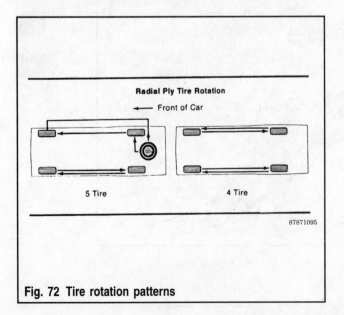

Fig. 72 Tire rotation patterns

Fig. 74 Always inspect the tires for any cuts or bulging

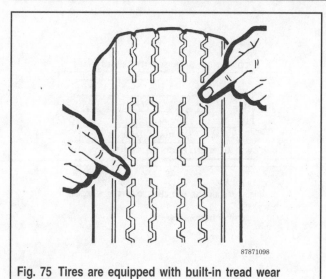

Fig. 75 Tires are equipped with built-in tread wear indicators

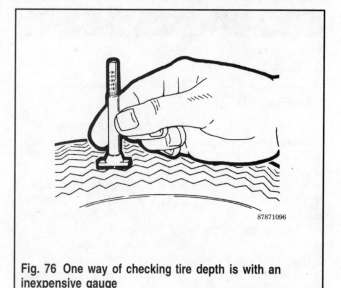

Fig. 76 One way of checking tire depth is with an inexpensive gauge

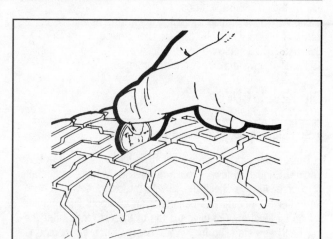

Fig. 77 Tread depth can also be roughly checked with a Lincoln head penny. If the top of the head is visible, replace the tire

across the tire when ¹/₁₆ in. (2mm) of tread remains. The appearance of tread wear indicators means that the tires should be replaced. In fact, many states have laws prohibiting the use of tires with less than ¹/₁₆ in. (2mm) tread.

You can check your own tread depth with an inexpensive gauge or by using a Lincoln head penny. Slip the Lincoln penny into several tread grooves. If you can see the top of Lincoln's head in 2 adjacent grooves, the tires have less than ¹/₁₆ in. (2mm) tread left and should be replaced. You can measure snow tires in the same manner by using the "tails" side of the Lincoln penny. If you can see the top of the Lincoln memorial, it's time to replace the snow tires.

FLUIDS AND LUBRICANTS

Fluid Disposal

Used fluids such as engine oil, transaxle fluid, antifreeze and brake fluid are hazardous wastes which must be disposed of properly. Before draining any fluids, consult with local authorities; in many cases, waste oil, etc., is accepted in recycling programs. A number of service stations and auto parts stores are also accepting waste fluids for recycling.

Be sure of the recycling center's policies before draining the fluids, as many will not accept mixed fluids such as oil and antifreeze.

Fuel Recommendations

Only gasoline with a 91 Research Octane Number (RON) or an octane value of 87 (or higher) if using the (R+M)/2 method, should be used. Unleaded gasoline must be used in those cars with a catalytic converter. These cars have specially designed filler necks that prevent the direct insertion of the leaded gasoline pump nozzle.

Avoid the constant use of fuel system cleaning agents. Many of these materials contain highly active solvents that will deteriorate the gasket and diaphragm materials used on these carburetors.

Engine

FLUID RECOMMENDATIONS

▶ **See Figures 78 and 79**

Oils and lubricants are classified and graded according to standards established by the Society of Automotive Engineers (SAE), American Petroleum Institute (API), and the National Lubricating Grease Institute (NLGI).

Oils are classified by the SAE and API designations, found on the top of the oil can, such as SAE 5W-30, SAE 10W-30, etc. The SAE grade number indicates the viscosity of engine oils. Chrysler prefers the use of SAE 5W-30 for when minimum temperatures consistently fall below -10°F (-23°C). Chrysler does not recommend the use of SAE 5W-30 and 5W-40 in turbocharged engines in ambient temperatures above 60°F (15°C). or the use of SAE 10W-40 or SAE 10W-50 in any of their 1988-89 vehicles.

The API classification system defines oil performance in terms of usage. Only oils designed for service SF or SF/CD, SG or SG/CD should be used. These oils provide sufficient additives to give maximum engine protection.

OIL LEVEL CHECK

▶ **See Figures 80, 81, 82 and 83**

The engine oil dipstick is located on the radiator side of the engine. Engine oil level should be checked weekly as a matter of course. Always check the oil with the car on level ground and after the engine has been shut off for about five minutes.

The oil level may read at the top of the full range after the car has been standing for several hours. When the engine is started, the level will drop, due to oil passages filling, but the level should never be allowed to remain below the ADD mark.

1. Remove the dipstick and wipe it clean.
2. Reinsert the dipstick.

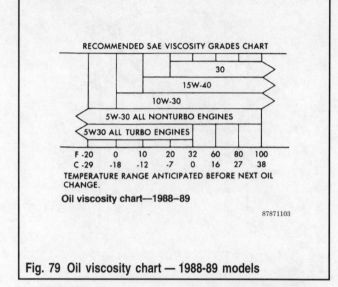

Fig. 79 Oil viscosity chart — 1988-89 models

Fig. 80 The engine oil dipstick is located on the radiator side of the engine, pull it out to check the level

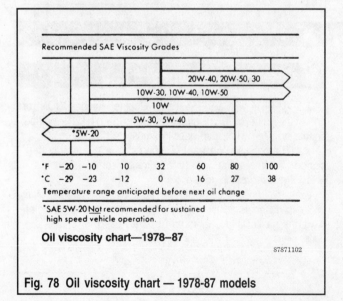

Fig. 78 Oil viscosity chart — 1978-87 models

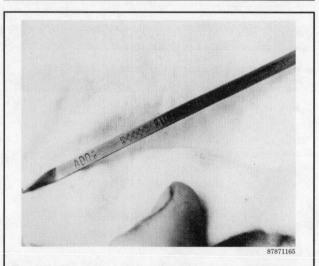

Fig. 81 After removing the dipstick, wipe it clean and reinsert it

3. Remove the dipstick again. The oil level should be between the two marks. The difference between the marks is one quart.

4. Add oil through the capped opening on the top of the valve cover.

5. After inserting oil, recheck the level again.

OIL AND FILTER CHANGE

▶ See Figures 84, 85, 86 and 87

Under normal service, the engine oil and filter should be changed every 12 months or 7500 miles (12,067 km), whichever comes first.

Under the following conditions, change the engine oil and filter every 3 months or 3000 miles (4827 km), whichever comes first:

- Frequent driving in dusty conditions
- Frequent trailer pulling
- Extensive idling
- Frequent short trip driving, less than 10 miles (16 km)
- More than 50% operation at sustained high speeds, over 70 mph (112 km)

➡ Drain the engine oil when the engine is at normal operating temperature.

To change the oil, the vehicle should be on a level surface at normal operating temperature. This ensures that you will drain away the foreign matter in the oil, which will not happen if the engine is cold. Oil which is slightly dirty when drained is a good sign. This means that the contaminants are being drained away and not being left behind to form sludge.

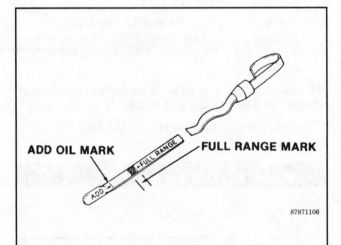

Fig. 82 Remove the dipstick again. The oil level should be between the two marks

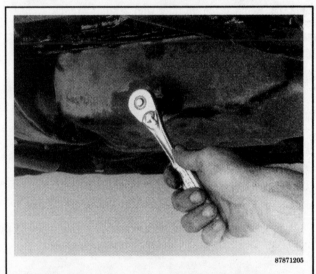

Fig. 84 Loosen, but do not remove the drain plug

Fig. 83 If necessary, add the oil through the opening of the valve cover.

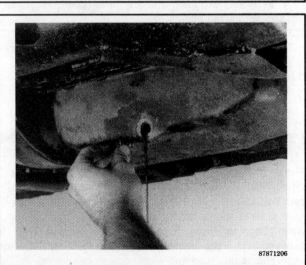

Fig. 85 Keep inward pressure while unscrewing the plug, then quickly pull it away

Fig. 86 Remove the oil filter with a strap wrench

Fig. 87 Before installing a new oil filter, coat the rubber gasket with clean engine oil

You should have available some means to support the car, a ½ in. (13 mm) wrench, a filter wrench, 4 quarts of oil, a drain pan and some rags.

1. Jack up the front of the car and support it.
2. Position the drain pan under the drain plug, which is located at the rear of the oil pan.

❋❋CAUTION

The EPA warns that prolonged contact with used engine oil may cause a number of skin disorders, including cancer! You should make every effort to minimize your exposure to used engine oil. Protective gloves should be worn when changing the oil. Wash your hands and any other exposed skin areas as soon as possible after exposure to used engine oil. Soap and water, or waterless hand cleaner should be used.

3. Loosen, but do not remove the drain plug. Cover your hand with a heavy rag and slowly unscrew the drain plug. Pushing the plug against the threads in the oil pan will prevent hot oil from running down your arm. As the drain plug comes to the end of the threads, quickly pull it away and allow all of the oil to drain into the pan.

4. When all the oil has drained, replace the drain plug and tighten it.

➡**Be sure to dispose of the old oil in an environmentally safe manner.**

5. Remove the oil filter. It can only be removed with the tools shown, from below the car. Once the filter is loose, cover your hand with a thick rag and spin it off by hand.

➡**On May 29, 1979, the assembly plant began installing 4 in. (101mm) diameter oil filters in place of the previously used 3 in. (76mm) diameter filters. The 4 in. (101mm) filters are the same as those used on other Chrysler vehicles and should be used for service.**

6. Coat the rubber gasket on a new filter with clean engine oil and install the new filter. Tighten it by hand until the gasket contacts the mounting base and then ¾-1 turn further.

7. Refill the engine with 4 quarts of fresh oil of the proper viscosity according to the anticipated temperatures before the next oil change.

➡**It requires 4 quarts of oil to fill the engine regardless of whether the filter was changed or not.**

8. Run the engine for a few minutes and check the oil level.

Manual Transaxle

FLUID RECOMMENDATIONS

◆ **See Figure 88**

The A-412 transaxle is a VW design and is the only model to use Hypoid gear lubricant. The A-412 transaxle can be easily identified from the Chrysler design models because the starter motor is located on the radiator side of the engine compartment. If it becomes necessary to add or change the fluid to the unit, lubricant conforming to API GL 4 specifications should be used. The recommended SAE grade should be selected from the chart.

All other manual transaxles through 1986, use only automatic transaxle fluid labeled DEXRON®II or it's superseding type. Starting in 1987, Chrysler recommends using SAE 5W-30 SF engine oil in all their manual transaxles.

LEVEL CHECK

◆ **See Figure 89**

The fluid level in the manual transaxle should be checked twice a year. Maintain the fluid level at the bottom of the filler plug opening.

To check the fluid level, position the car on a level surface and clean the dirt from around the transaxle filler plug. Remove the filler plug. The level should at least reach the bottom of the hole. You can check the level with your finger or a piece of bent wire.

Anticipated Temperature Range	Recommended SAE Grade
Above — 10° F.	90, 80W–90, 85W–90
As low as — 30° F.	80W, 80W–90, 85W–90
Below — 30° F.	75W

87871111

Fig. 88 A-412 transaxle lubricant recommendations

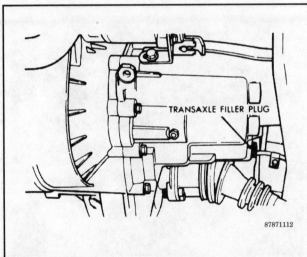

87871112

Fig. 89 Once you have located the plug, remove it. The level should at least reach the bottom of the hole

DRAIN AND REFILL

Under normal conditions, the manual transaxle fluid will never need changing. Rare circumstances, such as the fluid becoming contaminated with water will necessitate fluid replacement.

It is relatively easy to change your own transaxle oil. The only equipment required is a drain pan, a wrench to fit the filler and drain plugs, and an oil suction gun. Gear oil and automatic transaxle fluid can be purchased in both quart and gallon cans at automotive supply stores.

To change the oil:

1. Jack up the front of the car and support it safely on stands.
2. Slide drain pan under the transaxle.
3. Remove the filler plug and then the drain plug.
4. When the oil has been completely drained, install the drain plug. Tighten to 18 ft. lbs. (24 Nm).

5. Using the suction gun, refill the transaxle up to the level of the filler plug.
6. Install and tighten the filler plug.

Automatic Transaxle Differential

LEVEL CHECK

On 1978-82 models, the automatic transaxle and differential are contained in the same housing, but the units are sealed from each other. The 1983 and later automatic transaxles are filled as one unit. The transaxle does not have a conventional filler tube, but is filled through a die-cast opening in the case.

The filler hole is plugged during operation by the transaxle dipstick.

The fluid level should be checked every 6 months when the engine and transaxle fluid are warmed to normal operating temperature.

1. Position the car on a level surface.
2. Idle the engine and engage the parking brake.
3. Shift the lever through each gear momentarily and return the lever to PARK.
4. Remove the dipstick and wipe it clean.
5. Reinsert the dipstick and remove it again. The level should be between the ADD and FULL marks on the dipstick. If necessary, add DEXRON®II or it's superseding type automatic transaxle fluid. Do not overfill.

While you are checking the fluid level, check the condition of the fluid. The condition of the fluid will often reveal potential problems.

If the fluid level is consistently low, suspect a leak. The easiest way is to slip a piece of clean newspaper under the car overnight, but this is not always an accurate indication, since some leaks will occur only when the transaxle is operating.

Other leaks can be located by driving the car. Wipe the underside of the transaxle clean and drive the car for several miles/kilometers to bring the fluid temperature to normal. Stop the car, shut off the engine and look for leakage, but remember, that where the fluid is located may not be the source of the leak. Airflow around the transaxle while the car is moving may carry the fluid to other parts of the car.

Automatic Transaxle

FLUID RECOMMENDATIONS

Dexron®II or it's superseding type transaxle fluid is used in the automatic transaxles.

LEVEL CHECK

▶ See Figure 90

Vehicles 1978 through 1982 automatic transaxles have 2 separate reservoirs that require filling separately. The 1983 and later models fill as one unit. Most models have a drain and fill plug in the differential cover; some models will have only a fill plug. Should it become necessary to drain the differential and the cover has only a fill plug, simply remove the cover to drain. A service gasket, should be formed from RTV sealant when the cover is installed. Use a ¹⁄₁₆ in. (2mm) bead of RTV sealant on the cover.

To check the fluid level, remove the filler plug. The level should be at the bottom of the hole, which can be checked with your finger or a piece of bent wire.

DRAIN AND REFILL

▶ **See Figures 91, 92 and 93**

➡**RTV silicone sealer is used in place of a pan gasket.**

Chrysler recommends no fluid or filter changes under normal usage of the car. Severe usage requires a fluid and filter change every 15,000 miles (24,135 km). Severe usage is defined as:

• More than 50% heavy city traffic during 90° or higher weather.

• Police, taxi or commercial operation or trailer towing.

When changing the fluid, only Dexron®II or it's superseding type fluid should be used. A filter change should be performed at every fluid change.

1. Raise the vehicle and support it on jackstands.

2. Place a large container under the pan, loosen the pan bolts and tap at one corner to break it loose. Drain the fluid.

3. When the fluid is drained remove the pan bolts.

4. Remove the retaining screws and replace the filter. Tighten the screws to 35 inch lbs. (4 Nm).

5. Clean the fluid pan, peel off the old RTV silicone sealer and install the pan, using a ¹⁄₈ in. (3mm) bead of new RTV sealer. Always run the sealer bead inside the bolt holes. Tighten the pan bolts to 10-12 ft. lbs. (13-16 Nm).

6. Pour four quarts of Dexron®II or it's superseding type. fluid through the filler tube.

7. Start the engine and idle it for at least 2 minutes. Set the parking brake and move the selector through each position, ending in Park.

Fig. 91 An extension is helpful in removing the pan bolts

Fig. 92 Once the fluid is drained, remove the pan

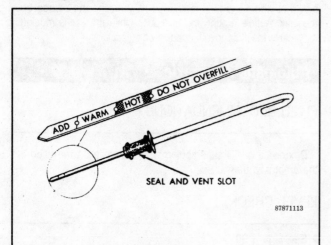
Fig. 90 The level should be between the ADD and FULL marks on the dipstick

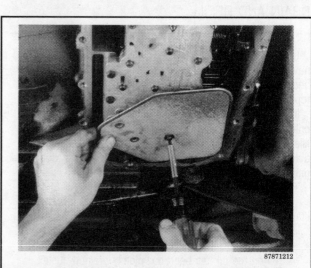
Fig. 93 Remove the retaining screw, then replace the filter with a new one

8. Add sufficient fluid to bring the level to the FULL mark on the dipstick. The level should be checked in Park, with the engine idling at normal operating temperature.

Brake Master Cylinder

LEVEL CHECK

▶ **See Figures 94 and 95**

The brake fluid level should be checked every 6 months.
1. Wipe the area around the master cylinder clean.
2. Remove the master cylinder cap. The fluid level should be within 1/4 in. (6mm) of the top of the reservoir.
3. If necessary, add brake fluid identified on the container as conforming to DOT 3 specifications.

Power Steering Reservoir

LEVEL CHECK

▶ **See Figures 96, 97, 98 and 99**

The power steering reservoir fluid level should be checked with the engine **OFF**. Check the level every 6 months. The fluid level can be checked with the engine either hot or cold.
1. Position the car on a level surface.
2. Wipe the area around the power steering reservoir cap clean and remove the cap.
3. The power steering pump cap has a dipstick attached. Fluid level should be kept at the level indicated on the dipstick.
4. The fluid can be checked with the car cold or hot. The dipstick has markings on both sides.
5. If it is necessary to add fluid, use only MOPAR Power Steering Fluid or the equivalent. DO NOT USE AUTOMATIC TRANSAXLE FLUID.

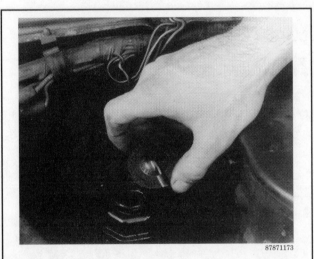

Fig. 94 Once the area around the cap is clean, remove it

Fig. 96 Wipe the area around the power steering reservoir cap clean and remove the cap

Fig. 95 If necessary, add fluid with a clean funnel

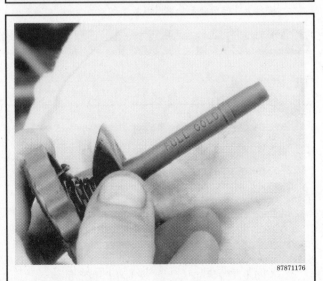

Fig. 97 Cold side marking on the power steering cap

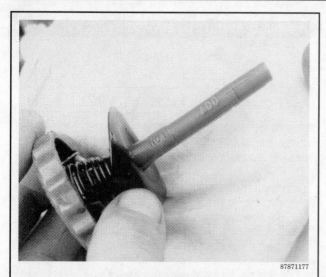

Fig. 98 Hot side marking on the power steering cap

Fig. 99 Add fluid if needed. Use a funnel to help prevent spilling the fluid

6. Replace the cap and tighten in place.

Chassis Greasing

TIE ROD ENDS

There are only 2 points on the car that require periodic greasing. The tie-rod end ball joints are semi-permanently lubricated and should be lubricated every 3 years or 30,000 miles (48,270 km), whichever occurs first. These joints should also be inspected whenever the car is serviced for other reasons. Damaged seals should be replaced.

To lubricate the tie rod end ball joints:
1. Clean the accumulated dirt and grease from the outside of the seal area to permit a close inspection.
2. Clean the grease fitting and surrounding area.
3. Using a grease gun fill the joint with fresh grease.

4. Stop filling when the grease begins to flow freely from the areas at the base of the seal or when the seal begins to balloon.
5. Wipe off the excess grease.

STEERING SHAFT SEAL

The steering shaft seal where the steering shaft passes through the dash is lubricated at manufacture. If the seal becomes noisy when the steering shaft is turned, it should be relubricated with multi-purpose chassis grease, NLGI Grade 2 EP.

BALL JOINTS

The 2 lower front suspension ball joints are permanently lubricated at the factory. Inspect the joints whenever the car is serviced for other reasons. Damaged seals should be replaced to prevent leakage of grease.

CLUTCH CABLE

▶ **See Figure 100**

If the clutch cable begins to make odd noises or if the effort to depress the clutch becomes excessive, lubricate the clutch cable ball end with multi-purpose chassis grease NLGI Grade 2 EP.

FLOORSHIFT CONTROL LINKAGE

▶ **See Figure 101**

The gearshift control linkage should be lubricated whenever the shifting effort becomes excessive or if the linkage exhibits a rattling noise. Use a multi-purpose chassis grease NLGI Grade 2 EP. Remove the unit and lubricate the spherical balls,

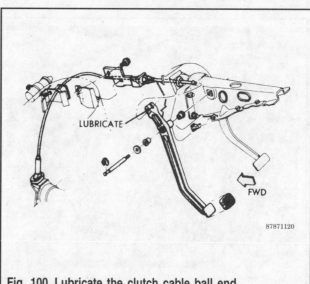

Fig. 100 Lubricate the clutch cable ball end

metal caps and shaft and lubricate each plastic grommet or bushing.

DRIVESHAFT CV-JOINTS

The car has 4 constant velocity joints. No periodic lubrication is required, but the joint seals should be inspected for damage or leakage whenever the car is serviced. If damage is found, replace the CV-joint boot and seal and fill with fresh grease immediately. Failure to do so will eventually require complete replacement of the constant velocity joint.

PARTS REQUIRING NO LUBRICATION

Some components are permanently lubricated. Some parts will be adversely affected by lubricants. In particular, rubber bushings should not be lubricated, since it will destroy their frictional characteristics. Parts that should not be lubricated are:

- Alternator bearings
- Drive belts
- Fan idler belt pulley
- Front wheel bearings
- Rubber bushings
- Starter bearings
- Suspension strut bearing
- Throttle cable control
- Throttle linkage
- Water pump bearings

Body Lubrication

Operating mechanisms of the body should be inspected, cleaned and lubricated as necessary. This will provide maximum protection against rust and wear.

Prior to lubricating, wipe the parts clean of dirt and old lubricant. When Lubriplate® is specified, use a smooth, white body lubricant of NLGI Grade 1. When Door-Ease is specified, use a stainless, wax-type lubricant.

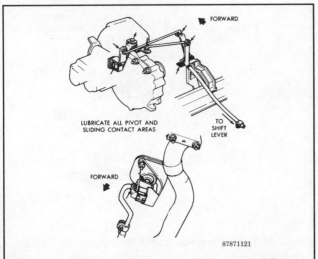

Fig. 101 Lubricate the linkage at all pivot and sliding contact areas

HOOD LATCH AND RELEASE

▶ **See Figure 102**

Apply Lubriplate®, or the equivalent to all pivot and sliding contact areas. Work the lubricant into the lock mechanism. Apply a thin film of the same lubricant to the safety catch.

BODY HINGES

▶ **See Figures 103 and 104**

These parts should be lubricated with engine oil at the points shown in the illustration.

DOOR CHECK STRAPS

▶ **See Figure 104**

Apply Lubriplate® or the equivalent whenever the car is serviced.

LOCK CYLINDERS

Pay particular attention to the lock cylinders when the temperature is around the freezing mark. When necessary, apply a thin film of Lubriplate®, or the equivalent directly to the key and insert the key in the lock. Work the lock several times and wipe the key dry.

Another alternative is to use a commercial spray that is sprayed directly into the lock to prevent freezing.

LIFTGATE PROP PIVOTS AND LATCH

▶ **See Figure 105**

Lubricate at the points illustrated with Lubriplate® or the equivalent.

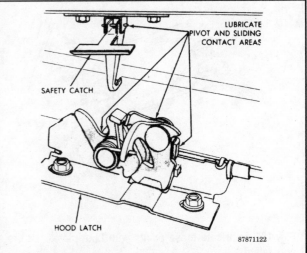

Fig. 102 Apply Lubriplate®, or the equivalent to all pivot and sliding contact areas

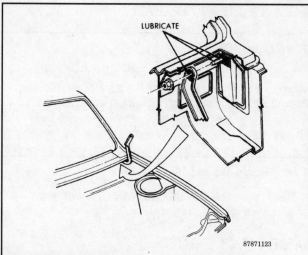

Fig. 103 Lubricate the hood hinges with engine oil at the points shown

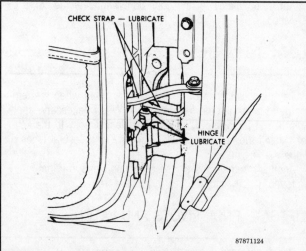

Fig. 104 Lubricate the door hinges and check straps in these locations

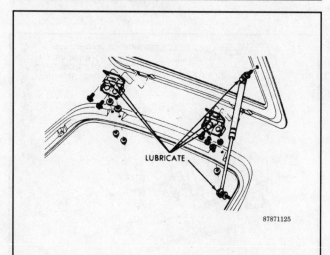

Fig. 105 Lubricate these points with Lubriplate® or the equivalent

DOOR LATCH, LOCK CONTROL, LINKAGE AND WINDOW REGULATOR

To lubricate these parts it is necessary to remove the trim panel. Lubricate all pivot and sliding contact areas with Lubriplate® or the equivalent.

PARKING BRAKE MECHANISM

▶ See Figure 106

Lubricate all parking brake sliding and pivot contact areas with Lubriplate® or the equivalent.

DOOR LATCH AND STRIKER PLATE

▶ See Figure 107

Lubricate the striker plate contact area and the ratchet pivot areas with a stainless, wax-type lubricant such as Door Ease®.

Rear Wheel Bearings

▶ See Figure 108

The front wheel bearings are permanently sealed and require no periodic lubrication.

The rear wheel bearings should be inspected and relubricated whenever the rear brakes are serviced or at least every 30,000 miles (48,270 km). Repack the bearings with high temperature multi-purpose grease.

Check the lubricant to see if it is contaminated. If it contains dirt or has a milky appearance indicating the presence of water, the bearings should be cleaned and repacked.

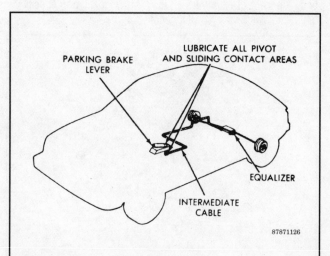

Fig. 106 Lubricate these points with Lubriplate® or the equivalent

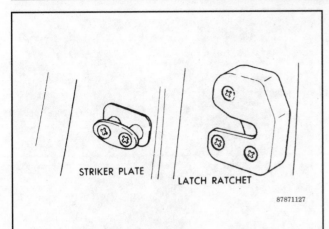

Fig. 107 Lubricate the striker plate contact area and the ratchet pivot areas with a stainless, wax-type lubricant such as Door Ease

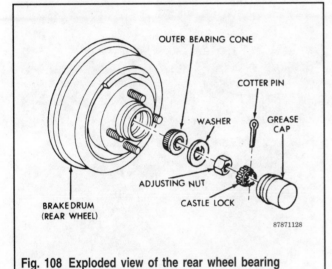

Fig. 108 Exploded view of the rear wheel bearing assembly

Clean the bearings in kerosene, mineral spirits or other suitable cleaning fluid. Do not dry them by spinning the bearings. Allow them to air dry.

➡Sodium-based grease is not compatible with lithium-based grease. Read the package labels and be careful not to mix the two types. If there is any doubt as to the type of grease used, completely clean the old grease from the bearing and hub before replacing.

Before handling the bearings, there are a few things that you should remember to do and not to do.

Remember to DO the following:
- Remove all outside dirt from the housing before exposing the bearing.
- Treat a used bearing as gently as you would a new one.
- Work with clean tools in clean surroundings.
- Use clean, dry canvas gloves, or at least clean, dry hands.
- Clean solvents and flushing fluids are a must.
- Use clean paper when laying out the bearings to dry.

- Protect disassembled bearings from rust and dirt. Cover them up.
- Use clean rags to wipe bearings.
- Keep the bearings in oil-proof paper when they are to be stored or are not in use.
- Clean the inside of the housing before replacing the bearing.

Do NOT do the following:
- Don't work in dirty surroundings.
- Don't use dirty, chipped or damaged tools.
- Try not to work on wooden work benches or use wooden mallets.
- Don't handle bearings with dirty or moist hands.
- Do not use gasoline for cleaning; use a safe solvent.
- Do not spin-dry bearings with compressed air. They will be damaged.
- Do not spin dirty bearings.
- Avoid using cotton waste or dirty cloths to wipe bearings.
- Try not to scratch or nick bearing surfaces.
- Do not allow the bearing to come in contact with dirt or rust at any time.

REMOVAL & INSTALLATION

▶ **See Figures 109, 110, 111, 112, 113, 114, 115 and 116**

For complete removal of the bearing races, please refer to Section 8.

1. Raise and support the car with the rear wheels off the floor.
2. Remove the wheel grease cap, cotter pin, nut lock and bearing adjusting nut.
3. Remove the thrust washer and bearing.
4. Remove the drum from the spindle.
5. Thoroughly clean the old lubricant from the bearings and hub cavity. Inspect the bearing rollers for pitting or other signs of wear. Light discoloration is normal.
6. Repack the bearings with high temperature multi-purpose EP grease and add a small amount of new grease to the hub cavity. Be sure to force the lubricant between all rollers in the bearing.

Fig. 109 Remove the grease cap.

Fig. 110 With pliers, remove the cotter pin, then discard it. Never reuse a cotter pin

Fig. 111 Once the cotter pin is removed, the nut lock can come off

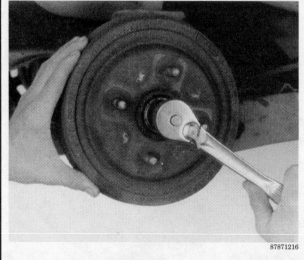

Fig. 112 Loosen and remove the bearing adjusting nut

Fig. 113 Remove the washer . . .

Fig. 114 . . . and the bearing

Fig. 115 Remove the drum from the spindle

TCCS8033

Fig. 116 Thoroughly pack the bearings with fresh, high temperature wheel bearing grease

To install:

7. Install the drum on the spindle after coating the polished spindle surfaces with wheel bearing lubricant.

8. Install the outer bearing cone, thrust washer and adjusting nut.

9. Tighten the adjusting nut to 20-25 ft. lbs. (27-34 Nm) while rotating the wheel.

10. Back off the adjusting nut to completely release the preload from the bearing.

11. Tighten the adjusting nut finger-tight.

12. Position the nut-lock with one pair of slots in line with the cotter pin hole. Install the cotter pin.

13. Clean and install the grease cap and wheel.

14. Lower the car.

TRAILER TOWING

General Recommendations

Your car was primarily designed to carry passengers and cargo. It is important to remember that towing a trailer will place additional loads on your vehicle's engine, drivetrain, steering, braking and other systems. However, if you find it necessary to tow a trailer, using the proper equipment is a must.

Local laws may require specific equipment such as trailer brakes or fender mounted mirrors. Check your local laws.

Trailer Weight

The weight of the trailer is the most important factor. A good weight-to-horsepower ratio is about 35:1, 35 lbs. (16 kg) of GCW (Gross Combined Weight) for every horsepower your engine develops. Multiply the engine's rated horsepower by 35 and subtract the weight of the car passengers and luggage. The result is the approximate ideal maximum weight you should tow, although a a numerically higher axle ratio can help compensate for heavier weight.

Hitch Weight

Figure the hitch weight to select a proper hitch. Hitch weight is usually 9-11% of the trailer gross weight and should be measured with the trailer loaded. Hitches fall into three types: those that mount on the frame and rear bumper or the bolt-on or weld-on distribution type used for larger trailers. Axle mounted or clamp-on bumper hitches should never be used.

Check the gross weight rating of your trailer. Tongue weight is usually figured as 10% of gross trailer weight. Therefore, a trailer with a maximum gross weight of 2000 lb. (907 kg) will

have a maximum tongue weight of 200 lb. Class I trailers fall into this category. Class II trailers are those with a gross weight rating of 2000-3500 lb. (907-1588 kg) Class III trailers fall into the 3500-6000 lb. (1588-2721 kg) category. Class IV trailers are those over 6000 lb. (2721 kg) and are for use with fifth wheel trucks, only.

When you've determined the hitch that you'll need, follow the manufacturer's installation instructions, exactly, especially when it comes to fastener torques. The hitch will subjected to a lot of stress and good hitches come with hardened bolts. Never substitute an inferior bolt for a hardened bolt.

Cooling

ENGINE

One of the most common, if not THE most common, problems associated with trailer towing is engine overheating.

If you have a standard cooling system, without an expansion tank, you'll definitely need to get an aftermarket expansion tank kit, preferably one with at least a 2 quart capacity. These kits are easily installed on the radiator's overflow hose, and come with a pressure cap designed for expansion tanks.

Aftermarket engine oil coolers are helpful for prolonging engine oil life and reducing overall engine temperatures. Both of these factors increase engine life.

While not absolutely necessary in towing Class I and some Class II trailers, they are recommended for heavier Class II and all Class III towing.

Engine oil cooler systems consist of an adapter, screwed on in place of the oil filter, a remote filter mounting and a multi-tube, finned heat exchanger, which is mounted in front of the radiator or air conditioning condenser.

TRANSAXLE

An automatic transaxle is usually recommended for trailer towing. Modern automatics have proven reliable and, of course, easy to operate, in trailer towing.

The increased load of a trailer, however, causes an increase in the temperature of the automatic transaxle fluid. Heat is the worst enemy of an automatic transaxle. As the temperature of the fluid increases, the life of the fluid decreases.

It is essential, therefore, that you install an automatic transaxle cooler.

The cooler, which consists of a multi-tube, finned heat exchanger, is usually installed in front of the radiator or air conditioning compressor, and hooked inline with the transaxle cooler tank inlet line. Follow the cooler manufacturer's installation instructions.

Select a cooler of at least adequate capacity, based upon the combined gross weights of the car and trailer.

Cooler manufacturers recommend that you use an aftermarket cooler in addition to, and not instead of, the present cooling tank in your radiator. If you do want to use it in place of the radiator cooling tank, get a cooler at least two sizes larger than normally necessary.

➡**A transaxle cooler can, sometimes, cause slow or harsh shifting in the transaxle during cold weather, until the fluid has a chance to come up to normal operating temperature. Some coolers can be purchased with or retrofitted with a temperature bypass valve which will allow fluid flow through the cooler only when the fluid has reached operating temperature, or above.**

Handling A Trailer

Towing a trailer with ease and safety requires a certain amount of experience. It's a good idea to learn the feel of a trailer by practicing turning, stopping and backing in an open area such as an empty parking lot.

PUSHING AND TOWING

If your car is equipped with a manual transaxle, it may be push started in an extreme emergency, but there is the possibility of damaging bumpers and/or fenders of both cars. Make sure that the bumpers of both cars are evenly matched. Depress the clutch pedal, select Second or Third gear, and switch the ignition **ON**. When the car reaches a speed of approximately 10 or 15 mph, release the clutch to start the engine. DO NOT ATTEMPT TO PUSH START AN AUTOMATIC

Manual transaxle models may be flat-towed short distances. Attach tow lines to the towing eye on the front suspension or the left or right bumper bracket at the rear. Flat-towing automatic transaxle models is not recommended more than 15 miles (7 km) at more than 30 mph (14 km), and this only in an emergency. Cars equipped with t he automatic should only be towed from the rear when the front wheels are on towing dollies.

JACKING

◗ **See Figures 117, 118 and 119**

Floor jacks can be used to raise the car at the locations shown. Four door models only can be jacked at the extreme rear provided a 2x4x25 in. (minimum dimensions) wood spacer is positioned against the ledge of the rear bumper.

Jack receptacles are located at the front and rear of the body sill for use with jack supplied with a car. Do not use these lift points as bearing points for a floor jack.

TCCS1202

Fig. 117 A hydraulic floor jack and a set of jackstands are essential for lifting and supporting the vehicle

JUMP STARTING A DEAD BATTERY

The chemical reaction in a battery produces explosive hydrogen gas. This is the safe way to jump start a dead battery, reducing the chances of an accidental spark that could cause an explosion.

Fig. 118 Four door models may be raised from the rear bumper

Jump Starting Precautions

- Be sure both batteries are of the same voltage.
- Be sure both batteries are of the same polarity (have the same grounded terminal).
- Be sure the vehicles are not touching.

- Be sure the vent cap holes are not obstructed.
- Do not smoke or allow sparks around the battery.
- In cold weather, check for frozen electrolyte in the battery.
- Do not allow electrolyte on your skin or clothing.
- Be sure the electrolyte is not frozen.

Jump Starting Procedure

1. Determine voltages of the two batteries, they must be the same.
2. Bring the starting vehicle close (they must not touch) so that the batteries can be reached easily.
3. Turn off all accessories and both engines. Put both cars in Neutral or Park and set the handbrake.
4. Cover the cell caps with a rag, do not cover terminals.
5. If the terminals on the run-down battery are heavily corroded, clean them.
6. Identify the positive and negative posts on both batteries and connect the cables in the order shown.
7. Start the engine of the starting vehicle and run it at fast idle. Try to start the car with the dead battery. Crank it for no more than 10 seconds at a time and let it cool off for 20 seconds in between tries.
8. If it doesn't start in 3 tries, there is something else wrong. Or the battery is evenly discharged.
9. Disconnect the cables in the reverse order.
10. Replace the cell covers and dispose of the rags.

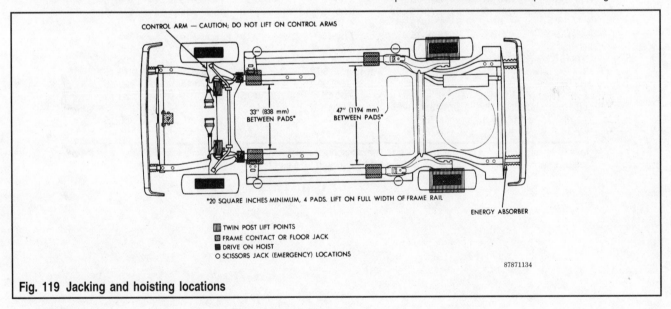

CONTROL ARM — CAUTION; DO NOT LIFT ON CONTROL ARMS

33" (838 mm) BETWEEN PADS*

47" (1194 mm) BETWEEN PADS*

*20 SQUARE INCHES MINIMUM, 4 PADS. LIFT ON FULL WIDTH OF FRAME RAIL

ENERGY ABSORBER

TWIN POST LIFT POINTS
FRAME CONTACT OR FLOOR JACK
DRIVE ON HOIST
O SCISSORS JACK (EMERGENCY) LOCATIONS

Fig. 119 Jacking and hoisting locations

TIRE SIZE COMPARISON

"Letter" sizes			Inch Sizes	Metric-inch Sizes		
"60 Series"	"70 Series"	"78 Series"	1965–77	"60 Series"	"70 Series"	"80 Series"
		Y78-12	5.50-12, 5.60-12 6.00-12	165/60-12	165/70-12	155-12
		W78-13	5.20-13	165/60-13	145/70-13	135-13
		Y78-13	5.60-13	175/60-13	155/70-13	145-13
			6.15-13	185/60-13	165/70-13	155-13, P155/80-13
A60-13	A70-13	A78-13	6.40-13	195/60-13	175/70-13	165-13
B60-13	B70-13	B78-13	6.70-13 6.90-13	205/60-13	185/70-13	175-13
C60-13	C70-13	C78-13	7.00-13	215/60-13	195/70-13	185-13
D60-13	D70-13	D78-13	7.25-13			
E60-13	E70-13	E78-13	7.75-13			195-13
			5.20-14	165/60-14	145/70-14	135-14
			5.60-14	175/60-14	155/70-14	145-14
			5.90-14			
A60-14	A70-14	A78-14	6.15-14	185/60-14	165/70-14	155-14
	B70-14	B78-14	6.45-14	195/60-14	175/70-14	165-14
	C70-14	C78-14	6.95-14	205/60-14	185/70-14	175-14
D60-14	D70-14	D78-14				
E60-14	E70-14	E78-14	7.35-14	215/60-14	195/70-14	185-14
F60-14	F70-14	F78-14, F83-14	7.75-14	225/60-14	200/70-14	195-14
G60-14	G70-14	G77-14, G78-14	8.25-14	235/60-14	205/70-14	205-14
H60-14	H70-14	H78-14	8.55-14	245/60-14	215/70-14	215-14
J60-14	J70-14	J78-14	8.85-14	255/60-14	225/70-14	225-14
L60-14	L70-14		9.15-14	265/60-14	235/70-14	
	A70-15	A78-15	5.60-15	185/60-15	165/70-15	155-15
B60-15	B70-15	B78-15	6.35-15	195/60-15	175/70-15	165-15
C60-15	C70-15	C78-15	6.85-15	205/60-15	185/70-15	175-15
	D70-15	D78-15				
E60-15	E70-15	E78-15	7.35-15	215/60-15	195/70-15	185-15
F60-15	F70-15	F78-15	7.75-15	225/60-15	205/70-15	195-15
G60-15	G70-15	G78-15	8.15-15/8.25-15	235/60-15	215/70-15	205-15
H60-15	H70-15	H78-15	8.45-15/8.55-15	245/60-15	225/70-15	215-15
J60-15	J70-15	J78-15	8.85-15/8.90-15	255/60-15	235/70-15	225-15
	K70-15		9.00-15	265/60-15	245/70-15	230-15
L60-15	L70-15	L78-15, L84-15	9.15-15			235-15
	M70-15	M78-15				255-15
		N78-15				

Note: Every size tire is not listed and many size comparisons are approximate, based on load ratings. Wider tires than those supplied new with the vehicle, should always be checked for clearance.

87871140

Normal Service Maintenance			Miles—in thousands					
			7.5	15	22.5	30	37.5	45
Brake Linings	Inspect front brakes			●		●		●
	Inspect rear brakes					●		
*Cooling System	First drain, flush and refill at 24 months	or				●		
	Subsequent drain, flush and refill every 12 months	or						●
	Check and service system every 12 months	or		●		●		●
*Drive Belts	Check tension and condition		●	●	●	●	●	●
*Engine Oil	Change every 12 months	or	●	●	●	●	●	●
*Engine Oil Filter	Change every 12 months	or	●		●		●	
Rear Wheel Bearings	Inspect	or			●			●
Clutch Pedal Free Play	Adjust every 6 months	or	●	●	●	●	●	●
Steering Linkage Tie Rod Ends	Lubricate every 6 months	or				●		
Automatic Choke	Check and adjust			●		●		●
Carburetor Choke Shaft	Apply solvent every six months	or	●	●	●	●	●	●
Carburetor Air Filter	Replace	at				●		
Fast Idle Cam and Pivot Pin	Apply solvent every six months	or	●	●	●	●	●	●
Fuel Filter	Replace	at	●		●		●	
Idle Speed Air-Fuel Mixture	Check and adjust	at		●		●		●
Ignition Cables	Check and replace as required at time of spark replacement							
Ignition Timing	Check and adjust if necessary			●		●		●
PCV Valve	Check and adjust if necessary			●		●		●
PCV Valve	Replace					●		
Spark Plugs	Replace			●		●		●
Valve Lash	Check and adjust if necessary	at		●		●		●
Underhood Rubber & Plastic Components (Emission Hoses)	Inspect and replace	at		●		●		●

Inspect and Service should also be performed any time a malfunction is observed or suspected.
*Also an emission control service.

87871144

Severe Service Maintenance			Miles—in thousands														
			3	6	9	12	15	18	21	24	27	30	33	36	39	42	45	48
Brake Linings	Inspect	Front		●		●		●		●		●		●		●		●
		Rear				●				●				●				●
Change Oil	Change every 3 months	or	●	●	●	●	●	●	●	●	●	●	●	●	●	●	●	●
Engine Oil Filter	Change at initial oil change and every second oil change thereafter																	
Rear Wheel Bearings	Inspect and Relubricate whenever drums are removed to inspect or service brakes or every				●			●				●			●			●	
Front Suspension Ball Joints	Inspect at every oil change																	
Steering Linkage Tie Rod Ends	Lubricate every 18 months	or				●						●						●
Transmission Fluid "Automatic"	Change					●						●						●
Constant Velocity Universal Joints	Inspect at every oil change																	

*Driving under any of the following operating conditions: Stop and go driving, driving in dusty conditions, extensive idling, frequent short trips, operating at sustained high speeds during hot weather (above +90°F, +32°C).

87871145

Capacities

Year	Model	Engine Displacement	Crankcase Incl. Filter (qts)	Transmission Pints to Refill after Draining		Final Drive (pts)	Gasoline Tank (gals)	Cooling System (qts)	
				Manual	Automatic			W/AC	WO/AC
1978	All	1.7L	4.0	2.65	13.0	2.0	13.0	6.5	8.0
1979	All	1.7L	4.0	2.65	13.0	2.0	13.0	6.0	6.0
1980	All	1.7L	4.0	2.65	13.0	2.0	13.0	6.0	6.0
1981–1982	All	1.7L	4.0	2.65	14.5	2.37	13.0	6.0	6.0
	All	2.2L	4.0	3.75	15.0	2.37	13.0	8.7	8.7
1983–1986	All	1.6L	3.5	①	18.0	—	13.0	6.8	6.8
	All	1.7L	4.0	①	16.8	—	13.0	6.0	6.0
	All	2.2L	4②	①	18.0	—	13.0	9.0	9.0
1987–1989	All	2.2L	4②	③	18.0	—	13.0	9.0	9.0

① 4-speed; 3.75
   5-speed; 4.55
② turbo: 5 qts
③ A525: 4.6
   A520, A555: 5.0

87871146

2

ENGINE PERFORMANCE AND TUNE-UP

TUNE-UP PROCEDURES

An engine tune-up is a service designed to restore the maximum capability of power, performance, economy and reliability in an engine, and, at the same time, assure the owner of a complete check and more lasting results in efficiency and trouble-free performance. Engine tune-up becomes increasingly important each year, to ensure that pollutant levels are in compliance with federal emissions standards.

It is advisable to follow a definite and thorough tune-up procedure. Tune-up consists of three separate steps: Analysis, the process of determining whether normal wear is responsible for performance loss, and whether parts require replacement or service; Parts Replacement or Service; and Adjustment, where engine adjustments are returned to the original factory specifications.

The extent of an engine tune-up is usually determined by the length of time since the previous service, although the type of driving and the general mechanical condition of the engine must be considered. Specific maintenance should also be performed at regular intervals, depending on operating conditions.

Troubleshooting is a logical sequence of procedures designed to lead the owner or service man to the particular cause of trouble. The troubleshooting section of this manual is general in nature, yet specific enough to locate the problem. Service usually comprises two areas; diagnosis and repair. While the apparent cause of trouble, in many cases, is worn or damaged parts, performance problems are less obvious. The first job is to locate the problem and cause. Once the problem has been isolated, refer to the appropriate section for repair, removal or adjustment procedures.

It is advisable to read the entire section before beginning a tune-up, although those who are more familiar with tune-up procedures may wish to go directly to the instructions.

Tune-Up Specifications

Part numbers listed in this reference are not recommendations by Chilton for any product by brand name. They are references that can be used with interchange manuals and after market supplier catalogs to locate each brand supplier's discrete part number.

NOTE: *When analyzing compression test results, look for uniformity among cylinders rather than specific pressures. The lowest reading cylinder should be within 20% of the highest.*

Year	Displ	Spark Plugs Orig Type	Gap (in.)	Ignition Timing (deg) ▲ Man Trans	Auto Trans	Intake Valve Opens (deg) ■	Fuel Pump Pressure (psi)	Idle Speed (rpm) ▲ Man Trans	Auto Trans	Valve Lash (in.) ▲ Intake	Exhaust
'78	1.7L	RN-12Y	.035	15B	15B	23	4.5–6	900	900	.008–.012H	.016–.020H
'79	1.7L	RN-12Y	.035	15B	15B	14	4.4–5.8	900	900	.008–.012H	.016–.020H
'80	1.7L	RN-12Y	.035	12B ⑤	12B ⑤	14	4.4–5.8	900	900	.008–.012H	.016–.020H
'81	1.7L	P65-PR4 ①	.048 ②	12B ③	10B ④	14	4.4–5.8	900	900	.008–.012H	.016–.020H
	2.2L	P65-PR	.035	10B	10B	12	4.5–6.0	900	900	Hyd.	Hyd.
'82	1.7L	P65-PR	.035	20B	12B	14	4.4–5.8	900	900	.008–.012H	.016–.020H
	2.2L	P65-PR	.035	12B	12B	12	4.5–6.0	900	900	Hyd.	Hyd.
'83	1.7L	RN-12YC ⑥	.035	20°	12°	14	4.4–5.8	850	900	.008–.012H	.016–.020H
	2.2L	RN-12YC ⑥	.035	12° ⑦	12° ⑦	12	4.5–6.0	850	900	Hyd.	Hyd.
'84–'86	1.6L	RN-12YC ⑥	.035	12°	12°	16	4.5–6.0	850	1000	.012C	.014C
	2.2L	RN-12YC ⑥	.035	10° ⑧	10° ⑧	12	4.5–6.0	900 ⑧	900 ⑧	Hyd.	Hyd.
'87	2.2L	RN12YC ⑥	.035	12°	12°	16° ⑩		900	700 ⑨	Hyd.	Hyd.
'88–'89	2.2L	RN12YC ⑥	.035	12°	12°	0°		850	850	Hyd.	Hyd.

NOTE: *The underhood specifications sticker often reflects tune-up specification changes made in production. Sticker figures must be used if they disagree with those in this chart.*
▲ See text for procedure
■ Before Top Dead Center
① Canada: P65-PR
② Canada: .035
③ Canada: 5B
④ Canada: 10B
⑤ California: 10B
⑥ Replacement plug: RN-12Y
⑦ High-altitude: 6B
⑧ High-performance engine: 15°B @ 850 RPM—refer to VECI label under hood.
⑨ Turbocharged: 800

87872002

Spark Plugs

Spark plugs ignite the air and fuel mixture in the cylinder as the piston reaches the top of the compression stroke. The controlled explosion that results forces the piston down, turning the crankshaft and the rest of the drivetrain.

The average life of a spark plug is dependent on a number of factors:

- Mechanical condition of the engine
- Type of engine
- Type of fuel
- Driving conditions
- The driver

When you remove the spark plugs, check their condition. They are a good indicator of the condition of the engine. It isa good idea to remove the spark plugs at regular intervals, such as every 2000-3000 miles (3218-4827 km), just so you can keep an eye on the mechanical state of your engine.

A small deposit of light tan or gray material on a spark plug that has been used for any period of time is to be considered normal.

The gap between the center electrode and the side or ground electrode can be expected to increase not more than 0.001 in. (.025mm) every 1,000 miles (1609 km) under normal conditions.

When a spark plug is functioning normally or, more accurately, when the plug is installed in an engine that is functioning properly, the plugs can be taken out, cleaned, regapped, and reinstalled in the engine without doing the engine any harm.

When, and if, a plug fouls and beings to misfire, you will have to investigate, correct the cause of the fouling, and either clean or replace the plug.

Spark plug heat range is the ability of the plug to dissipate heat. The longer the insulator (or the farther it extends into the engine), the hotter the plug will operate; the shorter the insulator the cooler it will operate. A plug that absorbs little heat and remains too cool will quickly accumulate deposits of oil and carbon since it is not hot enough to burn them off. This leads to plug fouling and consequently to misfiring. A plug that absorbs too much heat will have no deposits, but, due to the excessive heat, the electrodes will burn away quickly and in some instances, preignition may result. Preignition takes place when plug tips get so hot that they glow sufficiently to ignite the fuel/air mixture before the actual spark occurs. This early ignition will usually cause a pinging during low speeds and heavy loads.

The general rule of thumb for choosing the correct heat range when picking a spark plug is: if most of your driving is long distance or high speed travel, use a colder plug. If most of your driving is stop and go, use a hotter plug. Original equipment plugs are compromise plugs, but most people never have occasion to change their plugs from the factory recommended heat range.

REMOVAL & INSTALLATION

▶ **See Figures 1, 2, 3, 4 and 5**

A set of spark plugs usually requires replacement after about 10,000 miles (16,090 km) on cars with conventional ignition systems and after about 20,000-30,000 miles (32,180-48,270 km) on cars with electronic ignition, depending on your style of driving. In normal operation, plug gap increases about 0.001 in. (0.025mm) for every 1000-2500 miles (1609-4023 km). As the gap increases, the plug's voltage requirement also increases. It requires a greater voltage to jump the wider gap and about two to three times as much voltage to fire a plug at high speeds than at idle.

When you're removing spark plugs, you should work on one at a time. Don't start by removing the plug wires all at once, because unless you number them, they may become mixed up. Take a minute before you begin and number the wires with tape. The best location for numbering is near where the wires come out of the cap.

1. Twist the spark plug boot and remove the boot and wire from the plug. Do not pull on the wire itself as this will ruin the wire.

2. If possible, use a brush or rag to clean the area around the spark plug. Make sure that all the dirt is removed so that none will enter the cylinder after the plug is removed.

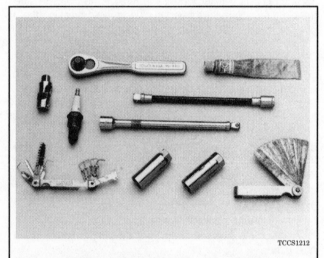

TCCS1212

Fig. 1 A variety of tools and gauges are needed for spark plug service

87872200

Fig. 2 An extension is useful for reaching the spark plug

Fig. 3 Once the plug is removed, inspect it

3. Remove the spark plug using the proper size socket. Turn the socket counterclockwise to remove the plug. Be sure to hold the socket straight on the plug to avoid breaking the plug, or rounding off the hex on the plug.

To install:

4. Use a wire feeler gauge to check the plug gap. The correct size gauge should pass through the electrode gap with a slight drag. If you're in doubt, try one size smaller and one larger. The smaller gauge should go through easily while the larger one shouldn't go through at all. If the gap is incorrect, use the electrode bending tool on the end of the gauge to adjust the gap. When adjusting the gap, always bend the side electrode. The center electrode is non-adjustable.

5. Squirt a drop of penetrating oil on the threads of the new plug and install it. Don't oil the threads too heavily. Turn the plug in clockwise by hand until it is snug.

6. Tighten the plug with a wrench.

7. Install the plug boot firmly over the plug. Proceed to the next plug.

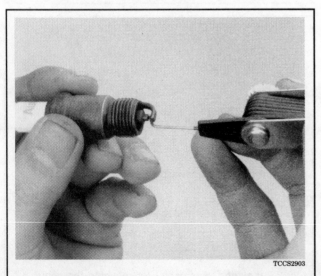

Fig. 4 Checking the spark plug gap with a feeler gauge

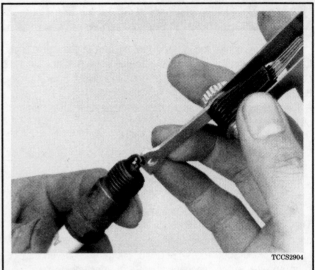

Fig. 5 Adjusting the spark plug gap

INSPECTION

▶ **See Figures 6 and 7**

Check the plugs for deposits and wear. If they are not going to be replaced, clean the plugs thoroughly. Remember that any kind of deposit will decrease the efficiency of the plug. Plugs can be cleaned on a spark plug cleaning machine, which can sometimes be found in service stations, or you can do an acceptable job of cleaning with a stiff brush.

Check spark plug gap before installation. The ground electrode must be aligned with the center electrode and the specified size wire gauge should pass through the gap with a slight drag. If the electrodes are worn, it is possible to file them level.

Spark Plug Wires

INSPECTION & TESTING

➡**On 1980 and later models, DO NOT pull the wires from the distributor cap. They must be released from inside the cap.**

Visually inspect the spark plug cables for burns, cuts, or breaks in the insulation. Check the spark plug boots and the nipples on the distributor cap and coil. Replace any damaged wiring. If no physical damage is obvious, the wires can be checked with an ohmmeter for excessive resistance.

REMOVAL & INSTALLATION

▶ **See Figures 8 and 9**

➡**Replace the cables one at a time to avoid confusion.**

1. Unplug the wire from the spark plug.

2. On 1978-79 models, unplug the wire from the distributor cap. On later models, remove the distributor cap and disengage the retaining tabs securing the wire to the cap.

Tracking Arc
High voltage arcs between a fouling deposit on the insulator tip and spark plug shell. This ignites the fuel/air mixture at some point along the insulator tip, retarding the ignition timing which causes a power and fuel loss.

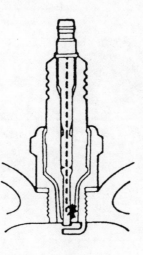

Wide Gap
Spark plug electrodes are worn so that the high voltage charge cannot arc across the electrodes. Improper gapping of electrodes on new or "cleaned" spark plugs could cause a similar condition. Fuel remains unburned and a power loss results.

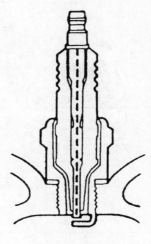

Flashover
A damaged spark plug boot, along with dirt and moisture, could permit the high voltage charge to short over the insulator to the spark plug shell or the engine. A buttress insulator design helps prevent high voltage flashover.

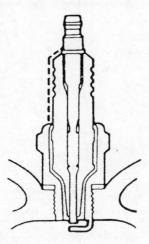

Fouled Spark Plug
Deposits that have formed on the insulator tip may become conductive and provide a "shunt" path to the shell. This prevents the high voltage from arcing between the electrodes. A power and fuel loss is the result.

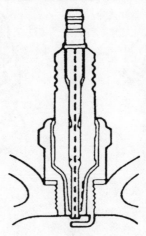

Bridged Electrodes
Fouling deposits between the electrodes "ground out" the high voltage needed to fire the spark plug. The arc between the electrodes does not occur and the fuel air mixture is not ignited. This causes a power loss and exhausting of raw fuel.

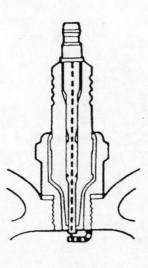

Cracked Insulator
A crack in the spark plug insulator could cause the high voltage charge to "ground out." Here, the spark does not jump the electrode gap and the fuel air mixture is not ignited. This causes a power loss and raw fuel is exhausted.

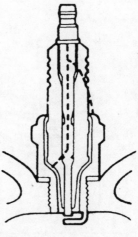

TCCS201A

Fig. 6 Used spark plugs which show damage may indicate engine problems

GAP BRIDGED

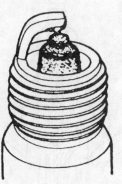

IDENTIFIED BY DEPOSIT BUILD—UP CLOSING GAP BETWEEN ELECTRODES.

CAUSED BY OIL OR CARBON FOULING. REPLACE PLUG, OR, IF DEPOSITS ARE NOT EXCESSIVE THE PLUG CAN BE CLEANED.

OIL FOULED

IDENTIFIED BY WET BLACK DEPOSITS ON THE INSULATOR SHELL BORE ELECTRODES.

CAUSED BY EXCESSIVE OIL ENTERING COMBUSTION CHAMBER THROUGH WORN RINGS AND PISTONS. EXCESSIVE CLEARANCE BETWEEN VALVE GUIDES AND STEMS, OR WORN OR LOOSE BEARINGS. CORRECT OIL PROBLEM. REPLACE THE PLUG.

CARBON FOULED

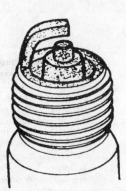

IDENTIFIED BY BLACK, DRY FLUFFY CARBON DEPOSITS ON INSULATOR TIPS, EXPOSED SHELL SURFACES AND ELECTRODES.

CAUSED BY TOO COLD A PLUG, WEAK IGNITION, DIRTY AIR CLEANER, DEFECTIVE FUEL PUMP, TOO RICH A FUEL MIXTURE, IMPROPERLY OPERATING HEAT RISER OR EXCESSIVE IDLING. CAN BE CLEANED.

NORMAL

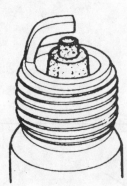

IDENTIFIED BY LIGHT TAN OR GRAY DEPOSITS ON THE FIRING TIP.

PRE-IGNITION

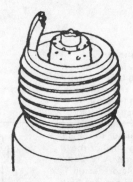

IDENTIFIED BY MELTED ELECTRODES AND POSSIBLY BLISTERED INSULATOR. METALIC DEPOSITS ON INSULATOR INDICATE ENGINE DAMAGE.

CAUSED BY WRONG TYPE OF FUEL, INCORRECT IGNITION TIMING OR ADVANCE, TOO HOT A PLUG, BURNT VALVES OR ENGINE OVERHEATING. REPLACE THE PLUG.

OVERHEATING

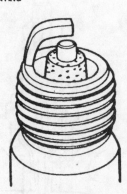

IDENTIFIED BY A WHITE OR LIGHT GRAY INSULATOR WITH SMALL BLACK OR GRAY BROWN SPOTS AND WITH BLUISH-BURNT APPEARANCE OF ELECTRODES.

CAUSED BY ENGINE OVER-HEATING, WRONG TYPE OF FUEL, LOOSE SPARK PLUGS, TOO HOT A PLUG, LOW FUEL PUMP PRESSURE OR INCORRECT IGNITION TIMING. REPLACE THE PLUG.

FUSED SPOT DEPOSIT

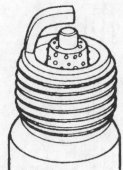

IDENTIFIED BY MELTED OR SPOTTY DEPOSITS RESEMBLING BUBBLES OR BLISTERS.

CAUSED BY SUDDEN ACCELERATION. CAN BE CLEANED IF NOT EXCESSIVE, OTHERWISE REPLACE PLUG.

TCCS2002

Fig. 7 Inspect the spark plug to determine engine running conditions

To install:

3. Install the boot firmly over the spark plug and distributor cap terminal. Route the wire exactly the same as the original.

4. Repeat the process for each cable.

Distributor Cap

REMOVAL & INSTALLATION

▶ **See Figures 10 and 11**

1. Remove the hold-down screws for the cap.
2. Lift the cap off the distributor.
3. Tag the wires and cap before removing them, then disassemble.

To install:

4. Install the new cap.
5. Attach the tagged wires on the cap.

Fig. 10 Remove the hold-down screws for the cap

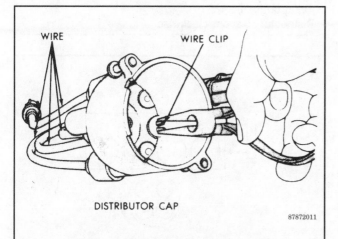

Fig. 8 On some engines, when removing the wires from the cap, you may need to use pliers to squeeze the electrode, then push through the opening of the cap

Fig. 11 Lift the cap off the distributor

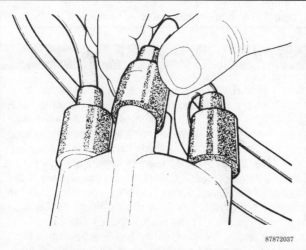

Fig. 9 On other engines use your fingers and grasp around the plug nipple, then pull

FIRING ORDERS

▶ **See Figures 12, 13 and 14**

To avoid confusion, replace spark plug wires or spark plugs one at a time, for replacement.

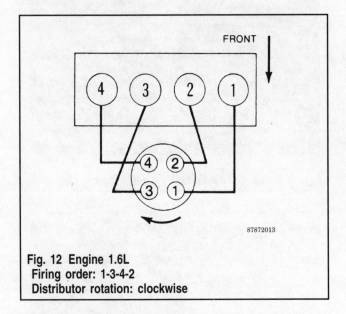

Fig. 12 Engine 1.6L
Firing order: 1-3-4-2
Distributor rotation: clockwise

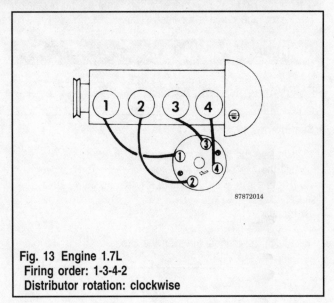

Fig. 13 Engine 1.7L
Firing order: 1-3-4-2
Distributor rotation: clockwise

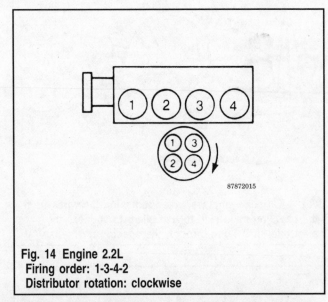

Fig. 14 Engine 2.2L
Firing order: 1-3-4-2
Distributor rotation: clockwise

ELECTRONIC IGNITION

Description and Operation

Omni's and Horizon's are equipped with the Electronic Fuel Control system. This consists of a spark control computer, various engine sensors, and a specially calibrated carburetor with an electronically controlled fuel metering system. On fuel injected engines, the computer controls the total amount of fuel injected by slightly modifying the pulses that operate the injectors. The function of this system is to provide a way for the engine to burn a correct air-fuel mixture.

The spark control computer is the heart of the entire system. It has the capability of igniting the fuel mixture according to different models of engine operation by delivering an infinite number of different variable advance curves. The computer consists of one electronic printed circuit board, which simultaneously received signals from all the sensors and within milliseconds, analyzes them to determine how the engine is operating and then advances or retards the timing.

For 1988, this system has been renamed the Single Module Engine Controller (SMEC) system. It functions similarly to the Electronic Fuel Control system, using coolant temperature, engine rpm, and available manifold vacuum for inputs. On turbo engines, it synchronizes the injection pulses with the ignition pulses by reading signals from the Hall Effect pickup in the distributor. Both systems use the oxygen sensor to fine-tune the mixture to actual operating conditions.

Testing

The electronic ignition system is controlled by the Chrysler Corporation Lean Burn system, which is actually an emission control system.

The ignition coil can be tested on a conventional coil tester. The ballast resistor, mounted on the firewall, must be included in all tests. Refer to the beginning of Engine and Engine Overhaul for coil testing.

➡**Some of the procedures in this section refer to an adjustable timing light. This is also known as a spark advance tester, i.e., a device that will measure how much spark advance is present going from one point, a base figure, to another. Since precise timing is very important to the Lean Burn System, do not attempt to perform any of the tests calling for an adjustable timing light without one.**

CARBURETED ENGINES

Spark Test

▶ **See Figure 15**

1. Remove the coil wire from the distributor cap and hold it cautiously about ¼ in. (6mm) away from an engine ground, then have someone crank the engine while you check for spark.

2. If you have a good spark, slowly move the coil wire away from the engine and check for arcing at the coil while cranking.

3. If you have good spark and it is not arcing at the coil, check the rest of the parts of the ignition system.

No Start

1978-80 MODELS

▶ **See Figures 16, 17 and 18**

1. Measure the battery specific gravity. It must be at least 1.220, temperature corrected. Measure the battery voltage and make a note of it.

2. Disconnect the thin wire from the negative coil terminal.

3. Remove the coil high tension lead at the distributor cap.

4. Turn the ignition **ON**. While holding the coil high tension lead ¼ in. (6mm) from a ground, connect a jumper wire from the negative coil terminal to a ground. A spark should be obtained from the high tension lead.

5. If there is no spark, use a voltmeter to test for at least 9 volts at the positive coil terminal (ignition **ON**). If so, the coil must be replaced. If less than 9 volts is obtained, check the ballast resistor, wiring, and connections. If the car still won't start, proceed to the next step.

6. If there was a spark in Step 4, turn the ignition **OFF**, reconnect the wire to the negative coil terminal, and disconnect the distributor pick-up coil connection.

7. Turn the ignition **ON**, and measure voltage between pin **B** of the pick-up coil connector on the spark control computer side, and a good engine ground. Voltage should be the same as the battery voltage measured in the first step. If it is, go to Step 11. If not, go to the next step.

➡**Malfunction of the distributor pick-up coil can be the result of the rotor not properly grounded to the distributor shaft. Remove the rotor and check the metal grounding tab to be sure it is not covered with plastic. If so, replace the rotor with a new one. Clean the top of the distributor shaft and install the rotor, pushing it onto the shaft so the metal tab contacts the shaft. Check for continuity between the interrupter vane and distributor housing. Do not try to start the engine with no continuity.**

8. Turn the ignition **OFF** and disconnect the terminal connector at the spark control computer.

➡**Do not remove grease from the 10-wire harness connector.**

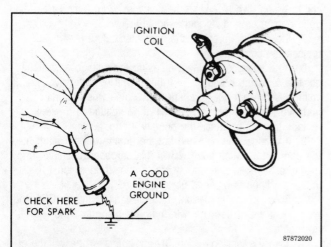

87872020

Fig. 15 Remove the coil wire from the distributor cap and hold it cautiously about ¼ in. (6mm) away from an engine ground

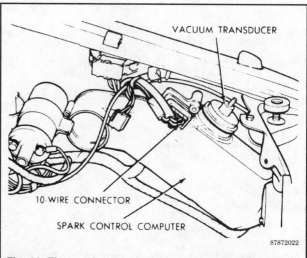

87872022

Fig. 16 The spark control computer is located in the left front of the vehicle

9. Check for continuity between pin **B** of the pick-up coil connector on the computer side, and terminal **3** of the computer connector. If there is no continuity, the wire must be replaced. If continuity exists, go to the next step.

10. With the ignition **ON**, connect a voltmeter between terminals **2** and **10** of the computer connector. Voltage should be the same as measured in the first step. If so, the computer is defective and must be replaced.

11. Secure the 10 wire computer connector. Turn the ignition **ON**. Hold the coil high tension lead (disconnected at the distributor cap) about ¼ in. (6mm) from a ground. Connect a jumper wire between pins **A** and **C** of the distributor pick-up coil connector. If a spark is obtained, the distributor pick-up is defective and must be replaced. If not, go to the next step.

12. Turn the ignition **OFF**. Disconnect the 10 wire computer connection.

13. Check for continuity between pin **C** of the distributor connector and terminal **9** of the computer connector. Also check for continuity between pin **A** of the distributor connector and terminal **5** of the computer connector. If continuity exists, the computer is defective and must be replaced. If not, the wires are damaged. Repair them and recheck, starting at Step 11.

1981 AND LATER

▶ See Figures 19, 20 and 21

1. Make sure the battery is fully charged, then measure and record the battery voltage.

2. Remove the coil secondary wire from the distributor cap.

3. With the key **ON**, use the special jumper wire and momentarily connect the negative terminal of the ignition coil to ground while holding the coil secondary wire (using insulated pliers and heavy gloves) about ¼ from a good ground. A spark should fire.

4. If spark was obtained, go to Step 9.

5. If no spark was obtained, turn **OFF** the ignition and disconnect the 10-wire harness going into the Spark Control Computer. Do not remove the grease from the connection.

6. With the ignition key **ON**, use the special jumper wire and momentarily connect the negative terminal of the ignition

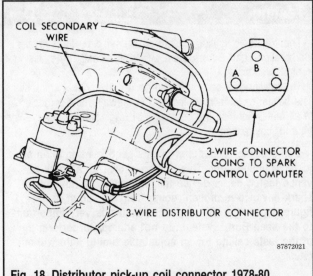

Fig. 18 Distributor pick-up coil connector 1978-80

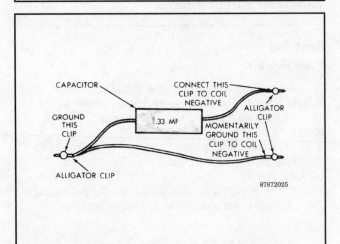

Fig. 19 Use this special jumper wire, then momentarily connect the negative terminal of the ignition coil to ground while holding the coil secondary wire

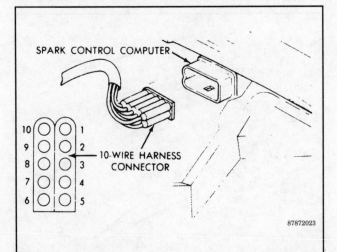

Fig. 17 The 10 wire connector is plugged into the spark control computer

coil to ground while holding the coil wire ¼ in. (6mm) from a good engine ground. A spark should fire.

7. If a spark is present, the computer output is shorted: replace the computer.

8. If no spark is obtained, measure the voltage at the coil positive terminal. It should be within 1 volt of battery voltage. If voltage is present but no spark is available when shorting negative terminal, replace the coil. If no voltage is present, replace the coil or check the primary wiring.

9. If voltage was obtained but the engine will not start, hold the carburetor switch open with a thin cardboard insulator and measure the voltage at the switch. It should be at least 5 volts. If voltage is present, go to Step 16.

10. If no voltage is present, turn the ignition switch **OFF** and disconnect the 10 terminal wire harness going into the computer.

11. Turn the ignition switch **ON** and measure the voltage at terminal **2** of the harness. It should be within 1 volt of battery voltage.

12. If no battery voltage is present, check for continuity between the battery and terminal **2** of the harness. If no continuity, repair fault and repeat the previous step.

13. If voltage is present turn ignition switch **OFF** and check for continuity between the carburetor switch and terminal **7** on connector. If no continuity is present, check for open wire between terminal **7** and the carburetor switch.

14. If continuity is present, check continuity between terminal **10** and ground. If continuity is present here, replace the computer. Repeat Step 9.

15. If no continuity is present, check for an open wire. If wiring is OK but the engine still won't start, go to next step.

16. Plug the 10 terminal dual connector back into the computer and turn the ignition switch **ON**, hold the secondary coil wire near a good ground and disconnect the distributor harness connector. Using a regular jumper wire (not the special one mentioned earlier), jump terminal **2** to terminal **3** of the connector. A spark should fire at the coil wire. Make and break the connection at terminal **2** or **3** several times and check for good spark at the coil wire.

17. If spark is present at the coil wire but the engine won't start, replace the Hall Effect pick-up and check the rotor for cracks or burning. Replace as necessary.

➡ **When replacing a pick-up, always make sure rotor blades are grounded using an ohmmeter.**

18. If no spark is present at the coil wire, measure the voltage at terminal 1 of the distributor harness connector: it should be within 1 volt of battery voltage.

19. If correct, disconnect the 10 terminal dual connector from the computer and check for continuity between terminal **2** of distributor harness and terminal **9** of the dual connector. Repeat test on terminal **3** of distributor harness and terminal **5** of dual connector. If no continuity, repair the harness. If continuity is present, replace the computer and repeat Step 16.

20. If no battery voltage is present in Step 18, turn **OFF** the ignition switch, disconnect the 10 terminal dual connector from the computer and check for continuity between terminal **1** of distributor harness and terminal **3** of dual connector. If no continuity, repair wire and repeat Step 16.

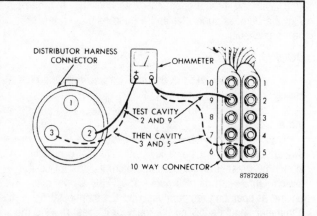

Fig. 21 Check for continuity between terminal 2 of distributor harness and terminal 9 of the dual connector. Repeat test on terminal 3 of distributor harness and terminal 5 of dual connector

21. If continuity is present, turn the ignition switch **ON** and check for battery voltage between terminal **2** and terminal **10** of the dual connector. If voltage is present, replace the computer and repeat Step 16. If no battery voltage is present, the computer is not grounded. Check and repair the ground wire and repeat Step 16.

Poor Performance

Before proceeding with these tests, be sure the ignition timing and idle speed are as specified.

CARBURETOR SWITCH

▶ **See Figures 22, 23 and 24**

1. With the key **OFF**, disconnect the 10-wire harness from the Spark Control Computer.

2. With the throttle completely closed, check for continuity between pin **7** of the harness connector and a good ground. If there is no continuity, check the carburetor switch and wire. Recheck the timing.

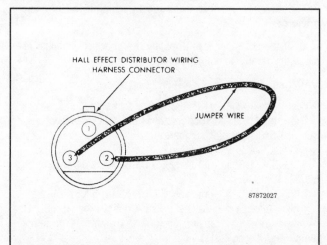

Fig. 20 Using a regular jumper wire, jump terminal 2 terminal 3 of the connector. A spark should fire at the coil wire

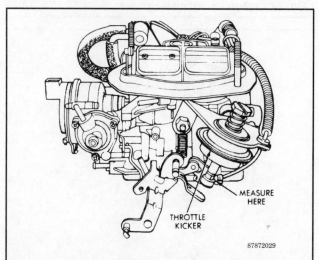

Fig. 22 Carburetor continuity test is similar on the 1.6L and 1.7L — 2.2L shown

3. With the throttle open, check for continuity between pin **7** of the harness connector and a good ground. There should be no continuity.

COOLANT SWITCH

1. With the key **OFF**, disconnect the wire from the coolant switch.

2. Connect one lead of an ohmmeter to a good ground, on the engine.

3. Connect the other lead to the terminal of the coolant switch. On a cold engine, below 150°F (66°C) continuity should be present at the coolant switch. If not, replace the switch. On a warm engine above 150°F (66°C) or on an engine at operating temperature, with the thermostat open, the ohmmeter should show no continuity. If it does, replace the coolant switch.

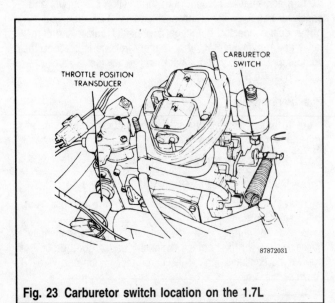

Fig. 23 Carburetor switch location on the 1.7L

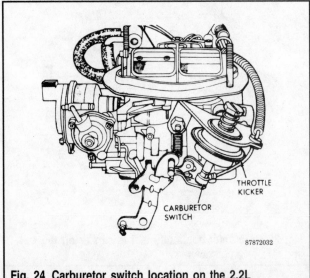

Fig. 24 Carburetor switch location on the 2.2L

START-UP ADVANCE

For vehicles built in 1978-79, follow this procedure:

1. Connect an adjustable timing light to the engine so that the total timing advance can be checked.

2. Connect a jumper wire from the carburetor switch to a ground.

3. Start the engine and immediately adjust the timing light so that the basic timing light is seen on the timing plate of the engine. The meter (on the timing light) should show an 8° advance. Continue to observe the mark for 90 seconds, adjusting the light as necessary. The basic timing signal over a period of about one minute. If not, replace the Spark Control Computer and recheck. If it is ok, go on to the next test. Do not remove the timing light or jumper wire. They will be used for the next test.

SPEED ADVANCE

For vehicles built in 1978-80, follow this procedure:

1. Start and run the engine for 2 minutes.

2. Adjust the timing light so that the basic timing is shown at the timing indicator. Additional advance shown on the timing light meter should be:

- 0-3° @ 1100 rpm
- 8-12° @ 2000 rpm

If not, replace the spark control computer and repeat the test. If as specified, go to the next test.

SPARK ADVANCE

For vehicles built in 1980 on, follow this procedure:

1. Check basic ignition timing and adjust if necessary.

2. Run the engine to obtain normal operating temperature. Check the operation of the coolant temperature sensor, refer to the coolant switch test in this section.

3. Remove and plug the vacuum hose at the vacuum transducer.

4. Connect an auxiliary vacuum pump to the vacuum transducer and apply 16 in. Hg (54 kPa) of vacuum.

5. Increase the engine speed to 2000 rpm, wait one minute then check specifications.

➡**The advance specifications are in addition to the basic advance.**

6. If the computer fails to obtain the specified settings, replace the Spark Control Computer.

VACUUM ADVANCE

For vehicles built in 1979-80, follow this procedure:

The program for each computer is different. Specifications for individual computer numbers are:

- 18-22° @ 2000 rpm (all part numbers)
- 23-27° @ 3000 rpm (nos. 5206721, 5206784 and 5206793)
- 28-32° @ 3000 rpm (nos. 5206785 and 5206790)

While performing these tests, use a metal exhaust tube. Use of rubber tube may cause a fire due to extremely high temperatures and a long test period.

If the spark control computer fails to meet these tests, it should be replaced.

1. Connect an adjustable timing light and tachometer.

2. Start the engine and warm it to normal operating temperature. Wait at least 1 minute for start up advance to return to

basic timing. Place the transaxle in Neutral and apply the parking brake.

3. Check, and, if necessary, adjust the basic timing.

4. Remove the vacuum line from the vacuum transducer and plug the line.

5. Ground the carburetor switch.

6. Increase the engine speed to 1100 rpm.

7. Check the speed advance timing.

8. Increase speed to 2000 rpm. Remove the carburetor switch ground and connect the vacuum line to the vacuum transducer.

9. Check the Zero Time Offset. Timing should be:
- 6-10° — computer number 5206721
- 2-6° — computer number 5206784
- 3-7° — computer number 5206785
- 0-3° — computer number 5206790, 5206793

10. Allow the accumulator in the computer to clock-up for 8 minutes.

11. With the accumulator clocked-up and the speed at 1100 rpm, check the vacuum advance. It should be 0-3° at 1100 rpm.

12. Disconnect and plug the vacuum line from the transducer and increase the engine speed to 3000 rpm. Note the speed advance timing.

13. Reconnect the vacuum line to the transducer and recheck the vacuum advance.

14. Return the engine to curb idle. Connect the wire to the carburetor switch if applicable.

FUEL INJECTION

Spark Test

▶ See Figure 15

1. Remove the coil wire from the distributor cap and hold it cautiously about ¼ in. (6mm) away from an engine ground, then have someone crank the engine while you check for spark.

2. If you have a good spark, slowly move the coil wire away from the engine and check for arcing at the coil while cranking.

3. If you have good spark and it is not arcing at the coil, check the rest of the parts of the ignition system.

Failure To Start

SINGLE MODULE ENGINE CONTROLLER (SMEC)

1. Test for spark at the coil.

2. Determine that the battery has sufficient voltage, (12.4 volts) for the cranking and ignition systems.

3. Crank the engine for seconds while monitoring the voltage at the coil positive (+). If the voltage remains near zero during the entire period of cranking, check the Single Module Engine Controller (SMEC) and the auto shutdown relay.

4. If the voltage is at '"near battery" voltage and drops to zero after 1-2 seconds of cranking check the distributor reference pickup circuit to the SMEC.

5. If the voltage remains at '"near battery" voltage during the entire 5 seconds, with the key **OFF**, remove the 14-way connector from the SMEC. Check the connector for any spread terminals.

6. Remove the lead-to-coil (+) and connect a jumper wire between battery (+) and coil (+).

7. Using a special jumper, momentarily ground the terminal no. 12 of the 14-way connector. A spark should be generated when the ground is removed.

8. If the spark is generated, replace the SMEC.

9. If no spark is seen, use the special jumper to ground the coil (-) terminal directly.

10. If spark is produced, repair the wiring harness for an open condition.

11. If no spark is produced, replace the ignition coil.

SINGLE BOARD ENGINE CONTROLLER (SBEC)

1. Test for spark at the coil.

2. Determine that sufficient battery voltage (12.4) volts is present for the cranking and ignitions systems.

3. Crank the engine for 5 seconds while monitoring the voltage at the coil (+). If the voltage remains near zero during the entire period of cranking, check the SBEC and the auto shutdown relay.

4. If the voltage is at '"near battery" voltage and drops to zero after 1-2 seconds of cranking check the distributor reference pickup circuit to the SBEC.

5. If the voltage remains at '"near battery" voltage during the entire 5 seconds, with the key **OFF**, remove the 60-way connector from the SMEC. Check the 60-way for any loose terminals from the connector.

6. Remove the lead-to-coil (+) and connect a jumper wire between battery (+) and coil (+).

7. Using a special jumper, momentarily ground the terminal no. 19 of the 60-way connector. A spark should be generated when the ground is removed.

8. If the spark is generated, replace the SBEC.

9. If no spark is seen, use the special jumper to ground the coil (-) terminal directly.

10. If spark is produced, repair the wiring harness for an open condition.

11. If no spark is produced, replace the ignition coil.

COMPONENT REPLACEMENT

Hall Effect Pickup

▶ See Figure 25

1. Loosen the distributor cap retaining screws and remove the cap.

2. Pull straight up on the rotor and remove it from the shaft.

3. Disconnect the pickup assembly lead.

4. Remove the pickup lead hold down screw.

5. Remove the pickup assembly lock springs and lift off the pickup.

To install:

6. Install the new pickup assembly onto the distributor housing and fasten it into place with the lock springs.

7. Fasten the pickup lead to the housing with the hold down screw.

8. Reconnect the lead to the harness.

9. Press the rotor back into place on the shaft. Do not wipe off the silicone grease on the metal portion of the rotor.

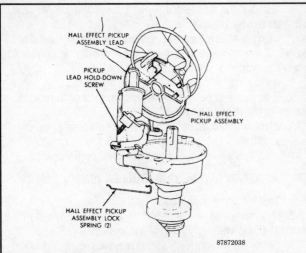

Fig. 25 Remove the pickup assembly lock springs and lift off the hall effect pickup

IGNITION TIMING

Inspection and Adjustment

▶ **See Figures 26, 27, 28, 29, 30, 31 and 32**

The engine is timed on No. 1 cylinder, which is the passenger's side of the car.

1. Connect a timing light according to the manufacturer's instructions.

2. Run the engine to normal operating temperature.

3. Make sure the idle speed is correct.

4. Loosen the distributor hold-down screw just enough so that the distributor can be rotated.

5. Ground the carburetor switch on models so equipped.

6. Disconnect and plug the vacuum line at the Spark Control Computer (if so equipped).

7. Remove the timing hole access cover and aim the timing light at the hole in the clutch housing. Carefully rotate the distributor until the mark is aligned with the pointer on the flywheel housing.

8. Tighten the distributor and recheck the timing.

9. Check, and if necessary adjust, the idle speed.

10. Replace the distributor cap and tighten the retaining screws.

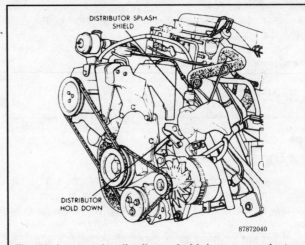

Fig. 26 Loosen the distributor hold-down screw just enough so that the distributor can be rotated — 1.6L shown

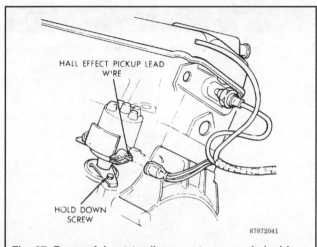

Fig. 27 Be careful not to disconnect any needed wiring at the distributor while loosening the hold-down bolt — 1.7L shown

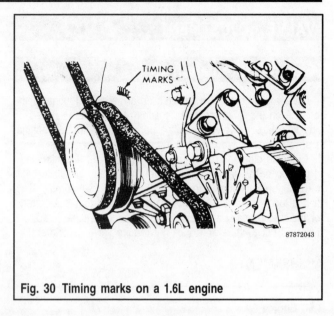

Fig. 30 Timing marks on a 1.6L engine

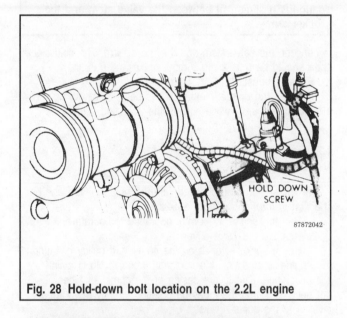

Fig. 28 Hold-down bolt location on the 2.2L engine

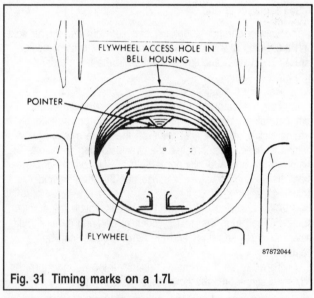

Fig. 31 Timing marks on a 1.7L

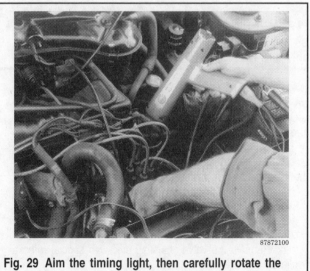

Fig. 29 Aim the timing light, then carefully rotate the distributor until the mark is aligned with the pointer

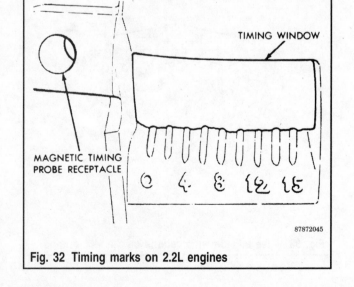

Fig. 32 Timing marks on 2.2L engines

VALVE ADJUSTMENT

General Information

Valve adjustment is not required as a matter of routine maintenance on the 1.6L and 1.7L engines. It is, however, necessary to check the valve clearance periodically. The 1.6L engine is an overhead valve design with adjustable rocker arms. The 1.7L engine clearance is adjusted by substituting discs located at the top of the cam followers. The discs are available in 0.01 in. (0.05mm) increments from 0.12-0.17 in. (3.00-4.25mm). One disc is located in each cam follower. A special tool is required for the disc removal and installation. The 2.2L engine uses hydraulic valve lifters and does not require valve adjustment.

ADJUSTMENT

1.6L Engine

▶ See Figures 33 and 34

The valve clearance should be checked with the engine cold and the piston at TDC (top dead center) on the compression stroke. The valves should be checked in the firing order 1-3-4-2.

1. Remove the valve cover.
2. Turn the crankshaft and watch the movement of the exhaust valves. When one is closing (moving upward) continue turning slowly until the inlet valve on the same cylinder just begins to open. This is called the "valve rocking" position. The piston in the opposite cylinder is then at TDC on the compression stroke, and its valve clearance can be checked and adjusted.
3. After checking both valve clearances, rotate the crankshaft one half turn, the next cylinder in the firing order should have its valves "rocking" and the pared cylinder can be adjusted.
4. To make an adjustment, loosen the locknut and turn the adjusting screw until the correct size feeler gauge is a sliding

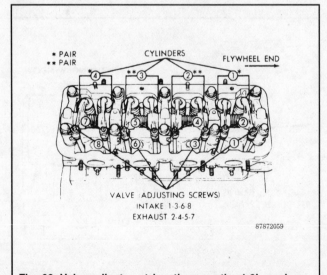

Fig. 33 Valve adjustment locations on the 1.6L engine

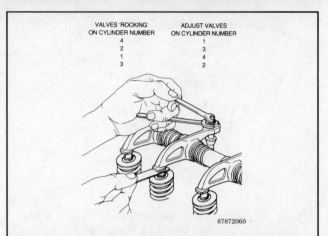

Fig. 34 To make an adjustment, loosen the locknut and turn the adjusting screw until the correct size feeler gauge is a sliding fit between the valve stem and the rocker arm

fit between the valve stem and the rocker arm. The cold clearance should be 0.01 in. (0.25mm) intake and 0.02 in. (0.35mm) exhaust.

5. When the correct clearance has been obtained, tighten the locknut securely while holding the adjusting screw.
6. Reinstall the valve cover.

1.7L Engine

▶ See Figures 35 and 36

The valve should be checked with the engine warm and be checked in the firing order 1-3-4-2.

1. Run the engine to normal operating temperature.
2. Remove the valve cover.
3. Use a socket wrench on the crankshaft pulley or bump the engine around until the camshaft lobes of No. 1 cylinder are positioned. Due to the design of the camshaft lobes, it is not necessary that the lobes be pointing directly away (perpendicular) to the adjusting disc.

✳✳WARNING

Do not turn the engine using the camshaft pulley, and only turn the engine in the direction of normal rotation.

4. Using a feeler gauge, check the valve clearance between the camshaft lobe and the valve adjusting disc.
   Clearance should be 0.007-0.011 in. (0.20-0.30mm) intake and 0.015-0.019 in. (0.40-0.50mm) exhaust.
5. If the measure clearance is not as specified, the valve adjusting disc can be removed and replaced with another of the proper size to give the correct valve clearance.
6. To remove the disc:
   a. Depress the cam follower with Tool L-4417. This tool is necessary to remove the disc without damaging the camshaft or cylinder head.
   b. Remove the valve adjusting disc with special removal pliers.

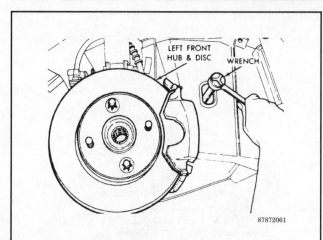

Fig. 35 Use a socket wrench on the crankshaft pulley or bump the engine around until the camshaft lobes of No. 1 cylinder are positioned

Valve Adjusting Discs, 1.7

Thickness (mm)	Part Number	Thickness (mm)	Part Number
3.00	5240946	3.65	5240580
3.05	5240945	3.70	5240581
3.10	5240944	3.75	5240582
3.15	5240943	3.80	5240583
3.20	5240942	3.85	5240584
3.25	5240941	3.90	5240585
3.30	5240573	3.95	5240586
3.35	5240574	4.00	5240587
3.40	5240575	4.05	5240588
3.45	5240576	4.10	5240589
3.50	5240577	4.15	5240590
3.55	5240578	4.20	5240591
3.60	5240579	4.25	5240592

87872064

Fig. 36 Valve adjusting discs are available in different thicknesses

c. Calculate the thickness of a new disc and install one of the proper size. Be sure the number indicating the thickness of the disc faces down when installed.

d. Recheck the valve clearance.

7. Recheck or adjust all other valves in the same manner.

➡ **When the camshaft is in position to check the valves of No. 1 cylinder, cylinders No. 3 and 4 can also be checked or adjusted. It is only necessary to turn the engine one time to position the camshaft to check No. 2 cylinder.**

8. Reinstall the camshaft cover.

2.2L Engine

This engine has hydraulic valve lifter and no adjustment is required.

IDLE SPEED AND MIXTURE ADJUSTMENTS

Idle Speed And Mixture Adjustment

CARBURETED ENGINES

▸ **See Figures 37, 38 and 39**

Chrysler recommends the use of a propane enrichment procedure to adjust the mixture. The equipment needed for this procedure is not readily available to the general public. An alternate method recommended by Chrysler is with the use of an exhaust gas analyzer. If this equipment is not available, and a mixture adjustment must be performed, follow this procedure:

1. Connect the red lead of the test tachometer to the negative primary terminal of the coil and the black lead to a good ground.

2. Turn the selector switch to the appropriate cylinder position and read the idle on the 1000 rpm scale, if so equipped.

3. With the engine at normal operating temperature momentarily open the throttle to check for binding in the linkage. Make sure that the idle screw is against its stop.

4. Place the transaxle in Neutral (MT) or Drive (AT), turn off the lights and air conditioning and make certain that the electric cooling fan is operating.

5. Disconnect the EGR vacuum line, disconnect the distributor electrical advance connector, and ground the carburetor idle stop switch (if equipped) with a jumper wire.

6. Adjust the idle screw to achieve the curb idle figure listed on the underhood sticker.

7. Back out the mixture screw to achieve the fastest possible idle.

8. Adjust the idle screw to the specified curb idle speed.

FUEL INJECTED ENGINES

The idle speed is controlled by the automatic idle speed (AIS) motor which is controlled by the logic module. The logic module gathers data from the various sensors and switches in the system and adjusts the engine idle to a predetermined speed. Idle specifications can be found on the vehicle emission control information (VECI) label located in the engine compartment.

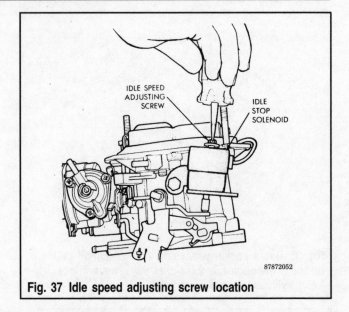

Fig. 37 Idle speed adjusting screw location

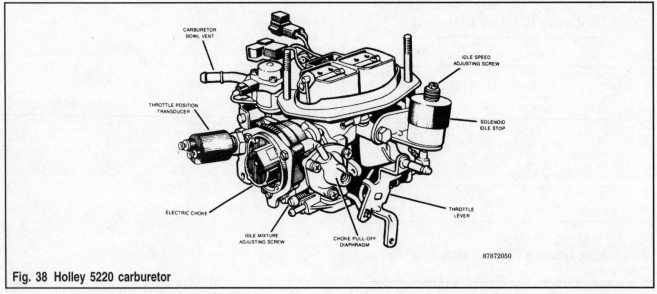

Fig. 38 Holley 5220 carburetor

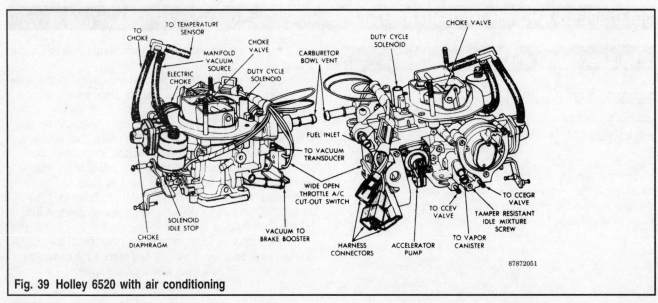

Fig. 39 Holley 6520 with air conditioning

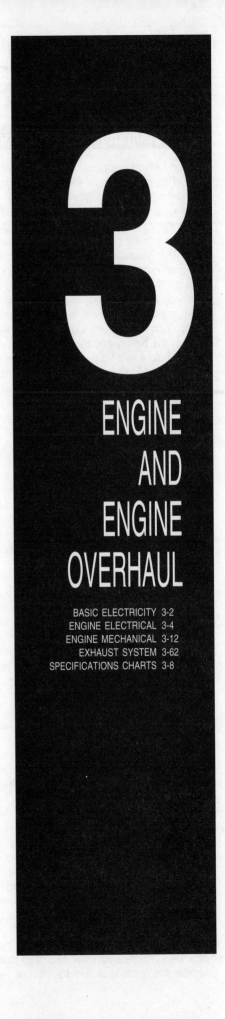

3

ENGINE
AND
ENGINE
OVERHAUL

BASIC ELECTRICITY

Understanding Basic Electricity

For any electrical system to operate, it must be a complete circuit. This simply means that the power flow from the battery must make a full circle. When an electrical component is operating, power flows from the battery to the components, passes through the component (load) causing it to function, and returns to the battery through the ground path of the circuit. This ground may be either another wire or the actual metal part of the vehicle depending upon how the component is designed.

Perhaps the easiest way to visualize this is to think of connecting a light bulb with two wires attached to it to the battery. If one of the two wires was attached to the negative (-) post of the battery and the other wire to the positive (+) post, the light bulb would light and the circuit would be complete. Electricity could follow a path from the battery to the bulb and back to the battery. It's not hard to see that with longer wires on our light bulb, it could be mounted anywhere on the vehicle. Further, one wire could be fitted with a switch so that the light could be turned on and off at will. Various other items could be added to our primitive circuit to make the light flash, become brighter or dimmer under certain conditions, or advise the user that it's burned out.

Some automotive components are grounded through their mounting points. The electrical current runs through the chassis of the vehicle and returns to the battery through the ground (-) cable; if you look, you'll see that the battery ground cable connects between the battery and the body of the vehicle.

Every complete circuit must include a "load" (something to use the electricity coming from the source). If you were to connect a wire between the two terminals of the battery (DON'T do this) without the light bulb, the battery would attempt to deliver its entire power supply from one pole to another almost instantly. This is a short circuit. The electricity is taking a short cut to get to ground and is not being used by any load in the circuit. This sudden and uncontrolled electrical flow can cause great damage to other components in the circuit and can develop a tremendous amount of heat. A short in an automotive wiring harness can develop sufficient heat to melt the insulation on all the surrounding wires and reduce a multiple wire cable to one sad lump of plastic and copper. Two common causes of shorts are broken insulation (thereby exposing the wire to contact with surrounding metal surfaces or other wires) or a failed switch (the pins inside the switch come out of place and touch each other).

Some electrical components which require a large amount of current to operate also have a relay in their circuit. Since these circuits carry a large amount of current (amperage or amps), the thickness of the wire in the circuit (wire gauge) is also greater. If this large wire were connected from the load to the control switch on the dash, the switch would have to carry the high amperage load and the dash would be twice as large to accommodate wiring harnesses as thick as your wrist. To prevent these problems, a relay is used. The large wires in the circuit are connected from the battery to one side of the relay and from the opposite side of the relay to the load. The relay is normally open, preventing current from passing through the circuit. An additional, smaller wire is connected from the relay to the control switch for the circuit. When the control switch is turned on, it grounds the smaller wire to the relay and completes its circuit. The main switch inside the relay closes, sending power to the component without routing the main power through the inside of the vehicle. Some common circuits which may use relays are the horn, headlights, starter and rear window defogger systems.

It is possible for larger surges of current to pass through the electrical system of your vehicle. If this surge of current were to reach the load in the circuit, it could burn it out or severely damage it. To prevent this, fuses, circuit breakers and/or fusible links are connected into the supply wires of the electrical system. These items are nothing more than a built-in weak spot in the system. It's much easier to go to a known location (the fusebox) to see why a circuit is inoperative than to dissect 15 feet of wiring under the dashboard, looking for what happened.

When an electrical current of excessive power passes through the fuse, the fuse blows and breaks the circuit, preventing the passage of current and protecting the components.

A circuit breaker is basically a self repairing fuse. It will open the circuit in the same fashion as a fuse, but when either the short is removed or the surge subsides, the circuit breaker resets itself and does not need replacement.

A fuse link (fusible link or main link) is a wire that acts as a fuse. One of these is normally connected between the starter relay and the main wiring harness under the hood. Since the starter is the highest electrical draw on the vehicle, an internal short during starting could direct about 130 amps into the wrong places. Consider the damage potential of introducing this current into a system whose wiring is rated at 15 amps and you'll understand the need for protection. Since this link is very early in the electrical path, it's the first place to look if nothing on the vehicle works, but the battery seems to be charged and is properly connected.

Electrical problems generally fall into one of three areas:
• The component that is not functioning is not receiving current.
• The component is receiving power but not using it or using it incorrectly (component failure).
• The component is improperly grounded.

The circuit can be can be checked with a test light and a jumper wire. The test light is a device that looks like a pointed screwdriver with a wire on one end and a bulb in its handle. A jumper wire is simply a piece of wire with alligator clips on each end. If a component is not working, you must follow a systematic plan to determine which of the three causes is the villain.

1. Turn on the switch that controls the item not working.

➡**Some items only work when the ignition switch is turned ON.**

2. Disconnect the power supply wire from the component.
3. Attach the ground wire on the test light to a good metal ground.

4. Touch the end probe of the test light to the power wire; if there is current in the wire, the light in the test light will come on. You have now established that current is getting to the component.

5. Turn the ignition or dash switch **OFF** and reconnect the wire to the component.

If the test light did not go on, then the problem is between the battery and the component. This includes all the switches, fuses, relays and the battery itself. The next place to look is the fusebox; check carefully either by eye or by using the test light across the fuse clips. The easiest way to check is to simply replace the fuse. If the fuse is blown, and upon replacement, immediately blows again, there is a short between the fuse and the component. This is generally (not always) a sign of an internal short in the component. Disconnect the power wire at the component again and replace the fuse; if the fuse holds, the component is the problem.

If all the fuses are good and the component is not receiving power, find the switch for the circuit. Bypass the switch with the jumper wire. This is done by connecting one end of the jumper to the power wire coming into the switch and the other end to the wire leaving the switch. If the component comes to life, the switch has failed.

✳✳WARNING

Never substitute the jumper for the component. The circuit needs the electrical load of the component. If you bypass it, you will cause a short circuit.

Checking the ground for any circuit can mean tracing wires to the body, cleaning connections or tightening mounting bolts for the component itself. If the jumper wire can be connected to the case of the component or the ground connector, you can ground the other end to a piece of clean, solid metal on the vehicle. Again, if the component starts working, you've found the problem.

A systematic search through the fuse, connectors, switches and the component itself will almost always yield an answer. Loose and/or corroded connectors, particularly in ground circuits, are becoming a larger problem in modern vehicles. The computers and on-board electronic (solid state) systems are highly sensitive to improper grounds and will change their function drastically if one occurs.

Remember that for any electrical circuit to work, ALL the connections must be clean and tight.

Battery, Starting and Charging Systems

BASIC OPERATING PRINCIPLES

Battery

The battery is the first link in the chain of mechanisms which work together to provide cranking of the automobile engine. In most modern vehicles, the battery is a lead/acid electrochemical device consisting of six 2v subsections (cells) connected in series so the unit is capable of producing approximately 12v of electrical pressure. Each subsection consists of a series of positive and negative plates held a short distance apart in a solution of sulfuric acid and water.

The two types of plates are of dissimilar metals. This causes a chemical reaction to be set up, and it is this reaction which produces current flow from the battery when its positive and negative terminals are connected to an electrical appliance such as a lamp or motor. The continued transfer of electrons would eventually convert the sulfuric acid to water, and make the two plates identical in chemical composition. As electrical energy is removed from the battery, its voltage output tends to drop. Thus, measuring battery voltage and battery electrolyte composition are two ways of checking the ability of the unit to supply power. During the starting of the engine, electrical energy is removed from the battery. However, if the charging circuit is in good condition and the operating conditions are normal, the power removed from the battery will be replaced by the alternator which will force electrons back through the battery, reversing the normal flow, and restoring the battery to its original chemical state.

Starting System

The battery and starting motor are linked by very heavy electrical cables designed to minimize resistance to the flow of current. Generally, the major power supply cable that leaves the battery goes directly to the starter, while other electrical system needs are supplied by a smaller cable. During starter operation, power flows from the battery to the starter and is grounded through the vehicle's frame and the battery's negative ground strap.

The starting motor is a specially designed, direct current electric motor capable of producing a great amount of power for its size. One thing that allows the motor to produce a great deal of power is its tremendous rotating speed. It drives the engine through a tiny pinion gear (attached to the starter's armature), which drives the very large flywheel ring gear at a greatly reduced speed. Another factor allowing it to produce so much power is that only intermittent operation is required of it. Thus, little allowance for air circulation is required, and the windings can be built into a very small space.

The starter solenoid is a magnetic device which employs the small current supplied by the start circuit of the ignition switch. This magnetic action moves a plunger which mechanically engages the starter and closes the heavy switch connecting it to the battery. The starting switch circuit consists of the starting switch contained within the ignition switch, a transaxle neutral safety switch or clutch pedal switch, and the wiring necessary to connect these in series with the starter solenoid or relay.

The pinion, a small gear, is mounted to a one way drive clutch. This clutch is splined to the starter armature shaft. When the ignition switch is moved to the **START** position, the solenoid plunger slides the pinion toward the flywheel ring gear via a collar and spring. If the teeth on the pinion and flywheel match properly, the pinion will engage the flywheel immediately. If the gear teeth butt one another, the spring will be compressed and will force the gears to mesh as soon as the starter turns far enough to allow them to do so. As the solenoid plunger reaches the end of its travel, it closes the contacts that connect the battery and starter and then the engine is cranked.

As soon as the engine starts, the flywheel ring gear begins turning fast enough to drive the pinion at an extremely high rate of speed. At this point, the one-way clutch begins allowing the pinion to spin faster than the starter shaft so that the starter will not operate at excessive speed. When the ignition switch is released from the starter position, the solenoid is de-energized, and a spring pulls the gear out of mesh interrupting the current flow to the starter.

Some starters employ a separate relay, mounted away from the starter, to switch the motor and solenoid current on and off. The relay replaces the solenoid electrical switch, but does not eliminate the need for a solenoid mounted on the starter used to mechanically engage the starter drive gears. The relay is used to reduce the amount of current the starting switch must carry.

Charging System

The automobile charging system provides electrical power for operation of the vehicle's ignition system, starting system and all the electrical accessories. The battery serves as an electrical surge or storage tank, storing (in chemical form) the energy originally produced by the engine driven generator. The system also provides a means of regulating output to protect the battery from being overcharged and to avoid excessive voltage to the accessories.

The storage battery is a chemical device incorporating parallel lead plates in a tank containing a sulfuric acid/water solution. Adjacent plates are slightly dissimilar, and the chemical reaction of the two dissimilar plates produces electrical energy when the battery is connected to a load such as the starter motor. The chemical reaction is reversible, so that when the generator is producing a voltage (electrical pressure) greater than that produced by the battery, electricity is forced into the battery, and the battery is returned to its fully charged state.

Newer automobiles use alternating current generators or alternators, because they are more efficient, can be rotated at higher speeds, and have fewer brush problems. In an alternator, the field rotates while all the current produced passes only through the stator winding. The brushes bear against continuous slip rings. This causes the current produced to periodically reverse the direction of its flow. Diodes (electrical one way valves) block the flow of current from traveling in the wrong direction. A series of diodes is wired together to permit the alternating flow of the stator to be rectified back to 12 volts DC for use by the vehicles's electrical system.

The voltage regulating function is performed by a regulator. The regulator is often built in to the alternator; this system is termed an integrated or internal regulator.

ENGINE ELECTRICAL

Ignition Coil

TESTING

▶ See Figure 1

➡To perform a reliable test of the coil, you must make up several jumper wires. You'll need two simple wires several feet long with alligator clips on the ends. A third wire must incorporate a capacitor of 0.33 Micro Farad capacitance. The materials and components needed to make up such jumpers should be available at a reasonable price in a local electronics store.

1. Turn the ignition key **OFF**. Disconnect the negative battery cable. Then, carefully remove the retaining nuts and disconnect the two coil primary leads. Wrap the positive (+) lead in electrician's tape or otherwise ensure that it cannot accidentally ground during the test.

2. Run a jumper wire from the battery positive (+) terminal directly to the coil positive (+) terminal. Run the jumper wire incorporating the capacitor from the coil negative terminal to a good ground. Reconnect the battery negative cable. Fasten one end of the remaining standard jumper wire in a position where the clip cannot ground. Then connect the other end of it to the coil negative terminal. Turn **ON** the ignition key.

3. Unclip the coil high tension lead from inside the distributor cap and pull it out. Hold the distributor end of the lead ¼ in. (6mm) from a good ground. Ground the standard jumper wire coming from the coil negative terminal.

4. Break the ground in the standard lead coming from the coil negative as you watch for spark. The coil should produce

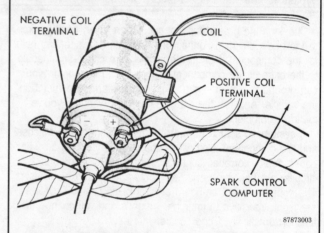

Fig. 1 The ignition coil has two primary terminals, positive and negative. Make sure they are free of corrosion prior to testing

a hot, blue-white spark. Repeat the test looking at the coil tower. If sparks are visible there, replace the ignition wires if the rubber boots are deteriorated, or the coil, if the tower is burned and tracked.

5. If the coil tower and wire boots are okay, and this test fails to produce a spark, replace the coil.

On 1987-89 cars, you can confirm the problem with an ohmmeter. Turn **OFF** the ignition switch, and disconnect the negative battery cable. With the coil primary wires still disconnected, test the resistance between positive and negative primary terminals. It must be 1.35-1.55 ohms. For secondary resistance, first determine whether the coil is a Chrysler Prestolite, Chrysler Essex, or Diamond brand coil by wiping off the coil and looking for appropriate lettering. Then, pull the high tension lead out of the coil tower and run the ohmmeter lead between the coil negative primary terminal and the brass connector down inside the tower. Resistance ranges must be as follows:

- Chrysler Prestolite — 9,400-11,700 ohms
- Chrysler Essex — 9,000-12,200 ohms
- Diamond — 15,000-19,000 ohms

✳✳WARNING

If the coil tests okay, you must be sure to turn OFF the ignition switch and have the battery negative cable disconnected before reconnecting the primary leads.

REMOVAL & INSTALLATION

▶ See Figures 2, 3 and 4

1. Disconnect the negative battery cable.
2. Remove the coil wire.
3. Tag the negative and positive wire leads to the coil.
4. Remove the wire lead connections.
5. Take off the wire leads from the coil.
6. Loosen the mounting screw, then slide the coil from the mounting brace.

Fig. 2 Carefully unplug the secondary terminal wire

Fig. 3 Tag the wires, then remove the nuts securing them

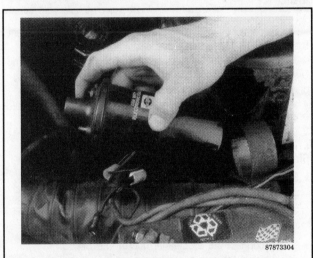

Fig. 4 After the mounting screw is loosened, the coil can be removed from the brace

To install:
7. Insert the coil into the mounting brace.
8. Attach the wiring leads to the coil.
9. Tighten down the brace if needed.
10. Attach the coil wire.
11. Connect the negative battery cable.

Ignition Module

REMOVAL & INSTALLATION

Spark Control Computer (SCC)

The Ignition Module is called the Spark Control Computer (SCC) on 1978-87 models.

✳✳WARNING

The grease located in the 10 or 14 way connector cavity in the computer is necessary to prevent moisture from corroding the terminals. Not only should this grease be left in place, but if the layer is less than 1/8 in. (3mm) thick, spread Mopar Multi-purpose grease part No. 2932524 or an equivalent available in the aftermarket in an even layer over the end of each connector plug before reconnecting them.

1. Disconnect the negative battery cable. Then, disconnect the 10 and 14-way dual connectors.
2. Disconnect the outside air duct at the computer housing. Disconnect the vacuum line at the vacuum transducer on top of the housing.
3. Remove the 3 mounting screws that fasten the computer to the inside of the left front fender and remove it.
4. Installation is the reverse of removal.

Single Module Engine Controller (SMEC)
▶ See Figure 5

The Single Module Engine Controller (SMEC) is used on 1988-89 models.
1. Disconnect both battery cables (negative first).
2. Disconnect the air cleaner duct at the SMEC.
3. Remove the two mounting screws by which the module hangs onto the fender well.

4. Move the unit out slightly for access, then detach both the 14 and 60-way wiring connectors. Remove the SMEC from the engine compartment.
5. Install the module in reverse order. Attach the electrical connectors before attempting to mount it.

Distributor

✳✳WARNING

1980 and later models have a different distributor cap. Never pull the wire from the cap. The wires are retained in the cap by means of internal clips in the wire towers. To remove a wire, first remove the distributor cap, then squeeze the clips ends together while gently removing the wire from the cap. Failure to follow this procedure will damage the core of the wire.

Chrysler recommends that the wires not be removed from the cap for any reason other than replacement of a damaged wire or a wire that shows too much resistance.

REMOVAL & INSTALLATION

▶ See Figures 6, 7, 8 and 9

1. Disconnect the distributor pickup lead wire at the harness. If so equipped, remove the splash shield.
2. Remove the distributor cap.
3. Matchmark the position of the rotor to the distributor, then the distributor to the block.
4. Remove the distributor hold-down bolt.
5. Carefully lift the distributor from the engine. The shaft will rotate slightly as the distributor is removed.
   To install:
6. If the engine has been cranked over while the distributor was removed, rotate the crankshaft until the number one piston is at TDC on the compression stroke. This will be indicated by the O mark on the flywheel aligning with the pointer on the clutch housing. Position the rotor just ahead of the No. 1

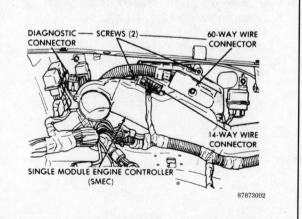

Fig. 5 The Single Module Engine Controller (SMEC) replaces the Spark Control Computer in the earlier models

Fig. 6 Remove the distributor cap and position it aside

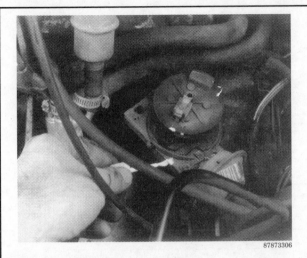

Fig. 7 Mark the position of the rotor and distributor for easier installation

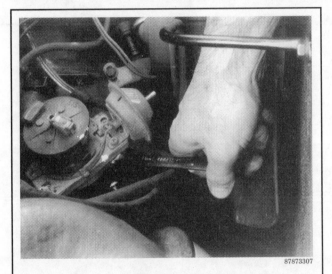

Fig. 8 Remove the distributor hold-down bolt

Fig. 9 Carefully lift the distributor from the engine. The shaft will rotate slightly as the distributor is removed

terminal of the cap and lower the distributor into the engine. With the distributor fully seated, the rotor should be directly under the No. 1 terminal.

7. If the engine was not disturbed while the distributor was out, lower the distributor into the engine, engaging the gears and making sure that the gasket is properly seated in the block. The rotor should line up with the mark made before removal.

8. Tighten the hold-down bolt and connect the wires. Install the distributor splash shield on models so equipped.

9. Check and adjust the ignition timing.

Alternator

A conventional alternator is used. It has six built-in rectifiers which convert AC current to DC current. Current at the output terminal is DC. The main components of the alternator are: the rotor, stator, rectifiers, end shields and the drive pulley.

The electronic voltage regulator is a device which regulates the vehicle electrical system voltage by limiting the output voltage that is generated by the alternator. This is accomplished by controlling the amount of current that is allowed to pass through the alternator field windings. The regulator has no moving parts and requires no adjustment.

PRECAUTIONS

To prevent damage to the alternator and regulator, the following precautions should be taken when working with the electrical system.

- Never reverse the battery connections.
- Booster batteries for starting must be connected properly, positive-to-positive and negative-to-negative.
- Disconnect the battery cables before using a fast charger. The charger has a tendency to force current through the diodes in the opposite direction for which they were designed. This burns out the diodes.
- Never use a fast charger as a booster for starting the vehicle.
- Never adjust an alternator with the engine running.
- Never disconnect the voltage regulator while the engine is running.
- Avoid long soldering times when replacing diodes or transistors. Prolonged heat is damaging to AC generators.
- Do not use test lamps of more than 12 volts (V) for checking diode continuity.
- Do not short across or ground any of the terminals on the AC generator.
- The polarity of the battery, generator, and regulator must be matched and considered before making any electrical connections within the system.
- Never operate the alternator on an open circuit. Make sure that all connections within the circuit are clean and tight.
- Disconnect the battery terminals when performing any service on the electrical system. This will eliminate the possibility of accidental reversal of polarity.
- Disconnect the battery ground cable if arc welding is to be done on any part of the car.

Alternator and Regulator Specifications

	Alternator				Regulator	
Year	Manufacturer	Identification	Field Current @ 12v (amp)	Output (amps)	Manufacturer	Volts @ 75°F
'79–'81	Chrysler	Yellow Tag	4.5–6.5	60	Chrysler Electronic	13.9
	Chrysler	Brown Tag	4.5–6.5	65	Chrysler Electronic	13.9
'82–'83	Chrysler	Yellow Tag	4.5–6.5	60	Chrysler Electronic	13.9
	Chrysler	Brown Tag	4.5–6.5	78	Chrysler Electronic	13.9
'84–'86	Chrysler	Yellow Tag	2.5–5.0	60	Chrysler Electronic	13.9
	Chrysler	Brown Tag	2.5–5.0	78	Chrysler Electronic	13.9
	Bosch	K1	2.5–5.0	65	Chrysler Electronic	13.9
	Bosch	N1	—	90	Bosch Integral	14.1
'87	Chrysler	5213763	2.5–5.0	78	Chrysler Electronics	13.9
	Chrysler	5226135	2.5–5.0	78	——— ① ———	
	Chrysler	5227100	2.5–5.0	40/90	——— ① ———	
	Bosch	522600	2.5–5.0	40/90	——— ① ———	
'88–'89	Bosch	5227469	2.5–5.0	35/75	——— ① ———	
	Bosch	5227474	2.5–5.0	40/90	——— ① ———	
	Bosch	5227749	2.5–5.0	40/90	——— ① ———	
	Chrysler	5233474	2.5–5.0	40/90	——— ① ———	
	Chrysler	5233508	2.5–5.0	50/120	——— ① ———	

① Contained within engine electronics Power Module and Logic Module

87873caa

REMOVAL & INSTALLATION

▶ See Figures 10, 11 and 12

1. Disconnect the negative battery cable.
2. Remove the wires from the alternator.
3. Support the alternator, remove the mounting bolts and brackets if needed.
4. Slide the belt off the unit.
5. Lift the alternator out of the vehicle.

To install:

6. Position the alternator on the engine.
7. Install the mounting bolts (and brackets) if removed.
8. Install the belt on the alternator.
9. Adjust the belt by tightening the adjusting bolt.

➡**Never adjust a belt with the engine running.**

10. Tighten the mounting bolts, attach the wiring to the alternator.

11. Connect the negative battery cable.
12. Start the engine and observe the operation.

Regulator

REMOVAL & INSTALLATION

▶ See Figures 13, 14 and 15

1. Disconnect the negative battery cable.
2. Remove the wires from the regulator.
3. Remove the two sheet metal screws securing the regulator to the right side fender skirt.

To install:

4. Attach the regulator to the vehicle with the mounting screws.
5. Attach the wiring harness to the regulator.
6. Connect the negative battery cable.

Fig. 10 Loosen . . .

Fig. 11 . . . then remove the alternator mounting bolts

Fig. 12 After the mounting bolts are removed, the alternator can be removed from the vehicle

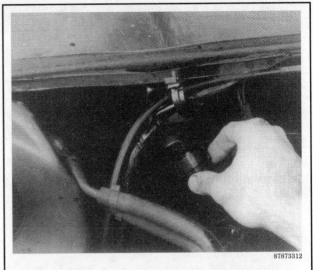

Fig. 13 Unplug the wiring harness from the regulator

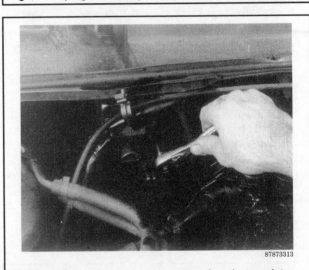

Fig. 14 Remove the two screws securing the regulator to the body of the vehicle

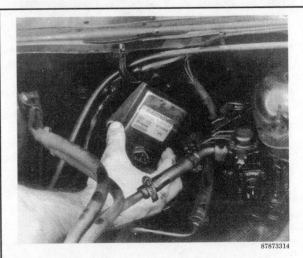

Fig. 15 The regulator can now be removed from the vehicle

Battery

REMOVAL & INSTALLATION

▶ See Figure 16

✳✳WARNING

In the event of the battery case is cracked or leaking, protect your hands with a suitable pair of rubber gloves. The common household type are not recommended for this.

1. Make sure the ignition is in the **OFF** position and all battery feed accessories are off.
2. Open the hood.
3. Disconnect the negative battery cable first, then the positive.
4. Unfasten the hold-down clamp, then remove the battery.
To install:
5. If necessary, replace any damaged cables before installing the battery.
6. Clean the top of the battery with a solution of water and baking soda. Scrub the area using a stiff bristle brush, then wipe off with a cloth moistened in the baking soda solution. Throw away all used rags when done.
7. Inspect the battery tray for any damage, clean with the baking soda solution or replace if needed.
8. If the old battery is being put back in the vehicle, clean the posts with a suitable tool. With a new or old battery, make sure to clean the inside surfaces of the terminal ends of the cables.
9. Position the battery on the tray.
10. Attach the hold down clamp, tighten the bolts to 250 inch lbs. (28 Nm).

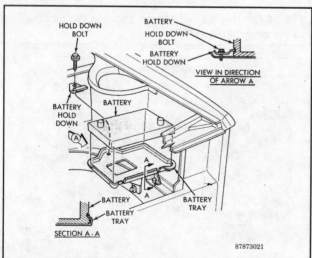

Fig. 16 Common battery mounting found on models covered by this manual

11. Connect the battery cables. Make sure the top of the clamps are flush with the top of the post.
12. Tighten the clamp nut securely.
13. Coat the terminal ends with a light mineral grease after tightening.
14. Close the hood.
15. Start the vehicle, run for about 15-20 min. to make sure you have a good charge.

Starter

The starter is an overrunning clutch drive type with a solenoid mounted on the starter motor. Six different type starters are used on these models. Two each are built by Nippondenso, Bosch and Mitsubishi for manual and automatic transaxle applications. Removal and installation procedures are the same for all units.

Some early production models may experience starter motor damage due to improper fit of the upper and lower steering column shrouds. Irregularities in the mating surface of the key cylinder area may cause the ignition key to bind, causing the starter to be continuously engaged. The condition can be corrected by loosening the shroud cover screws about 1½ turns.

If loosening the screws does not solve the problem, the covers will have to be replaced with new parts, which are available only in black and must be painted to match interior trim.

REMOVAL & INSTALLATION

▶ See Figures 17, 18, 19 and 20

1. Disconnect the negative battery cable.
2. If equipped, remove the heat shield.
3. On the 2.2L loosen the air pump tube at the exhaust manifold, then swivel the bracket away from the starter.
4. Remove the wires from the starter and solenoid.
5. Support the starter, remove the bolts and lift the unit out from the flywheel housing.
6. Installation is the reverse of removal.

SOLENOID REPLACEMENT

1. Remove the starter from the vehicle.
2. Disconnect any wiring that may be connecting the solenoid and starter.
3. Loosen the solenoid mounting screws, then slide it off the starter.
To install:
4. Position the new solenoid on the starter, tighten the mounting screws.
5. Connect any wiring from the starter to the solenoid.
6. Install the starter.

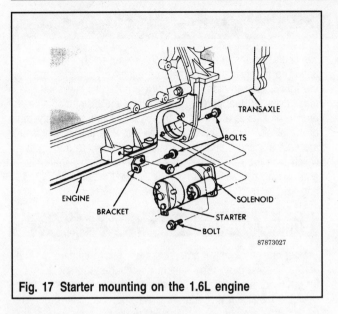

Fig. 17 Starter mounting on the 1.6L engine

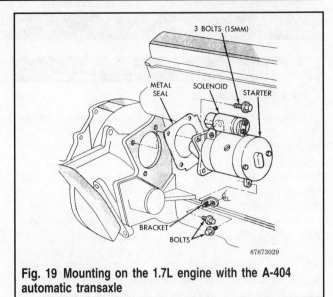

Fig. 19 Mounting on the 1.7L engine with the A-404 automatic transaxle

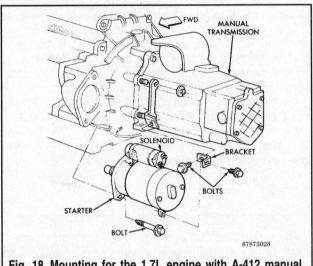

Fig. 18 Mounting for the 1.7L engine with A-412 manual transaxle

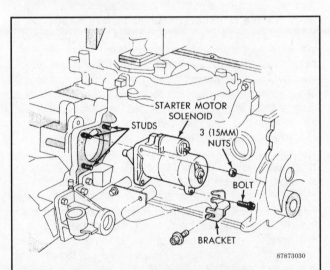

Fig. 20 Mounting for the 1.7L A-460 manual transaxle and the 2.2L manual or automatic transaxle

STARTER SPECIFICATIONS

Year	Engine	Trans.	Manufacturer	Load Test*		Torque (ft. lb.)	No-Load Test		
				Amps	Volts		Amps	Volts	RPM
'78–'83	All	All	Bosch or Nippondenso	120–160	12	—	47	11	6600
'84–'86	1.6	All	Mitsubishi	120–160	12	—	47	11	6600
	2.2	All	Bosch or Nippondenso	120–160	12	—	47	11	6600
'87	2.2	All	Bosch ①	120–160	12	—	47	11	6600
	2.2	All	Bosch ②	150–210	12	—	75	11	4020
	2.2	All	Nippondenso ②	150–210	12	—	75	11	4020
'88–'89	2.2	All	Nippondenso ②	150–220	12	—	82	11	3625

*To perform the load test, the engine should be up to operating temperature. Extremely heavy oil or tight engine will increase starter amperage draw.
① Direct Drive starter
② Reduction Gear starter

ENGINE MECHANICAL

Description

♦ **See Figures 21 and 22**

There are three different engines used in these body styles. The 1.7L, basically a Volkswagen design, is used during the 1978 thru 1983 model years. The 2.2L engine, a Chrysler refined version of the 1.7L engine was introduced during the 1981 model year. In 1984 the 1.6L engine was introduced to replace the 1.7L engine. Below is a description of each of these engines.

The 1.6L displacement engine is a four cylinder overhead valve engine with a cast iron block and an aluminum cylinder head. Five main bearings support the forged steel crankshaft with number three being the thrust bearing. The cast iron dual timing chain sprocket on the crankshaft, not only provides power for the timing chains, but it also acts as a vibration damper. The cast iron camshaft is mounted on three babbitt bearings and a thrust plate located at the front bearing controls the camshaft end-play. The camshaft itself is positioned left of the crankshaft, or toward the front of the car. The camshaft is driven by dual timing chains. These chains are enclosed by a cast aluminum timing cover which has the strobe ignition timing marks embossed on it. The cylinder head material is an aluminum alloy. The head is a crossflow design with inline valves. The valve train design incorporates the use of mechanical tappets, pushrods, and adjustable rocker arms. The spark plugs are located on the left side of the engine opposite the valves. The intake manifold is made of a cast aluminum alloy, cored with coolant passages for carburetor warm up. This manifold is located on the left side of the head. Embossed on the intake manifold is the cylinder number identification, firing order, and the direction of the distributor rotation. The exhaust manifold is made of nodular iron and is attached to the right side of the head (towards the rear of the car) and is held on by eight bolts.

The 1.7L displacement engine is a four cylinder, overhead camshaft engine. The block is cast iron and the head is aluminum. A five main bearing forged steel crankshaft using no vibration damper is employed, rotated by cast aluminum pistons. A sintered iron timing belt sprocket is mounted on the end of the crankshaft. The intake manifold and oil filter base are aluminum. A steel reinforced belt drives the intermediate shaft and camshaft. The intermediate shaft drives the oil pump, distributor, and fuel pump. The cylinder head is lightweight aluminum alloy. The intake and exhaust manifolds are mounted on the same side of the cylinder head. The valves are opened and closed by the camshaft lobes operating on cupped cam followers which fit over the valves and springs. This design results in lighter valve train weight and fewer moving parts.

The 2.2L displacement engine is a four cylinder, overhead camshaft design powerplant with a cast iron block and an aluminum cylinder head. The cast iron crankshaft is supported by five main bearings. No vibration dampener is used. The iron camshaft also has five bearing journals and there are flanges at the rear journal to control the camshaft end-play. Sintered iron timing sprockets are mounted on both the camshaft and the crankshaft which are driven by the timing belt. The timing belt also drives an accessory shaft, housed in the forward facing side of the block. The accessory shaft, in turn drives the fuel pump, oil pump and the distributor. The engine oil filter is attached to the base located at the left front of the block, toward the front of the car. The intake manifolds are cast aluminum and the exhaust manifolds are iron, both of which face the rear of the vehicle. The distributor, spark plugs and oil filter are all located on the forward facing side of the engine.

Engine Overhaul Tips

Most engine overhaul procedures are fairly standard. In addition to specific parts replacement procedures and specifications for your individual engine, this section also is a guide to acceptable rebuilding procedures. Examples of standard rebuilding practice are shown and should be used along with specific details concerning your particular engine.

Competent and accurate machine shop services will ensure maximum performance, reliability and engine life. In most instances it is more profitable for the do-it-yourself mechanic to remove, clean and inspect the component, buy the necessary parts and deliver these to a shop for actual machine work.

On the other hand, much of the rebuilding work (crankshaft, block, bearings, piston rods, and other components) is well within the scope of the do-it-yourself mechanic's tools and abilities. You will have to decide for yourself the depth of involvement you desire in an engine repair or rebuild.

TOOLS

The tools required for an engine overhaul or parts replacement will depend on the depth of your involvement. With a few exceptions, they will be the tools found in a mechanic's tool kit (see Section 1 of this manual). More in-depth work will require some or all of the following:
- a dial indicator (reading in thousandths) mounted on a universal base
- micrometers and telescope gauges
- jaw and screw-type pullers
- scraper
- valve spring compressor
- ring groove cleaner
- piston ring expander and compressor
- ridge reamer
- cylinder hone or glaze breaker
- Plastigage®
- engine stand

The use of most of these tools is illustrated in this chapter. Many can be rented for a one-time use from a local parts jobber or tool supply house specializing in automotive work.

Occasionally, the use of special tools is called for. See the information on Special Tools and the Safety Notice in the front of this book before substituting another tool.

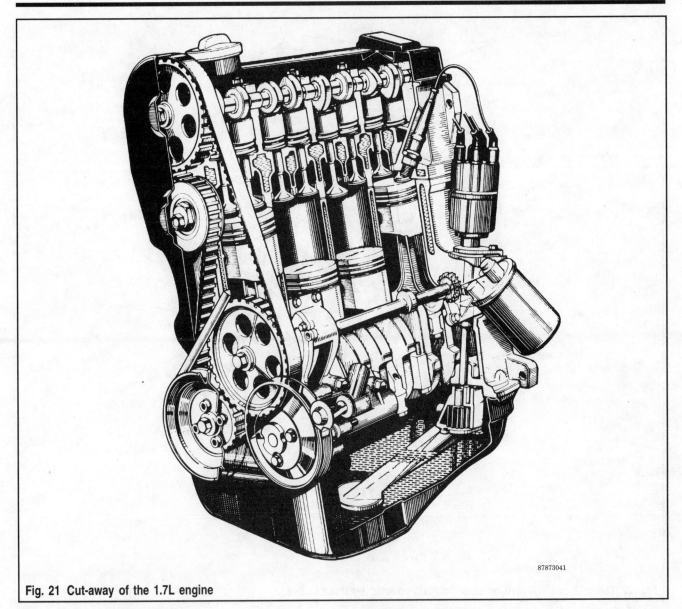

Fig. 21 Cut-away of the 1.7L engine

87873041

INSPECTION TECHNIQUES

Procedures and specifications are given in this chapter for inspecting, cleaning and assessing the wear limits of most major components. Other procedures such as Magnaflux® and Zyglo® can be used to locate material flaws and stress cracks. Magnaflux® is a magnetic process applicable only to ferrous materials. The Zyglo® process coats the material with a fluorescent dye penetrant and can be used on any material. Checking for suspected surface cracks can be more readily made using spot check dye. The dye is sprayed onto the suspected area, wiped off and the area sprayed with a developer. Cracks will show up brightly.

OVERHAUL TIPS

Aluminum has become extremely popular for use in engines, due to its low weight. Observe the following precautions when handling aluminum parts:
• Never hot tank aluminum parts (the caustic hot tank solution will eat the aluminum.
• Remove all aluminum parts (identification tag, etc.) from engine parts prior to the tanking.
• Always coat threads lightly with engine oil or anti-seize compounds before installation, to prevent seizure.
• Never overtighten bolts or spark plugs especially in aluminum threads.

Stripped threads in any component can be repaired using any of several commercial repair kits (Heli-Coil®, Microdot®, Keenserts®, etc.).

When assembling the engine, any parts that will be exposed to frictional contact, the parts must be prelubed to provide lubrication at initial start-up. Any product specifically formulated

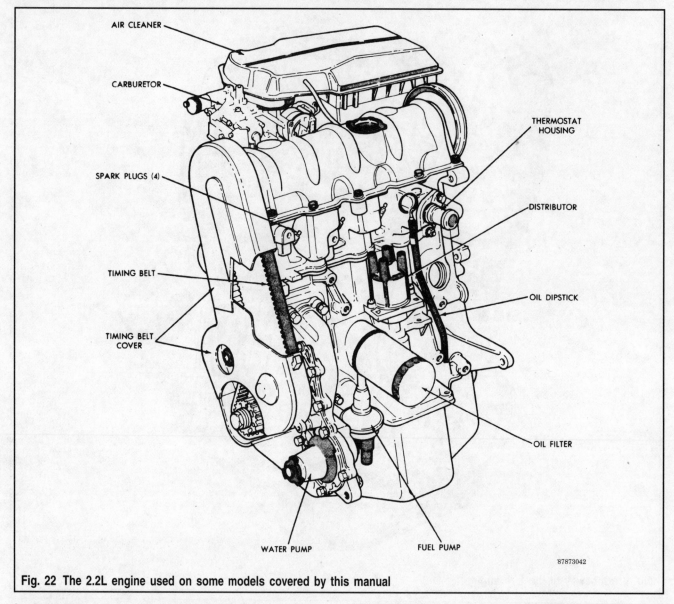

AIR CLEANER

CARBURETOR

THERMOSTAT HOUSING

SPARK PLUGS (4)

DISTRIBUTOR

TIMING BELT

OIL DIPSTICK

TIMING BELT COVER

OIL FILTER

WATER PUMP

FUEL PUMP

87873042

Fig. 22 The 2.2L engine used on some models covered by this manual

for this purpose can be used, but engine oil is not recommended as a prelube in most cases.

When semi-permanent (locked, but removable) installation of bolts or nuts is desired, threads should be cleaned and coated with Loctite® or other similar, commercial non-hardening sealant.

REPAIRING DAMAGED THREADS

▶ **See Figures 23, 24, 25, 26 and 27**

Several methods of repairing damaged threads are available. Heli-Coil® (shown here), Keenserts® and Microdot® are among the most widely used. All involve basically the same principle — drilling out stripped threads, tapping the hole and installing a prewound insert — making welding, plugging and oversize fasteners unnecessary.

Two types of thread repair inserts are usually supplied: a standard type for most inch coarse, inch fine, metric course and metric fine thread sizes and a spark lug type to fit most spark plug port sizes. Consult the individual manufacturer's

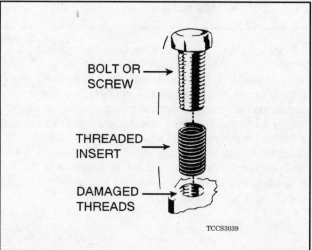

BOLT OR SCREW

THREADED INSERT

DAMAGED THREADS

TCCS3039

Fig. 23 Damaged bolt hole threads can be replaced with thread repair inserts

Fig. 24 Standard thread repair insert (left), and spark plug thread insert

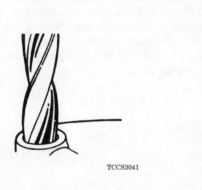

Fig. 25 Drill out the damaged threads with the specified drill. Be sure to drill completely through the hole or to the bottom of a blind hole

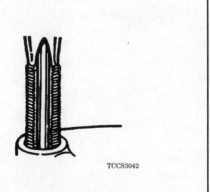

Fig. 26 Using the kit, tap the hole in order to receive the thread insert. Keep the tap well oiled and back it out frequently to avoid clogging the threads.

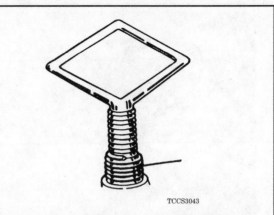

Fig. 27 Screw the threaded insert onto the installer tool until the tang engages the slot. Thread the insert into the hole until it is ¼ or ½ turn below the top surface, then remove the tool and break off the tang using a punch.

catalog to determine exact applications. Typical thread repair kits will contain a selection of prewound threaded inserts, a tap (corresponding to the outside diameter threads of the insert) and an installation tool. Spark plug inserts usually differ because they require a tap equipped with pilot threads and a combined reamer/tap section. Most manufacturers also supply blister-packed thread repair inserts separately in addition to a master kit containing a variety of taps and inserts plus installation tools.

Before attempting to repair a threaded hole, remove any snapped, broken or damaged bolts or studs. Penetrating oil can be used to free frozen threads. The offending item can be removed with locking pliers or using a screw/stud extractor. After the hole is clear, the thread can be repaired.

Checking Engine Compression

▶ See Figure 28

A noticeable lack of engine power, excessive oil consumption and/or poor fuel mileage measured over an extended period are all indicators of internal engine wear. Worn piston rings, scored or worn cylinder bores, blown head gaskets, sticking or burnt valves and worn valve seats are all possible culprits here. A check of each cylinder's compression will help you locate the problems.

As mentioned in the Tools and Equipment section, a screw-in type compression gauge is more accurate that the type you simply hold against the spark plug hole, although it takes slightly longer to use. It's worth it to obtain a more accurate reading. Follow the procedures below.

1. Warm up the engine to normal operating temperature.
2. Remove all the spark plugs.
3. Disconnect the high tension lead from the ignition coil.
4. Fully open the throttle either by operating the throttle linkage by hand or by having an assistant floor the accelerator pedal.

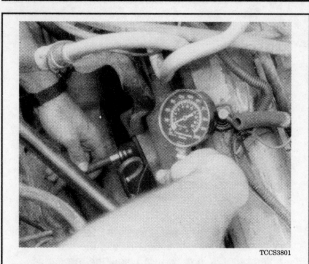

TCCS3801

Fig. 28 A screw-in type compression gauge is more accurate and easier to use without an assistant

5. Screw the compression gauge into the No.1 spark plug hole until the fitting is snug.

✴✴WARNING

Be careful not to crossthread the plug hole. On aluminum cylinder heads use extra care, as the threads in these heads are easily ruined.

6. Ask an assistant to depress the accelerator pedal fully on both carbureted and fuel injected vehicles. Then, while you read the compression gauge, ask the assistant to crank the engine two or three times in short bursts using the ignition switch.

7. Read the compression gauge at the end of each series of cranks, and record the highest of these readings. Repeat this procedure for each of the engine's cylinders. Compare the highest reading of each cylinder to the compression pressure specification in the Tune-Up Specifications chart. The specs in this chart are maximum values.

A cylinder's compression pressure is acceptable on these cars if it is not less than 75% of maximum. The minimum pressure for these engines is 100 psi. (690 kPa).

8. If a cylinder is unusually low, pour a tablespoon of clean engine oil into the cylinder through the spark plug hole and repeat the compression test. If the compression comes up after adding the oil, it appears that the cylinder's piston rings or bore are damaged or worn. If the pressure remains low, the valves may not be seating properly (a valve job is needed), or the head gasket may be blown near that cylinder. If compression in any two adjacent cylinders is low, and if the addition of oil doesn't help the compression, there is leakage past the head gasket. Oil and coolant water in the combustion chamber can result from this problem. There may be evidence of water droplets in the oil film on the engine dipstick when a head gasket has blown.

GENERAL ENGINE SPECIFICATIONS

Engine	Year	Carb. Type	Horsepower @ rpm	Torque ft. lb. @ rpm	Bore x Stroke	Comp. Ratio	Oil. Press. (psi.) @ 2000 rpm
1.6L	'84	2 bbl.	64 @ 4800	87 @ 2800	3.17 x 3.07	8.8:1	58–87
1.7L	'78	2 bbl.	75 @ 5600	90 @ 3200	3.13 x 3.40	8.2:1	60–90
	'79	2 bbl.	70 @ 5200	85 @ 2800	3.13 x 3.40	8.2:1	60–90
	'80	2 bbl.	65 @ 5200	85 @ 2400	3.13 x 3.40	8.2:1	60–90
	'81–'82	2 bbl	63 @ 5200	83 @ 2400	3.13 x 3.40	8.2:1	60–90
	'83	2 bbl.	63 @ 4800	83 @ 2400	3.13 x 3.40	8.2:1	60–90
2.2L	'81–'82	2 bbl.	84 @ 4800	111 @ 2800	3.44 x 3.62	8.5:1	50
	'83	2 bbl.	94 @ 5200	117 @ 3200	3.44 x 3.62	9.0:1	50
	①	2 bbl.	100 @ 5200	122 @ 3200	3.44 x 3.62	9.0:1	50
	②	2 bbl.	107 @ 5600	126 @ 3600	3.44 x 3.62	9.6:1	50
	'84–'86	2 bbl.	96 @ 5200	119 @ 3200	3.44 x 3.62	9.0:1	50
	①	2 bbl.	101 @ 5200	124 @ 3200	3.44 x 3.62	9.0:1	50
	②	2 bbl.	110 @ 5600	129 @ 3600	3.44 x 3.62	9.6:1	50
	③	EFI	110 @ 5600	129 @ 3600	3.44 x 3.62	—	50
	④	Turbo	146 @ 5200	170 @ 3600	3.44 x 3.62	—	50
	'87	2 bbl.	96 @ 5200	119 @ 3200	3.44 x 3.62	9.0:1	50
		Turbo.	146 @ 5200	170 @ 3600	3.44 x 3.62	8.0:1	50
	'88–'89	EFI	93 @ 4800	121 @ 3200	3.44 x 3.62	9.5:1	50

① Standard engine in the Charger & Turismo 2.2 models
② High output engine used in the Shelby Charger
③ High output GLH
④ Turbo GLH

87873044

VALVE SPECIFICATIONS

Engine	Seat Angle (deg)	Face Angle (deg)	Spring Test Pressure (lbs. @ in.)	Spring Installed Height (in.)	Stem to Guide Clearance (in.) Intake	Stem to Guide Clearance (in.) Exhaust	Stem Diameter (in.) Intake	Stem Diameter (in.) Exhaust
1.6L	46	45	—	—	.0015–.0027	.0022–.0035	.3137–.3143	.3129–.3136
1.7L	45	①	②	③	.020 ④ max	.027 ④ max	.3140	.3140
2.2L (1981–82)	45	45.5	⑤	1.65	.001–.003	.002–.004	.312–.313	.311–.312
2.2L (1983–89)	45	45	⑤	1.65	.0009–.0026	.0030–.0047	.3124	.3103

① Intake: 45° 33' Exhaust: 43° 33'
② Outer: 101 @ .878 Inner: 49 @ .720
③ Outer: 1.28 Inner: 1.13
④ Measurement is made with the valve in the cylinder head positioned .400 in. above the cylinder head gasket surface.
⑤ Standard: 150 lbs. @ 122. Turbo: 175 @ 1.22

87873045

CRANKSHAFT AND CONNECTING ROD SPECIFICATIONS

	Crankshaft				Connecting Rod		
Engine	Main Bearing Journal Dia.	Main Bearing Oil Clearance	Shaft End Play	Thrust on No.	Journal Dia.	Oil Clearance	Side Clearance
1.6L	2.046–2.047	.0009–.0031	.003–.011	3	1.612–1.613	.0010–.0025	.006–.009
1.7L	2.124–2.128	.0008–.0030	.003–.007	3	1.809–1.813	.0011–.0034	.015
2.2L	2.362–2.363	.0003–.0031	.002–.007	3	1.968–1.969	.0008–.0034 ①	.005–.013

① Turbocharged: .0008–.0031

87873046

PISTON AND RING SPECIFICATIONS

		Ring Gap			Ring Side Clearance			
Engine	Year	Top Compr.	Bottom Compr.	Oil Control	Top Compr.	Bottom Compr.	Oil Control	Piston Clearance
1.6L	'84	.012–.018	.012–.018	.010–.016	.0018–.0028	.0018–.0028	.008 max	.0016–.0020
1.7L	'78–'79	.012–.018	.012–.018	.010–.016	.0008–.0020	.0008–.0020	.0008–.0020	.0011–.0270
	'80	.012–.018	.012–.018	.016–.045	.0016–.0028	.0008–.0020	.0008–.0020	.0004–.0015
	'81–'83	.012–.018	.012–.018	.016–.055	.0016–.0028	.0008–.0020	.008 max	.0004–.0015
2.2L	'81–'83	.011–.021	.011–.021	.015–.055	.0015–.0031	.0015–.0037	.008 max	.0005–.0015
2.2L	'84–'89	.010–.020	.009–.019	.015–.055	.0015–.0031	.0015–.0037	.008 max	.0015–.0025

87873047

TORQUE SPECIFICATIONS

Engine	Cyl. Head	Conn. Rod	Main Bearing	Crankshaft Bolt	Flywheel	Camshaft Cap Bolts	Camshaft Sprocket Bolts
1.6L	52	28	48	110	—	—	—
1.7L	60 ①	35 ③	47	58	55 ②	14	58
2.2L	45 ①	40 ①	30 ①	50	65	14	65

① Thru 1986; 4 step sequence: 30, 45, 45 plus ¼ turn more
  1987–89: 4 step sequence: 45, 65, 65 plus ½ turn more
② 50 ft. lbs. with auto. trans.
③ 1978 33 ft. lbs.
④ 1986–89 all transaxles: 70 ft. lbs.

87873048

Engine

REMOVAL & INSTALLATION

◆ **See Figures 29, 30, 31, 32, 33 and 34**

1. Disconnect the negative battery cable.
2. Scribe the hood hinge outline and remove the hood.
3. Drain the cooling system.

✳✳CAUTION

When draining the coolant, keep in mind that cats and dogs are attracted by ethylene glycol antifreeze, and are quite likely to drink any that is left in an uncovered container or in puddles on the ground. This will prove fatal in sufficient quantity. Always drain the coolant into a sealable container. Coolant should be reused unless it is contaminated or several years old.

4. Remove the radiator hoses and remove the radiator and shroud assembly.
5. Remove the air cleaner and hoses.
6. On cars equipped with air conditioning, the compressor does not have to be disconnected. Remove it from its bracket and position it out of the way. Securing it with a piece of wire is the best method.

➡**On air conditioned, cars do not disconnect any hoses from the air conditioning system. Disconnect the compressor from the bracket with the hoses attached.**

7. Remove the power steering pump and position it out of the way.
8. Drain the engine oil and remove the oil filter.

✳✳CAUTION

The EPA warns that prolonged contact with used engine oil may cause a number of skin disorders, including cancer! You should make every effort to minimize your exposure to used engine oil. Protective gloves should be worn when changing the oil. Wash your hands and any other exposed skin areas as soon as possible after exposure to used engine oil. Soap and water, or waterless hand cleaner should be used.

9. Disconnect all the wiring from the engine and alternator.
10. Disconnect the fuel line, heater hose and the accelerator cable.
11. Remove the alternator.
12. On manual transaxle models:
    a. Disconnect the clutch cable.
    b. Remove the transaxle case lower cover.
    c. Disconnect the exhaust pipe at the manifold.
    d. Remove the starter.
    e. Install a transaxle holding fixture to support the transaxle when the engine is removed.
13. On automatic transaxle models:
    a. Disconnect the exhaust pipe at the manifold.
    b. Remove the starter.
    c. Remove the transaxle case lower cover.

d. Mark the flex plate to the torque converter for reassembly.
    e. Attach a C-clamp on the front bottom of the torque converter housing to prevent the torque converter from coming out.
    f. Install a transaxle holding fixture to support the transaxle when the engine is removed.
14. Attach a lifting fixture and a shop crane to the engine. Raise the engine slightly to take up the weight of the engine.

✳✳WARNING

On models with the A-460 transaxle, the left front engine mount is attached with two different types of mounting bolts. Two of the three bolts are of the pilot type with extended tips. Damage to the shift cover or difficult shifting may occur if the bolts are incorrectly installed.

15. Remove the right inner splash shield.
16. Remove the ground strap.
17. To raise the engine remove the long bolts through the yoke and insulator.

➡**If the insulator screws are to be removed, mark the insulator position on the side rail to insure an exact reinstallation.**

18. Remove the transaxle case to engine mounting screws.
19. Disconnect the clutch cable.
20. Take off the screw and nut from the front engine mount.
21. Remove the manual transaxle anti-roll strut.
22. Withdraw the left engine mount insulator through-bolt (from the inside of the wheelhouse) or the insulator bracket to transaxle screws.
23. Lift the engine out of the vehicle.
   To install:
24. Carefully lower the engine into place and loosely install all the mounting bolts. When all the mounting bolts have been hand tightened, then tighten each to 40 ft. lbs. (54 Nm).
25. Install the transaxle case to the engine and tighten the mounting bolts to 70 ft. lbs. (95 Nm).
26. Remove the engine sling and the transaxle holding fixture.
27. Install the ground strap.
28. Install the right inner splash shield.
29. Install the starter.
30. Connect the exhaust pipe to the manifold.
31. On manual transaxle models, install the lower case cover and connect the clutch cable.
32. On automatic transaxle models, remove the C-clamp from the torque converter housing. Align the flex plate to the torque converter, install the mounting screws and tighten to 40 ft. lbs. (54 Nm).
33. Reinstall the power steering pump and alternator.
34. Connect the fuel line, heater hose and the accelerator cable.
35. Connect all wiring.
36. Install the oil filter and refill the engine crankcase with the proper oil to the correct level.
37. If equipped with air conditioning, reinstall the A/C compressor.
38. Reinstall the air cleaner and hoses.
39. Install the radiator and hoses.

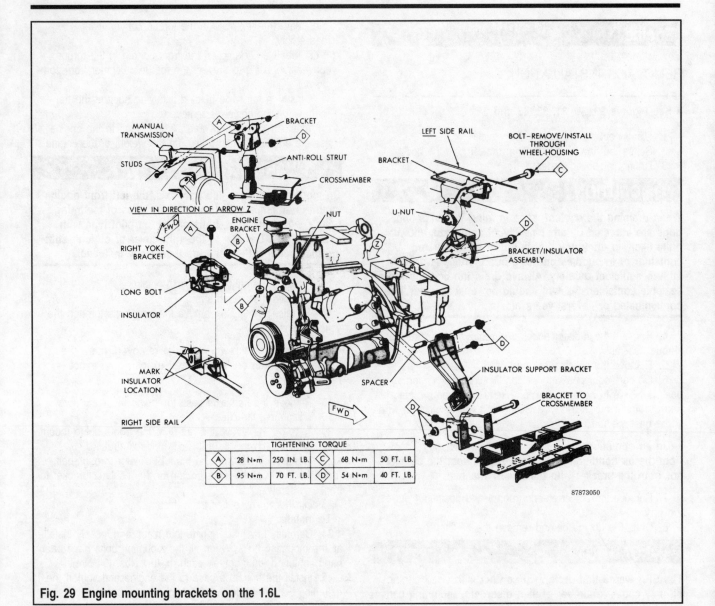

Fig. 29 Engine mounting brackets on the 1.6L

TIGHTENING TORQUE				
Ⓐ	28 N•m	250 IN. LB.	Ⓒ	68 N•m	50 FT. LB.
Ⓑ	95 N•m	70 FT. LB.	Ⓓ	54 N•m	40 FT. LB.

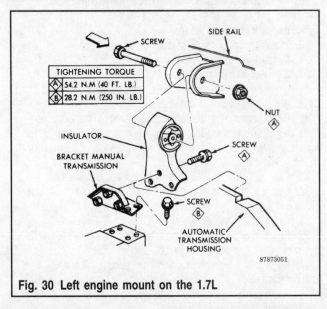

TIGHTENING TORQUE	
Ⓐ	54.2 N.M (40 FT. LB.)
Ⓑ	28.2 N.M (250 IN. LB.)

Fig. 30 Left engine mount on the 1.7L

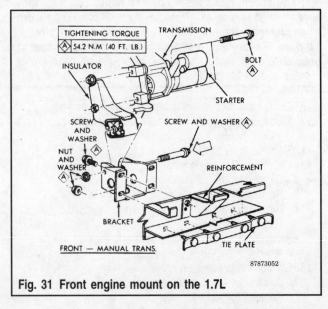

TIGHTENING TORQUE	
Ⓐ	54.2 N.M (40 FT. LB.)

Fig. 31 Front engine mount on the 1.7L

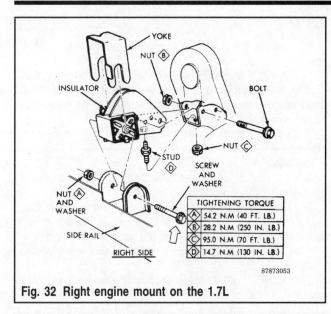

Fig. 32 Right engine mount on the 1.7L

	TIGHTENING TORQUE	
A	54.2 N.M (40 FT. LB.)	
B	28.2 N.M (250 IN. LB.)	
C	95.0 N.M (70 FT. LBS.)	
D	14.7 N.M (130 IN. LB.)	

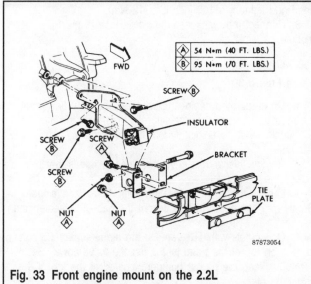

A	54 N•m (40 FT. LBS.)
B	95 N•m (70 FT. LBS.)

Fig. 33 Front engine mount on the 2.2L

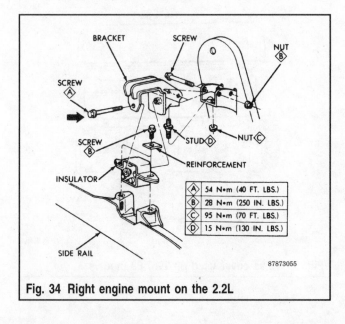

A	54 N•m (40 FT. LBS.)
B	28 N•m (250 IN. LBS.)
C	95 N•m (70 FT. LBS.)
D	15 N•m (130 IN. LBS.)

Fig. 34 Right engine mount on the 2.2L

40. Fill the cooling system.
41. Install the hood.
42. Connect the battery cables.
43. Start the engine and run it to normal operating temperature.
44. If necessary, adjust the transaxle linkage.

Rocker Arm\Valve\Camshaft Cover

REMOVAL & INSTALLATION

1978-86 Models

1.6L ENGINE

▶ **See Figure 35**

1. Separate the crankcase ventilator hose from the valve cover.
2. Disconnect the diverter hose from the bracket.
3. Remove the six screws that retain the cover to the cylinder head and remove the cover.

To install:

4. Clean the cylinder head cover thoroughly, ensure that the cover rails are straight and then, install a new gasket.
5. Install the six screws and tighten to 44 inch lbs. (5 Nm).
6. Connect the diverter hose to the bracket and the crankcase ventilator hose to the valve cover.

1.7L ENGINE

▶ **See Figures 36, 37 and 38**

1. Separate the crankcase ventilator hose from the valve cover.
2. Remove the eight nuts that retain the cover to the cylinder head and remove the cover.

To install:

3. Clean the cylinder head cover thoroughly, ensure that the cover rails are straight, and then, install a new gasket.
4. Install the eight nuts and tighten to 48 inch lbs. (5 Nm).
5. Connect the crankcase ventilator hose to the valve cover.

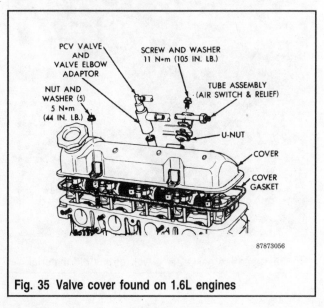

Fig. 35 Valve cover found on 1.6L engines

Fig. 36 After removing the PCV hose, remove the screws retaining the cover

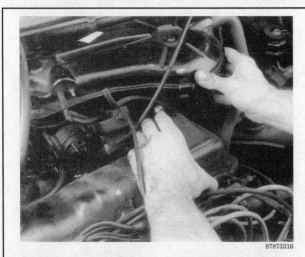

Fig. 37 Once all of the nuts are removed you can lift the cover off of the studs on the head

Fig. 38 Clean the gasket area well of any old material

2.2L ENGINE

1. Separate the crankcase ventilator hose from the PCV module.

2. Depress the retaining clip on the PCV module, turn the module counterclockwise and remove it from the cylinder head cover taking care not to damage the module of the cylinder head cover during the removal.

3. Remove the ten screws that retain the cover to the cylinder head and remove the cover.

To install:

4. Clean the cylinder head cover and its mating surface on the cylinder head thoroughly.

5. Depress the retaining clip on the PCV module, turn the module clockwise, then install the PCV module into the cylinder head cover, check to see that the snorkel is positioned so that the open end is facing up. The snorkel should not be free to rotate.

6. Apply RTV gasket sealer in a continuous bead approximately $\frac{1}{8}$ in. (3mm) in diameter.

7. Install the ten screws that retain the cover to the cylinder head and tighten to 105 inch lbs. (12 Nm).

8. Connect the crankcase ventilator hose to the PCV module.

1987-89 Models

▶ **See Figure 39**

1. On carbureted engines, disconnect the PCV line from the module, depress the retaining clip, then turn the module counterclockwise to unlock it from the valve cover, and remove.

2. Remove/disconnect any other lines or hoses that run across the cam cover.

3. Loosen the cover installation bolts, then remove them. Gently rock the cover to free it from the gasket or sealer, then remove.

4. On models with TBI, remove the air/oil separating curtain located on top of the head just under the valve cover. Be careful to keep the rubber bumpers located at the top of the curtain in place.

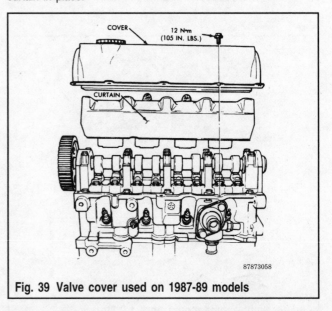

Fig. 39 Valve cover used on 1987-89 models

5. On 1987 covers, replace the two end seals, forcing the locating tabs into the matching holes in the cover.

To install:

6. If the engine has the air/oil separating curtain, install it as described below (otherwise, proceed to the next step):

  a. Position the curtain manifold side first with the upper surface contacting the cylinder head and the cutouts over the cam towers. The cutouts must face the manifold.

  b. Press the distributor side of the curtain into position below the cylinder head rail.

  c. Make sure both rubber bumpers are in place at the top.

7. On 1987 engines, form a gasket on the sealing surface of the head. It is necessary to use an RTV silicone aerobic gasket material (Chrysler Part No. 4318025 or equivalent).

8. On 1988-89 engines, install the gasket onto the cam cover (on normally aspirated engines with Single Point Injection, fasten the gasket in place by forcing the tabs through the holes in the cover).

9. On 1987 engines, install the reinforcements over both sides. Install the mounting bolts, then tighten them alternately and evenly to 105 inch lbs. (12 Nm).

Rocker Arm/Shaft

REMOVAL & INSTALLATION

1.6L Engine

♦ **See Figures 40, 41, 42 and 43**

➡**Allow the cylinder head to cool before performing this procedure.**

1. Remove the cylinder head cover as previously described in Rocker Arm (Valve) Cover.

2. Loosen the cylinder head bolts evenly, beginning at the ends and working towards the center.

3. Tie the rocker arm assembly together with safety wire or equivalent.

Fig. 41 Tie the rocker arm assembly together with safety wire or an equivalent

4. Remove the bolts and lift the rocker arm assembly off the cylinder head.

➡**Before disassembly of the rocker arm assemblies, mark the component positions so they be installed in their original order.**

5. To disassemble, remove the retaining wire from the assembly. Slide the rocker shaft end brackets, rockers, and springs from the rocker shafts.

6. Check the fit of the rockers on the shafts, also check to see that the oil holes in the shafts are clear. Replace any worn components. If replacing the rocker shafts, the roll pin that secures it to the center bracket (No. 2 or No. 4) must be driven out.

To install:

7. To assemble, position the closed end of each rocker shaft so that they are at the outer ends of the assembly. Insert the rocker shaft into its center bracket (No. 2 or No. 4) with the flat on the shaft aligned with the hole in the bracket, and the plugged end right or left as required. Drive the rollpins back into the brackets.

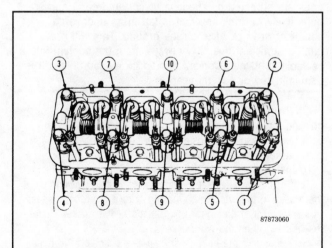

Fig. 40 Loosen the cylinder head bolts using this sequence

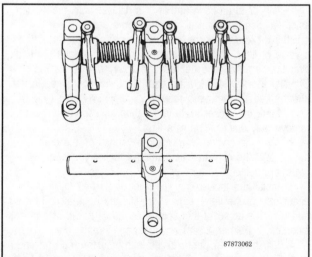

Fig. 42 If disassembling the shaft, keep all parts in order

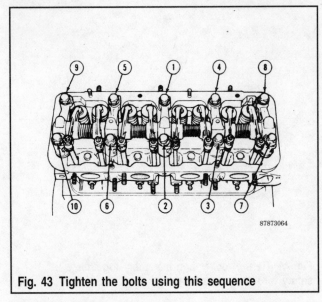

Fig. 43 Tighten the bolts using this sequence

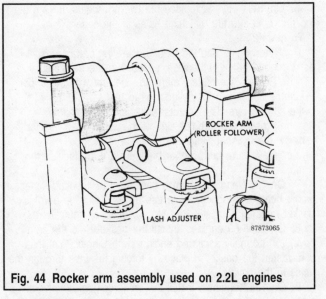

Fig. 44 Rocker arm assembly used on 2.2L engines

8. Lubricate the components and assemblies with engine oil.

9. Tie the end brackets with wire to retain them as one assembly.

10. Position each rocker arm assembly on its dowel.

11. Lubricate the head bolt threads with engine oil, then install through the rocker shaft brackets. Screw the bolts down finger-tight while checking to see that each rocker adjusting screw engages its pushrod. Remove the retaining wire.

12. Tighten the head bolts in progressive steps to 52 ft. lbs. (6 Nm).

13. Start and run the engine to normal operating temperature, allow to cool down and retighten as described in the previous step. Check valve clearance and adjust as necessary.

14. Install the cylinder head cover as previously described in Rocker Arm (Valve) Cover.

2.2L Engine

▶ **See Figure 44**

The rocker arms may be removed very easily after camshaft removal. In case they are to be removed as a group for inspection or to proceed further with disassembly, mark each as to location for installation in the same position.

If the rockers are to be removed in order to gain access to a valve or lifter, you will need a special tool designed to hook over the camshaft and depress the applicable valve. Use Chrysler tool No. 4682 or an equivalent tool purchased in the aftermarket. To remove a rocker:

1. Mark the rocker as to its location, unless you expect to remove only one, or one at a time.

2. Turn the engine over, using a wrench on the crankshaft pulley, until the cam that actuates the rocker you want to remove it pointing straight up.

3. Install the tool so that the jaws on its fulcrum fit on either side of the valve cap. Then, clip the hook at its forward end over the adjacent thin section of the camshaft (a part not incorporating either a cam or a bearing journal).

4. Lift the rocker gently at the lash adjuster end (the end opposite the tool). Pull downward gently on the outer end of the tool lever just until the rocker can be disengaged from the lifter. Pull it out from between the valve and camshaft.

To install:

5. Install the new rocker or reinstall the old one in reverse. Depress the valve just far enough to slide the lever in between the top of the valve stem and the camshaft and still clear the lifter. When the rocker is located on the valve stem and lifter, gradually release the tension on the tool.

6. Repeat the procedure until all the necessary rockers have been replaced.

Thermostat

REMOVAL & INSTALLATION

▶ **See Figures 45, 46, 47, 48 and 49**

1. Drain the cooling system to a level below the thermostat.

✳✳CAUTION

When draining the coolant, keep in mind that cats and dogs are attracted by ethylene glycol antifreeze, and are quite likely to drink any that is left in an uncovered container or in puddles on the ground. This will prove fatal in sufficient quantity. Always drain the coolant into a sealable container. Coolant should be reused unless it is contaminated or several years old.

2. Remove the two mounting bolts, then the thermostat housing.

3. Remove the thermostat and discard the gasket. Clean both gasket surfaces thoroughly.

To install:

4. Dip the new gasket in water, then install. Position the thermostat in the water box, making sure it is properly seated by centering it in the water box, on top of the gasket. Install the housing, then the two bolts.

5. Reconnect the hose, then install and tighten the hose clamp.

6. Refill the cooling system, start the engine, and check for leaks. After the engine has reached operating temperature,

Fig. 45 Remove the two mounting bolts

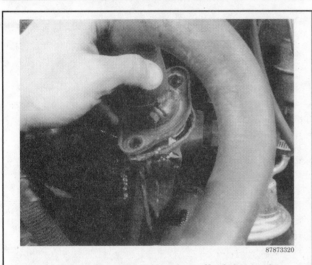

Fig. 46 Lift the thermostat housing off of the mating area, and position it aside

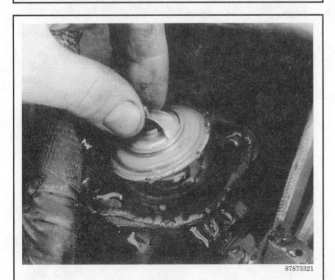

Fig. 47 Remove the thermostat . . .

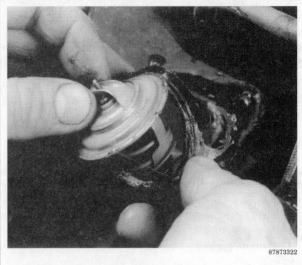

Fig. 48 . . . and the gasket

Fig. 49 Clean the mating area thoroughly

allow it to cool. Then, recheck coolant level in the radiator, refilling as necessary.

Intake Manifold

REMOVAL & INSTALLATION

1.6L Engine

1. Disconnect the negative battery cable.
2. Remove the air cleaner and detach all vacuum lines, electrical connections and fuel line from the carburetor.

3. Drain the cooling system. Remove the inlet hose from the water box to the heated intake manifold, then the outlet hose to the heater.

☀☀CAUTION

When draining the coolant, keep in mind that cats and dogs are attracted by ethylene glycol antifreeze, and are quite likely to drink any that is left in an uncovered container or in puddles on the ground. This will prove fatal in sufficient quantity. Always drain the coolant into a sealable container. Coolant should be reused unless it is contaminated or several years old.

4. Disconnect the EGR tube at the manifold.
5. Remove the eight mounting nuts and washers from the manifold and remove it from the engine.
6. Remove the carburetor from the manifold.
 To install:
7. Clean all gasket surfaces, install new gaskets and tighten the mounting nuts to 15 ft. lbs. (20 Nm). The remaining procedures are reverse the removal.

Exhaust Manifold

REMOVAL & INSTALLATION

1.6L Engine

▶ **See Figure 50**

1. Disconnect the negative battery cable.
2. Separate the carburetor air heater tube from the manifold stove.
3. Remove the oxygen sensor form the manifold.
4. Disconnect the air injection pipe from the manifold and separate the EGR assembly.
5. Raise the vehicle and support on jackstands, remove the exhaust pipe from the manifold.
6. Remove the exhaust manifold retaining nuts and remove the assembly.
7. Remove the carburetor air heater from the manifold.
 To install:
8. Clean all gasket surfaces, install new gaskets, then tighten the mounting nuts to 15 ft. lbs. (20 Nm). The remaining procedures are reverse the removal.

Combination Manifold

REMOVAL & INSTALLATION

1.7L Engine

▶ **See Figures 51, 52 and 53**

➡**You will need to raise and lower the vehicle several times for this procedure.**

1. Disconnect the battery.
2. Remove the air cleaner assembly. Disconnect all vacuum lines, electrical wiring and fuel lines to the carburetor.

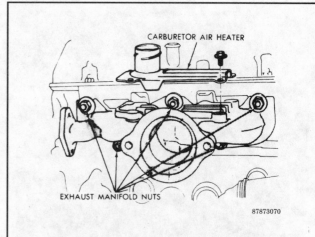

Fig. 50 Do not forget to remove the air heater from the old manifold. It will have to be installed on the new manifold

3. Remove the throttle linkage.
4. Loosen the power steering pump, then remove it.
5. Remove the power brake hose from the intake manifold.
6. Raise and support the vehicle.
7. Remove the exhaust pipe from the manifold.
8. Take off the power steering pump.
9. Remove the intake and exhaust manifold retaining nuts and bolts.
10. Lower the vehicle.
11. Remove the carburetor and manifold assembly.
12. Remove the carburetor and gasket.
13. Separate the manifolds.
 To install:
14. Transfer the studs to the new intake manifold.
15. Clean the manifolds and cylinder head.
16. Assemble the intake and exhaust manifolds loosely.
17. Attach the carburetor to the manifold assembly, then place on the engine.
18. Raise and support the vehicle, tighten all the intake and exhaust nuts and bolts to the cylinder head 10-15 inch lbs. (1-2 Nm).

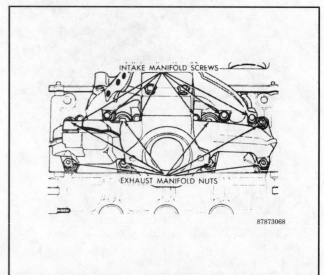

Fig. 51 Combination manifold fastener locations

Fig. 52 Lift the carburetor and manifold assembly off the engine

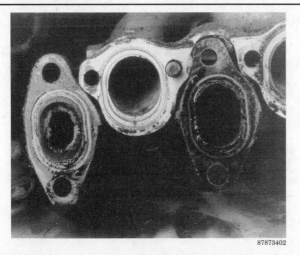

Fig. 53 Be sure to clean the manifolds thoroughly of any carbon deposits and gasket material

19. Tighten the inboard intake to the exhaust manifold nut to 150 inch lbs. (17 Nm). Tighten the outboard intake to exhaust manifold nuts to 200 inch lbs. (23 Nm). Repeat this step until all the intake and exhaust nuts are tightened.

20. Tighten the intake and exhaust manifold port flange nuts at the cylinder head, starting at the center and progressing outwards in both directions. Exhaust nuts 150 inch lbs. (17 Nm) and intake 200 inch lbs. (23 Nm). Repeat this step until all the nuts are tightened.

2.2L Engine

▶ See Figure 54

➡These engines use a combined intake/exhaust manifold gasket. Therefore, the manifolds must always be removed and replaced together.

1. Disconnect the negative battery cable. Drain the cooling system.

✳✳CAUTION

When draining the coolant, keep in mind that cats and dogs are attracted by ethylene glycol antifreeze, and are quite likely to drink any that is left in an uncovered container or in puddles on the ground. This will prove fatal in sufficient quantity. Always drain the coolant into a sealable container. Coolant should be reused unless it is contaminated or several years old.

2. Remove the air cleaner and hoses.
3. If the engine is fuel injected, depressurize the fuel system. Remove all wiring and any hoses connected to the carburetor or injection throttle body and the manifold.
4. Disconnect the accelerator linkage.
5. Loosen the power steering pump mounting bolts and remove the belt. Disconnect the power brake vacuum hose at the manifold.
6. On Canadian cars, only remove the coupling hose connecting the diverter valve and the exhaust manifold air injection tube.
7. Disconnect the water hose from the water crossover.
8. Raise the vehicle and support it securely. Disconnect the exhaust pipe at the manifold.
9. Remove the power steering pump, leaving lines connected, and hang it to one side so the hoses are not stressed.
10. Remove the intake manifold support bracket.
11. Remove the intake manifold-to-head bolts.
12. Lower the vehicle to the floor. Remove the intake manifold.
13. Remove the exhaust manifold retaining nuts and remove the exhaust manifold.

To install:

14. Clean all gasket surfaces and reposition the intake and exhaust manifolds using new gaskets. A composition gasket is installed as-is; a steel gasket must be coated with a sealer such as Chrysler Part No. 3419115 or equivalent.

15. Put the exhaust manifold into position, then install the retaining nuts just finger-tight. Put the intake manifold into posi-

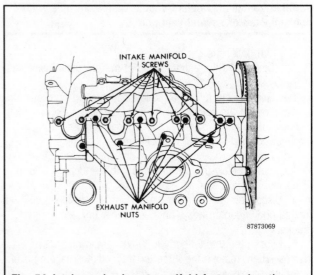

Fig. 54 Intake and exhaust manifold fastener locations

tion, then install all accessible bolts. Raise the car and support it securely.

16. Install all the manifold-to-head bolts finger-tight. Install the intake manifold support bracket. Install the power steering pump, bolting it into position with bolts just finger-tight. Connect the exhaust pipe at the manifold, using a new seal, and tighten the bolts and nuts to 21 ft. lbs. (28 Nm).

17. Lower the car to the floor. Tighten the manifold nuts and bolts in three stages, starting at the center and progressing outward.

18. Connect the power brake vacuum hose to the manifold. Connect the water hose to the water crossover.

19. On Canadian cars only: Install the coupling hose connecting the diverter valve and the exhaust manifold air injection tube.

20. Install the power steering pump belt and adjust tension.

21. Connect the accelerator linkage. Install the air cleaner and hoses.

22. Install all wiring and any hoses disconnected from the carburetor or injection throttle body and the manifold. Refill the cooling system, reconnect the battery, start the engine and run it to check for leaks. Refill the cooling system after the engine has reached operating temperature (air has been bled out) and it has cooled off again.

Turbocharger

REMOVAL & INSTALLATION

▶ **See Figures 55 and 56**

1. Disconnect the negative battery cable.
2. Drain the cooling system.

❄❄CAUTION

When draining the coolant, keep in mind that cats and dogs are attracted by ethylene glycol antifreeze, and are quite likely to drink any that is left in an uncovered container or in puddles on the ground. This will prove fatal in sufficient quantity. Always drain the coolant into a sealable container. Coolant should be reused unless it is contaminated or several years old.

3. From under the car:
   a. Disconnect the exhaust pipe at the articulated joint and the O_2 sensor.
   b. Remove the turbocharger-to-block support bracket.
   c. Loosen the clamps for the oil drain-back tube and then move the tube downward onto the block fitting so it no longer connects with the turbocharger.
   d. Disconnect the turbocharger coolant supply tube at the block outlet below the power steering pump bracket and at the tube support bracket.

4. Disconnect and remove the air cleaner complete with the throttle body adaptor, hose, and air cleaner box and support bracket.

5. Loosen the throttle body to turbocharger inlet hose clamps. Then, remove the three throttle body-to-intake manifold attaching screws and remove the throttle body.

6. Loosen the turbocharger discharge hose end clamps, leaving the center band in place to retain the de-swirler.

7. Pull the fuel rail out of the way after removing the hose retaining bracket screw, four bracket screws from the intake manifold, and two bracket-to-heat shield retaining clips. The rail, injectors, wiring harness, and fuel lines will be moved as an assembly.

8. Disconnect the oil feed line at the turbocharger bearing housing.

9. Remove the three screws attaching the heat shield to the intake manifold and remove the shield.

10. Disconnect the coolant return tube and hose assembly at the turbocharger and water box. Remove the tube support bracket from the cylinder head and remove the assembly.

11. Remove the four nuts attaching the turbocharger to the exhaust manifold. Then, remove the turbocharger by lifting it off the exhaust manifold studs, tilting it downward toward the passenger side of the car, and then pulling it up and out of the car, and out of the engine compartment.

To install:

12. When repositioning the turbo on the mounting studs, make sure the discharge tube goes in position so it's properly connected to both the intake manifold and turbocharger. Apply an anti-seize compound such as Loctite® 771-64 or equivalent to the threads. Tighten the nuts to 30 ft. lbs. (41 Nm). Observe the following torques:
   • Oil feed line nuts — 10 ft. lbs. (14 Nm)
   • Heat shield to intake manifold screws — 105 ft. lbs. (142 Nm)
   • Coolant tube nuts — 30 ft. lbs. (10 Nm)
   • Fuel rail bracket-to-intake manifold retaining screws — 21 ft. lbs. (28 Nm)
   • Discharge tube hose clamp — 35 inch lbs. (4 Nm)
   • Throttle body-to-intake manifold screws — 21 ft. lbs. (28 Nm)
   • Throttle body hose clamps — 35 inch lbs. (4 Nm)
   • Hose adapter-to-throttle body screws — 55 inch lbs. (6 Nm)
   • Air cleaner box support bracket screws — 40 ft. lbs. (54 Nm)
   • Coolant tube nut-to-block connector — 30 ft. lbs. (41 Nm)

13. When installing the turbocharger-to-block support bracket, first install screws finger-tight. Tighten the block screw to 40 ft. lbs. (54 Nm), then tighten the screw going into the turbocharger housing to 20 ft. lbs. (27 Nm). Tighten the articulated ball joint shoulder bolts to 21 ft. lbs. (28 Nm).

14. Make sure to fill the cooling system back up before starting the engine, recheck the level after the coolant begins circulating through the radiator, and check for leaks after you install the pressure cap. Check the turbocharger carefully for any oil leaks and correct if necessary.

Radiator

REMOVAL & INSTALLATION

▶ **See Figures 57, 58, 59, 60, 61, 62, 63 and 64**

1. Disconnect the negative battery cable.
2. Move the temperature selector to full on.

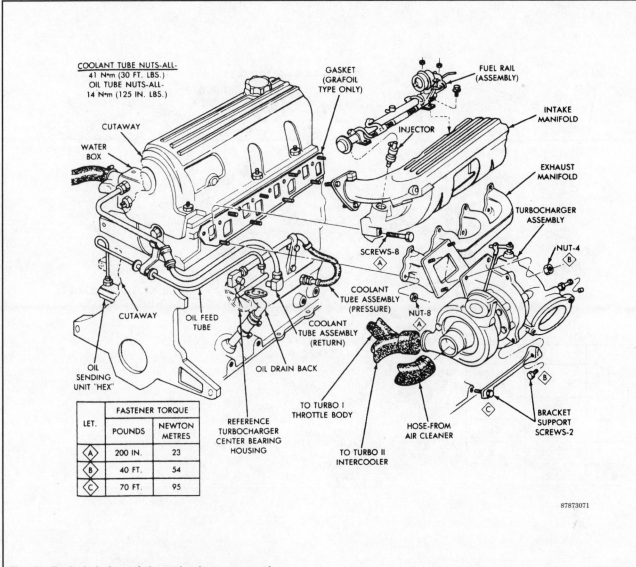

Fig. 55 Exploded view of the turbocharger mounting

3. Open the radiator drain cock.

✳✳CAUTION

When draining the coolant, keep in mind that cats and dogs are attracted by ethylene glycol antifreeze, and are quite likely to drink any that is left in an uncovered container or in puddles on the ground. This will prove fatal in sufficient quantity. Always drain the coolant into a sealable container. Coolant should be reused unless it is contaminated or several years old.

4. When the coolant reserve tank is empty, remove the hose leading to the radiator.

5. Loosen the radiator cap.

6. Remove the radiator hoses.

7. Disconnect the fan.

8. Remove the fan shroud/motor attaching bolts. Be careful not to damage the fan blades, remove the shroud by pulling it upward and out of the attachment clips at the bottom.

9. Disconnect the radiator fan switch wiring harness if equipped. This is located in the radiator.

10. If equipped with automatic transaxle, disconnect and plug the fluid cooler lines.

11. Remove the upper and lower mounting brackets. Remove the top radiator attaching bolt.

12. Remove the bottom radiator attaching bolts on 1981-85 models only.

13. Lift the radiator from the engine compartment.

To install:

14. Installation is the reverse of removal. On 1987-89 models without rubber grommets at the top, preload the upper mounting brackets with 10 lbs. (5 kg.) of force downward. Tighten all mounting bolts to 105 inch lbs. (12 Nm). Make sure the hoses are fully installed onto the fittings and that clamps are properly tightened. Refill the cooling system with 50/50 water/antifreeze mix by filling the radiator to the top and the overflow tank to the fill line.

15. Connect the negative battery cable.

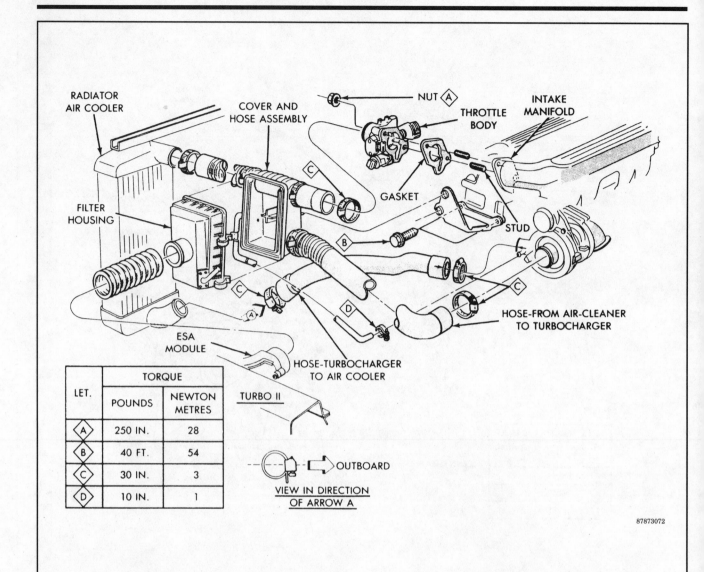

LET.	TORQUE	
	POUNDS	NEWTON METRES
A	250 IN.	28
B	40 FT.	54
C	30 IN.	3
D	10 IN.	1

Fig. 56 Turbocharger air duct routing

Fig. 57 Disconnect the coolant reserve tank hose . . .

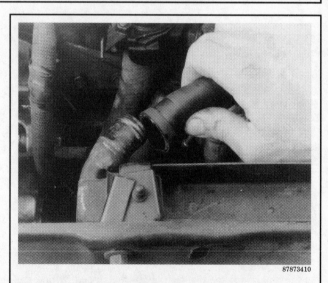

Fig. 58 . . . and the radiator hoses

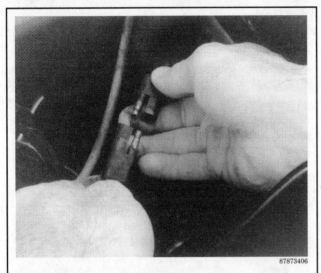

Fig. 59 Disconnect the fan wiring

Fig. 62 If equipped with automatic transaxle, disconnect and plug the fluid cooler lines

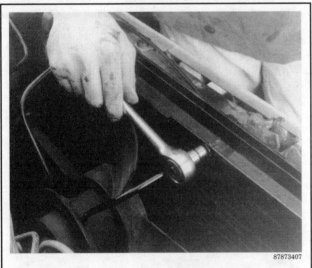

Fig. 60 Unbolt the fan shroud bracket

Fig. 63 Once you have unscrewed the upper radiator bolts, set aside the brackets

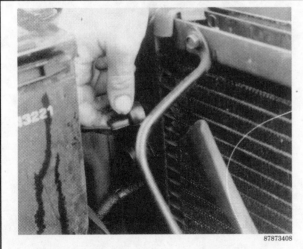

Fig. 61 Disconnect the radiator fan switch wiring harness if equipped

Fig. 64 Lift the radiator from the engine compartment

16. If there is no overflow tank, recheck the coolant level after the system has reached operating temperature and has then cooled.

Water Pump

REMOVAL & INSTALLATION

1.6L Engine

▶ See Figure 65

1. Remove the radiator cap and drain the cooling system.

✳✳CAUTION

When draining the coolant, keep in mind that cats and dogs are attracted by ethylene glycol antifreeze, and are quite likely to drink any that is left in an uncovered container or in puddles on the ground. This will prove fatal in sufficient quantity. Always drain the coolant into a sealable container. Coolant should be reused unless it is contaminated or several years old.

2. Remove the drive belts.
3. Disconnect the water pump to block coolant hose at the pump.
4. Remove the water pump pulley.
5. Remove the four water pump to crankcase extension bolts and remove the water pump assembly.
6. Installation is the reverse of removal. Be sure to use a new gasket.

1.7L Engine

▶ See Figures 66, 67 and 68

1. Drain the cooling system.

✳✳CAUTION

When draining the coolant, keep in mind that cats and dogs are attracted by ethylene glycol antifreeze, and are quite likely to drink any that is left in an uncovered container or in puddles on the ground. This will prove fatal in sufficient quantity. Always drain the coolant into a sealable container. Coolant should be reused unless it is contaminated or several years old.

2. Remove the upper radiator hose.
3. Unbolt the compressor and/or air pump brackets from the water pump and secure them out of the way.
4. Remove the alternator completely from the vehicle.
5. Unbolt the water pump pulley.
6. If equipped, remove the diverter valve hose at the valve. Remove the rear air pump bracket, then the front bracket.
7. Remove the alternator bracket attached to the water pump.
8. Disconnect the lower radiator hose, bypass hose and unbolt the timing cover bolt. Unbolt and remove the water pump. Discard the gasket and clean the gasket surfaces.
9. Installation is the reverse of removal. Tighten the water pump bolts to 25 ft. lbs. (34 Nm), the alternator adjusting bolt to 30-50 ft. lbs. (41-68 Nm) and the pulley bolts to 85-125 inch lbs. (9-14 Nm).

2.2L Engine

▶ See Figure 69

1. Disconnect the battery negative cable.

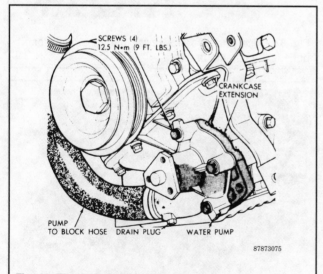

Fig. 65 The 1.6L water pump mounting

Fig. 66 Remove the rear air pump bracket, then the front bracket

Fig. 67 Remove the alternator bracket attached to the water pump

Fig. 68 Unbolt the water pump and remove it

2. Drain the cooling system.

✳✳CAUTION

When draining the coolant, keep in mind that cats and dogs are attracted by ethylene glycol antifreeze, and are quite likely to drink any that is left in an uncovered container or in puddles on the ground. This will prove fatal in sufficient quantity. Always drain the coolant into a sealable container. Coolant should be reused unless it is contaminated or several years old.

3. Remove the upper radiator hose.

4. Remove the alternator.

➡**Do not disconnect the air conditioner compressor lines in the next step. The compressor can be moved far enough out of the way to remove the water pump without disturbing the refrigerant filled lines.**

5. Unbolt the air conditioning compressor brackets from the water pump and secure the compressor out of the way. Support the compressor so it will not put stress on the lines.

6. Disconnect the bypass hose, heater return hose, and lower radiator hose.

7. Unbolt and remove the water pump assembly. Disassemble the pump as follows:

   a. Remove the three bolts fastening the drive pulley to the water pump.

   b. Remove the 9 bolts fastening the water pump body to the housing. Then, use a chisel to gently break the bond between the pump and housing.

   c. Clean the gasket surfaces on the pump body and housing. Remove the O-ring gasket and discard it. Clean the O-ring groove.

   d. Apply RTV sealer to the sealing surface of the water pump body. The bead should be $1/8$ in. (3mm) in diameter and should encircle all bolt holes. Assemble the pump body to the housing, install the 9 bolts, and tighten them to 105 inch lbs. (12 Nm). Make sure the gasket material has set (as per package instructions) before actually filling the system.

8. Position a new O-ring in the O-ring groove. Then, put the pulley on the pump, install the 3 attaching bolts, then tighten them to 105 inch lbs. (12 Nm).

9. Installation is the reverse of removal. Tighten the top 3 water pump bolts to 21 ft. lbs. (28 Nm) and the lower bolt to 50 ft. lbs. (68 Nm). Make sure to refill the system with 50/50 antifreeze/water mix.

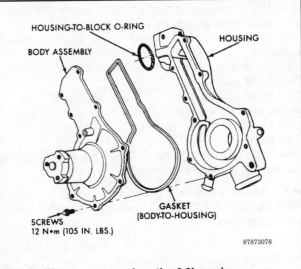

Fig. 69 Water pump used on the 2.2L engine

Cylinder Head

REMOVAL & INSTALLATION

1.6L Engine
◆ See Figures 70, 71, 72 and 73

✳✳WARNING

The cylinder head must be cool before removing to avoid distortion.

1. Disconnect the negative battery cable.
2. Drain the cooling system.

✳✳CAUTION

When draining the coolant, keep in mind that cats and dogs are attracted by ethylene glycol antifreeze, and are quite likely to drink any that is left in an uncovered container or in puddles on the ground. This will prove fatal in sufficient quantity. Always drain the coolant into a sealable container. Coolant should be reused unless it is contaminated or several years old.

3. Remove the air cleaner assembly.
4. Disconnect all lines, hoses and wires from the head, manifold and carburetor.
5. Disconnect the accelerator linkage.
6. Remove the intake and exhaust manifolds.
7. If equipped with air conditioning, remove the compressor from the mounting brackets and support it out of the way. DO NOT remove the hoses from the compressor.
8. Remove the valve cover as previously described.
9. Loosen the cylinder head bolts evenly, beginning at the ends and working towards the center.
10. Tie the rocker arm assembly together with safety wire or equivalent.
11. Remove the bolts and lift the rocker arm assembly off the cylinder head.
12. Label all the pushrods so they be reinstalled in their original locations and remove them from the cylinder head.
13. Lift off the cylinder head and discard the gasket.
To install:
14. Make certain the gasket surfaces are thoroughly cleaned and are free of nicks or scratches.

➡**Always use a new head gasket and make certain the word DESSUS or TOP faces up when the gasket is laid on the engine block.**

15. Lubricate the head bolt threads with engine oil and install through the rocker shaft brackets.
16. Screw the bolts down finger-tight while checking to see that each rocker adjusting screw engages its pushrod.
17. Tighten the head bolts in progressive steps to 52 ft. lbs. (71 Nm). Start and run the engine to normal operating temperature, allow to cool down and retighten as described above.
18. Check valve clearance and adjust as necessary.
19. Install the air conditioning compressor.
20. Install the intake and exhaust manifolds.

21. Connect the accelerator linkage.
22. Connect all lines, hoses and wires to the head, manifold and carburetor.
23. Install the air cleaner assembly.
24. Fill the cooling system.
25. Connect the negative battery cable.

1.7L Engine
◆ See Figures 74, 75 and 76

The engine should be cold before the cylinder head is removed. The head is retained by 10 socket head bolts.
1. Disconnect the negative battery cable.
2. Drain the cooling system.

✳✳CAUTION

When draining the coolant, keep in mind that cats and dogs are attracted by ethylene glycol antifreeze, and are quite likely to drink any that is left in an uncovered container or in puddles on the ground. This will prove fatal in sufficient quantity. Always drain the coolant into a sealable container. Coolant should be reused unless it is contaminated or several years old.

3. Remove the air cleaner assembly.
4. Disconnect all lines, hoses and wires from the head, manifold and carburetor.
5. Disconnect the accelerator linkage.
6. Remove the distributor cap.
7. Disconnect the exhaust pipe.
8. Remove the carburetor.
9. Remove the intake and exhaust manifolds.
10. Remove the upper portion of the front cover.
11. Turn the engine by hand until all gear timing marks are aligned.
12. Loosen the drive belt tensioner and slip the belt off the camshaft gear.

➡**The camshaft timing mark is on the back of the gear and is properly positioned when it is in line with the left corner of the camshaft cover at the head.**

13. If equipped with air conditioning, remove the compressor from the mounting brackets and support it out of the way with wires. Remove the mounting brackets from the head.
14. Remove the valve cover, gaskets and seals.
15. Remove head bolts in reverse order of the tightening sequence.
16. Lift off the head and discard the gasket.
To install:
17. Make certain all gasket surfaces are thoroughly cleaned and are free of deep nicks or scratches.

➡**Always use new gaskets and seals. Never reuse a gasket or seal, even if it looks good.**

18. When positioning the head on the block, insert bolts 8 and 10 to align the head.
19. Tighten bolts in the order. Bolts should be tightened to 30 ft. lbs. (41 Nm). in rotation, then tightened to 60 ft. lbs. (81 Nm). When all bolts are at 60 ft. lbs. (81 Nm), tighten each ¼ turn more in sequence.
20. Install the valve cover, gaskets and seals.

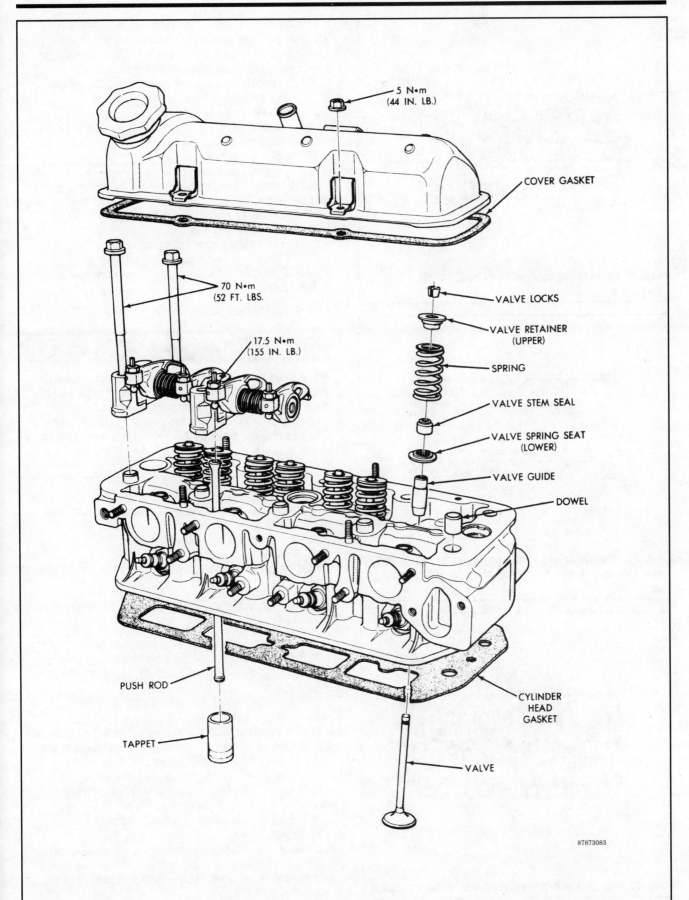

Fig. 70 Exploded view of the 1.6L cylinder head

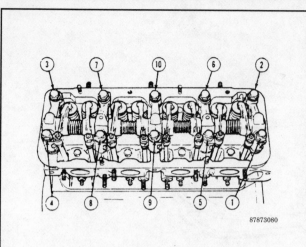

Fig. 71 Remove the cylinder head bolts in this sequence

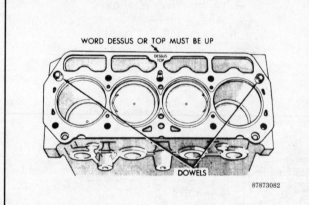

Fig. 72 When installing a new gasket, place the gasket over the dowels with the words DESSUS or TOP facing up

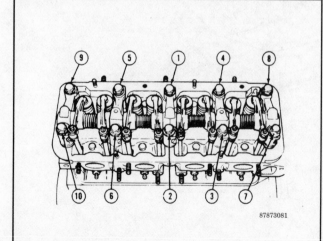

Fig. 73 Tighten the cylinder head bolts in this sequence

21. Make sure all timing marks are aligned before installing the drive belt. The drive belt is correctly tensioned when it can be twisted 90° with the thumb and index finger midway between the camshaft and intermediate shaft.

22. If equipped with air conditioning, install the compressor.

23. Install the upper portion of the front cover.

24. Install the intake and exhaust manifolds.

25. Install the carburetor.

26. Connect the exhaust pipe.

27. Install the distributor cap.

28. Connect the accelerator linkage.

29. Connect all lines, hoses and wires to the head, manifold and carburetor.

30. Install the air cleaner assembly.

31. Fill the cooling system.

32. Connect the negative battery cable.

2.2L Engine

◗ **See Figures 77 and 78**

1. Disconnect the negative battery cable.

2. Drain the cooling system.

✳✳CAUTION

When draining the coolant, keep in mind that cats and dogs are attracted by ethylene glycol antifreeze, and are quite likely to drink any that is left in an uncovered container or in puddles on the ground. This will prove fatal in sufficient quantity. Always drain the coolant into a sealable container. Coolant should be reused unless it is contaminated or several years old.

3. Remove the air cleaner assembly.

4. Disconnect all lines, hoses and wires from the head, manifold and carburetor.

5. Disconnect the accelerator linkage.

6. Remove the distributor cap.

7. Disconnect the exhaust pipe.

8. Remove the carburetor or throttle body.

➡**If equipped with fuel injection, release the fuel system pressure.**

9. Remove the intake and exhaust manifolds.

10. Remove the upper portion of the front cover.

11. Turn the engine by hand until all gear timing marks are aligned.

12. Loosen the drive belt tensioner and slip the belt off the camshaft gear.

13. If equipped with air conditioning, remove the compressor from the mounting brackets and support it out of the way with wires. Remove the mounting brackets from the head.

14. Remove the valve cover, gaskets and seals.

15. Remove head bolts in reverse order of tightening sequence.

16. Lift off the head and discard the gasket.

To install:

17. Make certain all gasket surfaces are thoroughly cleaned and are free of deep nicks or scratches. Always use new gaskets and seals. Never reuse a gasket or seal, even if it looks good.

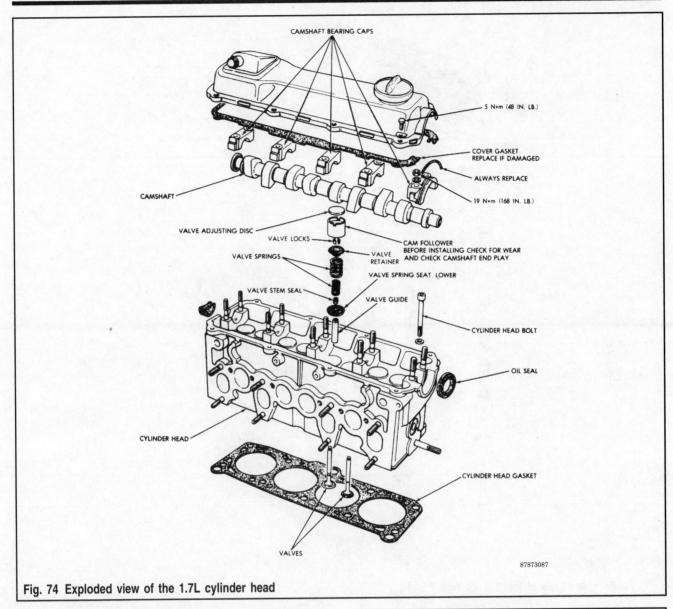

Fig. 74 Exploded view of the 1.7L cylinder head

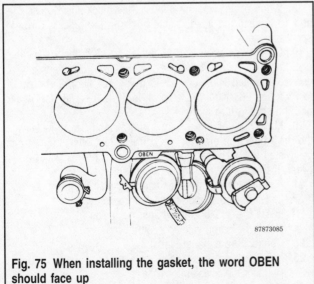

Fig. 75 When installing the gasket, the word OBEN should face up

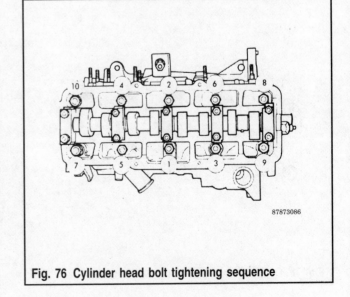

Fig. 76 Cylinder head bolt tightening sequence

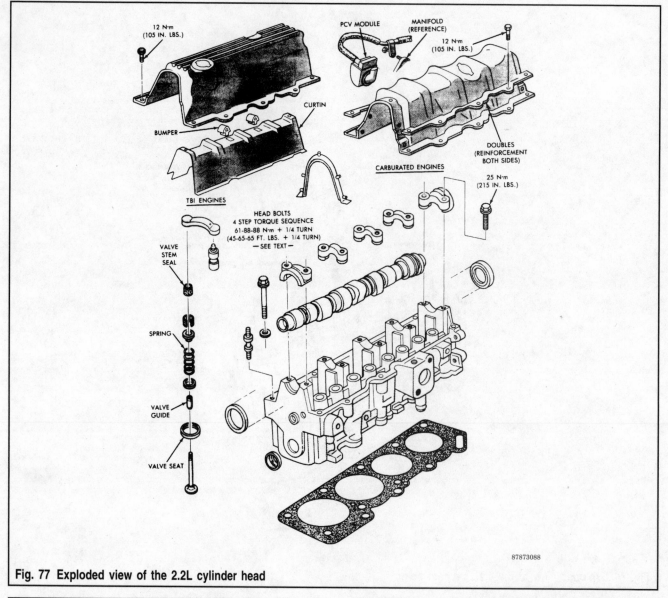

Fig. 77 Exploded view of the 2.2L cylinder head

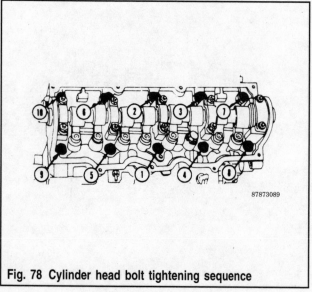

Fig. 78 Cylinder head bolt tightening sequence

18. When positioning the head on the block, insert bolts 8 and 10 to align the head. Tighten bolts in the order shown to specifications.

19. On models through 1986 tighten to 45 ft. lbs. (61 Nm) plus ¼ turn. On 1987-89 models tighten in a four step sequence. 1st step tighten all to 45 ft. lbs. (61 Nm), 2nd step all to 65 ft. lbs. (88 Nm), 3rd step all to 65 ft. lbs. (88 Nm) again and 4th step ¼ turn more.

20. Make sure all timing marks are aligned before installing the drive belt. The drive belt is correctly tensioned when it can be twisted 90° with the thumb and index finger midway between the camshaft and the intermediate shaft.

21. If equipped with air conditioning, install the compressor.

22. Install the upper portion of the front cover.

23. Install the intake and exhaust manifolds.

24. Install the carburetor or throttle body.

25. Connect the exhaust pipe.

26. Install the distributor cap.

27. Connect the accelerator linkage.

28. Connect all lines, hoses and wires to the head, manifold and carburetor.

29. Install the air cleaner assembly.
30. Fill the cooling system.
31. Connect the negative battery cable.

CLEANING AND INSPECTION

▶ See Figures 79 and 80

➡With the cylinder head removed from the engine, the rocker arm assemblies and camshaft removed, the valves, valve springs and valve stem oil seals can now be serviced.

Since the machining of valve seats and valves, and the insertion of new valve guides or valve seats may tax the experience and equipment resources of the car owner, it is suggested that the cylinder head be taken to an automotive machine shop for rebuilding.

1. Remove the cylinder head from the car engine (see Cylinder Head Removal). Place the head on a workbench and

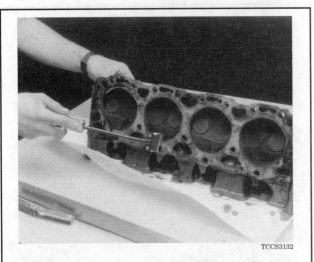

TCCS3132

Fig. 79 Use a gasket scraper to remove the bulk of the old head gasket from the mating surface

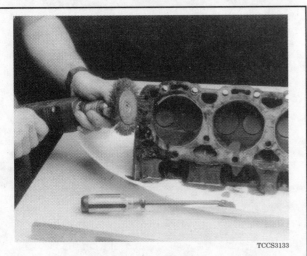

TCCS3133

Fig. 80 An electric drill equipped with a wire wheel will expedite complete gasket removal

remove any manifolds that are still connected. Remove all rocker arm assembly parts, if still installed and the camshaft (see Camshaft Removal).

2. Turn the cylinder head over so that the mounting surface is facing up and support evenly on wooden blocks.

3. Use a scraper and remove all of the gasket material and carbon stuck to the head mounting surface. Mount a wire carbon removal brush in an electric drill and clean away the carbon on the valve heads and head combustion chambers.

✳✳WARNING

When scraping or decarbonizing the cylinder head, take care not to damage or nick the gasket mounting surface or combustion chamber.

4. Number the valve heads with a permanent felt-tipped marker for cylinder location.

RESURFACING

▶ See Figures 81 and 82

If the cylinder head is warped, resurfacing by an automotive machine shop will be required. After cleaning the gasket surface, place a straightedge across the mounting surface of the head. Using feeler gauges, determine the clearance at the center and along the lengths of both diagonals. If warpage exceeds 0.003 in. (0.08mm) in a 6 in. (152mm) span, or 0.006 in. (0.15mm) over the total length, the cylinder head must be resurfaced.

Valves and Springs

REMOVAL & INSTALLATION

▶ See Figures 83, 84 and 85

1.6L Engine

1. Remove the cylinder head.
2. Compress the valve with a spring compressor tool.
3. Before removing the valves, remove any burrs from the valve stem lock grooves to prevent damage the valve guides. Mark all the valves so they may be installed in their original position.

To install:

4. Coat the valve stems with oil and insert in the cylinder head. Install the spring seat on each guide.
5. Place a protective cap over the end of the valve, or wrap the lock grooves with tape to prevent the edges of the valve from damaging the oil seals.
6. Install the new valve stem seals on all of the valves. The seals should be pushed firmly and squarely over the valve guide and down until it bottoms out.
7. Install the valve springs and retainers. Compress the valve spring only enough to install the locks, being careful not to misalign the direction of compression.
8. The remaining procedures are reverse the removal.
9. Remove the valve retaining locks, spring retainer, spring, valve seals, and the spring seat.

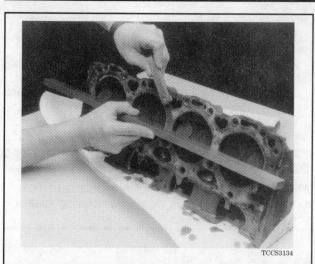

Fig. 81 Check the cylinder head for warpage along the center using a straightedge and a feeler gauge

Fig. 82 Be sure to check for warpage across the cylinder head at both diagonals

Fig. 83 Use a valve spring compressor tool to relieve spring tension from the valve caps

Fig. 84 A small magnet will help in removal of the valve keys

Fig. 85 Remove the valve stem seal from the cylinder head

1.7L Engine

1. Remove the cylinder head.
2. Compress the valve spring with tool L-4419 or equivalent.
3. Remove the adjusting disc, valve keeper, spring retainer, valve spring and valve.
4. Remove the seal by pulling side-to-side with a pair of long nose pliers or the C-4745 Seal Remover tool may be used.
5. Place a protective cap over the end of the valve, or wrap the lock grooves with tape to prevent the edges of the valve from damaging the oil seals.

To install:
6. Install the valves in the cylinder head.
7. Install the new valve stem seals on all of the valves. The seals should be pushed firmly and squarely over the valve guide with tool L-4421 or equivalent and down until it bottoms out.
8. The remainder of the installation is the reverse the removal procedures.

2.2L Engine

1. Remove the rocker arms, camshaft and cylinder head.
2. Using tool 4682 or equivalent compress the valve spring and remove the valve locks.
3. Remove the valve spring and valve.
4. Remove the seal by pulling side-to-side with a pair of long nose pliers.

To install:
5. Install the spring seat on each guide.
6. Place a protective cap over the end of the valve, or wrap the lock grooves with tape to prevent the edges of the valve from damaging the oil seals.
7. Install the new valve stem seals on all of the valves. The seals should be pushed firmly and squarely over the valve guide and down until it bottoms out.

➡ **When using tool 4682 the valve locks can become dislocated. Check to be certain that both locks are in position after removing the tool.**

8. Install the valve springs and retainers. Compress the valve spring with tool 4682 or equivalent, only enough to install the locks being careful not to misalign the direction of compression.
9. Check the installed spring height of the springs. This measurement should be made from the lower edge of the spring to its upper edge, not including the spring seat.
10. Install the cylinder head, camshaft and rocker arms.

VALVE INSPECTION

▶ **See Figures 86, 87, 88 and 89**

1. Clean the valves thoroughly and discard burned, warped, or cracked valves.
2. If the valve face is only lightly pitted, the valve may be refaced to an angle of 45° by a qualified machine shop.
3. Measure the valve stem for wear at various points and check it against the specifications shown in the Valve Specifications chart.

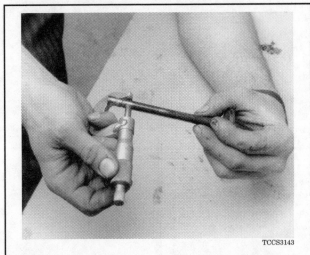

Fig. 88 Use a micrometer to measure the valve stem diameter

Fig. 86 A dial gauge may be used to check valve stem-to-guide clearance

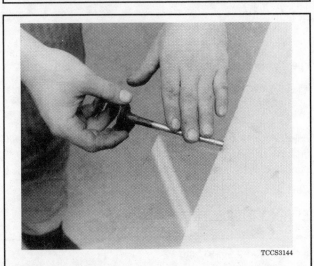

Fig. 87 Valve stems may be rolled on a flat surface to check for bends

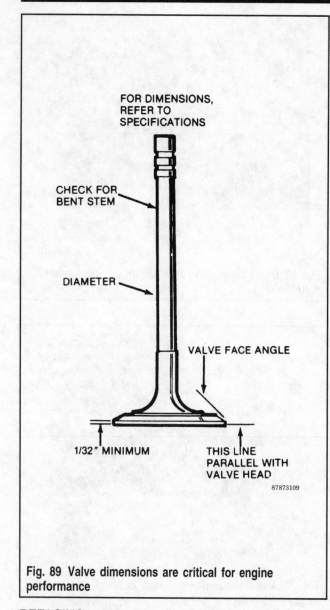

FOR DIMENSIONS,
REFER TO
SPECIFICATIONS

CHECK FOR
BENT STEM

DIAMETER

VALVE FACE ANGLE

1/32" MINIMUM

THIS LINE
PARALLEL WITH
VALVE HEAD

87873109

Fig. 89 Valve dimensions are critical for engine performance

REFACING

Using a valve grinder, resurface the valves according to the specifications given in the Valve Specifications chart.

➡The valve face angle is not always identical to the valve seat angle.

A minimum margin of 0.03 in. (0.8mm) should remain after grinding the valve. The valve stem top should also be squared and resurfaced, by placing the stem in the V-block of the grinder, and turning it while pressing lightly against the grinding wheel.

SPRING INSPECTION

▶ See Figures 90, 91 and 92

Whenever the valves have been removed for inspection, reconditioning or replacement, the valve springs should be tested. To test the spring tension you will need special tool

C-647 or equivalent. Place the spring over the stud on the table and lift the compressing lever to set the tone device. Pull on the torque wrench until a ping is heard. Take a reading on the torque wrench at this instant. Multiply this reading by two. The resulting specification is the spring load at the test length. Refer to the Valve Specifications chart for specifications. Inspect each valve spring for squareness with a steel square and a surface plate, test the springs from both ends. If the spring is more than 0.06 in. (1.5mm) out of square, replace the spring.

Valve Guides

REMOVAL & INSTALLATION

Valve guides are replaceable, but they should not be replaced in a cylinder head in which the valve seats cannot be refaced.

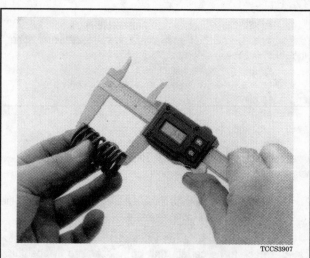

TCCS3907

Fig. 90 Use a caliper gauge to check the valve spring free-length

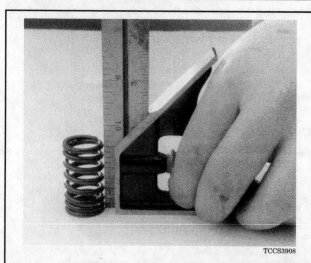

TCCS3908

Fig. 91 Check the valve spring for squareness on a flat service, a carpenters square can be used

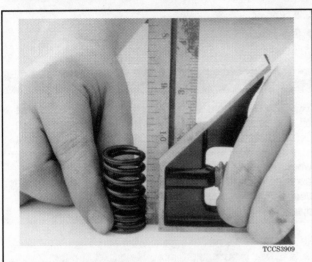

Fig. 92 The valve spring should be straight up and down when placed like this

Worn guides should be pressed out from the combustion chamber side and new guides pressed in as far as they will go.

✳✳WARNING

Service valve guides have a shoulder. Once the guide is seated, do not use more than 1 ton pressure or the guide shoulder could break.

Valve Seats

REMOVAL & INSTALLATION

Valve seats can be refaced if they are worn or burned, but the correction angle and seat width must be maintained. If not, the cylinder head must be replaced.

Intake valve seats should be ground to a 45° angle and the valve margin should not be less than 0.02 in. (0.5mm). Check the valve stem diameter.

Exhaust valves are sodium filled and should not be ground by machine. Use lapping compound and lap by hand. Valve margin should be at least 0.02 in. (0.5mm). Check the stem diameter. The exhaust valve seat should be ground to a 45° angle.

On 1.7L engines the intake and exhaust valves are available with stems 0.02 in. (0.5mm) shorter than production valves. If the seats are cut too much during repairs, these shorter valves should be installed to allow the use of proper sized valve adjusting discs.

Oil Pan

REMOVAL & INSTALLATION

1.6L and 1.7L Engines
◗ **See Figures 93, 94, 95 and 96**

1. Raise and support the vehicle.
2. Drain the oil pan.

✳✳CAUTION

The EPA warns that prolonged contact with used engine oil may cause a number of skin disorders, including cancer! You should make every effort to minimize your exposure to used engine oil. Protective gloves should be worn when changing the oil. Wash your hands and any other exposed skin areas as soon as possible after exposure to used engine oil. Soap and water, or waterless hand cleaner should be used.

3. On some engines it may be necessary to remove a shield in front of the flywheel. This shield needs to be removed to access some of the oil pan mounting bolts.
4. Remove the attaching bolts, you may need to support the pan.
5. Lower the pan and discard the gaskets.
   To install:
6. Clean all gasket surfaces thoroughly, then install the pan using gasket sealer and a new gasket.
7. Tighten the pan bolts to 7 ft. lbs. (9 Nm).
8. Refill the pan, start the engine, and check for leaks.

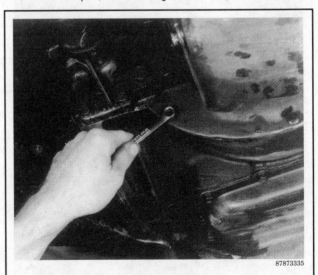

Fig. 93 Remove the flywheel shield

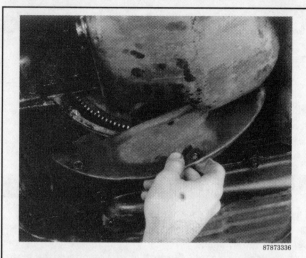

Fig. 94 After removing this shield, the mounting bolts are accessible

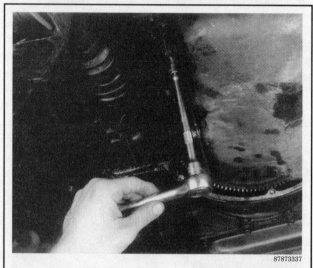

Fig. 95 Remove the attaching bolts all the way around

Fig. 96 Lower the pan

2.2L Engine

▶ See Figure 97

1. Drain the engine oil.

✳✳CAUTION

The EPA warns that prolonged contact with used engine oil may cause a number of skin disorders, including cancer! You should make every effort to minimize your exposure to used engine oil. Protective gloves should be worn when changing the oil. Wash your hands and any other exposed skin areas as soon as possible after exposure to used engine oil. Soap and water, or waterless hand cleaner should be used.

2. Support the pan and remove the attaching bolts.
3. Lower the pan and remove the gasket, if it has one.
To install:
4. Clean all gasket surfaces thoroughly.
5. On all engines from 1981-87, use new end seals and apply a 1 in. (25mm) bead of sealer to the rest of the pan. Make sure to apply sealer where the end seals meet the block. On 1988-89 engines, replace the end seals and the side gaskets. Apply RTV to the parting lines between end and side seals on these engines. If necessary, use grease or RTV to hold the side seals in place.
6. Tighten the pan bolts to 200 inch lbs. (22 Nm).
7. Refill the engine with oil, start the engine, and check for leaks.

Oil Pump

REMOVAL & INSTALLATION

1.6L Engine

▶ See Figure 98

1. Drain the crankcase oil and remove the oil filter.

✳✳CAUTION

The EPA warns that prolonged contact with used engine oil may cause a number of skin disorders, including cancer! You should make every effort to minimize your exposure to used engine oil. Protective gloves should be worn when changing the oil. Wash your hands and any other exposed skin areas as soon as possible after exposure to used engine oil. Soap and water, or waterless hand cleaner should be used.

2. While holding the cover and housing together, remove the seven mounting bolts and pull the assembly from the engine block.
To install:
3. Seal all the oil pump attaching bolt threads with an oil resistant sealer.
4. Install new gaskets on the pump, housing to block and housing to cover.
5. Place the cover on the housing and insert two bolts to maintain alignment.

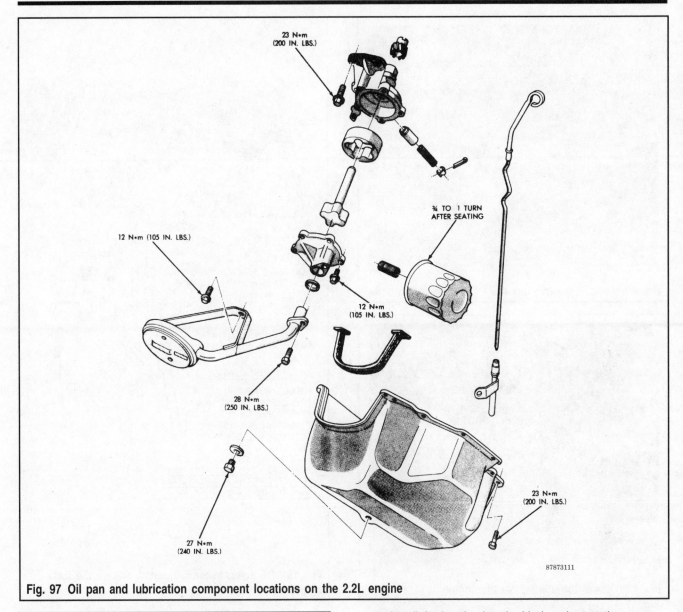

23 N•m (200 IN. LBS.)

12 N•m (105 IN. LBS.)

¾ TO 1 TURN AFTER SEATING

12 N•m (105 IN. LBS.)

28 N•m (250 IN. LBS.)

23 N•m (200 IN. LBS.)

27 N•m (240 IN. LBS.)

87873111

Fig. 97 Oil pan and lubrication component locations on the 2.2L engine

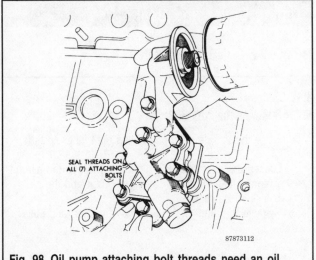

SEAL THREADS ON ALL (7) ATTACHING BOLTS

87873112

Fig. 98 Oil pump attaching bolt threads need an oil resistant sealer

6. Install the housing into the block and rotate the assembly until the driving gear shaft engages the slot in the driveshaft.

7. Align the bolt pattern to the block, install the remaining five bolts and tighten to 9 ft. lbs. (12 Nm).

8. Install the oil filter and refill the crankcase.

1.7L Engine

▶ **See Figures 99 and 100**

1. Remove the oil pan.
2. Remove the two hex head pump mounting bolts.
3. Pull the oil pump down and out of the engine.
4. Installation is the reverse of removal. Tighten pump mounting bolts to 14 ft. lbs. (19 Nm).

2.2L Engine

▶ **See Figure 101**

1. Remove the oil pan.
2. Remove the two pump mounting bolts.
3. Pull the pump down and out of the engine.

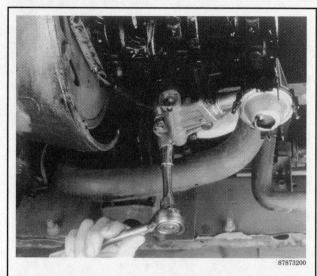

Fig. 99 Remove the two hex head pump mounting bolts

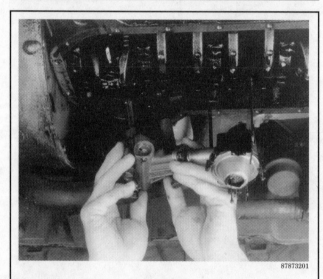

Fig. 100 Lower the pump from the engine

To install:

4. Apply a sealer such as Loctite 515® to the pump/block sealing surfaces.

5. Lubricate the pump rotor, shaft, and drive gear.

6. When installing the pump, rotate the shaft back and forth slightly so the drive mechanism will engage fully and permit the pump to sit squarely against the block.

7. Make sure the pump body is fully seated in the block before installing the mounting bolts. Tighten the pump mounting bolts to 200 inch lbs. (22 Nm).

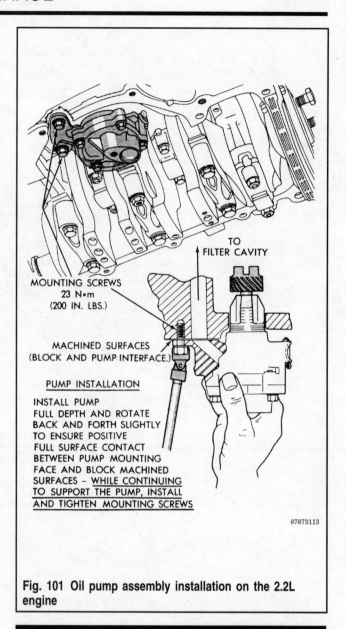

Fig. 101 Oil pump assembly installation on the 2.2L engine

Timing Cover and Seal

REMOVAL & INSTALLATION

1.6L Engine

▶ **See Figures 102, 103 and 104**

1. Raise the vehicle and remove the right inner splash shield.

2. Loosen the alternator adjusting screw. Move the alternator and remove the alternator/water pump belt and the air pump belt (if so equipped).

3. Remove the crankshaft pulley bolt, washer, and pulley.

4. Drain the cooling system through the water pump drain plug and remove the water pump to timing cover hose.

✳✳CAUTION

When draining the coolant, keep in mind that cats and dogs are attracted by ethylene glycol antifreeze, and are quite likely to drink any that is left in an uncovered container or in puddles on the ground. This will prove fatal in sufficient quantity. Always drain the coolant into a sealable container. Coolant should be reused unless it is contaminated or several years old.

5. Raise the timing cover end of the engine and carefully support.
6. Remove the bolts supporting the engine mount bracket to the timing cover and block.

✳✳WARNING

Two of the cover to block screws pass through the tubular locating dowels. Make sure the dowels DO NOT fall into the crankcase extension during the cover removal.

7. Remove the crankcase extension to cover and the cover to block screws and remove the cover.
8. Clean the mating surface of any gasket material.
9. To remove the oil seal, install the seal removal tool C-748 or equivalent over the crankshaft nose and turn tightly into the seal.
To install:
10. Install the gasket on the clean mating surface.
11. Position tool C-4761 or equivalent on the seal and drive the seal into the timing cover until the tool stops against the cover.
12. To install the timing cover, reverse the removal procedures.

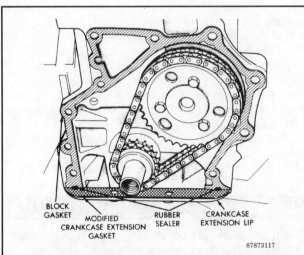

Fig. 102 Before installing the cover, attach the gasket to the block. Ensure the gasket is seated properly

BLOCK GASKET — MODIFIED CRANKCASE EXTENSION GASKET — RUBBER SEALER — CRANKCASE EXTENSION LIP

87873117

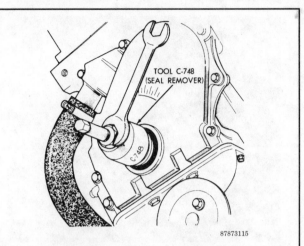

Fig. 103 To remove the oil seal, install the seal removal tool C-748 or equivalent over the crankshaft nose and turn tightly into the seal.

TOOL C-748 (SEAL REMOVER)

87873115

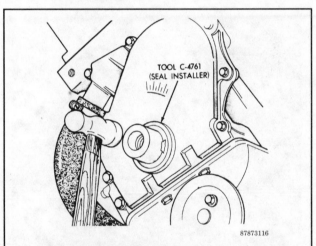

Fig. 104 Position tool C-4761 or equivalent on the seal and drive the seal into the timing cover until the tool stops against the cover

TOOL C-4761 (SEAL INSTALLER)

87873116

1.7L Engine

▶ See Figures 105, 106 and 107

1. Loosen the alternator mounting bolts, pivot the alternator and remove the drive belt.
2. Do the same thing with the air conditioning compressor.
3. Unfasten the cover retaining nuts, washers and spacers.
4. Remove the cover.
5. Clean all mating surfaces.
6. Installation is the reverse of removal.

2.2L Engine

1. Loosen the alternator mounting bolts, pivot the alternator and remove the drive belt.
2. Do the same thing with the air conditioning compressor.
3. Remove the cover retaining nuts, washers and spacers.
4. Remove the cover.
5. Installation is the reverse of removal.

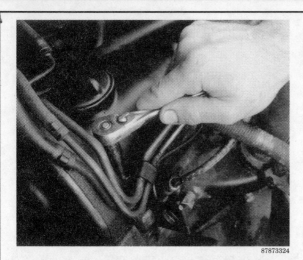

Fig. 105 Remove the cover retaining nuts along the top . . .

Fig. 106 . . . and the sides

Fig. 107 Lift off the cover

Timing Chain and Gears

REMOVAL & INSTALLATION

1.6L Engine

1. Remove the timing cover as outlined earlier.
2. Remove the camshaft sprocket bolts and remove the sprocket and chain.
3. Remove the crankshaft gear with a pilot adapter tool C-4760 and gear puller C-3894-A or equivalent.

To install:

4. Align the crankshaft sprocket with the key and drive it onto the shaft.
5. Position the camshaft sprocket into place and turn it so that the timing marks on both sprockets are on a line passing through the sprocket centers.
6. Remove the camshaft sprocket without turning the camshaft, place the timing chain over it and reinstall the camshaft sprocket.
7. Recheck the timing marks. Install and tighten the camshaft sprocket bolts to 113 inch lbs. (13 Nm).
8. Install the timing cover.

Timing Belt

REMOVAL & INSTALLATION

1.7L Engine

▶ See Figure 108

The timing belt is designed to last a long time without requiring tension adjustments. If the belt is removed or replaced, basic valve timing must be checked and the belt retensioned.

1. Remove the timing belt cover.
2. While holding the large hex on the tension pulley, loosen the pulley nut.
3. Remove the belt from the tensioner.
4. Slide the belt off the three toothed pulleys.
5. Using the larger bolt on the crankshaft pulley, turn the engine until the No. 1 cylinder is at TDC of the compression stroke. At this point the valves for the No. 1 cylinder will be closed and the timing mark will be aligned with the pointer on the flywheel housing. Make sure that the timing mark on the rear face of the camshaft pulley is aligned with the lower left corner of the valve cover.
6. Check that the V-notch in the crankshaft pulley aligns with the dot mark on the intermediate shaft.

✳✳WARNING

If the timing marks are not perfectly aligned, poor engine performance and probably engine damage will result!

To install:

7. Install the belt on the pulleys.
8. Adjust the tension by turning the large tensioner hex to the right. Tension is correct when the belt can be twisted 90°

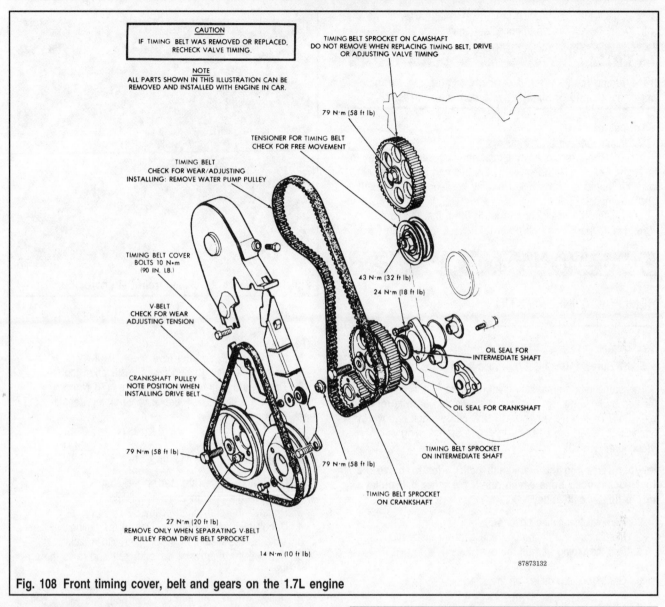

CAUTION
IF TIMING BELT WAS REMOVED OR REPLACED, RECHECK VALVE TIMING.

NOTE
ALL PARTS SHOWN IN THIS ILLUSTRATION CAN BE REMOVED AND INSTALLED WITH ENGINE IN CAR.

TIMING BELT SPROCKET ON CAMSHAFT
DO NOT REMOVE WHEN REPLACING TIMING BELT, DRIVE OR ADJUSTING VALVE TIMING

79 N·m (58 ft lb)

TENSIONER FOR TIMING BELT
CHECK FOR FREE MOVEMENT

TIMING BELT
CHECK FOR WEAR/ADJUSTING
INSTALLING: REMOVE WATER PUMP PULLEY

TIMING BELT COVER
BOLTS 10 N·m (90 IN. LB.)

43 N·m (32 ft lb)
24 N·m (18 ft lb)

V-BELT
CHECK FOR WEAR
ADJUSTING TENSION

OIL SEAL FOR INTERMEDIATE SHAFT

CRANKSHAFT PULLEY
NOTE POSITION WHEN INSTALLING DRIVE BELT

OIL SEAL FOR CRANKSHAFT

79 N·m (58 ft lb)

79 N·m (58 ft lb)

TIMING BELT SPROCKET ON INTERMEDIATE SHAFT

TIMING BELT SPROCKET ON CRANKSHAFT

27 N·m (20 ft lb)
REMOVE ONLY WHEN SEPARATING V-BELT PULLEY FROM DRIVE BELT SPROCKET

14 N·m (10 ft lb)

87873132

Fig. 108 Front timing cover, belt and gears on the 1.7L engine

with the thumb and forefinger, midway between the camshaft and intermediate pulleys.

9. Tighten the tensioner locknut to 32 ft. lbs. (43 Nm).

10. Install the timing belt cover and check the ignition timing.

2.2L Engine

▶ See Figure 109

1. Remove the timing belt cover.

2. While holding the large hex on the tension pulley, loosen the pulley nut.

3. Remove the belt from the tensioner.

4. Slide the belt off the three toothed pulleys.

5. Using the larger bolt on the crankshaft pulley, turn the engine until the No. 1 cylinder is at TDC of the compression stroke. At this point the valves for the No. 1 cylinder will be closed and the timing mark will be aligned with the pointer on the flywheel housing. Make sure that the dots on the cam sprocket and cylinder head are aligned.

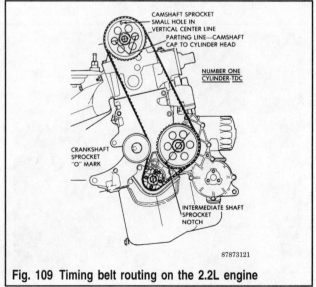

CAMSHAFT SPROCKET
SMALL HOLE IN VERTICAL CENTER LINE
PARTING LINE—CAMSHAFT CAP TO CYLINDER HEAD

NUMBER ONE CYLINDER-TDC

CRANKSHAFT SPROCKET "O" MARK

INTERMEDIATE SHAFT SPROCKET NOTCH

87873121

Fig. 109 Timing belt routing on the 2.2L engine

6. Check that the V-notch in the crankshaft pulley aligns with the dot mark on the intermediate shaft.

✳✳WARNING

If the timing marks are not perfectly aligned, poor engine performance and probably engine damage will result!

To install:

7. Install the belt on the pulleys.

8. Adjust the tensioner by turning the large tensioner hex to the right. Tension is correct when the belt can be twisted 90° with the thumb and forefinger, midway between the camshaft and intermediate pulleys.

9. Tighten the tensioner locknut to 32 ft. lbs. (43 Nm).

10. Install the timing belt cover and check the ignition timing.

Timing Sprockets and Oil Seal

REMOVAL & INSTALLATION

1.7L Engine

▶ **See Figures 110, 111, 112, 113 and 114**

The camshaft, intermediate shaft, and crankshaft pulleys are located by keys on their respective shafts and each is retained by a bolt. To remove any or all of the pulleys, first remove the timing belt cover and belt and then use the following procedure.

➡**When removing the crankshaft pulley, don't remove the four socket head bolts which retain the outer belt pulley to the timing belt pulley.**

1. Remove the timing cover(s).
2. Matchmark the timing belt and gear for installation.
3. Pull the timing belt off the gear.
4. Remove the center bolt.
5. Gently pry the pulley off the shaft.
6. If the pulley is stubborn in coming off, use a gear puller. Do not hammer on the pulley.

Fig. 111 Remove the pulley from the shaft

7. Remove the pulley and key. The oil seal may now be removed.

To install:

8. Install the pulley in the reverse order of removal.

9. Install a new seal using a seal installation tool.

10. Tighten the center bolt to 58 ft. lbs. (78 Nm).

11. Install the timing belt, check valve timing, tension belt, then install the cover.

2.2L Engine

▶ **See Figures 115, 116, 117 and 118**

1. Raise and support the car on jackstands.
2. Remove the right inner splash shield.
3. Remove the crankshaft pulley.
4. Unbolt and remove both halves of the timing belt cover.
5. Take up the weight of the engine with a jack.
6. Remove the right engine mount bolt and raise the engine slightly.
7. Remove the timing belt tensioner and remove the belt.
8. Remove the crankshaft sprocket bolt, and with a puller, remove the sprocket.

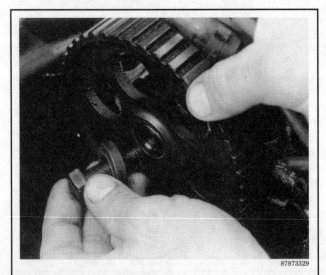
Fig. 110 Remove the center bolt

Fig. 112 The oil seal can now be removed

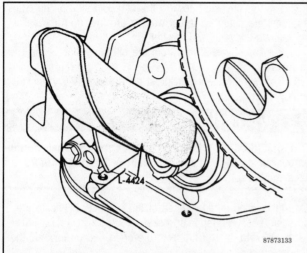

Fig. 113 Use tool L-4424 or an equivalent, to remove the front oil seal on the 1.7L engine

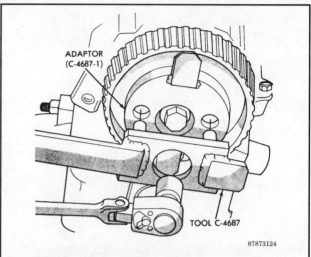

Fig. 115 Using tools C-4687 and C-4687-1, remove the camshaft and intermediate shaft sprockets

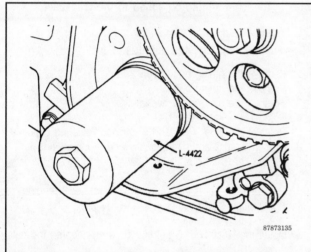

Fig. 114 To install the seal, use tool L-4422 or an equivalent

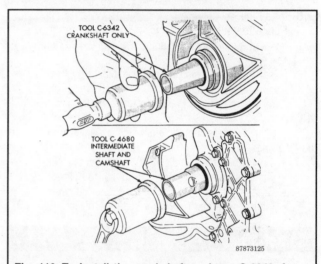

Fig. 116 To install the crankshaft seal use C-6342, for the intermediate and camshaft seal use tool C-4680

9. Using special Tool C-4679 or its equivalent, remove the crankshaft seal.

10. Unbolt and remove the camshaft and intermediate shaft sprockets.

To install:

11. To install the crankshaft seal, first polish the shaft with 400 grit emery paper. If the seal has a steel case, lightly coat the OD of the seal with Loctite® Stud N' Bearing Mount or its equivalent. If the seal case is rubber coated, generously apply a soap and water solution to facilitate installation. Install the seal with a seal driver.

12. Install the sprockets making sure that the timing marks are aligned as illustrated. When installing the camshaft sprocket, make certain that the arrows on the sprocket are in line with the No. 1 camshaft bearing cap-to-cylinder head line.

13. The small hole in the camshaft sprocket must be at the top and in line with the vertical center line of the engine.

14. Rotate the engine two full revolutions and recheck timing mark positioning.

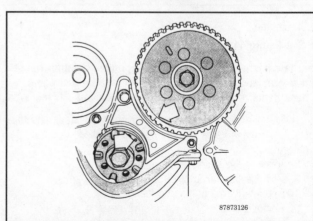

Fig. 117 Install the sprockets making sure that the timing marks are aligned as illustrated. When installing the camshaft sprocket, make certain that the arrows on the sprocket are in line with the No. 1 camshaft bearing cap-to-cylinder head line

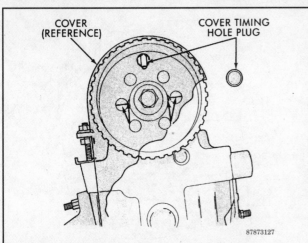

Fig. 118 When installing the camshaft sprocket, make certain that the arrows on the sprocket are in line with the No. 1 camshaft bearing cap-to-cylinder head line

15. Install the belt.

16. Rotate the engine to the No. 1 piston TDC position.

17. Install the belt tensioner and place tool C-4703 on the large hex nut.

18. Reset the belt tension so that the axis of the tool is about 15° off of horizontal.

19. Turn the engine clockwise two full revolutions to No. 1 TDC.

20. Tighten the tensioner locknut using a weighted wrench to the following:

- Timing belt cover bolts — 105 inch lbs. (12 Nm)
- Camshaft sprocket bolt — 65 ft. lbs. (88 Nm)
- Crankshaft sprocket bolt — 50 ft. lbs. (68 Nm)
- Intermediate shaft sprocket bolt — 65 ft. lbs. (88 Nm)

Camshaft

REMOVAL & INSTALLATION

1.6L Engine

▶ See Figure 119

➡The camshaft has an integral oil pump/distributor helical drive gear and an eccentric which drives the fuel pump. These items must be removed to enable camshaft removal.

1. Remove the valve cover, rocker arms, pushrods and tappets. Label these items so they may be installed in their original locations.

2. Remove the timing cover.

3. Remove the timing chain and sprockets.

4. Remove the oil pump and fuel pump.

5. Remove the distributor and drive housing, mark the crankcase in relation to the distributor drive slot.

6. With a magnet, remove the distributor drive from the driveshaft spindle.

7. Remove the oil pump shaft drive gear circlip.

➡Place a clean rag in the cavity around the gear to prevent the circlip from falling into the crankcase.

8. Tap the driveshaft toward the oil pump side of the crankcase until the gear and thrust washer are free from the spline, and remove the gear and washer.

9. Pull the driveshaft out from the oil pump side of the crankcase.

10. Remove the camshaft thrust plate and carefully remove the camshaft.

✳✳WARNING

Care should be exercised not to cock the camshaft during removal or damage to the camshaft or bearing thrust surfaces may result.

11. Installation is the reverse of the removal. Lubricate the camshaft, bearings, tappets, rockers and pushrods. Lubricate the thrust plate, then install with the open end up towards the cylinder head.

➡If a new camshaft or tappets have been installed, one pint of Chrysler oil conditioner 3419130 or an equivalent break in lubricant should be added to the crankcase.

1.7L Engine

▶ See Figures 120, 121, 122 and 123

1. Remove the timing belt cover.
2. Remove the timing belt.
3. Remove the air cleaner assembly.
4. Remove the valve cover.
5. Remove the Nos. 1, 3, and 5 camshaft bearing caps.
6. Loosen caps 2 and 4 diagonally and in increments.
7. Lift the camshaft out.

To install:

8. Lubricate the camshaft journals and lobes with engine assembly lubricant and position it in the head.

9. Install a new oil seal.

10. Install the Nos. 1, 3, 5 bearing caps and tighten the nuts to 14 ft. lbs. (19 Nm).

➡All bearing caps are slightly offset. They should be installed so that the numbers on the cap read right side up from the driver's seat.

11. Install the Nos. 2 and 4 caps and diagonally tighten the nuts to 14 ft. lbs. (19 Nm).

12. Position a dial indicator so that the feeler touches the front end of the camshaft. Check for end-play. Play should not exceed 0.01 in. (0.15mm).

13. Place a new seal on the No. 1 bearing cap. If necessary, replace the end plug in the head.

14. Follow the procedures under Timing Belt Removal and Installation for belt installation and timing.

15. Check the valve clearance and ignition.

2.2L Engine

▶ See Figure 124

1. Remove the timing belt.
2. Mark the rocker arms for installation identification.
3. Loosen the camshaft bearing capnuts several turns each.
4. Using a wooden or rubber mallet, rap the rear of the camshaft a few times to break it loose.

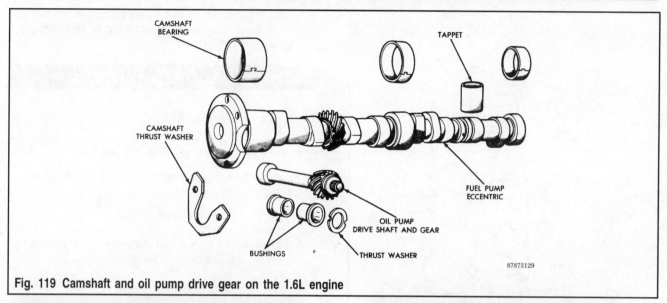

Fig. 119 Camshaft and oil pump drive gear on the 1.6L engine

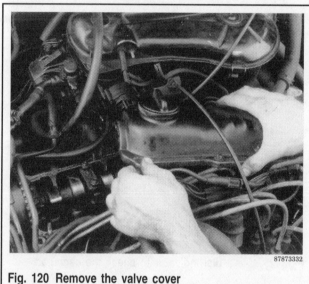

Fig. 120 Remove the valve cover

Fig. 122 The camshaft can now be removed from the engine

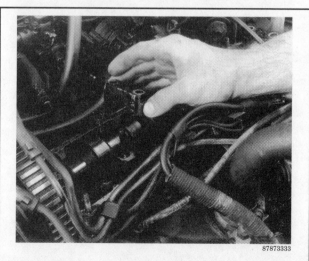

Fig. 121 Remove the bearing caps one at a time in the correct order

5. Remove the capnuts and caps being very careful that the camshaft does not cock. Cocking the camshaft could cause irreparable damage to the bearings.

To install:

6. Check all oil holes for blockage.

7. Install the bearing caps with No. 1 at the timing belt end and No. 5 at the transaxle end. Caps are numbered and have arrows facing forward. Tighten the cap nut to 14 ft. lbs. (19 Nm).

8. Apply RTV silicone gasket material as per the accompanying picture.

9. Install the bearing caps before the seals are installed.

10. The rest of the procedure is the reverse of disassembly.

CAMSHAFT END-PLAY CHECK

▶ **See Figure 125**

1. Move the camshaft as far forward as possible.
2. Install a dial indicator as per the accompanying picture.

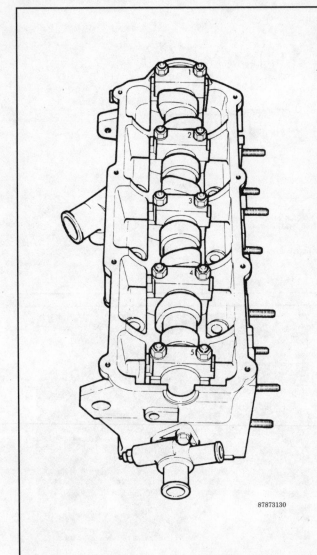

Fig. 123 Camshaft bearing cap identification on the 1.7L engine

Fig. 124 Bearing caps are marked and must be placed in their proper locations. The caps are placed in this order

3. Zero the indicator, push the camshaft backward, then forward as far as possible and record the play. Maximum play should be 0.006 in. (0.15mm).

Pistons and Connecting Rods

REMOVAL & INSTALLATION

▶ See Figures 126, 127, 128, 129, 130 and 131

➡This procedure is much easier performed with the engine out of the car.

1. Remove the cylinder head.
2. Remove the oil pan.
3. Pistons should be removed in the order: 1-3-4-2. Turn the crankshaft until the piston to be removed is at the bottom of its stroke.

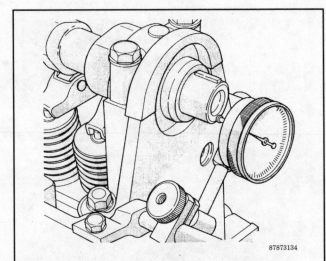

Fig. 125 Use a dial indicator to check the camshaft end-play

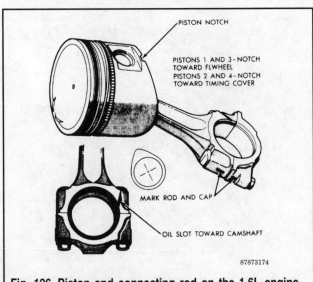

Fig. 126 Piston and connecting rod on the 1.6L engine

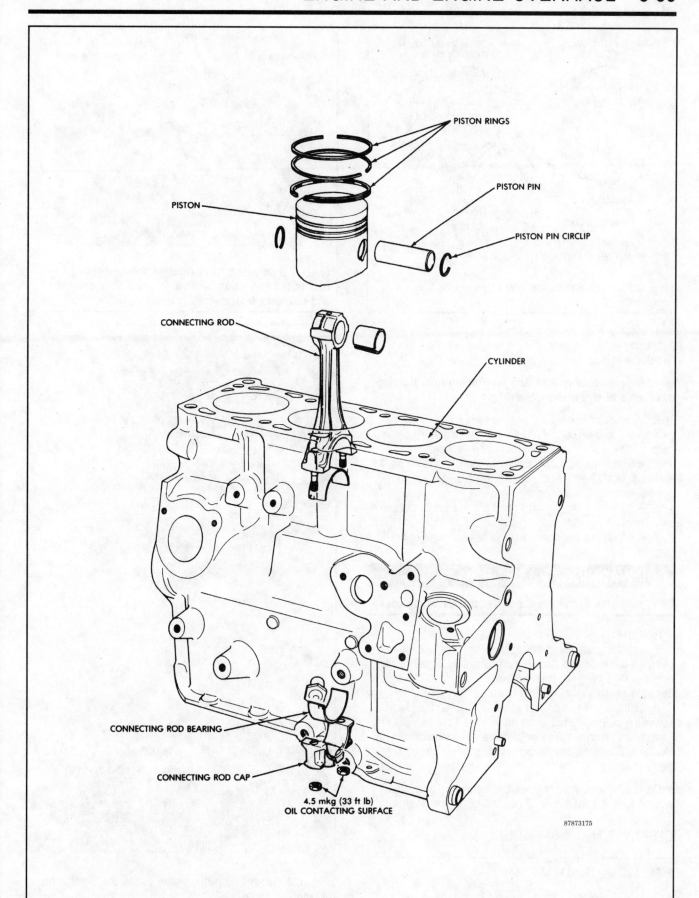

Fig. 127 Piston and connecting rod on the 1.7L engine

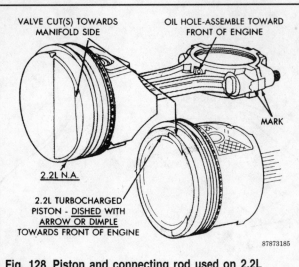

Fig. 128 Piston and connecting rod used on 2.2L engines

Fig. 129 Place lengths of rubber hose over the connecting rod studs in order to protect the crankshaft and cylinders from damage

4. Place a cloth on the head of the piston to be removed and, using a ridge reamer, remove the deposits from the upper end of the cylinder bore.

➡**Never remove more than 0.03 in. (0.8mm) from the ring travel area when removing the ridges.**

5. Mark all connecting rod bearing caps so that they may be returned to their original locations in the engine. The connecting rod caps are marked with rectangular forge marks which must be mated during assembly and be installed on the intermediate shaft side of the engine. Mark all pistons so they can be returned to their original cylinders.

6. Remove the bearing caps, then place a length of hose over the studs.

7. Carefully tap the piston and rod assembly out of the bore.

❊❊WARNING

Don't score the cylinder walls or the crankshaft journal.

To install:

8. Install the pistons in their original bores, if you are reusing the same pistons. Install short lengths of rubber hose over the connecting rod bolts to prevent damage to the cylinder walls or rod journal.

9. Install a ring compressor over the rings on the piston. Lower the piston and rod assembly into the bore until the ring compressor contacts the block. Using a wooden hammer handle, push the piston into the bore while guiding the rod onto the journal.

➡**On the 1.7 and 2.2L engines the arrow on the piston should face toward the front (drive belt) of the engine.**

CLEANING AND INSPECTION

▶ **See Figures 132, 133 and 134**

1. Use a piston ring expander and remove the rings from the piston.

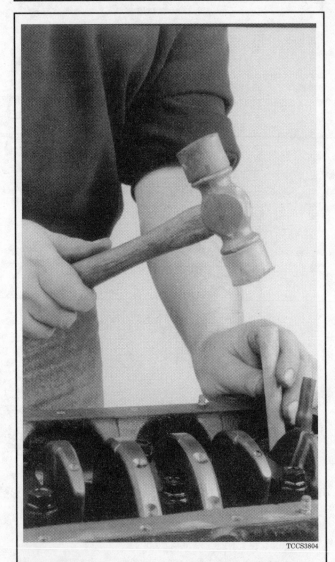

Fig. 130 Carefully tap the piston out of the bore using a wooden dowel

Fig. 131 Installing the piston into the block using a ring compressor and the handle of a hammer

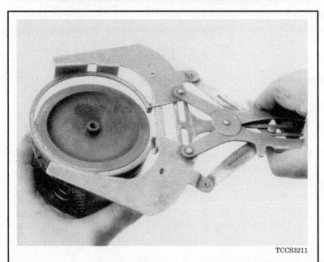

Fig. 132 Use a ring expander tool to remove the piston rings

Fig. 133 Clean the piston grooves using a ring groove cleaner

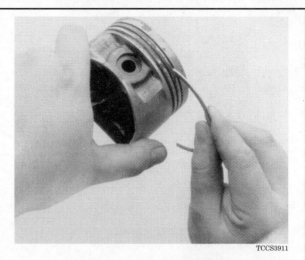

Fig. 134 You can use a piece of an old ring to clean the ring grooves, BUT be careful the ring is sharp

2. Clean the ring grooves using an appropriate cleaning tool, exercise care to avoid cutting too deeply.

3. Clean all varnish and carbon from the piston with a safe solvent. Do not use a wire brush or caustic solution on the pistons.

4. Inspect the pistons for scuffing, scoring, cracks, pitting or excessive ring groove wear. If wear is evident, the piston must be replaced.

5. Have the piston and connecting rod assembly checked by a machine shop for correct alignment, piston pin wear and piston diameter. If the piston has collapsed it will have to be replaced or knurled to restore original diameter. Connecting rod bushing replacement, piston pin fitting and piston changing can be handled by the machine shop.

CYLINDER BORE

▶ See Figures 135 and 136

Check the cylinder bore for wearing using a telescope gauge and a micrometer, measure the cylinder bore diameter perpendicular to the piston pin at a point 2½ in. (63.5mm) below the top of the engine block. Measure the piston skirt perpendicular to the piston pin. The difference between the two measurements is the piston clearance. If the clearance is within specifications, finish honing or glaze breaking is all that is required. If clearance is excessive a slightly oversize piston may be required. If greatly oversize, the engine will have to be bored and 0.01 in. (0.25mm) or larger oversized pistons installed.

PISTON PINS

The pin connecting the piston and connecting rod is press fitted. If too much free-play develops take the piston assemblies to the machine shop and have oversize pins installed. Installing new rods or pistons requires the use of a press; have the machine shop handle the job for you.

Fig. 135 Measure the piston's outer diameter using a micrometer

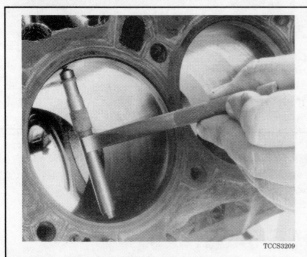

Fig. 136 A telescoping gauge may be used to measure the cylinder bore diameter

FITTING PISTON RINGS

▶ See Figures 137 and 138

1. Take the new piston rings and compress them, one at a time into the cylinder that they will be used in. Press the ring about 1 in. (25mm) below the top of the cylinder block using an inverted piston.

2. Use a feeler gauge and measure the distance between the ends of the ring, this is called, measuring the ring end-gap. Compare the reading to the one called for in the specifications table. File the ends of the ring with a fine file to obtain necessary clearance.

✳✳WARNING

If inadequate ring end-gap is utilized ring breakage will result.

3. Inspect the ring grooves on the piston for excessive wear or taper. If necessary have the grooves recut for use with a standard ring and spacer. The machine shop can handle the job for you.

4. Check the ring groove by rolling the new piston ring around the groove to check for burrs or carbon deposits. If any are found, remove with a fine file. Hold the ring in the groove and measure side clearance with a feeler gauge. If clearance is excessive, spacer(s) will have to be added.

➡**Always add spacers above the piston ring.**

5. Install the rings on the piston, lower ring first using a ring installing tool. Consult the instruction sheet that comes with the rings to be sure they are installed with the correct side up. A mark on the ring usually faces upward.

6. When installing oil rings, first install the ring in the groove. Hold the ends of the ring butted together (they must not overlap) and install the bottom rail (scraper) with the end about 1 in. (25mm) away from the butted end of the control ring. Install the top rail about 1 in. (25mm) away from the

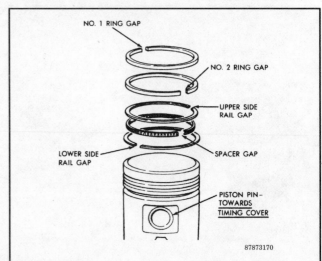

Fig. 137 Piston rings must be installed in a specific order

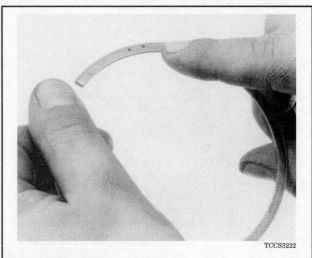

Fig. 138 Most rings are marked to show which side should face upward

butted end of the control but on the opposite side from the lower rail.

7. Install the two compression rings.

8. Consult the illustration with piston ring set instruction sheet for ring positioning, arrange the rings, then install a ring compressor and insert the piston and rod assembly into the engine.

Freeze Plugs

REMOVAL & INSTALLATION

▶ See Figures 139 and 140

1. Drain the cooling system.

2. Using a drift and a hammer, strike the bottom edge of the cup plug.

3. With the plug rotated, grasp firmly with pliers or an equivalent, and remove the plug.

❄❄WARNING

Do not drive the plug into the casting, restricted cooling can result and cause serious engine problems.

To install:

4. Thoroughly clean the inside of the plug hole in the cylinder block or head. Be sure to remove any old sealer.

5. Lightly coat the inside of the plug hole with Loctite® or an equivalent. Make certain the new plug is clean before insertion.

6. Using a drive tool, insert the plug into the hole so that the sharp edge of the plug is at least 0.02 in. (0.5mm) inside the chamfer.

7. It will not be necessary to wait for curing of the sealant. The cooling system can be refilled and the vehicle driven immediately.

Fig. 140 After the plug is loosened, it can be removed from the block

Block Heaters

REMOVAL & INSTALLATION

▶ See Figure 141

1. Drain the cooling system.

2. Detach the electrical connection from the heater unit.

3. Loosen the screw in the center of the heater unit, then remove the assembly.

To install:

4. Clean the core hole and heater seat thoroughly.

5. Insert the heater assembly with the element loop in the upward position.

6. With the heater seated, tighten the center screw.

7. Fill the cooling system, start the engine.

8. Check for leaks.

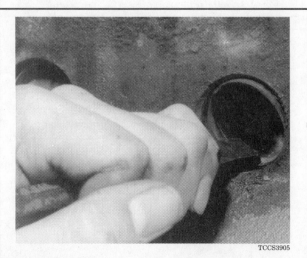
Fig. 139 Using a punch and hammer, the freeze plug can be loosened in the block

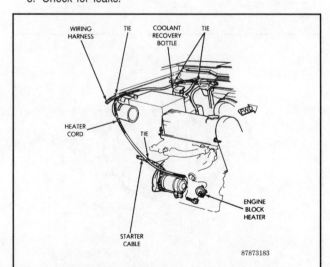
Fig. 141 The engine block heater is usually located in the lower portion of the block

Rear Main Seal

REMOVAL & INSTALLATION

▶ **See Figure 142**

The rear main seal is located in a housing on the rear of the block.

1. Remove the transaxle and flywheel.

➡**Before removing the transaxle, align the dimple on the flywheel with the pointer on the flywheel housing. The transaxle will not mate with the engine during installation unless this alignment is observed.**

2. Very carefully, pry the old seal out of the support ring with a suitable tool.

To install:

3. Coat the new seal with clean engine oil and press it into place with a flat piece of metal. Take great care not to scratch the seal or crankshaft.

4. Install the flywheel and transaxle.

Crankshaft and Bearings

REMOVAL & INSTALLATION

Rod bearings can be installed when the pistons have been removed for servicing (rings etc) or, in most cases, while the engine is still in the car. Bearing replacement, however, is far easier with the engine out of the car and disassembled.

Engine In The Car

▶ **See Figures 143 and 144**

1. Remove the transaxle and flywheel.
2. Remove the oil pan, spark plugs and front cover if necessary.

3. Turn the engine until the connecting rod to be serviced is at the bottom of its travel. Remove the bearing cap, place two pieces of rubber hose over the rod cap bolts and push the piston and rod assembly up the cylinder bore until enough room is gained for bearing insert removal. Take care not to push the rod assembly up too far or the top ring will engage the cylinder ridge or come out of the cylinder and require head removal for reinstallation.

4. Main bearings may be replaced while the engine is still in the car by rolling them out and in.

5. Special roll-out pins are available from automotive parts houses or can be fabricated from a cotter pin. The roll out pin fits in the oil hole of the main bearing journal. When the crankshaft is rotated opposite the direction of the bearing lock tab, the pin engages the end of the bearing and rolls out the insert.

6. Remove main bearing cap and roll out upper bearing insert. Remove insert from main bearing cap. Clean the inside of the bearing cap and crankshaft journal.

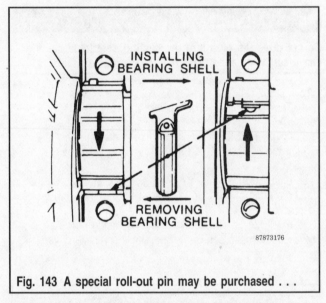

Fig. 143 A special roll-out pin may be purchased . . .

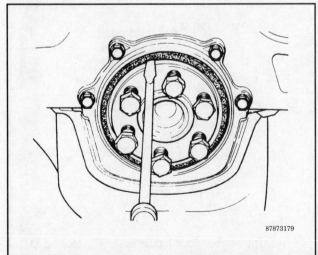

Fig. 142 Very carefully, pry the old seal out of the support ring — 2.2L shown

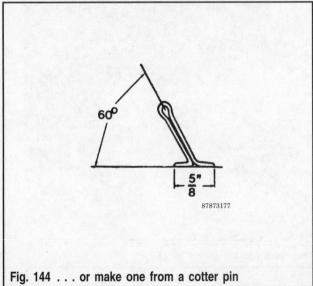

Fig. 144 . . . or make one from a cotter pin

To install:

7. Lubricate and roll upper insert into position, make sure the lock tab is anchored and the insert is not cocked. Install the lower bearing insert into the cap; lubricate and install on the engine. Make sure the main bearing cap is installed facing in the correct direction and tighten to specifications.

8. Clean the rod journal, the connecting rod end and the bearing cap after removing the old bearing inserts. Install the new inserts in the rod and bearing cap, lubricate them with oil. Position the rod over the crankshaft journal, then install the rod caps. Make sure the cap and rod numbers match, tighten the rod nuts to specifications.

9. Install the oil pan, spark plugs and front cover.

10. Install the flywheel and transaxle.

Engine Out Of The Car

1. Remove the engine from the vehicle.

2. Remove the intake manifold, cylinder head, front cover, timing gears and/or chain, oil pan, oil pump and flywheel.

3. Remove the piston and rod assemblies. Remove the main bearing caps after marking them for position and direction.

4. Remove the crankshaft bearing inserts and rear main oil seal. Clean the engine block and cap bearing saddles. Clean the crankshaft and inspect for wear. Check the bearing journals with a micrometer for out-of-round condition and to determine what size rod and main bearing inserts to install.

To install:

5. Install the main bearing upper inserts and rear main oil seal half into the engine block.

6. Lubricate the bearing insets and the crankshaft journals. Slowly and carefully lower the crankshaft into position.

7. Install the bearing inserts and rear main seal into the bearing caps, install the caps working from the middle out. Tighten the cap bolts to specifications in stages, rotate the crankshaft after each stage.

8. Remove bearing caps, one at a time and check the oil clearance with Plastigage®. Reinstall if clearance is within specifications. Check the crankshaft end-play, if within specifications, install connecting rod and piston assemblies with new rod bearing inserts. Check connecting rod bearing oil clearance and rod side-play, if correct and assemble the rest of the engine.

BEARING OIL CLEARANCE

▶ See Figure 145

Remove cap from the bearing to be checked. Using a clean, dry rag, thoroughly clean all oil from crankshaft journal and bearing insert.

➡Plastigage® is soluble in oil, therefore oil on the journal or bearing could result in erroneous readings.

Place a piece of Plastigage® along the full width of the insert, reinstall cap, then tighten to specifications.

➡Specifications are given in the engine specifications earlier in this section.

Remove bearing cap, and determine clearance by comparing width of Plastigage® to the scale on Plastigage® envelope.

Journal taper is determined by comparing width of the Plastigage® strip near its ends. Rotate crankshaft 90° and retest, to determine journal eccentricity.

➡Do not rotate crankshaft with Plastigage® installed. If bearing insert and journal appear intact, and are within tolerances, no further main bearing service is required. If bearing or journal appear defective, cause of failure should be determined before replacement.

CRANKSHAFT END-PLAY/CONNECTING ROD SIDE-PLAY

▶ See Figures 146 and 147

Place a pry bar between a main bearing cap and crankshaft casting taking care not to damage any journals. Pry backward and forward measure the distance between the thrust bearing (center main 3) and crankshaft with a feeler gauge. Compare reading with specifications. If too great a clearance is determined, a larger thrust bearing or crank machining may be

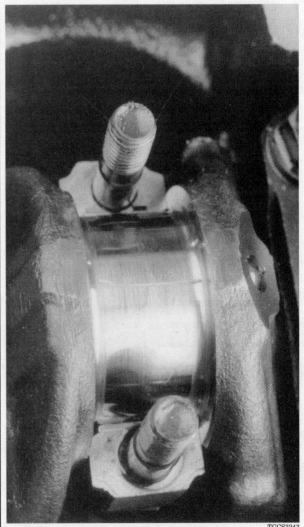

Fig. 145 Apply a strip of gauging material to the bearing journal, then install and tighten the cap

required. Check with an automotive machine shop for their advice.

Connecting rod clearance between the rod and crankthrow casting can be checked with a feeler gauge. Pry the rod carefully to one side as far as possible and measure the distance on the other side of the rod.

CRANKSHAFT REPAIRS

If a journal is damaged on the crankshaft, repair is possible by having the crankshaft machined, after removal from engine to a standard undersize. Consult the machine shop for their advice.

Flywheel and Ring Gear

REMOVAL & INSTALLATION

The flywheel on manual transaxle cars serves as the forward clutch engagement surface. It also serves as the ring gear with

Fig. 146 A dial gauge may be used to check crankshaft end-play

Fig. 147 Carefully pry the shaft back and forth while reading the dial gauge for play

which the starter pinion engages to crank the engine. The most common reason to replace the flywheel is broken teeth on the starter ring gear. To remove it, remove the transaxle. Then, unbolt and remove the clutch and pressure plate. Finally, support the flywheel in a secure manner and then remove the eight attaching bolts and remove the flywheel.

On automatic transaxle cars, the torque converter actually forms part of the flywheel. It is bolted to a thin flexplate which, in turn, is bolted to the crankshaft. The flex plate also serves as the ring gear with which the starter pinion engages in engine cranking. The flex plate occasionally cracks, the teeth on the ring gear may also break, especially if the starter is often engaged while the pinion is still spinning. The torque converter and flex plate are separated so the converter and transaxle can be removed together. Remove the automatic transaxle. Then, remove the attaching bolts and remove the flexplate from the flywheel.

Install the flywheel in reverse order, tightening the flywheel-to-crankshaft mounting bolts to the specifications.

When the flywheel or flexplate is back in position, reinstall the transaxle.

EXHAUST SYSTEM

General Information

→Safety glasses should be worn at all times when working on or near the exhaust system. Older exhaust systems will almost always be covered with loose rust particles which will shower you when disturbed. These particles are more than a nuisance and could injure your eye.

Whenever working on the exhaust system always keep the following in mind:

• Check the complete exhaust system for open seams, holes loose connections, or other deterioration which could permit exhaust fumes to seep into the passenger compartment.

• The exhaust system is usually supported by free-hanging rubber mountings which permit some movement of the exhaust system, but does not permit transfer of noise and vibration into the passenger compartment. Do not replace the rubber mounts with solid ones.

• Before removing any component of the exhaust system, ALWAYS squirt a liquid rust dissolving agent onto the fasteners for ease of removal. A lot of knuckle skin will be saved by following this rule. It may even be wise to spray the fasteners and allow them to sit overnight.

• Annoying rattles and noise vibrations in the exhaust system are usually caused by misalignment of the parts. When aligning the system, leave all bolts and nuts loose until all parts are properly aligned, then tighten, working from front to rear.

• When installing exhaust system parts, make sure there is enough clearance between the hot exhaust parts and pipes and hoses that would be adversely affected by excessive heat. Also make sure there is adequate clearance from the floor pan to avoid possible overheating of the floor.

• Support the car extra securely. Not only will you often be working directly under it, but you'll frequently be using a lot of force, heavy hammer blows, to dislodge rusted parts. This can cause a car that's improperly supported to shift and possibly fall.

• Wear goggles. Exhaust system parts are always rusty. Metal chips can be dislodged, even when you're only turning rusted bolts. Attempting to pry pipes apart with a chisel makes chips fly even more frequently.

• If you're using a cutting torch, keep it at a great distance from either the fuel tank or lines. Stop what you're doing and feel the temperature of fuel bearing pipes or the tank frequently. Even slight heat can expand or vaporize the fuel, resulting in accumulated vapor or even a liquid leak near your torch.

SPECIAL TOOLS

A number of special exhaust system tools can be rented from auto supply houses or local stores that rent special equipment. A common one is a tail pipe expander, designed to enable you to join pipes of identical diameter.

It may also be quite helpful to use solvents designed to loosen rusted bolts or flanges. Soaking rusted parts the night before you do the job can speed the work of freeing rusted parts considerably. Remember that these solvents are often flammable. Apply them only after the parts are cool.

Note that a special flexible coupling is used to connect the exhaust pipe to the exhaust manifold. If this important coupling should develop a leak, be sure to replace the seal ring with a quality part, install it in the proper direction, and tighten the bolts to specifications. Check also for any cracks in the exhaust pipe, exhaust manifold, or flanges and replace such parts as necessary.

Extension Pipe and Catalytic Converters

REMOVAL & INSTALLATION

▶ **See Figure 148**

1. Raise and support the vehicle.
2. Disconnect the extension pipe from the exhaust manifold.
3. Remove the clamp securing the extension pipe to the tailpipe.
4. Remove any supporting hardware, then remove the extension pipe and catalytic converter assembly from the vehicle.
5. Installation is the reverse of removal.

Tailpipes and Mufflers

REMOVAL & INSTALLATION

▶ **See Figures 148, 149 and 150**

1. Support the vehicle securely. Apply penetrating oil to all clamp bolts and nuts you will be working on. Support the vehicle by the body, if possible, to increase working clearances.
2. If the tailpipe is integral with the muffler, and the muffler must be replaced, cut the tail pipe with a hacksaw right near the front of the muffler. The replacement muffler is then installed using a clamp to attach to the tailpipe.
3. Loosen clamps and supports to permit alignment of all parts, and then retighten. Make sure there is adequate clearance so exhaust parts stay clear of underbody parts.
4. Clean the mating surfaces of pipes or the muffler to ensure a tight seal. Use new insulators, clamps, and supports unless the condition of old parts is very good. Note that the slip joint at the front of the muffler uses a U-clamp. The bolts should be tightened to 270 inch lbs. (30 Nm) on cars with normally aspirated engines and to 360 inch lbs. (40 Nm) on turbocharged cars.

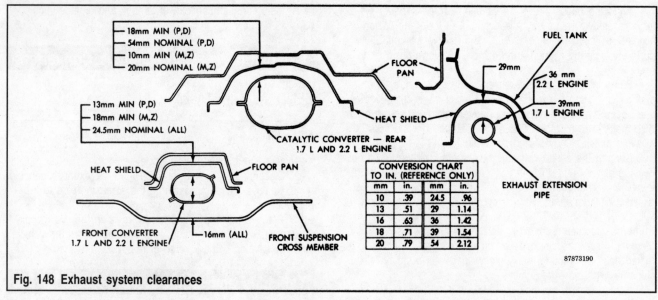

Fig. 148 Exhaust system clearances

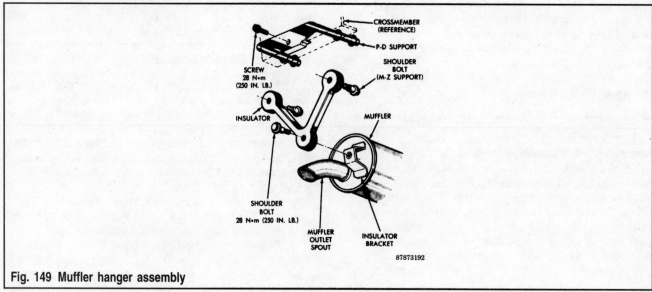

Fig. 149 Muffler hanger assembly

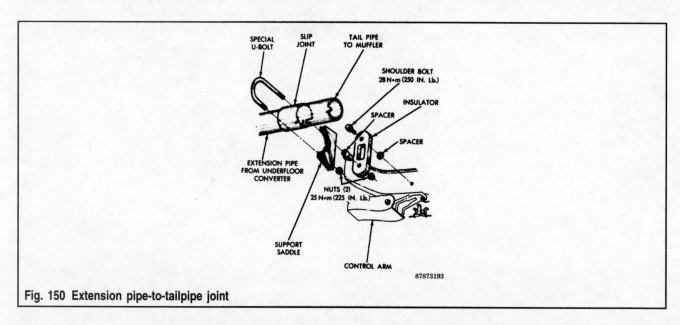

Fig. 150 Extension pipe-to-tailpipe joint

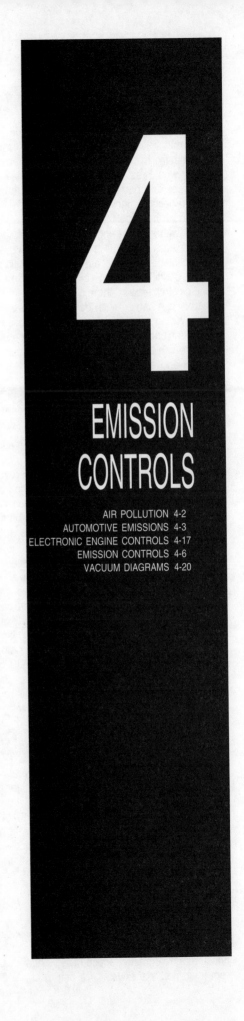

4

EMISSION CONTROLS

AIR POLLUTION

The earth's atmosphere, at or near sea level, consists of 78% nitrogen, 21% oxygen and 1% other gases, approximately. If it were possible to remain in this state, 100% clean air would result. However, many varied causes allow other gases and particulates to mix with the clean air, causing the air to become unclean or polluted.

Certain of these pollutants are visible while others are invisible, with each having the capability of causing distress to the eyes, ears, throat, skin and respiratory system. Should these pollutants be concentrated in a specific area and under the right conditions, death could result due to the displacement or chemical change of the oxygen content in the air. These pollutants can cause much damage to the environment and to the many man made objects that are exposed to the elements.

To better understand the causes of air pollution, the pollutants can be categorized into 3 separate types: natural, industrial and automotive.

Natural Pollutants

Natural pollution has been present on earth before man appeared and is still a factor to be considered when discussing air pollution, although it causes only a small percentage of the present overall pollution problem existing in our country. It is the direct result of decaying organic matter, wind born smoke and particulates from such natural events as plains and forest fires (ignited by heat or lightning), volcanic ash, sand and dust which can spread over a large area of the countryside.

Such a phenomenon of natural pollution has been recent volcanic eruptions, with the resulting plume of smoke, steam and volcanic ash blotting out the sun's rays as it spreads and rises higher into the atmosphere, where the upper air currents catch and carry the smoke and ash, while condensing the steam back into water vapor. As the water vapor, smoke and ash traveled on their journey, the smoke dissipates into the atmosphere while the ash and moisture settle back to earth in a trail hundred of miles long. In many cases, lives are lost and millions of dollars of property damage result, and ironically, man can only stand by and watch it happen.

Industrial Pollutants

Industrial pollution is caused primarily by industrial processes, the burning of coal, oil and natural gas, which in turn produces smoke and fumes. Because the burning fuels contain much sulfur, the principal ingredients of smoke and fumes are sulfur dioxide (SO_2) and particulate matter. This type of pollutant occurs most severely during still, damp and cool weather, such as at night. Even in its less severe form, this pollutant is not confined to just cities. Because of air movements, the pollutants move for miles over the surrounding countryside, leaving in its path a barren and unhealthy environment for all living things.

Working with Federal, State and Local mandated rules, regulations and by carefully monitoring the emissions, industries have greatly reduced the amount of pollutant emitted from their industrial sources, striving to obtain an acceptable level. Because of the mandated industrial emission clean up, many land areas and streams in and around the cities that were formerly barren of vegetation and life, have now begun to move back in the direction of nature's intended balance.

Automotive Pollutants

The third major source of air pollution is the automotive emissions. The emissions from the internal combustion engine were not an appreciable problem years ago because of the small number of registered vehicles and the nation's small highway system. However, during the early 1950's, the trend of the American people was to move from the cities to the surrounding suburbs. This caused an immediate problem in the transportation areas because the majority of the suburbs were not afforded mass transit conveniences. This lack of transportation created an attractive market for the automobile manufacturers, which resulted in a dramatic increase in the number of vehicles produced and sold, along with a marked increase in highway construction between cities and the suburbs. Multi-vehicle families emerged with much emphasis placed on the individual vehicle per family member. As the increase in vehicle ownership and usage occurred, so did the pollutant levels in and around the cities, as the suburbanites drove daily to their businesses and employment in the city and its fringe area, returning at the end of the day to their homes in the suburbs.

It was noted that a fog and smoke type haze was being formed and at times, remained in suspension over the cities and did not quickly dissipate. At first this "smog," derived from the words "smoke" and "fog," was thought to result from industrial pollution but it was determined that the automobile emissions were largely to blame. It was discovered that as normal automobile emissions were exposed to sunlight for a period of time, complex chemical reactions would take place.

It was found the smog was a photo chemical layer and was developed when certain oxides of nitrogen (NOx) and unburned hydrocarbons (HC) from the automobile emissions were exposed to sunlight and was more severe when the smog would remain stagnant over an area in which a warm layer of air would settle over the top of a cooler air mass at ground level, trapping and holding the automobile emissions, instead of the emissions being dispersed and diluted through normal air flows. This type of air stagnation was given the name "Temperature Inversion."

Temperature Inversion

In normal weather situations, the surface air is warmed by the heat radiating from the earth's surface and the sun's rays and will rise upward, into the atmosphere, to be cooled through a convection type heat expands with the cooler upper air. As the warm air rises, the surface pollutants are carried upward and dissipated into the atmosphere.

When a temperature inversion occurs, we find the higher air is no longer cooler but warmer than the surface air, causing the cooler surface air to become trapped and unable to move. This warm air blanket can extend from above ground level to a few hundred or even a few thousand feet into the air. As the surface air is trapped, so are the pollutants, causing a severe smog condition. Should this stagnant air mass extend to a few thousand feet high, enough air movement with the inversion takes place to allow the smog layer to rise above ground level but the pollutants still cannot dissipate. This inversion can remain for days over an area, with only the smog level rising or lowering from ground level to a few hundred feet high. Meanwhile, the pollutant levels increases, causing eye irritation, respirator problems, reduced visibility, plant damage and in some cases, cancer type diseases.

This inversion phenomenon was first noted in the Los Angeles, California area. The city lies in a basin type of terrain and during certain weather conditions, a cold air mass is held in the basin while a warmer air mass covers it like a lid.

Because this type of condition was first documented as prevalent in the Los Angeles area, this type of smog was named Los Angeles Smog, although it occurs in other areas where a large concentration of automobiles are used and the air remains stagnant for any length of time.

Internal Combustion Engine Pollutants

Consider the internal combustion engine as a machine in which raw materials must be placed so a finished product comes out. As in any machine operation, a certain amount of wasted material is formed. When we relate this to the internal combustion engine, we find that by putting in air and fuel, we obtain power from this mixture during the combustion process to drive the vehicle. The by-product or waste of this power is, in part, heat and exhaust gases with which we must concern ourselves.

AUTOMOTIVE EMISSIONS

Before emission controls were mandated on the internal combustion engines, other sources of engine pollutants were discovered, along with the exhaust emission. It was determined the engine combustion exhaust produced 60% of the total emission pollutants, fuel evaporation from the fuel tank and carburetor vents produced 20%, with the another 20% being produced through the crankcase as a by-product of the combustion process.

Exhaust Gases

The exhaust gases emitted into the atmosphere are a combination of burned and unburned fuel. To understand the exhaust emission and its composition review some basic chemistry.

When the air/fuel mixture is introduced into the engine, we are mixing air, composed of nitrogen (78%), oxygen (21%) and other gases (1%) with the fuel, which is 100% hydrocarbons (HC), in a semi-controlled ratio. As the combustion process is accomplished, power is produced to move the vehicle while the heat of combustion is transferred to the cooling system. The exhaust gases are then composed of nitrogen, a diatomic gas (N_2), the same as was introduced in the engine, carbon dioxide (CO_2), the same gas that is used in beverage carbonation and water vapor (H_2O). The nitrogen (N_2), for the

HEAT TRANSFER

The heat from the combustion process can rise to over 4000°F (2204°C). The dissipation of this heat is controlled by a ram air effect, the use of cooling fans to cause air flow and having a liquid coolant solution surrounding the combustion area and transferring the heat of combustion through the cylinder walls and into the coolant. The coolant is then directed to a thin-finned, multi-tubed radiator, from which the excess heat is transferred to the outside air by one or all of the 3 heat transfer methods: conduction, convection or radiation.

The cooling of the combustion area is an important part in the control of exhaust emissions. To understand the behavior of the combustion and transfer of its heat, consider the air/fuel charge. It is ignited and the flame front burns progressively across the combustion chamber until the burning charge reaches the cylinder walls. Some of the fuel in contact with the walls is not hot enough to burn, thereby snuffing out or quenching the combustion process. This leaves unburned fuel in the combustion chamber. This unburned fuel is then forced out of the cylinder along with the exhaust gases and into the exhaust system.

Many attempts have been made to minimize the amount of unburned fuel in the combustion chambers due to the snuffing out or quenching, by increasing the coolant temperature and lessening the contact area of the coolant around the combustion area. Design limitations within the combustion chambers prevent the complete burning of the air/fuel charge, so a certain amount of the unburned fuel is still expelled into the exhaust system, regardless of modifications to the engine.

most part passes through the engine unchanged, while the oxygen (O_2) reacts (burns) with the hydrocarbons (HC) and produces the carbon dioxide (CO_2) and the water vapors (H_2O). If this chemical process would be the only process to take place, the exhaust emissions would be harmless. However, during the combustion process, other pollutants are formed and are considered dangerous. These pollutants are carbon monoxide (CO), hydrocarbons (HC), oxides of nitrogen (NOx) oxides of sulfur (SOx) and engine particulates.

Lead (Pb), is considered 1 of the particulates and is present in the exhaust gases whenever leaded fuels are used. Lead (Pb) does not dissipate easily. Levels can be high along roadways when it is emitted from vehicles and can pose a health threat. Since the increased usage of unleaded gasoline and the phasing out of leaded gasoline for fuel, this pollutant is gradually diminishing. While not considered a major threat lead is still considered a dangerous pollutant.

HYDROCARBONS

Hydrocarbons (HC) are essentially unburned fuel that have not been successfully burned during the combustion process or have escaped into the atmosphere through fuel evaporation. The main sources of incomplete combustion are rich air/fuel mixtures, low engine temperatures and improper spark timing.

The main sources of hydrocarbon emission through fuel evaporation come from the vehicle's fuel tank and carburetor bowl.

To reduce combustion hydrocarbon emission, engine modifications were made to minimize dead space and surface area in the combustion chamber. In addition the air/fuel mixture was made more lean through improved carburetion, fuel injection and by the addition of external controls to aid in further combustion of the hydrocarbons outside the engine. Two such methods were the addition of an air injection system, to inject fresh air into the exhaust manifolds and the installation of a catalytic converter, a unit that is able to burn traces of hydrocarbons without affecting the internal combustion process or fuel economy.

To control hydrocarbon emissions through fuel evaporation, modifications were made to the fuel tank and carburetor bowl to allow storage of the fuel vapors during periods of engine shut-down, and at specific times during engine operation, to purge and burn these same vapors by blending them with the air/fuel mixture.

CARBON MONOXIDE

Carbon monoxide is formed when not enough oxygen is present during the combustion process to convert carbon (C) to carbon dioxide (CO_2). An increase in the carbon monoxide (CO) emission is normally accompanied by an increase in the hydrocarbon (HC) emission because of the lack of oxygen to completely burn all of the fuel mixture.

Carbon monoxide (CO) also increases the rate at which the photochemical smog is formed by speeding up the conversion of nitric oxide (NO) to nitrogen dioxide (NO_2). To accomplish this, carbon monoxide (CO) combines with oxygen (O_2) and nitric oxide (NO) to produce carbon dioxide (CO_2) and nitrogen dioxide (NO_2). ($CO + O_2S + NO = CO_2 + NO_2$).

The dangers of carbon monoxide, which is an odorless, colorless toxic gas are many. When carbon monoxide is inhaled into the lungs and passed into the blood stream, oxygen is replaced by the carbon monoxide in the red blood cells, causing a reduction in the amount of oxygen being supplied to the many parts of the body. This lack of oxygen causes headaches, lack of coordination, reduced mental alertness and should the carbon monoxide concentration be high enough, death could result.

NITROGEN

Normally, nitrogen is an inert gas. When heated to approximately 2500°F (1371°C) through the combustion process, this gas becomes active and causes an increase in the nitric oxide (NOx) emission.

Oxides of nitrogen (NOx) are composed of approximately 97-98% nitric oxide (NO_2). Nitric oxide is a colorless gas but when it is passed into the atmosphere, it combines with oxygen and forms nitrogen dioxide (NO_2). The nitrogen dioxide then combines with chemically active hydrocarbons (HC) and when in the presence of sunlight, causes the formation of photo chemical smog.

OZONE

To further complicate matters, some of the nitrogen dioxide (NO_2) is broken apart by the sunlight to form nitric oxide and oxygen. (NO_2 + sunlight = NO + O). This single atom of oxygen then combines with diatomic (meaning 2 atoms) oxygen (O_2S) to form ozone (O_3). Ozone is 1 of the smells associated with smog. It has a pungent and offensive odor, irritates the eyes and lung tissues, affects the growth of plant life and causes rapid deterioration of rubber products. Ozone can be formed by sunlight as well as electrical discharge into the air.

The most common discharge area on the automobile engine is the secondary ignition electrical system, especially when inferior quality spark plug cables are used. As the surge of high voltage is routed through the secondary cable, the circuit builds up an electrical field around the wire, acting upon the oxygen in the surrounding air to form the ozone. The faint glow along the cable with the engine running that may be visible on a dark night, is called the "corona discharge." It is the result of the electrical field passing from a high along the cable, to a low in the surrounding air, which forms the ozone gas. The combination of corona and ozone has been a major cause of cable deterioration. Recently, different types and better quality insulating materials have lengthened the life of the electrical cables.

Although ozone at ground level can be harmful, ozone is beneficial to the earth's inhabitants. By having a concentrated ozone layer called the "ozonosphere," between 10 and 20 miles (16-32 km) up in the atmosphere much of the ultra violet radiation from the sun's rays are absorbed and screened. If this ozone layer were not present, much of the earth's surface would be burned, dried and unfit for human life.

There is much discussion concerning the ozone layer and its density. A feeling exists that this protective layer of ozone is slowly diminishing and corrective action must be directed to this problem. Much experimenting is presently being conducted to determine if a problem exists and if so, the short and long term effects of the problem and how it can be remedied.

OXIDES OF SULFUR

Oxides of sulfur (SOx) were initially ignored in the exhaust system emissions, since the sulfur content of gasoline as a fuel is less than $\frac{1}{10}$ of 1%. Because of this small amount, it was felt that it contributed very little to the overall pollution problem. However, because of the difficulty in solving the sulfur emissions in industrial pollutions and the introduction of catalytic converter to the automobile exhaust systems, a change was mandated. The automobile exhaust system, when equipped with a catalytic converter, changes the sulfur dioxide (SO_2) into the sulfur trioxide (SO_3).

When this combines with water vapors (H_2O), a sulfuric acid mist (H_2SO_4) is formed and is a very difficult pollutant to handle and is extremely corrosive. This sulfuric acid mist that is formed, is the same mist that rises from the vents of an automobile storage battery when an active chemical reaction takes place within the battery cells.

When a large concentration of vehicles equipped with catalytic converters are operating in an area, this acid mist will rise and be distributed over a large ground area causing land, plant, crop, paints and building damage.

PARTICULATE MATTER

A certain amount of particulate matter is present in the burning of any fuel, with carbon constituting the largest percentage of the particulates. In gasoline, the remaining percentage of particulates is the burned remains of the various other compounds used in its manufacture. When a gasoline engine is in good internal condition, the particulate emissions are low but as the engine wears internally, the particulate emissions increase. By visually inspecting the tail pipe emissions, a determination can be made as to where an engine defect may exist. An engine with light gray smoke emitting from the tail pipe normally indicates an increase in the oil consumption through burning due to internal engine wear. Black smoke would indicate a defective fuel delivery system, causing the engine to operate in a rich mode. Regardless of the color of the smoke, the internal part of the engine or the fuel delivery system should be repaired to a "like new" condition to prevent excess particulate emissions.

Diesel and turbine engines emit a darkened plume of smoke from the exhaust system because of the type of fuel used. Emission control regulations are mandated for this type of emission and more stringent measures are being used to prevent excess emission of the particulate matter. Electronic components are being introduced to control the injection of the fuel at precisely the proper time of piston travel, to achieve the optimum in fuel ignition and fuel usage. Other particulate after-burning components are being tested to achieve a cleaner particular emission.

Good grades of engine lubricating oils should be used, meeting the manufacturers specification. "Cut-rate" oils can contribute to the particulate emission problem because of their low "flash" or ignition temperature point. Such oils burn prematurely during the combustion process causing emissions of particulate matter.

The cooling system is an important factor in the reduction of particulate matter. With the cooling system operating at a temperature specified by the manufacturer, the optimum of combustion will occur. The cooling system must be maintained in the same manner as the engine oiling system, as each system is required to perform properly in order for the engine to operate efficiently for a long time.

Crankcase Emissions

Crankcase emissions are made up of water, acids, unburned fuel, oil fumes and particulates. The emissions are classified as hydrocarbons (HC) and are formed by the small amount of unburned, compressed air/fuel mixture entering the crankcase from the combustion area during the compression and power strokes, between the cylinder walls and piston rings. The head of the compression and combustion help to form the remaining crankcase emissions.

Since the first engines, crankcase emissions were allowed to go into the air through a road draft tube, mounted on the lower side of the engine block. Fresh air came in through an open oil filler cap or breather. The air passed through the crankcase mixing with blow-by gases. The motion of the vehicle and the air blowing past the open end of the road draft tube caused a low pressure area at the end of the tube. Crankcase emissions were simply drawn out of the road draft tube into the air.

To control the crankcase emission, the road draft tube was deleted. A hose and/or tubing was routed from the crankcase to the intake manifold so the blow-by emission could be burned with the air/fuel mixture. However, it was found that intake manifold vacuum, used to draw the crankcase emissions into the manifold, would vary in strength at the wrong time and not allow the proper emission flow. A regulating type valve was needed to control the flow of air through the crankcase.

Testing, showed the removal of the blow-by gases from the crankcase as quickly as possible, was most important to the longevity of the engine. Should large accumulations of blow-by gases remain and condense, dilution of the engine oil would occur to form water, soots, resins, acids and lead salts, resulting in the formation of sludge and varnishes. This condensation of the blow-by gases occur more frequently on vehicles used in numerous starting and stopping conditions, excessive idling and when the engine is not allowed to attain normal operating temperature through short runs. The crankcase purge control or PCV system will be described in detail later in this section.

Evaporative Emissions

Gasoline fuel is a major source of pollution, before and after it is burned in the automobile engine. From the time the fuel is refined, stored, pumped and transported, again stored until it is pumped into the fuel tank of the vehicle, the gasoline gives off unburned hydrocarbons (HC) into the atmosphere. Through redesigning of the storage areas and venting systems, the pollution factor has been diminished but not eliminated, from the refinery standpoint. However, the automobile still remained the primary source of vaporized, unburned hydrocarbon (HC) emissions.

Fuel pumped form an underground storage tank is cool but when exposed to a warmer ambient temperature, will expand. Before controls were mandated, an owner would fill the fuel tank with fuel from an underground storage tank and park the vehicle for some time in warm area, such as a parking lot. As the fuel would warm, it would expand and should no provisions or area be provided for the expansion, the fuel would spill out the filler neck and onto the ground, causing hydrocarbon (HC) pollution and creating a severe fire hazard. To correct this condition, the vehicle manufacturers added overflow plumbing and/or gasoline tanks with built in expansion areas or domes.

However, this did not control the fuel vapor emission from the fuel tank and the carburetor bowl. It was determined that most of the fuel evaporation occurred when the vehicle was stationary and the engine not operating. Most vehicles carry 5-25 gallons (19-95 liters) of gasoline. Should a large concentration of vehicles be parked in one area, such as a large parking lot, excessive fuel vapor emissions would take place, increasing as the temperature increases.

To prevent the vapor emission from escaping into the atmosphere, the fuel system is designed to trap the fuel vapors while the vehicle is stationary, by sealing the fuel system from the atmosphere. A storage system is used to collect and hold the fuel vapors from the carburetor and the fuel tank when the engine is not operating. When the engine is started, the storage system is then purged of the fuel vapors, which are drawn into the engine and burned with the air/fuel mixture.

The components of the fuel evaporative system will be described in detail later in this section.

EMISSION CONTROLS

Crankcase Ventilation System

OPERATION

These models are equipped with a closed crankcase ventilation system. The PCV valve is located in a line running between the cylinder head cover and the air cleaner.

Blowby gasses or crankcase vapors must be removed from the crankcase to prevent oil dilution and to prevent the formation of sludge. Traditionally, this was accomplished with a road draft tube. Air entered the rocker arm cover through an open oil filler cap and flowed down past the pushrods, mixing with the blow-by gases in the crankcase. It was finally routed into the road draft tube where a partial vacuum was created, drawing the mixture into the road draft tube and out into the atmosphere.

The open PCV system replaced the road draft tube and engine manifold vacuum was used instead of the action of a moving vehicle to create a low pressure area. Air flowed into an open oil filler cap, which is characteristic of an open PCV system, and mixed with the crankcase fumes. These vapors were then drawn into the intake manifold and burned in the combustion chamber. Under heavy acceleration, however, manifold vacuum would decrease and crankcase pressure would build up. When this happened, a portion of the crankcase vapors were forced back out of the oil filter cap, creating a system which was only about 75% efficient.

The closed PCV system operates in a similar manner as the open system, except that a sealed oil filler cap and dipstick are used in place of a vented oil filler cap. In addition, an air intake hose is installed between the carburetor air filter and crankcase opening in the valve cover. A separate PCV air filter is used when the air intake hose is connected to the "dirty" side of the carburetor air cleaner. This filter is located where the intake air line connects to the valve cover.

Under normal engine operation, the closed PCV system operates the way an open system does, except that air enters through the intake hose via the air filter. Under heavy acceleration, any excess vapors back up through the air intake hose. They are forced to mix with incoming air from the carburetor and are burned in the combustion chamber. Back-up fumes cannot escape into the atmosphere, thereby creating a closed system.

The PCV valve is used to control the rate at which crankcase vapors are returned to the intake manifold. The action of the valve plunger is controlled by intake manifold vacuum and the spring. During deceleration and idle (when manifold vacuum is high), it overcomes the tension of the valve spring and the plunger bottoms in the manifold end of the valve housing. Because of the valve construction, it reduces (but does not stop) the passage of vapors to the intake manifold. When the engine is lightly accelerated or operated at constant speed, spring tension matches intake manifold vacuum pull, and the plunger takes a mid-position in the valve body, allowing more vapors to flow into the manifold.

An inoperative PCV system will cause rough idling, sludge and oil dilution. In the event of erratic idle, never attempt to compensate by disconnecting the PCV system. Disconnecting the PCV system will adversely shorten engine life through the buildup of sludge.

The PCV valve must be kept clean for optimum engine performance and fuel economy. The PCV valve should be inspected every 15,000 miles (25,395 km) and replaced every 30,000 miles (48,279 km). In extremely dusty conditions or if the car is subjected to extensive idling or short trip operation, the interval should be halved.

COMPONENT TESTING

▶ See Figures 1 and 2

1. With the engine idling, remove the PCV valve from the rocker arm cover. If the valve is not plugged, a hissing sound will be heard. A strong vacuum should be felt when you place your finger over the valve.

2. Reinstall the PCV valve and allow about a minute for pressure to drop.

3. Remove the crankcase intake air cleaner. Cover the opening in the rocker arm cover with a piece of stiff paper. The paper should be sucked against the opening with noticeable force. With a new PCV valve installed, if the paper is not sucked against the crankcase air intake opening, it will be necessary to clean the PCV valve hose and the passage in the lower part of the carburetor. If the hose is cracked, oil

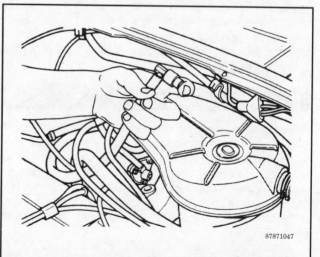

87871047

Fig. 1 A strong vacuum should be felt at the end of the valve

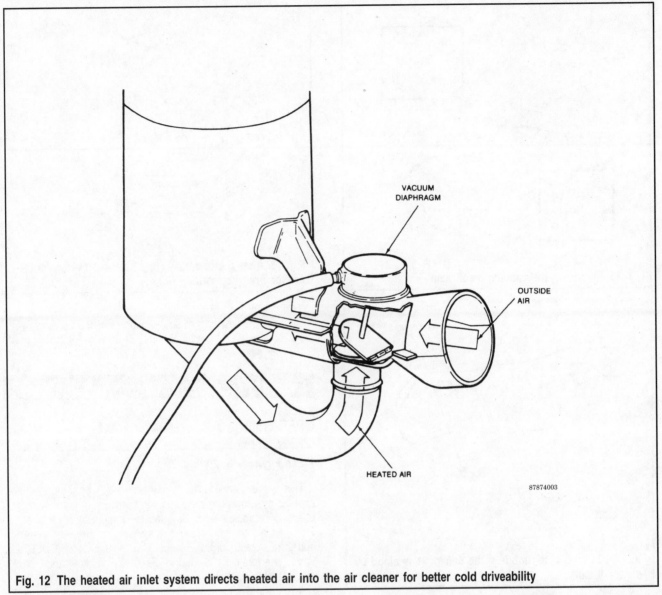

VACUUM
DIAPHRAGM

OUTSIDE
AIR

HEATED AIR

87874003

Fig. 12 The heated air inlet system directs heated air into the air cleaner for better cold driveability

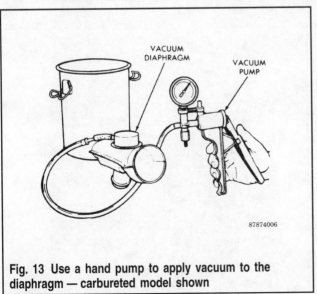

VACUUM
DIAPHRAGM

VACUUM
PUMP

87874006

Fig. 13 Use a hand pump to apply vacuum to the diaphragm — carbureted model shown

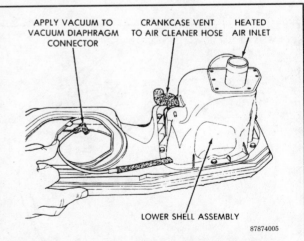

APPLY VACUUM TO
VACUUM DIAPHRAGM
CONNECTOR

CRANKCASE VENT
TO AIR CLEANER HOSE

HEATED
AIR INLET

LOWER SHELL ASSEMBLY

87874005

Fig. 14 Fuel injected models can be tested the same way. Simply apply vacuum to the vacuum diaphragm connector

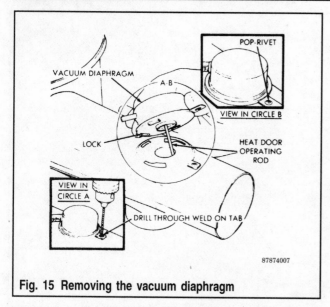

Fig. 15 Removing the vacuum diaphragm

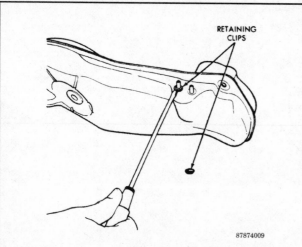

Fig. 16 On carbureted models, the sensor is retained by two small clips

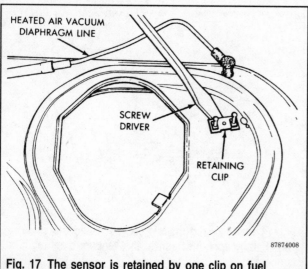

Fig. 17 The sensor is retained by one clip on fuel injected models

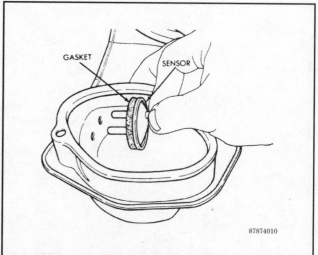

Fig. 18 After the retaining clip(s) are removed, pull the sensor from its mouting boss

To install:

4. Install a new gasket and sensor. Hold the sensor in place and install new retainer clips. Be sure the gasket forms a tight air seal. Do not attempt to adjust the sensor.

Exhaust Gas Recirculation System (EGR)

OPERATION

▶ **See Figures 19, 20 and 21**

This system reduces the amount of oxides of nitrogen in the exhaust by allowing a predetermined amount of hot exhaust gases to recirculate and dilute the incoming fuel/air mixture. The principal components of the system are the EGR valve and the Coolant Control Exhaust Gas Recirculation (CCEGR) valve. The former is located in the intake manifold and directly regulates the flow of exhaust gases into the intake. The latter is located in the thermostat housing and overrides the EGR valve when coolant temperature is below 125°F (52°C).

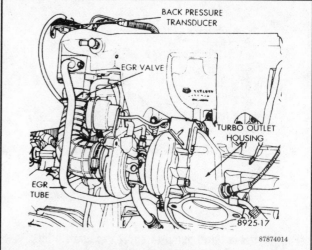

Fig. 19 The EGR mounting on the 2.2L turbocharged engine

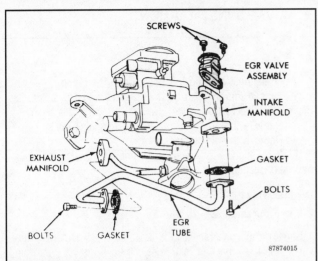

Fig. 20 The EGR mounting on single point fuel injected engines

Ported vacuum uses a slot in the carburetor throttle body which is exposed to an increasing percentage of manifold vacuum as the throttle opens. The throttle bore port is connected to the EGR valve. The flow rate of recirculation is dependent on manifold vacuum, throttle position and exhaust gas back pressure. Recycling at wide open throttle is eliminated, by calibrating the valve opening point above the manifold vacuum available at wide open throttle, which provides maximum performance.

TESTING

EGR Valve

1. Inspect all hose connections between the carburetor, intake manifold and EGR valve.
2. Check the valve with the engine warmed and running.
3. Allow the engine to idle in Neutral for 70 seconds, with the throttle closed. Abruptly accelerate the engine to about 2000 rpm, but not more than 3000 rpm.

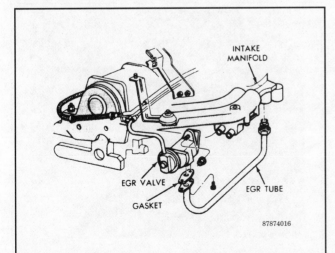

Fig. 21 The EGR mounting found on the carbureted engines

4. Visible movement of the EGR valve stem should occur during this operation. Movement can be seen by the position of the groove on the EGR valve stem. You may have to repeat the operation several times to definitely ascertain movement.

Inspect the EGR valve for deposits, particularly around the poppet and seat area. If deposits amount to more than a thin film, the valve should be cleaned. Apply a liberal amount of manifold heat control valve solvent to the poppet and seat area and allow the deposits to soften. Open the valve with an external vacuum source and remove the deposits, with a suitable sharp tool.

✳✳WARNING

During the cleaning operation, do not spill solvent on the valve diaphragm or it will cause failure of the diaphragm. Do not push on the diaphragm to operate the valve, use an external vacuum source.

An alternate procedure to this messy operation is to simply replace the valve if it is extremely clogged.

➡**A new EGR valve was used on models built after February 20, 1978. Vehicles built prior to the change can increase fuel economy slightly by using the new EGR valve (part no. 4131219) and gasket (part no. 3671425).**

Coolant Control Exhaust Gas Recirculation (CCEGR) Valve

This valve is mounted in the thermostat housing and is color coded yellow.

1. Remove the vacuum connection to the sensor.
2. Remove the valve from the housing.
3. Place it in an ice bath below 40°F (4°C) so that the threaded portion of the valve is covered.
4. Connect a hand vacuum pump to the valve nipple corresponding to the yellow stripe hose. Apply 10 in. Hg (34 kPa) of vacuum. There should be no more than 1 in. Hg (3 kPa) drop in vacuum in 1 minute. If the vacuum reading falls off, the valve should be replaced.

REMOVAL & INSTALLATION

EGR Valve

1. Disconnect the vacuum line to the EGR valve. Inspect for damage.
2. Remove the EGR valve bolts from the intake manifold.
3. Remove the EGR valve from the intake manifold.
4. Clean the gasket surfaces, then discard the old gasket. Check for any signs of leakage or cracked surfaces.
   To install:
5. Assemble the EGR valve with a new gasket onto the intake manifold.
6. Insert the mounting screws, then tighten them to 17 ft. lbs. (22 Nm).
7. Connect the vacuum lines to the EGR valve.

CCEGR Valve

1. Disconnect the vacuum hose from the valve.

2. Using an appropriate sized wrench, remove the valve from the housing.

3. Installation is the reverse of removal. Use a non-hardening sealer on the threads and tighten until snug.

Air Injection System

OPERATION

▶ **See Figure 22**

This system's job is to reduce carbon monoxide and hydrocarbons to required levels. The system adds a controlled amount of air to exhaust gases, via an air pump and induction tubes, causing oxidation of the gases. The system is composed of an air pump, a combination diverter/pressure-relief valve, hoses, a check valve to protect the hoses from exhaust gas, and an injection tube.

➡**The system is not noiseless. A certain squeal is present in pump operation.**

SERVICE

For proper operation of the system, the drive belt should be in good condition and properly tensioned. The air pump is not a serviceable item; if necessary, it should be replaced.

❊❊WARNING

Do not attempt to disassemble the pump or clamp it in a vise.

Complaints of road surge at about 40-60 mph on 1978 Federal models equipped with manual transaxle and AIR pump can be corrected, in most cases, by installing a kit (Chrysler part No. 4131207). The kit consists of a vacuum bleed, an idle air bleed, a carburetor ID tag, main metering jet, air horn gasket and hose routing label.

REMOVAL & INSTALLATION

Air Pump

1. Disconnect and tag the hoses from the pump.
2. Loosen the air pump idler pivot and adjusting bolts. Remove the drive belt.
3. Remove the air pump pulley and attaching bolts.
4. Remove the air pump.
5. Installation is the reverse of removal. Tension the drive belt, see Section 1.

Diverter Valve
▶ **See Figures 23, 24, 25 and 26**

Servicing the diverter valve is limited to replacement. If the valve fails it will become extremely noisy. If air escapes from the silencer at idle speed, either the diverter valve or the relief valve has failed and the entire valve assembly should be replaced.

1. Remove the air and vacuum hoses.
2. Remove the bolts securing the diverter valve to the mounting flange and remove the valve.
3. Remove the old gasket.
4. Installation is the reverse of removal. Use a new gasket and connect the hoses properly.

Check Valve

The check valve is not repairable. If it is necessary to service it, replace it with a new one. The valve can be tested by removing the hose from the valve inlet tube. If exhaust gasses escape from the inlet tube the valve has failed. On California cars, if the tube nut joint is leaking, retighten the nut to 25-35 ft. lbs. (34-47 Nm). If the adapter to the exhaust manifold joint is leaking, retighten the connection to a maximum of 40 ft. lbs. (54 Nm). On Canadian cars, if the air injection tube to the head joint is leaking, retighten the hollow bolts to 20 ft. lbs. (27 Nm).

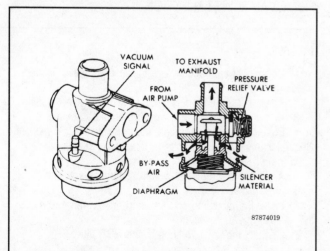

Fig. 22 The diverter valve prevents backfire in the exhaust system during deceleration

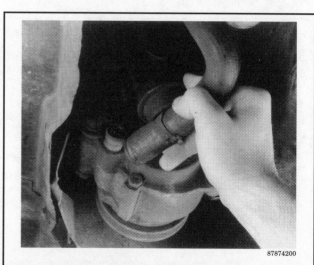

Fig. 23 Remove the hose leading to the air pump for better access to the diverter valve

Fig. 24 Now disconnect the vacuum hose leading to the valve

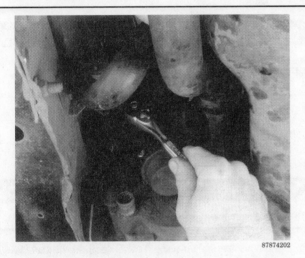

Fig. 25 Remove the bolts securing the diverter valve and remove the valve

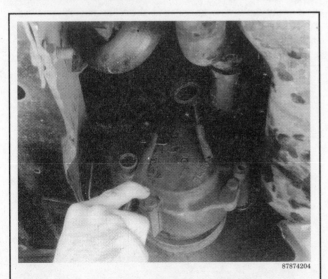

Fig. 26 Be sure to clean the gasket mating area well

EXCEPT CANADA

1. Release the clamp and disconnect the air hose from the check valve.
2. Remove the tube nut holding the injection tube to the exhaust manifold.
3. Remove the injection tube from the engine.
4. Installation is the reverse of removal.

CANADA

1. Release the clamp and remove the air hose from the check valve inlet.
2. On air conditioned cars, remove the air conditioning compressor from the mount.

✴✴CAUTION

Do not disconnect any air conditioning system hoses.

3. Remove the 4 isolated rubber compressor mounting bracket bolts and the compressor-to-cylinder head bolt. Set the compressor aside and keep it upright.
4. Drain the cooling system to a level below the thermostat housing.
5. Remove the housing from the bypass hose.
6. Remove the 4 hollow bolts holding the injection tube assembly to the cylinder head.

To install:

7. Install the injection tube assembly on the cylinder head. The 4 copper washers must be used between the tube assembly and the cylinder head.
8. Install the 4 hollow bolts with copper washers between each bolt and the injection tube assembly. The washers must be used. Tighten the bolts to 20 ft. lbs. (27 Nm).
9. Install the thermostat housing and connect the bypass hose.
10. On engines with air conditioning, reinstall the compressor. Adjust the drive belt.
11. Reconnect the air hose to the check valve inlet.
12. Refill the cooling system.

Air Aspirator System

OPERATION

▶ See Figure 27

The aspirator valve utilizes exhaust pressure pulsation to draw clean air from the inside of the air cleaner into the exhaust system. The function is to reduce HC (hydrocarbon) emissions.

TESTING

To determine if the air aspirator valve has failed, disconnect the hose from the aspirator inlet. With the engine idling in Neutral, vacuum exhaust pulses can be felt at the aspirator inlet. If hot exhaust gas is escaping from the aspirator inlet, the valve has failed and should be replaced.

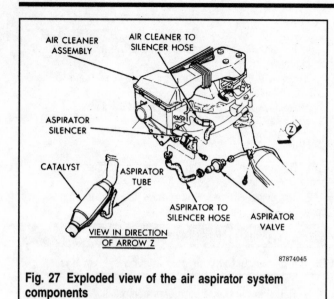

Fig. 27 Exploded view of the air aspirator system components

REMOVAL & INSTALLATION

Aspirator Valve

1. Disconnect the air hose from the aspirator valve inlet.
2. Unscrew the valve from the aspirator tube assembly.
To install:
3. Install the aspirators tube, then tighten the tube nut to 25-40 ft. lbs. (54 Nm).
4. Install the aspirator tube bracket screw, tighten to 95 inch lbs. (11 Nm).
5. Connect the air hose to the aspirator valve inlet and the air cleaner nipple.

Aspirator Tube Assembly

1. Disconnect the air hose fro the aspirator valve inlet.
2. Remove the nut securing the aspirator tube assembly to the engine.
3. Remove the aspirator tube.
4. Installation is the reverse of removal. Tighten the tube nut to 25-40 ft. lbs. (34-54 Nm).

Catalytic Converter

OPERATION

▶ **See Figure 28**

Two catalysts are used. A small one located just after the exhaust manifold and a larger one located under the car body.

Catalysts promote complete oxidation of exhaust gases through the effect of a platinum coated mass in the catalyst shell. Two things act to destroy the catalyst, functionally: excessive heat and leaded gas. Excessive heat during misfiring and prolonged testing with the ignition system in any way altered is the most common occurrence. Test procedures should be accomplished as quickly as possible, and the car should not be driven when misfiring is noted.

✳✳WARNING

Operation of any type including idling should be avoided if engine misfiring occurs. Alteration or deterioration of the ignition system or fuel system must be avoided to prevent overheating the catalytic converter.

These cars are equipped with a special fuel filler neck that prevents the use of any filler nozzle except those designed for unleaded fuel. As a reminder to the operator, a decal '"UNLEADED GASOLINE" is located near the filler neck, and on the dash.

Oxygen Sensor

REMOVAL & INSTALLATION

▶ **See Figures 29 and 30**

The oxygen sensor is mounted in the exhaust manifold.
1. Disconnect the engine harness connector from the sensor.

✳✳WARNING

Do not pull on the sensor wire.

2. Remove the sensor using Tool C-4589 on the carbureted engine and Tool C-4907 or their equivalents, for the fuel injected and turbo engines.
To install:
3. After the sensor is removed clean the exhaust manifold threads with an 0.7 in. x 0.06 in. x 6E (18mm x 1.5mm x 6E) tap. If the old sensor is to be reinstalled, the sensor threads must be coated with an anti seize compound such as Loctite® 771-64 or equivalent on the threads. New sensors are packaged with compound on the threads and no additional compound is required.
4. Tighten the sensor to 20 ft. lbs. (27 Nm).

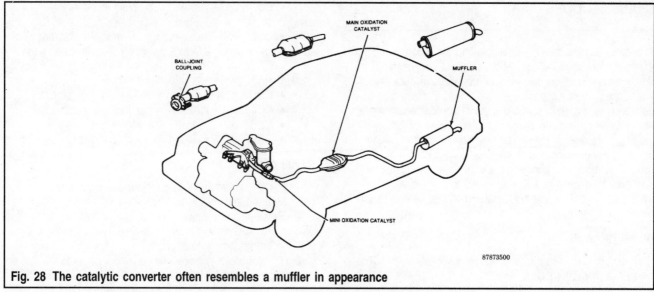

Fig. 28 The catalytic converter often resembles a muffler in appearance

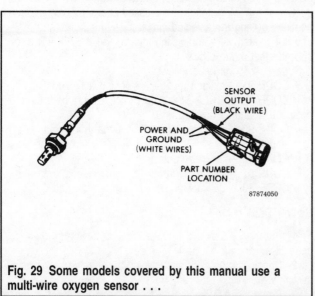

Fig. 29 Some models covered by this manual use a multi-wire oxygen sensor . . .

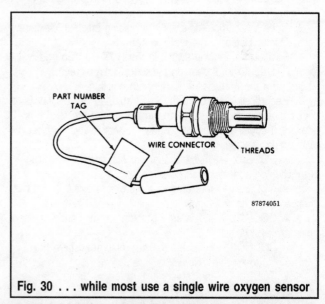

Fig. 30 . . . while most use a single wire oxygen sensor

ELECTRONIC ENGINE CONTROLS

Electronic Feedback Carburetor (EFC) System

GENERAL INFORMATION

The EFC system is essentially an emissions control system which utilizes an electronic signal, generated by an exhaust gas oxygen sensor, to precisely control the air-fuel mixture ratio in the carburetor. This allows the engine to produce exhaust gases of the proper composition to permit the use of a three-way catalyst. The three-way catalyst is designed to convert the three pollutants (1) Hydrocarbons (HC), (2) Carbon Monoxide (CO), and (3) Oxides of Nitrogen (NO_x) into harmless substances.

There are two operating modes in the EFC system:
- Open Loop — Air fuel ratio is controlled by information programmed into the computer at manufacture.
- Closed Loop — Air fuel ratio is varied by the computer based on information supplied by the oxygen sensor.

When the engine is cold, the system will be operating in the open loop mode. During that time, the air fuel ratio will be fixed at a richer level. This will allow proper engine warm-up. Also during this period, air injection (from the air injection pump) will be injected upstream in the exhaust manifold.

The computer has been programmed to monitor various component systems. If a malfunction of a system occurs, a fault code will be stored in the computer. If the problem is repaired or corrects itself, the computer will erase the code after thirty ignition cycles.

READING CODES

In order to read the computer and find the fault code, diagnostic readout tool C-4805 or equivalent will be needed. If a fault code appears on the read-out tool, perform a careful visual check of all vacuum lines and electrical connections before doing any repairs to the system. The diagnostic readout tool can be used to check out three different problem modes. They are the diagnostic test mode, circuit actuation test mode and switch test mode. The diagnostic test mode is used to retrieve fault codes that are stored in the computer. The circuit actuation test mode is used to analyze various systems. The switch test mode is used to test various switch circuits.

Diagnostic Mode

1. Install the readout tool to the wiring connector which is located on the left shock tower.
2. Position the read/hold switch on the tool to the read position.
3. Open the carburetor switch by placing the fast idle screw on the highest step of the fast idle cam.
4. Position the ignition switch in the **RUN** position and wait for fault code 00 to appear on the tool display screen.
5. Move the read/switch to the hold position.
6. Record all fault codes that may appear. The display fault codes may be stopped by switching the tool to the read position. Fault codes will continue when the tool is switched back to the hold position.

- CODE 00 — indicates that the diagnostic readout tool is functioning and receiving power
- CODE 11 — indicates that a problem exists in the oxygen solenoid control circuit
- CODE 12 — indicates a problem in the transmission unlock relay
- CODE 13 — indicates that a problem exists in the canister purge solenoid circuit
- CODE 14 — indicates that the vehicle battery has been disconnected
- CODE 16 — indicates that there is a problem in the radiator fan control circuit in vehicles equipped with the 2.2L engines. If vehicle is equipped with air condition disregard this fault code
- CODE 17 — indicates that a problem exists in the electronic throttle control vacuum solenoid system on vehicles equipped with a 2.2L engine
- CODE 18 — indicates a problem in the vacuum operated secondary control solenoid system on vehicles equipped with the 2.2L engine
- CODE 21 — indicates a problem in the distributor pick up system
- CODE 22 — indicates that the oxygen system is stuck in full lean position
- CODE 23 — indicates that the oxygen sensor is stuck in the full rich position
- CODE 24 — indicates a problem in the computer
- CODE 25 — indicates a problem in the radiator fan coolant sensor portion of the engine temperature dual sensor system on vehicles equipped with the 2.2L engine

- CODE 26 — indicates a problem in the engine temperature portion of the engine temperature dual sensor system
- CODE 28 — indicates a problem in the distance sensor system on vehicles equipped with manual transmission
- CODE 31 — indicates that the engine has not been cranked since the battery was disconnected
- CODE 32 — indicates a problem in the computer
- CODE 33 — indicates a problem in the computer
- CODE 55 — indicates the end of a message
- CODE 88 — indicates the end of a message

Circuit Actuation Testing

1. Put the system into diagnostic mode testing and wait for code 55 to appear on the tool test screen.
2. Press the ATM function button on the tool to activate the display. If a specific ATM test is desired, hold the button down until the proper test code appears.
3. The computer will continue to turn the selected circuit on and off for as long as five minutes or until the ATM button is pressed again or if the ignition switch is turned **OFF**.
4. If the ATM button is not pressed again, the computer will continue cycling the selected circuit for five minutes and then shut the system off. Turning the ignition switch **OFF** will also shut the test mode off.

Code description is as follows:

- CODE 91 — oxygen feedback solenoid activated
- CODE 92 — shift indicator light on the instrument panel activated (manual transmission)
- CODE 93 — vacuum operated secondary solenoid activated
- CODE 96 — fan relay activated
- CODE 97 — electronic throttle control solenoid activated
- CODE 98 — canister purge solenoid is activated

Switch Testing Mode

1. Put the system into diagnostic mode testing and wait for code 55 to appear on the test screen.
2. Check that both air conditioning and heated rear window switches are in the off position.
3. Press the ATM button on the tool and immediately move the read/hold switch to the read position.
4. Wait for code 00 to appear on the test screen.
5. Turn the air conditioning switch to the on position. If the computer is receiving input, the display will change to 88 when the switch is turned on and switch back to 00 when the switch is turned off. Repeat the test for the heated rear window switch.

Code description is as follows:

- CODE — 00 air conditioning and heated rear window switches are off
- CODE — 88 air conditioning or heated rear window switches are on

CLEARING CODES

The computer will automatically erase the code(s) thirty ignition cycles after the problem has been repaired. The code(s) may also be erased manually by disconnecting the negative battery cable for 30 seconds.

Electronic Fuel Injection

GENERAL INFORMATION

Single Point Injection

This system is a continuous flow, single point, fully electronically controlled system. A single system electronically monitors the ratio of air to fuel and compares it to an ideal ratio by adjusting it automatically to changing environmental and engine conditions. This system also provides an integrated and pre-programed computer that commands ignition timing, monitors air/fuel ratio and emission control systems. The system also has the ability to update its programing to suite the current engine operating conditions, as required.

The computer has been programmed to monitor various component systems. If a malfunction of a system occurs, a fault code will be stored in the computer. If the problem is repaired or corrects itself, the computer will erase the code after 20 to 40 vehicle starts.

Mult-Point Injection

This fuel injection system is made up of an electronic fuel injection and spark advance control system. The multi-point fuel injection system uses an injector for each cylinder, where the single point fuel injection system has one injector that is positioned in the throttle body assembly. With the multi-point fuel injection system, fuel is pumped to the fuel rail by using an electric fuel pump that is mounted in the fuel tank. The injectors are secured to the fuel rail with lock rings. The rail and the injector assembly is bolted in position with the injectors inserted in the recessed holes of the intake manifold. The fuel rail takes the fuel from the fuel pump and distributes it to the injectors, the injectors then atomize the fuel and spray it into the air entering the individual cylinder combustion chambers.

The computer has been programmed to monitor various component systems. If a malfunction of a system occurs, a fault code will be stored in the computer. If the problem is repaired or corrects itself, the computer will erase the code after 20 to 40 vehicle starts.

READING CODES

The fault codes can be read using diagnostic readout tool C-4805 (or equivalent) or through the Power Loss/Limited lamp. If a fault code appears, perform a careful visual check of all vacuum lines and electrical connections before doing any repairs to the system. The diagnostic read-out tool can be used to check out two other problem modes. They are the circuit actuation test mode and switch test mode. The circuit actuation test mode is used to analyze various systems. The switch test mode is used to test various switch circuits.

Diagnostic Mode

1. If available, connect Diagnostic Readout Box tool C-4805 or equivalent, to the diagnostic connector located in the engine compartment near the passenger side strut tower.

2. Start the engine if possible. Cycle the transmission selector and the A/C switch if applicable. Shut off the engine. Cycle the ignition switch three times within five seconds.

➡**When cycling the ignition switch, do not turn to the START position.**

3. Record all the diagnostic codes shown on the readout tool or Power Loss/Limited lamp. Codes can be read from the Power Loss/Limited lamp by counting the number of flashes. For example, a code 35 would be three flashes, a pause, then five more flashes.

Code description is as follows:

SINGLE POINT FAULT CODES

- CODE 88 — Start of the test
- CODE 11 — Engine not cranked since the battery was disconnected
- CODE 12 — Memory Standby power lost
- CODE 13 — MAP sensor pneumatic circuit (Power loss/limited lamp on)
- CODE 14 — MAP sensor electrical circuit (Power loss/limited lamp on)
- CODE 15 — Vehicle speed/distance sensor
- CODE 16 — Loss of battery voltage sense (Power loss/limited lamp on)
- CODE 17 — Engine running too cool (trouble in the cooling system)
- CODE 21 — Oxygen sensor circuit
- CODE 22 — Coolant temperature sensor circuit (Power loss/limited lamp on)
- CODE 23 — Throttle body temperature sensor circuit
- CODE 24 — Throttle position sensor
- CODE 25 — AIS motor driven circuit
- CODE 26 — Peak injection current has not been reached
- CODE 27 — Internal problem in logic module fuel circuit
- ODE 31 — Purge solenoid circuit
- CODE 33 — A/C cutout relay circuit
- CODE 35 — Fan control relay circuit
- CODE 37 — Shift indicator light circuit
- CODE 41 — Charging system excess or no field circuit
- CODE 42 — Auto shutdown relay driver
- CODE 43 — Spark interface circuit
- CODE 44 — Battery temperature is out of range
- CODE 46 — Battery voltage is too high (Power loss/limited lamp on)
- CODE 47 — Battery voltage is too low
- CODE 51 — Oxygen feedback system stuck in the lean position
- CODE 52 — Oxygen feedback system stuck in the rich position
- CODE 53 — Internal logic module problem
- CODE 55 — End of message

MULTI-POINT FAULT CODES

- CODE 88 — Start of the test
- CODE 11 — Engine not cranked since the battery was disconnected
- CODE 12 — Memory standby power lost
- CODE 13 — MAP sensor pneumatic circuit (Power loss/limited lamp on)

- CODE 14 — MAP sensor electrical circuit (Power loss/limited lamp on)
- CODE 15 — Vehicle speed/distance sensor
- CODE 16 — Loss of battery voltage sense (Power loss/limited lamp on)
- CODE 17 — Engine running too cool (trouble in the cooling system)
- CODE 21 — Oxygen sensor circuit
- CODE 22 — Coolant temperature sensor circuit (Power loss/limited lamp on)
- CODE 23 — Charge temperature sensor circuit (Power loss/limited lamp on)
- CODE 24 — Throttle position sensor
- CODE 25 — AIS motor driven circuit
- CODE 26 — Number one injector circuit
- CODE 27 — Number two injector circuit
- CODE 31 — Purge solenoid circuit
- CODE 33 — A/C cutout relay circuit
- CODE 34 — EGR solenoid circuit
- CODE 35 — Fan control relay circuit
- CODE 36 — Wastegate solenoid circuit (Power loss/limited lamp on)
- CODE 37 — Barometric read solenoid circuit
- CODE 41 — Charging system excess or no field circuit
- CODE 42 — Auto shutdown relay driver
- CODE 43 — Spark interface circuit
- CODE 44 — Battery temperature is out of range
- CODE 45 — Overboost shut-off circuit
- CODE 46 — Battery voltage is too high (Power loss/limited lamp on)
- CODE 47 — Battery voltage is too low
- CODE 51 — Oxygen feedback system stuck in the lean position
- CODE 52 — Oxygen feedback system stuck in the rich position
- CODE 53 — Internal logic module problem
- CODE 54 — Distributor sync pick-up circuit (Power loss/limited lamp on)
- CODE 55 — End of message

Circuit Actuation Testing

1. Put the system into diagnostic mode testing and wait for code 55 to appear on the test screen. Press the ATM button on the diagnostic tool to activate the display.

2. If a specific ATM test is desired, hold the ATM button down until the desired test code appears.

3. The computer will continue to turn the selected circuit on and off for as long as five minutes or until the ATM button is pressed again or if the ignition switch is turned **OFF**.

4. If the ATM button is not pressed again, the computer will continue cycling the selected circuit for five minutes and then shut the system off. Turning the ignition switch **OFF** will also shut the test mode off.

Code description is as follows:
- CODE 01 — Spark Activation, once every two seconds
- CODE 02 — Injector Activation, once every two seconds
- CODE 03 — Automatic Idle Speed System (AIS) Activation, one step open/one step closed every four seconds
- CODE 04 — Radiator Fan Relay, once every two seconds
- CODE 05 — A/C Wide Open Throttle Cut Out Relay, once every two seconds
- CODE 06 — Automatic Shut Down Relay (ASD) Activation, once every two seconds
- CODE 07 — Purge Solenoid Activation, one toggle every two seconds

Switch Testing Mode

1. Put the system into diagnostic mode testing and wait for code 55 to appear on the test screen.

2. After code 55 appears, actuate the following component switches. The digital display must change its numbers when the switch is activated and released:
- Brake pedal
- Gear shift selector
- A/C switch
- Blower switch
- Speed sensor

CLEARING CODES

The computer will automatically erase the code(s) after 20 to 40 vehicle starts after the problem has been repaired. The code(s) may also be erased manually by disconnecting the negative battery cable for 30 seconds.

VACUUM DIAGRAMS

Following is a listing of vacuum diagrams for most of the engine and emissions package combinations covered by this manual. Because vacuum circuits will vary based on various engine and vehicle options, always refer first to the vehicle emission control information label, if present. Should the label be missing, or should vehicle be equipped with a different engine from the original equipment, refer to the diagrams below for the same or similar configuration.

If you wish to obtain a replacement emissions label, most manufacturers make the labels available for purchase. The labels can usually be ordered from a local dealer.

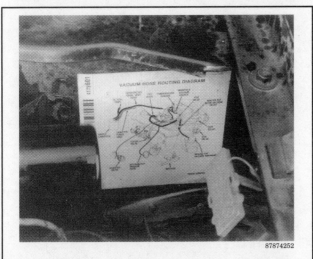

Fig. 31 The vacuum hose routing label can usually be found in the engine compartment

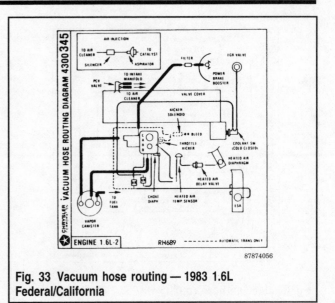

Fig. 33 Vacuum hose routing — 1983 1.6L Federal/California

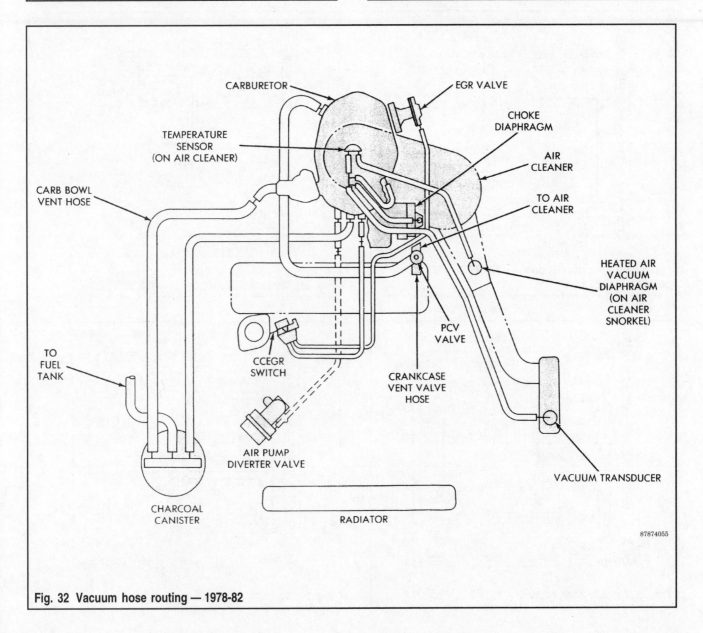

Fig. 32 Vacuum hose routing — 1978-82

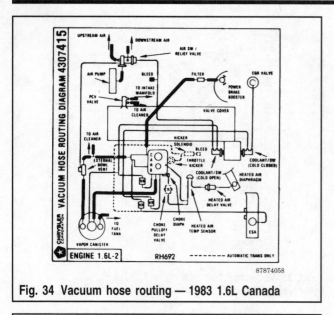

Fig. 34 Vacuum hose routing — 1983 1.6L Canada

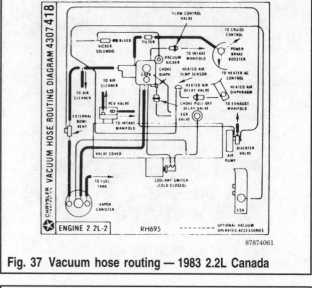

Fig. 37 Vacuum hose routing — 1983 2.2L Canada

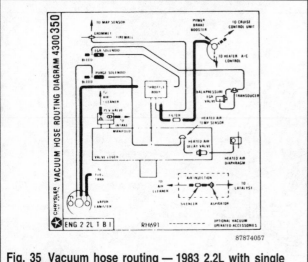

Fig. 35 Vacuum hose routing — 1983 2.2L with single point fuel injection

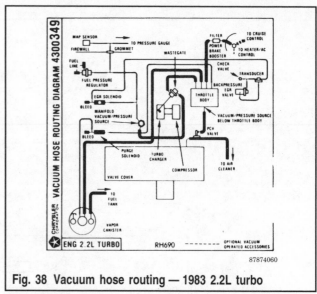

Fig. 38 Vacuum hose routing — 1983 2.2L turbo

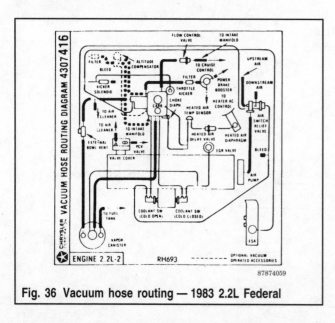

Fig. 36 Vacuum hose routing — 1983 2.2L Federal

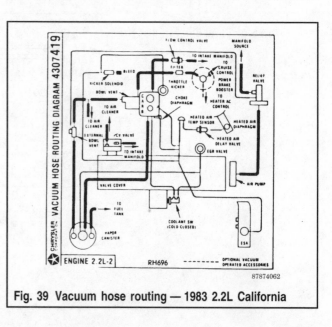

Fig. 39 Vacuum hose routing — 1983 2.2L California

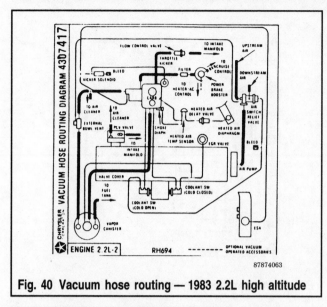

Fig. 40 Vacuum hose routing — 1983 2.2L high altitude

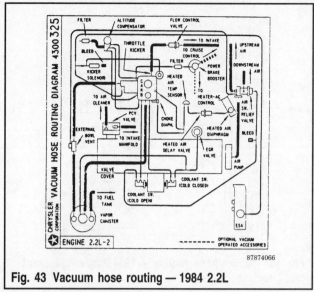

Fig. 43 Vacuum hose routing — 1984 2.2L

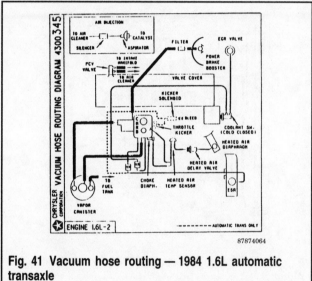

Fig. 41 Vacuum hose routing — 1984 1.6L automatic transaxle

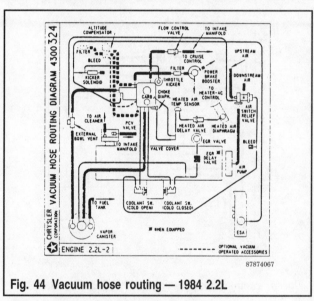

Fig. 44 Vacuum hose routing — 1984 2.2L

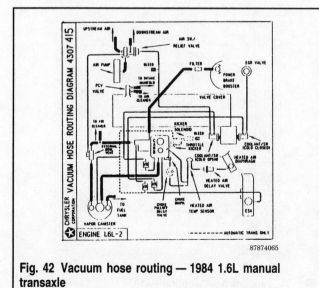

Fig. 42 Vacuum hose routing — 1984 1.6L manual transaxle

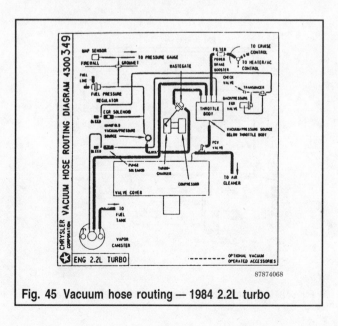

Fig. 45 Vacuum hose routing — 1984 2.2L turbo

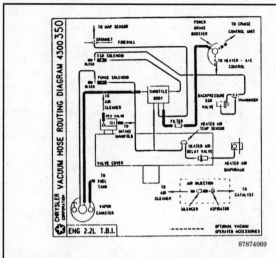

Fig. 46 Vacuum hose routing — 1984 2.2L single point fuel injection

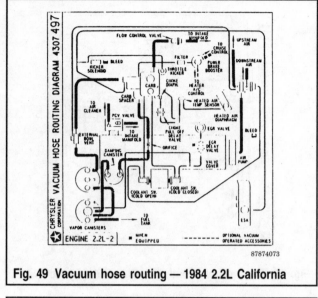

Fig. 49 Vacuum hose routing — 1984 2.2L California

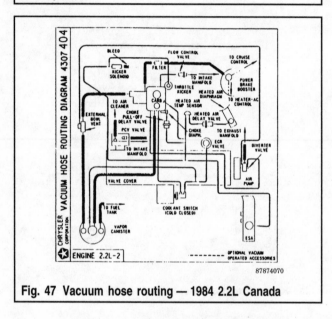

Fig. 47 Vacuum hose routing — 1984 2.2L Canada

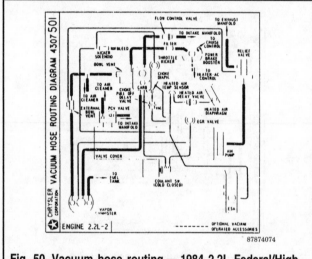

Fig. 50 Vacuum hose routing — 1984 2.2L Federal/High Altitude

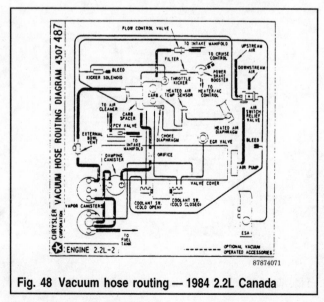

Fig. 48 Vacuum hose routing — 1984 2.2L Canada

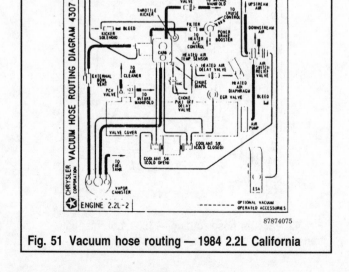

Fig. 51 Vacuum hose routing — 1984 2.2L California

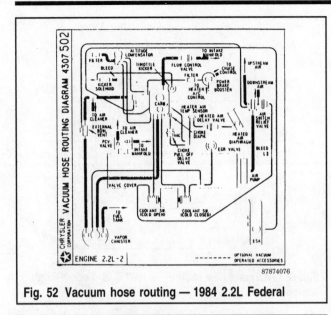

Fig. 52 Vacuum hose routing — 1984 2.2L Federal

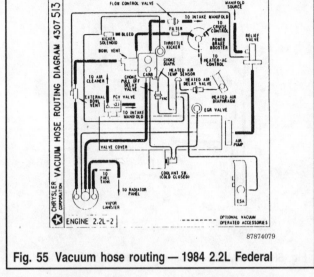

Fig. 55 Vacuum hose routing — 1984 2.2L Federal

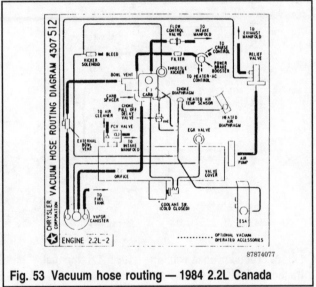

Fig. 53 Vacuum hose routing — 1984 2.2L Canada

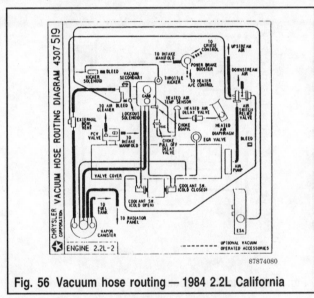

Fig. 56 Vacuum hose routing — 1984 2.2L California

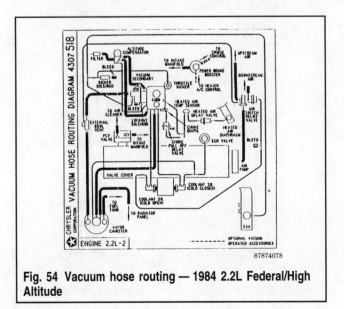

Fig. 54 Vacuum hose routing — 1984 2.2L Federal/High Altitude

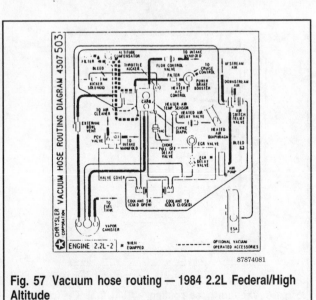

Fig. 57 Vacuum hose routing — 1984 2.2L Federal/High Altitude

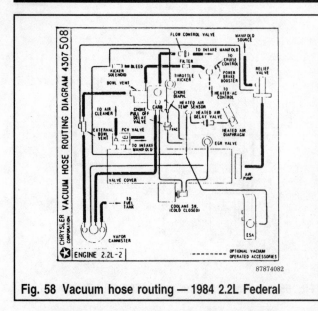

Fig. 58 Vacuum hose routing — 1984 2.2L Federal

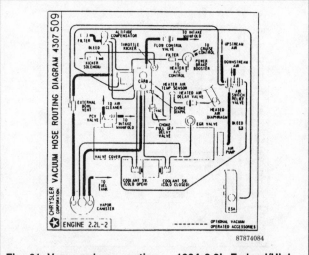

Fig. 61 Vacuum hose routing — 1984 2.2L Federal/High Altitude

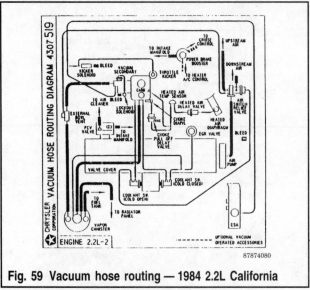

Fig. 59 Vacuum hose routing — 1984 2.2L California

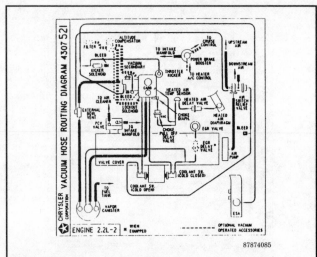

Fig. 62 Vacuum hose routing — 1984 2.2L manual transaxle, Federal/High Altitude

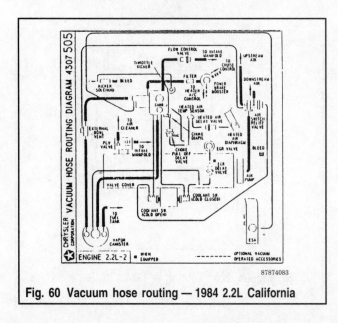

Fig. 60 Vacuum hose routing — 1984 2.2L California

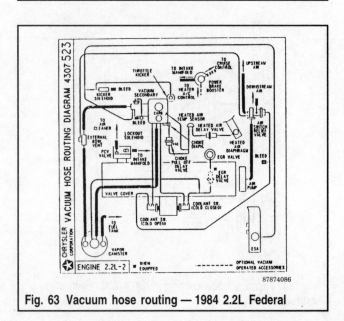

Fig. 63 Vacuum hose routing — 1984 2.2L Federal

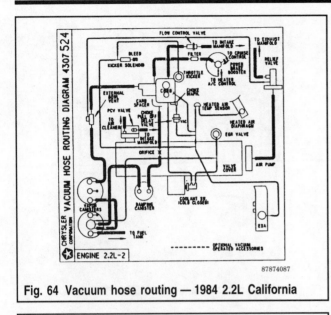

Fig. 64 Vacuum hose routing — 1984 2.2L California

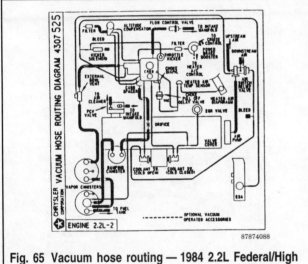

Fig. 65 Vacuum hose routing — 1984 2.2L Federal/High Altitude

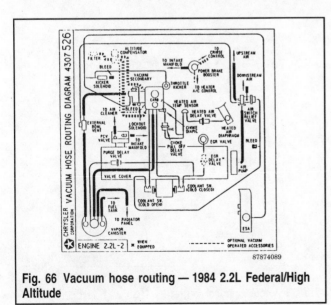

Fig. 66 Vacuum hose routing — 1984 2.2L Federal/High Altitude

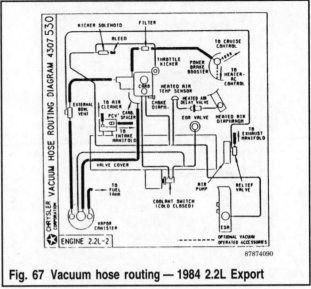

Fig. 67 Vacuum hose routing — 1984 2.2L Export

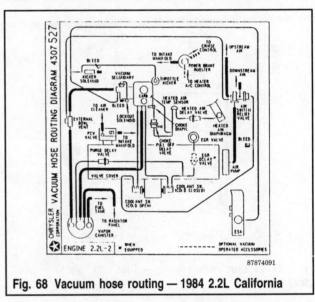

Fig. 68 Vacuum hose routing — 1984 2.2L California

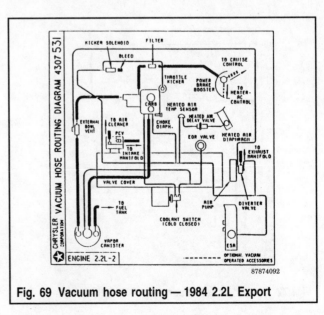

Fig. 69 Vacuum hose routing — 1984 2.2L Export

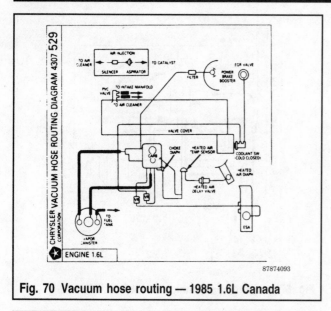

Fig. 70 Vacuum hose routing — 1985 1.6L Canada

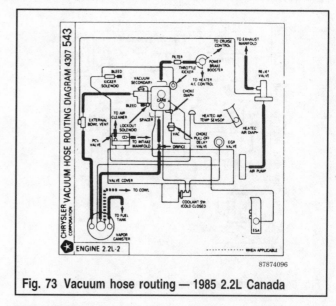

Fig. 73 Vacuum hose routing — 1985 2.2L Canada

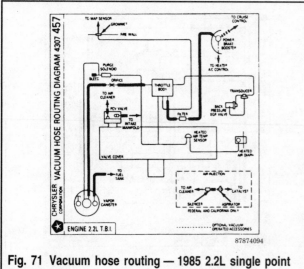

Fig. 71 Vacuum hose routing — 1985 2.2L single point fuel injection

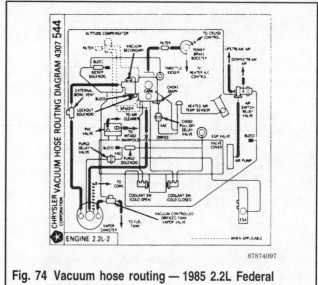

Fig. 74 Vacuum hose routing — 1985 2.2L Federal

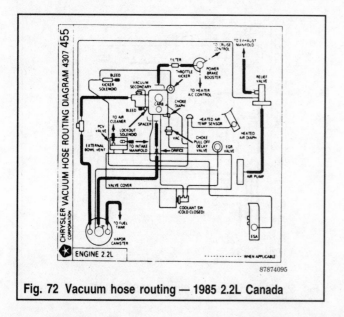

Fig. 72 Vacuum hose routing — 1985 2.2L Canada

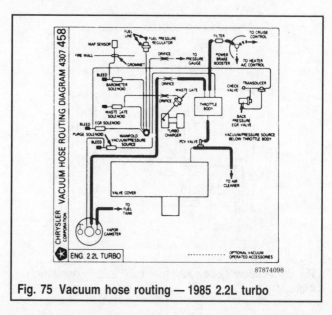

Fig. 75 Vacuum hose routing — 1985 2.2L turbo

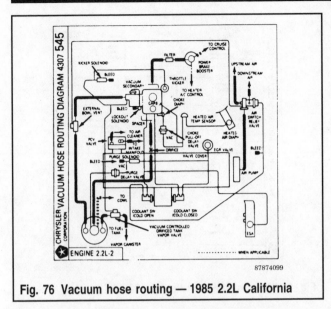

Fig. 76 Vacuum hose routing — 1985 2.2L California

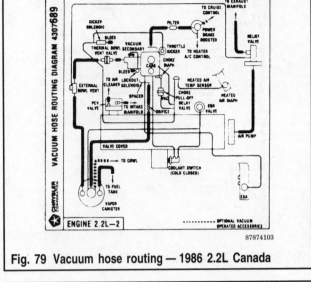

Fig. 79 Vacuum hose routing — 1986 2.2L Canada

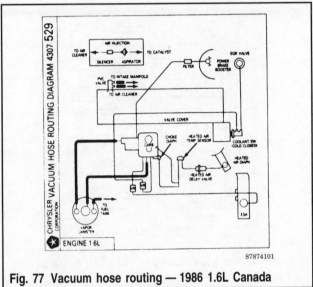

Fig. 77 Vacuum hose routing — 1986 1.6L Canada

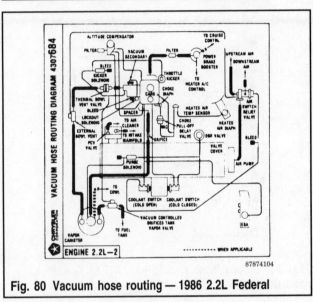

Fig. 80 Vacuum hose routing — 1986 2.2L Federal

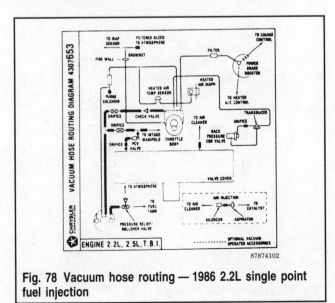

Fig. 78 Vacuum hose routing — 1986 2.2L single point fuel injection

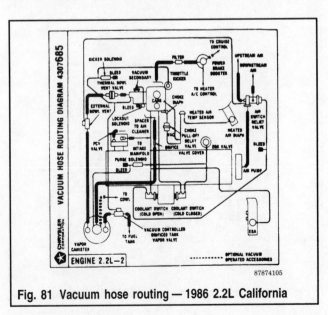

Fig. 81 Vacuum hose routing — 1986 2.2L California

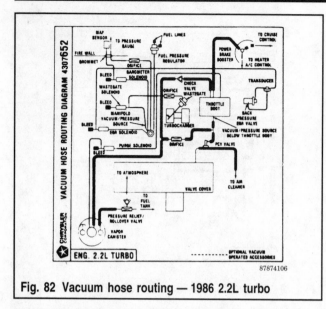

Fig. 82 Vacuum hose routing — 1986 2.2L turbo

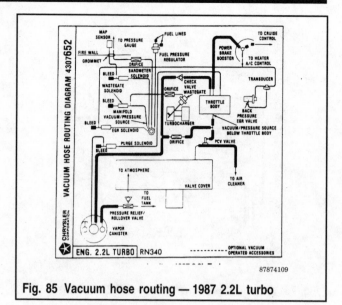

Fig. 85 Vacuum hose routing — 1987 2.2L turbo

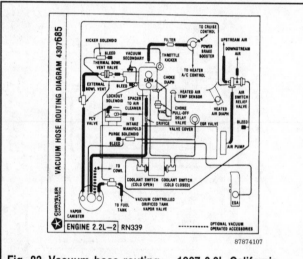

Fig. 83 Vacuum hose routing — 1987 2.2L California and Canada

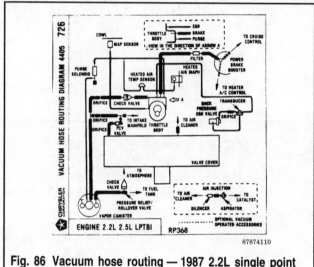

Fig. 86 Vacuum hose routing — 1987 2.2L single point fuel injection

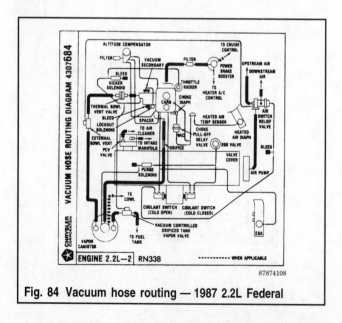

Fig. 84 Vacuum hose routing — 1987 2.2L Federal

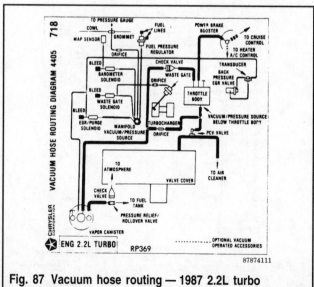

Fig. 87 Vacuum hose routing — 1987 2.2L turbo

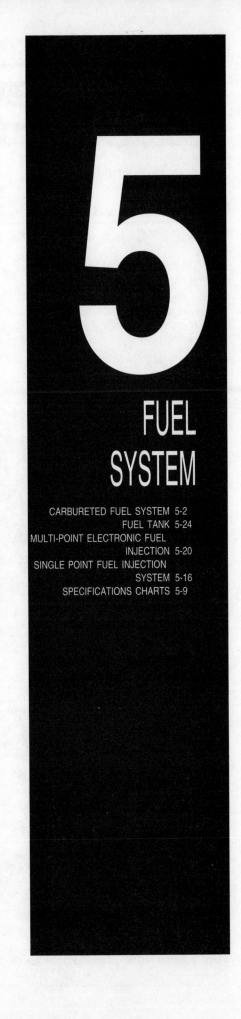

5

FUEL SYSTEM

CARBURETED FUEL SYSTEM

Mechanical Fuel Pump

REMOVAL & INSTALLATION

▶ **See Figures 1, 2, 3 and 4**

A mechanical fuel pump is located on the left side of the engine.

1. Disconnect the fuel and vapor lines.
2. Remove the attaching bolts.
3. Remove the insulator block from the old pump. This may be reused if it is good condition.
4. Remove any gasket mating material that may have adhered to the block.

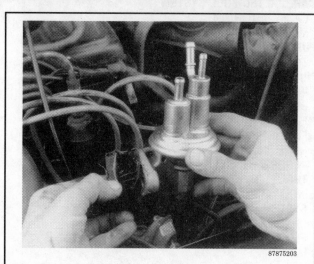

Fig. 3 Remove the insulator block from the old pump. This may be reused if it is good condition

5. Installation is the reverse of removal. Always use a new gasket when installing the pump, then make certain the gasket surfaces are clean.

TESTING

▶ **See Figure 5**

The fuel pump can be tested in a variety of ways, depending on the equipment available.

Volume

1. Disconnect the fuel supply line from the carburetor (leave it connected to the fuel pump).
2. Crank the engine. The fuel pump should supply 1 quart of fuel in 1 minute or less. Do not catch the fuel in a styrofoam container.
3. Reconnect the line to the carburetor.

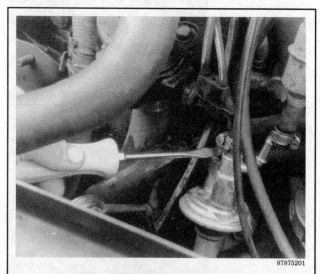

Fig. 1 Disconnect the fuel and vapor lines

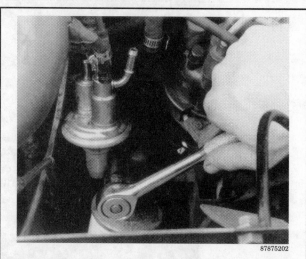

Fig. 2 Remove the attaching bolts for the pump to the block

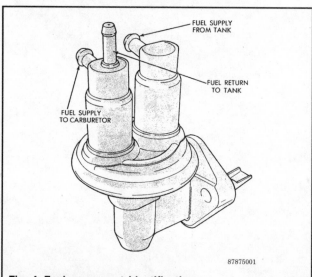

Fig. 4 Fuel pump port identification

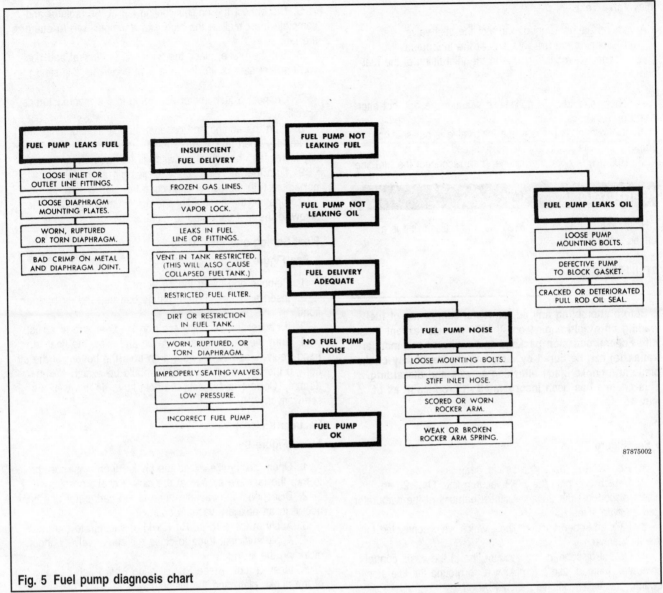

Fig. 5 Fuel pump diagnosis chart

Pressure

▶ **See Figure 6**

1. Insert a tee fitting in the fuel line at the carburetor.
2. Connect a 6 in. (152mm) maximum piece of hose between the tee and a pressure gauge.
3. Vent the pump for a few seconds to relieve air trapped in the fuel chamber. This will allow the pump to operate at full capacity.
4. Operate the engine at idle. The pressure should be 4-6 psi (27-41 kPa) and remain constant or return slowly to zero when the engine is stopped. An instant drop to zero when the engine is stopped indicates a leaking outlet valve. If the pressure is too high, the main spring is too strong or the air vent is plugged.

Vacuum

The vacuum test should be made with the fuel line disconnected. The minimum reading should be at least 10 in. Hg with the fuel line disconnected at the carburetor.

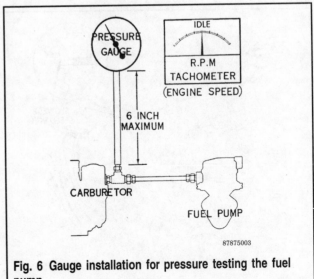

Fig. 6 Gauge installation for pressure testing the fuel pump

Inlet Valve Test

A vacuum gauge is needed to test the inlet valve.

1. Disconnect the fuel inlet line at the fuel pump.
2. Connect a vacuum gauge to the inlet fitting of the fuel pump.
3. Crank the engine.
4. There should be a noticeable vacuum present, not alternated by blowback.
5. If blowback is present, the inlet valve is not seating properly and the pump should be replaced.
6. Remove the vacuum gauge, then reconnect the fuel line.

Carburetor

Holley models 5220 and 6520 are used. Each unit is a staged 2-barrel unit.

ADJUSTMENTS

➡Before attempting any adjustments, complaints of fuel loading on a cold engine on all 1978 models (except those with Federal emission package and aspirator and manual transaxle) can be cured by removing the secondary choke blade and choke blade attaching screws and discarding. This change has been incorporated in production as of May 15, 1978.

Fast Idle
▶ See Figure 7

1. Remove the top of the air cleaner.
2. Detach and plug the EGR vacuum line. On 2.2L engines, disconnect the 2-way electrical harness at the carburetor (red and tan wires).
3. Plug any open vacuum lines, which were connected to the air cleaner.
4. Do not disconnect the vacuum line to the spark control computer. Instead, use a jumper wire to ground the idle stop switch. The air conditioning should be off.

5. Disconnect the engine cooling fan at the radiator and complete the circuit at the plug with a jumper wire to energize the fan.
6. Set the brake, place the transaxle in Neutral and position the first step of the fast idle cam under the adjusting screw.
7. Connect a tachometer according to the manufacturer's specifications.
8. Start the engine and observe the idle speed. With the choke fully open, the speed should remain steady. If it gradually increases, the idle stop switch is not properly grounded.
9. Turn the adjusting screw to give the specified rpm. Do not adjust with the screw contacting the plastic cam.
10. Operate the throttle linkage a few times and return the screw to the first cam step to recheck rpm.

Float Setting and Float Drop
▶ See Figure 8

1. Remove and invert the air horn.
2. Insert a $^{15}/_{32}$ in. (12mm) gauge between the air horn and float.
3. If necessary, bend the tang on the float arm to adjust.
4. Turn the air horn right side up and allow the float to hang freely. Measure the float drop from the bottom of the air horn to the bottom of the float. It should be exactly $^{55}/_{64}$ in. (22mm). Correct by bending the float tang, do this with a screwdriver.

Vacuum Kick
▶ See Figure 9

1. Open the throttle, close the choke, then close the throttle to trap the fast idle system at the closed choke position.
2. Disconnect the vacuum hose to the carburetor and connect it to an auxiliary vacuum source.
3. Apply at least 15 in. Hg (51 kPa) vacuum to the unit.
4. Apply sufficient force to close the choke valve without distorting the linkage.
5. Insert a gauge (see Specification Chart) between the top of the choke plate and the air horn wall.

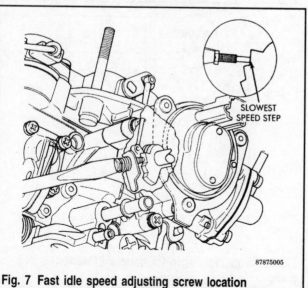

Fig. 7 Fast idle speed adjusting screw location

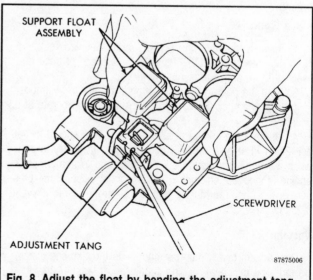

Fig. 8 Adjust the float by bending the adjustment tang

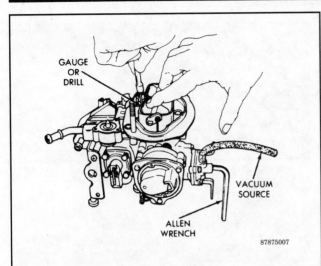

Fig. 9 Insert the specified gauge between the top of the choke plate and the air horn wall

6. Adjust by rotating the Allen screw in the center diaphragm housing.

7. Replace the vacuum hose.

Throttle Position Transducer

▶ See Figure 10

This is only used on the 1978 vehicles with a manual transaxle.

1. Disconnect the wire from the transducer.
2. Loosen the locknut.
3. Place a $^{21}/_{32}$ in. (17mm) gauge between the outer portion of the transducer and the mounting bracket.
4. To adjust the gap, turn the transducer.
5. Tighten the locknut.

Throttle Stop Speed

▶ See Figure 11

This applies to models without air conditioning.

1. The engine should be fully warmed.
2. Put the transaxle in Neutral and set the parking brake.

3. Turn the headlights off.
4. Using a jumper wire, ground the idle stop carburetor switch.
5. Disconnect the idle stop solenoid wire.
6. Adjust the throttle stop speed screw to 700 rpm.
7. Reconnect the idle stop solenoid wire.
8. Disconnect the jumper wire from the carburetor switch.

REMOVAL & INSTALLATION

▶ See Figures 12, 13, 14, 15, 16 and 17

Do not attempt to remove the carburetor from a hot engine that has just been run. Allow the engine to cool sufficiently. When removing the carburetor, it should not be necessary to disturb the intake manifold isolator mounting screws, unless you have determined that a leak exists in the isolator.

1. Disconnect the negative battery cable.
2. Remove the air cleaner.
3. Remove the fuel filler cap to relieve pressure.
4. Disconnect the fuel inlet fitting, then catch any excess fuel that may flow out.
5. Tag and detach all electrical connections.
6. Disconnect the throttle linkage.
7. Disconnect and tag all air hoses.
8. Remove the carburetor mounting nuts, then the carburetor. Hold the carburetor level to avoid spilling fuel on a hot engine.
9. Installation is the reverse of removal. Be careful when installing the mounting nut nearest the fast idle lever. It is very easy to bend the lever. Tighten the mounting nuts evenly until snug to prevent vacuum leaks.

Check to be sure the choke plate opens and closes fully and that full throttle travel is obtained.

OVERHAUL

Efficient carburetion depends greatly on careful cleaning and inspection during overhaul, since dirt, gum, varnish, water in or

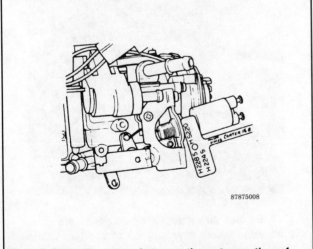

Fig. 10 Place the gauge between the outer portion of the transducer and the mounting bracket

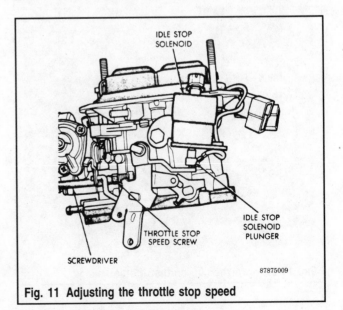

Fig. 11 Adjusting the throttle stop speed

Fig. 12 With a rag at hand, disconnect all the fuel lines

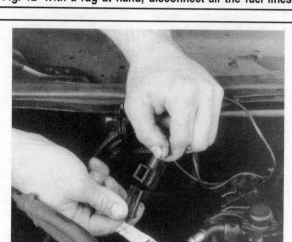

Fig. 13 Tag all the electrical leads to the carburetor, then disconnect them

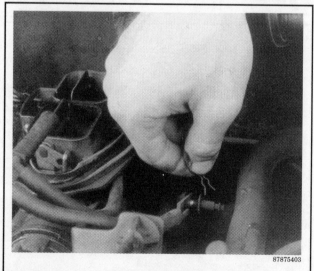

Fig. 14 Remove the clip on the throttle linkage

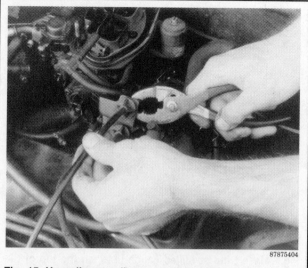

Fig. 15 Use pliers to disengage the cable

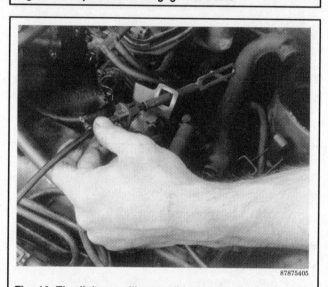

Fig. 16 The linkage will now slide out easily

Fig. 17 Be sure all vacuum lines and wires are disconnected before removing the carburetor from the engine

on the carburetor parts are mainly responsible for poor performance.

Carburetor overhaul should be performed in a clean, dust-free area. Carefully disassemble the carburetor, keeping look-alike parts segregated. Note all jet sizes.

Once the carburetor is disassembled, wash all parts (except diaphragms, electric choke units, pump plunger and any other plastic, leather or fiber parts) in clean carburetor solvent. Do not leave the parts in solvent any longer than necessary to sufficiently loosen the deposits. Excessive cleaning may remove the special finish from the float bowl and choke valve bodies, leaving them unfit for service. Rinse all parts in clean solvent and blow dry with compressed air. Wipe all plastic, leather or fiber parts with a clean, lint-free cloth.

Blow out all passages and jets with compressed air and be sure there are no restrictions or blockages. Never use wire to clean jets, fuel passages or air bleeds.

Check all parts for wear or damage. If wear or damage is found, replace the complete assembly. Especially check the following:

• Check the float and needle seat for wear. If any is found, replace the assembly.

• Check the float hinge pin for wear and the floats for distortion or dents. Replace the float if fuel has leaked into it.

• Check the throttle and choke shaft bores for out-of-round. Damage or wear to the throttle arm, shaft or shaft bore will often require replacement of the throttle body. These parts require close tolerances and an air leak here can cause poor starting and idling.

• Inspect the idle mixture adjusting needles for burrs or grooves. Burrs or grooves will usually require replacement of the needles since a satisfactory idle cannot be obtained.

• Test the accelerator pump check valves. They should pass air one way only. Test for proper seating by blowing and sucking on the valve. If the valve is satisfactory, wash the valve again to remove breath moisture.

• Check the bowl cover for warping with a straightedge.

• Closely inspect the valves and seats for wear or damage, replacing as necessary.

• After the carburetor is assembled, check the choke valve for freedom of operation.

Carburetor overhaul kits are recommended for each overhaul. These kits contain all gaskets and new parts to replace those that deteriorate most rapidly. Failure to replace all parts supplied with the kit (especially gaskets) can result in poor performance later.

Some carburetor manufacturers supply overhaul kits of three types: minor repair, major repair and gasket kits. They basically consist of:

Minor Repair Kits:
• All gaskets
• Float needle valve
• Volume control screw
• All diaphragms
• Pump diaphragm spring

Major Repair Kits:
• All jets and gaskets
• All diaphragms
• Float needle valve
• Volume control screw
• Pump ball valve

• Main jet carrier
• Float
• Complete intermediate rod
• Intermediate pump lever
• Complete injector tube
• Assorted screws and washers

Gasket Kits:
• All gaskets

After cleaning and checking all components, reassemble the carburetor using new parts, using the exploded views in the car sections, if necessary. Make sure that all screws and jets are tight in their seats, but do not overtighten or the tips will be distorted. Do not tighten needle valves into their seats or uneven jetting will result. Always use new gaskets and adjust the float.

Disassembly

▶ See Figures 18, 19, 20, 21, 22, 23, 24, 25, 26, 27, 28, 29, 30, 31, 32, 33, 34, 35, 36, 37, 38, 39 and 40

1. Remove the fuel inlet fitting from the air horn.
2. Disconnect and remove the choke operating rod and seal.
3. Remove the solenoid retaining screws and the idle stop from the carburetor.
4. Loosen and remove the air horn mounting screws, then separate the air horn assembly from the carburetor body.
5. Remove the float level pin, float and float inlet needle.
6. Separate the assembly from the air horn, remove the power valve diaphragm mounting screws.
7. A socket can be used to remove the needle and seat, also discard the gasket.
8. Remove the power valve.
9. Next remove the secondary main metering jet. Be sure to note the size so that it can be installed in its proper position.
10. Take out the primary main metering jet. Be sure to note the size so that it can be installed in its proper position.
11. Remove the secondary high speed bleed and secondary main well tube. Note the sizes for installation.
12. Remove the primary high speed bleed and primary main well tube. Note the sizes for installation

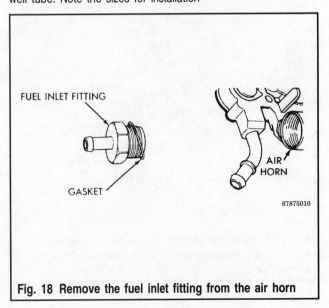

Fig. 18 Remove the fuel inlet fitting from the air horn

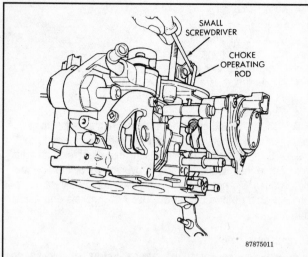

Fig. 19 Disconnect and remove the choke operating rod and seal

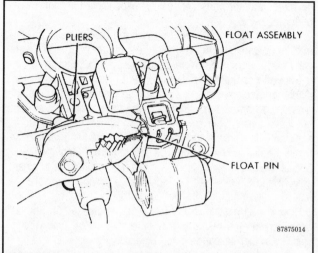

Fig. 22 Remove the float level pin, float and float inlet needle

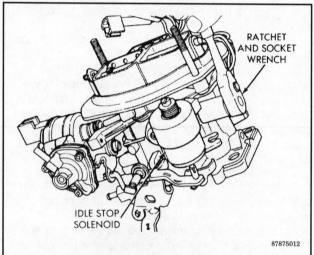

Fig. 20 Remove the solenoid retaining screws and the idle stop from the carburetor

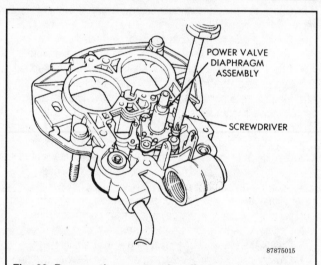

Fig. 23 Remove the power valve diaphragm mounting screws

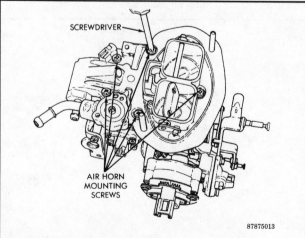

Fig. 21 Loosen and remove the air horn mounting screws, then separate the air horn assembly from the carburetor body

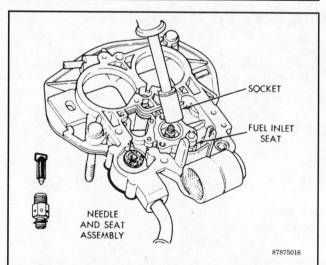

Fig. 24 A socket can be used to remove the needle and seat, also discard the gasket

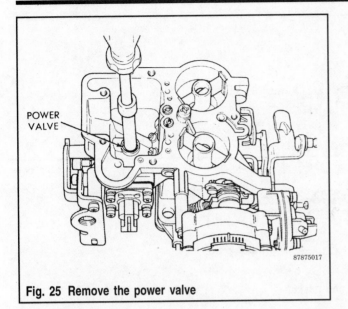

Fig. 25 Remove the power valve

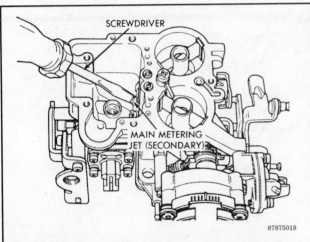

Fig. 26 Next remove the secondary main metering jet. Be sure to note the size so that it can be installed in its proper position

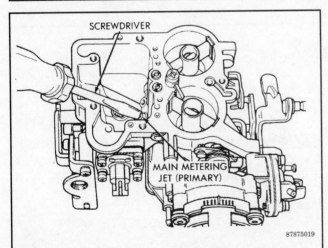

Fig. 27 Remove the primary main metering jet. Be sure to note the size so that it can be installed in its proper position

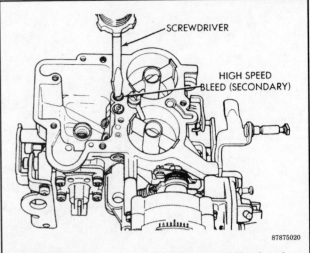

Fig. 28 Remove the secondary high speed bleed and secondary main well tube. Note the sizes for installation

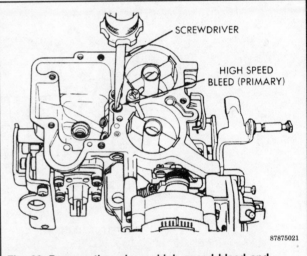

Fig. 29 Remove the primary high speed bleed and primary main well tube. Note the sizes for installation

13. Remove the discharge nozzle screw, then the discharge nozzle and gasket.

14. Invert the carburetor and drop out the accelerator pump discharge weight ball and checkball. You will notice that both of the balls are the same size.

15. Remove the upper choke diaphragm cover screws. Grind or file the head from the lower mounting screw, then remove the cover and spring.

16. Rotate the choke shaft diaphragm assembly clockwise, then remove from the housing. Remove end of lower screw from the housing. If the choke diaphragm is to be replaced, the diaphragm cover must also be replaced.

17. Remove the wide open cut-out switch mounting screws. Mark the location for assembly, then remove the harness mounting screws and open the retaining clip. Remove the wires from the connector, then thread through the clip.

18. Remove the idle mixture screw.

19. Clean and inspect the carburetor, then reassemble. In the reverse of disassembly.

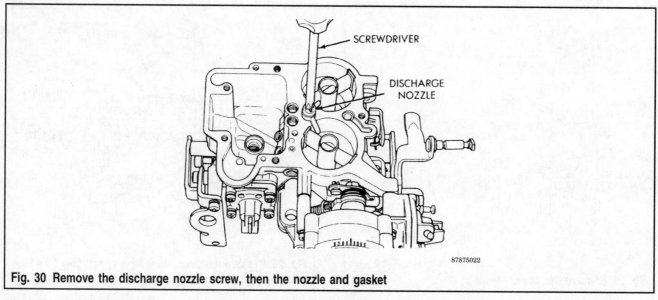

Fig. 30 Remove the discharge nozzle screw, then the nozzle and gasket

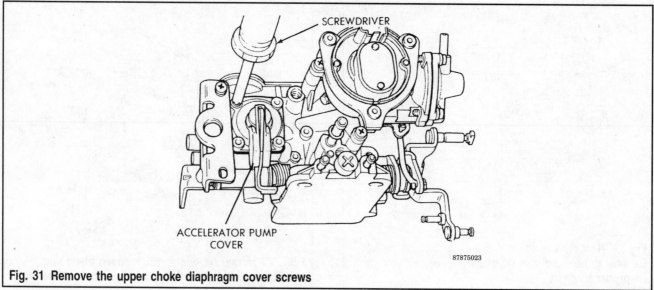

Fig. 31 Remove the upper choke diaphragm cover screws

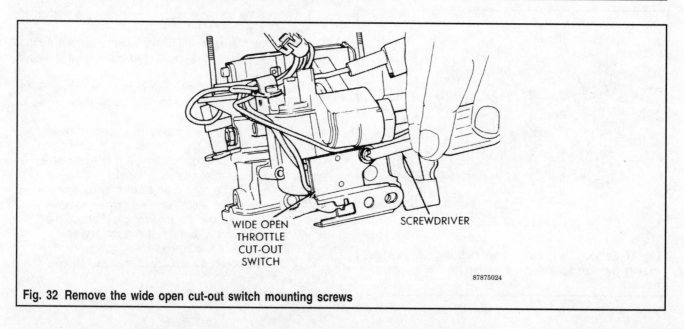

Fig. 32 Remove the wide open cut-out switch mounting screws

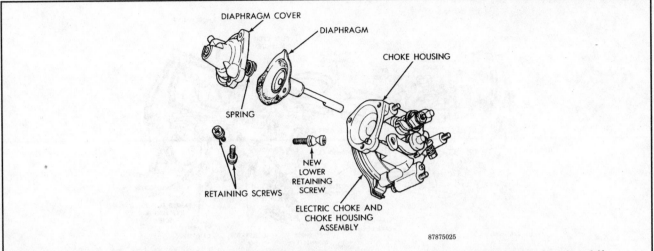

Fig. 33 The choke housing contains few parts, the diaphragm can go bad and should be checked and replaced if needed.

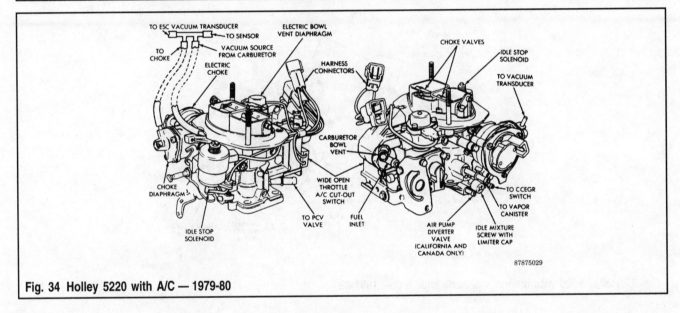

Fig. 34 Holley 5220 with A/C — 1979-80

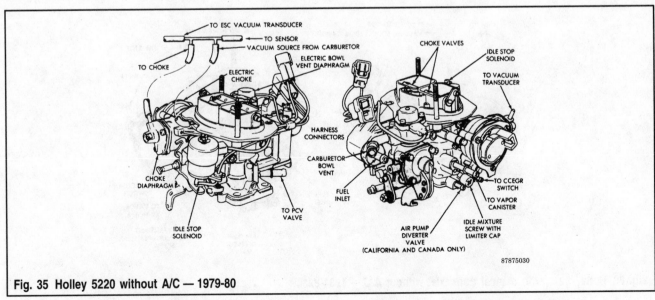

Fig. 35 Holley 5220 without A/C — 1979-80

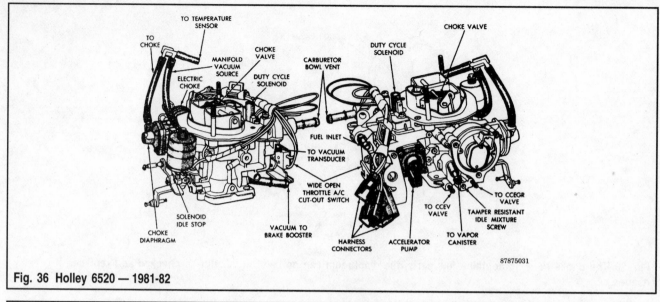

Fig. 36 Holley 6520 — 1981-82

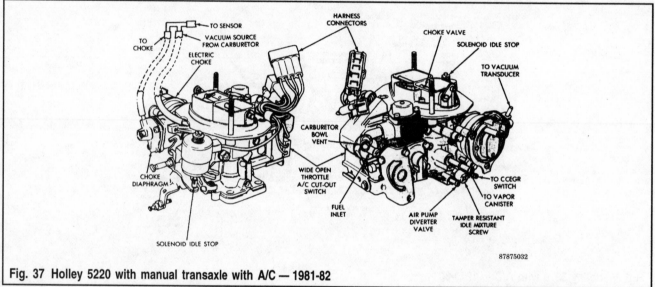

Fig. 37 Holley 5220 with manual transaxle with A/C — 1981-82

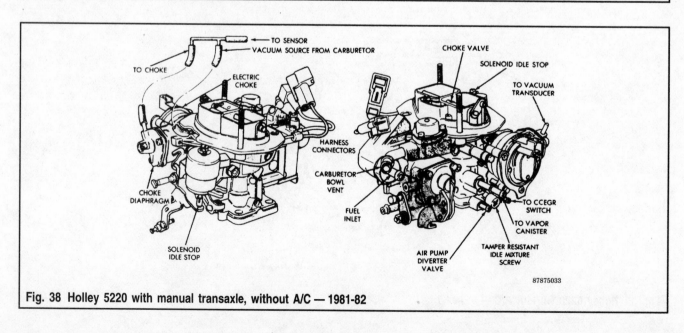

Fig. 38 Holley 5220 with manual transaxle, without A/C — 1981-82

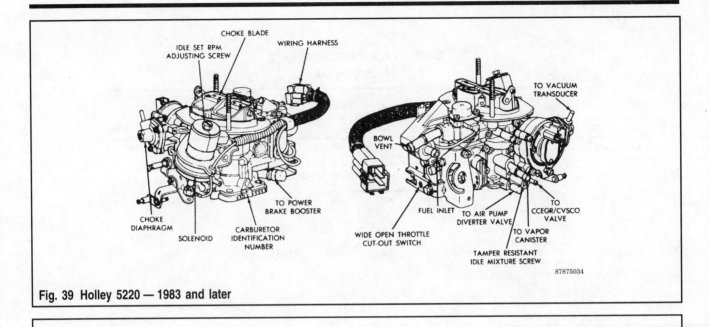

Fig. 39 Holley 5220 — 1983 and later

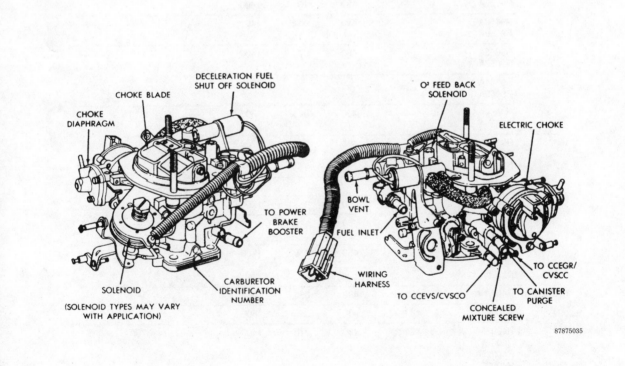

Fig. 40 Holley 6520 — 1983 and later

Carburetor Specifications
Holley 5220

Year	Carb Part No.	Accelerator Pump	Dry Float Level (in.)	Vacuum Kick (in.)	Fast Idle RPM (w/fan)	Throttle Position Transducer (in.)	Throttle Stop Speed RPM	Choke
1978	R-8376A, 8378A, 8384A, 8439A, 8441A, 8505A, 8507A	#2 hole	.480	.070	1100	.547	700	2 Rich
1979	R-8524A, 8526A, 8532A, 8534A, 8528A, 8530A	#2 hole	.480	.040	1700	—	700	2 Rich
	R8525A, 8541A, 8531A, 8533A, 8527A, 8529A	#2 hole	.480	.070	1400	—	700	2 Rich
1980	R8838A R8839A R9110A R9111A	—	.480	.040	1700	—	700	—
	R8726A R8727A R9108A	—	.480	.070	1400	—	700	—
	R9109A	—	.480	.100	1400	—	700	—
1981	R9058A R9059A	—	.480	.040	1400	—	850	—
	R9056A R9057A	—	.480	.070	1400	—	850	—
	R9064A R9065A				1300			
	R9684A R9685A	—	.480	.060	1300	—	850	—
1982	R9582A R9583A R9584A	—	.480	.060	1200	—	—	—
	R9585A				1500			
	R9820A	—	.480	.080	1200	—	—	—
	R9513A R9514A	—	.480	.120	1400	—	—	—
	R9499A R9511A R9512A	—	.480	.130	1200	—	—	—
1983	R40020A	#3 hole	.480	.055	1300	—	—	—
	R40022A	#3 hole	.480	.055	1500	—	—	—
	R40023A R40024 R40025A R40026A	#2 hole	.480	.070	1400	—	700	—
1984	R400601A	#2 hole	.480	.055	1200	—	—	—
	R400851A	#2 hole	.480	.040	1500	—	—	—
	R40170A	#3 hole	.480	.060	1650	—	—	—
	R40171A	#3 hole	.480	.060	1700	—	—	—
	R400671A	#3 hole	.480	.070	1500	—	—	—
	R400681A	#3 hole	.480	.070	1700	—	—	—

87875036

Carburetor Specifications
Holley 6520

Year	Carb. Part No.	Dry Float Setting (in.)	Solenoid Idle Stop (rpm)	Fast Idle Speed (rpm)	Vacuum Kick (in.)
1981	R9060A R9061A	.480	850	1100	.030
	R9125A R9126A	.480	850	1200	.030
	R9052A R9053A	.480	850	1400	.070
	R9054A R9055A	.480	850	1400	.040
	R9602A R9603A	.480	850	1500	.065
	R9604A R9605A	.480	850	1600	.065
1982	R9824A	.480	900	1400	.065
	R9503A R9504A R9750A R9751A	.480	850	1300	.085
	R9822A R9823A	.480	850	1400	.080
	R9505A R9506A R9752A R9753A	.480	900	1600	.100
1983	R40080A R40081A	.480	850	1400	.045
	R40003A R40007A	.480	775	1400	.070
	R40010A R40004A	.480	900	1500	.080
	R40012A R4008A	.480	900	1600	.070
	R40014A R40006A	.480	850	1275	.080
1984	R400581A	.480	850	1400	.070
	R401071A	.480	1000	1600	.055
	R400641A R400811A	.480	800	1500	.080
	R400651A R400821A	.480	900	1600	.080
	R40071A R40122A	.480	850	1500	.080

87875037

Carburetor Specifications
Holley 5220/6520

Year/ Part No.	Dry Float Setting	Solenoid Idle Stop	Fast Idle Speed (rpm)	Vacuum Kick (in.)
1985				
R40058A	.480	①	①	.070
R40060A	.480	①	①	.055
R40116A	.480	①	①	.095
R40117A	.480	①	①	.095
R40134A	.480	①	①	.075
R40135A	.480	①	①	.075
R40138A	.480	①	①	.075
R40139A	.480	①	①	.075
1986				
R400581A	.480	①	①	.070
R400602A	.480	①	①	.055
R401341A	.480	①	①	.075
R401351A	.480	①	①	.075
R401381A	.480	①	①	.075
R401391A	.480	①	①	.075
R401161A	.480	①	①	.095
R401171A	.480	①	①	.095
1987				
R40295A	.480	①	①	.075
R40296A	.480	①	①	.075

① Refer to specification on VECI label under the hood.

87875038

SINGLE POINT FUEL INJECTION SYSTEM

Description of System

This electronic fuel injection system is a computer regulated single point fuel injection system that provides precise air/fuel ratio for all driving conditions. At the center of this system is a digital pre-programmed computer known as a logic module that regulates ignition timing, air-fuel ratio, emission control devices and idle speed. This component has the ability to update and revise its programming to meet changing operating conditions. This system is also sometimes refered to as a Throttle Body Injection (TBI) system.

Various sensors provide the input necessary for the logic module to correctly regulate the fuel flow at the fuel injector. These include the manifold absolute pressure, throttle position, oxygen feedback, coolant temperature, charge temperature and vehicle speed sensors. In addition to the sensors, various switches also provide important information. These include the neutral-safety, heated rear window, air conditioning, air conditioning clutch switches, and an electronic idle switch.

All inputs to the logic module are converted into signals sent to the power module. These signals cause the power module to change either the fuel flow at the injector or ignition timing or both.

The logic module tests many of its own input and output circuits. If a fault is found in a major system this information is stored in the logic module. Information on this fault can be displayed tool by connecting a diagnostic readout and reading a numbered display code which directly relates to a specific fault.

➡**Experience has shown that many complaints that may occur with EFI can be traced to poor wiring or hose connections. A visual check will help spot these most common faults and save unnecessary test and diagnosis time.**

Relieving Fuel System Pressure

▶ **See Figure 41**

1. Loosen the fuel cap to release tank pressure.
2. Disconnect the injector wiring harness from the engine harness.
3. Connect a jumper wire to the ground terminal number 1 of the injector harness to the engine ground.
4. Connect a jumper wire to the positive terminal of number 2 of the injector harness. Touch the battery positive post for no longer then 5 seconds. This releases system pressure.
5. Remove the jumper wires.

Electric Fuel Pump

REMOVAL & INSTALLATION

▶ **See Figure 42**

An electric fuel pump is used with fuel injection systems in order to provide higher and more uniform fuel pressures. It is located in the tank.

1. Relive the fuel pressure.
2. Disconnect the negative battery cable.
3. Remove the tank from the vehicle.
4. With a soft head hammer and non-metallic punch, tap the fuel pump lockring counterclockwise to release the pump.
   To install:
5. Wipe the seal area of the tank clean and install a new O-ring seal.
6. Replace the filter on the end of the pump if it appears to be damaged.
7. Position the pump in the tank and install the locking ring.
8. Tighten the ring in the same general way in which you loosened it. Do not overtighten it, as this can cause leakage.
9. Install the tank.
10. Connect the negative battery cable.

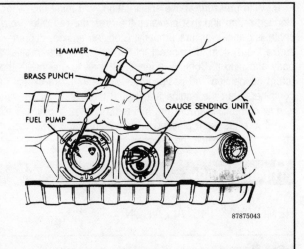

Fig. 42 Using a hammer and brass drift punch, carefully tap the lockring counterclockwise to release the pump

TESTING

➡ **To perform this procedure, you will need a gauge capable of reading 10-20 psi (69-138 kPa) and the extra length of hose, clamps and fittings necessary to tee the gauge into a $\frac{5}{16}$ in. (8mm) fuel line. Have a metal container handy to collect any fuel that may spill.**

1. Release the fuel system pressure.
2. Disconnect the fuel supply line at the throttle body.
3. Tee in the gauge between the fuel supply line and the fuel supply nipple on the throttle body, connecting the inlet side of the tee to the fuel supply line and the throttle body side of the tee to the throttle body with a rubber hose and clamps.

✳✳WARNING

At the beginning of the next step, watch carefully for fuel leaks. Shut the engine off immediately at any sign of leakage.

4. Start the engine and run it at idle. Read the fuel pressure gauge. Pressure should be 14.5 psi. (100 kPa). If pressure is correct, the pump is okay and you should depressurize the system, remove the gauge, and restore the normal fuel line connections. If the pressure is low, proceed with the next step to test for filter clogging. If the pressure is too high, proceed with Step 6.
5. Stop the engine and then depressurize the system. Remove the gauge tee from the line going into the throttle body and restore the normal connections. Then, tee the gauge into the line going into the fuel filter. Run the test again. If the pressure is now okay, depressurize the system, replace the fuel filter, and restore normal connections. If the pressure is still low, pinch the fuel return hose closed with your fingers. If pressure now increases to above 14.5 psi (100 kPa), replace the fuel pressure regulator. If no change is observed, the problem is either a defective pump or a clogged filter sock in the tank. Make repairs as necessary.

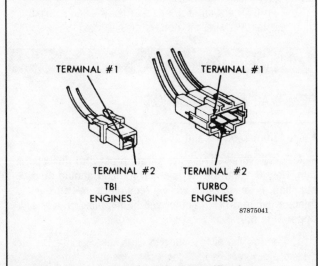

Fig. 41 Injector harness terminal identification

6. With pressure above specification, you must check for a clogged return line that prevents the pressure regulator from controlling fuel pressure properly. Stop the engine, depressurize the system, disconnect the return line at the throttle body and plug it. Connect a length of hose to the throttle body return connection and position the open end into a clean container. Start the engine and repeat the test. If the pressure is now correct, clean out the fuel return line or repair it. Relocate it if it has been pinched or damaged. If the pressure is still too high, replace the pressure regulator.

Throttle Body

REMOVAL & INSTALLATION

▶ **See Figure 43**

➡**To perform this operation, you'll need a new throttle body-to-manifold gasket and new original equipment-type fuel hose clamps (with rolled edges).**

1. Allow the engine to cool completely. Perform the fuel system pressure release procedure.
2. Disconnect the negative battery cable. Remove the air cleaner and those air hoses which might restrict access to the throttle body.
3. Label and then disconnect all the vacuum hoses and electrical harnesses to the throttle body.
4. Disconnect the throttle cable and, on automatic transaxle-equipped cars the transaxle kickdown cable. Remove the throttle return spring.
5. Disconnect the fuel supply and return hoses by wrapping a rag around the hose and twisting. Collect any fuel that drains in a metal cup. Remove the copper washers and supply new ones.
6. Remove the throttle body mounting bolts and remove the throttle body from the manifold. Remove the gasket and clean both gasket surfaces.
   To install:
7. Install the new gasket and carefully put the throttle body into position with the bolt holes in it and the manifold lined up.
8. Install the mounting bolts and tighten them alternately and evenly to 16 ft. lbs. (22 Nm).
9. Install the throttle return spring. Reconnect the throttle and, if necessary, transaxle cable linkages.
10. Reconnect the wiring and vacuum hoses.
11. Reconnect the fuel hose to the supply on the throttle body, using a new copper washer. Reattach the return hose to the return connection with a new copper washer. Use new clamps and tighten to 10 inch lbs. (1 Nm).
12. Install the air cleaner and hoses. Reconnect the negative battery cable.
13. Start the engine and check for fuel leaks.

ADJUSTMENT

Idle Speed

➡**This procedure applies to vehicles built through 1986. Later models require a "Throttle Body Minimum Airflow Check Procedure". This cannot be performed without utilizing an expensive electronic test system. If airflow is incorrect on these models, the throttle body must be replaced.**

1. Before adjusting the idle on an electronic fuel injected vehicle the following items must be checked.
   a. AIS motor has been checked for operation.
   b. Engine has been checked for vacuum or EGR leaks.
   c. Engine timing has been checked and set to specifications.
   d. Coolant temperature sensor has been checked for operation.
2. Connect a tachometer and timing light to engine.
3. Disconnect throttle body 6-way harness. Remove the brown with white trace AIS wire from the connector and reattach.
4. Connect one end of a jumper wire to AIS wire and other end to battery positive post for 5 seconds.
5. Connect a jumper to radiator fan so that it will run continuously.
6. Start and run engine for 3 minutes to allow speed to stabilize.
7. Using tool C-4804 or equivalent, turn idle speed adjusting screw to obtain 790-810 rpm on Manuals and 715-735 rpm on Automatics in neutral.

➡**If idle will not adjust down, check for binding linkage, speed control servo cable adjustments, or throttle shaft binding.**

8. Check that the timing is 16°-20° BTDC on Manuals and 10°-14° BTDC on Automatics.
9. If timing is not to above specifications, adjust the timing and turn the idle speed adjusting screw until correct idle speed and ignition timing are obtained.
10. Turn **OFF** engine, disconnect tachometer and timing light, reinstall AIS wire and remove jumper wire.

Fuel Injector

REMOVAL & INSTALLATION

▶ **See Figures 44, 45 and 46**

➡**A Torx® screwdriver is required to perform this operation. New O-rings for the injector and cap should also be supplied. A set of three will be required to re-use the old injector, while a new injector will be supplied with a new upper O-ring.**

1. Remove the air cleaner and air hoses. Release the fuel system pressure. Then, disconnect the negative battery cable.
2. Remove the Torx® head screw. With two screwdrivers positioned in the slots on either side, gently and evenly pry upward to remove the injector cap.

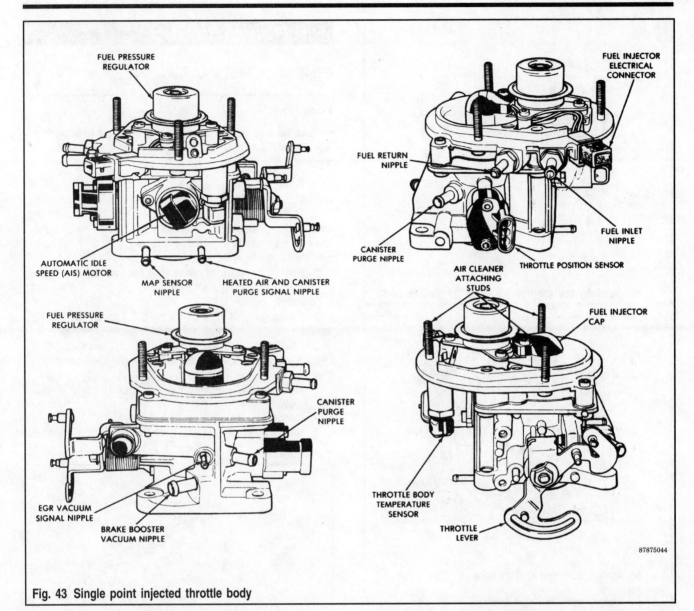

Fig. 43 Single point injected throttle body

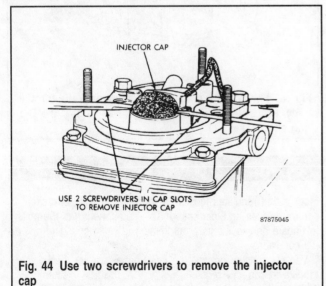

Fig. 44 Use two screwdrivers to remove the injector cap

3. Gently and evenly pry the injector upward and out of the throttle body unit using a screwdriver. Once the injector is removed, check that the lower O-ring has been removed from the throttle body unit.

4. Remove the two O-rings from the injector body and the single O-ring from the cap and replace them. If the injector is being replaced, a new upper O-ring will already be installed.

To install:

5. Carefully assemble the injector and cap together with the keyway and key aligned. Then, align the cap and injector so the cap's hole aligns with the bolt hole in the throttle body. Start the injector/cap assembly into the throttle body without applying downward pressure.

6. With the assembly almost seated, rotate the cap as necessary to ensure perfect alignment of the cap and throttle body. Then apply gentle, downward pressure on both sides to seat the injector and cap.

7. Install the Torx® screw and tighten it to 30-35 inch lbs. (41-47 Nm).

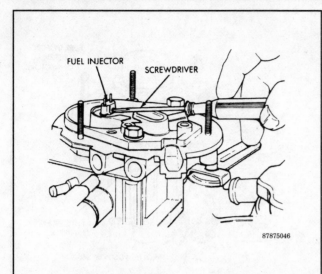

Fig. 45 Carefully pry the injector from the throttle body

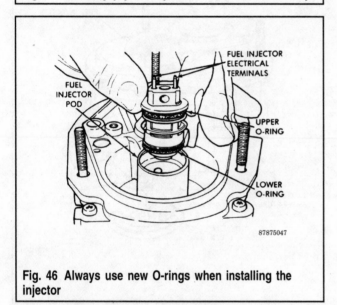

Fig. 46 Always use new O-rings when installing the injector

8. Connect the battery. Start the engine and check for leaks with the air cleaner off. Then, replace the air cleaner and hoses.

Fuel Pressure Regulator

REMOVAL & INSTALLATION

◗ See Figure 47

➡ **Make sure to have a towel or rag on hand to absorb fuel. Supply a new O-ring and gasket for the pressure regulator.**

1. Remove the air cleaner and air hoses. Release the fuel system pressure. Then, disconnect the negative battery cable.
2. Remove the three screws which attach the pressure regulator to the throttle body. Then, quickly place a rag over the fuel inlet chamber to absorb any fuel that remains in the system. When fuel is absorbed, dispose of the rag safely.
3. Pull the pressure regulator from the throttle body. Carefully remove the O-ring and gasket.
   To install:
4. Carefully install the new O-ring and gasket onto the regulator.
5. Position the pressure regulator onto the throttle body. Press it into place squarely so as to seal the O-ring and gasket.
6. Install the three attaching screws and tighten to 40 inch lbs. (4 Nm).
7. Connect the battery.
8. Start the engine and check for leaks with the air cleaner off. Then, replace the air cleaner and hoses.

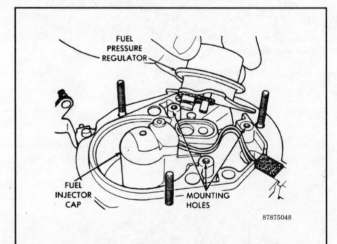

Fig. 47 Position the pressure regulator onto the throttle body. Press it into place squarely so as to seal the O-ring and gasket

MULTI-POINT ELECTRONIC FUEL INJECTION

Description of System

◗ See Figure 48

The turbocharged Multi-point Electronic Fuel Injection system combines an electronic fuel and spark advance control system with a turbocharged intake system. At the center of this system is a digital, pre-programmed computer known as a Logic Module that regulates ignition timing, air-fuel ratio, emission control devices and idle speed. This component has the ability to update and revise its programming to meet changing operating conditions.

Various sensors provide the input necessary for the Logic Module to correctly regulate fuel flow at the fuel injectors. These include the Manifold Absolute Pressure, Throttle Position, Oxygen Feedback, Coolant Temperature, Charge Temperature, and Vehicle Speed Sensors. In addition to the sensors, various switches also provide important information. These include the Transaxle Neutral-Safety, Heated Rear Window, Air Conditioning, and the Air Conditioning Clutch Switches.

Inputs to the Logic Module are converted into signals sent to the Power Module. These signals cause the Power Module to change either the fuel flow at the injector or ignition timing or both. The Logic Module tests many of its own input and output circuits. if a fault is found in a major circuit, this information is stored in the Logic Module. Information on this fault can be displayed by means of the instrument panel power loss lamp or by connecting a diagnostic readout tool and observing a numbered display code which directly relates to a general fault.

➡**Most complaints that may occur with this system can be traced to poor wiring or hose connections. A visual check will help stop these faults and save unnecessary test and diagnosis time.**

Relieving Fuel System Pressure

▶ **See Figure 41**

1. Loosen the fuel cap to release tank pressure.
2. Disconnect the injector wiring harness from the engine harness.
3. Connect a jumper wire to the ground terminal number 1 of the injector harness to the engine ground.
4. Connect a jumper wire to the positive terminal of number 2 of the injector harness. Touch the battery positive post for no longer then 5 seconds. This releases system pressure.
5. Remove the jumper wires.

Electric Fuel Pump

REMOVAL & INSTALLATION

An electric fuel pump is used with fuel injection systems in order to provide higher and more uniform fuel pressures. It is located in the tank.

1. Relive the fuel pressure.
2. Disconnect the negative battery cable.
3. Remove the tank from the vehicle.
4. With a soft headed hammer and non-metallic punch, tap the fuel pump lockring counterclockwise to release the pump.

To install:

5. Wipe the seal area of the tank clean and install a new O-ring seal.
6. Replace the filter on the end of the pump if it appears to be damaged.
7. Position the pump in the tank and install the locking ring.
8. Tighten the ring in the same general way in which you loosened it. Do not overtighten it, as this can cause leakage.
9. Install the tank.
10. Connect the negative battery cable.

TESTING

➡**To perform this test, you will need a pressure gauge capable of reading pressures above 55 psi (379 kPa). The gauge must have a connection that will fit the fuel rail service valve. The gauge should be compatible with Chrysler part No. C-3292 and the connector fitting compatible with C-4805. You may also need a tee and fittings necessary to tee the gauge into the fuel supply line at the tank, and a 2 gallon container suitable for collecting fuel.**

1. Release the fuel system pressure. Remove the protective cover from the service valve on the fuel rail.
2. Connect the gauge to the pressure tap on the fuel rail. Hold the gauge and have someone start the engine. Run the

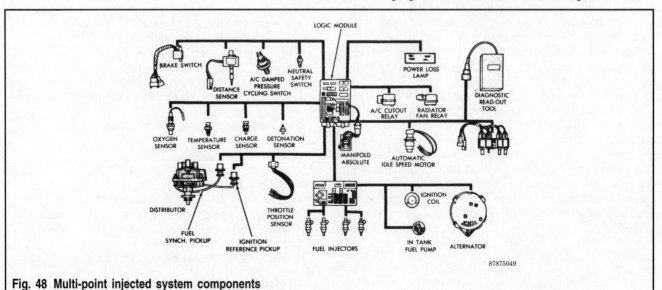

Fig. 48 Multi-point injected system components

engine at idle speed in Neutral (manual transaxles) or Park (automatic transaxles).

3. Read the pressure. It should be 53-57 psi. (365-393 kPa). If it is outside the range, take note of it. Stop the engine, depressurize the system, then disconnect the gauge and replace the protective cover. If the pressure is correct, the test is complete. If the pressure is below the range, proceed with the steps following; if it is too high, proceed with Step 7.

✳✳WARNING

In the next step, note that fuel may drain from the lines as you disconnect them. Make sure all surrounding exhaust system parts are cool and that all sources of ignition are removed from the area. Collect fuel and dispose of it safely.

4. Connect the gauge into the fuel supply line running between the tank and the filter which is located at the rear of the vehicle.

➡**Make sure all connections are secure.**

5. Have someone start the engine. Read the pressure gauge. If the pressure has risen more than 5 psi, (34 kPa) replace the filter. If the pressure is now within range:
   a. Allow the engine to cool
   b. Remove all sources of ignition
   c. Depressurize the system
   d. Disconnect the gauge from the lines
   e. Replace the fuel filter
   f. Restore connections

6. If the pressure is still too low, gently and gradually pinch the fuel return line closed as you watch the gauge. If the pressure increases, the fuel pressure regulator is at fault. If there is no change, the problem is either clogging of the filter sock mounted on the pump itself or a defective pump.

7. If the pressure is too high, shut off the engine, allow it to cool, depressurize the system and then disconnect the fuel return hose at the chassis, near the fuel tank. Connect a 3 foot length of hose to the open end of the line running along the chassis. Position the open end of the line into a container suitable for collecting fuel. Have a helper start the engine and check the pressure. If it is now correct, check the in-tank fuel return hose for kinking. If the hose is okay, and the system still exhibits excessive pressure with the tank half full or more, the fuel pump reservoir check valve or aspirator jet may be obstructed and the assembly must be replaced.

8. If the pressure is still too high, shut off the engine, and allow it to cool. Depressurize the system and then reconnect the fuel lines at the rear. Disconnect the fuel return hose at the pressure regulator. Collect all fuel that drains. Then, run the open connection into a large metal container. Connect the fuel gauge back into the fuel rail. Start the engine and repeat the test. If the fuel pressure is now correct, clean a clogged return line or replace pinched or kinked sections of the return line. If no such problems exist, replace the fuel pressure regulator.

Throttle Body

REMOVAL & INSTALLATION

▶ **See Figure 49**

1. Disconnect the negative battery cable. Remove the nuts attaching the air cleaner adaptor to the throttle body, loosen the hose clamps, and remove the air cleaner adaptor.

2. Remove the three control cables accelerator, accelerator and, if so-equipped, automatic transaxle kickdown and speed control cables. Then remove the throttle cable bracket from the throttle body.

3. Note locations and then disconnect the electrical wiring.

4. Note their locations or, if necessary, label them and then disconnect the vacuum hoses from the throttle body.

5. Remove the throttle body-to-adaptor attaching nuts. Then, remove the throttle body and its gasket.

To install:

6. Clean gasket surfaces and install a new gasket. Install the throttle body-to-adaptor attaching nuts and tighten them alternately and evenly.

7. Reconnect the vacuum hoses, checking the routing and making certain the connections are secure. Reconnect each electrical harness to its location on the throttle body.

8. Install the throttle and, as necessary, transaxle kickdown and speed control cables. Install the air cleaner adaptor. Reconnect the battery.

ADJUSTMENTS

Idle Speed

➡**This procedure applies to vehicles built through 1986. Later models require a "Throttle Body Minimum Airflow Check Procedure". This cannot be performed without utilizing an expensive electronic test system. If airflow is incorrect on these models, the throttle body must be replaced.**

Before adjusting the idle on an electronic fuel injected vehicle the following items must be checked:
- AIS motor has been checked for operation.
- Engine has been checked for vacuum or EGR leaks.
- Engine timing has been checked and set to specifications.
- Coolant temperature sensor has been checked for operation.

Once these checks have been made and you know these components are performing satisfactorily:

1. Install a tachometer.

2. Warm up engine to normal operating temperature (accessories off).

3. Shut the engine **OFF** and disconnect the radiator fan.

4. Disconnect the throttle body 6-way harness. Remove the brown with white tracer AIS wire from the connector and reattach.

5. Start the engine with the transaxle selector in park or neutral.

6. Apply 12 volts to AIS brown with white tracer wire. This will drive the AIS fully closed and the idle should drop.

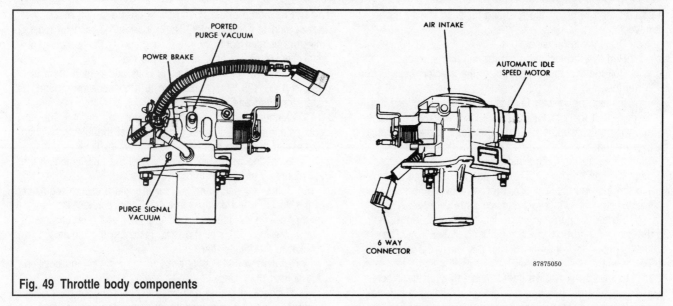

Fig. 49 Throttle body components

7. Disconnect then reattach the coolant temperature sensor.

8. With transaxle in neutral, idle speed should be 750-800 rpm, (725-775 rpm green engine).

9. If idle is not to specifications adjust idle air bypass screw.

10. If idle will not adjust down, check for vacuum leaks, AIS motor damage, throttle body damage, or speed control cable adjustment.

Fuel Rail and Injectors

REMOVAL & INSTALLATION

▶ See Figures 50 and 51

➡You should have a set of four injector nozzle protective caps and a set of new O-rings before removing the injectors.

1. Release fuel system pressure. Disconnect the negative battery cable.

2. Loosen the hose clamp on the fuel supply hose at the fuel rail inlet and disconnect it. Collect any fuel that may drain out into a metal cup and dispose of it safely.

3. Disconnect the fuel pressure regulator vacuum hose at the intake manifold vacuum tree.

4. Remove the 2 fuel pressure regulator-to-intake manifold bracket screws.

5. Loosen the clamp at the rail end of the fuel rail-to-pressure regulator hose and then remove the regulator and hose. Collect any fuel that may drain out into a metal cup and dispose of it safely.

6. Remove the bolt from the fuel rail-to-valve cover bracket.

7. Remove the fuel injector head shield clips. Then, remove the four intake manifold-to-rail mounting bolts. Note that one bolt retains a ground strap.

8. Pull the rail away from the manifold in such a way as to pull the injectors straight out of their mounting holes. Pull the injectors out straight so as to avoid damaging their O-rings.

9. To remove individual injectors from the rail, first position the rail on a bench or other surfaces so that the injectors are

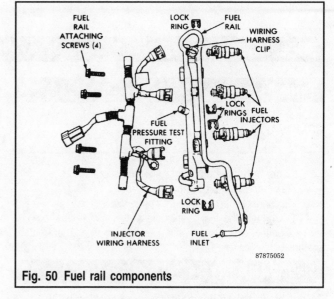

Fig. 50 Fuel rail components

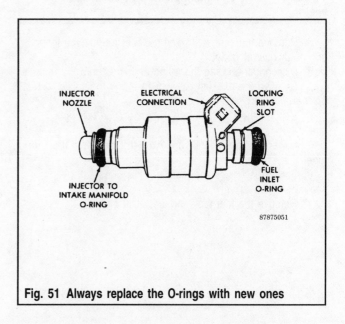

Fig. 51 Always replace the O-rings with new ones

easily reached. Perform the following for each injector to be removed:

   a. Disconnect the wiring.

   b. Remove the lockring from the rail and injector.

   c. Pull the injector straight out of the injector receiver cup in the fuel rail.

   d. Inspect the injector O-rings for damage. Replace it if necessary. If the injector will be re-used and will be off the rail while other work is performed, install a protective cap over the nozzle.

   e. Lubricate the O-ring that seals the upper end with a drop of clean engine oil. Then, install the inlet end carefully into the fuel rail receiver cup. Proceed slowly and insert the injector straight in to avoid damaging the O-ring.

   f. Slide the open end of the injector lockring down over the injector, and onto the ridge in the receiver cup. The lockring must lock into the slot on the top of the injector.

To install:

10. Remove all protective covers installed over the injector tips. Make sure the bores of the injector mounting holes are clean.

11. Put a drop of clean engine oil on the O-ring at the nozzle end of each injector. Then position the rail with the injectors headed squarely into their mounting holes and gently and evenly slide all four injectors into place.

12. Install the four rail mounting bolts and tighten them to 250 inch lbs. (28 Nm). Make sure to reconnect the ground strap removed earlier.

13. Connect each plug to its corresponding injector. Install each wiring harness into its clips. Connect the injector wiring harness to the main harness.

14. Install the heat shield clips. Install the bolt fastening the rail mounting bracket to the valve cover.

15. Connect the vacuum line for the fuel pressure regulator to the vacuum tree on the manifold. Then, connect the fuel return hose to the fuel pressure regulator and position and tighten the clamp. Install the bolts fastening the regulator bracket to the intake manifold.

16. Attach the fuel supply hose to the fuel rail and position and tighten the clamp.

17. Recheck all wiring and hose connections for routing and tightness. Then, connect the battery, start the engine, and check for leaks.

FUEL TANK

Tank Assembly

REMOVAL & INSTALLATION

1. Perform the fuel pressure relief procedure.
2. Raise and support the car.
3. Disconnect the negative battery cable.
4. Disconnect the fuel supply line at the right front shock tower. Connect a drain or siphon line and empty the tank into another container.

❋❋WARNING

Do not begin the siphoning process by sucking on the line.

5. Remove the screws holding the filler tube to the inner and outer quarter panel.
6. Disconnect and tag the wiring and lines from the tank.
7. Remove the exhaust pipe shield. Allow the shield to rest on the exhaust pipe.
8. Support the fuel tank and disconnect the fuel tank straps.
9. Lower the tank slightly and work the tank from the filler tube.
10. Lower the tank some more and disconnect the vapor separator roll-over valve hose.
11. Remove the fuel tank and insulating pad.

12. Installation is the reverse of removal. Be sure the vapor vent hose is clipped to the tank and not pinched between the tank and floorpan. Also be sure the fuel tank straps are not twisted when they are installed.

SENDING UNIT REPLACEMENT

It is necessary to remove the fuel tank for replacement of the sending unit.

1. Relieve the fuel pressure.
2. Disconnect the negative battery cable.
3. Remove the tank from the vehicle.
4. With a hammer and non-metallic punch, tap the fuel pump lockring counterclockwise to release the pump.
5. Lift the sending unit and O-ring out of the tank. On fuel injected models remove the internal return line from the end of the sending unit.

To install:

6. Wipe the seal area of the tank clean and install a new O-ring seal.
7. On fuel injected engines inspect the internal fuel line hose and its attachment to the reservoir. Make sure the line does not interfere with the float travel.
8. Position the sending unit in the tank and install the locking ring.
9. Tighten the ring in the same general way in which you loosened it. Do not overtighten it, as this can cause leakage.
10. Install the tank.

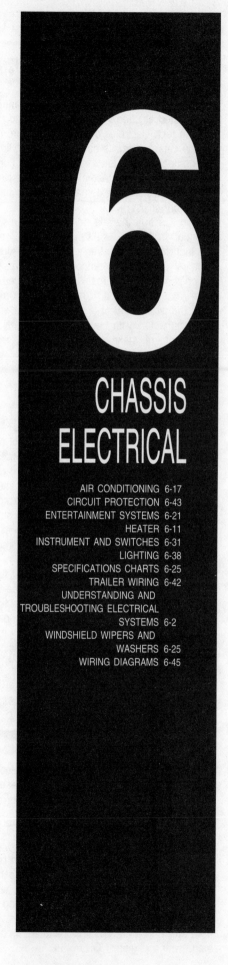

6

CHASSIS ELECTRICAL

UNDERSTANDING AND TROUBLESHOOTING ELECTRICAL SYSTEMS

Over the years import and domestic manufacturers have incorporated electronic control systems into their production lines. In fact, electronic control systems are so prevalent that all new cars and trucks built today are equipped with at least one on-board computer. These electronic components (with no moving parts) should theoretically last the life of the vehicle, provided that nothing external happens to damage the circuits or memory chips.

While it is true that electronic components should never wear out, in the real world malfunctions do occur. It is also true that any computer-based system is extremely sensitive to electrical voltages and cannot tolerate careless or haphazard testing/service procedures. An inexperienced individual can literally cause major damage looking for a minor problem by using the wrong kind of test equipment or connecting test leads/connectors with the ignition switch **ON**. When selecting test equipment, make sure the manufacturer's instructions state that the tester is compatible with whatever type of system is being serviced. Read all instructions carefully and double check all test points before installing probes or making any test connections.

The following section outlines basic diagnosis techniques for dealing with automotive electrical systems. Along with a general explanation of the various types of test equipment available to aid in servicing modern automotive systems, basic repair techniques for wiring harnesses and connectors are also given. Read the basic information before attempting any repairs or testing. This will provide the background of information necessary to avoid the most common and obvious mistakes that can cost both time and money. Although the replacement and testing procedures are simple in themselves, the systems are not, and unless one has a thorough understanding of all components and their function within a particular system, the logical test sequence these systems demand cannot be followed. Minor malfunctions can make a big difference, so it is important to know how each component affects the operation of the overall system in order to find the ultimate cause of a problem without replacing good components unnecessarily. It is not enough to use the correct test equipment; the test equipment must be used correctly.

Safety Precautions

✸✸CAUTION

Whenever working on or around any electrical or electronic systems, always observe these general precautions to prevent the possibility of personal injury or damage to electronic components.

• Never install or remove battery cables with the key **ON** or the engine running. Jumper cables should be connected with the key **OFF** to avoid power surges that can damage electronic control units. Engines equipped with computer controlled systems should avoid both giving and getting jump starts due to the possibility of serious damage to components from arcing in the engine compartment if connections are made with the ignition **ON**.

• Always remove the battery cables before charging the battery. Never use a high output charger on an installed battery or attempt to use any type of "hot shot" (24 volt) starting aid.

• Exercise care when inserting test probes into connectors to insure good contact without damaging the connector or spreading the pins. Always probe connectors from the rear (wire) side, NOT the pin side, to avoid accidental shorting of terminals during test procedures.

• Never remove or attach wiring harness connectors with the ignition switch **ON**, especially to an electronic control unit.

• Do not drop any components during service procedures and never apply 12 volts directly to any component (like a solenoid or relay) unless instructed specifically to do so. Some component electrical windings are designed to safely handle only 4 or 5 volts and can be destroyed in seconds if 12 volts are applied directly to the connector.

• Remove the electronic control unit if the vehicle is to be placed in an environment where temperatures exceed approximately 176°F (80°C), such as a paint spray booth or when arc/gas welding near the control unit location.

Understanding Basic Electricity

Understanding the basic theory of electricity makes electrical troubleshooting much easier. Several gauges are used in electrical troubleshooting to see inside the circuit being tested. Without a basic understanding, it will be difficult to understand testing procedures.

THE WATER ANALOGY

Electricity is the flow of electrons — hypothetical particles thought to constitute the basic stuff of electricity. Many people have been taught electrical theory using an analogy with water. In a comparison with water flowing in a pipe, the electrons would be the water. As the flow of water can be measured, the flow of electricity can be measured. The unit of measurement is amperes, frequently abbreviated amps. An ammeter will measure the actual amount of current flowing in the circuit.

Just as the water pressure is measured in units such as pounds per square inch, electrical pressure is measured in volts. When a voltmeter's two probes are placed on two live portions of an electrical circuit with different electrical pressures, current will flow through the voltmeter and produce a reading which indicates the difference in electrical pressure between the two parts of the circuit.

While increasing the voltage in a circuit will increase the flow of current, the actual flow depends not only on voltage, but on the resistance of the circuit. The standard unit for measuring circuit resistance is an ohm, measured by an ohmmeter. The ohmmeter is somewhat similar to an ammeter, but incorporates its own source of power so that a standard voltage is always present.

CIRCUITS

An actual electric circuit consists of four basic parts. These are: the power source, such as a generator or battery; a hot wire, which conducts the electricity under a relatively high voltage to the component supplied by the circuit; the load, such as a lamp, motor, resistor or relay coil; and the ground wire, which carries the current back to the source under very low voltage. In such a circuit the bulk of the resistance exists between the point where the hot wire is connected to the load, and the point where the load is grounded. In an automobile, the vehicle's frame or body, which is made of steel, is used as a part of the ground circuit for many of the electrical devices.

Remember that, in electrical testing, the voltmeter is connected in parallel with the circuit being tested (without disconnecting any wires) and measures the difference in voltage between the locations of the two probes; that the ammeter is connected in series with the load (the circuit is separated at one point and the ammeter inserted so it becomes a part of the circuit); and the ohmmeter is self-powered, so that all the power in the circuit should be off and the portion of the circuit to be measured contacted at either end by one of the probes of the meter.

For any electrical system to operate, it must make a complete circuit. This simply means that the power flow from the battery must make a complete circle. When an electrical component is operating, power flows from the battery to the component, passes through the component causing it to perform it to function (such as lighting a light bulb) and then returns to the battery through the ground of the circuit. This ground is usually (but not always) the metal part of the vehicle on which the electrical component is mounted.

Perhaps the easiest way to visualize this is to think of connecting a light bulb with two wires attached to it to your vehicle's battery. The battery in your vehicle has two posts (negative and positive). If one of the two wires attached to the light bulb was attached to the negative post of the battery and the other wire was attached to the positive post of the battery, you would have a complete circuit. Current from the battery would flow out one post, through the wire attached to it and then to the light bulb, where it would pass through causing it to light. It would then leave the light bulb, travel through the other wire, and return to the other post of the battery.

AUTOMOTIVE CIRCUITS

The normal automotive circuit differs from this simple example in two ways. First, instead of having a return wire from the bulb to the battery, the light bulb return the current to the battery through the chassis of the vehicle. Since the negative battery cable is attached to the chassis and the chassis is made of electrically conductive metal, the chassis of the vehicle can serve as a ground wire to complete the circuit. Secondly, most automotive circuits contain switches to turn components on and off.

Some electrical components which require a large amount of current to operate also have a relay in their circuit. Since these circuits carry a large amount of current, the thickness of the wire in the circuit (gauge size) is also greater. If this large wire were connected from the component to the control switch on the instrument panel, and then back to the component, a voltage drop would occur in the circuit. To prevent this potential drop in voltage, an electromagnetic switch (relay) is used. The large wires in the circuit are connected from the vehicle battery to one side of the relay, and from the opposite side of the relay to the component. The relay is normally open, preventing current from passing through the circuit. An additional, smaller wire is connected from the relay to the control switch for the circuit. When the control switch is turned on, it grounds the smaller wire from the relay and completes the circuit.

SHORT CIRCUITS

If you were to disconnect the light bulb (from the previous example of a light-bulb being connected to the battery by two wires) from the wires and touch the two wires together (please take our word for this; don't try it), the result will be a shower of sparks. A similar thing happens (on a smaller scale) when the power supply wire to a component or the electrical component itself becomes grounded before the normal ground connection for the circuit. To prevent damage to the system, the fuse for the circuit blows to interrupt the circuit — protecting the components from damage. Because grounding a wire from a power source makes a complete circuit — less the required component to use the power — the phenomenon is called a short circuit. The most common causes of short circuits are: the rubber insulation on a wire breaking or rubbing through to expose the current carrying core of the wire to a metal part of the car, or a shorted switch.

Some electrical systems on the vehicle are protected by a circuit breaker which is, basically, a self-repairing fuse. When either of the described events takes place in a system which is protected by a circuit breaker, the circuit breaker opens the circuit the same way a fuse does. However, when either the short is removed from the circuit or the surge subsides, the circuit breaker resets itself and does not have to be replaced as a fuse does.

Troubleshooting

When diagnosing a specific problem, organized troubleshooting is a must. The complexity of a modern automobile demands that you approach any problem in a logical, organized manner. There are certain troubleshooting techniques that are standard:

1. Establish when the problem occurs. Does the problem appear only under certain conditions? Were there any noises, odors, or other unusual symptoms?

2. Isolate the problem area. To do this, make some simple tests and observations; then eliminate the systems that are working properly. Check for obvious problems such as broken wires, dirty connections or split/disconnected vacuum hoses. Always check the obvious before assuming something complicated is the cause.

3. Test for problems systematically to determine the cause once the problem area is isolated. Are all the components functioning properly? Is there power going to electrical switches and motors? Is there vacuum at vacuum switches and/or actuators? Is there a mechanical problem such as bent linkage

or loose mounting screws? Performing careful, systematic checks will often turn up most causes on the first inspection without wasting time checking components that have little or no relationship to the problem.

4. Test all repairs after the work is done to make sure that the problem is fixed. Some causes can be traced to more than one component, so a careful verification of repair work is important in order to pick up additional malfunctions that may cause a problem to reappear or a different problem to arise. A blown fuse, for example, is a simple problem that may require more than another fuse to repair. If you don't look for a problem that caused a fuse to blow, a shorted wire (for example) may go undetected.

Experience has shown that most problems tend to be the result of a fairly simple and obvious cause, such as loose or corroded connectors or air leaks in the intake system. This makes careful inspection of components during testing essential to quick and accurate troubleshooting.

BASIC TROUBLESHOOTING THEORY

Electrical problems generally fall into one of three areas:
• The component that is not functioning is not receiving current.
• The component itself is not functioning.
• The component is not properly grounded.

Problems that fall into the first category are by far the most complicated. It is the current supply system to the component which contains all the switches, relay, fuses, etc.

The electrical system can be checked with a test light and a jumper wire. A test light is a device that looks like a pointed screwdriver with a wire attached to it. It has a light bulb in its handle. A jumper wire is a piece of insulated wire with an alligator clip attached to each end.

If a light bulb is not working, you must follow a systematic plan to determine which of the three causes is the villain.

1. Turn on the switch that controls the inoperable bulb.
2. Disconnect the power supply wire from the bulb.
3. Attach the ground wire to the test light to a good metal ground.
4. Touch the probe end of the test light to the end of the power supply wire that was disconnected from the bulb. If the bulb is receiving current, the test light will go on.

➡**If the bulb is one which works only when the ignition key is turned on (turn signal), make sure the key is turned on.**

If the test light does not go on, then the problem is in the circuit between the battery and the bulb. As mentioned before, this includes all the switches, fuses, and relays in the system. Turn to a wiring diagram and find the bulb on the diagram. Follow the wire that runs back to the battery. The problem is an open circuit between the battery and the bulb. If the fuse is blown and, when replaced, immediately blows again, there is a short circuit in the system which must be located and repaired. If there is a switch in the system, bypass it with a jumper wire. This is done by connecting one end of the jumper wire to the power supply wire into the switch and the other end of the jumper wire to the wire coming out of the switch. If the test

light illuminates with the jumper wire installed, the switch or whatever was bypassed is defective.

➡**Never substitute the jumper wire for the bulb, as the bulb is the component required to use the power from the power source.**

5. If the bulb in the test light goes on, then the current is getting to the bulb that is not working in the car. This eliminates the first of the three possible causes. Connect the power supply wire and connect a jumper wire from the bulb to a good metal ground. Do this with the switch which controls the bulb works with jumper wire installed, then it has a bad ground. This is usually caused by the metal area on which the bulb mounts to the vehicle being coated with some type of foreign matter.

6. If neither test located the source of the trouble, then the light bulb itself is defective.

The above test procedure can be applied to any of the components of the chassis electrical system by substituting the component that is not working for the light bulb. Remember that for any electrical system to work, all connections must be clean and tight.

TEST EQUIPMENT

➡**Pinpointing the exact cause of trouble in an electrical system can sometimes only be accomplished by the use of special test equipment. The following describes different types of commonly used test equipment and explains how to use them in diagnosis. In addition to the information covered below, the tool manufacturer's instructions booklet (provided with the tester) should be read and clearly understood before attempting any test procedures.**

Jumper Wires

Jumper wires are simple, yet extremely valuable, pieces of test equipment. They are basically test wires which are used to bypass sections of a circuit. The simplest type of jumper wire is a length of multi-strand wire with an alligator clip at each end. Jumper wires are usually fabricated from lengths of standard automotive wire and whatever type of connector (alligator clip, spade connector or pin connector) that is required for the particular vehicle being tested. The well equipped tool box will have several different styles of jumper wires in several different lengths. Some jumper wires are made with three or more terminals coming from a common splice for special purpose testing. In cramped, hard-to-reach areas it is advisable to have insulated boots over the jumper wire terminals in order to prevent accidental grounding, sparks, and possible fire, especially when testing fuel system components.

Jumper wires are used primarily to locate open electrical circuits, on either the ground (-) side of the circuit or on the hot (+) side. If an electrical component fails to operate, connect the jumper wire between the component and a good ground. If the component operates only with the jumper installed, the ground circuit is open. If the ground circuit is good, but the component does not operate, the circuit between the power feed and component may be open. By moving the jumper wire successively back from the lamp toward the power source, you can isolate the area of the circuit where the open is located. When the component stops functioning, or the power is cut off, the open is in the segment of wire between the jumper and the point previously tested.

You can sometimes connect the jumper wire directly from the battery to the hot terminal of the component, but first make sure the component uses 12 volts in operation. Some electrical components, such as fuel injectors, are designed to operate on about 4 volts and running 12 volts directly to the injector terminals can cause damage.

By inserting an in-line fuse holder between a set of test leads, a fused jumper wire can be used for bypassing open circuits. Use a 5 amp fuse to provide protection against voltage spikes. When in doubt, use a voltmeter to check the voltage input to the component and measure how much voltage is normally being applied.

✳✳CAUTION

Never use jumpers made from wire that is of lighter gauge than that which is used in the circuit under test. If the jumper wire is of too small a gauge, it may overheat and possibly melt. Never use jumpers to bypass high resistance loads in a circuit. Bypassing resistances, in effect, creates a short circuit. This may, in turn, cause damage and fire. Jumper wires should only be used to bypass lengths of wire.

Unpowered Test Lights

The 12 volt test light is used to check circuits and components while electrical current is flowing through them. It is used for voltage and ground tests. Twelve volt test lights come in different styles but all have three main parts; a ground clip, a probe, and a light. The most commonly used 12 volt test lights have pick-type probes. To use a 12 volt test light, connect the ground clip to a good ground and probe wherever necessary with the pick. The pick should be sharp so that it can be probed into tight spaces.

✳✳CAUTION

Do not use a test light to probe electronic ignition spark plug or coil wires. Never use a pick-type test light to probe wiring on computer controlled systems unless specifically instructed to do so. Any wire insulation that is pierced by the test light probe should be taped and sealed with silicone after testing.

Like the jumper wire, the 12 volt test light is used to isolate opens in circuits. But, whereas the jumper wire is used to bypass the open to operate the load, the 12 volt test light is used to locate the presence of voltage in a circuit. If the test light glows, you know that there is power up to that point; if the 12 volt test light does not glow when its probe is inserted into the wire or connector, you know that there is an open circuit (no power). Move the test light in successive steps back toward the power source until the light in the handle does

glow. When it glows, the open is between the probe and point which was probed previously.

➡The test light does not detect that 12 volts (or any particular amount of voltage) is present; it only detects that some voltage is present. It is advisable before using the test light to touch its terminals across the battery posts to make sure the light is operating properly.

Self-Powered Test Lights

The self-powered test light usually contains a 1.5 volt penlight battery. One type of self-powered test light is similar in design to the 12 volt unit. This type has both the battery and the light in the handle, along with a pick-type probe tip. The second type has the light toward the open tip, so that the light illuminates the contact point. The self-powered test light is a dual purpose piece of test equipment. It can be used to test for either open or short circuits when power is isolated from the circuit (continuity test). A powered test light should not be used on any computer controlled system or component unless specifically instructed to do so. Many engine sensors can be destroyed by even this small amount of voltage applied directly to the terminals.

Voltmeters

A voltmeter is used to measure voltage at any point in a circuit, or to measure the voltage drop across any part of a circuit. It can also be used to check continuity in a wire or circuit by indicating current flow from one end to the other. Analog voltmeters usually have various scales on the meter dial and a selector switch to allow the selection of different voltages. The voltmeter has a positive and a negative lead. To avoid damage to the meter, always connect the negative lead to the negative (-) side of the circuit (to ground or nearest the ground side of the circuit) and connect the positive lead to the positive (+) side of the circuit (to the power source or the nearest power source). Note that the negative voltmeter lead will always be black and that the positive voltmeter will always be some color other than black (usually red).

Depending on how the voltmeter is connected into the circuit, it has several uses. A voltmeter can be connected either in parallel or in series with a circuit and it has a very high resistance to current flow. When connected in parallel, only a small amount of current will flow through the voltmeter current path; the rest will flow through the normal circuit current path and the circuit will work normally. When the voltmeter is connected in series with a circuit, only a small amount of current can flow through the circuit. The circuit will not work properly, but the voltmeter reading will show if the circuit is complete or not.

Ohmmeters

The ohmmeter is designed to read resistance (which is measured in ohms or Ω) in a circuit or component. Although there are several different styles of ohmmeters, all analog meters will usually have a selector switch which permits the measurement of different ranges of resistance (usually the selector switch allows the multiplication of the meter reading by 10, 100, 1000, and 10,000). A calibration knob allows the meter to be set at zero for accurate measurement. Since all ohmmeters are powered by an internal battery, the ohmmeter can be used as a self-powered test light. When the ohmmeter is connected, current from the ohmmeter flows through the circuit or component being tested. Since the ohmmeter's internal resistance and voltage are known values, the amount of current flow through the meter depends on the resistance of the circuit or component being tested.

The ohmmeter can be used to perform a continuity test for opens or shorts (either by observation of the meter needle or as a self-powered test light), and to read actual resistance in a circuit. It should be noted that the ohmmeter is used to check the resistance of a component or wire while there is no voltage applied to the circuit. Current flow from an outside voltage source (such as the vehicle battery) can damage the ohmmeter, so the circuit or component should be isolated from the vehicle electrical system before any testing is done. Since the ohmmeter uses its own voltage source, either lead can be connected to any test point.

➡**When checking diodes or other solid state components, the ohmmeter leads can only be connected one way in order to measure current flow in a single direction. Make sure the positive (+) and negative (-) terminal connections are as described in the test procedures to verify the one-way diode operation.**

In using the meter for making continuity checks, do not be concerned with the actual resistance readings. Zero resistance, or any ohm reading, indicates continuity in the circuit. Infinite resistance indicates an open in the circuit. A high resistance reading where there should be none indicates a problem in the circuit. Checks for short circuits are made in the same manner as checks for open circuits except that the circuit must be isolated from both power and normal ground. Infinite resistance indicates no continuity to ground, while zero resistance indicates a dead short to ground.

Ammeters

An ammeter measures the amount of current flowing through a circuit in units called amperes or amps. Amperes are units of electron flow which indicate how fast the electrons are flowing through the circuit. Since Ohms Law dictates that current flow in a circuit is equal to the circuit voltage divided by the total circuit resistance, increasing voltage also increases the current level (amps). Likewise, any decrease in resistance will increase the amount of amps in a circuit. At normal operating voltage, most circuits have a characteristic amount of amperes, called "current draw" which can be measured using an ammeter. By referring to a specified current draw rating, measuring the amperes, and comparing the two values, one can determine what is happening within the circuit to aid in diagnosis. An open circuit, for example, will not allow any current to flow so the ammeter reading will be zero. More current flows through a heavily loaded circuit or when the charging system is operating.

An ammeter is always connected in series with the circuit being tested. All of the current that normally flows through the circuit must also flow through the ammeter; if there is any other path for the current to follow, the ammeter reading will not be accurate. The ammeter itself has very little resistance to current flow and therefore will not affect the circuit, but it will measure current draw only when the circuit is closed and electricity is flowing. Excessive current draw can blow fuses

and drain the battery, while a reduced current draw can cause motors to run slowly, lights to dim and other components to not operate properly. The ammeter can help diagnose these conditions by locating the cause of the high or low reading.

Multimeters

Different combinations of test meters can be built into a single unit designed for specific tests. Some of the more common combination test devices are known as Volt/Amp testers, Tach/Dwell meters, or Digital Multimeters. The Volt/Amp tester is used for charging system, starting system or battery tests and consists of a voltmeter, an ammeter and a variable resistance carbon pile. The voltmeter will usually have at least two ranges for use with 6, 12 and/or 24 volt systems. The ammeter also has more than one range for testing various levels of battery loads and starter current draw. The carbon pile can be adjusted to offer different amounts of resistance. The Volt/Amp tester has heavy leads to carry large amounts of current and many later models have an inductive ammeter pickup that clamps around the wire to simplify test connections. On some models, the ammeter also has a zero-center scale to allow testing of charging and starting systems without switching leads or polarity. A digital multimeter is a voltmeter, ammeter and ohmmeter combined in an instrument which gives a digital readout. These are often used when testing solid state circuits because of their high input impedance (usually 10 megohms or more).

The tach/dwell meter that combines a tachometer and a dwell (cam angle) meter is a specialized kind of voltmeter. The tachometer scale is marked to show engine speed in rpm and the dwell scale is marked to show degrees of distributor shaft rotation. In most electronic ignition systems, dwell is determined by the control unit, but the dwell meter can also be used to check the duty cycle (operation) of some electronic engine control systems. Some tach/dwell meters are powered by an internal battery, while others take their power from the vehicle battery in use. The battery powered testers usually require calibration (much like an ohmmeter) before testing.

TESTING

Open Circuits

To use the self-powered test light or a multimeter to check for open circuits, first isolate the circuit from the vehicle's 12 volt power source by disconnecting the battery or wiring harness connector. Connect the test light or ohmmeter ground clip to a good ground and probe sections of the circuit sequentially with the test light. (start from either end of the circuit). If the light is out/or there is infinite resistance, the open is between the probe and the circuit ground. If the light is on/or the meter shows continuity, the open is between the probe and end of the circuit toward the power source.

Short Circuits

By isolating the circuit both from power and from ground, and using a self-powered test light or multimeter, you can check for shorts to ground in the circuit. Isolate the circuit from power and ground. Connect the test light or ohmmeter ground clip to a good ground and probe any easy-to-reach test point in the circuit. If the light comes on or there is continuity, there is a short somewhere in the circuit. To isolate the short, probe a test point at either end of the isolated circuit (the light should be on/there should be continuity). Leave the test light probe engaged and open connectors, switches, remove parts, etc., sequentially, until the light goes out/continuity is broken. When the light goes out, the short is between the last circuit component opened and the previous circuit opened.

➡**The battery in the test light and does not provide much current. A weak battery may not provide enough power to illuminate the test light even when a complete circuit is made (especially if there are high resistances in the circuit). Always make sure that the test battery is strong. To check the battery, briefly touch the ground clip to the probe; if the light glows brightly the battery is strong enough for testing. Never use a self-powered test light to perform checks for opens or shorts when power is applied to the electrical system under test. The 12 volt vehicle power will quickly burn out the light bulb in the test light.**

Available Voltage Measurement

Set the voltmeter selector switch to the 20V position and connect the meter negative lead to the negative post of the battery. Connect the positive meter lead to the positive post of the battery and turn the ignition switch **ON** to provide a load. Read the voltage on the meter or digital display. A well charged battery should register over 12 volts. If the meter reads below 11.5 volts, the battery power may be insufficient to operate the electrical system properly. This test determines voltage available from the battery and should be the first step in any electrical trouble diagnosis procedure. Many electrical problems, especially on computer controlled systems, can be caused by a low state of charge in the battery. Excessive corrosion at the battery cable terminals can cause a poor contact that will prevent proper charging and full battery current flow.

Normal battery voltage is 12 volts when fully charged. When the battery is supplying current to one or more circuits it is said to be "under load." When everything is off the electrical system is under a "no-load" condition. A fully charged battery may show about 12.5 volts at no load; will drop to 12 volts under medium load; and will drop even lower under heavy load. If the battery is partially discharged the voltage decrease under heavy load may be excessive, even though the battery shows 12 volts or more at no load. When allowed to discharge further, the battery's available voltage under load will decrease more severely. For this reason, it is important that the battery be fully charged during all testing procedures to avoid errors in diagnosis and incorrect test results.

Voltage Drop

When current flows through a resistance, the voltage beyond the resistance is reduced (the larger the current, the greater the reduction in voltage). When no current is flowing, there is no voltage drop because there is no current flow. All points in the circuit which are connected to the power source are at the same voltage as the power source. The total voltage drop always equals the total source voltage. In a long circuit with many connectors, a series of small, unwanted voltage drops

due to corrosion at the connectors can add up to a total loss of voltage which impairs the operation of the normal loads in the circuit. The maximum allowable voltage drop under load is critical, especially if there is more than one high resistance problem in a circuit because all voltage drops are cumulative. A small drop is normal due to the resistance of the conductors.

INDIRECT COMPUTATION OF VOLTAGE DROPS

1. Set the voltmeter selector switch to the 20 volt position.
2. Connect the meter negative lead to a good ground.
3. While operating the circuit, probe all loads in the circuit with the positive meter lead and observe the voltage readings. A drop should be noticed after the first load. But, there should be little or no voltage drop before the first load.

DIRECT MEASUREMENT OF VOLTAGE DROPS

1. Set the voltmeter switch to the 20 volt position.
2. Connect the voltmeter negative lead to the ground side of the load to be measured.
3. Connect the positive lead to the positive side of the resistance or load to be measured.
4. Read the voltage drop directly on the 20 volt scale.

Too high a voltage indicates too high a resistance. If, for example, a blower motor runs too slowly, you can determine if perhaps there is too high a resistance in the resistor pack. By taking voltage drop readings in all parts of the circuit, you can isolate the problem. Too low a voltage drop indicates too low a resistance. Take the blower motor for example again. If a blower motor runs too fast in the MED and/or LOW position, the problem might be isolated in the resistor pack by taking voltage drop readings in all parts of the circuit to locate a possibly shorted resistor.

HIGH RESISTANCE TESTING

1. Set the voltmeter selector switch to the 4 volt position.
2. Connect the voltmeter positive lead to the positive post of the battery.
3. Turn on the headlights and heater blower to provide a load.
4. Probe various points in the circuit with the negative voltmeter lead.
5. Read the voltage drop on the 4 volt scale. Some average maximum allowable voltage drops are:
   - FUSE PANEL: 0.7 volts
   - IGNITION SWITCH: 0.5 volts
   - HEADLIGHT SWITCH: 0.7 volts
   - IGNITION COIL (+): 0.5 volts
   - ANY OTHER LOAD: 1.3 volts

➡**Voltage drops are all measured while a load is operating; without current flow, there will be no voltage drop.**

Resistance Measurement

The batteries in an ohmmeter will weaken with age and temperature, so the ohmmeter must be calibrated or "zeroed" before taking measurements. To zero the meter, place the selector switch in its lowest range and touch the two ohmmeter leads together. Turn the calibration knob until the meter needle is exactly on zero.

➡**All analog (needle) type ohmmeters must be zeroed before use, but some digital ohmmeter models are automatically calibrated when the switch is turned on. Self-calibrating digital ohmmeters do not have an adjusting knob, but its a good idea to check for a zero readout before use by touching the leads together. All computer controlled systems require the use of a digital ohmmeter with at least 10 megohms impedance for testing. Before any test procedures are attempted, make sure the ohmmeter used is compatible with the electrical system or damage to the on-board computer could result.**

To measure resistance, first isolate the circuit from the vehicle power source by disconnecting the battery cables or the harness connector. Make sure the key is **OFF** when disconnecting any components or the battery. Where necessary, also isolate at least one side of the circuit to be checked in order to avoid reading parallel resistances. Parallel circuit resistances will always give a lower reading than the actual resistance of either of the branches. When measuring the resistance of parallel circuits, the total resistance will always be lower than the smallest resistance in the circuit. Connect the meter leads to both sides of the circuit (wire or component) and read the actual measured ohms on the meter scale. Make sure the selector switch is set to the proper ohm scale for the circuit being tested to avoid misreading the ohmmeter test value.

✳✳WARNING

Never use an ohmmeter with power applied to the circuit. Like the self-powered test light, the ohmmeter is designed to operate on its own power supply. The normal 12 volt automotive electrical system current could damage the meter!

Wiring Harnesses

The average automobile contains about ½ mile of wiring, with hundreds of individual connections. To protect the many wires from damage and to keep them from becoming a confusing tangle, they are organized into bundles, enclosed in plastic or taped together and called wiring harnesses. Different harnesses serve different parts of the vehicle. Individual wires are color coded to help trace them through a harness where sections are hidden from view.

Automotive wiring or circuit conductors can be in any one of three forms:
1. Single strand wire
2. Multi-strand wire
3. Printed circuitry

Single strand wire has a solid metal core and is usually used inside such components as alternators, motors, relays and other devices. Multi-strand wire has a core made of many small strands of wire twisted together into a single conductor. Most of the wiring in an automotive electrical system is made up of multi-strand wire, either as a single conductor or grouped together in a harness. All wiring is color coded on the insulator, either as a solid color or as a colored wire with an identification stripe. A printed circuit is a thin film of copper or other conductor that is printed on an insulator backing. Occasionally, a printed circuit is sandwiched between two sheets of plastic for more protection and flexibility. A complete printed circuit, consisting of conductors, insulating material and connectors for lamps or other components is called a printed circuit board. Printed circuitry is used in place of individual wires or harnesses in places where space is limited, such as behind instrument panels.

Since automotive electrical systems are very sensitive to changes in resistance, the selection of properly sized wires is critical when systems are repaired. A loose or corroded connection or a replacement wire that is too small for the circuit will add extra resistance and an additional voltage drop to the circuit. A ten percent voltage drop can result in slow or erratic motor operation, for example, even though the circuit is complete. The wire gauge number is an expression of the cross-section area of the conductor. The most common system for expressing wire size is the American Wire Gauge (AWG) system.

Gauge numbers are assigned to conductors of various cross-section areas. As gauge number increases, area decreases and the conductor becomes smaller. A 5 gauge conductor is smaller than a 1 gauge conductor and a 10 gauge is smaller than a 5 gauge. As the cross-section area of a conductor decreases, resistance increases and so does the gauge number. A conductor with a higher gauge number will carry less current than a conductor with a lower gauge number.

➡**Gauge wire size refers to the size of the conductor, not the size of the complete wire. It is possible to have two wires of the same gauge with different diameters because one may have thicker insulation than the other.**

12 volt automotive electrical systems generally use 10, 12, 14, 16 and 18 gauge wire. Main power distribution circuits and larger accessories usually use 10 and 12 gauge wire. Battery cables are usually 4 or 6 gauge, although 1 and 2 gauge wires are occasionally used. Wire length must also be considered when making repairs to a circuit. As conductor length increases, so does resistance. An 18 gauge wire, for example, can carry a 10 amp load for 10 feet without excessive voltage drop; however if a 15 foot wire is required for the same 10 amp load, it must be a 16 gauge wire.

An electrical schematic shows the electrical current paths when a circuit is operating properly. It is essential to understand how a circuit works before trying to figure out why it doesn't. Schematics break the entire electrical system down into individual circuits and show only one particular circuit. In a schematic, no attempt is made to represent wiring and components as they physically appear on the vehicle; switches and other components are shown as simply as possible. Face views of harness connectors show the cavity or terminal locations in all multi-pin connectors to help locate test points.

If you need to backprobe a connector while it is on the component, the order of the terminals must be mentally reversed. The wire color code can help in this situation, as well as a keyway, lock tab or other reference mark.

WIRING REPAIR

Soldering is a quick, efficient method of joining metals permanently. Everyone who has the occasion to make wiring repairs should know how to solder. Electrical connections that are soldered are far less likely to come apart and will conduct electricity much better than connections that are only "pig-tailed" together. The most popular (and preferred) method of soldering is with an electrical soldering gun. Soldering irons are available in many sizes and wattage ratings. Irons with higher wattage ratings deliver higher temperatures and recover lost heat faster. A small soldering iron rated for no more than 50 watts is recommended, especially on electrical systems where excess heat can damage the components being soldered.

There are three ingredients necessary for successful soldering; proper flux, good solder and sufficient heat. A soldering flux is necessary to clean the metal of tarnish, prepare it for soldering and to enable the solder to spread into tiny crevices. When soldering, always use a rosin core solder which is non-corrosive and will not attract moisture once the job is finished. Other types of flux (acid core) will leave a residue that will attract moisture and cause the wires to corrode. Tin is a unique metal with a low melting point. In a molten state, it dissolves and alloys easily with many metals. Solder is made by mixing tin with lead. The most common proportions are 40/60, 50/50 and 60/40, with the percentage of tin listed first. Low priced solders usually contain less tin, making them very difficult for a beginner to use because more heat is required to melt the solder. A common solder is 40/60 which is well suited for all-around general use, but 60/40 melts easier and is preferred for electrical work.

Soldering Techniques

Successful soldering requires that the metals to be joined be heated to a temperature that will melt the solder, usually 360-460°F (182-238°C). Contrary to popular belief, the purpose of the soldering iron is not to melt the solder itself, but to heat the parts being soldered to a temperature high enough to melt the solder when it is touched to the work. Melting flux-cored solder on the soldering iron will usually destroy the effectiveness of the flux.

➡**Soldering tips are made of copper for good heat conductivity, but must be "tinned" regularly for quick transference of heat to the project and to prevent the solder from sticking to the iron. To "tin" the iron, simply heat it and touch the flux-cored solder to the tip; the solder will flow over the hot tip. Wipe the excess off with a clean rag, but be careful as the iron will be hot.**

After some use, the tip may become pitted. If so, simply dress the tip smooth with a smooth file and "tin" the tip again. Flux-cored solder will remove oxides but rust, bits of insulation and oil or grease must be removed with a wire brush or emery cloth. For maximum strength in soldered parts, the joint must start off clean and tight. Weak joints will result in gaps too wide for the solder to bridge.

If a separate soldering flux is used, it should be brushed or swabbed on only those areas that are to be soldered. Most solders contain a core of flux and separate fluxing is unnecessary. Hold the work to be soldered firmly. It is best to solder on a wooden board, because a metal vise will only rob the piece to be soldered of heat and make it difficult to melt the solder. Hold the soldering tip with the broadest face against the work to be soldered. Apply solder under the tip close to the work, using enough solder to give a heavy film between the iron and the piece being soldered, while moving slowly and making sure the solder melts properly. Keep the work level or the solder will run to the lowest part and favor the thicker parts, because these require more heat to melt the solder. If the soldering tip overheats (the solder coating on the face of the tip burns up), it should be retinned. Once the soldering is completed, let the soldered joint stand until cool. Tape and seal all soldered wire splices after the repair has cooled.

Wire Harness Connectors

Most connectors in the engine compartment or that are otherwise exposed to the elements are protected against moisture and dirt which could create oxidation and deposits on the terminals.

These special connectors are weather-proof. All repairs require the use of a special terminal and the tool required to service it. This tool is used to remove the pin and sleeve terminals. If removal is attempted with an ordinary pick, there is a good chance that the terminal will be bent or deformed. Unlike standard blade type terminals, these weather-proof terminals cannot be straightened once they are bent. Make certain that the connectors are properly seated and all of the sealing rings are in place when connecting leads. On some models, a hinge-type flap provides a backup or secondary locking feature for the terminals. Most secondary locks are used to improve connector reliability by retaining the terminals if the small terminal lock tangs are not positioned properly.

Molded-on connectors require complete replacement of the connection. This means splicing a new connector assembly into the harness. All splices should be soldered to insure proper contact. Use care when probing the connections or replacing terminals in them as it is possible to short between opposite terminals. If this happens to the wrong terminal pair, it is possible to damage certain components. Always use jumper wires between connectors for circuit checking and never probe through weatherproof seals.

Open circuits are often difficult to locate by sight because corrosion or terminal misalignment are hidden by the connectors. Merely wiggling a connector on a sensor or in the wiring harness may correct the open circuit condition. This should always be considered when an open circuit or a failed sensor is indicated. Intermittent problems may also be caused by oxidized or loose connections. When using a circuit tester for diagnosis, always probe connections from the wire side. Be careful not to damage sealed connectors with test probes.

All wiring harnesses should be replaced with identical parts, using the same gauge wire and connectors. When signal wires are spliced into a harness, use wire with high temperature insulation only. It is seldom necessary to replace a complete harness. If replacement is necessary, pay close attention to insure proper harness routing. Secure the harness with suitable plastic wire clamps to prevent vibrations from causing the harness to wear in spots or contact any hot components.

➡ **Weatherproof connectors cannot be replaced with standard connectors. Instructions are provided with replacement connector and terminal packages. Some wire harnesses have mounting indicators (usually pieces of colored tape) to mark where the harness is to be secured.**

In making wiring repairs, its important that you always replace damaged wires with wiring of the same gauge as the wire being replaced. The heavier the wire, the smaller the gauge number. Wires are color-coded to aid in identification and whenever possible the same color coded wire should be used for replacement. A wire stripping and crimping tool is necessary to install solderless terminal connectors. Test all crimps by pulling on the wires; it should not be possible to pull the wires out of a good crimp.

Wires which are open, exposed or otherwise damaged are repaired by simple splicing. Where possible, if the wiring harness is accessible and the damaged place in the wire can be located, it is best to open the harness and check for all possible damage. In an inaccessible harness, the wire must be bypassed with a new insert, usually taped to the outside of the old harness.

When replacing fusible links, be sure to use fusible link wire, NOT ordinary automotive wire. Make sure the fusible segment is of the same gauge and construction as the one being replaced and double the stripped end when crimping the terminal connector for a good contact. The melted (open) fusible link segment of the wiring harness should be cut off as close to the harness as possible, then a new segment spliced in as described. In the case of a damaged fusible link that feeds two harness wires, the harness connections should be replaced with two fusible link wires so that each circuit will have its own separate protection.

➡ **Most of the problems caused in the wiring harness are due to bad ground connections. Always check all vehicle ground connections for corrosion or looseness before performing any power feed checks to eliminate the chance of a bad ground affecting the circuit.**

Hard-Shell Connectors

Unlike molded connectors, the terminal contacts in hard-shell connectors can be replaced. Weatherproof hard-shell connectors with the leads molded into the shell have non-replaceable terminal ends. Replacement usually involves the use of a special terminal removal tool that depresses the locking tangs (barbs) on the connector terminal and allows the connector to be removed from the rear of the shell. The connector shell should be replaced if it shows any evidence of burning, melting, cracks, or breaks. Replace individual terminals that are burnt, corroded, distorted or loose.

➡ **The insulation crimp must be tight to prevent the insulation from sliding back on the wire when the wire is pulled. The insulation must be visibly compressed under the crimp tabs, and the ends of the crimp should be turned in for a firm grip on the insulation.**

The wire crimp must be made with all wire strands inside the crimp. The terminal must be fully compressed on the wire strands with the ends of the crimp tabs turned in to make a

firm grip on the wire. Check all connections with an ohmmeter to insure a good contact. There should be no measurable resistance between the wire and the terminal when connected.

Fusible Links

The fuse link is a short length of special, Hypalon (high temperature) insulated wire, integral with the engine compartment wiring harness and should not be confused with standard wire. It is several wire gauges smaller than the circuit which it protects. Under no circumstances should a fuse link replacement repair be made using a length of standard wire cut from bulk stock or from another wiring harness.

To repair any blown fuse link use the following procedure:

1. Determine which circuit is damaged, its location and the cause of the open fuse link. If the damaged fuse link is one of three fed by a common No. 10 or 12 gauge feed wire, determine the specific affected circuit.

2. Disconnect the negative battery cable.

3. Cut the damaged fuse link from the wiring harness and discard it. If the fuse link is one of three circuits fed by a single feed wire, cut it out of the harness at each splice end and discard it.

4. Identify and procure the proper fuse link with butt connectors for attaching the fuse link to the harness.

➡ **Heat shrink tubing must be slipped over the wire before crimping and soldering the connection.**

5. To repair any fuse link in a 3-link group with one feed:

   a. After cutting the open link out of the harness, cut each of the remaining undamaged fuse links close to the feed wire weld.

   b. Strip approximately ½ in. (13mm) of insulation from the detached ends of the two good fuse links. Insert two wire ends into one end of a butt connector, then carefully push one stripped end of the replacement fuse link into the same end of the butt connector and crimp all three firmly together.

➡ **Care must be taken when fitting the three fuse links into the butt connector as the internal diameter is a snug fit for three wires. Make sure to use a proper crimping tool. Pliers, side cutters, etc. will not apply the proper crimp to retain the wires and withstand a pull test.**

   c. After crimping the butt connector to the three fuse links, cut the weld portion from the feed wire and strip approximately ½ in. (13mm) of insulation from the cut end. Insert the stripped end into the open end of the butt connector and crimp very firmly.

   d. To attach the remaining end of the replacement fuse link, strip approximately ½ in. (13mm) of insulation from the wire end of the circuit from which the blown fuse link was removed, and firmly crimp a butt connector or equivalent to the stripped wire. Then, insert the end of the replacement link into the other end of the butt connector and crimp firmly.

   e. Using rosin core solder with a consistency of 60 percent tin and 40 percent lead, solder the connectors and the wires at the repairs then insulate with electrical tape or heat shrink tubing.

6. To replace any fuse link on a single circuit in a harness, cut out the damaged portion, strip approximately ½ in. (13mm) of insulation from the two wire ends and attach the appropriate replacement fuse link to the stripped wire ends with two proper

size butt connectors. Solder the connectors and wires, then insulate.

7. To repair any fuse link which has an eyelet terminal on one end such as the charging circuit, cut off the open fuse link behind the weld, strip approximately ½ in. (13mm) of insulation from the cut end and attach the appropriate new eyelet fuse link to the cut stripped wire with an appropriate size butt connector. Solder the connectors and wires at the repair, then insulate.

8. Connect the negative battery cable to the battery and test the system for proper operation.

➡**Do not mistake a resistor wire for a fuse link. The resistor wire is generally longer and has print stating, "Resistor-don't cut or splice."**

When attaching a single No. 16, 17, 18 or 20 gauge fuse link to a heavy gauge wire, always double the stripped wire end of the fuse link before inserting and crimping it into the butt connector for positive wire retention.

Add-On Electrical Equipment

The electrical system in your vehicle is designed to perform under reasonable operating conditions without interference between components. Before any additional electrical equipment is installed, it is recommended that you consult your dealer or a reputable repair facility that is familiar with the vehicle and its systems.

If the vehicle is equipped with mobile radio equipment and/or mobile telephone, it may have an effect upon the operation of any on-board computer control modules. Radio Frequency Interference (RFI) from the communications system can be picked up by the vehicle's wiring harnesses and conducted into the control module, giving it the wrong messages at the wrong time. Although well shielded against RFI, the computer should be further protected by taking the following measures:

• Install the antenna as far as possible from the control module. For instance, if the module is located behind the center console area, then the antenna should be mounted at the rear of the vehicle.

• Keep the antenna wiring a minimum of eight inches away from any wiring running to control modules and from the module itself. NEVER wind the antenna wire around any other wiring.

• Mount the equipment as far from the control module as possible. Be very careful during installation not to drill through any wires or short a wire harness with a mounting screw.

• Insure that the electrical feed wire(s) to the equipment are properly and tightly connected. Loose connectors can cause interference.

• Make certain that the equipment is properly grounded to the vehicle. Poor grounding can damage expensive equipment.

HEATER

Blower Motor

REMOVAL & INSTALLATION

▶ **See Figures 1, 2, 3 and 4**

The blower motor is located under the instrument panel on the left side of the heater assembly.
1. Disconnect the motor wiring.
2. Remove the left outlet duct.
3. Remove the motor retaining screws, then remove the motor.
4. Installation is the reverse of removal.

Heater Case Assembly

REMOVAL & INSTALLATION

1978-80 Models
▶ **See Figures 5, 6, 7, 8, 9, 10, 11 and 12**

1. Disconnect the negative battery cable.
2. Drain the cooling system.

✳✳CAUTION

When draining the coolant, keep in mind that cats and dogs are attracted by ethylene glycol antifreeze, and are quite likely to drink any that is left in an uncovered

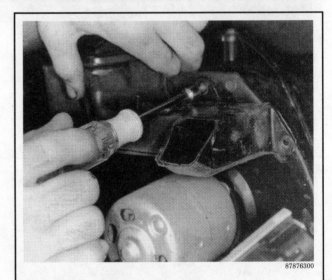

Fig. 1 Remove the left outlet duct

container or in puddles on the ground. This will prove fatal in sufficient quantity. Always drain the coolant into a sealable container. Coolant should be reused unless it is contaminated or several years old.

3. Remove the center outside air floor vent housing.
4. Remove the ash tray.
5. Remove the two defroster duct adapter screws. The left one is reached through the ash tray opening.
6. Remove the defrost duct adapter and push the flexible hose up out of the way.

Fig. 2 Unscrew the heater motor

Fig. 5 Unfasten the floor vent

Fig. 3 Pull the motor out of its casing

Fig. 6 Pull the vent out

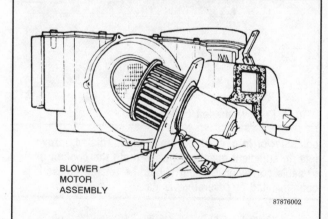

Fig. 4 Be careful when removing the blower motor not to damage the blower fan; always pull the motor straight outward from the casing

Fig. 7 Remove the ash tray

Fig. 8 Remove the screw in the ashtray opening, then the other duct adapter screw

Fig. 10 Remove the glove compartment door

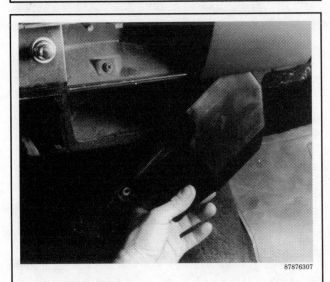

Fig. 9 Take out the duct

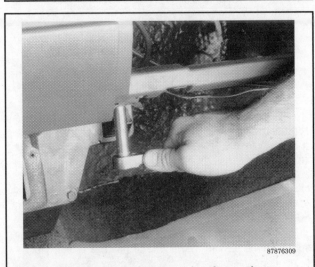

Fig. 11 Unscrew the heater brace bracket to the instrument panel

7. Disconnect the temperature control cable.

8. Disengage the blower motor wiring connector.

9. Part the hoses from the heater core and plug the core openings.

10. Remove the two nuts retaining the heater unit to the firewall.

11. Remove the glove compartment and door.

12. Remove the screw attaching the heater brace bracket to the instrument panel.

13. Remove the heater assembly support strap nut. Disconnect the strap from the plenum stud and lower the heater from the instrument panel.

14. Disconnect the control cable and remove the unit from the car.

To install:

15. Connect the control cable and raise the unit into position so that the core tubes and mounting studs fit through their holes in the firewall.

16. Install the support strap and hand-tighten the nut.

17. Install and tighten the two heater-to-firewall nuts.

Fig. 12 Remove the unit from the vehicle

18. Unplug and connect the core tubes.
19. Install the defroster duct adaptor.
20. Install the ash tray.
21. Install the center outside air floor vent housing.
22. Attach the glove compartment.
23. Refill the cooling system.

1981-89 Models

▶ **See Figure 13**

1. Disconnect the negative battery cable.
2. Drain the cooling system.

✳✳CAUTION

When draining the coolant, keep in mind that cats and dogs are attracted by ethylene glycol antifreeze, and are quite likely to drink any that is left in an uncovered container or in puddles on the ground. This will prove fatal in sufficient quantity. Always drain the coolant into a sealable container. Coolant should be reused unless it is contaminated or several years old.

3. Disconnect the blower motor wiring.
4. Remove the ash tray.
5. Depress the retaining tab and pull the temperature control cable out of the receptacle on the heater.
6. Remove the glove compartment and door.
7. Part the heater hoses at the core tubes, and cover the tube openings to prevent spillage.
8. Remove the two nuts holding the heater case to the firewall.
9. Take off the wire connector from the blower motor resistor block.
10. Remove the bolt holding the heater support brace to the instrument panel.
11. Remove the heater support bracket nut. Disconnect the strap from the plenum stud and lower the heater from the instrument panel.
12. Depress the tab on the retainer and pull the mode control door cable from the heater.
13. Move the heater to the right and remove it from the car.

14. Installation is the reverse of removal.

Heater Core

REMOVAL & INSTALLATION

1. Remove the heater assembly as described earlier.
2. Take off the left outlet duct.
3. Remove the blower motor.
4. Remove the defroster duct adapter.
5. Withdraw the outside air and defroster door cover.
6. Remove the defroster door.
7. Remove the defroster door control rod.
8. Remove the core cover.
9. Lift the core from the unit.
10. Installation is the reverse of removal.

Control Panel

REMOVAL & INSTALLATION

▶ **See Figures 14, 15 and 16**

1. Reach under the left panel to the extreme left end, disengage the headlamp switch knob release button on the switch lower surface. Pull out the knob and shaft assembly.
2. Remove the bezel attachment screws.
3. Extract the left bezel.
4. Remove the control mounting screws.
5. Slide the control rearwards, disconnect the cables, vacuum hose and wiring. Next remove the control assembly.
   To install:
6. Position the control at the panel, connect the cables, vacuum hose and wiring.
7. Install the control to the panel, attaching with the mounting screws.
8. Push the headlamp knob stem all the way into the headlamp switch.

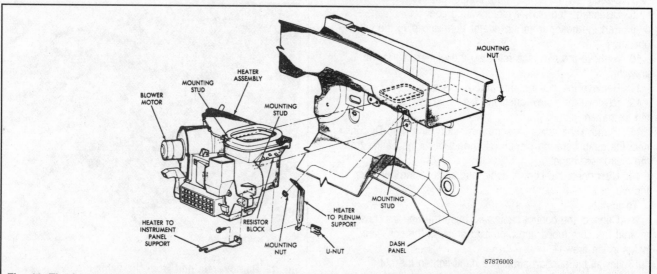

Fig. 13 The heater system components are mainly on the inside of the vehicle — drivers side

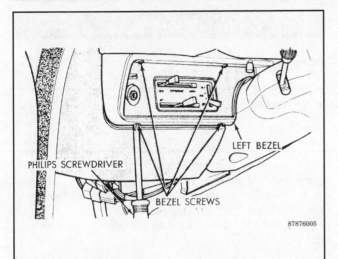

Fig. 14 The bezel has to be removed, notice the mounting locations

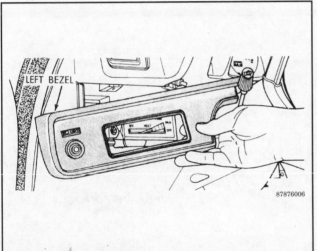

Fig. 15 Once the bezel is removed you will have access to the control assembly

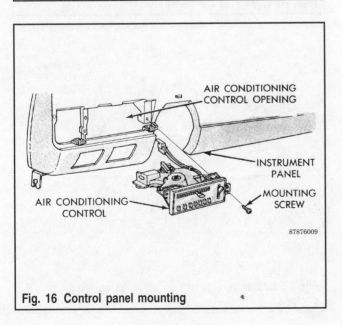

Fig. 16 Control panel mounting

Control Cables

REMOVAL, INSTALLATION AND ADJUSTMENT

▶ **See Figures 17, 18, 19, 20 and 21**

1. Remove the control assembly from the vehicle.

2. Depress the tab on the flag, then pull the temperature control cable out of the receiver on the heater control.

3. Depress the tab on the flag, then pull the temperature control cable out of the receiver on the heater assembly.

4. Pull the heater assembly end of the cable towards the right of the vehicle through the middle holes in the brake support bracket.

5. Place a ¼ in. (7mm) tube over the clip and pry the self-adjusting clip off of the core wire.

To install and adjust:

6. Position the self-adjusting clip on the cable core a 2 in. (50mm) from the small loop at the heater assembly flag end.

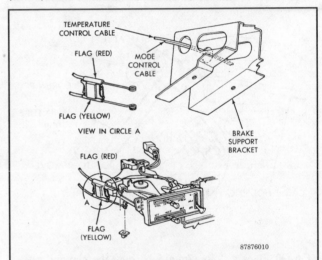

Fig. 17 Depress the flag tab, then pull the temperature control cable out of the heater control receiver

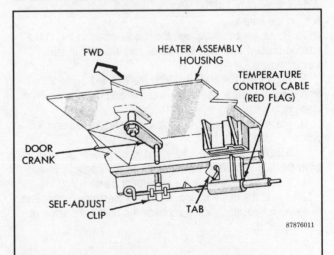

Fig. 18 Depress the flag tab, then pull the temperature control cable out of the heater \assembly

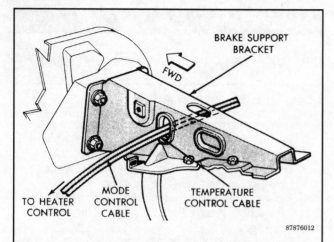

Fig. 19 Pull the heater assembly end of the cable towards the right of the vehicle through the middle holes in the brake support bracket

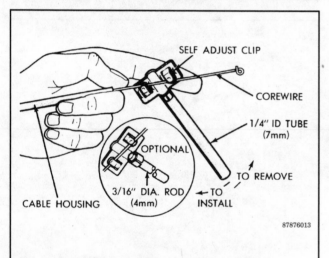

Fig. 20 Place a ¼ in. (7mm) tube over the clip and pry the self-adjusting clip off of the core wire

With a ¼ in. (7mm) tube, twist the self-adjusting clip into position on the core wire.

7. Route the cable through the middle holes in the brake support bracket and then forward of and around the main wiring harness.

8. Align the door crank pin with the clip and at the same time. Seat the cable flag in the receiver and the clip over the crank pin.

9. Place the temperature control lever in the extreme left position (cool).

10. Join the cable core wire to the control lever pin and snap the flag into the receiver on the heater control.

11. Install the heater control instrument panel.

12. Adjust the cable by moving the temperature control lever to the warm position, until it contacts the right hand edge of the bezel slot.

Heater Control (Water) Valve

REMOVAL & INSTALLATION

▶ See Figure 22

Non-Turbo

1. Drain the cooling system.
2. Locate and loosen the clamps for the control valve. Some fluid may still flow out, have a rag handy.
3. Disconnect the vacuum line and heater hoses from the valve. Mark the hoses for installation.
4. Reverse to install. Fill the cooling system, check for leaks.

Turbo

▶ See Figure 23

1. Remove the battery and tray.

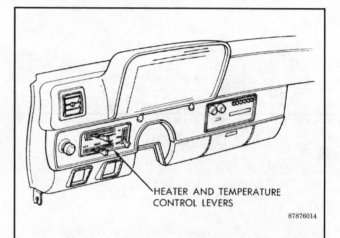

Fig. 21 Adjust the cable by moving the temperature control lever to the warm position, until it contacts the right hand edge of the bezel slot

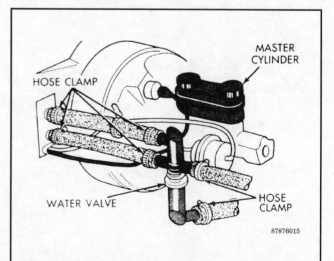

Fig. 22 Heater control (water) valve on non-turbo engines

2. Drain the engine cooling system.

3. Loosen the hose clamps to the heater control valve.

4. Disconnect the vacuum line and heater hoses from the control valve. Mark the hoses for installation.

5. Remove the attaching bolt and separate the valve from the vehicle.

6. Reverse to install.

7. Fill the cooling system and check for leaks.

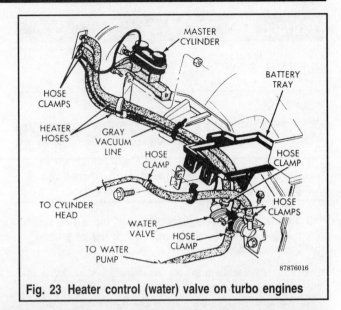

Fig. 23 Heater control (water) valve on turbo engines

AIR CONDITIONING

Compressor

REMOVAL & INSTALLATION

▶ See Figure 24

➡If a refrigerant recovery/recycling machine is not available, this job should be performed at a dealer or a shop that has this equipment.

➡Be sure to consult the laws in your area before servicing the air conditioning system. In some states, it is illegal to perform repairs involving refrigerant unless the work is done by a certified technician.

1. Properly discharge the air conditioning system into a recovery/recycling machine.

2. Disconnect the negative battery cable.

3. Disconnect the clutch electrical wiring.

4. Once the system has been discharged, unbolt the connections at the compressor and plug all four openings.

5. Loosen the A/C compressor belt idler pulley tensioning bracket mounting and pivot bolts. Remove the tension from the compressor drive belt and then remove the belt.

6. Support the compressor. Remove the two mounting bolts from the lower side of the compressor, then the two mounting nuts from above it. Remove the compressor.

To install:

7. Install the compressor in reverse order, noting these points:

   a. Tighten the attaching nuts and bolts to 40 ft. lbs. (54 Nm).

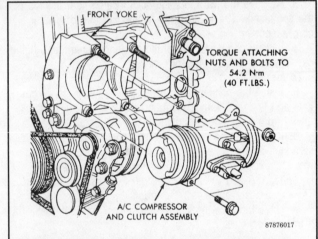

Fig. 24 The A/C compressor and clutch assembly fits on the mounted studs as seen here on the 2.2L engine — 1989 shown

   b. Make sure sealing surfaces are clean and free of scratches and replace gaskets. Gaskets are specific to suction and discharge fittings, so fit them according to the number of pilots on the fitting and/or number of holes in the gasket. Make the connections, install the bolts, then tighten them to 170-230 inch lbs. (19-26 Nm).

   c. Have the system thoroughly evacuated at a repair shop and then have it recharged.

Condenser

REMOVAL & INSTALLATION

▶ See Figure 25

> **✳✳CAUTION**
>
> The air conditioning system in filled with refrigerant under high pressure. The refrigerant must be discharged before you can safely work on any of the components.

➡️ If a refrigerant recovery/recycling machine is not available, this job should be performed at a dealer or a shop that has this equipment.

1. Properly discharge the air conditioning system into a recovery/recycling machine.
2. Remove the refrigerant line attaching nut and separate the lines at the condenser sealing plate. Immediately cap the ends with a plastic cap designed for this purpose or with plastic sheeting and tape.
3. Remove the two mounting bolts located near the top of the condenser. These attach the condenser to the radiator core support.
4. Lift the condenser out of the engine compartment, being careful not to damage fins or piping.

To install:

5. Install the condenser in reverse order. Replace all gaskets and O-rings. O-rings must be coated with refrigerant oil drawn from an unopened container prior to installation.
6. If the condenser used is a new one, make sure to have oil added to the system to replace that which was removed with the old compressor. This requires specialized service knowledge. A 500 SUS viscosity, wax-free oil must be used. The compressor holds 198-212 grams.
7. Have the system evacuated, charged and leak tested by a trained technician.

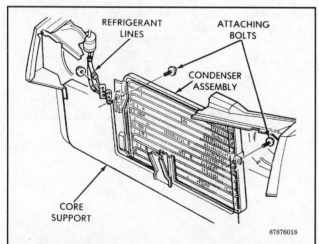

Fig. 25 Remove the two mounting bolts located near the top of the condenser. These attach the condenser to the radiator core support

Blower Motor

1. Disconnect the negative battery cable.
2. Remove the three screws securing the glovebox to the instrument panel.
3. Disconnect the wiring from the blower and case.
4. Remove the blower vent tube from the case.
5. Loosen the recirculating door from the bracket and remove the actuator from the housing. Leave the vacuum lines attached.
6. Remove the seven screws attaching the recirculating housing to the air conditioning unit and remove the housing.
7. Remove the three mounting flange nuts and washers.
8. Remove the blower motor from the unit.
9. Installation is the reverse of removal. Replace any damaged sealer.

Evaporator Case

REMOVAL & INSTALLATION

1978-79 Models

➡️ If a refrigerant recovery/recycling machine is not available, this job should be performed at a dealer or a shop that has this equipment. During installation, a small can of refrigerant oil will be necessary.

1. Properly discharge the air conditioning system into a recovery/recycling machine.
2. Disconnect the negative battery cable.
3. Drain the coolant.

> **✳✳CAUTION**
>
> When draining the coolant, keep in mind that cats and dogs are attracted by ethylene glycol antifreeze, and are quite likely to drink any that is left in an uncovered container or in puddles on the ground. This will prove fatal in sufficient quantity. Always drain the coolant into a sealable container. Coolant should be reused unless it is contaminated or several years old.

4. Part the temperature door cable from the heater-evaporator unit.
5. Disconnect the temperature door cable from the retaining clips.
6. Remove the glove box.
7. Disconnect the vacuum harness from the control head.
8. Disconnect the blower motor lead and anti-diesel relay wire.
9. Remove the seven screws fastening the right trim bezel to the instrument panel. Starting at the right side, swing the bezel clear and remove it.
10. Remove the three screws on the bottom of the center distribution duct cover and slide the cover rearward and remove it.
11. Remove the center distribution duct.
12. Remove the defroster duct adaptor.

13. Remove the H-type expansion valve, located on the right side of the firewall:

   a. Remove the 5/16 in. bolt in the center of the plumbing sealing plate.

   b. Carefully pull the refrigerant lines toward the front of the car, taking care to avoid scratching the valve sealing surfaces.

   c. Remove the two 1/4-20 Allen head cap screws and remove the valve.

14. Cap the pipe openings at once. Wrap the valve in a plastic bag.

15. Disconnect the hoses from the core tubes.

16. Disconnect the vacuum lines at the intake manifold and water valve.

17. Remove the unit-to-firewall retaining nuts.

18. Take off the panel support bracket.

19. Remove the right cowl lower panel.

20. Take off the instrument panel pivot bracket screw from the right side.

21. Remove the screws securing the lower instrument panel at the steering column.

22. Pull back the carpet from under the unit as far as possible.

23. Remove the nut from the evaporator-heater unit-to-plenum mounting brace and blower motor ground cable. While supporting the unit, remove the brace from its stud.

24. Lift the unit, pulling it rearward to allow clearance. These operations may require two people.

25. Slowly lower the unit taking care to keep the studs from hanging-up on the insulation.

26. When the unit reaches the floor, slide it rearward until it is out from under the instrument panel.

27. Remove the unit from the car.

To install:

❄❄WARNING

When installing the unit in the car, care must be taken that the vacuum lines to the engine compartment do not hang-up on the accelerator or become trapped between the unit and the firewall. If this happens, kinked lines will result and the unit will have to be removed to free them. Proper routing of these lines will require two people. The portion of the vacuum harness which is routed through the steering column support MUST be positioned BEFORE the distribution housing is installed. The harness MUST be routed ABOVE the temperature control cable.

28. Place the unit on the floor as far under the panel as possible.

29. Raise the unit carefully, at the same time pull the lower instrument panel rearward as far as possible.

30. Position the unit in place and attach the brace to the stud.

31. Install the lower ground cable and attach the nut.

32. Install and tighten the unit-to-firewall nuts.

33. Reposition the carpet and install, but do not tighten the right instrument panel pivot bracket screw.

34. Place a piece of sheet metal or thin cardboard against the evaporator-heater assembly to center the assembly duct seal.

35. Position the center distributor duct in place making sure that the upper left tab comes in through the left center air conditioning outlet opening and that each air take-off is properly inserted in its respective outlet.

➡**Make sure that the radio wiring connector does not interfere with the duct.**

36. Install and tighten the screw securing the upper left tab of the center air distribution duct to the instrument panel.

37. Take out the sheet metal or cardboard from between the unit and the duct.

➡**Make sure that the unit seal is properly aligned with the duct opening.**

38. Install and tighten the two lower screws fastening the center distribution duct to the instrument panel.

39. Place and tighten the screws securing the lower instrument panel at the steering column.

40. Install and tighten the nut securing the instrument panel to the support bracket.

41. Make sure that the seal on the unit is properly aligned and seated against the distribution duct assembly.

42. Tighten the instrument panel pivot bracket screw and install the right cowl lower trim.

43. Slide the distributor duct cover assembly onto the center distribution duct so that the notches lock into the tabs and the tabs slide over the rear and side ledges of the center duct assembly.

44. Install the three screws securing the ducting.

45. Install the right trim bezel.

46. Join the vacuum harness to the control head.

47. Connect the blower lead and the anti-diesel wire.

48. Install the glove box.

49. Connect the temperature door cable.

50. Install new O-rings on the evaporator plate and the plumbing plate. Coat the new O-rings with clean refrigerant oil.

51. Place the H-valve against the evaporator sealing plate surface, then install the two 1/2-20 through-bolts. Tighten to 6-10 ft. lbs. (8-14 Nm).

52. Carefully hold the refrigerant line connector against the valve, then install the 5/16-18 bolt. Tighten to 14-20 ft. lbs. (19-27 Nm).

53. Install the heater hoses at the core tubes.

54. Connect the vacuum lines at the manifold and water valve.

55. Install the condensate drain tube.

56. Have the system evacuated, charged and leak tested by a trained technician.

1980-89 Models

➡**If a refrigerant recovery/recycling machine is not available, this job should be performed at a dealer or a shop that has this equipment.**

1. Properly discharge the air conditioning system into a recovery/recycling machine.

2. Drain the cooling system.

❋❋CAUTION

When draining the coolant, keep in mind that cats and dogs are attracted by ethylene glycol antifreeze, and are quite likely to drink any that is left in an uncovered container or in puddles on the ground. This will prove fatal in sufficient quantity. Always drain the coolant into a sealable container. Coolant should be reused unless it is contaminated or several years old.

3. Disconnect the negative battery cable.
4. Disengage the heater hoses at the core tubes. Cap the tube openings to prevent spillage.
5. Separate the vacuum lines at the intake manifold and the water valve. Tag the lines for installation.
6. Remove the "H" valve:
   a. Disconnect the wire from the low pressure cut-off switch.
   b. Remove the bolt in the center of the plumbing sealing plate.
   c. Pull the refrigerant line assembly toward the front of the car. Take care to avoid scratching the valve sealing surfaces with the tube pilots.
   d. Hold the "H" valve, remove the two Allen head screws and lift out the valve.
7. Unclamp and remove the condensation drain.
8. Remove the nuts holding the heater/evaporator case to the firewall.
9. Depress the tab and unhook the cable retainer from the case.
10. Remove the glove compartment.
11. Disconnect the vacuum harness from the air conditioning control head.
12. Separate the blower feed wire and the anti-diesel solenoid wires.
13. Remove the seven screws retaining the right trim bezel to the instrument panel. Starting at the right side, swing the trim bezel clear of the panel and remove it.
14. Remove the three screws securing the center distribution duct to the instrument panel and remove it.
15. Remove the defroster duct adapter.
16. Take off the instrument panel support bracket.
17. Remove the instrument panel pivot bracket screw from the right side.
18. Extract the screws securing the instrument panel to the steering column.
19. Pull the carpet away from the case.
20. Remove the nut securing the case to the plenum and ground cable.
21. Support the case and remove the plenum bracket.
22. Lift the case and pull it rearward as far as possible to clear the panel. The lower panel may have to be pulled rearward to aid in case removal.

➡Two people will make this job a lot easier.

23. When the case clears the panel, lower it slowly so that the studs don't hang up in the panel liner.

24. Lower the case to the floor and remove it from the car.

❋❋WARNING

When installing the unit, make sure that none of the vacuum lines are kinked. Kinked lines would require removal of the unit again.

25. Place the case on the floor as far forward as possible.
26. Lift the unit being careful of the studs. Manipulate the panel to aid installation of the case.
   To install:
27. Attach the brace to the stud. Install the ground wire and tighten the nut.
28. Install and tighten the case-to-firewall nuts.
29. Connect the drain tube.
30. Install the heater hoses.
31. Install the vacuum lines.
32. Install the "H" valve.
33. Reposition the carpet.
34. Install, but don't tighten the right side instrument panel pivot bracket screw.
35. Install the defroster duct adapter, making certain that the opening is properly aligned.
36. Place a piece of thin cardboard against the evaporator/heater assembly-to-center distribution duct seal.
37. Position the center distribution duct in place. Make sure that the upper left tab comes out through the left center duct. Each end air outlet must be properly aligned with its respective spot cooler.

➡Be certain that the radio wiring connector does not interfere with the center duct.

38. Install and tighten the screw retaining the upper left tab of the center duct.
39. Remove the cardboard. Make sure that the evaporator/heater seal is properly aligned with the top of the center duct opening.
40. Install and tighten the two lower center duct-to-panel screws.
41. Install all remaining parts in the reverse of the removal sequence. Fill the cooling system. Evacuate, charge and leak test the air conditioning system.

Evaporator Core

REMOVAL & INSTALLATION

➡Core removal requires removal of the entire heater assembly.

1. Remove the heater/evaporator assembly.
2. Place the unit on a workbench. On the inside-the-car side, remove the $1/4$-20 in. nut from the mode door actuator on the top cover and the two retaining clips from the front edge of the cover. To remove the mode door actuator, remove the two screws securing it to the cover.
3. Remove the fifteen screws attaching the cover to the assembly and lift off the cover. Lift the mode door out of the unit.

4. Remove the screw from the core retaining bracket and lift out the core.

5. Place the core in the unit and install the bracket.

6. Install the actuator arm.

Receiver Drier

REMOVAL & INSTALLATION

➡If a refrigerant recovery/recycling machine is not available, this job should be performed at a dealer or a shop that has this equipment.

ENTERTAINMENT SYSTEMS

Radio, Receiver Assembly

REMOVAL & INSTALLATION

▶ **See Figures 26, 27, 28, 29, 30, 31 and 32**

1. Pull the radio knobs, mounting nuts and washers off the unit.

2. Slide the radio faceplate off.

3. Open the ashtray.

4. Remove the bezel attaching screws, then open the glove compartment.

5. Remove the bezel, guiding the right end around the glove compartment and away from the panel.

6. If equipped, remove the other faceplate on the radio.

7. Disconnect the radio ground strap and remove the two radio mounting screws.

8. Pull the radio from the panel and disconnect the wiring and antenna lead.

9. Installation is the reverse of removal.

1. Properly discharge the air conditioning system into a recovery/recycling machine.

2. Remove the two high pressure retaining nuts from the sides of the drier assembly. Carefully separate the lines from the drier.

3. Plug the open lines.

4. Remove the strap bolts, then lift the drier from the vehicle.

5. Replace all the O-rings and gaskets with new ones. Coat the sealing surfaces with wax free refrigerant oil, then reverse to install.

Fig. 27 Next remove the mounting nuts and washers from the front of the radio

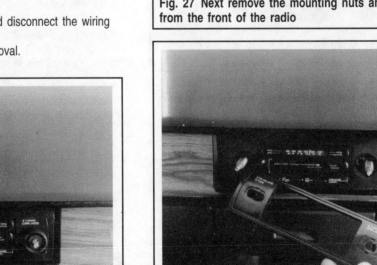

Fig. 28 Slide the radio faceplate off

Fig. 26 Pull the radio knobs off

AM, AM/FM monaural, or AM/FM stereo multiplex units are available.

Fig. 29 Unscrew the face plate mounting screws

Fig. 30 Open the glove compartment to access other screws, then remove the bezel

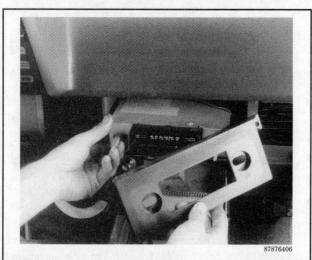
Fig. 31 If equipped, remove the other faceplate on the radio

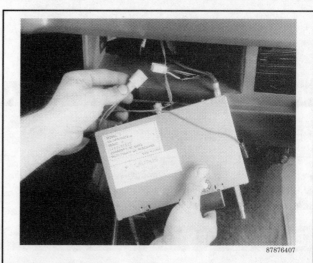
Fig. 32 Pull the radio from its mounting and disconnect the wiring

Antenna

TRIMMING

▶ See Figure 33

All radios are trimmed at the factory and should require no further adjustment. However, after a repair or if the antenna trim is to be verified, proceed as follows:
1. Turn radio on.
2. Manually tune the radio to a weak station between 1400 and 1600 KHz on AM.
3. Increase the volume and set the tone control to full treble (clockwise).
4. Viewing the radio from the front, the trimmer control is a slot-head located at the rear of the right side. Adjust it carefully by turning it back and forth with a flat-bladed tool until maximum loudness is achieved.

➡ Some 1978 and early production 1979 cars exhibit an ignition noise interfering with radio reception. This can be corrected by installing the following items:

• Ground strap, engine-mount-to-frame — Chrysler Part No. 5211212
• Ground strap, engine-to-cowl — Chrysler Part No. 5211211
• Ground strap, air conditioning evaporator-to-cowl — Chrysler Part No. 5211210
Ground straps can also be obtained in kit form from local radio or CB shops.

REMOVAL & INSTALLATION

▶ See Figures 34, 35, 36 and 37

1. Remove the radio from the vehicle.
2. Unplug the antenna lead from the radio.
3. Unscrew the antenna mast from the body of the vehicle.
4. Remove the cap nut, tool C-4816 or an equivalent may be used.

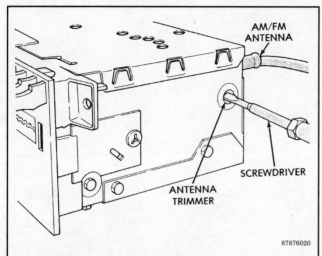

Fig. 33 The antenna trimmer is located on the side of the radio

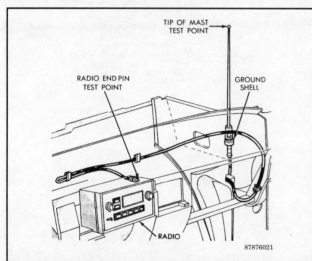

Fig. 34 As you can see the antenna wire leads from the mast to the radio

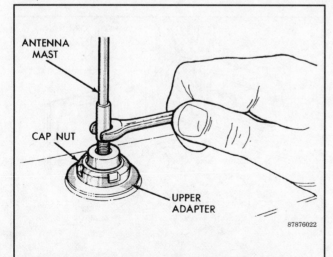

Fig. 35 Using a wrench, or your hands if it isn't too tight, unscrew the mast

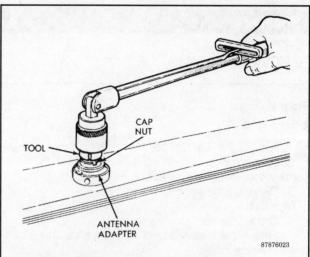

Fig. 36 Remove the cap nut, tool C-4816 or an equivalent may be used

5. Remove the antenna adapter and gasket.

6. Unfasten the pins from the rear of the plastic fender well, then bend the shield out of the way.

7. From under the fender, remove the antenna lead and body assembly.

To install:

8. Install the antenna body and cable from underneath the fender.

9. Install the gasket, adapter and cap nut. Tighten the cap nut to 125 inch lbs. (14 Nm). You may need tool C-4816 or an equivalent.

10. Attach the antenna mast to the body until the sleeve bottoms on thew antenna body.

11. Route the cable to the radio.

12. Install the radio.

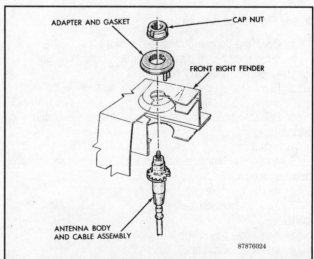

Fig. 37 Once the cap nut is removed, the cable body can be pulled from the inner fender well

Speakers

REMOVAL & INSTALLATION

Front Monaural
▶ **See Figure 38**

1. Remove the cowl trim pad.
2. Loosen the speaker mounting screws, then lift the speaker from the attaching panel.
3. Disengage the wiring to the speaker.

To install:

4. Connect the wiring for the speaker.
5. Position the speaker into its mounting place, then install and tighten the screws.
6. Attach the cowl trim pad.

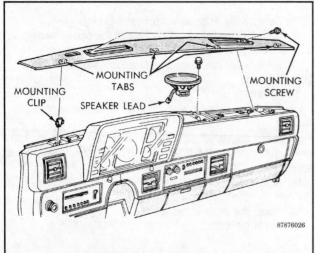

Fig. 38 After lifting the cowl trim pad, you can access the speaker

Door
▶ **See Figures 39 and 40**

1. Open the door and remove the trim panel.
2. If the door has a plastic sheet under the trim panel, carefully peel it aside. Try not to rip it.
3. Remove the screws attaching the speaker to the door shell.
4. Pull the speaker out of the door shell, unfasten the wiring.

To install:

5. Attach the wiring to the speaker, then insert the speaker into the door shell.
6. Install the mounting screws and tighten.
7. Test the speaker before replacing the plastic and trim panel.
8. Apply the plastic sheet in place.
9. Install the trim panel.

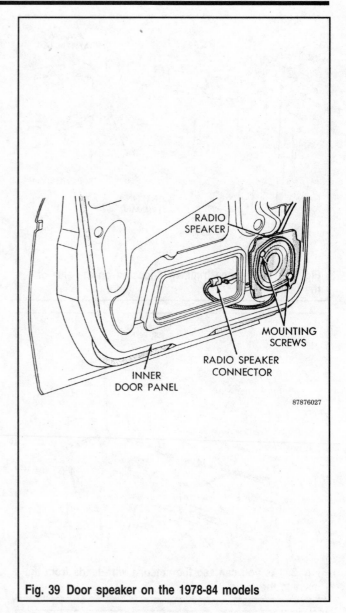

Fig. 39 Door speaker on the 1978-84 models

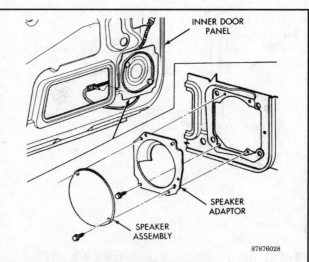

Fig. 40 For the 1984-89 models the speaker has an adapter which stays in place on removal

RADIO DIAGNOSIS

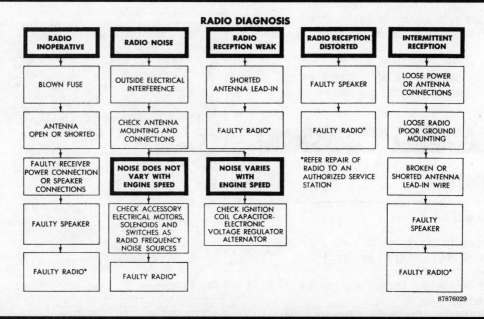

RADIO INOPERATIVE	RADIO NOISE	RADIO RECEPTION WEAK	RADIO RECEPTION DISTORTED	INTERMITTENT RECEPTION
BLOWN FUSE	OUTSIDE ELECTRICAL INTERFERENCE	SHORTED ANTENNA LEAD-IN	FAULTY SPEAKER	LOOSE POWER OR ANTENNA CONNECTIONS
ANTENNA OPEN OR SHORTED	CHECK ANTENNA MOUNTING AND CONNECTIONS	FAULTY RADIO*	FAULTY RADIO*	LOOSE RADIO (POOR GROUND) MOUNTING
FAULTY RECEIVER POWER CONNECTION OR SPEAKER CONNECTIONS	NOISE DOES NOT VARY WITH ENGINE SPEED	NOISE VARIES WITH ENGINE SPEED	*REFER REPAIR OF RADIO TO AN AUTHORIZED SERVICE STATION	BROKEN OR SHORTED ANTENNA LEAD-IN WIRE
FAULTY SPEAKER	CHECK ACCESSORY ELECTRICAL MOTORS, SOLENOIDS AND SWITCHES AS RADIO FREQUENCY NOISE SOURCES	CHECK IGNITION COIL CAPACITOR-ELECTRONIC VOLTAGE REGULATOR ALTERNATOR		FAULTY SPEAKER
FAULTY RADIO*	FAULTY RADIO*			FAULTY RADIO*

87876029

WINDSHIELD WIPERS AND WASHERS

Front Wiper Blade

REMOVAL & INSTALLATION

▶ **See Figure 41**

1. Lift the wiper arm away from the glass.
2. Depress the release lever on the bridge and remove the blade assembly from the arm.
3. Lift the tab and pinch the end bridge to release it from the center bridge.
4. Slide the end bridge from the blade element and the element from the opposite end bridge.
5. Assembly is the reverse of removal. Make sure that the element locking tabs are securely locked in position.

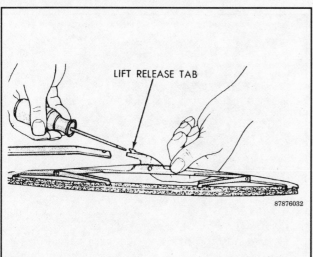

LIFT RELEASE TAB

87876032

Fig. 41 Depress the release lever on the bridge and remove the blade assembly from the arm

Front Wiper Arm

REMOVAL & INSTALLATION

▶ **See Figure 42**

1. Lift the arm to permit the latch to be pulled out to the holding position, then release.
2. Remove the arm from the pivot using a rocking motion.
3. The arm should be up off the windshield so not to scratch the surface.
   To install:
4. Position the arm on the pivot shaft.
5. Push down the arm in place, make sure it is secure.
6. Run the motor to the park position.

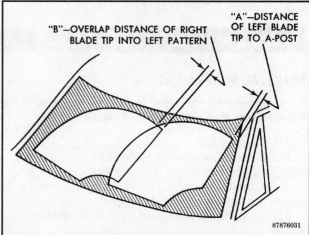

"B"—OVERLAP DISTANCE OF RIGHT BLADE TIP INTO LEFT PATTERN

"A"—DISTANCE OF LEFT BLADE TIP TO A-POST

87876031

Fig. 42 Check that the blades do not hit the outer windshield moulding, if they do, remove the arms and start the adjusting process over

7. Adjust the arm by measuring the distance from the bottom of the windshield moulding. The distance should be $\frac{1}{2}$-$2\frac{1}{2}$ in. (13-63mm).

8. Operate the wipers at low speed.

9. Check that the blades do not hit the outer windshield moulding, if they do, remove the arms and start the adjusting process over.

Rear Wiper Blade and Arm

REMOVAL & INSTALLATION

▶ See Figures 43 and 44

1. Turn the wipers on and position the blade at a convenient place on the glass by turning the ignition **OFF**.

2. Lift the wiper arm off the glass.

3. Depress the release lever on the center bridge and remove the center bridge.

4. Depress the release button on the end bridge to release it from the center bridge.

5. Remove the wiper blade from the end bridge.

6. To remove the arm, pull out the latch knob and remove the arm from the pivot.

7. Installation is the reverse of removal. Be sure the element is engaged in all 4 bridge claws.

Front Wiper Motor

REMOVAL & INSTALLATION

▶ See Figures 45, 46, 47, 48, 49 and 50

1. Disconnect the linkage from the motor crank arm.

2. Remove the wiper motor plastic cover.

3. Disengage the wiring harness from the motor.

4. Remove the three mounting bolts from the motor bracket and remove the motor.

5. Installation is the reverse of removal.

Rear Wiper Motor

REMOVAL & INSTALLATION

▶ See Figures 51, 52, 53, 54, 55, 56 and 57

1. Open the liftgate.

2. Remove the wiper motor plastic cover.

3. Take off the blade and arm assembly.

4. Remove the chrome nut from the pivot shaft and the chrome ring from the pivot shaft.

5. From inside the tailgate, remove the motor mounting screws.

6. Disconnect the main liftgate wiring harness from the motor pigtail wire.

7. Remove the motor.

8. Installation is the reverse of removal.

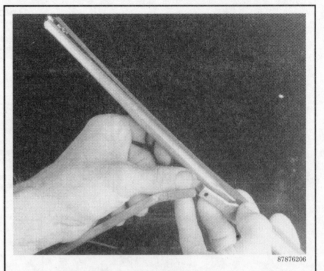

Fig. 43 Remove the wiper blade from the end bridge

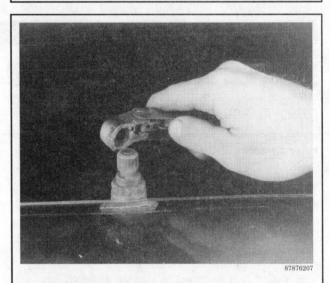

Fig. 44 Remove the arm from the pivot

Fig. 45 Disconnect the wiper linkage from the crank arm

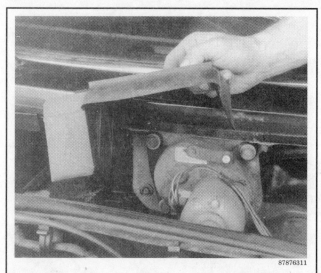

Fig. 46 Release the motor cover, then put aside

Fig. 47 Disconnect the wiring harness from the motor

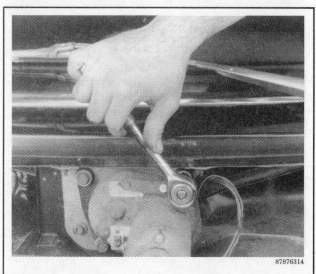

Fig. 48 Remove the wiper motor mounting screws

Windshield Washer Reservoir and Pump

REMOVAL & INSTALLATION

Front

▶ See Figure 58

1. Open the hood and disconnect the wiring harness from the pump.
2. Remove the sheet metal screws holding the reservoir to the inner fender shield.
3. Disconnect the washer hose and remove the reservoir. Keep your thumb over the liquid outlet to avoid spilling the washer solvent on painted surfaces.
4. Drain the reservoir to remove the pump. Insert a $^{19}/_{32}$ in. socket and extension through the filler opening and remove the pump filter and nut.
5. Disconnect the outside portion of the pump and remove the inner and outer portions of the pump.
6. Installation is the reverse of removal. Be sure the rubber grommet is in place when installing the pump.

Rear

▶ See Figure 59

1. Open the liftgate.
2. Remove the plastic cap and mounting retainer from the reservoir filler on the right side of the liftgate. Reach through the side drain and remove the sheet metal screws.
3. Disconnect the wiring from the pump.
4. Remove the 2 side panel reservoir mounting screws.
5. Disconnect the washer hose from the reservoir.
6. Remove the reservoir and pump from the side panel through the aperture panel access hole. Try not to spill windshield washer solvent on the paint.
7. Drain the reservoir to remove the pump. Insert a $^{19}/_{32}$ in. socket and extension through the filler opening and remove the pump filter and nut.
8. Disconnect the outside portion of the pump and remove the inner and outer parts of the pump.
9. Installation is the reverse of removal. Be sure the rubber grommet is in place when installing the pump.

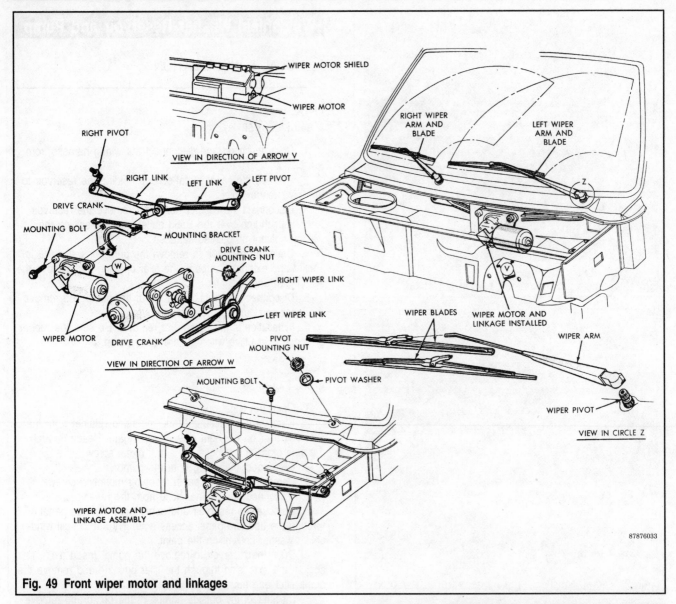

WIPER MOTOR SHIELD

WIPER MOTOR

VIEW IN DIRECTION OF ARROW V

RIGHT WIPER ARM AND BLADE

LEFT WIPER ARM AND BLADE

RIGHT PIVOT

RIGHT LINK

LEFT LINK

LEFT PIVOT

DRIVE CRANK

MOUNTING BOLT

MOUNTING BRACKET

DRIVE CRANK MOUNTING NUT

WIPER MOTOR

DRIVE CRANK

RIGHT WIPER LINK

LEFT WIPER LINK

VIEW IN DIRECTION OF ARROW W

WIPER BLADES

WIPER MOTOR AND LINKAGE INSTALLED

WIPER ARM

PIVOT MOUNTING NUT

MOUNTING BOLT

PIVOT WASHER

WIPER PIVOT

VIEW IN CIRCLE Z

WIPER MOTOR AND LINKAGE ASSEMBLY

87876033

Fig. 49 Front wiper motor and linkages

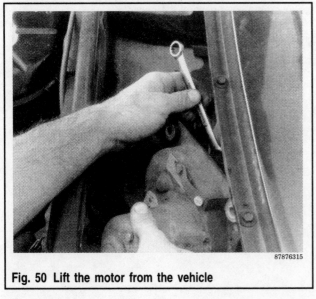

87876315

Fig. 50 Lift the motor from the vehicle

87876218

Fig. 51 Remove the wiper motor plastic cover

Fig. 52 Using a wrench, loosen the nut on the wiper shaft

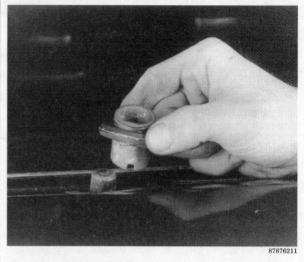

Fig. 55 Pull the shaft cover off

Fig. 53 Remove the chrome nut . . .

Fig. 56 From inside the tailgate, remove the motor mounting screws

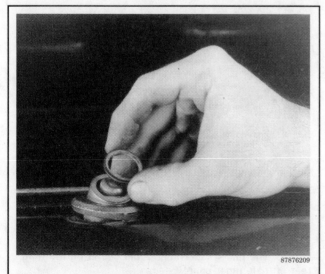

Fig. 54 . . . and the chrome ring

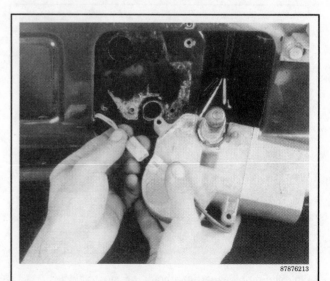

Fig. 57 Disconnect the wiring to the motor

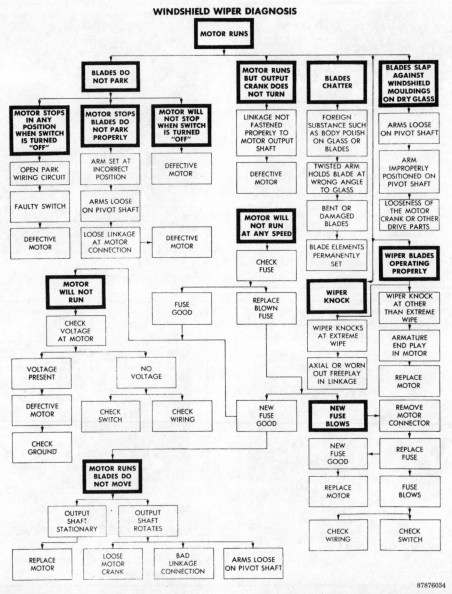

WINDSHIELD WIPER DIAGNOSIS

```
                              MOTOR RUNS
```

BLADES DO NOT PARK

- **MOTOR STOPS IN ANY POSITION WHEN SWITCH IS TURNED "OFF"**
  - OPEN PARK WIRING CIRCUIT
  - FAULTY SWITCH
  - DEFECTIVE MOTOR

- **MOTOR STOPS BLADES DO NOT PARK PROPERLY**
  - ARM SET AT INCORRECT POSITION
  - ARMS LOOSE ON PIVOT SHAFT
  - LOOSE LINKAGE AT MOTOR CONNECTION

- **MOTOR WILL NOT STOP WHEN SWITCH IS TURNED "OFF"**
  - DEFECTIVE MOTOR

- DEFECTIVE MOTOR

MOTOR WILL NOT RUN
- CHECK VOLTAGE AT MOTOR
  - VOLTAGE PRESENT
    - DEFECTIVE MOTOR
    - CHECK GROUND
  - NO VOLTAGE
    - CHECK SWITCH
    - CHECK WIRING

MOTOR RUNS BLADES DO NOT MOVE
- OUTPUT SHAFT STATIONARY
  - REPLACE MOTOR
- OUTPUT SHAFT ROTATES
  - LOOSE MOTOR CRANK
  - BAD LINKAGE CONNECTION
  - ARMS LOOSE ON PIVOT SHAFT

MOTOR RUNS BUT OUTPUT CRANK DOES NOT TURN
- LINKAGE NOT FASTENED PROPERLY TO MOTOR OUTPUT SHAFT
- DEFECTIVE MOTOR

MOTOR WILL NOT RUN AT ANY SPEED
- CHECK FUSE
  - FUSE GOOD
  - REPLACE BLOWN FUSE
    - NEW FUSE GOOD

BLADES CHATTER
- FOREIGN SUBSTANCE SUCH AS BODY POLISH ON GLASS OR BLADES
- TWISTED ARM HOLDS BLADE AT WRONG ANGLE TO GLASS
- BENT OR DAMAGED BLADES
- BLADE ELEMENTS PERMANENTLY SET

WIPER KNOCK
- WIPER KNOCKS AT EXTREME WIPE
- AXIAL OR WORN OUT FREEPLAY IN LINKAGE

NEW FUSE BLOWS
- NEW FUSE GOOD
  - REPLACE MOTOR
    - CHECK WIRING

BLADES SLAP AGAINST WINDSHIELD MOULDINGS ON DRY GLASS
- ARMS LOOSE ON PIVOT SHAFT
- ARM IMPROPERLY POSITIONED ON PIVOT SHAFT
- LOOSENESS OF THE MOTOR CRANK OR OTHER DRIVE PARTS

WIPER BLADES OPERATING PROPERLY
- WIPER KNOCK AT OTHER THAN EXTREME WIPE
- ARMATURE END PLAY IN MOTOR
- REPLACE MOTOR
- REMOVE MOTOR CONNECTOR
  - REPLACE FUSE
    - FUSE BLOWS
      - CHECK SWITCH

87876034

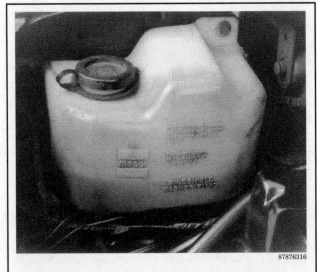

Fig. 58 Front washer fluid bottle on most vehicles

87876316

Fig. 59 The rear washer fluid bottle cap is on the right rear lift gate inner panel

87876317

INSTRUMENT AND SWITCHES

The fuel, temperature and oil pressure gauges work on the constant voltage principle through a common voltage limiter which pulses to provide intermittent current to the gauge system.

Instrument Cluster

REMOVAL & INSTALLATION

1978-83 Models

▶ **See Figures 60, 61 and 62**

1. Remove the two lens assembly lower attaching retaining springs by pulling rearward with a pliers.
2. Allow the lens assembly to drop as it is pulled rearward.
3. Remove the speedometer assembly, usually two screws.
4. Remove the two wiring harness connectors.
5. Remove the two (1978-79), or four (1980-83) cluster attaching screws.
6. In 1978-79 only, pull the two upper spring retainers away from the panel.
7. If equipped with a clock, reach behind the panel and disconnect the wires.
8. Remove the cluster assembly.
To install:
9. Installation is the reverse of removal.

Rattles in a 1978 or 1979 instrument cluster may be caused by loose or missing upper cluster mounting clips. To correct rattles, use a screw Chrysler Part No 9414172 in the screw holes provided in the upper part of the cluster.

1984-89 Models

▶ **See Figures 63 and 64**

1. Remove the two lower cluster bezel retaining screws.
2. Allow the bezel to drop slightly as it is moved rearward and remove the bezel.

Fig. 60 Instrument panel on the 1980 Omni

3. Remove the four screws attaching the cluster to the base panel.

4. Pull the cluster rearward and disconnect the speedometer cable and the wiring connector.
5. Remove the cluster assembly from the instrument panel.
6. To install, reverse the removal procedure.

Speedometer Head

REMOVAL & INSTALLATION

▶ **See Figure 65**

1. Remove the cluster bezel and mask assemblies.
2. On some models you will need to remove the voltmeter gauge.
3. If used, remove the head mounting screws, then slip the head from the cluster.
4. Pull the cluster rearward and disengage from the pins.
To install:
5. If head mounting screws are used, attach the head, then tighten securely. If not, position the speedometer head on the gauge pins, then push firmly until seated.
6. Secure the speedometer head to the cluster housing with the attaching screws.
7. Install the cluster mask and bezel.

Speedometer Cable

REMOVAL & INSTALLATION

▶ **See Figures 66 and 67**

1. Reach under the instrument panel and depress the spring clip retaining the cable to the speedometer head. Pull the cable back and away from the head.
2. If the core is broken, raise and support the vehicle and remove the cable retaining screw from the cable bracket. Carefully slide the cable out of the transaxle.
To install:
3. Coat the new core sparingly with speedometer cable lubricant, then insert it in the cable.
4. Install the cable at the transaxle.
5. Lower the car and insert the cable into the speedometer head.

Ammeter Gauge

REMOVAL & INSTALLATION

1978-82 Models

▶ **See Figure 68**

1. Remove the speedometer assembly.

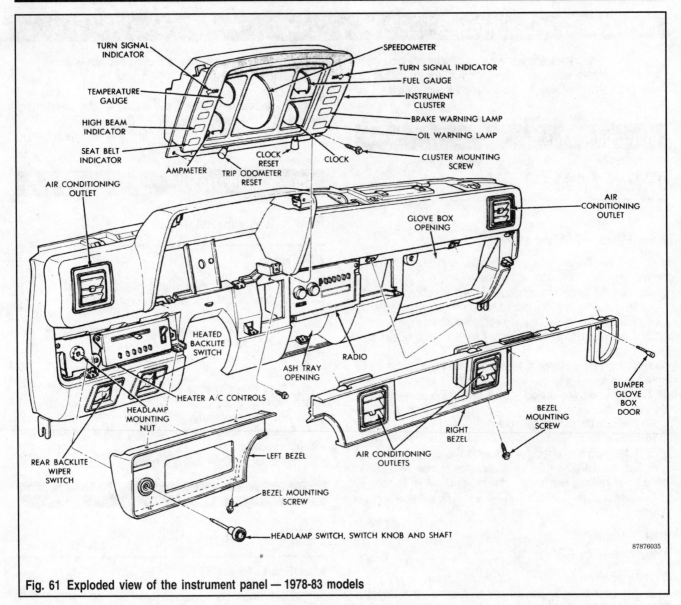

TURN SIGNAL INDICATOR
SPEEDOMETER
TURN SIGNAL INDICATOR
FUEL GAUGE
TEMPERATURE GAUGE
INSTRUMENT CLUSTER
HIGH BEAM INDICATOR
BRAKE WARNING LAMP
OIL WARNING LAMP
SEAT BELT INDICATOR
CLUSTER MOUNTING SCREW
AMPMETER
CLOCK RESET
TRIP ODOMETER RESET
CLOCK
AIR CONDITIONING OUTLET
GLOVE BOX OPENING
AIR CONDITIONING OUTLET
HEATED BACKLITE SWITCH
ASH TRAY OPENING
RADIO
BUMPER GLOVE BOX DOOR
HEADLAMP MOUNTING NUT
HEATER A/C CONTROLS
BEZEL MOUNTING SCREW
RIGHT BEZEL
REAR BACKLITE WIPER SWITCH
LEFT BEZEL
AIR CONDITIONING OUTLETS
BEZEL MOUNTING SCREW
HEADLAMP SWITCH, SWITCH KNOB AND SHAFT

87876035

Fig. 61 Exploded view of the instrument panel — 1978-83 models

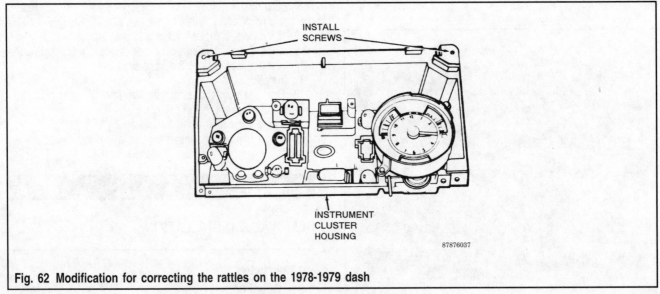

INSTALL SCREWS

INSTRUMENT CLUSTER HOUSING

87876037

Fig. 62 Modification for correcting the rattles on the 1978-1979 dash

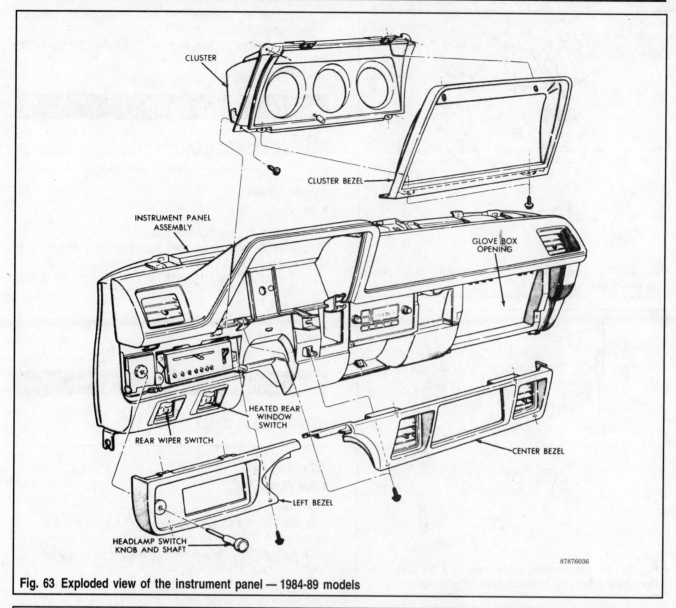

Fig. 63 Exploded view of the instrument panel — 1984-89 models

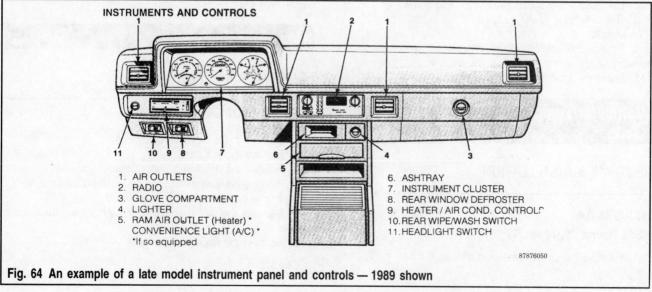

Fig. 64 An example of a late model instrument panel and controls — 1989 shown

INSTRUMENTS AND CONTROLS

1. AIR OUTLETS
2. RADIO
3. GLOVE COMPARTMENT
4. LIGHTER
5. RAM AIR OUTLET (Heater) *
   CONVENIENCE LIGHT (A/C) *
   *If so equipped

6. ASHTRAY
7. INSTRUMENT CLUSTER
8. REAR WINDOW DEFROSTER
9. HEATER / AIR COND. CONTROLS
10. REAR WIPE/WASH SWITCH
11. HEADLIGHT SWITCH

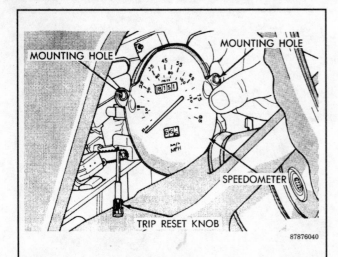

Fig. 65 The speedometer head is mounted into a hole on the cluster assembly

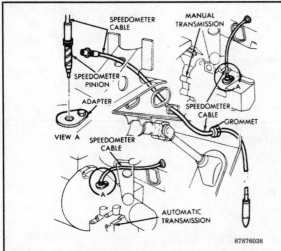

Fig. 66 The speedometer cable runs from the transaxle, through the firewall, to the speedometer head

2. Unthread the ammeter gauge mounting screws.
3. Remove the ammeter gauge from the cluster assembly.
To install:
4. Position the ammeter gauge into place in the cluster housing. Attach with the mounting screws.
5. Install the speedometer head assembly.

Voltmeter/Temperature/Oil Pressure Gauge

REMOVAL & INSTALLATION

1983-89 Models
▶ **See Figures 69, 70 and 71**

1. Remove the cluster bezel and mask.

2. Unscrew the attaching voltmeter/temperature/oil pressure gage assembly from the cluster.
3. Pull rearward to disengage the gauge from the mounting pins.
4. Reverse to install.

Fuel/Temperature Gauge

REMOVAL & INSTALLATION

1978-82 Models
▶ **See Figures 72 and 73**

1. Remove the speedometer assembly.
2. Unthread the fuel and temperature gauge mounting screws.
3. Remove the fuel and temperature gauge from the cluster assembly.
To install:
4. Position the gauge into place in the cluster housing. Attach with the mounting screws.
5. Install the speedometer head assembly.

Fuel/Tachometer Gauge

REMOVAL & INSTALLATION

1984-89 Models
▶ **See Figure 74**

1. Remove the cluster bezel and mask.
2. Remove the screws attaching the gauge to the cluster assembly.
3. Remove the fuel/tachometer assembly by pulling rearward to disengage the gauge from the mounting pins.
To install:
4. Position the gauge assembly on the cluster pins, then secure with the attaching screws.

Headlight Switch

REMOVAL & INSTALLATION

▶ **See Figures 75 and 76**

1. Disconnect the negative battery cable.
2. Remove the left bezel.
3. Remove the headlamp switch mounting screws.
4. Remove the switch from the panel and disconnect the wiring harness connector.
5. Separate the switch and bracket by removing the bracket retainer.
6. Install in the reverse of removal.

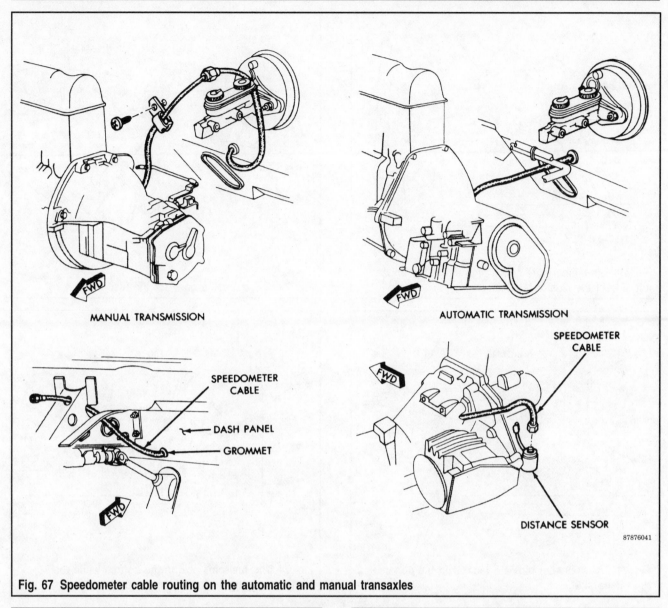

MANUAL TRANSMISSION

AUTOMATIC TRANSMISSION

SPEEDOMETER CABLE

DASH PANEL

GROMMET

SPEEDOMETER CABLE

DISTANCE SENSOR

87876041

Fig. 67 Speedometer cable routing on the automatic and manual transaxles

AMMETER

87876042

Fig. 68 With the aid of a ratchet you can remove the ammeter mounting screws

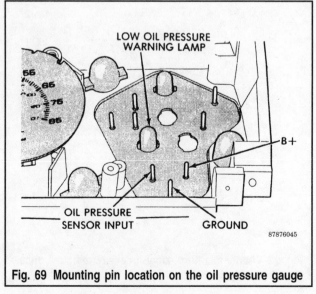

LOW OIL PRESSURE WARNING LAMP

B+

OIL PRESSURE SENSOR INPUT

GROUND

87876045

Fig. 69 Mounting pin location on the oil pressure gauge

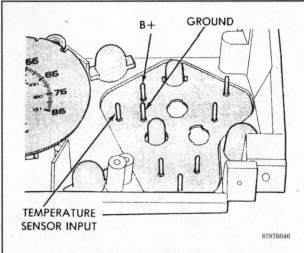

Fig. 70 The temperature gauge pins are in the upper left side of the cluster terminal

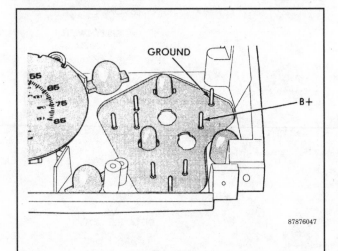

Fig. 71 The voltmeter pins are located in the upper right hand side

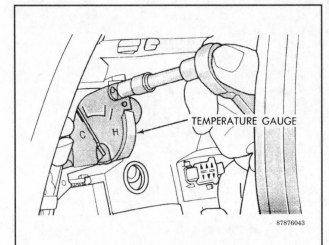

Fig. 72 The temperature gauge is easily removed once the cluster is exposed . . .

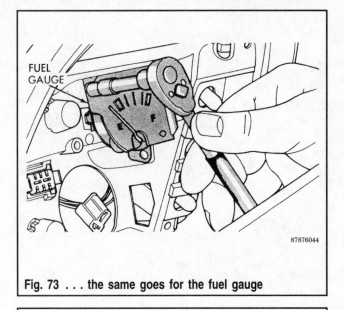

Fig. 73 . . . the same goes for the fuel gauge

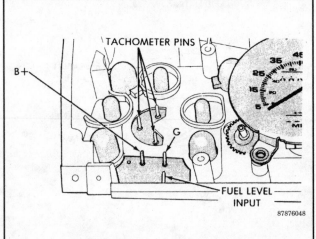

Fig. 74 The fuel pins are on the bottom while the tachometer pins are on the top of the cluster

Windshield Wiper Switch

REMOVAL & INSTALLATION

1. Disconnect the electrical switch wiring from both the wash/wipe switch and the turn signal switch.

2. Remove the lower column cover.

3. Remove the horn button by carefully lifting it with your fingers.

4. Remove the wash/wipe switch hider disc.

5. Rotate the ignition key to the **OFF** position and turn the steering wheel so that the access hole in the hub area is at the 9 o'clock position.

6. Using a flat bladed tool, loosen the turn signal lever screw through the access hole.

7. Disengage the dimmer push rod from the wash/wipe switch, unsnap the wiring clip and remove the switch.

FUEL GAUGE SYSTEM DIAGNOSIS

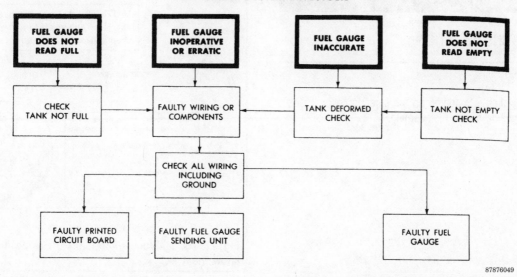

87876049

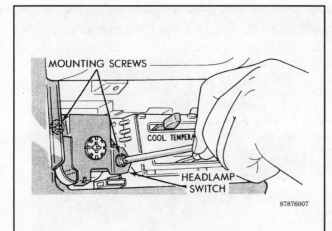

Fig. 75 Loosen and remove the headlamp switch mounting screws

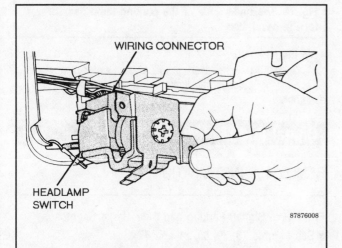

Fig. 76 Disconnect the harness as you remove the switch from the dash

8. When installing, properly position the dimmer push rod in the wash/wipe switch and secure the wiring clip. Install the wash/wipe hider disc.

Rear Wiper, Hatch Release and Defogger Switch

REMOVAL & INSTALLATION

1. With the aid of a thin bladed tool, depress the two spring clips on top of the bezel.
2. Tip the bezel rearward and remove the assembly.
3. Disconnect the wiring and remove the switch.
4. To install, reconnect the wiring and snap the switch into position.

Clock

REMOVAL & INSTALLATION

On earlier models the clock is in the instrument cluster and part of the fuel and alternator gauge assembly. On later models the electronic digital clock is built into the radio. Remove the cluster mounted clock as follows:

1. Remove the two mask/lens assembly lower attachment retaining spring pins by pulling rearward with pliers.
2. Allow the mask/lens assembly to drop slightly as it is moved rearward. Remove it from the cluster area.
3. Remove the clock/gauge assembly retaining screws then remove the clock from the gauge.
4. Installation is the reverse of removal.

Ignition Switch

REMOVAL & INSTALLATION

▶ **See Figure 77**

The ignition switch is mounted on the steering column. See Section 8 for ignition switch replacement.

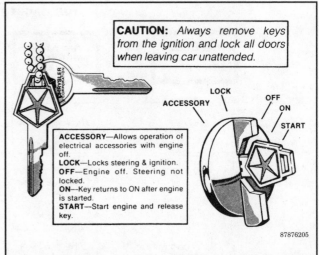

> **CAUTION:** *Always remove keys from the ignition and lock all doors when leaving car unattended.*

ACCESSORY—Allows operation of electrical accessories with engine off.
LOCK—Locks steering & ignition.
OFF—Engine off. Steering not locked.
ON—Key returns to ON after engine is started.
START—Start engine and release key.

87876205

Fig. 77 The ignition switch has various positions, get to know them well

LIGHTING

Headlights

REMOVAL & INSTALLATION

▶ **See Figures 78, 79, 80, 81, 82, 83 and 84**

1. Be sure the light switch is **OFF**.
2. Remove the screws that hold the headlight bezel in place, if used.
3. Remove the headlight bezel. Pull the bezel away, then disconnect the parking/turn signal light. Twist to remove the light and socket.
4. Set the bezel aside.
5. Remove the screws securing the headlight retainer and remove the retainer.
6. Pull the headlight out, then disconnect the socket.

87876319

Fig. 79 The under side of the parking lamp has screws for the bezel also

To install:
7. Install a new headlight in the reverse order of removal. Check the operation of the lights before completing the assembly.

Signal and Marker Lights

REMOVAL & INSTALLATION

Front Turn Signal, Parking and Side Marker Lights
▶ **See Figures 78, 79, 80, 81 and 85**

1. Remove the four headlamp bezel attaching screws and remove the bezel.
2. Twist out the socket from the rear.

87876318

Fig. 78 Unscrew the upper portion of the headlamp bezel

Fig. 80 Remove the headlight bezel by pulling it away from the vehicle

Fig. 81 Disconnect the parking/turn signal light by twisting, then pulling back to remove the light and socket

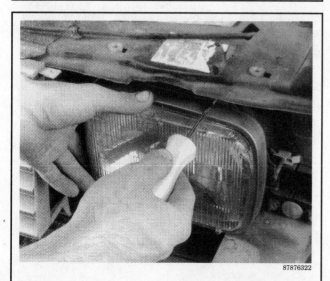

Fig. 82 Remove the screws securing the headlight

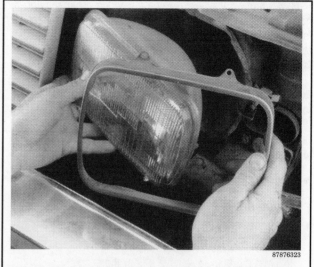

Fig. 83 Remove the retainer ring around the headlamp

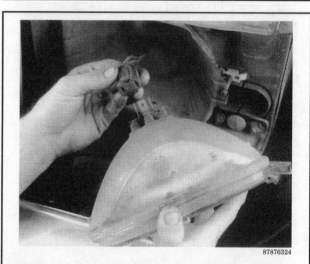

Fig. 84 Pull the headlight out, then disconnect the socket

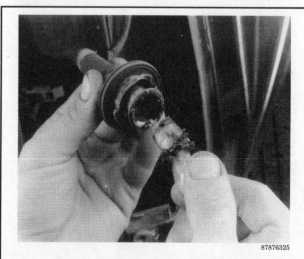

Fig. 85 To remove the bulb, twist slightly and pull it out of the socket

3. To remove the lens, extend a wooden dowel through the housing socket holes and push against the lens with a steady force until the lens is free from the housing, making sure to release the locking tabs.

To install:

4. Clean the housing gasket track and apply butyl tape adhesive to all corners and at the bottom overlap the tape ends approximately ½ in. (13mm).

5. Press the lens into position until the housing tabs snap over the lens.

6. Twist in the lamp socket.

7. Position the bezel and lamp assembly and install the four headlamp bezel attaching screws.

Rear Turn Signal, Brake and Parking Lights

▶ See Figures 86, 87 and 88

1. Snap or twist out the sockets.
2. Twist the bulb to remove it from the socket.
3. Remove the housing by depressing the four snap tabs and push against the housing with a steady force until the housing is free from the body.
4. With a small screwdriver release the lens locking tabs taking care not to damage the lens retaining tabs on the housing and remove the lens.

To install:

5. Clean both housing gasket tracks and apply butyl tape adhesive to all corners and overlap the tape ends approximately ½ in. (13mm).

6. Press the lens into position until the housing tabs snap over the lens.

7. Press the lamp assembly into the body until the four housing retainers snap into the body.

8. Twist in the lamp socket.

High-Mount Brake Light

▶ See Figure 89

1. Remove the two lens attaching screws and pull the lens from the lamp assembly.
2. The bulbs may be removed by pulling straight out.

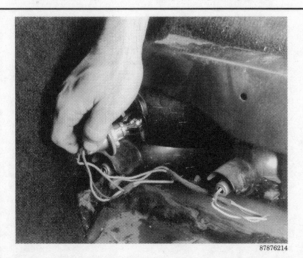

Fig. 86 In many cases the bulb can be replaced without removing the lamp from the vehicle

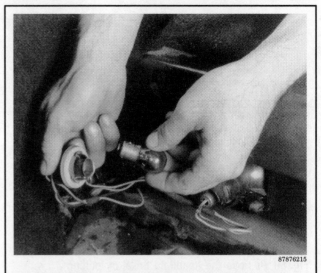

Fig. 87 Twist the bulb to remove it from the socket

Fig. 88 If the lamp is removed from the vehicle, a new gasket will be needed for replacement

3. To remove the lamp assembly, from under the deck lid remove the two attaching nuts and lift the lamp from the mounting.

4. Installation is the reverse of removal.

Licence Plate

▶ See Figures 90, 91, 92 and 93

1. Lift the rear tail gate or hatch.
2. Loosen and remove the lamp assembly hold-down screws.
3. Pull the lamp from the body of the vehicle.
4. The bulb and socket assembly will come out of the unit.
5. To remove the bulb, pull from the socket.

To install:

6. Place a new bulb in the socket.
7. Install the socket into the housing.
8. Attach the housing to the body of the vehicle.
9. Test the lamp.

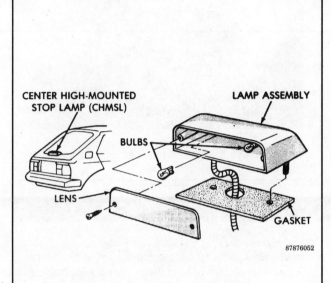

Fig. 89 Remove the two lens attaching screws and pull the lens from the lamp assembly

Fig. 90 Loosen and remove the lamp assembly hold-down screws

Fig. 91 Pull the lamp from the body of the vehicle

Fig. 92 The bulb and socket assembly will come out of the unit

Fig. 93 To remove the bulb, pull from the socket

Trunk Lamp

▶ **See Figures 94 and 95**

1. Open the hatch lid, locate the lamp.
2. Remove the lens cover.
3. Release the bulb by carefully pulling it out of the socket.
4. Install a new bulb, insert the socket into the housing.
5. Attach the lens to the vehicle.
6. Close the hatch.

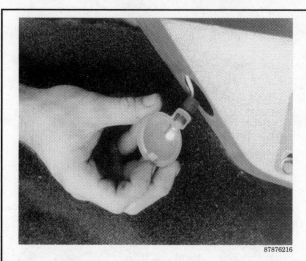

87876216

Fig. 94 Remove the lens cover, then pull the socket out of the housing

TRAILER WIRING

➡**For more information on towing a trailer, please refer to Section 1 of this manual.**

Wiring the vehicle for towing is fairly easy. There are a number of good wiring kits available and these should be used, rather than trying to design your own. All trailers will need brake lights and turn signals as well as tail lights and side marker lights. Most states require extra marker lights for overly wide trailers. Also, most states have recently required back-up lights for trailers, and most trailer manufacturers have been building trailers with back-up lights for several years.

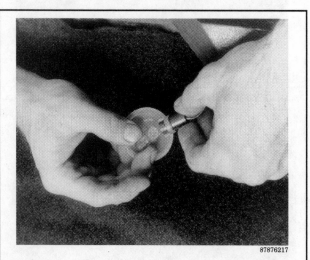

87876217

Fig. 95 Release the bulb by carefully pulling it out of the socket

Additionally, some Class I, most Class II and just about all Class III trailers will have electric brakes. Add to this number an accessories wire, to operate trailer internal equipment or to charge the trailer's battery, and you can have as many as seven wires in the harness.

Determine the equipment on your trailer and buy the wiring kit necessary. The kit will contain all the necessary wires, plus a plug adapter set which includes the female plug, mounted on the bumper or hitch, and the male plug, which is wired or plugged into the trailer harness. When installing the kit, follow the manufacturer's instructions. The color coding of the wires tends to be standard throughout the industry.

One point to note: some domestic vehicles, and most imported vehicles, have separate turn signals. On most domestic vehicles, however, the brake lights and rear turn signals operate with the same bulb. For those vehicles without separate turn signals, you can purchase an isolation unit so that the brake lights won't blink whenever the turn signals are operated, or you can go to your local electronics supply house and buy four diodes to wire in series with the brake and turn signal bulbs. Diodes will isolate the brake and turn signals. The choice is yours. The isolation units are simple and quick to install, but far more expensive than the diodes. The diodes, however, require more work to install properly, since they require the cutting of each bulb's wire and soldering the diode in place.

One final point: the best kits are those with a spring loaded cover on the vehicle mounted socket. This cover prevents dirt and moisture from corroding the terminals. Never let the vehicle socket hang loosely; always mount it securely to the bumper or hitch.

CIRCUIT PROTECTION

▶ **See Figures 96, 97 and 98**

Fuses

REPLACEMENT

The fuse block is located on the left side of the vehicle, beneath the end of the instrument panel. The circuit each fuse protects is indicated by numbers located on the fuse block.

A blade type fuse is used instead of a glass cartridge type. The amperage rating is on the top of the colored fuse.

✳✳WARNING

When you are replacing a blown fuse be sure to use only the specified fuse for that particular circuit. If one is not available only temporarily use one from another circuit that is not necessary to keep the vehicle running. For example a clock, radio or cigar lighter fuse is a good idea. Never use a fuse higher than specified, damage to the wiring circuit could occur.

Fusible Links

Fusible links are used to prevent major wire harness damage in the event of a short circuit or an overload condition in the electrical circuits. Each fusible link is of a fixed value for a specific electrical load. Should a link fail, the cause of a failure must be determined and repaired prior to installing a new link of the same value.

Fig. 96 Some breakers are located in the fuse block, shaped like a large metal fuse. The large round cylinders are flashers

Circuit Breakers

Circuit breakers are used along with fusible links to protect electrical system components such as headlamps, windshield wipers, electric windows, tailgate front and rear switches. The circuit breakers are located either in the switch or mounted on or near the lower lip of the instrument panel, to the right or left side of the steering column. Some breakers are located in the fuse block, shaped like a large metal fuse.

Fuse Panels

The fuse panel is used to house the fuses that protect the individual or combined electrical circuits within the vehicle. The turn signal flasher, the hazard warning flasher and the seat belt warning buzzer/timer are located on the fuse panel for quick identification and replacement. The fuses are usually identified by abbreviated circuit names or number, with the number of the rated fuse needed to protect the circuit printed below the fuse holder.

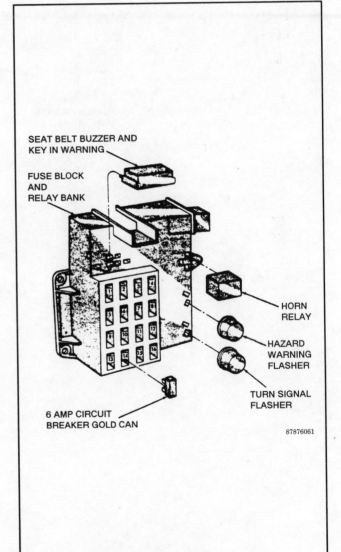

Fig. 97 Fuse block — 1980-89 models

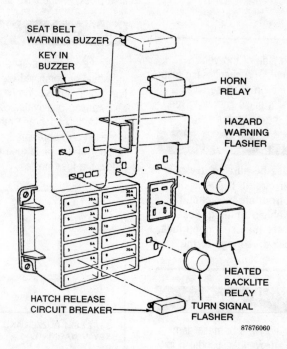

Fig. 98 Fuse block — 1978-79 models

WIRING DIAGRAMS

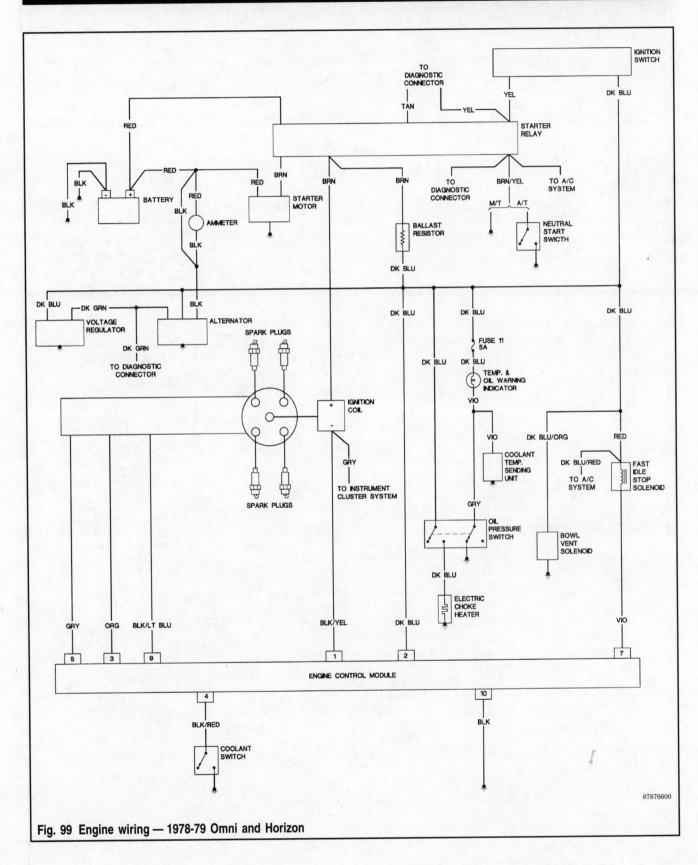

Fig. 99 Engine wiring — 1978-79 Omni and Horizon

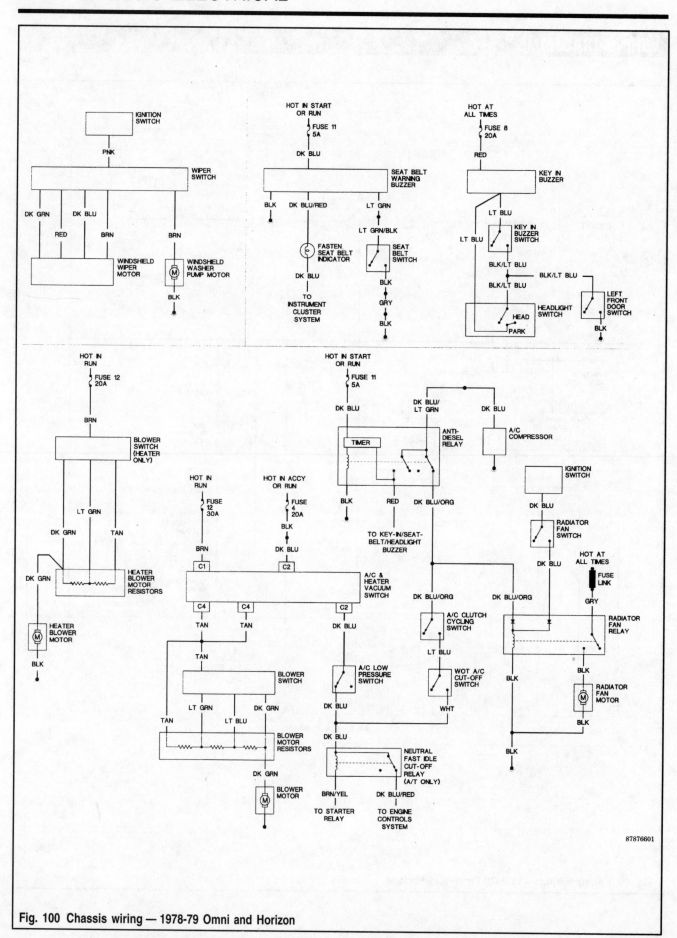

Fig. 100 Chassis wiring — 1978-79 Omni and Horizon

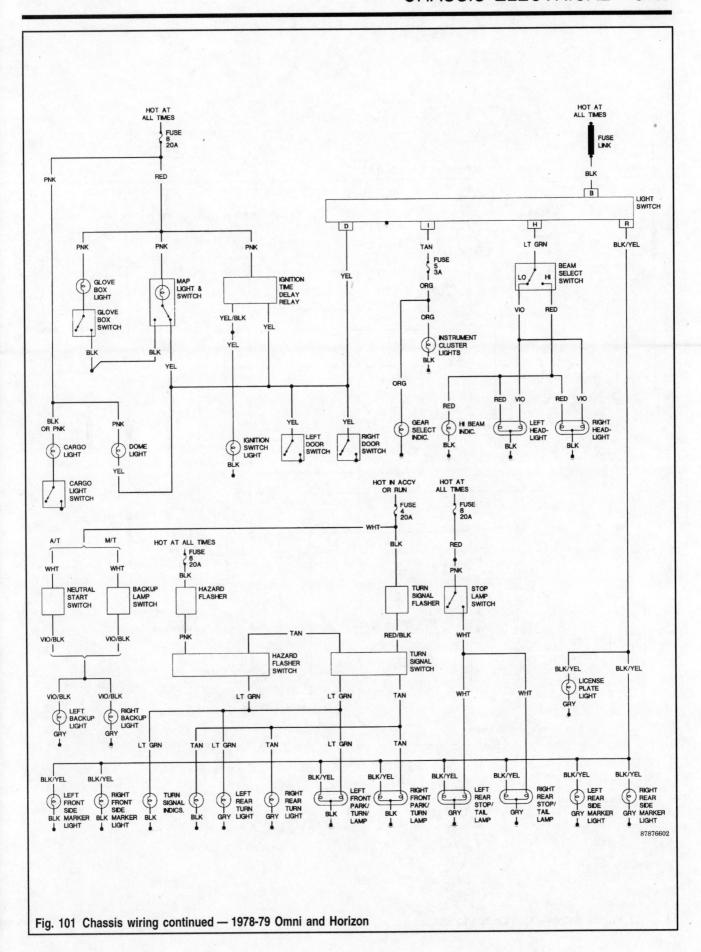

Fig. 101 Chassis wiring continued — 1978-79 Omni and Horizon

87876602

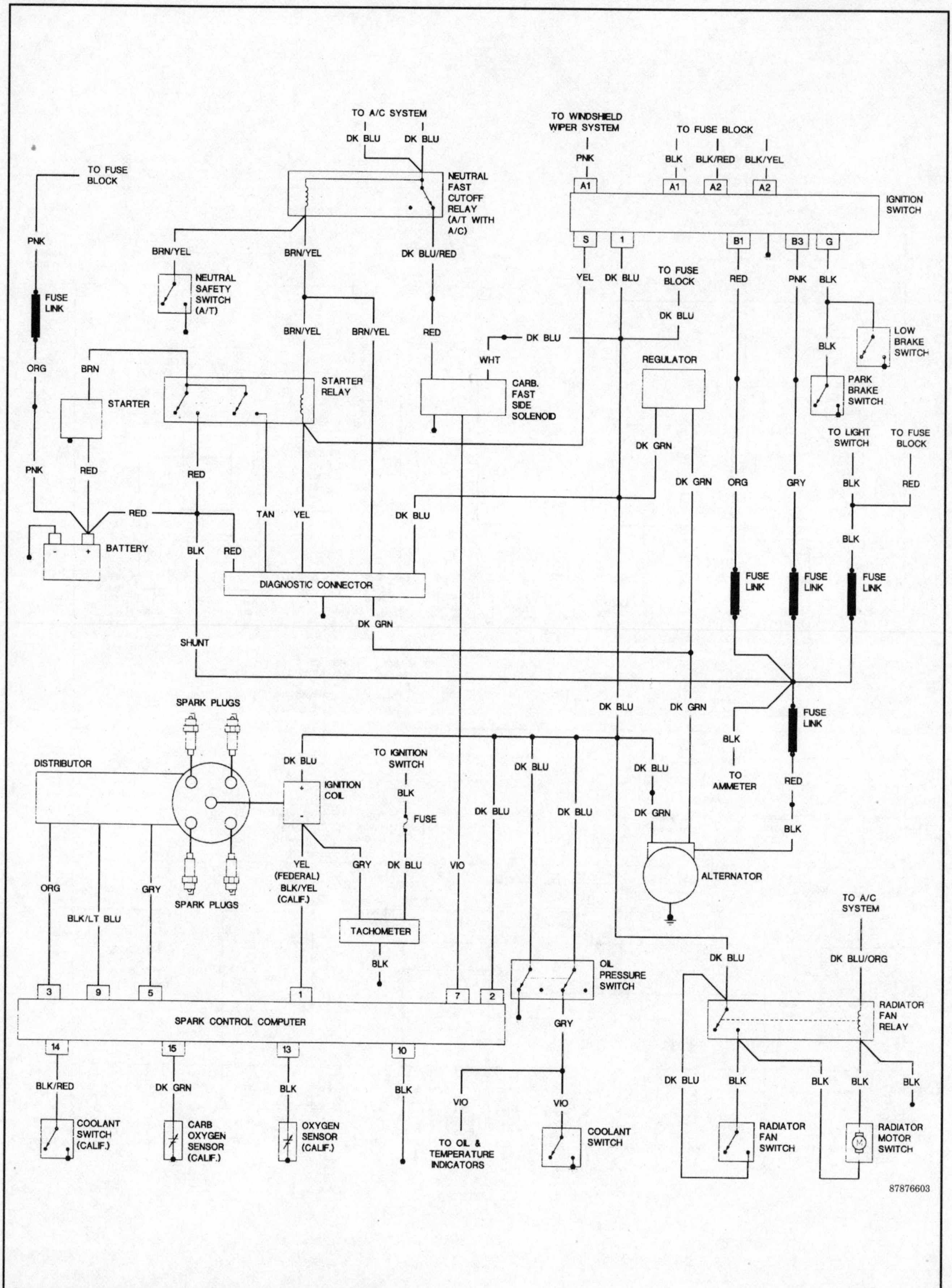

Fig. 102 Engine wiring — 1980 Omni and Horizon

87876603

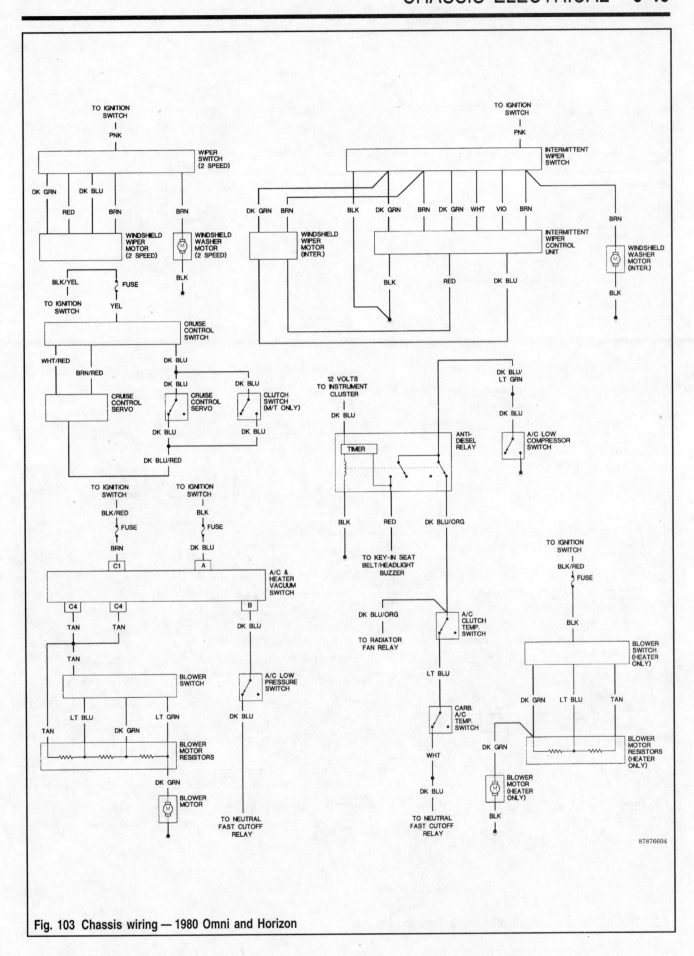

Fig. 103 Chassis wiring — 1980 Omni and Horizon

87876604

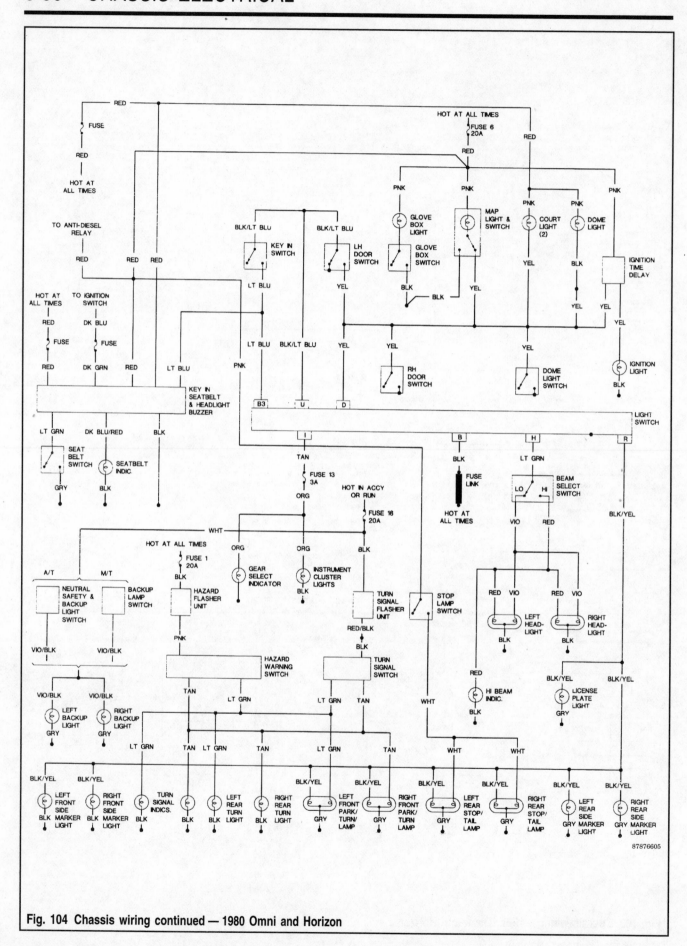

Fig. 104 Chassis wiring continued — 1980 Omni and Horizon

87876605

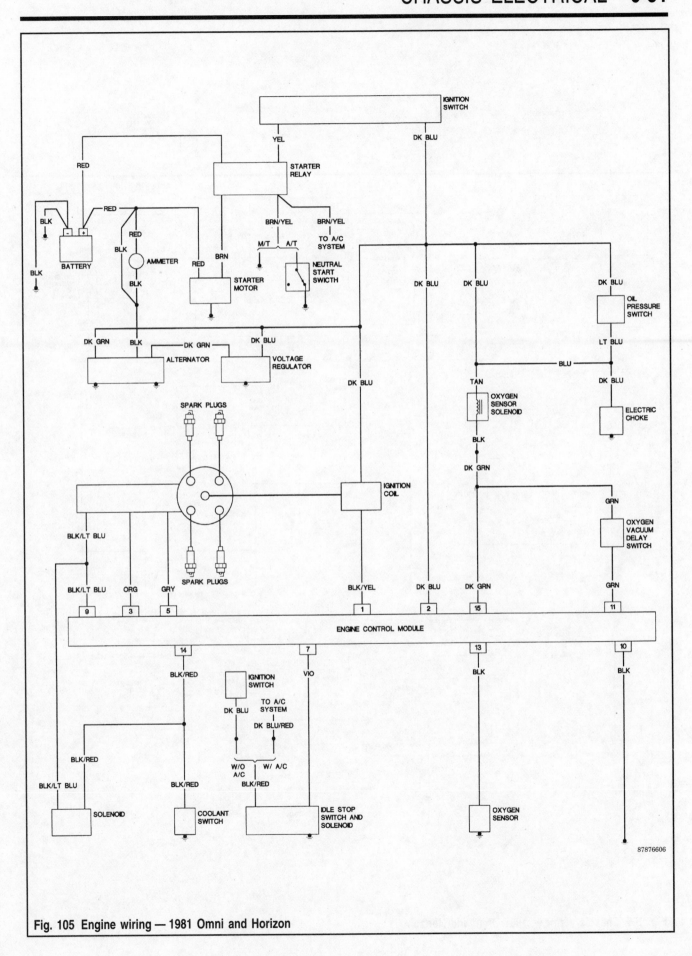

Fig. 105 Engine wiring — 1981 Omni and Horizon

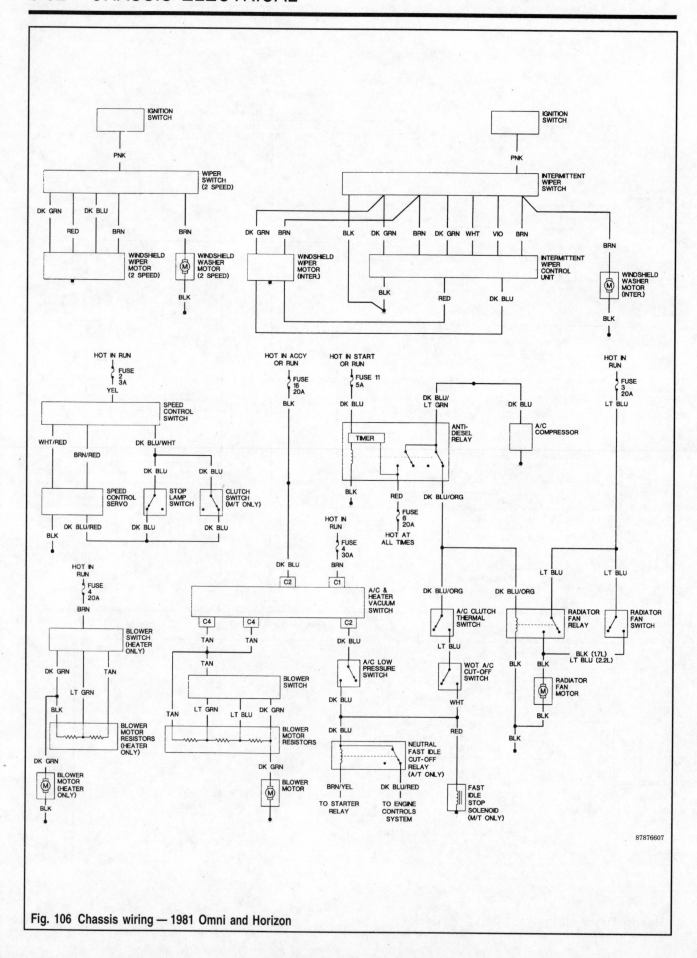

Fig. 106 Chassis wiring — 1981 Omni and Horizon

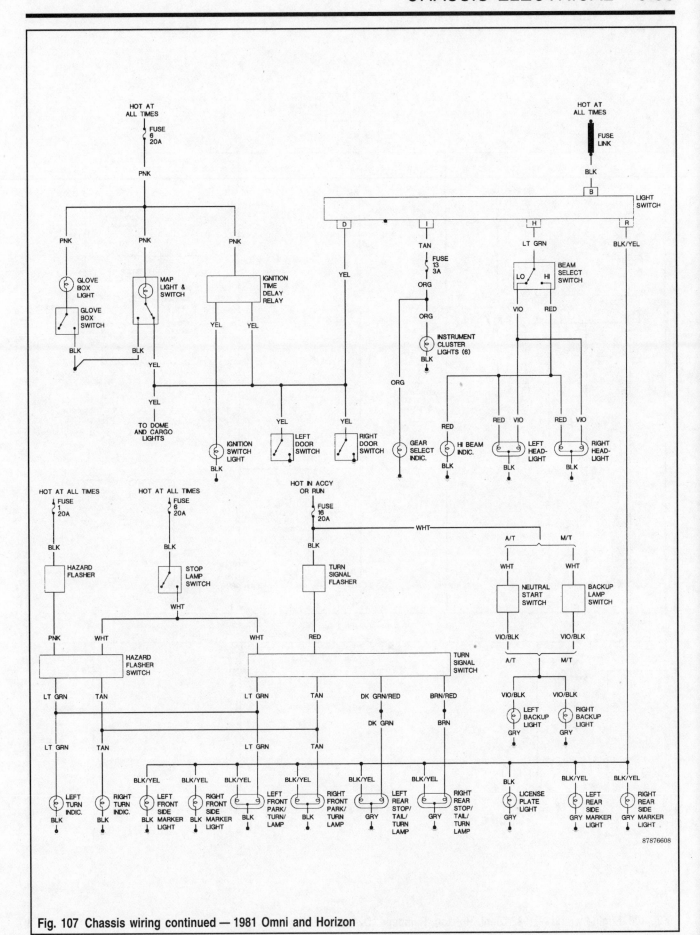

Fig. 107 Chassis wiring continued — 1981 Omni and Horizon

87876608

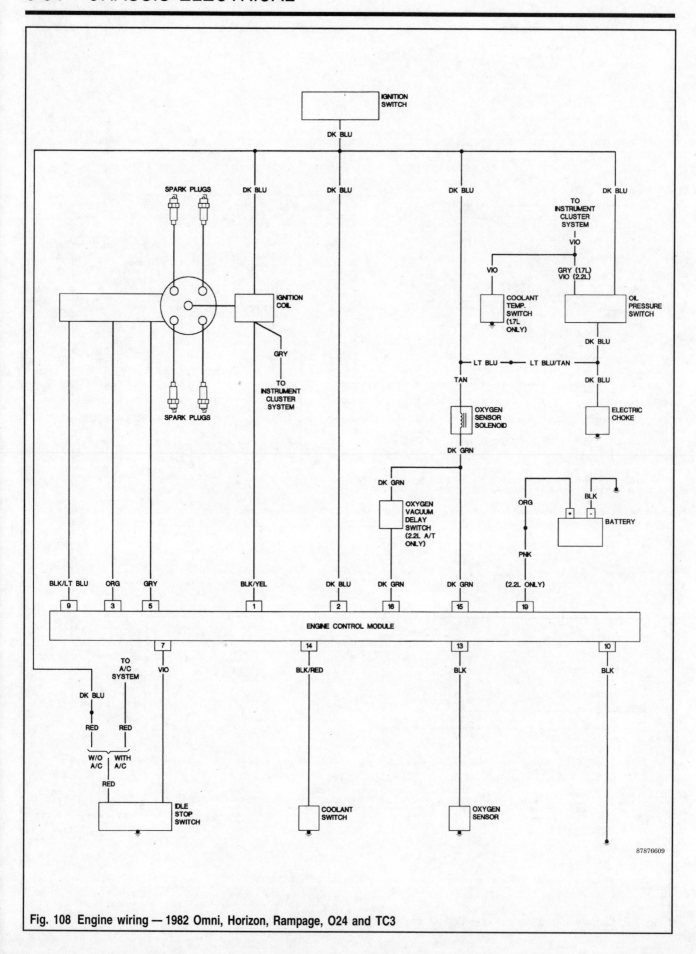

Fig. 108 *Engine wiring — 1982 Omni, Horizon, Rampage, O24 and TC3*

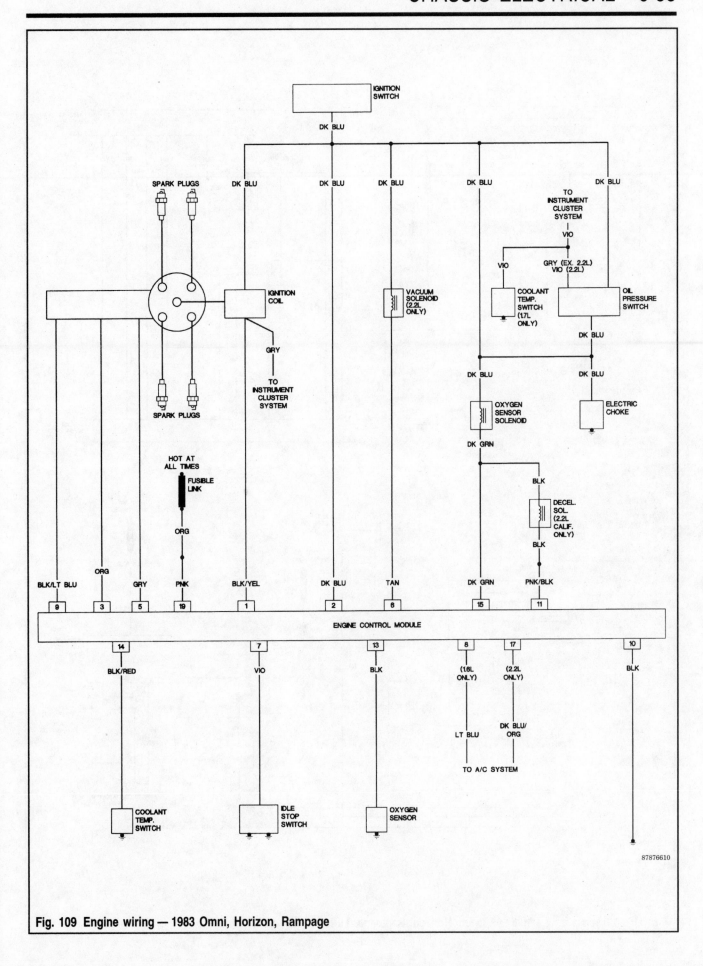

Fig. 109 Engine wiring — 1983 Omni, Horizon, Rampage

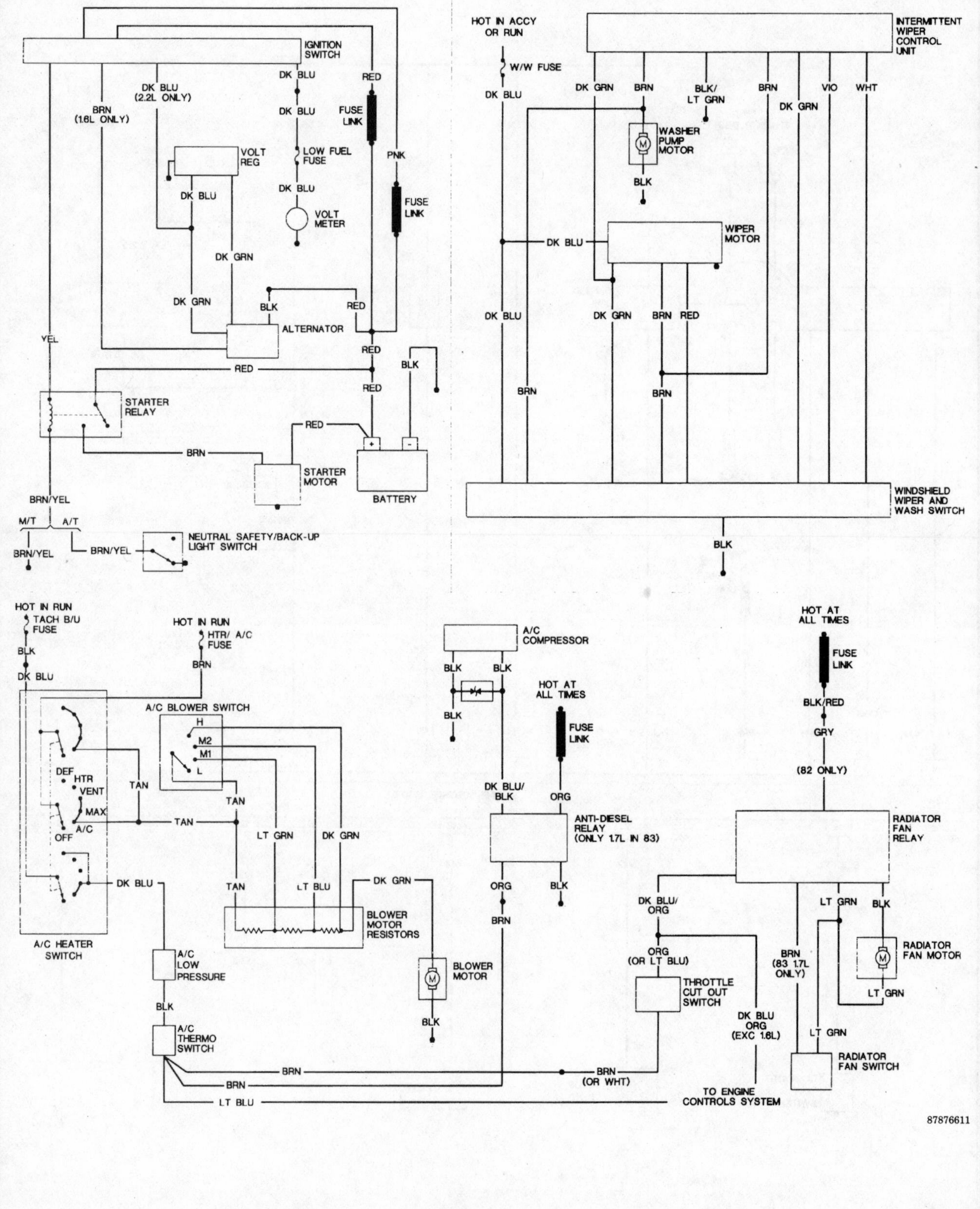

Fig. 110 Chassis wiring — 1982-83 Omni, Horizon, Rampage, Turismo, O24 and TC3

87876611

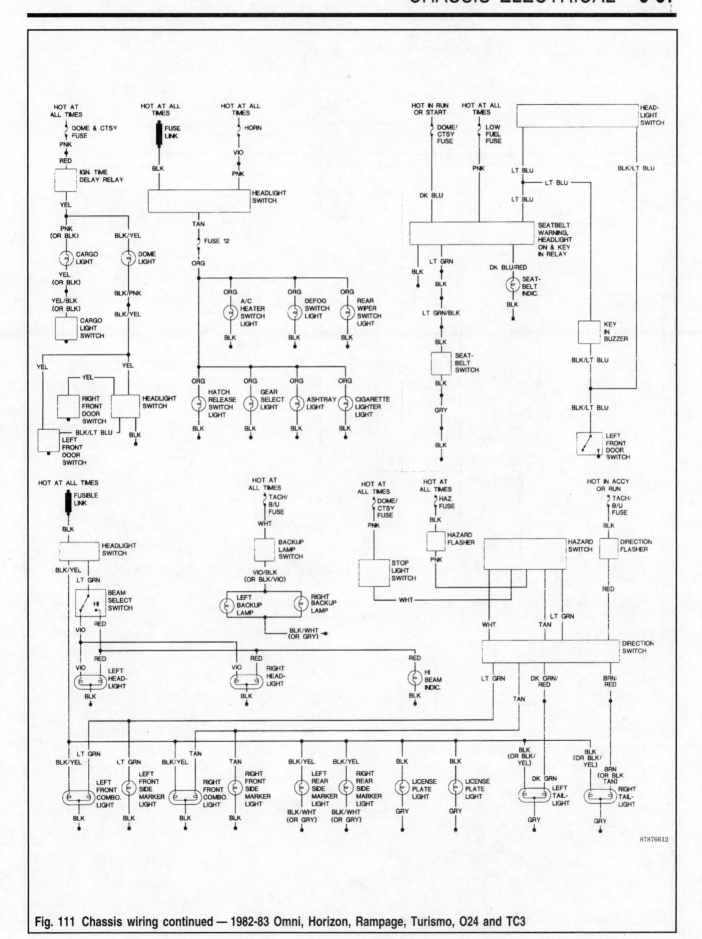

Fig. 111 Chassis wiring continued — 1982-83 Omni, Horizon, Rampage, Turismo, O24 and TC3

87876612

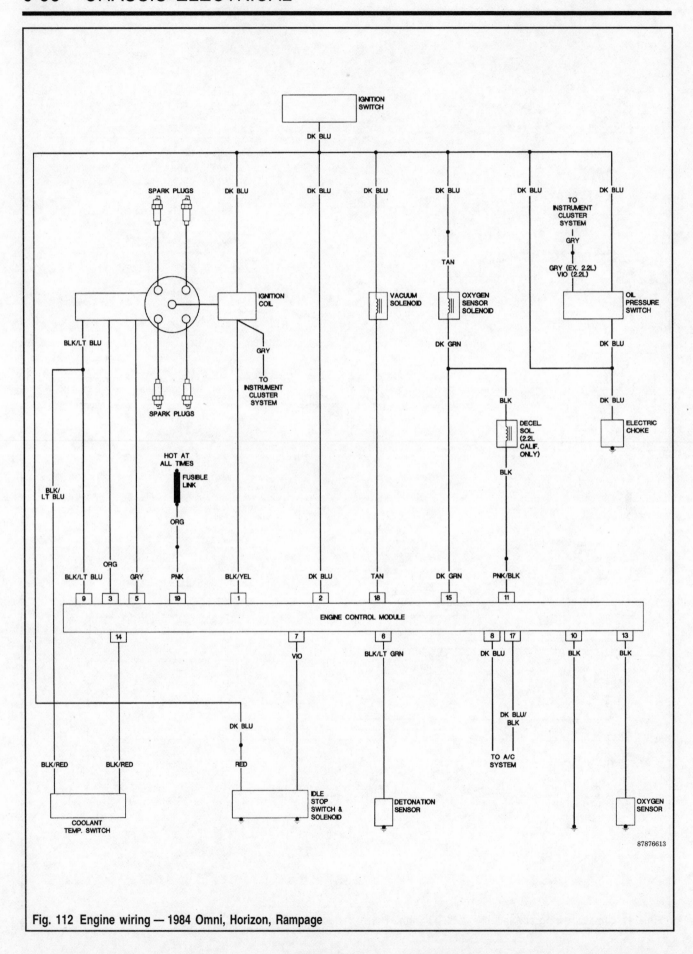

Fig. 112 Engine wiring — 1984 Omni, Horizon, Rampage

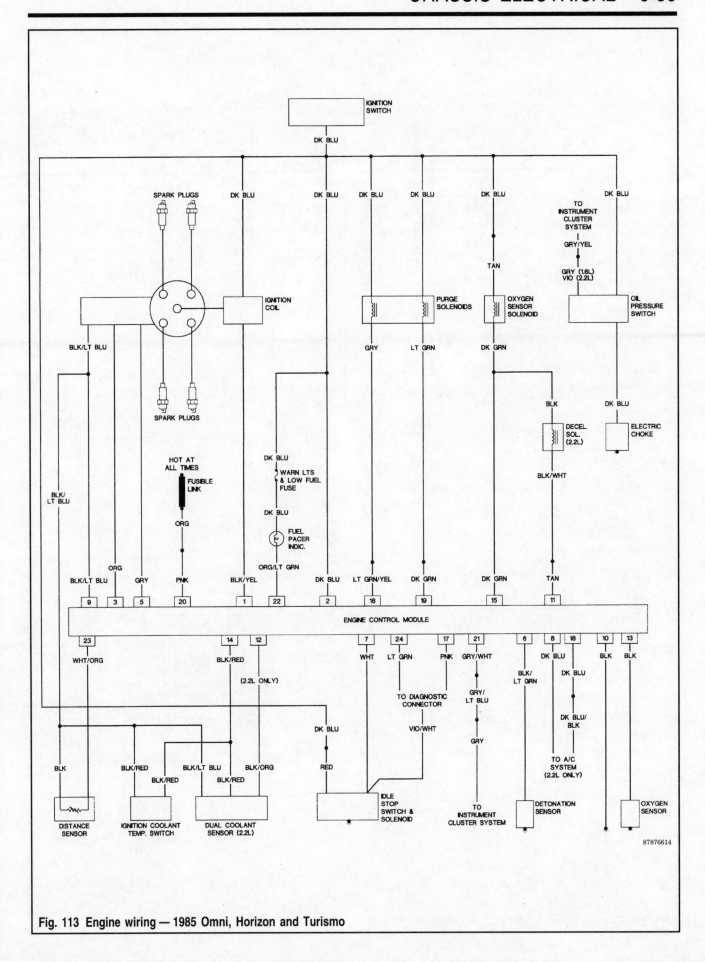

Fig. 113 Engine wiring — 1985 Omni, Horizon and Turismo

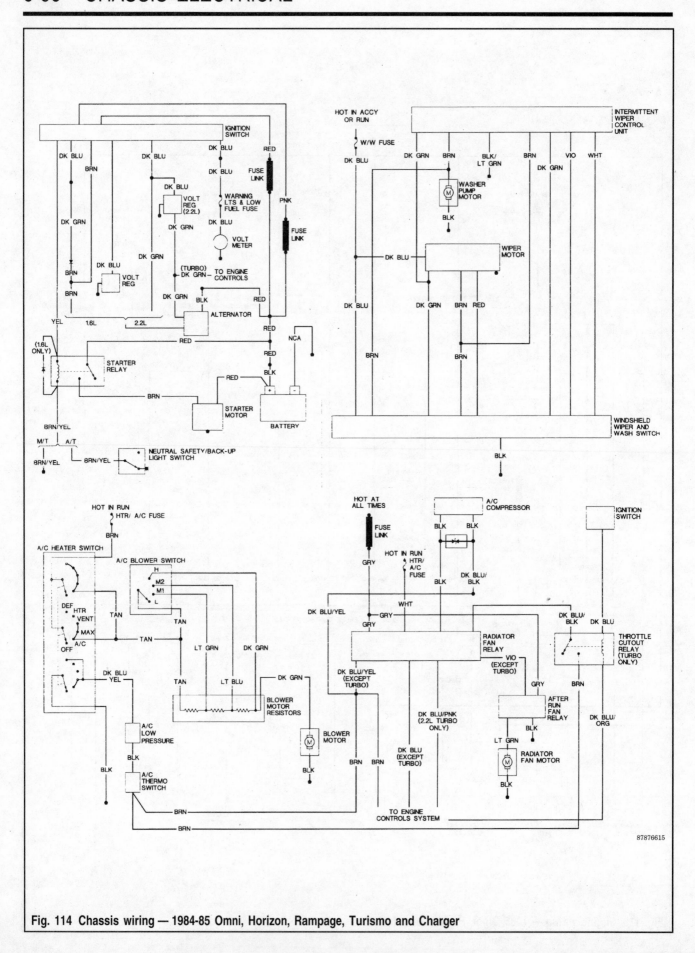

Fig. 114 Chassis wiring — 1984-85 Omni, Horizon, Rampage, Turismo and Charger

87876615

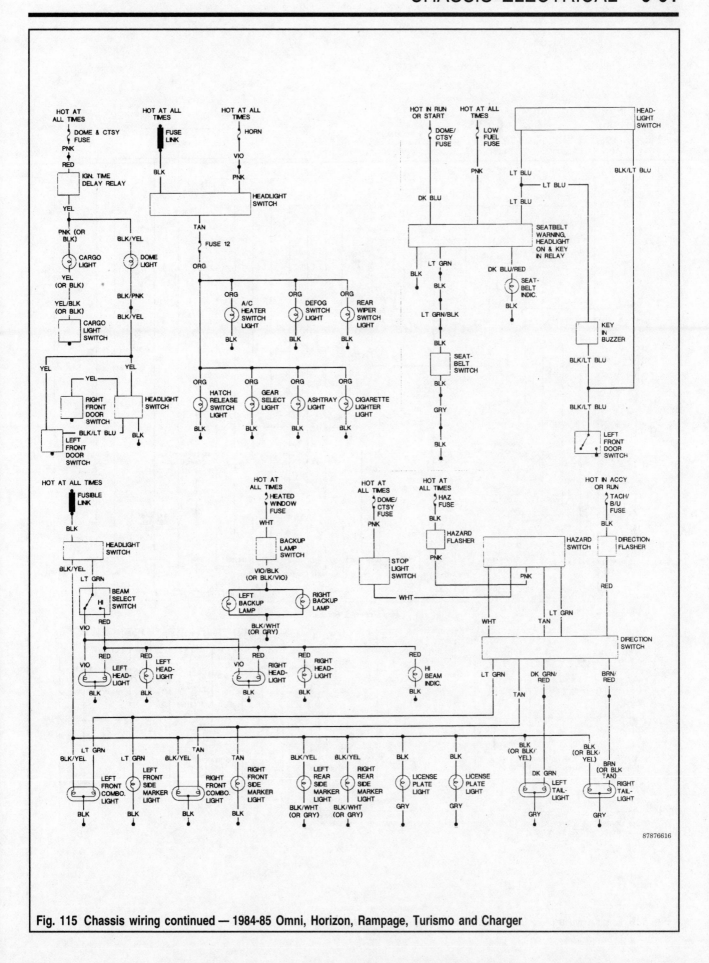

Fig. 115 Chassis wiring continued — 1984-85 Omni, Horizon, Rampage, Turismo and Charger

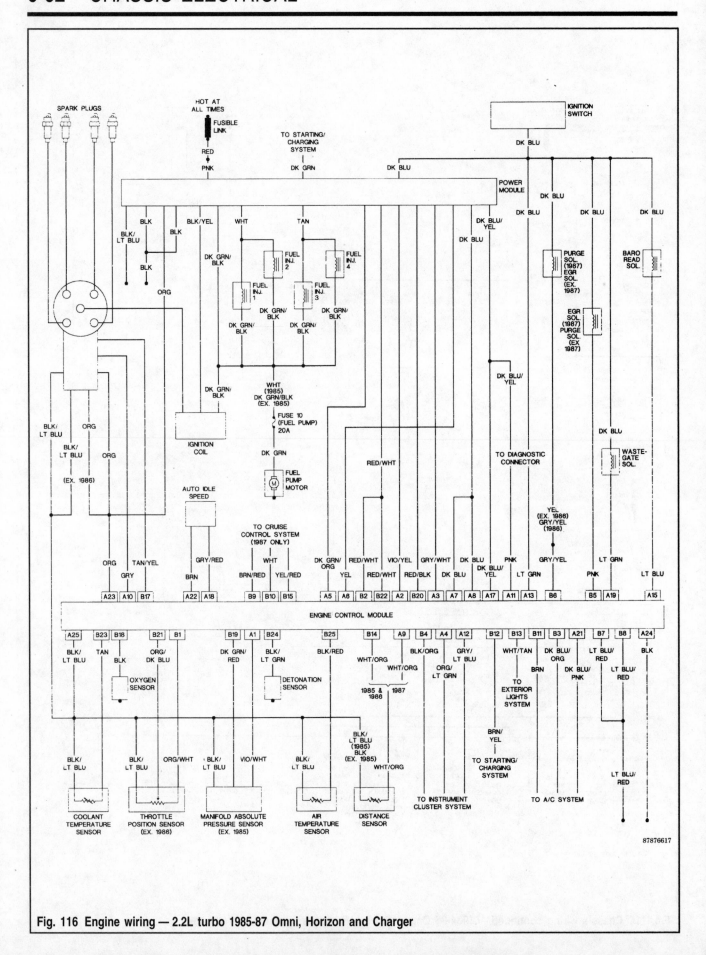

Fig. 116 Engine wiring — 2.2L turbo 1985-87 Omni, Horizon and Charger

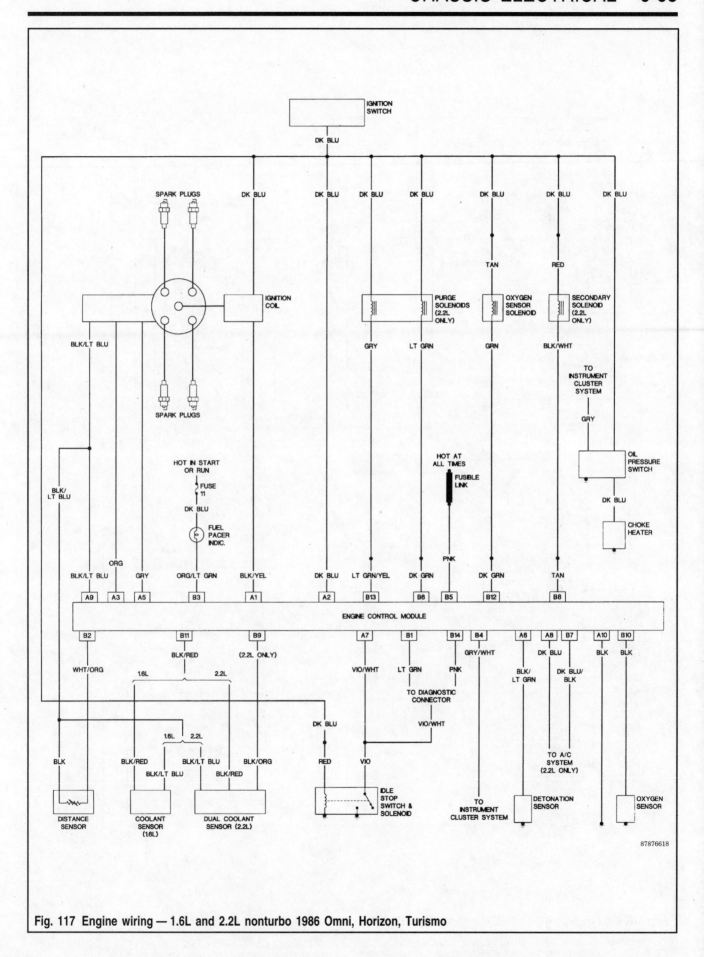

Fig. 117 Engine wiring — 1.6L and 2.2L nonturbo 1986 Omni, Horizon, Turismo

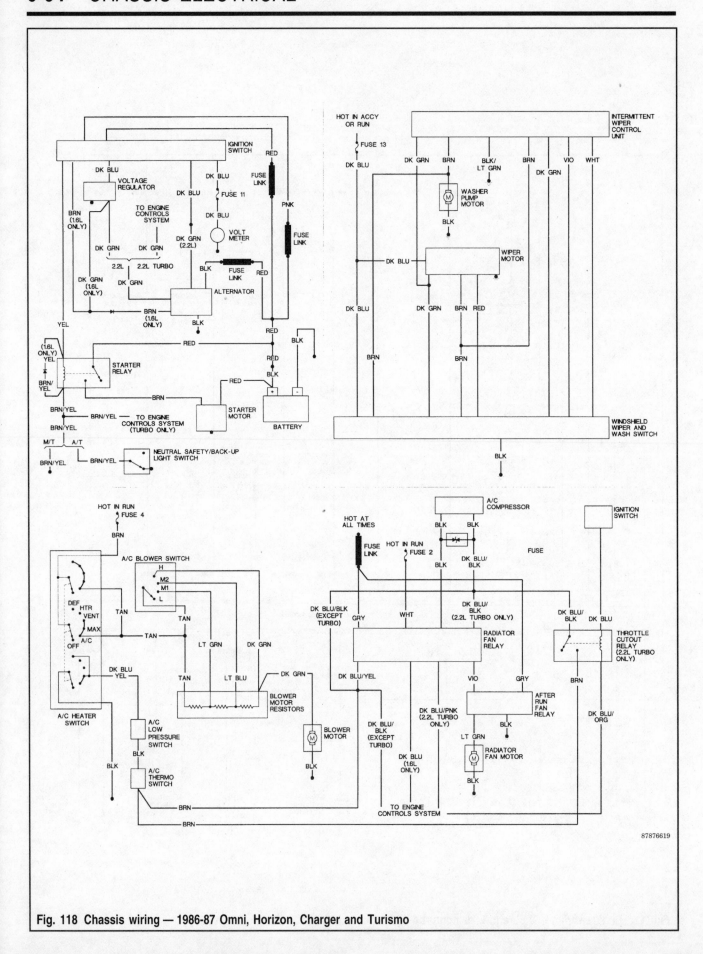

Fig. 118 Chassis wiring — 1986-87 Omni, Horizon, Charger and Turismo

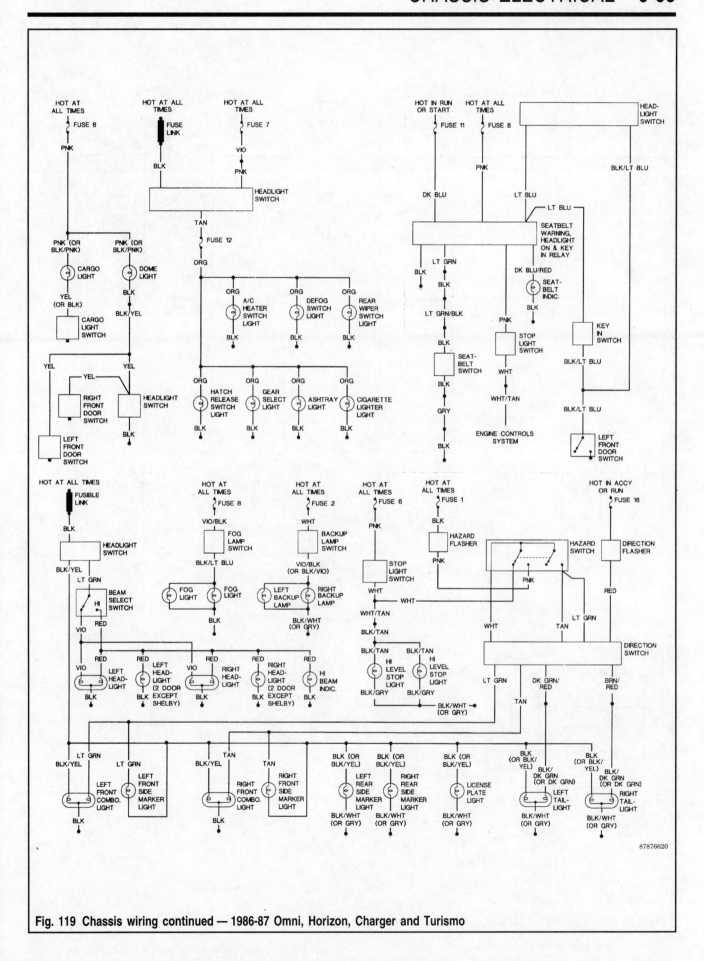

Fig. 119 Chassis wiring continued — 1986-87 Omni, Horizon, Charger and Turismo

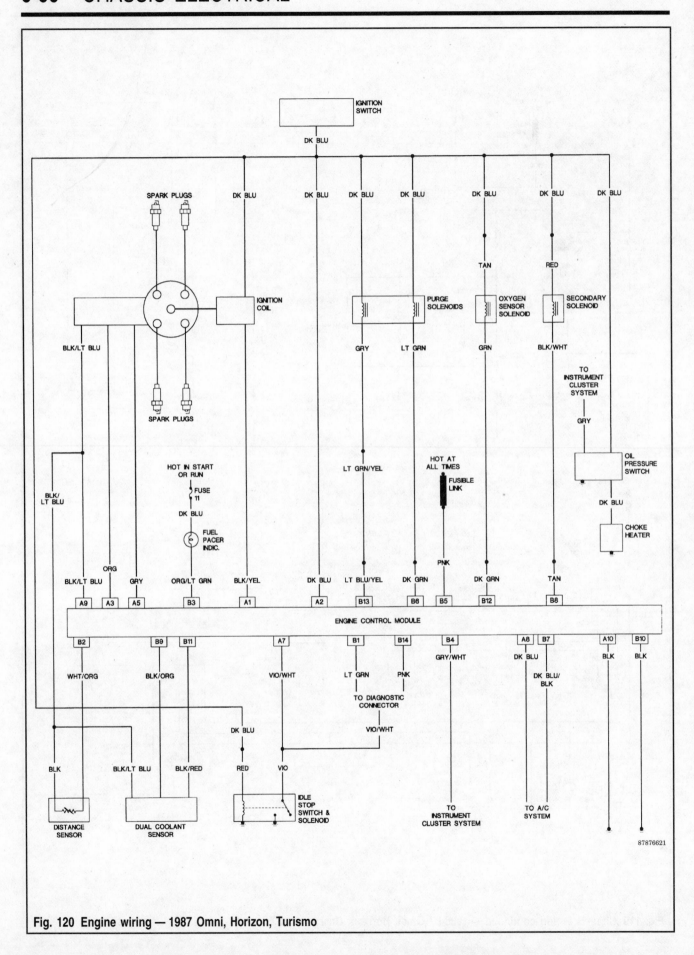

Fig. 120 Engine wiring — 1987 Omni, Horizon, Turismo

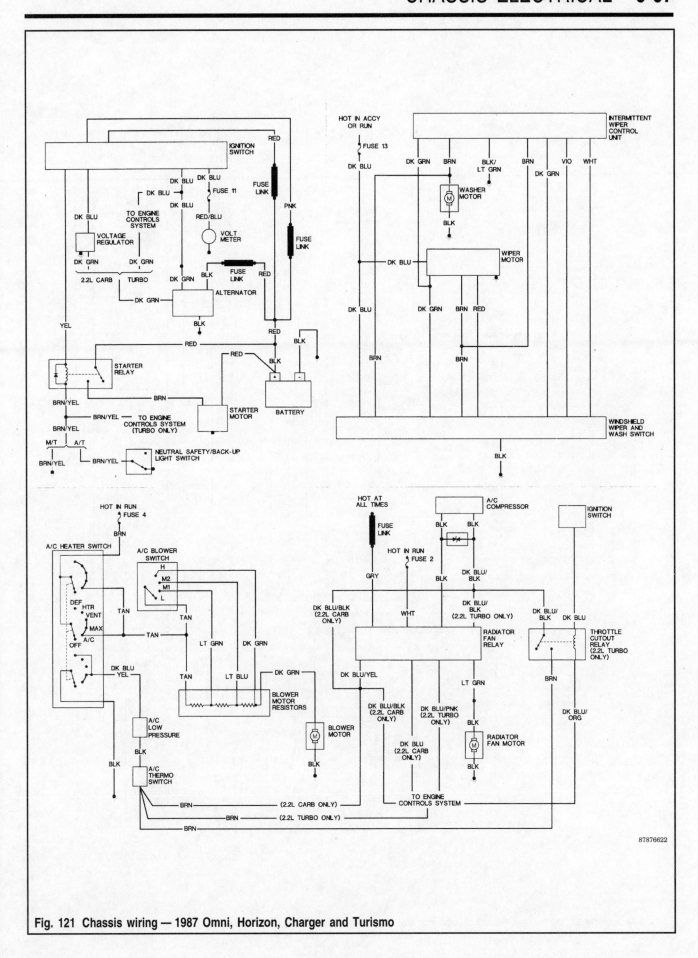

Fig. 121 Chassis wiring — 1987 Omni, Horizon, Charger and Turismo

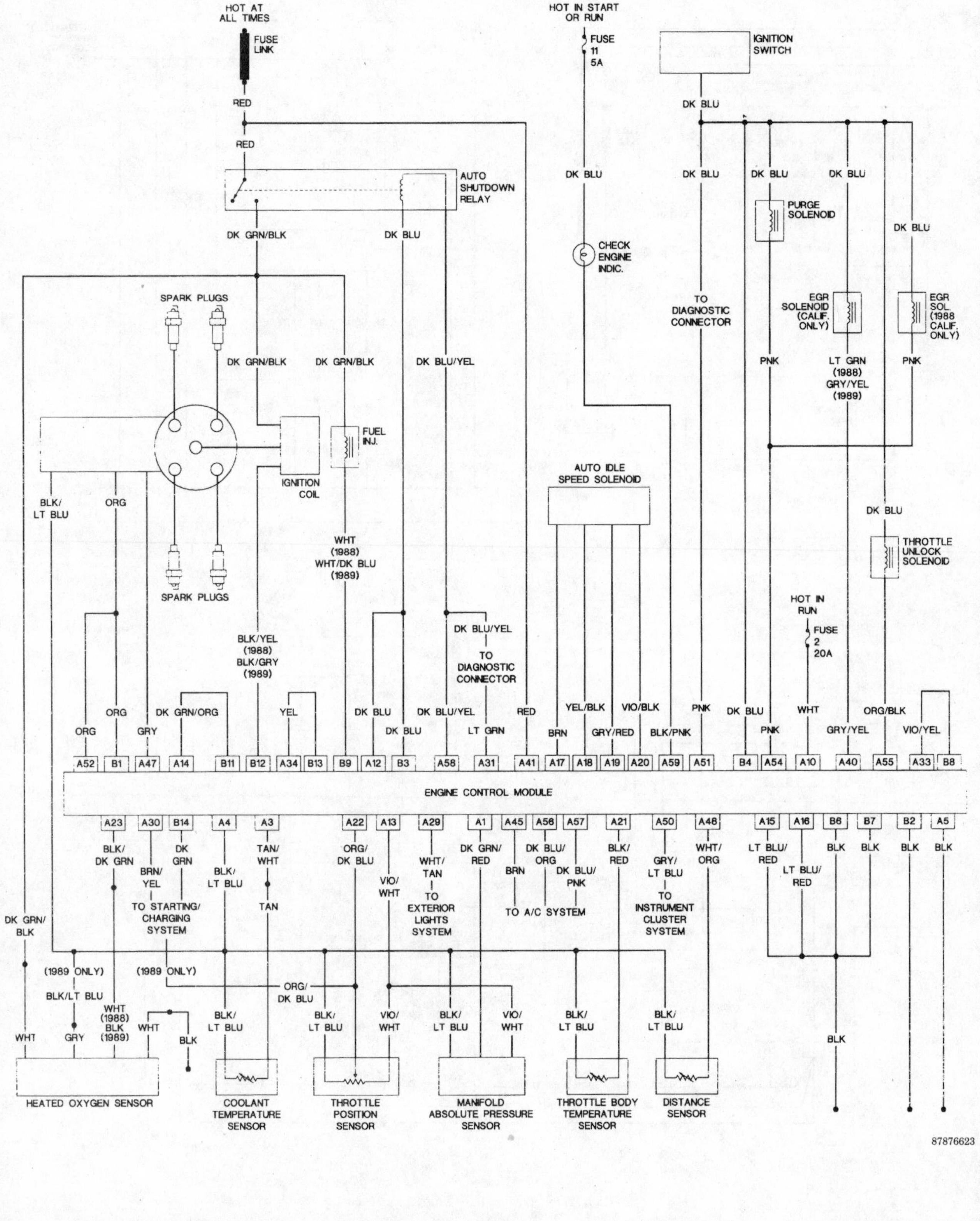

Fig. 122 Engine wiring — 1988-89 Omni and Horizon

87876623

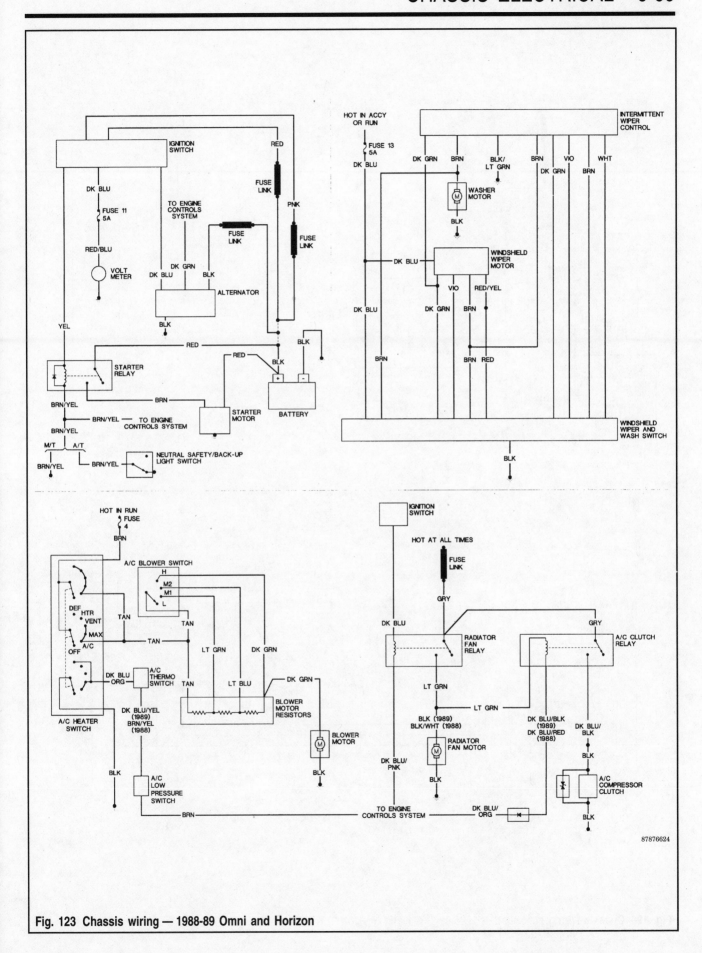

Fig. 123 Chassis wiring — 1988-89 Omni and Horizon

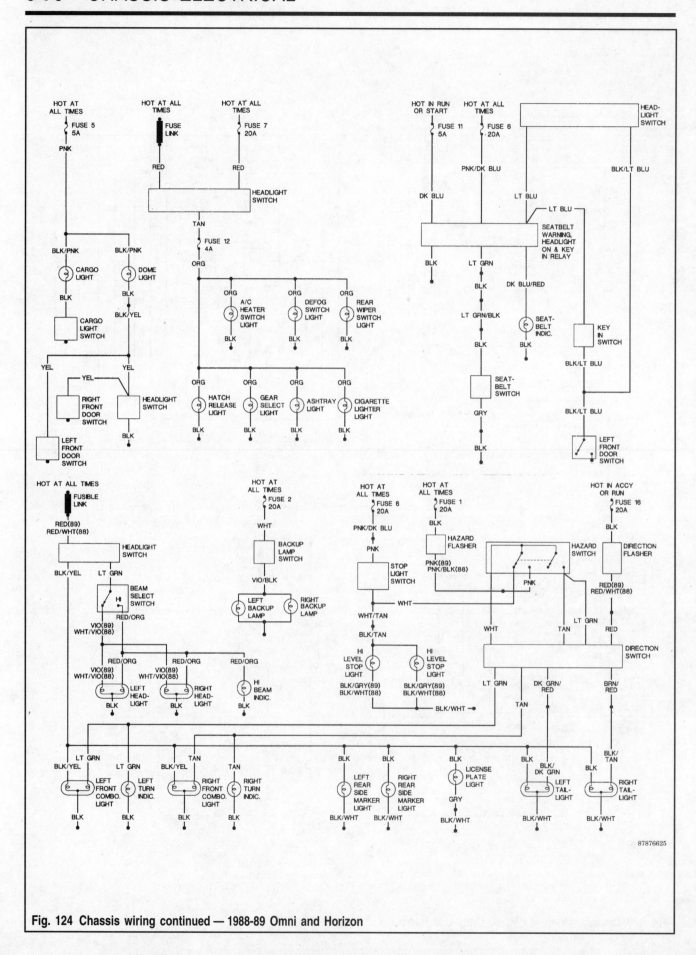

Fig. 124 Chassis wiring continued — 1988-89 Omni and Horizon

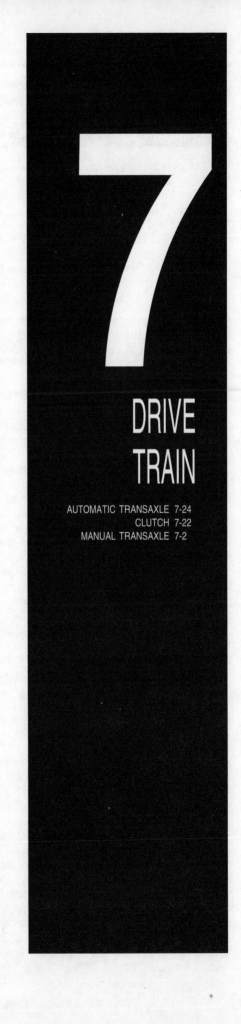

7

DRIVE
TRAIN

MANUAL TRANSAXLE

Identification

The models covered by this manual use four types of manual transaxles:
- A-412 Volkswagen designed 4-spd.
- Chrysler designed A-460 4-spd.
- A-465 5-spd.
- A-525 close ratio 5-spd. used in the high performance models.

A pad, located on top of the clutch housing contains the transaxle and Vehicle Identification Numbers (VIN). Please refer to Section 1 for further identification information.

Understanding the Manual Transaxle and Clutch

Because of the way an internal combustion engine breathes, it can produce torque, or twisting force, only within a narrow speed range. Most modern engines must turn at about 2500 rpm to produce their peak torque. By 4500 rpm they are producing so little torque that continued increases in engine speed produce no power increases.

The transaxle and clutch are employed to vary the relationship between engine speed and the speed of the wheels so that adequate engine power can be produced under all circumstances. The clutch allows engine torque to be applied to the transaxle input shaft gradually, due to mechanical slippage. The vehicle can, consequently, be started smoothly from a full stop.

The transaxle changes the ratio between the rotating speeds of the engine and the wheels by the use of gears. The lower gears allow full engine power to be applied to the rear wheels during acceleration at low speeds.

The clutch drive plate is a thin disc, the center of which is splined to the transaxle input shaft. Both sides of the disc are covered with a layer of material which is similar to brake lining and which is capable of allowing slippage without roughness or excessive noise.

The clutch cover is bolted to the engine flywheel and incorporates a diaphragm spring which provides the pressure to engage the clutch. The cover also houses the pressure plate. The driven disc is sandwiched between the pressure plate and the smooth surface of the flywheel when the clutch pedal is released, thus forcing it to turn at the same speed as the engine crankshaft.

The transaxle contains a main shaft which passes all the way through the transaxle, from the clutch to the driveshaft. This shaft is separated at one point, so that front and rear portions can turn at different speeds.

Power is transmitted by a countershaft in the lower gears and reverse. The gears of the countershaft mesh with gears on the main shaft, allowing power to be carried from one to the other. All the countershaft gears are integral with that shaft, while several of the main shaft gears can either rotate independently of the shaft or be locked to it. Shifting from one gear to the next causes one of the gears to be freed from rotating with the shaft and locks another to it. Gears are

locked and unlocked by internal dog clutches which slide between the center of the gear and the shaft. The forward gears usually employ synchronizers, friction members which smoothly bring gear and shaft to the same speed before the toothed dog clutches are engaged.

Adjustments

SHIFT LINKAGE

A-412 Models

▶ **See Figures 1, 2 and 3**

1. Place the transaxle in neutral at the 3-4 position.
2. Loosen the shift tube clamp. Align the hole in the blocker bracket with the tab in the slider.
3. Place a ⅝ in. (16mm) spacer between the shift tube flange and the yoke at the shift base.
4. Tighten the shift tube clamp and remove the spacer.

➡**It is possible for the manual transaxle to become locked in two gears at once. This will occur if the interlock blocker on the gearshift selector lever has spread apart. The result of operating like this will be clutch failure at the least, and driveline failure at the worst. To correctly diagnose the problem, the interlock should be checked using the following procedure:**

5. Disconnect the shift linkage operating lever from the transaxle selector shaft.
6. Remove the transaxle detent spring assembly and selector shaft boot.
7. Remove the aluminum selector shaft plug.
8. Place the transaxle in neutral and pull the selector shaft assembly out of the case.
9. Measure the interlock blocker gap **A**, in the accompanying picture. If gap **A** exceeds ⁵⁄₁₆ in. (8mm) replace the gearshift selector shaft assembly.

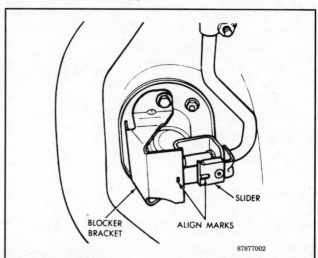

87877002

Fig. 1 Align the hole in the blocker bracket with the tab in the slider

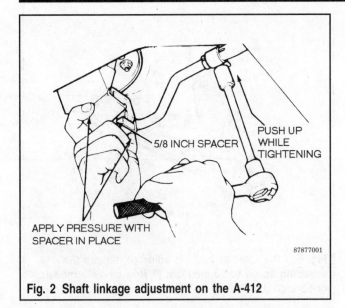

Fig. 2 Shaft linkage adjustment on the A-412

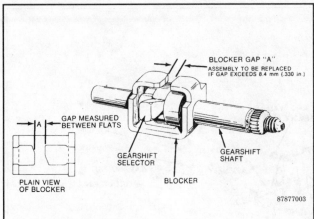

Fig. 3 If the interlock blocker gap (A) exceeds ⁵/₁₆ in. (8mm) replace the gearshift selector shaft assembly

10. Apply a thick coating of chassis grease to the selector shaft shoulder at the threaded end, then insert the shaft through the oil seal. Reverse steps 1-4 to install. Adjust the shift linkage.

A-460 Models
▶ See Figure 4

1. From the left side of the car, remove the lockpin from the transaxle selector shaft housing.
2. Reverse the lockpin and insert it in the same threaded hole while pushing the shaft into the selector housing. A hole in the shaft will align with the lockpin, allowing the pin to be threaded into the housing. This will lock the shaft in the 1-2 neutral position.
3. Raise and support the vehicle on jackstands.
4. Loosen the clamp bolt that secures the gearshift tube to the gearshift connector.
5. Make sure that the gearshift connector slides and turns freely in the gearshift tube.

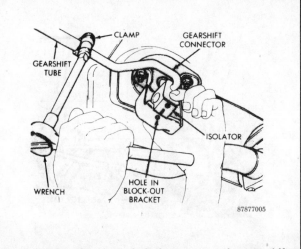

Fig. 4 Loosen the clamp bolt that secures the gearshift tube to the gearshift connector

6. Position the shift connector assembly so that the isolator is contacting the standing flange and the isolator rib is aligned front and back with the hole in the block-out bracket. Hold the connector in this position and tighten the gearshift tube clamp bolt to 14 ft. lbs. (19 Nm).
7. Lower the car.
8. Remove the lockpin from the selector shaft housing and install it the original way in the housing.
9. Tighten the lockpin to 105 inch lbs. (12 Nm).
10. Check shifter action.

A-465 and A-525 Models
▶ See Figures 5, 6, 7, 8, 9 and 10

1. From the left side of the car, remove the lockpin from the transaxle selector shaft housing.
2. Reverse the lockpin and insert it in the same threaded hole while pushing the selector shaft into the selector housing. A hole in the selector shaft will align with the lockpin, allowing the lockpin to be screwed into the housing. This will lock the selector shaft in the 1-2 neutral position.
3. Remove the gearshift knob, the retaining nut and the pull-up ring.
4. Remove the attaching screws and remove the console.
5. Make two cable adjusting pins.
6. Adjust the selector cable and tighten the adjusting screw to 60 inch lbs. (7 Nm) on 1983 models, or 55 inch lbs. (6 Nm) on 1984 models.

➡**Proper tension of the selector cable and the crossover cable adjusting screw is important for proper operation of the shift linkage.**

7. Adjust the crossover cable and tighten the adjusting screw to 60 inch lbs. (7 Nm) on 1983 models, or 55 inch lbs. (6 Nm) on 1984 models.
8. Remove the lock pin from the selector shaft housing and reinstall the pin in the housing so that the long end is pointing up. Tighten the pin to 105 inch lbs. (12 Nm).
9. Check for proper operation of the shift cables.
10. Reinstall the console, pull-up ring, retaining nut and the gearshift knob.

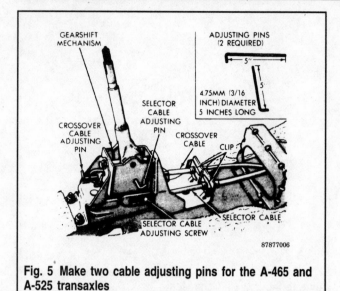

Fig. 5 Make two cable adjusting pins for the A-465 and A-525 transaxles

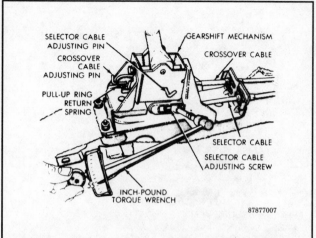

Fig. 6 If the selector cable is adjusted, tighten the adjusting screw to 60 inch lbs. (7 Nm) on 1983 models, or 55 inch lbs. (6 Nm) on 1984 models

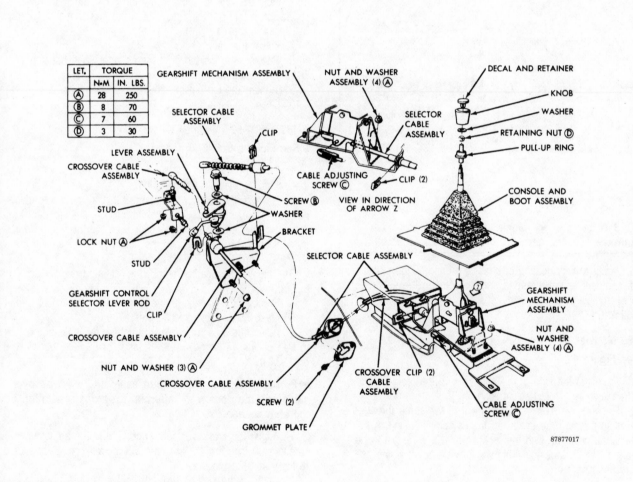

Fig. 7 Cable operated shift linkage — 1983 A-465 models

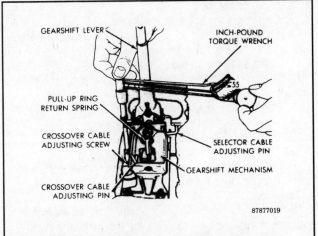

Fig. 8 Adjust the crossover cable and tighten the adjusting screw to 60 inch lbs. (7 Nm) on 1983 models, or 55 inch lbs. (6 Nm) on 1984 models

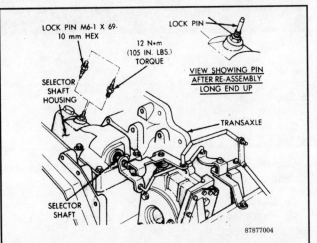

Fig. 9 Install the lock pin in the selector shaft housing so that the long end is pointing up, then tighten to 105 inch lbs. (12 Nm) — A-460, A-465 and A-525 shown

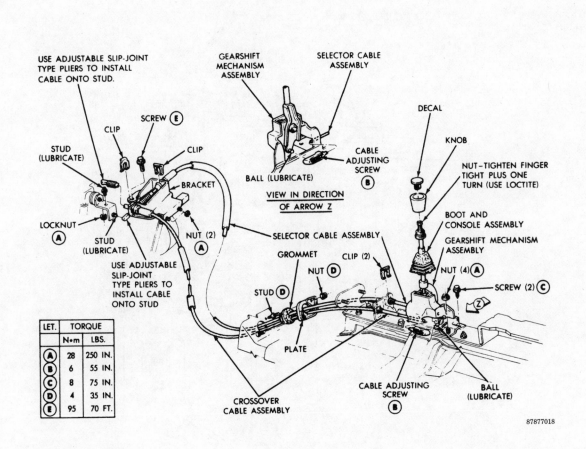

LET.	TORQUE	
	N•m	LBS.
A	28	250 IN.
B	6	55 IN.
C	8	75 IN.
D	4	35 IN.
E	95	70 FT.

Fig. 10 Cable operated shift linkage — 1984 A-465 and A-525 models

Transaxle Assembly

REMOVAL & INSTALLATION

▶ See Figure 11

A-412 Models

▶ See Figures 12 and 13

➡ **Any time the differential cover is removed, a new gasket should be formed from RTV sealant.**

1. Remove the engine timing mark access plug.
2. Rotate the engine to align the drilled mark on the flywheel with the pointer on the engine.
3. Disconnect the negative battery cable.
4. Part the shift linkage rods.
5. Detach the starter and ground wires.
6. Disconnect the backup light switch wire.
7. Remove the starter.
8. Separate the clutch cable.
9. Disconnect the speedometer cable.
10. Support the weight of the engine from above, preferably with a shop hoist or the fabricated holding fixture.
11. Raise and support the vehicle.
12. Disconnect the driveshafts and support them out of the way.
13. Remove the left splash shield.
14. Drain the transaxle.
15. Unbolt the left engine mount.
16. Remove the transaxle-to-engine bolts.
17. Slide the transaxle to the left until the mainshaft clears, then, carefully lower it from the car.

To install:

18. Position the transaxle so the mainshaft will slide straight into the center of the clutch. Turn the transaxle slightly, if necessary, and change the angle until the mainshaft engages, and then slide the transaxle to the right until the bell housing bolt-holes line up with the corresponding bores in the block.
19. Install the transaxle-to-engine bolts. Reinstall the through bolt for the left engine mount.

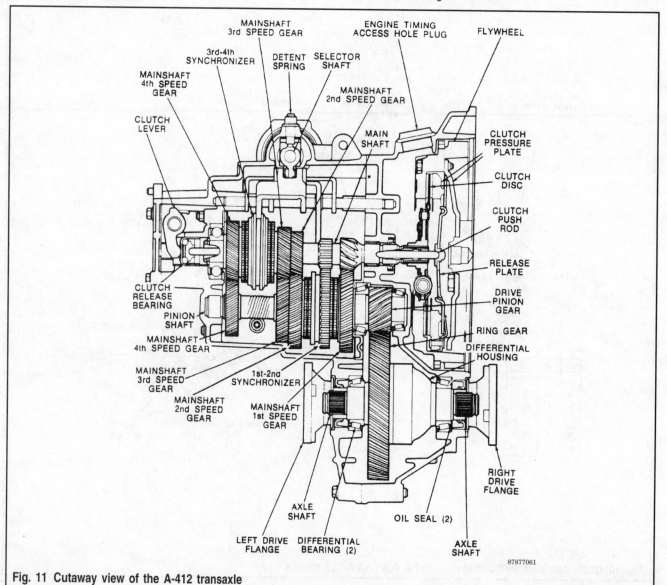

Fig. 11 Cutaway view of the A-412 transaxle

87877061

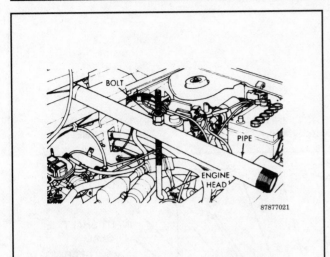

Fig. 12 Support the weight of the engine using a suitable holding fixture

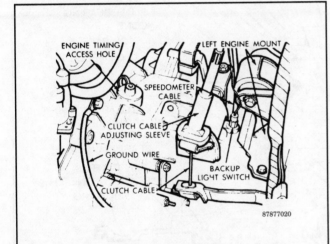

Fig. 13 Unbolt the left engine mount, if in the way remove the backup light switch

20. Install the left side splash shield.
21. Install the driveshafts back into the transaxle.
22. Lower the vehicle to the ground. Remove the engine support system.
23. Reconnect the speedometer and clutch cables.
24. Install the starter. Connect the backup light switch wire.
25. Reconnect the shift rods. Reconnect the battery cable. Install the engine timing mark access plug.
26. Adjust the clutch cable and the shift linkage.
27. Fill the transaxle with the recommended fluid. See Section 1.

A-460, A-465, A-525 Models
▶ **See Figures 14, 15 and 16**

1. Disconnect the negative battery cable.
2. Install a shop crane and lifting eye under the number 4 cylinder exhaust manifold bolt to securely support the engine.
3. Disconnect the shift linkage.
4. Remove both front wheels.

5. Remove the left front splash shield, and left engine mount.
6. Follow the procedures under Halfshaft Removal and Installation later in this section.
7. On 1987-89 models, disconnect the anti-rotation link or damper at the crossmember, leaving it connected at the transaxle.

➡ It will be easier to locate the transaxle, so as to align the bell housing bolt-holes with those in the block, if two locating pins are fabricated and are used in place of the top two locating bolts. To fabricate the pins: Buy two extra bolts. Hacksaw the heads off the bolts. Then, cut slots in the ends of the bolts for a flat-bladed screwdriver. Finally, remove all burrs with a grinding wheel.

8. Before installing the transaxle onto the engine block, install the two locating pins into the top two engine block holes.
9. Install a positive means of supporting the engine, such as a support fixture that runs across between the two front fenders.
10. Remove the upper bolts those that are accessible from above from the bell housing.
11. For 1986 and later vehicles, refer to the appropriate procedure in this section to remove or install the driveshafts. This will include removing both front wheels and raising the car and supporting it securely so it can be worked on from underneath. On 1985 and earlier vehicles, remove the driveshafts as follows:

   a. Remove the left splash shield. Drain the differential and remove the cover.
   b. Remove the speedometer adapter, cable and gear.
   c. Remove the sway bar.
   d. Remove both lower ball joint-to-steering knuckle bolts.
   e. Pry the lower ball joint from the steering knuckle.
   f. Remove the driveshaft from the hub.
   g. Rotate both driveshafts to expose the circlip ends. Note the flat surface on the inner ends of both axle tripod shafts. Pry the circlip out.
   h. Remove both driveshafts.

12. On 1986 and later vehicles, remove the left side splash shield.
13. Disconnect the plug for the neutral safety/backup light switch.
14. Remove the engine mount bracket from the front crossmember.
15. Support the transaxle from underneath.
16. Remove the front mount insulator through-bolts.
17. Remove the long through-bolt from the left hand engine mount.
18. Remove the starter. Then, remove any bell housing bolts that are still in position.
19. Slide the transaxle directly away from the engine so the transaxle input shaft will slide smoothly out of the bearing in the flywheel and the clutch disc. Lower the transaxle and remove it from the engine compartment.

To install:
20. Support the unit securely and raise it into precise alignment with the engine block. Then, move it toward the block, inserting the transaxle input shaft into the clutch disc. Turn the input shaft slightly, if necessary, to get the splines to engage.
21. Install the lower bell housing bolts and the starter. Bell housing bolts are tightened to 70 ft. lbs. (95 Nm).

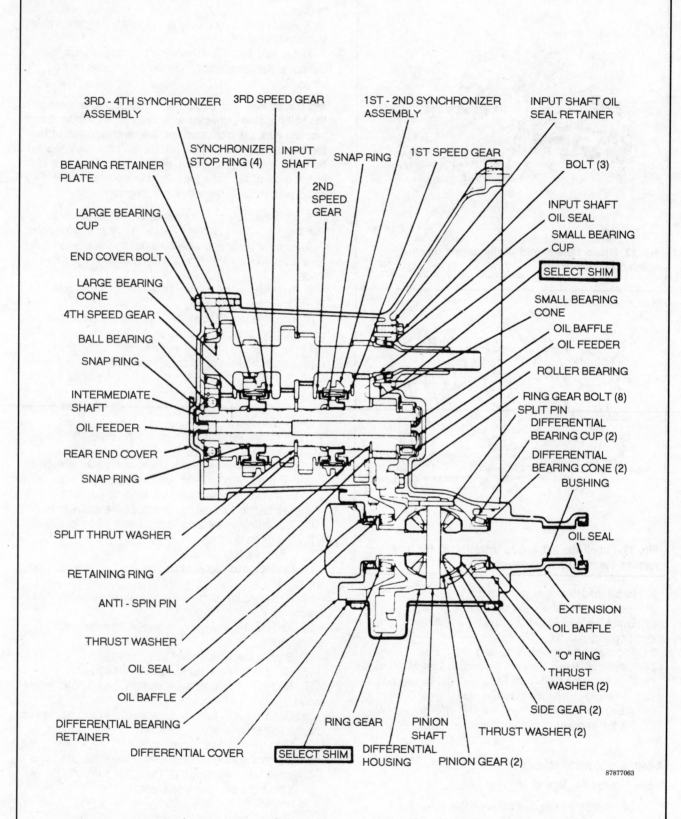

Fig. 14 Cross-section of the A-460 transaxle

87877063

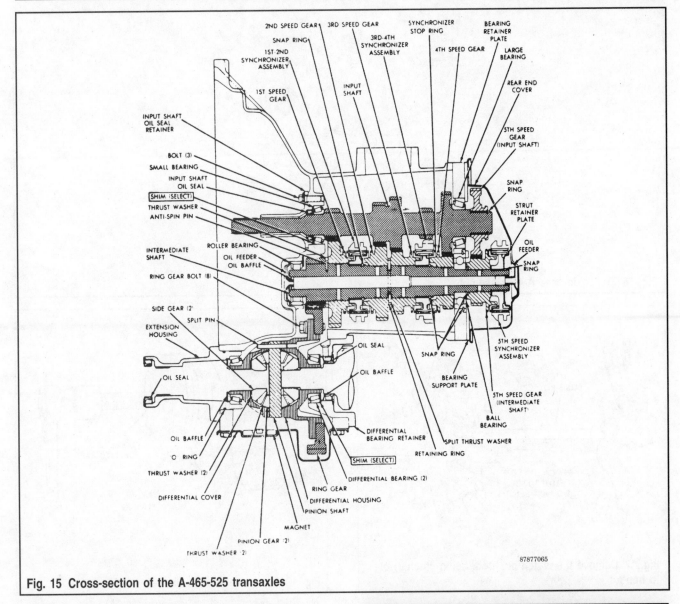

Fig. 15 Cross-section of the A-465-525 transaxles

22. Install the long through-bolt into the left hand engine mount.

23. Install the front mount insulator through-bolts.

24. Remove the jack supporting the transaxle. Then, install the engine mount bracket onto the front crossmember.

25. Reconnect the electrical connector for the backup light/neutral safety switch.

26. Install the driveshafts by reversing the removal procedure. Install the left side splash shield.

27. With the wheels remounted and the car back on the floor, install the remaining bell housing bolts and tighten them to 105 inch lbs. (12 Nm).

28. Remove the engine support fixture.

29. Connect the anti-rotation strut. Tighten the bolts to 70 ft. lbs. (95 Nm).

30. Connect the shift linkage. Always use new self-locking nuts on the shift linkage. Observe the following torques:
- Shift housing-to-case: 21 ft. lbs. (28 Nm)
- Strut-to-case: 70 ft. lbs. 95 Nm)
- Flywheel-to-crankshaft: 65 ft. lbs. (88 Nm)

Transaxle Overhaul

DISASSEMBLY & ASSEMBLY

A-412 Models

◗ See Figures 17, 18, 19, 20, 21, 22, 23, 24, 25, 26, 27, 28, 29, 30, 31, 32, 33, 34, 35, 36, 37, 38, 39, 40, 41, 42, 43, 44, 45, 46, 47, 48 and 49

➥**Final mainshaft adjustment requires a measurement made with a special tool.**

1. Remove the clutch pushrod, being careful not to bend it.

2. Remove the selector shaft plug from the case.

3. Using pliers, remove the snap-ring and cone washer.

4. With special tool L-4443 or an equivalent, remove the drive flange.

5. Next with special tool L-4445 or equivalent remove the drive flange seal.

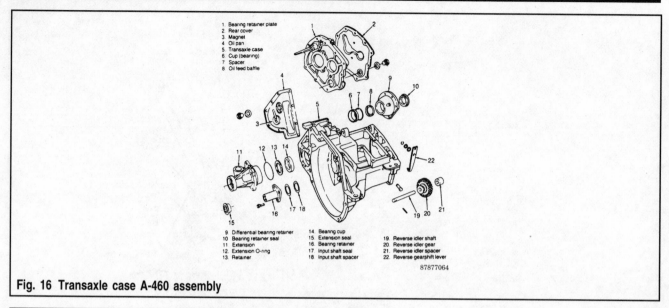

1. Bearing retainer plate
2. Rear cover
3. Magnet
4. Oil pan
5. Transaxle case
6. Cup (bearing)
7. Spacer
8. Oil feed baffle

9. Differential bearing retainer
10. Bearing retainer seal
11. Extension
12. Extension O-ring
13. Retainer

14. Bearing cup
15. Extension seal
16. Bearing retainer
17. Input shaft seal
18. Input shaft spacer

19. Reverse idler shaft
20. Reverse idler gear
21. Reverse idler spacer
22. Reverse gearshift lever

87877064

Fig. 16 Transaxle case A-460 assembly

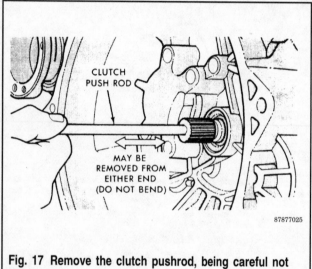

CLUTCH PUSH ROD

MAY BE REMOVED FROM EITHER END (DO NOT BEND)

87877025

Fig. 17 Remove the clutch pushrod, being careful not to bend it

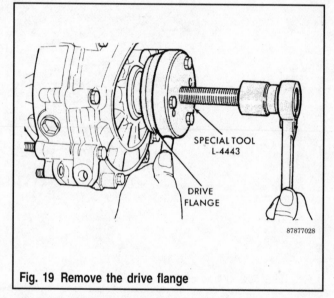

SPECIAL TOOL L-4443

DRIVE FLANGE

87877028

Fig. 19 Remove the drive flange

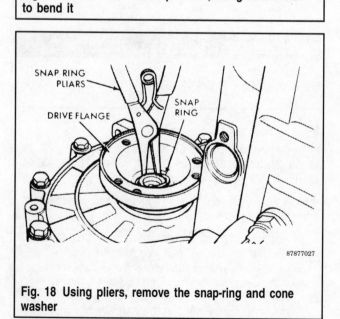

SNAP RING PLIARS

DRIVE FLANGE

SNAP RING

87877027

Fig. 18 Using pliers, remove the snap-ring and cone washer

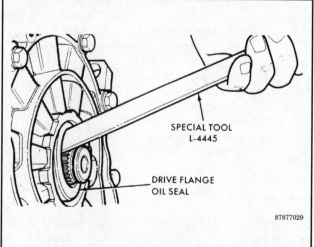

SPECIAL TOOL L-4445

DRIVE FLANGE OIL SEAL

87877029

Fig. 20 With special tool L-4445 or equivalent remove the drive flange seal

6. Disconnect the selector shaft cover from the transaxle.

7. Remove the detent spring assembly and rubber boot, then tap out the selector shaft and pry out the oil seal.

8. Push out the selector shaft, then remove it and the seal.

9. Using a small prybar, carefully pry out the two mainshaft bearing retaining nut rubber plugs.

10. Remove the four bolts and the clutch release bearing end cover. Hold the clutch release lever upwards while removing the cover to avoid loading or damage to the case threads. Take out the release bearing and plastic sleeve.

11. Using two small prybars, push the circlip off the clutch torque shaft. Pull the torque shaft out of the case, then remove the pedal return spring and release lever. Pry out the torque shaft oil seal.

12. Remove the three mainshaft bearing retainer nuts; two were under the rubber covers removed earlier and the 3rd is inside the clutch release housing. The three studs and clips will drop into the case.

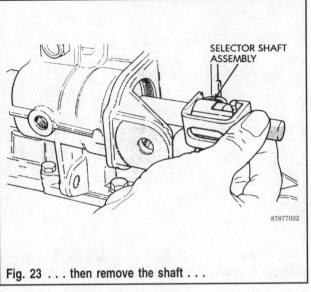

Fig. 23 . . . then remove the shaft . . .

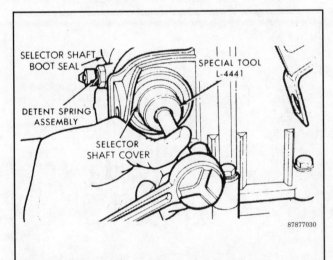

Fig. 21 **Disconnect the selector shaft cover from the transaxle**

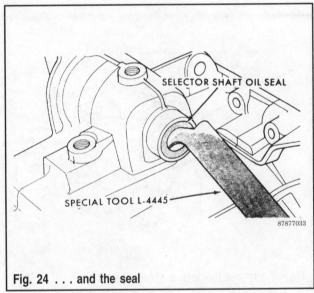

Fig. 24 . . . **and the seal**

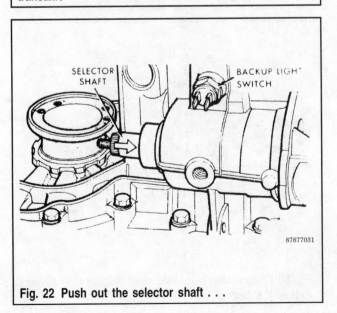

Fig. 22 **Push out the selector shaft . . .**

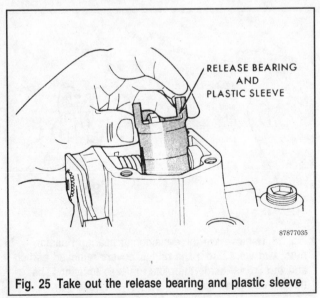

Fig. 25 **Take out the release bearing and plastic sleeve**

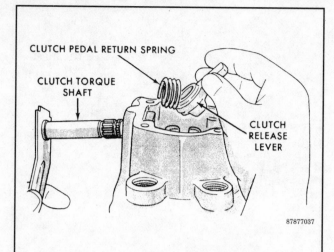

Fig. 26 Pull the torque shaft out of the case, then remove the pedal return spring and release lever

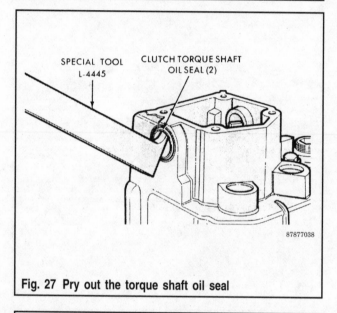

Fig. 27 Pry out the torque shaft oil seal

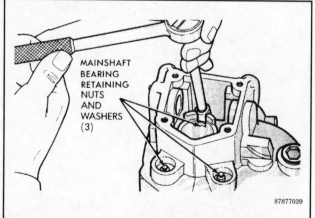

Fig. 28 Remove the three mainshaft bearing retainer nuts; two were under the rubber covers removed earlier and the 3rd is inside the clutch release housing. The three studs and clips will drop into the case

13. Remove the ten case bolts and the four stud nuts, then the transaxle case.

→**The factory uses a special tool to do this; it pushes against the end of the mainshaft. Make sure to tag the shims for reuse.**

14. Remove the transaxle case.

15. Remove the reverse idler set screw (bolt) and the backup light switch.

16. Remove the two bolts, the reverse shift fork and the supports.

17. Remove the snapring from the end of the pinion shaft.

18. Pull off the bearing and the 4th gear from the end of the mainshaft. Remove the 4th gear needle bearing.

19. Remove the 3rd-4th synchronizer and 3rd gear along with the needle bearing.

20. Using a small prybar, carefully pry off the shift rail E-clips, then remove the shift fork assembly.

21. Remove the mainshaft assembly; it can be disassembled by removing the snaprings and the components. The clutch

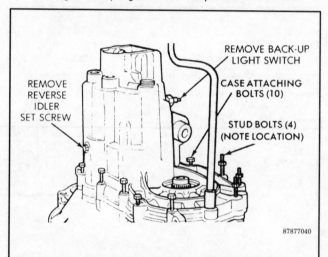

Fig. 29 Remove the ten case bolts and the four stud nuts, then remove the transaxle case

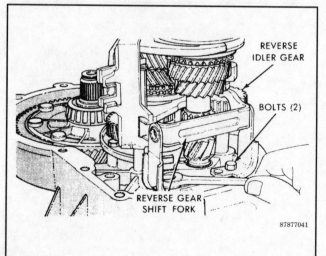

Fig. 30 Remove the two bolts, then remove the reverse shift fork supports

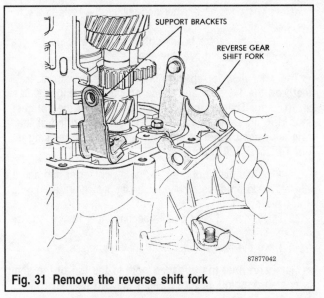

Fig. 31 Remove the reverse shift fork

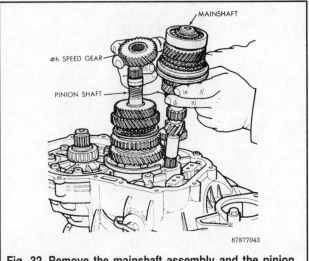

Fig. 32 Remove the mainshaft assembly and the pinion shaft 4th gear

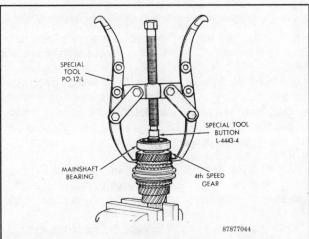

Fig. 33 Pull off the bearing and the 4th gear from the end of the mainshaft. Remove the 4th gear needle bearing

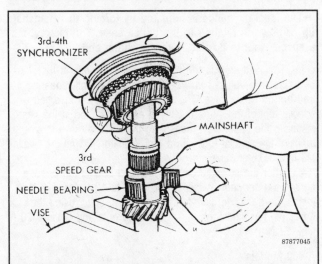

Fig. 34 Remove the 3rd-4th synchronizer and 3rd gear along with the needle bearing

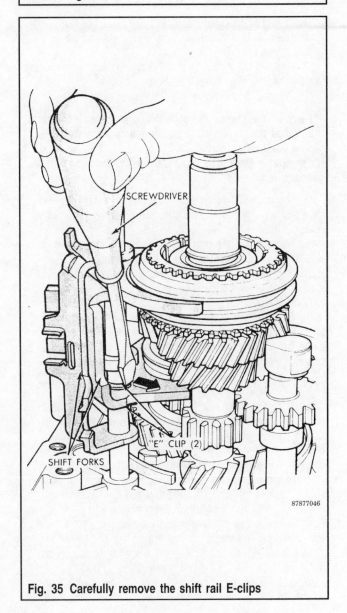

Fig. 35 Carefully remove the shift rail E-clips

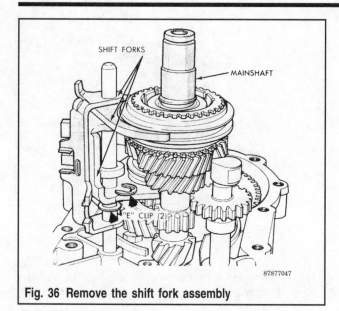

SHIFT FORKS
MAINSHAFT
"E" CLIP (2)
87877047

Fig. 36 Remove the shift fork assembly

pushrod seal and bushing assembly can be driven out of the shaft with a ⅜ in. (10mm) diameter brass rod. Replace it by driving it with a plastic hammer.

22. Remove the pinion shaft snapring and the 3rd gear, then the 2nd gear and its needle bearing.

23. Pry or pull out the reverse idler gear shaft.

➡**Remove the plastic thrust button and install a tool at the end of the pinion shaft before using the puller. The pinion shaft bearing retainer is notched in two locations for the puller jaws. The inner sleeve for 2nd gear and 1st gear are removed together.**

24. Using L-4534 or an equivalent puller, remove the 1st gear and the 1st-2nd synchronizer assembly from the pinion shaft.

25. Remove the 1st gear needle bearing and scribe a mark across the 1st-2nd synchronizer for reassembly.

26. Remove the pinion shaft bolts, the retainer, the thrust washer (the flat side goes up) and the pinion shaft.

To assemble:

27. Place a 0.02 in. (0.65mm) shim in the bearing housing and press the small bearing cup into the clutch housing, then move the pinion up and down, measuring the end-play with a dial indicator.

➡**Do not rotate the shaft while moving it up and down.**

28. The correct preload is determined by adding 0.008 in. (0.20mm) to the reading obtained from the dial indicator in Step 1, along with the shim thickness, 0.02 in. (0.65mm). For example: if the measurement is 0.02 in. (0.30mm), the correct shim to use is 0.05 in. (1.15mm) (0.65 + 0.03 + 0.20 = 1.15). Remove the pinion shaft ball bearing retainer and the pinion shaft. Remove the small bearing cup and the 0.02 in. (0.65mm) shim and install the correct shim.

29. If new bearings are installed on the pinion shaft, lubricate them with transaxle oil, install the shaft and check the shaft rotational pre-load with a torque wrench; it should be 4-13 inch lbs. (0.4-1.5 Nm), if not, reset the preload.

30. Install the pinion shaft and place the 1st gear thrust washer over the shaft, with the flat side up facing the gear.

Install the pinion shaft retainer and tighten the bolts to 29 ft. lbs. (39 Nm).

31. Install the needle bearing, the 1st gear and the 1st gear synchronizer stop ring over the shaft.

➡**The wear limit for spacing between the synchronizer teeth on the 1st gear and those on the stop ring is 0.02 in. (0.5mm). There is one tooth missing from the 1st gear stop ring on early models. The 1st gear will grind, if this ring isn't used. Later models have three teeth missing in three places, 120° apart.**

32. Align the marks on the 1st-2nd synchronizer hub and the sleeve, made on disassembly. Install the synchronizer, driving it into place.

33. Drive the 2nd gear needle bearing inner race into place over the shaft.

34. Drive the reverse idler gear shaft into place.

➡**Make sure that the threaded hole in the top of the shaft is centered, pointing out between the two nearest case edge bolt holes.**

35. Place the 2nd gear needle bearing over the pinion shaft, then the 2nd gear stop ring, the 2nd gear and the 3rd gear onto the shaft; make sure that the 3rd gear has the thrust face down.

36. Install the 3rd gear snap-ring. Measure the end-play between 3rd gear and the snapring with a feeler gauge; it should be 0-0.004 in. (0-0.1mm). The snaprings are available in thicknesses from 0.1-0.12 in. (2.5-3.0mm) for adjustment. Replace the snapring with the one selected.

37. Seat the mainshaft assembly.

38. Install the shift fork assemblies and the E-clips.

39. Install the 4th gear needle bearing over the mainshaft and place the 4th gear synchronizer stop ring in place. Install the 4th gear and the snapring.

40. Install the reverse shift fork and the support brackets, then tighten the bolts to 105 inch lbs. (12 Nm).

41. Using a feeler gauge, measure the clearance between the top of the pinion shaft 2nd gear and the bottom of the mainshaft 3rd gear.

➡**The ideal clearance is adjusted by forcing the mainshaft up or down in relation to the clutch case. The factory has a special tool to do this from the clutch end.**

42. The next step is to determine the thickness of the shim or shims to be placed between the mainshaft roller bearing and the transaxle case. The factory does this by inserting a special tool of the same thickness as the bearing in the case, installing the case, then measuring the up and down movement of the special tool with a dial indicator. Shims are available in 0.3-0.6mm sizes.

43. After the selected shim is installed behind the bearing, tighten the bearing retainer clamp bolts to 13 ft. lbs. (18 Nm). Install the transaxle case-to-clutch housing bolts, using the guide pin for alignment, and tighten the nuts and bolts to 20 ft. lbs. (27 Nm).

A-460 Models

The Chrysler designed and built A-460 (4-speed) fully synchronized manual transaxle combines gear reduction, ratio se-

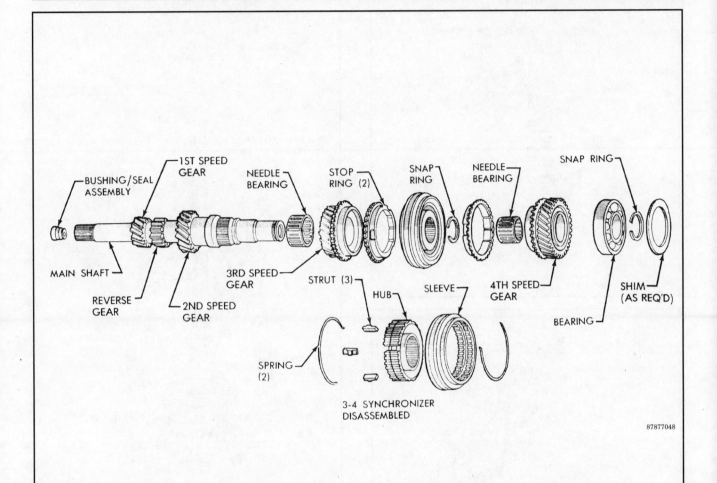

Fig. 37 Remove the mainshaft assembly; it can be disassembled by removing the snaprings and the components

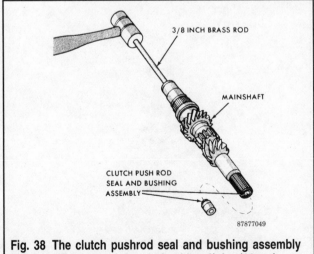

Fig. 38 The clutch pushrod seal and bushing assembly can be driven out of the shaft with a ⅜ in. (10mm) diameter brass rod

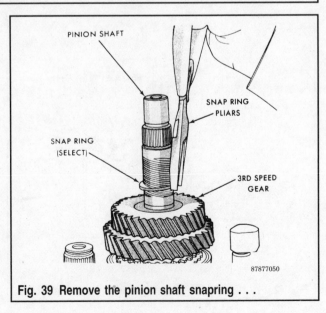

Fig. 39 Remove the pinion shaft snapring . . .

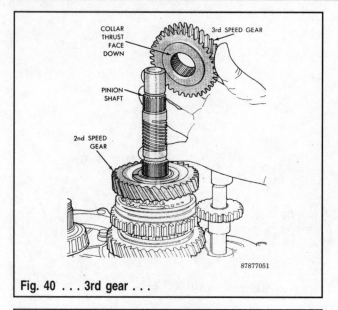

Fig. 40 . . . 3rd gear . . .

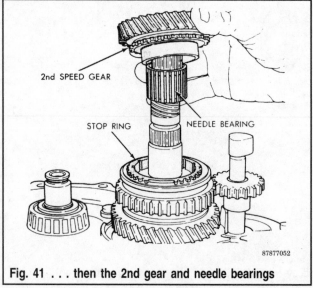

Fig. 41 . . . then the 2nd gear and needle bearings

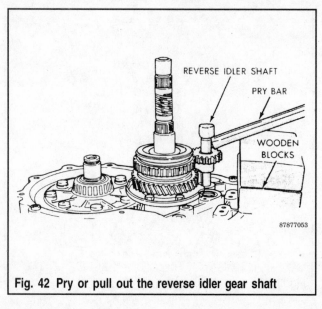

Fig. 42 Pry or pull out the reverse idler gear shaft

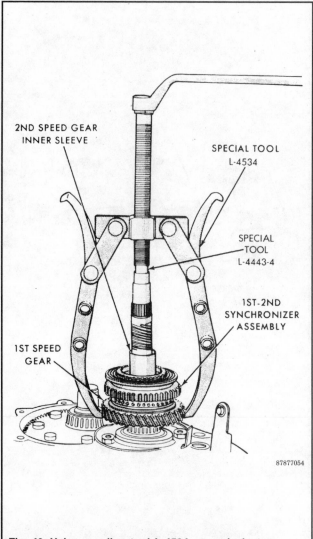

Fig. 43 Using a puller, tool L-4534 or equivalent, remove the 1st gear and the 1st-2nd synchronizer assembly from the pinion shaft

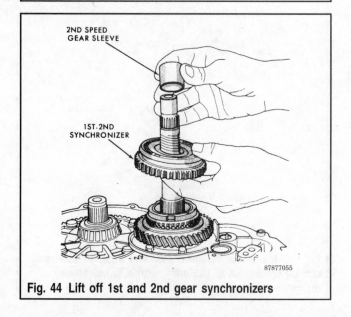

Fig. 44 Lift off 1st and 2nd gear synchronizers

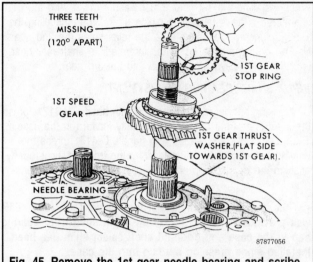

Fig. 45 Remove the 1st gear needle bearing and scribe a mark across the 1st-2nd synchronizer for reassembly

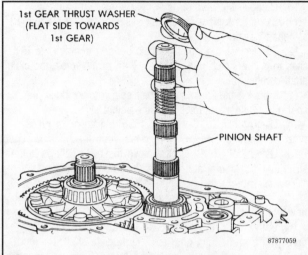

Fig. 48 . . . the thrust washer (the flat side goes up) . . .

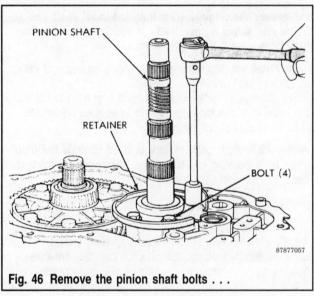

Fig. 46 Remove the pinion shaft bolts . . .

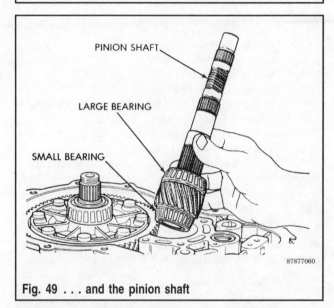

Fig. 49 . . . and the pinion shaft

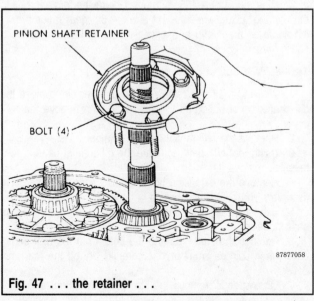

Fig. 47 . . . the retainer . . .

lection and differential functions in one unit housed in á die cast aluminum case.

1. With the transaxle removed from the vehicle, remove the differential cover bolts and the stud nuts, then remove the cover.

2. Remove the differential bearing retainer bolts.

3. Using tool No. L-4435, rotate the differential bearing retainer to remove it.

4. Remove the extension housing bolts, then the differential assembly and extension housing.

5. Take out the selector shaft housing bolts, then the selector shaft housing.

6. Remove the stud nuts and the bolts from the rear end cover, then using a small prybar, carefully pry off the rear end cover.

7. Using snaping pliers, remove the large snaping from the intermediate shaft rear ball bearing.

8. Take off the bearing retainer plate by tapping it with a plastic hammer.

9. Remove the 3rd-4th shift fork rail.

10. Remove the reverse idler gear shaft and gear.

11. Extract the input shaft gear assembly and the intermediate shaft gear assembly.

12. To remove the clutch release bearing, remove the E-clips from the clutch release shaft, then disassemble the clutch shaft components.

13. Take off the three input shaft seal retainer bolts, the seal, the retainer assembly and the select shim.

14. Using tools No. C-4171, C-4656 and an arbor press, press the input shaft front bearing cup from the transaxle case.

15. Using tool No. C-4660, remove the two bearing retainer strap bolts, then the intermediate shaft front bearing.

To assemble:

The assembly of the transaxle is the reverse of disassembly; however, please note the following:

16. Using tools No. C-4657, C-4171 and an arbor press, press the front bearing onto the intermediate shaft; the input shaft front bearing cup is installed with the same tools used for removal.

17. Determine the shim thickness for the correct bearing end-play only if any of the following parts are replaced:

    a. The transaxle case.

    b. The input shaft seal retainer.

    c. The bearing retainer plate.

    d. The rear end cover.

    e. The input shaft or bearings.

18. To determine proper shim thickness, refer to the Input Shaft Bearing End Play Adjustment.

19. Using tool No. C-4674 and a plastic hammer, install the input shaft oil seal.

20. Using a 0.1 in. (3mm) bead of RTV sealant, place it around the edge of the input shaft seal retainer and making sure the drain hole of the retainer is facing downward.

21. The differential bearing retainer is installed with the same special tool used for removal.

➡The rear end cover, the selector shaft housing and the differential cover are sealed with RTV sealant.

INTERMEDIATE SHAFT

➡The 1st-2nd, the 3rd-4th shift forks and the synchronizer stop rings are interchangeable. However, if parts are to be reused, reassemble them in their original position.

1. Remove the intermediate shaft rear bearing snapring.

2. Using the puller tool No. C-4693, remove the intermediate shaft rear bearing.

3. Using snapring pliers, remove the 3rd-4th synchronizer hub snapring.

4. Using the puller tool No. L-4534, remove the 3rd-4th synchronizer hub and the 3rd gear.

5. Remove the retaining ring, the split thrust washer, the 2nd gear and the synchronizer stop ring.

6. Using snapring pliers, remove the 1st-2nd synchronizer hub snapring.

7. Take off the 1st gear, the stop ring and the 1st-2nd synchronizer assembly.

8. Remove the 1st gear thrust washer and the anti-spin pin.

To assemble:

The assembly of the intermediate shaft is the reverse of the disassembly; however, please note the following: When assembling the intermediate shaft, make sure the speed gears turn freely and have a minimum of 0.003 in. (0.08mm) end-play.

When installing the 1st gear thrust washer make sure the chamfered edge is facing the pinion gear. When installing the 1st-2nd synchronizer make sure the relief faces the 2nd gear. Use an arbor press to install the intermediate shaft rear bearing, the 3rd-4th synchronizer hub and the 3rd gear.

INPUT SHAFT BEARING ADJUSTMENT

1. Using special tool No. L-4656 with handle C-4171, press the input shaft front bearing cup slightly forward in the case. Then, using tool No. L-4655 with handle C-4171, press the bearing cup back into the case, from the front, to the properly position the bearing cup before checking the input shaft end-play.

➡This step is not necessary if the special tool No. L-4655 was previously used to install the input shaft front bearing cup in the case and no input shaft select shim has been installed since pressing the cup into the case.

2. Select a gauging shim which will give 0.005-0.01 in. (0.025-0.50mm) end-play.

➡Measure the original shim from the input shaft seal retainer and select a shim 0.005 in. (0.25mm) thinner than the original for the gauging shim.

3. Install the gauging shim on the bearing cup and the input shaft seal retainer.

4. Alternately tighten the input shaft seal retainer bolts until the retainer is bottomed against the case, then tighten the bolts to 21 ft. lbs. (28 Nm).

➡The input shaft seal retainer is used to draw the input shaft front bearing cup the proper distance into the case bore.

A-465, A-525 Models

The Chrysler designed and built A-465 (1983-84) and the A-525 (1985-88) fully synchronized 5-speed manual transaxles combine gear reduction, ratio selection and differential functions in one unit housed in a die cast aluminum case. The A-525 has a close ratio gearset with different 2nd, 3rd and 4th gear ratios than the A-465, to provide better performance through the gears, while the 1st and the 5th gear ratios are the same as the A-465 to maintain the same launch and top gear characteristics.

1984-85 MODELS

1. With the transaxle removed from the vehicle, remove the differential cover bolts and the stud nuts, then remove the cover.

2. Remove the differential bearing retainer bolts.

3. Using tool No. L-4435, rotate the differential bearing retainer to remove it.

4. Remove the extension housing bolts, then the differential assembly and extension housing.

5. Extract the selector shaft housing bolts, then the selector shaft housing.

6. Remove the stud nuts and the bolts from the rear end cover, then using a small prybar, carefully pry off the rear end cover.

7. On 5-speeds, remove the 5th speed synchronizer strut retainer snapring, strut retainer plate, 5th gear synchronizer, shift fork with rail, intermediate shaft 5th gear, input shaft 5th

gear snapring and 5th gear. Then, use a puller such as C-4693 with legs C-4621-1 to remove the 5th gear synchronizer hub. On 4-speeds, remove the large snapring from the intermediate shaft rear ball bearing.

8. Remove the bearing retainer plate by tapping it with a plastic hammer.

9. Take off the 3rd-4th shift fork rail.

10. Remove the reverse idler gear shaft and gear.

11. Remove the input shaft gear assembly and the intermediate shaft gear assembly.

12. To remove the clutch release bearing, remove the E-clips from the clutch release shaft, then disassemble the clutch shaft components.

13. Remove the three input shaft seal retainer bolts, the seal, the retainer assembly and the select shim.

14. Using tools No. C-4171, C-4656 and an arbor press, press the input shaft front bearing cup from the transaxle case.

15. Using tool No. C-4660, remove the two bearing retainer strap bolts, then the intermediate shaft front bearing.

16. Remove the 5th gear shifter pin, the 5th gear detent ball and the spring.

17. Remove the 5th gear synchronizer strut retainer plate snapring and the 5th gear synchronizer strut retainer plate.

18. Remove the 5th gear synchronizer assembly and shift fork with shift rail.

19. Remove the intermediate shaft 5th gear, the input shaft 5th gear snapring and the 5th gear.

20. Remove the bearing support plate bolts and pry off the bearing support plate.

To assemble:

The assembly of the transaxle is the reverse of disassembly; however, please note the following:

21. Using tools No. C-4657, C-4171 and an arbor press, press the front bearing onto the intermediate shaft; the input shaft front bearing cup is installed with the same tools used for removal.

22. Determine the shim thickness for the correct bearing end-play only if any of the following parts are replaced:

    a. The transaxle case.

    b. The input shaft seal retainer.

    c. The bearing retainer plate.

    d. The rear end cover.

    e. The input shaft or bearings.

23. To determine proper shim thickness, refer to the Input Shaft Bearing End Play Adjustment at the end of this section.

24. Using tool No. C-4674 and a plastic hammer, install the input shaft oil seal.

25. Using a 0.1 in. (3mm) bead of RTV sealant, place it around the edge of the input shaft seal retainer and making sure the drain hole of the retainer is facing downward.

26. The differential bearing retainer is installed with the same special tool used for removal.

➡**The rear end cover, the selector shaft housing and the differential cover are sealed with RTV sealant.**

1986-89 MODELS

1. With the transaxle removed from the vehicle, remove the eight differential cover bolts and the two stud nuts and remove the cover.

2. Remove the eight differential bearing retainer bolts.

3. Using the L-4435 or equivalent spanner wrench, rotate the differential bearing retainer to remove it.

4. Remove the four extension housing bolts, then remove the differential assembly and extension housing.

5. Remove the six selector shaft housing assembly bolts and remove the selector shaft housing assembly.

6. Remove the ten rear end cover bolts and remove the rear end cover. Clean the bead of RTV sealer off the rear end cover.

7. Using snapring pliers, remove the snapring from the 5th gear synchronizer strut retainer plate.

8. Using an Allen wrench, unscrew and then remove the 5th gear shift fork set screw. Then, lift the 5th gear synchronizer sleeve and shift fork off the synchronizer hub. Retrieve the (3) winged struts and top synchronizer spring.

9. Use a puller such as C-4693 with legs C-4621-1 to remove the 5th gear synchronizer hub. Retrieve the remaining synchronizer spring.

10. Slide the 5th gear off the intermediate shaft. With snapring pliers, remove the copper colored snapring retaining the 5th gear to the input shaft. Then, using a pulley puller such as C-4333, pull the 5th gear off the input shaft.

11. Remove the two remaining bearing support plate bolts. Then, use a screwdriver to gently pry off the bearing support plate.

12. With snapring pliers, remove the large snapring from the intermediate shaft rear ball bearing. Then, gently tap the lower surface of the bearing retainer plate with a plastic hammer to free it and lift it off the transaxle case. Clean the RTV sealer from both surfaces.

13. With a socket wrench, unscrew the 5th gear shifter guide pin. Then, remove it. Do the same with the 1st-2nd shift fork setscrew. Then, slide out the 1-2, 3-4 shift fork rail.

14. Slide out the reverse idler gear shaft, gear, and plastic stop.

15. Rotate the 3-4 shift fork to the left, and the 5th gear shifter to the right. Pull out the 5th gear shift rail. Then, pull out the input shaft assembly. Finally, pull out the intermediate shaft assembly.

16. Now, remove the 1-2, 3-4, and 5th gear shift forks.

17. To remove the clutch release bearing, take off the E-clips from the clutch release shaft, then disassemble the clutch shaft components.

18. Remove the three input shaft seal retainer bolts, the seal, the retainer assembly and the select shim.

19. Using tools No. C-4171, C-4656 and an arbor press, press the input shaft front bearing cup from the transaxle case.

20. Using tool No. C-4660, remove the two bearing retainer strap bolts, then the intermediate shaft front bearing.

21. Remove the 5th gear shifter pin, the 5th gear detent ball and the spring.

22. Remove the 5th gear synchronizer strut retainer plate snapring and the 5th gear synchronizer strut retainer plate.

23. Take off the 5th gear synchronizer assembly and shift fork with shift rail.

24. Remove the intermediate shaft 5th gear, the input shaft 5th gear snapring and the 5th gear.

25. Take off the bearing support plate bolts and pry off the bearing support plate.

To assemble:

The assembly of the transaxle is the reverse of disassembly; however, please note the following:

26. Using tools No. C-4657, C-4171 and an arbor press, press the front bearing onto the intermediate shaft; the input shaft front bearing cup is installed with the same tools used for removal.

27. Determine the shim thickness for the correct bearing end-play only if any of the following parts are replaced:
   a. The transaxle case.
   b. The input shaft seal retainer.
   c. The bearing retainer plate.
   d. The rear end cover.
   e. The input shaft or bearings.

28. To determine proper shim thickness, refer to the Input Shaft Bearing End Play Adjustment at the end of this section.

29. Using tool No. C-4674 and a plastic hammer, install the input shaft oil seal.

30. Using a 0.12 in. (3mm) bead of RTV sealant, place it around the edge of the input shaft seal retainer and making sure the drain hole of the retainer is facing downward.

31. The differential bearing retainer is installed with the same special tool used for removal.

➡**The rear end cover, the selector shaft housing and the differential cover are sealed with RTV sealant.**

INTERMEDIATE SHAFT

➡**The 1st-2nd, the 3rd-4th shift forks and the synchronizer stop rings are interchangeable. However, if parts are to be reused reassemble in the original position.**

1. Remove the intermediate shaft rear bearing snapring.
2. Using the puller tool No. C-4693, remove the intermediate shaft rear bearing.
3. Using snapring pliers, remove the 3rd-4th synchronizer hub snapring.
4. Using the puller tool No. L-4534, remove the 3rd-4th synchronizer hub and the 3rd gear.
5. Extract the retaining ring, the split thrust washer, the 2nd gear and the synchronizer stop ring.
6. Using snapring pliers, remove the 1st-2nd synchronizer hub snapring.
7. Remove the 1st gear, the stop ring and the 1st-2nd synchronizer assembly.
8. Remove the 1st gear thrust washer and the anti-spin pin.

To assemble:

The assembly of the intermediate shaft is the Reverse of the disassembly, however please note the following:

• When assembling the intermediate shaft, make sure the speed gears turn freely and have a minimum of 0.003 in. (0.08mm) end-play.

• When installing the 1st gear thrust washer make sure the chamfered edge is facing the pinion gear.

• When installing the 1st-2nd synchronizer make sure the relief faces the 2nd gear.

• Use an arbor press to install the intermediate shaft rear bearing, the 3rd-4th synchronizer hub and the 3rd gear.

INPUT SHAFT BEARING END PLAY ADJUSTMENT

1. Using special tool No. L-4656 with handle C-4171, press the input shaft front bearing cup slightly forward in the case. Then, using tool No. L-4655 with handle C-4171, press the

bearing cup back into the case, from the front, to the properly position the bearing cup before checking the input shaft end-play.

➡**This step is not necessary if the special tool No. L-4655 was previously used to install the input shaft front bearing cup in the case and no input shaft select shim has been installed since pressing the cup into the case.**

2. Select a gauging shim which will give 0.001-0.196 in. (0.025-0.50mm) end-play.

➡**Measure the original shim from the input shaft seal retainer and select a shim 0.25mm thinner than the original for the gauging shim.**

3. Install the gauging shim on the bearing cup and the input shaft seal retainer.

4. Alternately tighten the input shaft seal retainer bolts until the retainer is bottomed against the case, then tighten the bolts to 21 ft. lbs. (28 Nm).

➡**The input shaft seal retainer is used to draw the input shaft front bearing cup the proper distance into the case bore.**

Halfshaft

REMOVAL & INSTALLATION

A-412 Models

◗ **See Figure 50**

➡**Any time the differential cover is removed, a new gasket should be formed from RTV sealant. Please refer to Section 1 for further information on differential fluid replacement.**

1. With the vehicle on the floor and the brakes applied, loosen the hub nut.

➡**The hub and driveshafts are splined together and retained by the hub nut which is tightened to at least 180 ft. lbs. (244 Nm).**

2. Raise and support the vehicle and remove the hub nut and washer.

➡**Always support both ends of the driveshaft during removal to prevent damage to the boots.**

3. Disconnect the lower control arm ball joint stud nut from the steering knuckle.

4. Remove the Allen head screws which secure the CV-joint to the transaxle flange.

5. Holding the CV-housing, push the outer joint and knuckle assembly outward while disengaging the inner housing from the flange face.

➡**The outer joint and shaft must be supported during disengagement of the inner joint.**

Quickly turn the open end of the joint upward to retain as much lubricant as possible, then carefully pull the outer joint

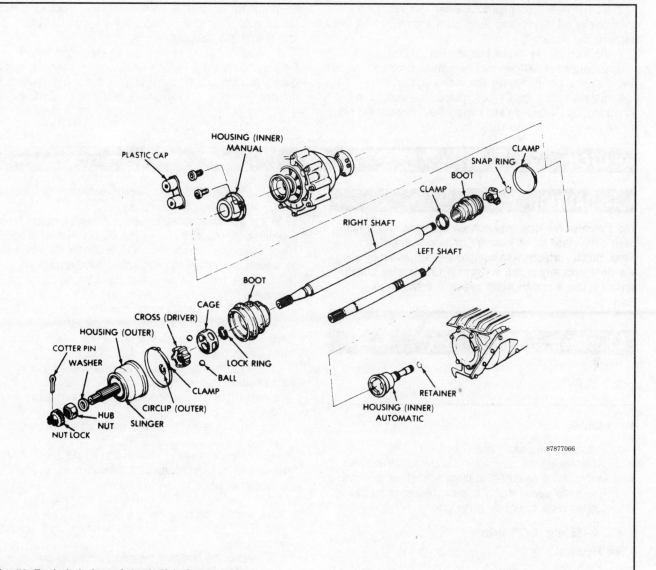

Fig. 50 Exploded view of the halfshaft assembly

spline out of the hub. Cover the joint with a clean towel to prevent dirt contamination.

6. Before installation, make sure that any lost lubricant is replaced. The only lubricant specified is Chrysler part number 4131389. No other lubricant of any type is to be used, as premature failure of the joint will result.

7. Clean the joint body and mating flange face.

8. Install the outer joint splined shaft into the hub. Do not secure with the nut and washer.

9. Early production vehicles were built with a cover plate between the hub and flange face. This cover is not necessary and should be discarded.

10. Position the inner joint in the transaxle drive flange and secure it with new screws. Tighten the screws to 37-40 ft. lbs. (50-54 Nm).

11. Connect the lower control arm to the knuckle.

12. Install the outer joint and secure it with a new nut and washer. Tighten the nut with the car on the ground and the brake set. Torque is:

- 200 ft. lbs. (271 Nm) — 1978
- 180 ft. lbs. (244 Nm) — 1979 and later

13. On 1978 models, stake the new nut to the joint spindle using a tool having a used end of 0.06 in. (1.6mm) and approximately 0.43 in. (11mm) wide. A sharp chisel should not be used since the collar will probably be split.

➡**1979 and later models use a cotter pin and nut-lock to retain the nut. Staking is unnecessary.**

14. After attaching the driveshaft, if the inboard boot appears to be collapsed or deformed, vent the inner boot by inserting a round-tipped, small diameter rod between the boot and the shaft. As venting occurs, boot will return to its original shape.

A-460, A-465, A-525 and Automatic Transaxle Models

1. With the car on the ground, loosen the hub nut, which has been tightened to 200 ft. lbs. (271 Nm).

2. Drain the transaxle differential and remove the cover.

➡**Any time the transaxle differential cover is removed, a new gasket should be formed from RTV sealant.**

3. To remove the right hand driveshaft, disconnect the speedometer cable and remove the cable and gear before removing the driveshaft.

4. Remove the clamp bolt from the ball stud and knuckle.

5. Separate the ball joint stud from the steering knuckle, by prying against the knuckle leg and control arm.

6. Separate the outer CV-joint splined shaft from the hub by holding the CV-housing and moving the hub away. Do not pry on the slinger or outer CV-joint.

CLUTCH

❋❋CAUTION

The clutch driven disc may contain asbestos, which has been determined to be a cancer causing agent. Never clean clutch surfaces with compressed air! Avoid inhaling any dust from any clutch surface! When cleaning clutch surfaces, use a commercially available brake cleaning fluid.

Adjustment

FREE-PLAY

A-412 Models

1. Pull up on the clutch plate.

2. While holding the cable up, rotate the adjusting sleeve downward until a snug contact is made against the grommet.

3. Rotate the sleeve slightly to allow the end of the sleeve to seat in the rectangular hole in the grommet.

A-460, A-465, and A-525 Models
▶ See Figure 51

This unit has a self-adjusting clutch. No manual adjustments are necessary or possible.

Driven Disc and Pressure Plate

REMOVAL & INSTALLATION

▶ See Figures 52, 53 and 54

1. Remove the transaxle as described earlier.

➡Chrysler recommends the use of special tool L-4533 for disc alignment on the A-412 and tool C-4676 for the A-460, A-465 and A-525 transaxles.

2. Loosen the flywheel-to-pressure plate bolts diagonally, one or two turns at a time to avoid warpage.

3. Remove the flywheel and clutch disc from the plate.

4. Remove the retaining ring and release plate.

5. Diagonally loosen the pressure plate-to-crankshaft bolts. Mark all parts for reassembly.

6. Remove the bolts, spacer and pressure plate.

7. Support the shaft at the CV-joints and remove the shaft. Do not pull on the shaft. If necessary use a prytool between the CV-joint and transaxle housing.

8. Installation is the reverse of removal. Insert the shaft into the transaxle housing, making sure the splines are engaged. A quick thrust will lock the circlip in the groove. Tighten the hub nut with the wheels on the ground to 180 ft. lbs. (244 Nm).

7. The flywheel and pressure plate surfaces should be cleaned thoroughly with fine sandpaper.

8. It is a false economy to replace either the clutch disc or pressure plate separately, since this will only lead to premature failure of the other component. In order to reuse any of the components, the following conditions should be met:

a. There should be no leakage from the rear main or transaxle front oil seals.

b. The friction surface of the pressure plate should have a uniform appearance over the entire contact area. The plate may be improperly mounted or sprung if a heavy wear pattern occurs directly opposite a light pattern.

c. The friction face of the flywheel should be free from discoloration, burned areas, cracks or grooves. The flywheel face must often be machined smooth before installing a new clutch.

d. The disc should be free of oil or grease. Replace the disc if it is worn within 0.01 in. (0.4mm) of the rivet heads.

e. Check the pressure plate for flatness. It should be flat within 0.02 in. (0.5mm) across the friction area, and be free from cracks, burns, grooves or ridges.

f. Inspect the cover outer mounting flange for flatness, burrs, nicks, or dents.

g. The 2 dowels in the flywheel should be tight and undamaged.

h. Inspect the center of the release plate for cracks or heavy wear. Wear up to 0.001 in. (0.25mm) is acceptable.

If the clutch assembly does not meet these conditions, it should be replaced.

To install:

9. Align marks and install the pressure plate, spacer and bolts. Coat the bolts with thread compound and tighten them to 55 ft. lbs. (75 Nm).

10. Install the release plate and retaining ring.

11. Using special tool L-4533, C-4676 or their equivalent, install the clutch disc and flywheel on the pressure plate.

❋❋WARNING

Make certain that the drilled mark on the flywheel is at the top, so that the two dowels on the flywheel align with the proper holes in the pressure plate.

12. Install the six flywheel bolts and tighten them to 15 ft. lbs. (20 Nm) on A-412 equipped models, and 21 ft. lbs. (28 Nm) on A-460, A-465, and A-525 equipped models.

13. Remove the aligning tool.

14. Install the transaxle.

15. If applicable, adjust the clutch free-play.

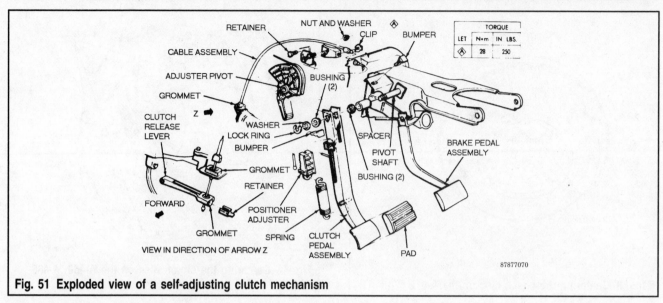

TORQUE		
LET	N•m	IN. LBS.
◇	28	250

RETAINER

NUT AND WASHER

CLIP

BUMPER

CABLE ASSEMBLY

ADJUSTER PIVOT

BUSHING (2)

GROMMET

CLUTCH RELEASE LEVER

Z

WASHER

LOCK RING

BUMPER

SPACER

PIVOT SHAFT

BUSHING (2)

BRAKE PEDAL ASSEMBLY

GROMMET

RETAINER

FORWARD

POSITIONER ADJUSTER

GROMMET

SPRING

CLUTCH PEDAL ASSEMBLY

PAD

VIEW IN DIRECTION OF ARROW Z

87877070

Fig. 51 Exploded view of a self-adjusting clutch mechanism

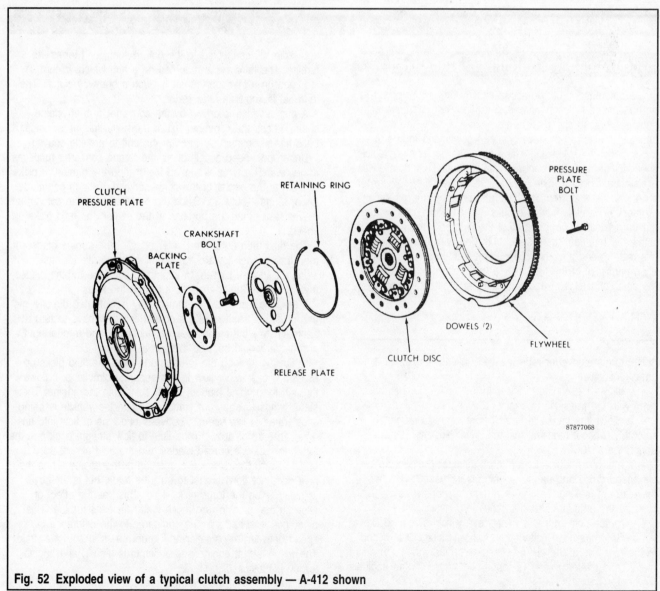

CLUTCH PRESSURE PLATE

BACKING PLATE

CRANKSHAFT BOLT

RETAINING RING

PRESSURE PLATE BOLT

RELEASE PLATE

CLUTCH DISC

DOWELS (2)

FLYWHEEL

87877068

Fig. 52 Exploded view of a typical clutch assembly — A-412 shown

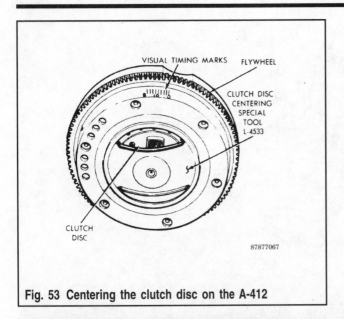

Fig. 53 Centering the clutch disc on the A-412

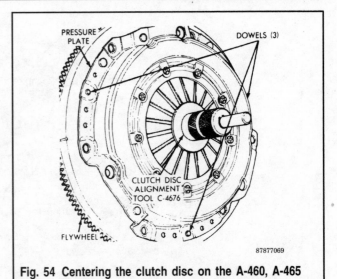

Fig. 54 Centering the clutch disc on the A-460, A-465 and the A-525

AUTOMATIC TRANSAXLE

Understanding Automatic Transaxles

The automatic transaxle allows engine torque and power to be transmitted to the front wheels within a narrow range of engine operating speeds. The transaxle will allow the engine to turn fast enough to produce plenty of power and torque at very low speeds, while keeping it at a sensible rpm at high vehicle speeds. The transaxle performs this job entirely without driver assistance. The transaxle uses a light fluid as the medium for the transaxle of power. This fluid also works in the operation of various hydraulic control circuits and as a lubricant. Because the transaxle fluid performs all of these three functions, trouble within the unit can easily travel from one part to another. For this reason, and because of the complexity and unusual operating principles of the transaxle, a very sound understanding of the basic principles of operation will simplify troubleshooting.

TORQUE CONVERTER

The torque converter replaces the conventional clutch. It has three functions:
- It allows the engine to idle with the vehicle at a standstill even with the transaxle in gear.
- It allows the transaxle to shift from range to range smoothly, without requiring that the driver close the throttle during the shift.
- It multiplies engine torque to an increasing extent as vehicle speed drops and throttle opening is increased. This has the effect of making the transaxle more responsive and reduces the amount of shifting required.

The torque converter is a metal case which is shaped like a sphere that has been flattened on opposite sides. It is bolted to the rear end of the engine's crankshaft. Generally, the entire metal case rotates at engine speed and serves as the engine's flywheel.

The case contains three sets of blades. One set is attached directly to the case. This set forms the torus or pump. Another set is directly connected to the output shaft, and forms the turbine. The third set is mounted on a hub which, in turn, is mounted on a stationary shaft through a one-way clutch. The third set is known as the stator.

A pump, which is driven by the converter hub at engine speed, keeps the converter full of transaxle fluid at all times. Fluid flows continuously through the unit to provide cooling.

Under low speed acceleration, the torque converter functions as follows: The torus is turning faster than the turbine. It picks up fluid at the center of the converter and, through centrifugal force, slings it outward. Since the outer edge of the converter moves faster than the portions at the center, the fluid picks up speed.

The fluid then enters the outer edge of the turbine blades. It then travels back toward the center of the converter case along the turbine blades. In impinging upon the turbine blades, the fluid loses the energy picked up in the torus.

If the fluid were now to immediately be returned directly into the torus, both halves of the converter would have to turn at approximately the same speed at all times, and torque input and output would both be the same.

In flowing through the torus and turbine, the fluid picks up two types of flow, or flow in two separate directions. It flows through the turbine blades, and it spins with the engine. The stator, whose blades are stationary when the vehicle is being accelerated at low speeds, converts one type of flow into another. Instead of allowing the fluid to flow straight back into the torus, the stator's curved blades turn the fluid almost 90 degrees toward the direction of rotation of the engine. Thus the fluid does not flow as fast toward the torus, but is already spinning when the torus picks it up. This has the effect of allowing the torus to turn much faster than the turbine. This difference is speed may be compared to the difference in speed between the smaller and larger gears in any gear train. The result is that engine power output is higher, and engine torque is multiplied.

As the speed of the turbine increases, the fluid spins faster and faster in the direction of engine rotation. As a result, the ability of the stator to redirect the fluid flow is reduced. Under cruising conditions, the stator is eventually forced to rotate on its one-way clutch in the direction of engine rotation. Under these conditions, the torque converter begins to behave almost like a solid shaft, with the torus and turbine speeds being almost equal.

PLANETARY GEARBOX

The ability of the torque converter to multiply engine torque is limited. Also, the unit tends to be more efficient when the turbine is rotating at relatively high speeds. Therefore, a planetary gearbox is used to carry the power output of the turbine to the driveshaft.

Planetary gears function very similarly to conventional transaxle gears. However, their construction is different in that three elements make up one gear system, and in that all three elements are different from one another,. The three elements are: an outer gear that is shaped like a hoop, with teeth cut into the inner surface. A sun gear, mounted on a shaft and located at the very center of the outer gear, and a set of three planet gears, held by pins in a ring-like planet carrier and meshing with both the sun gear and the outer gear. Either the outer gear or the sun gear may be held stationary, providing more than one possible torque multiplication factor for each set of gears. Also, if all three gears are forced to rotate the same speed, the gearset forms, in effect, a solid shaft.

Most modern automatics use the planetary gears to provide either a single reduction ratio of about 1.8:1, or two reduction gears: a low of about 2.5:1, and an intermediate of about l.5:1. Bands and clutches are used to hold various portions of the gearsets to the transaxle case or to the shaft on which they are mounted. Shifting is accomplished, then, by changing the portion of each planetary gearset which is held to the transaxle case or to the shaft.

SERVOS AND ACCUMULATORS

The servos are hydraulic pistons and cylinders. They resemble the hydraulic actuators used on many familiar machines, such as bulldozers. Hydraulic fluid enters the cylinder, under pressure, and forces the piston to move to engage the band or clutches.

The accumulators are used to cushion the engagement of the servos. The transaxle fluid must pass through the accumulator on the way to the servo. The accumulator housing contains a thin piston which is sprung away from the discharge passage of the accumulator. When fluid passes through the accumulator on the way to the servo, it must move the piston against spring pressure, and this action smooths out the action of the servo.

HYDRAULIC CONTROL SYSTEM

The hydraulic pressure used to operate the servos comes from the main transaxle oil pump. This fluid is channeled to the various servos through the shift valves. There is generally a manual shift valve which is operated by the transaxle selec-

tor level and an automatic shift valve for each automatic upshift the transaxle provides: i.e., 2-speed automatics have a low/high shift valve, while 3-speeds have a 1-2 valve, and a 2-3 valve.

There are two pressures which effect the operation of these valves. One is the governor pressure which is affected by vehicle sped. The other is the modulator pressure which is affected by intake manifold vacuum or throttle position. Governor pressure rises with an increase in vehicle sped, and modulator pressure rises as the throttle is opened wider. By responding to these two pressures, the shift valves cause the upshift points to be delayed with increased throttle opening to make the best use of the engine's power output.

Most transaxles also make use of an auxiliary circuit for downshifting. This circuit may be actuated by the throttle linkage or the vacuum line which actuates the modulator, or by a cable or solenoid. It applies pressure to a special downshift surface on the shift valve or valves.

The transaxle modulator also governs the line pressure, used to actuate the servos. In this way, the clutches and bands will be actuated with a force matching the torque output of the engine.

Identification

There are three automatic transaxle designations used in the Omni/Horizon model line, the A-404 used with the 1.7L engine 1978-83, the A-413 used with the 2.2L engine 1981-84, and the A-415 which is used with the 1.6L engine in 1984. All of these transaxles are Chrysler built Torqueflite Automatic Transaxles. See Section 1 for more information.

Fluid Pan

REMOVAL & INSTALLATION

➡**RTV silicone sealer is used in place of a pan gasket.**

Chrysler recommends no fluid or filter changes during the normal service life of the car. Severe usage requires a fluid and filter change every 15,000 miles (24,000 km). Severe usage is defined as:
- More than 50% heavy city traffic during 90°F (32°C) or warmer weather
- Police, taxi or commercial operation or trailer towing

When changing the fluid, only Dexron®II or it's superceding fluid should be used at every fluid change.

1. Raise the vehicle and support it on jackstands.
2. Place a large container under the pan, loosen the pan bolts and tap at one corner to break it loose. Drain the fluid.
3. When the fluid is drained remove the pan bolts.
4. Remove the retaining screws and replace the filter. Tighten the screws to 35 inch lbs. (4 Nm).
5. Clean the fluid pan, peel off the old RTV silicone sealer and install the pan, using a 0.12 in. (3mm) bead of new RTV sealer. Always run the sealer bead inside the bolt holes. Tighten the pan bolts to 10-12 ft. lbs. (14-16 Nm).
6. Pour the specified amount of Dexron®II or it's superceding fluid through the filler tube.

7. Turn the engine **ON** and idle it for at least 2 minutes. Set the parking brake and move the selector through each position, ending in Park.

8. Add sufficient fluid to bring the level to the FULL mark on the dipstick. The level should be checked in Park, with the engine idling at normal operating temperature.

Adjustments

SHIFT LINKAGE

▶ **See Figure 55**

➡**When it is necessary to disconnect the linkage cable from the lever, which uses plastic grommets as retainers, the grommets should be replaced.**

1. Make sure that the adjustable swivel block is free to slide on the shift cable.

2. Place the shift lever in Park.

3. With the linkage assembled, and the swivel lock bolt loose, move the shift arm on the transaxle into the Park position.

4. Hold the shift arm in position with a force of about 10 lbs. and tighten the adjuster swivel lock bolt to 8 ft. lbs. (11 Nm).

5. Check the linkage action.

➡**The automatic transaxle gear selector release button may pop up in the knob when shifting from Park to Drive. This is caused by inadequate retention of the selector release knob retaining tab. The release button will always work but the loose button can be annoying. A sleeve (Chrysler Part No. 5211984) and washers (Chrysler Part No. 6500380) are available to cure this condition. If these are unavailable, do the following:**

6. Remove the release button.

7. Cut and fold a standard paper match stem.

8. Using tweezers, insert the folded match as far as possible into the clearance slot. The match should be below the knob surface.

9. Insert the button, taking care not to break the button stem.

THROTTLE CABLE

▶ **See Figure 56**

1. Adjust the idle speed as previously described.

2. Run the engine to normal operating temperature.

3. Loosen the adjustment bracket lockscrew.

4. Make sure the adjustment bracket is free to slide in its slot.

5. Hold the transaxle lever firmly rearward against its internal stop and tighten the adjustment bracket lockscrew to 9 ft. lbs. (12 Nm).

6. Test the cable operation.

BAND

Front Kickdown

Chrysler recommends that the band be adjusted at each fluid change. The adjusting screw is located on the left side of the case.

1. Loosen the locknut and back off the nut above five full turns.

2. Tighten the band adjusting screw to 72 inch lbs. (8 Nm).

3. Back off the adjusting screw exactly 2½ turns except with 1.6L engine, back off 3 turns.

4. Hold the adjusting screw and tighten the locknut to 35 ft. lbs. (47 Nm).

Neutral Safety Switch

REMOVAL, TESTING & INSTALLATION

▶ **See Figure 57**

The neutral start circuit is the center contact of the three-terminal switch located in the transaxle case.

➡**Before removing the switch, position a drain pan to collect any transaxle fluid which may leak through the switch mounting hole in the transaxle case.**

1. Remove the wiring connector and test for continuity between the center pin and the case. Continuity should exist only in Park and Neutral.

2. Remove the switch and check that the operating lever fingers are centered in the switch opening.

To install:

3. Install the switch and a new seal, then tighten to 24 ft. lbs. (33 Nm). Retest with a lamp.

4. Replace the lost transaxle fluid.

5. If shift linkage adjustment is correct and the switch still malfunctions, replace the switch.

Transaxle Assembly

REMOVAL & INSTALLATION

The automatic transaxle can be removed with the engine installed in the car, but, the transaxle and torque converter must be removed as an assembly. Otherwise the drive plate, pump bushing or oil seal could be damaged. The drive plate will not support a load; no weight should be allowed to bear on the drive plate.

1. Disconnect the negative battery cable.

2. Disconnect the throttle and shift linkage from the transaxle.

3. Raise and support the car. Remove the front wheels. Refer to Halfshaft Removal and Installation to remove or install the halfshafts.

4. Take off the oil cooler hoses.

5. Remove the left splash shield. Drain the differential and remove the cover.

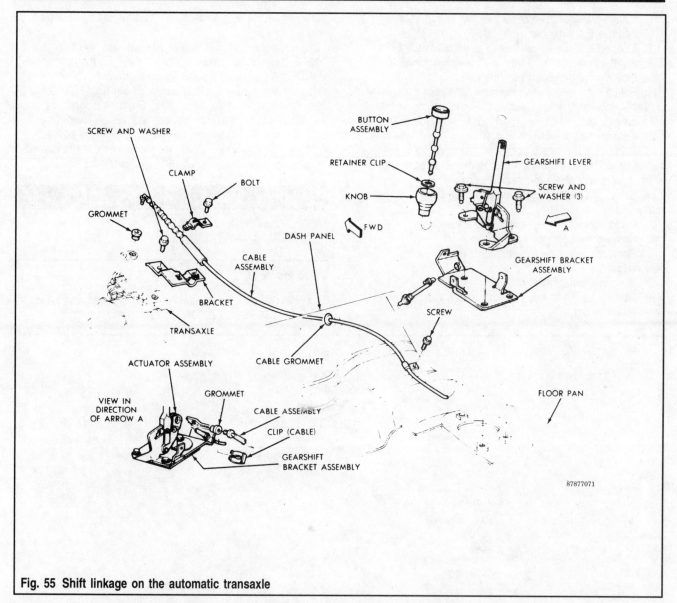

Fig. 55 Shift linkage on the automatic transaxle

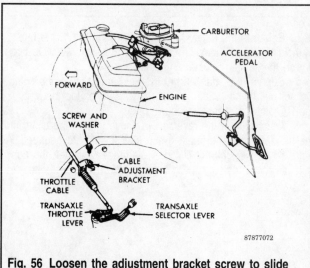

Fig. 56 Loosen the adjustment bracket screw to slide the bracket free

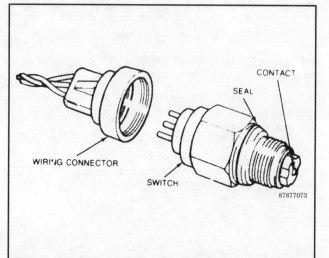

Fig. 57 Carefully disconnect the wiring, then unthread the switch from the transaxle case

6. Extract the speedometer adaptor, cable and gear.

7. Remove the sway bar.

8. Take off both lower ball joint-to-steering knuckle bolts.

9. Pry the lower ball joint from the steering knuckle.

10. Remove the driveshaft from the hub.

11. Rotate both driveshafts to expose the circlip ends. Note the flat surface on the inner ends of both axle tripod shafts. Pry the circlip out.

12. Remove both driveshafts.

13. Matchmark the torque converter and drive plate. Remove the torque converter mounting bolts. Remove the access plug in the right splash shield to rotate the engine.

14. Extract the lower cooler tube and the wire to the neutral safety switch.

15. Install some means of supporting the engine.

16. Remove the upper bellhousing bolts.

17. Remove the engine mount bracket from the front crossmember.

18. Support the transaxle.

19. Remove the front mount insulator through-bolts and the bell housing mount.

20. Extract the long through-bolt from the left hand engine mount.

21. Raise the transaxle and pry it away from the engine.

22. Installation is the reverse of removal. Fill the differential with DEXRON®II or it's superceding automatic transaxle fluid before lowering the car. Form a new gasket from RTV sealant when installing the differential cover. On 1978 models, be sure the auxiliary horn does not interfere with the oil cooler lines.

23. On the A-404, tighten the flex plate-to-torque converter to; 40 ft. lbs. (54 Nm), transfer-to-cylinder block; 70 ft. lbs. (95 Nm), cooler tube-to-transaxle; 150 inch lbs. (1339 Nm).

Halfshaft

REMOVAL & INSTALLATION

▶ See Figure 58

1. With the car on the ground, loosen the hub nut, which has been tightened to 200 ft. lbs. (271 Nm).

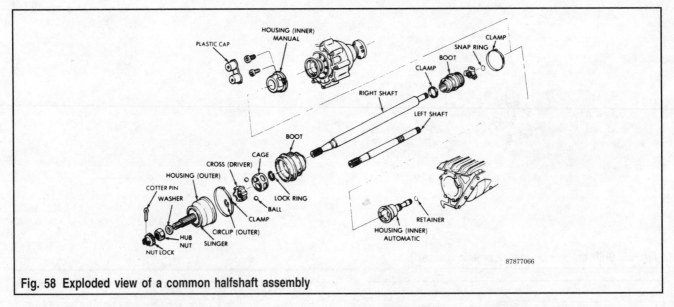

Fig. 58 Exploded view of a common halfshaft assembly

2. Drain the transaxle differential and remove the cover.

➡ **Any time the transaxle differential cover is removed, a new gasket should be formed from RTV sealant.**

3. To remove the right hand driveshaft, disconnect the speedometer cable and remove the cable and gear before removing the driveshaft.

4. Remove the clamp bolt from the ball stud and steering knuckle.

5. Separate the ball joint stud from the steering knuckle, by prying against the knuckle leg and control arm.

6. Separate the outer CV-joint splined shaft from the hub by holding the CV-housing and moving the hub away. Do not pry on the slinger or outer CV-joint.

7. Support the shaft at the CV-joints and remove the shaft. Do not pull on the shaft. If necessary use a prytool between the CV-joint and transaxle housing.

8. Installation is the reverse of removal. Insert the shaft into the transaxle housing, making sure the splines are engaged. A quick thrust will lock the circlip in the groove. Tighten the hub nut with the wheels on the ground to 180 ft. lbs. (244 Nm).

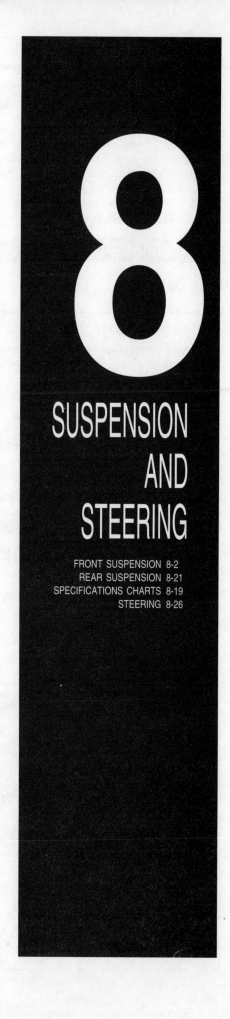

8

SUSPENSION AND STEERING

FRONT SUSPENSION

A MacPherson type front suspension, with vertical shock absorbers attached to the upper fender reinforcement and the steering knuckle, is used. Lower control arms, attached inboard to a cross-member and outboard to the steering knuckle through a ball joint, provide lower steering knuckle position. During steering maneuvers, the upper strut and steering knuckle turn as an assembly.

Coil Springs

REMOVAL & INSTALLATION

▶ See Figures 1, 2 and 3

➡A spring compressor is required to remove the spring from the strut. A crow's foot adaptor and torque wrench are also required.

1. Remove the strut and coil assembly from the vehicle.
2. Compress the spring, using a reliable coil spring compressor.
3. Hold the strut rod and remove the rod nut.
4. Remove the retainers and bushings.
5. Remove the spring.

➡Springs are not interchangeable from side to side.

✳✳CAUTION

When removing the spring from the compressor, open the compressor evenly and not more than 9¼ in. (235mm).

6. Assembly is the reverse of disassembly in the following order:
   a. Bumper dust shield
   b. Spring seat
   c. Upper spring retainer
   d. Bearing and spacer

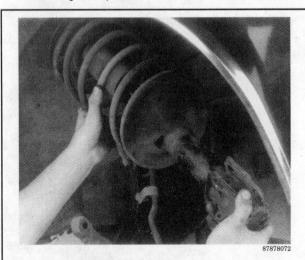
Fig. 1 Remove the strut and coil assembly from the vehicle.

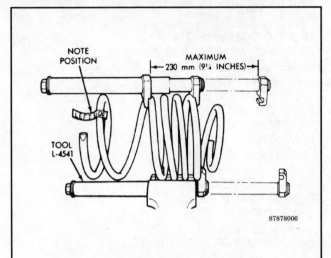
Fig. 2 Compress the spring, using a reliable coil spring compressor such as L-4541

   e. Mount assembly
   f. Rebound bumper
   g. Retainer
   h. Rod nut

➡Tighten rod nut to 55 ft. lbs. (75 Nm) before removing the spring compressor. Use a crow's foot adaptor to tighten the nut while holding the rod with an open end wrench.

➡Be sure the lower coil end of the spring is securely positioned in the seat recess.

MacPherson Struts

REMOVAL & INSTALLATION

▶ See Figures 4, 5, 6, 7 and 8

➡A new bonded mount assembly is used on late 1978 and later models, replacing the double nut, bearing retainer, isolator and strut retainer previously used. To remove the welded nut, grind the hex flats for proper wrench fit.

1. Loosen the lug nuts on the front wheels.
2. Raise and support the vehicle.
3. Remove the wheel.

➡If the original strut is to be assembled to the original knuckle, mark the cam adjusting bolt. Remove the cam adjusting bolt, through-bolt and brake hose bracket retaining screw.

4. Remove the cam bolt, knuckle bolts and washer plates.
5. Next, remove the brake hose to the dampener bracket retaining screw.
6. Inspect for evidence of fluid running from the upper end of the reservoir.

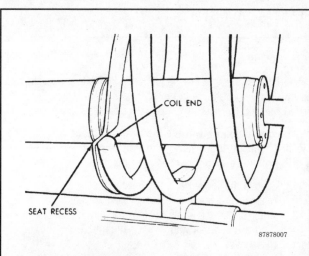

Fig. 3 Be sure the lower coil end of the spring is securely positioned in the seat recess

Fig. 4 If the original strut is to be reinstalled to the original knuckle, mark the cam adjusting bolt

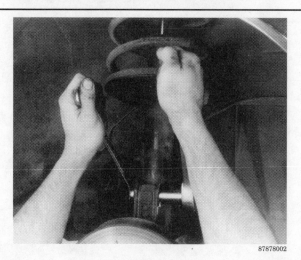

Fig. 5 Remove the cam bolt, knuckle bolts and washer plates

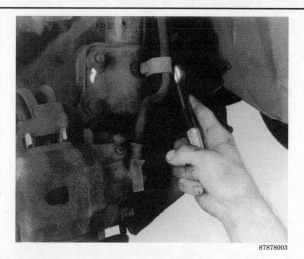

Fig. 6 Remove the bolt retaining the bracket for the brake hose

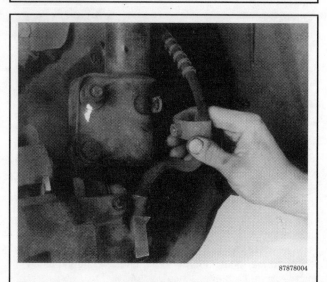

Fig. 7 Move the hose out of the way

To install:

  7. Attach the unit into the fender reinforcement, then install the retaining nut and washer assembly. Tighten to 20 ft. lbs. (27 Nm).

  8. Position the knuckle leg in the strut and install the upper (cam) and lower through-bolts.

  9. Attach the brake hose to the damper, tighten to 10 ft. lbs. (14 Nm).

  10. Index the cam bolt with the match marks.

  11. Place a C-clamp on the strut and knuckle, then tighten just enough to eliminate any looseness between the knuckle and the strut. Check the alignment of the index marks.

  12. Tighten the cam bolt to 45 ft. lbs. (61 Nm) plus ¼ turn.

  13. Remove the C-clamp, install the wheel.

  14. Lower the vehicle and tighten the lug nuts.

  15. Have the alignment checked as soon as possible.

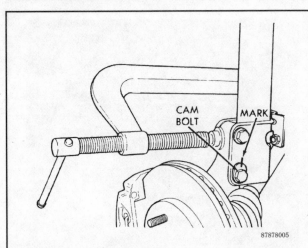

Fig. 8 Place a C-clamp on the strut and knuckle, then tighten just enough to eliminate any looseness between the knuckle and the strut

Ball Joints

INSPECTION

▶ **See Figure 9**

1. Raise and support the vehicle.
2. With the suspension fully extended (at full travel) clamp a dial indicator to the lower control arm with the plunger indexed against the steering knuckle leg.
3. Zero the dial indicator.
4. Use a stout bar to pry on the top of the ball joint housing-to-lower control arm bolt with the bar tip under the steering knuckle leg.
5. Measure the axial travel of the steering knuckle leg in relation to the control arm by raising and lowering the steering knuckle as in the previous step.
6. If the travel is more than 0.05 in. (1.25mm), the ball joint should be replaced.

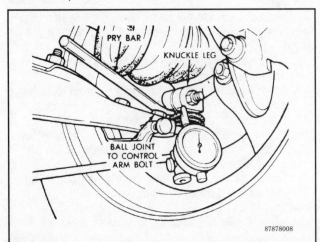

Fig. 9 With the suspension fully extended (at full travel) clamp a dial indicator to the lower control arm with the plunger indexed against the steering knuckle leg

REMOVAL & INSTALLATION

1978 Models

The lower ball joints are permanently lubricated, operate with no free-play, and are riveted in place. The rivets must be drilled out and replaced with special bolts.

➡**To avoid damage to the control arm surface adjacent to the ball joint during drilling, the use of a center punch and a drill press are strongly recommended.**

1. Remove the lower control arm.
2. Position the assembly with the ball joint up.
3. Center punch the rivets on the ball joint housing side.
4. Using a drill press with a ¼ in. (6mm) bit, drill out the center of the rivet.
5. Using a ½ in. (13mm) bit, drill the center of the rivet until the bit makes contact with the ball joint housing.
6. Using a ⅜ in. (9mm) bit, drill the center of the rivet. Remove the remainder of the rivet with a punch.

To install:

7. Position the new ball joint on the control arm and tighten the bolts to 60 ft. lbs. (81 Nm).
8. Install the control arm and tighten the ball joint clamp bolt to 50 ft. lbs. (68 Nm); the pivot bolt to 105 ft. lbs. (142 Nm) and the strut stub to 70 ft. lbs. (95 Nm).

1979-80 Models

▶ **See Figures 10, 11, 12, 13, 14, 15, 16 and 17**

The ball joint housing is bolted to the lower control arm with the joint stud retained in the steering knuckle by a clamp bolt.

1. Raise and support the car.
2. Remove the steering knuckle-to-ball joint stud clamp bolt and separate the stud from the knuckle leg.
3. Remove the 2 bolts holding the ball joint housing to the lower control arm.
4. Pry the ball joint arm from the control arm.
5. Remove the ball joint housing.

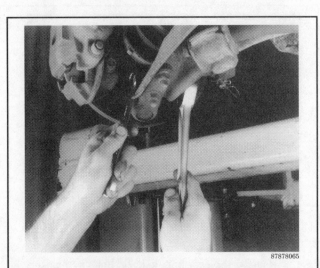

Fig. 10 Using a wrench and a socket, loosen the steering knuckle-to-ball joint stud clamp bolts . . .

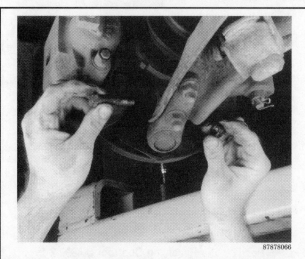

Fig. 11 . . . then remove the steering nut and clamp bolt from the vehicle

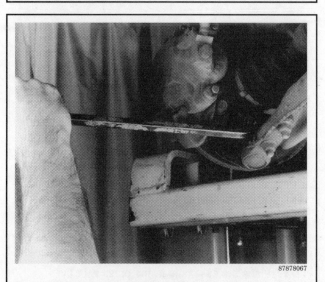

Fig. 12 Separate the stud from the knuckle leg

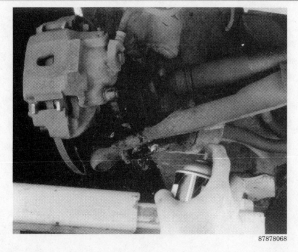

Fig. 13 Lubricate the ball joint retaining bolts to ease removal

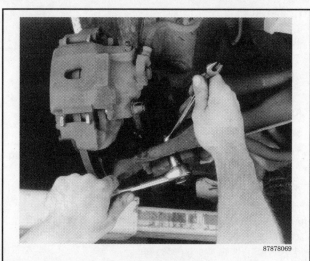

Fig. 14 Remove the 2 bolts holding the ball joint housing to the lower control arm

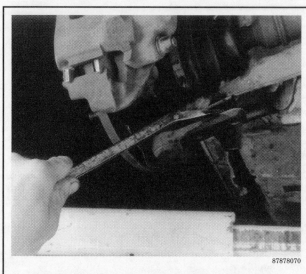

Fig. 15 Pry the ball joint arm from the control arm

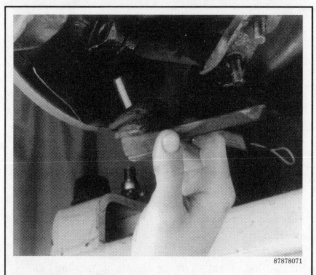

Fig. 16 Remove the ball joint housing

To install:

6. Install a new ball joint housing to the control arm. Tighten the retaining bolts to 60 ft. lbs. (81 Nm).

7. Install the ball joint stud in the steering knuckle. Tighten the clamp bolt to 50 ft. lbs. (68 Nm).

8. Lower the car.

1981-89 Models

▶ See Figures 18 and 19

➡This procedure requires special tools and machine shop services.

The ball joint is pressed into the lower control arm on these models and is retained to the steering knuckle by a clamp bolt. The lower control arm must be removed from the vehicle and placed in a press to perform this operation.

1. Pry off the rubber grease seal.

2. Position the receiving cup tool C-4699-2 to support the lower control arm while receiving the ball joint assembly.

3. Install a 1¹/₁₆ in. (27mm) deep socket over the stud and against the joint upper housing.

4. Apply pressure from the press to remove the joint from the arm.

To install:

5. Position the ball joint housing into the control arm cavity.

6. Place the assembly in the press with the installer tool C-4699-1 supporting the lower control arm.

7. Align and press the assembly until the ball joint bottoms against the control arm cavity down flange.

8. With a 1½ in. (3mm) socket, press the seal onto the ball joint housing so that it seats against the lower control arm.

Lower Control Arm

REMOVAL & INSTALLATION

▶ See Figures 20, 21 and 22

1. Raise and support the vehicle.

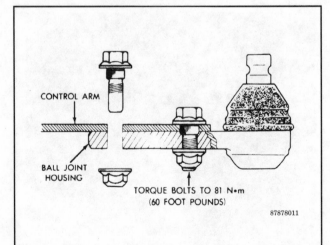

Fig. 17 During installation be sure to tighten the ball joint housing retainers using a torque wrench

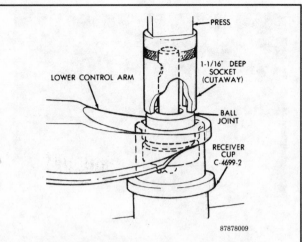

Fig. 18 Position the Receiving Cup tool C-4699-2 to support the lower control arm while receiving the ball joint assembly

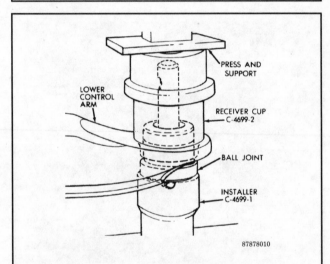

Fig. 19 Place the assembly in the press with the installer tool C-4699-1 supporting the lower control arm

Fig. 20 The vehicle must be raised and properly supported before beginning any suspension work

2. Remove the front inner pivot through-bolt, the rear stub strut nut, retainer and bushing, and the ball joint-to-steering knuckle clamp bolt.

3. Separate the ball joint stud from the steering knuckle by prying between the ball stud retainer on the knuckle and the lower control arm.

✳✳WARNING

Pulling the steering knuckle out from the vehicle after releasing it from the ball joint can separate the inner CV-joint.

4. Remove the sway bar-to-control arm nut and reinforcement and rotate the control arm over the sway bar. Remove the rear stub strut bushing, sleeve and retainer.

To install:

➡**The substitution of fasteners other than those of the grade originally used is not recommended.**

5. Install the retainer, bushing and sleeve on the stub strut.

6. Position the control arm over the sway bar and install the rear stub strut and front pivot into the crossmember.

7. Install the front pivot bolt and loosely install the nut.

8. Install the stub strut bushing and retainer and loosely assemble the nut.

9. Install the ball joint stud into the steering knuckle and install the clamp bolt. Tighten the clamp bolt to 50-70 ft. lbs. (68-95 Nm).

10. Position the sway bar bracket and stud through the control arm and install the retainer and nut. Tighten the nut to 10-25 ft. lbs. (14-34 Nm).

11. Lower the vehicle. With the suspension supporting the vehicle, tighten the front pivot bolts and the stub strut nuts.

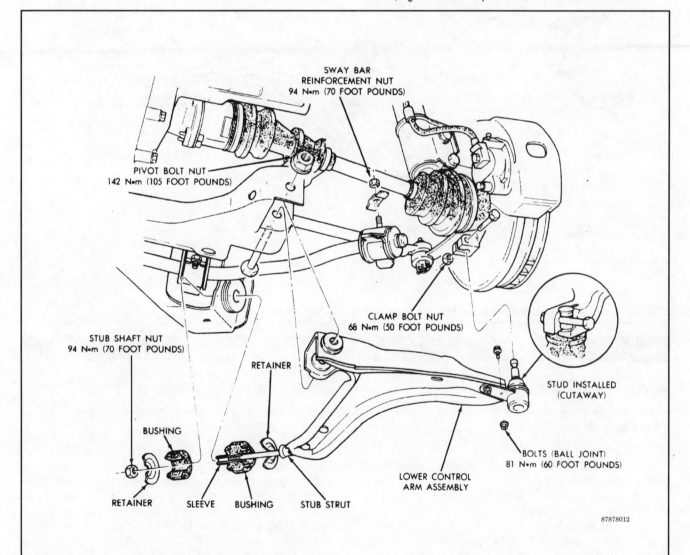

Fig. 21 Exploded view of the lower control arm mounting on 1978-80 models

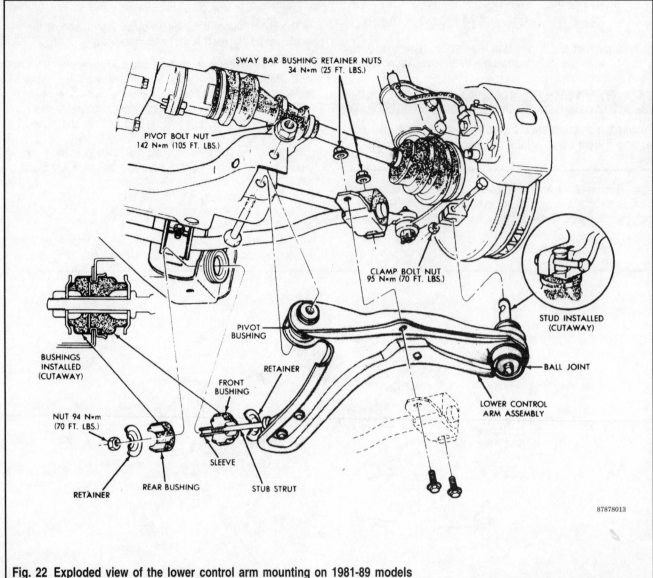

Fig. 22 Exploded view of the lower control arm mounting on 1981-89 models

Sway Bar

REMOVAL & INSTALLATION

♦ **See Figure 23**

1. Raise and support the car.
2. Take off the nut from the control arm end bushing and reinforcement plates.
3. Remove the nut retainers and insulator holding the sway bar to the crossmember linkage.
4. Take off the sway bar.
5. Inspect the sway bar for distortion or fatigue cracks in the metal. Replace any damaged or distorted bushings.
6. Installation is the reverse of removal.

Steering Knuckle

REMOVAL & INSTALLATION

♦ **See Figure 24**

Service or repair to the bearing, hub, brake dust shield or the steering knuckle itself will require removal of the knuckle. Before attempting this operation, be aware that to reassemble the components it is necessary to tighten the front hub nut to at least 180 ft. lbs. (244 Nm). You will need a large torque wrench to read that high and a great deal of strength to attain that much torque on the nut.

1. Remove the cotter pin and nut-lock.
2. Loosen the hub nut while the car is resting on the wheels with the brakes applied.

➡**The hub and driveshaft are splined together through the knuckle and retained by the hub nut.**

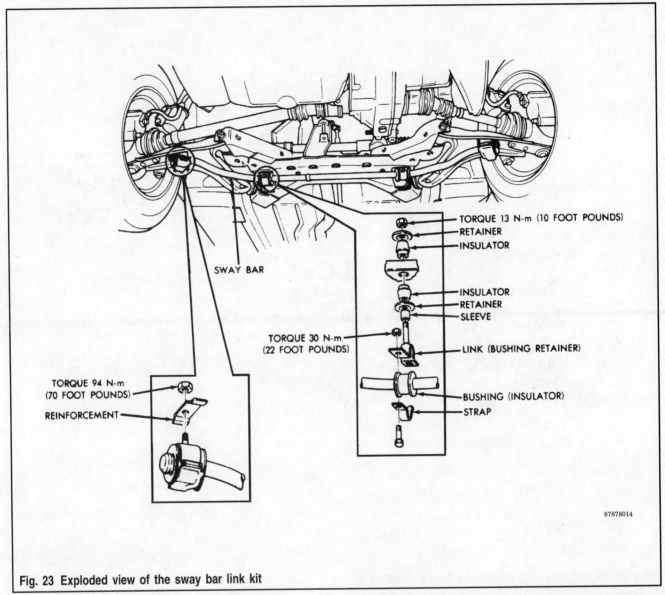

TORQUE 13 N-m (10 FOOT POUNDS)
RETAINER
INSULATOR

INSULATOR
RETAINER
SLEEVE

TORQUE 30 N-m
(22 FOOT POUNDS)

LINK (BUSHING RETAINER)

SWAY BAR

BUSHING (INSULATOR)
STRAP

TORQUE 94 N-m
(70 FOOT POUNDS)

REINFORCEMENT

87878014

Fig. 23 Exploded view of the sway bar link kit

3. Raise and support the car.

4. Remove the wheel and tire.

5. Remove the hub nut. Be sure the splined driveshaft is free to separate from the spline in hub when the knuckle is removed.

6. Disconnect the tie rod end from the steering arm.

7. Disconnect the brake hose retainer from the strut.

8. Remove the clamp bolt holding the ball joint stud in the steering knuckle.

9. Remove the brake caliper adaptor screw and washers.

10. Support the caliper on a wire hook.

11. Remove the brake disc.

12. Matchmark the camber adjusting cams and loosen both bolts.

13. Support the steering knuckle and remove the cam adjusting and through-bolts. Remove the upper knuckle leg out of the strut bracket and lift the knuckle from the ball joint stud.

WARNING

Do not allow the driveshaft to hang during this procedure.

14. Service procedures requiring hub removal also require that a new bearing be installed.

15. Installation is the reverse of removal. A new hub nut is required. When the car is resting in the wheels, with the brakes applied, tighten the hub nut to:

- 1978 models — 200 ft. lbs. (271 Nm)
- 1979-89 models — 180 ft. lbs. (244 Nm)

On 1978 models, stake the hub nut in place; on 1979 and later models, use a cotter pin and nut lock.

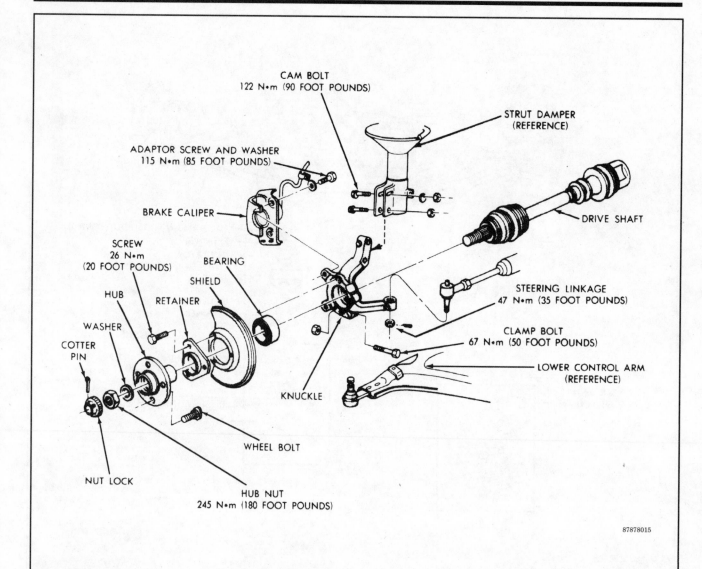

CAM BOLT
122 N•m (90 FOOT POUNDS)

STRUT DAMPER
(REFERENCE)

ADAPTOR SCREW AND WASHER
115 N•m (85 FOOT POUNDS)

BRAKE CALIPER

DRIVE SHAFT

SCREW
26 N•m
(20 FOOT POUNDS)

BEARING

SHIELD

HUB

RETAINER

WASHER

COTTER
PIN

STEERING LINKAGE
47 N•m (35 FOOT POUNDS)

CLAMP BOLT
67 N•m (50 FOOT POUNDS)

LOWER CONTROL ARM
(REFERENCE)

KNUCKLE

WHEEL BOLT

NUT LOCK

HUB NUT
245 N•m (180 FOOT POUNDS)

87878015

Fig. 24 Exploded view of the steering knuckle mounting

Front Hub and Bearings

REMOVAL & INSTALLATION

Pressed Type

▶ **See Figures 25, 26, 27, 28, 29, 30, 31, 32, 33, 34, 35, 36, 37, 38, 39, 40, 41, 42, 43, 44, 45, 46, 47, 48, 49 and 50**

The front wheel bearings are permanently sealed and require no periodic lubrication.

1. Remove the hub cap if equipped.
2. Remove the cotter pin, nut lock and spring washer.
3. Loosen the hub nut while the vehicle is on the floor, with the brakes applied.
4. Raise and support the vehicle.
5. Remove the wheel and tire assembly.
6. Take the hub nut off.
7. Disconnect the tie rod end from the steering arm with tool C-3894-A or an equivalent.

87878016

Fig. 25 Remove the hub cap

Fig. 26 Straighten the cotter pin using a pair of pliers . . .

Fig. 27 . . . then remove the pin to free the nut lock

Fig. 28 Next take off the nut lock and spring washer

Fig. 29 With a friend applying the brakes, loosen the hub nut while the vehicle is still on the floor

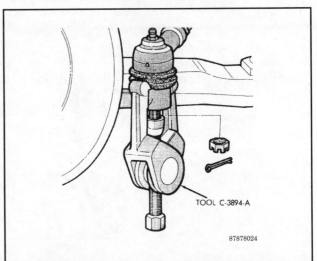

Fig. 30 Disconnect the tie rod end from the steering arm with tool C-3894-A or an equivalent

8. Disconnect the brake hose retainer from the strut damper.

9. Remove the clamp bolt securing ball joint stud into the steering knuckle and brake caliper or adapter screws and washer assemblies.

10. Support the caliper with a wire.

➡Do not allow the caliper to hang from the brake hose.

11. Remove the brake disc.

12. Separate the ball joint stud from the knuckle. Pull the knuckle out and away from the driveshaft.

➡A new bearing will need to installed when removing the hub.

13. Remove the hub out of the bearing with tool kit C-4811 or equivalent, as follows:

    a. Back out one of the bearing retainer screws and install the bracket C-4811-17 or equivalent, between the screw head and the retainer.

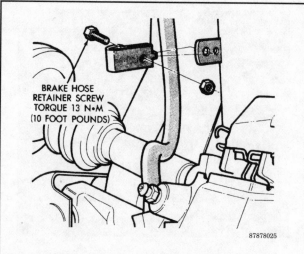

Fig. 31 Disconnect the brake hose retainer from the strut damper

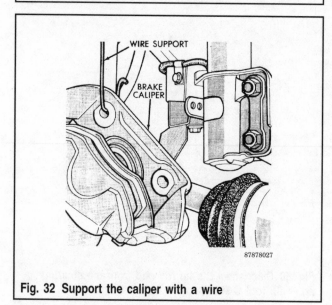

Fig. 32 Support the caliper with a wire

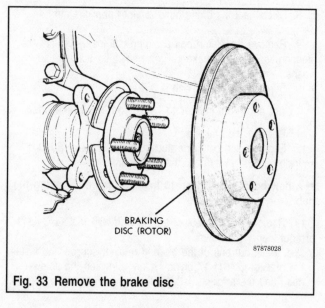

Fig. 33 Remove the brake disc

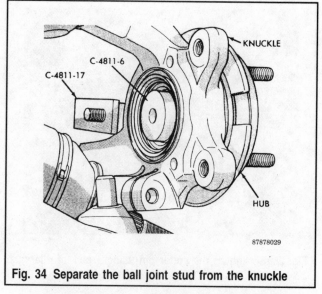

Fig. 34 Separate the ball joint stud from the knuckle

b. Place a thrust button, tool C-4811-6 or equivalent, inside the hub bore.

c. Position the tool C-4811-14 or equivalent, and install the two screws firmly into the tapped brake adapter extensions. Also the nut and washer on the bracket screw.

d. Tighten the screw on tool C-4811-14 or equivalent, to remove the hub and bearing.

e. Should the outboard inner race remain on the hub, it can be removed by using a universal puller, C-clamp and thrust washer.

f. Remove the tool C-4811-14 or equivalent, and the attaching screws from the steering knuckle.

14. Take off the three screws and the bearing retainer from the knuckle.

15. Pry the bearing seal from the machined recess in the knuckle, then clean the recess thoroughly.

16. Install C-4811-5 or equivalent, until the bearing is removed from the knuckle, and into ring C-4811-3A or equivalent. Discard the bearing and seal.

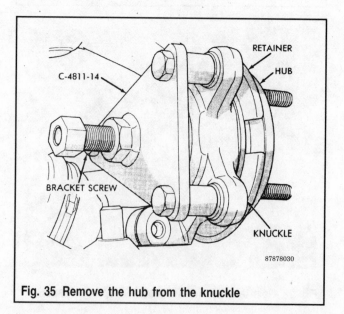

Fig. 35 Remove the hub from the knuckle

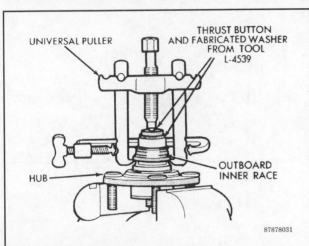

Fig. 36 Should the outboard inner race remain on the hub, it can be removed by using a universal puller, C-clamp and thrust washer

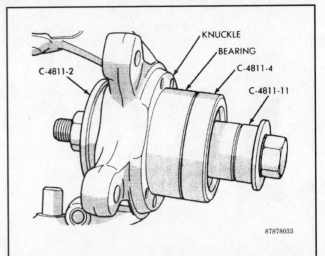

Fig. 38 Press the new bearing into the knuckle until it seats using tool C-4811 or equivalent

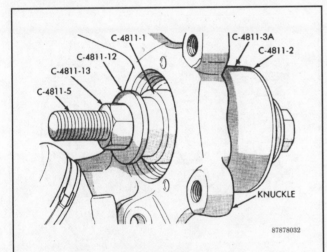

Fig. 37 With all of the attaching tools, remove the bearing from the knuckle

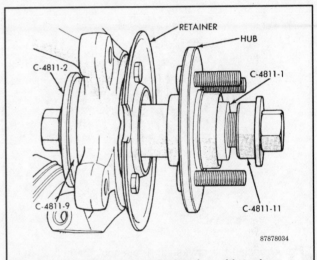

Fig. 39 Press the hub into the bearing with tools C-4811-1, 2, 9, and 11 or equivalent

To install:

17. Press the new bearing into the knuckle until it seats using tool C-4811 or equivalent.

18. Install the new gasket and bearing retainer, tighten the retainer screws to 20 ft. lbs. (27 Nm).

19. Press the hub into the bearing with tools C-4811-1, 2, 9, and 11 or equivalent.

20. Position the new seal in the recess, then assemble installer tool C-4698 or equivalent. Install the seal.

21. Lubricate the full circumference of the seal with multi-purpose grease.

22. Install the driveshaft throughout the hub, then install the steering knuckle on the lower control arm ball joint stud.

23. Attach the ball joint to the knuckle clamp, tighten to 70 ft. lbs. (95 Nm).

24. Install the tie rod end into the steering arm, tighten the nut to 35 ft. lbs. (47 Nm). Install a new cotter pin.

25. Install the brake disc.

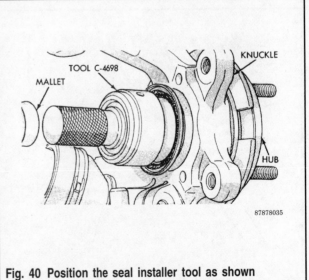

Fig. 40 Position the seal installer tool as shown

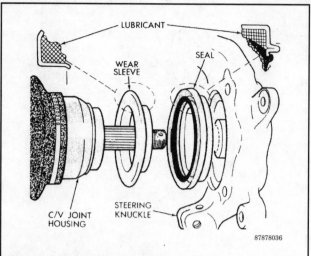

Fig. 41 Apply lubricant to the full circumference of the seal with multi-purpose grease

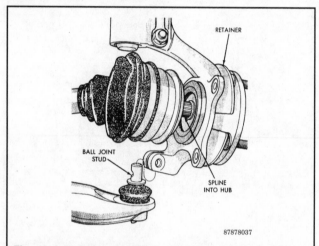

Fig. 42 Install the driveshaft throughout the hub, then install the steering knuckle on the lower control arm ball joint stud

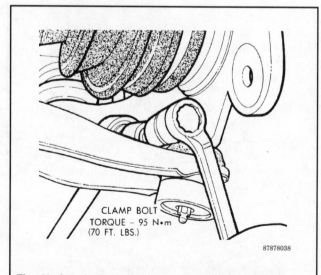

Fig. 43 Attach the ball joint to the knuckle clamp

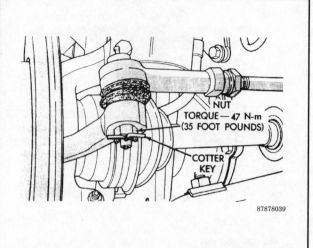

Fig. 44 Once the tie rod end is properly torqued, install a new cotter pin

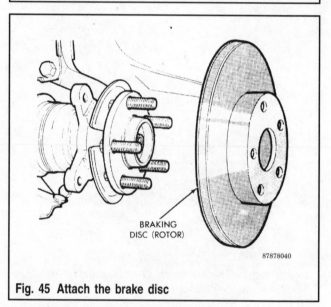

Fig. 45 Attach the brake disc

26. Attach the caliper assembly over the disc, position the adapter to the knuckle. Install the adapter to the knuckle bolts and tighten to 160 ft. lbs. (216 Nm).

27. Attach the brake hose retainer to strut damper, then tighten the screw to 10 ft. lbs. (13 Nm).

28. Install the washer and hub nut.

29. With the brakes applied, tighten the hub nut to 180 ft. lbs. (245 Nm).

30. Install the spring washer, nut lock and a new cotter pin. Wrap the cotter pin tightly against the nut lock.

31. Install the wheel and tire assembly, and lug nuts.

32. Lower the vehicle, then tighten the lug nuts.

Bolted Type

▶ **See Figures 51, 52, 53, 54, 55, 56, 57, 58, 59, 60, 61 and 63**

1. Loosen the lug nuts, raise and support the vehicle.

2. Remove the cotter pin, nut lock and spring washer.

3. Loosen the hub nut while the vehicle is on the ground, with the brakes applied.

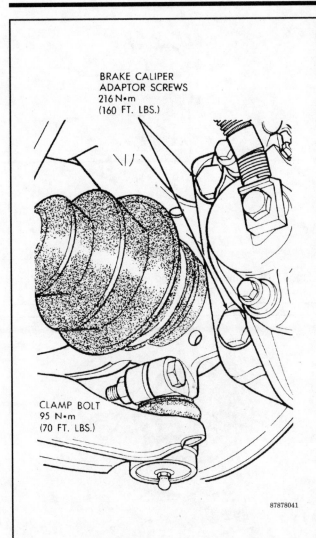

Fig. 46 Attach the caliper assembly over the disc, position the adapter to the knuckle. Install the adapter to the knuckle bolts and tighten

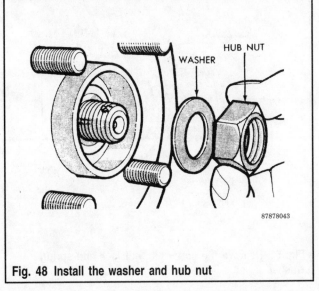

Fig. 48 Install the washer and hub nut

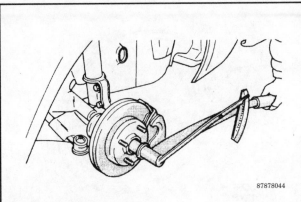

Fig. 49 With the brakes applied, tighten the hub nut (if the proper torque cannot be achieved this way, the wheel must be installed and the vehicle lowered before tightening the nut)

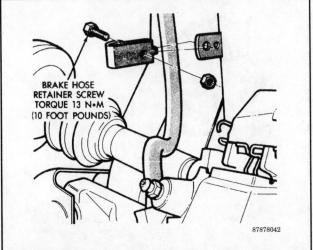

Fig. 47 Attach the brake hose retainer to strut damper, then tighten the screw

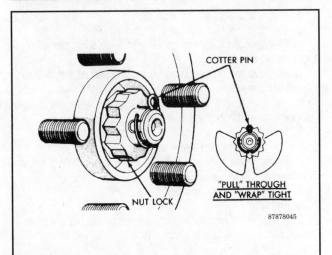

Fig. 50 Install the washer, nut lock and a new cotter pin. Wrap the pin ends tightly against the nut lock

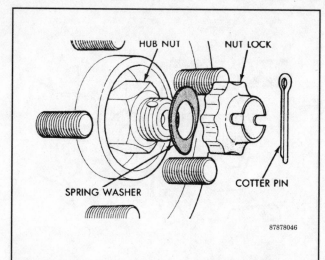

Fig. 51 Remove the cotter pin, nut lock and spring washer

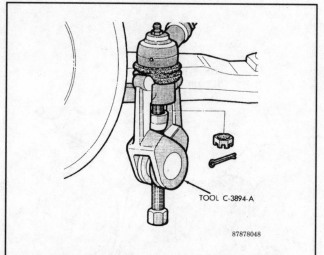

Fig. 53 Disconnect the tie rod end from the steering arm with tool C-3894-A

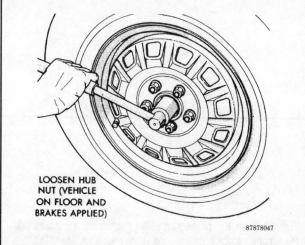

Fig. 52 Loosen the hub nut while the vehicle is on the ground, with the brakes applied

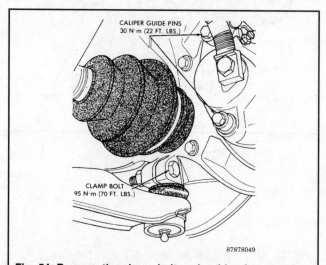

Fig. 54 Remove the clamp bolt and guide pins securing the ball joint stud into the steering knuckle

4. Raise and support the vehicle.

5. Remove the hub nut, washer and wheel.

6. Disconnect the tie rod end from the steering arm with tool C-3894-A

7. Remove the clamp bolt securing the ball joint stud into the steering knuckle.

8. Remove the caliper guide pins, then separate the caliper assembly from the braking disc. Remove the disc.

9. Separate the ball joint stud from the steering knuckle, pull the knuckle out and away from the driveshaft.

10. Remove the hub and bearing assembly mounting screws from the rear of the knuckle.

11. Remove the hub and bearing assembly.

To install:

12. Install the new hub and bearing assembly, then tighten the screws in a crisscross pattern to 45 ft. lbs. (65 Nm).

➡The knuckle and bearing surfaces must be free from all foreign materials or nicks

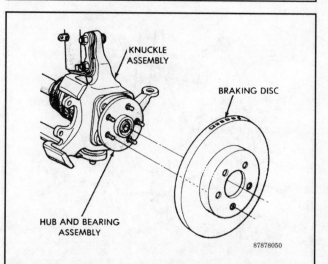

Fig. 55 Separate the disc from the hub and bearing assembly

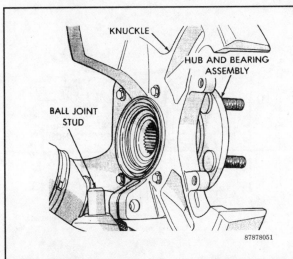

Fig. 56 Separate the ball joint stud from the steering knuckle

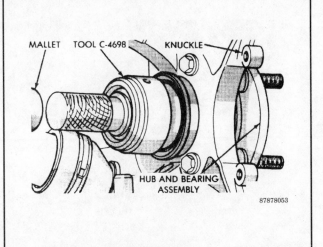

Fig. 58 Position the new seal in recess, then assemble the installer tool. Install the seal

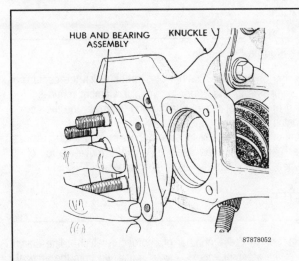

Fig. 57 Remove the hub and bearing assembly mounting screws from the rear of the knuckle

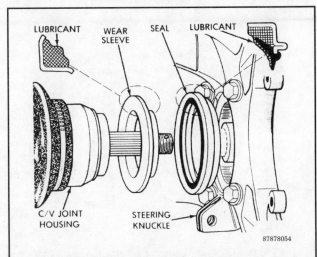

Fig. 59 Apply lubricant to the full circumference of the seal with multi-purpose grease

13. Position the new seal in recess, then assemble the installer tool. Install the seal.

14. Lubricate the full circumference of the seal with multi-purpose grease.

15. Install the driveshaft throughout the hub, then install the steering knuckle on the lower control arm ball joint stud.

16. Attach the ball joint to the knuckle clamp, tighten to 70 ft. lbs. (95 Nm).

17. Install the tie rod end into the steering arm, tighten the nut to 35 ft. lbs. (47 Nm). Install a new cotter pin.

18. Install the brake disc.

19. Carefully lower the caliper over the disc, then guide the hold-down spring under the machined abutment on the knuckle.

20. Install the washer and hub nut.

21. With the brakes applied, tighten the hub nut to 180 ft. lbs. (245 Nm).

22. Install the spring washer, nut lock and a new cotter pin. Wrap the cotter pin tightly against the nut lock.

23. Install the wheel and tire assembly, and lug nuts.

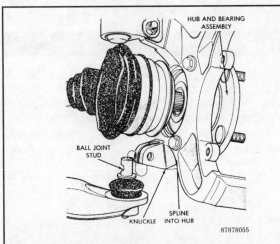

Fig. 60 Install the driveshaft throughout the hub, then install the steering knuckle on the lower control arm ball joint stud

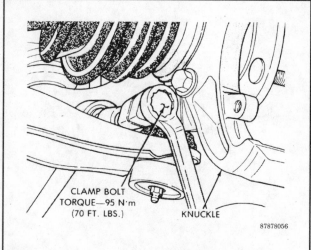

Fig. 61 Attach the ball joint to the knuckle clamp, then tighten

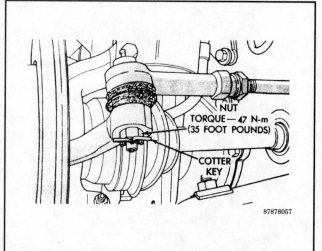

Fig. 62 Once the tie rod end nut is properly torqued, install a new cotter pin

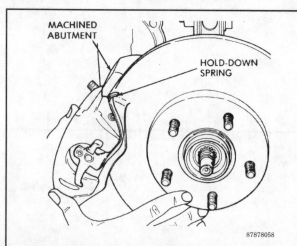

Fig. 63 Carefully lower the caliper over the disc, then guide the hold-down spring under the machined abutment on the knuckle

24. Lower the vehicle, then tighten the lug nuts.

Front End Alignment

Wheel alignment requires the use of sophisticated equipment to accurately measure the geometry of the front end. The information is given here so that the owner will be aware of what is involved, not so that he can do the work himself.

Before the wheels are aligned, the following checks should be made, since these are factors that will influence the wheel alignment settings.

• All tires should be of the same size and up to the recommended pressures.
• Check the lower ball joints and steering linkage.
• Check the struts for extremely stiff or spongy operation.
• Check for broken or sagged springs.
• The wheel alignment should be made with a full tank of gas, and no passenger or luggage compartment load.

CAMBER

▶ **See Figures 64 and 65**

Camber angle is the number of degrees which the centerline of the wheel is inclined from the vertical. Camber reduces loading of the outer wheel bearing and improves the tire contact patch while cornering.

Camber is adjusted by loosening the cam and through-bolts on each side. Rotate the upper cam bolt to move the top of the wheel in or out to the specified camber.

CASTER

Caster angle is the number of degrees in which a line drawn through the steering knuckle pivots is inclined from the vertical, toward the front or rear of the car. Positive cater improves directional stability and decreases susceptibility to crosswinds or road surface deviations. Other than the replacement of damaged suspension components, caster is not adjustable.

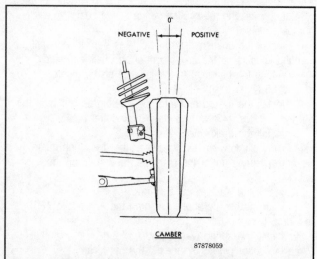

Fig. 64 Camber angle is the number of degrees which the centerline of the wheel is inclined from the vertical

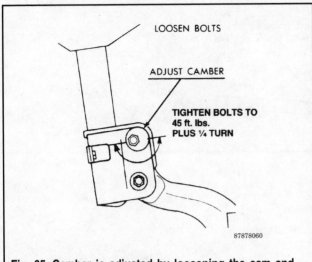

LOOSEN BOLTS

ADJUST CAMBER

**TIGHTEN BOLTS TO
45 ft. lbs.
PLUS ¼ TURN**

87878060

Fig. 65 Camber is adjusted by loosening the cam and through-bolts on each side

TOE-OUT

▶ **See Figures 66 and 67**

The front wheels on these models are set with a slight toe out, as on most front wheel drive cars, to counteract the tendency of the driving wheels to toe-in excessively. Toe out is the amount, that the wheels are closer together at the rear than at the front. Toe is checked with the wheels straight ahead. The tie-rod linkage is adjustable. Loosen the nuts and clamps and adjust the length of the tie-rod for correct toe out.

Wheel Alignment Specifications
(caster is not adjustable)

Year	Front Camber		Toe-Out (in.)		Rear Camber	
	Range (deg)	Preferred	Front	Rear	Range (deg)	Preferred
'78	¼N to ¾P	5/16P	⅛ out to 0	5/32 out to 1/32 in	1½N to ½N	1N
'79–'81	¼N to ¾P	5/16P	5/32 out to ⅛ in	5/32 out to 11/32 in	1½N to ½N	1N
'82–'89	¼N to ¾P	5/16P	7/32 in to ⅛ out	5/32 out to 11/32 in	1¼N to ¼N ①	½N

① Rampage/Scamp: 1⅛N to ⅛N

87878063

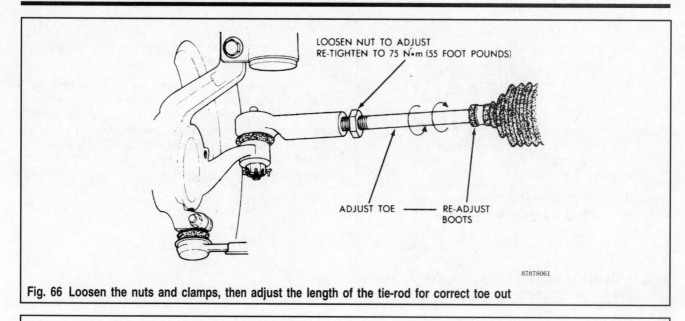

LOOSEN NUT TO ADJUST
RE-TIGHTEN TO 75 N•m (55 FOOT POUNDS)

ADJUST TOE — **RE-ADJUST BOOTS**

87878061

Fig. 66 Loosen the nuts and clamps, then adjust the length of the tie-rod for correct toe out

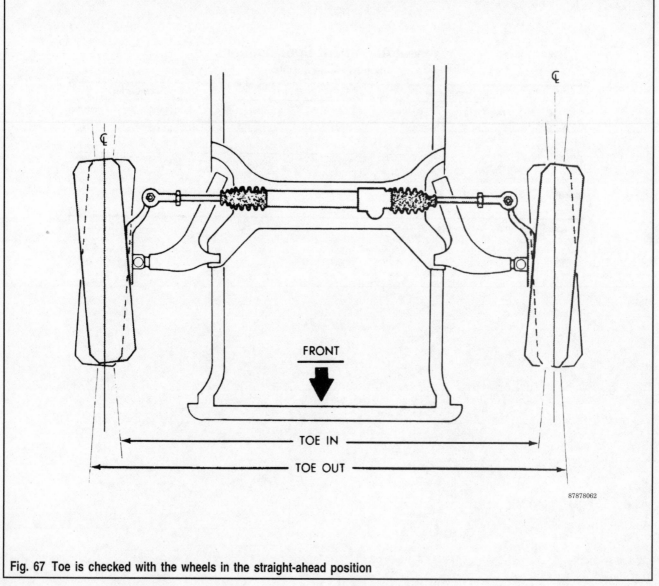

FRONT

TOE IN

TOE OUT

87878062

Fig. 67 Toe is checked with the wheels in the straight-ahead position

REAR SUSPENSION

On all models (except pickups) a trailing, independent arm assembly, with integral sway bar is used. The wheel spindles are attached to two trailing arms which extend rearward from mounting points on the body where they are attached with shock absorbing, oval bushings. A crossmember is welded to the trailing arms, just to the rear of the bushings. A coil spring over shock absorber strut assembly, similar to the front suspension, is used.

The rear suspension on the Rampage and Scamp pickup models uses leaf springs mounted to a tubular axle. The conventional type rear shock absorbers are mounted on an angle, outboard at the bottom and inboard at the top. This design is used to provide greater side-to-side stability and weight carrying capacity in addition to controlling ride motion. The wheel spindles are attached to the axle assembly and supported by the leaf springs.

➡It is important that aftermarket load leveling devices are NOT installed on this suspension system. The installation of these devices will cause the rear brake height sensing proportioning valve to sense a light load condition that is actually a loaded condition being created by these add-on devices.

Rear Springs

REMOVAL & INSTALLATION

Except Pickup Models
▶ **See Figure 68**

The use of a coil spring compressor, such as Chrysler part #L-4514, is necessary.

1. Remove the shock and spring assembly.
2. Install the spring compressor on the spring and place it in a vise.

➡**Always grip 4 or 5 coils and never extend the retractors beyond 9¼ in. (235mm).**

3. Tighten the retractors evenly until pressure is removed from the upper spring seat.
4. Loosen the retaining nut.

✳✳CAUTION

Be very careful when loosening the retaining nut. If the spring is not properly compressed, serious injury could result.

5. Remove the lower isolator, pushrod sleeve, and upper spring seat.
6. Carefully slip the strut from the spring.
7. Remove the rebound bumper and dust shield from the strut.

8. Remove the lower spring seat.
9. Carefully and evenly, remove the compressor from the spring.

To install:

10. Install the compressor on the spring, gripping four or five coils.
11. Compress the spring.
12. Install the lower spring seat, dust shield and rebound bumper on the strut.
13. Slip the unit inside the coil spring and install the upper spring seat.
14. Make sure that the level surfaces on the seats are in position with the spring.
15. Install the sleeve on the pushrod and install the retaining nut. Tighten the nut to 20 ft. lbs. (47 Nm).
16. Install the lower isolator.
17. Install the strut and spring assembly.

Rampage and Scamp Pickup Models

1. Raise the vehicle and support the frame on jackstands while relieving the weight on the rear springs.
2. Disconnect the rear brake proportioning valve spring. Disconnect the lower ends of the shock absorbers at the axle brackets.
3. Loosen and remove the U-bolt nuts and remove the U-bolts and spring plates.
4. Lower the rear axle assembly, allowing the springs to hang free.
5. Loosen and remove the front pivot bolt from the front spring hanger.
6. Loosen and remove the rear spring shackle nuts and remove the shackles from the spring.
7. Installation is the reverse of the removal procedure, tighten the U-bolts to 601 ft. lbs. (80 Nm).

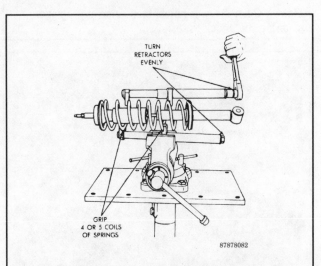

Fig. 68 Use a coil spring compressor to remove the spring

Shock Absorber

REMOVAL & INSTALLATION

Except Pickup Models

▶ **See Figures 69, 70, 71, 72, 73, 74 and 75**

1. Take off the protective cap from the upper mounting nut.
2. Remove the insulator, upper mounting nut and retainer.
3. Raise and support the vehicle.
4. Take off the lower shock mounting bolt.
5. Take off the shock and spring assembly.
6. Installation is the reverse of removal. Tighten the lower mounting bolt to 40 ft. lbs. (54 Nm), the upper nut to 20 ft. lbs. (27 Nm).

Fig. 71 . . . mounting nut. . .

Fig. 69 Open the rear hatch, then remove the cap covering the shock tower . . .

Fig. 72 . . . and retainer

Fig. 70 . . . the insulator . . .

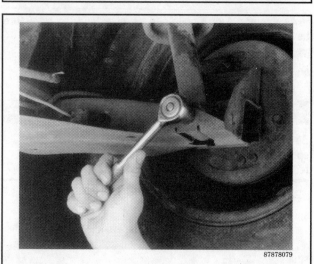

Fig. 73 Raise and support the vehicle, then remove the lower shock bolt

Fig. 74 Lift the shock/spring up . . .

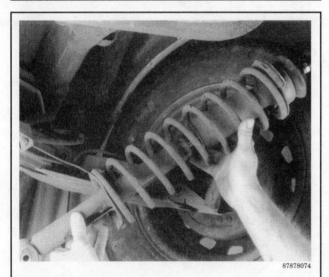

Fig. 75 . . . and lower the shock out of the vehicle

Rampage and Scamp Pickup Models
♦ **See Figure 76**

1. Raise and support the truck.
2. Take off the nuts and bolts securing the upper and lower ends of the shock absorber.
3. Remove the shock absorber and inspect the rubber eye and bushings. If these are defective, replace the shock absorber assembly.
4. Installation is the reverse of the removal.
5. Refer to the illustration for tightening specifications.

Rear Wheel Bearings

The rear wheel bearings should be inspected and relubricated whenever the rear brakes are serviced or at least every 30,000 miles (13,608 km). Repack the bearings with high temperature multi-purpose grease.

Check the lubricant to see if it is contaminated. If it contains dirt or has a milky appearance indicating the presence of water, the bearings should be cleaned and repacked.

Clean the bearings in kerosene, mineral spirits or other suitable cleaning fluid. Do not dry them by spinning the bearings. Allow them to air dry.

➡**Sodium-based grease is not compatible with lithium-based grease. Read the package labels and be careful not to mix the two types. If there is any doubt as to the type of grease used, completely clean the old grease from the bearing and hub before replacing.**

Before handling the bearings, there are a few things that you should remember to do and not to do.
Remember to DO the following:
• Remove all outside dirt from the housing before exposing the bearing.
• Treat a used bearing as gently as you would a new one.
• Work with clean tools in clean surroundings.
• Use clean, dry canvas gloves, or at least clean, dry hands.
• Clean solvents and flushing fluids are a must.
• Use clean paper when laying out the bearings to dry.
• Protect disassembled bearings from rust and dirt. Cover them up.
• Use clean rags to wipe bearings.
• Keep the bearings in oil-proof paper when they are to be stored or are not in use.
• Clean the inside of the housing before replacing the bearing.
Do NOT do the following:
• Don't work in dirty surroundings.
• Don't use dirty, chipped or damaged tools.
• Try not to work on wooden work benches or use wooden mallets.
• Don't handle bearings with dirty or moist hands.
• Do not use gasoline for cleaning; use a safe solvent.
• Do not spin-dry bearings with compressed air. They will be damaged.
• Do not spin dirty bearings.
• Avoid using cotton waste or dirty cloths to wipe bearings.
• Try not to scratch or nick bearing surfaces.
• Do not allow the bearing to come in contact with dirt or rust at any time.

REMOVAL & INSTALLATION

1. Raise and support the car with the rear wheels off the floor.
2. Remove the wheel grease cap, cotter pin, nut-lock and bearing adjusting nut.
3. Take off the thrust washer and bearing.
4. Take off the drum from the spindle.
5. Use a brass drift to drive the old races from the hub.
To install:
6. Thoroughly clean the old lubricant from the hub cavity.
7. Drive the new races into the hub assembly.
8. Pack the bearings with high temperature multi-purpose EP grease and add a small amount of new grease to the hub

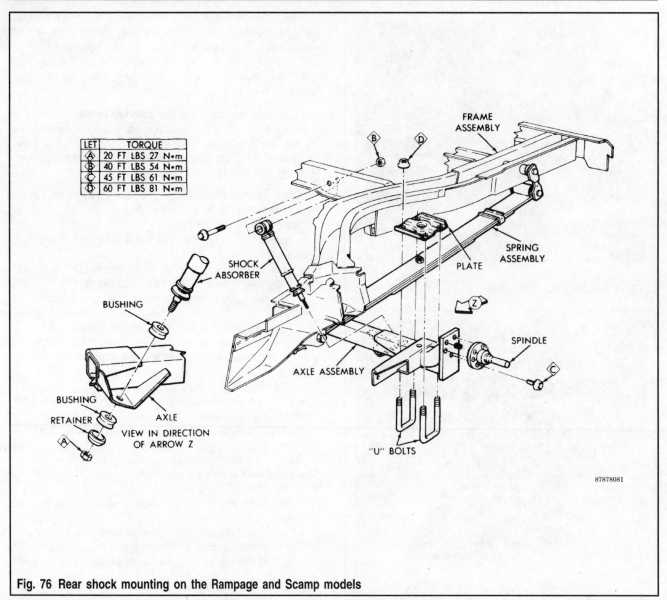

LET	TORQUE
△	20 FT LBS 27 N•m
◇	40 FT LBS 54 N•m
◇	45 FT LBS 61 N•m
◇	60 FT LBS 81 N•m

FRAME ASSEMBLY

SHOCK ABSORBER

BUSHING

BUSHING

RETAINER

AXLE

VIEW IN DIRECTION OF ARROW Z

AXLE ASSEMBLY

"U" BOLTS

PLATE

SPRING ASSEMBLY

SPINDLE

87878081

Fig. 76 Rear shock mounting on the Rampage and Scamp models

cavity. Be sure to force the lubricant between all rollers in the bearing.

9. Install the drum on the spindle after coating the polished spindle surfaces with wheel bearing lubricant.

10. Install the outer bearing cone, thrust washer and adjusting nut.

11. Tighten the adjusting nut to 20-25 ft. lbs. (27-34 Nm) while rotating the wheel.

12. Back off the adjusting nut to completely release the preload from the bearing.

13. Tighten the adjusting nut finger-tight.

14. Position the nut-lock with one pair of slots in line with the cotter pin hole. Install the cotter pin.

15. Clean and install the grease cap and wheel.

16. Lower the car.

Rear Wheel Alignment

▶ **See Figures 77, 78, 79 and 80**

Due to the design of the rear suspension, it is possible to adjust both the camber and toe-in of the rear wheels. Alignment is controlled by inserting 0.01 in. (0.25mm) shim stock between the spindle mounting surface and the spindle mounting plate. Each 0.01 in. (0.25mm) shim stock changes wheel alignment by approximately 0° at 18 min. per shim. Be sure to adjust the rear wheel bearings. Refer to Front Wheel Alignment for a description of alignment angles.

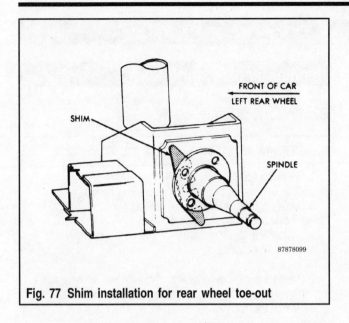

Fig. 77 Shim installation for rear wheel toe-out

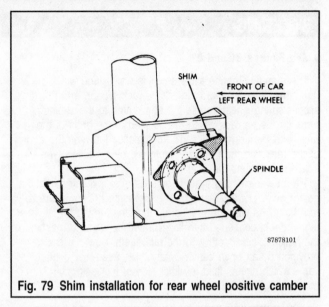

Fig. 79 Shim installation for rear wheel positive camber

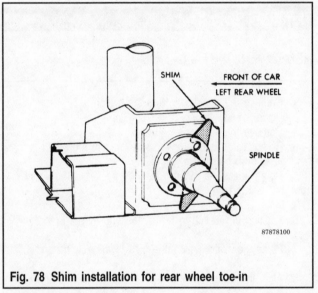

Fig. 78 Shim installation for rear wheel toe-in

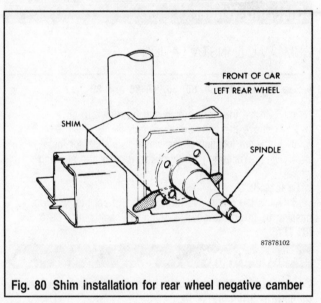

Fig. 80 Shim installation for rear wheel negative camber

STEERING

▶ **See Figures 81 and 82**

The manual steering system consists of a tube which contains the toothed rack, a pinion, the rack slipper, and the rack slipper spring. Steering effort is transmitted to the steering arms by the tie rods which are coupled to the ends of the rack, and the tie rod ends. The connection between the ends of the rack and the tie rod is protected by a bellows type oil seal which retains the gear lubricant.

The power steering system consists of four major parts: the power gear, power steering pump, pressure hose and the return hose. As with the manual system, the turning of the steering wheel is converted into linear travel through the meshing of the helical pinion teeth with the rack teeth. Power assist is provided by an open center, rotary type, three-way control valve which directs fluid to either side of the rack control piston.

Steering Wheel

REMOVAL & INSTALLATION

▶ **See Figures 83, 84, 85, 86, 87, 88 and 89**

1. Remove the horn button and horn switch.
2. Remove the steering wheel nut.
3. Mark the location of the wheel and shaft for installation.
4. Using a steering wheel puller, remove the steering wheel.

To install:

5. Align the master serration in the wheel hub with the missing tooth on the shaft. Tighten the shaft nut to 60 ft. lbs. (81 Nm).

✳✳WARNING

Do not tighten the nut against the steering column lock or damage will occur.

6. Install the horn switch and button.

Turn Signal Switch

REMOVAL & INSTALLATION

▶ **See Figures 83, 84, 85, 86, 87, 88, 89, 90 and 91**

1. Disconnect the electrical connector at column.
2. Remove the steering wheel as described earlier.
3. Remove the lower column cover.
4. Remove the wash/wipe switch.
5. Remove the wiring clip and the three screws securing the turn signal switch.
6. Installation is the reverse of removal.

Ignition and Steering Lock

REMOVAL & INSTALLATION

▶ **See Figures 83, 84, 85, 86, 87, 88, 89, 90 and 92**

1. Remove the steering wheel.
2. Remove the upper and lower column covers.
3. Using a hacksaw blade, cut the upper 1/4 in. (6mm) from the key cylinder retainer pin boot.
4. Using a drift, drive the roll pin from the housing and remove the key cylinder.

To install:

5. Insert the new cylinder into the housing, making sure that it engages the lug on the ignition switch driver.
6. Install the roll pin.

Ignition Switch

REMOVAL & INSTALLATION

1. Remove the connector from the switch.
2. Place the key in the LOCK position.
3. Remove the key.
4. Remove the two mounting screws from the switch and pushrod to drop below the jacket.
5. Rotate the switch 90° to permit removal of the switch from the pushrod.

To install:

6. Position the switch in LOCK (second detent from the top).
7. Place the switch at right angles to the column and insert the pushrod.
8. Align the switch on the bracket and install the screws.
9. With a light rearward load on the switch, tighten the screws. Check for proper operation.

Tie Rod End

REMOVAL & INSTALLATION

▶ **See Figures 93, 94, 95, 96, 97, 98 and 99**

1. Loosen the nut on the end of the tie rod end to the steering arm.
2. Mark the tie rod position on the threads.
3. Remove the cotter pin on the end of the tie rod end.
4. Loosen the nut on the tie rod end.
5. Using a ball joint separator, remove the tie rod end from the knuckle.
6. Slip the tie rod end out of the knuckle.
7. Unscrew the end from the steering shaft.

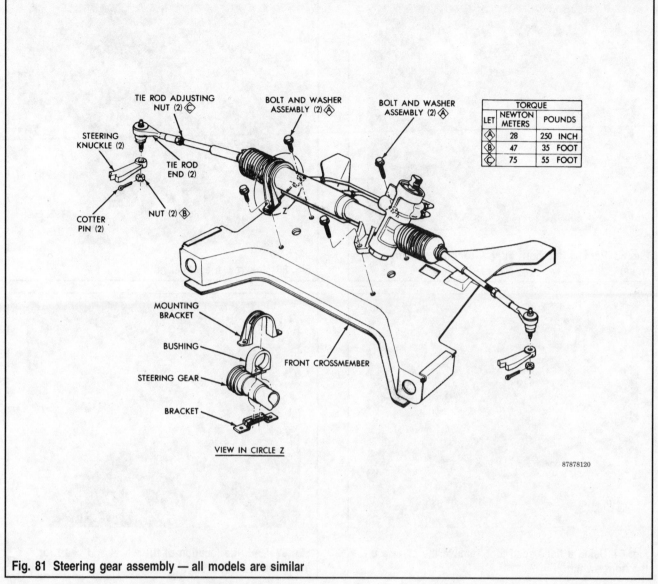

Fig. 81 Steering gear assembly — all models are similar

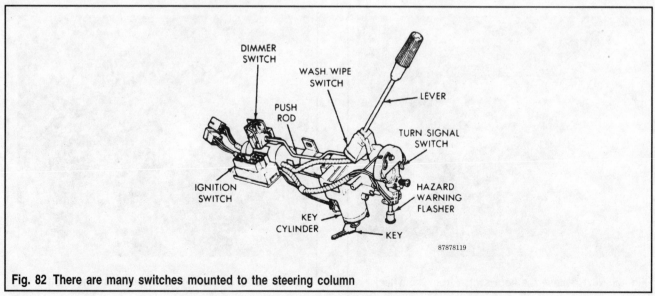

Fig. 82 There are many switches mounted to the steering column

Fig. 83 Remove the horn button from the steering wheel

Fig. 84 Using a flat-bladed tool, remove the screws on the horn switch

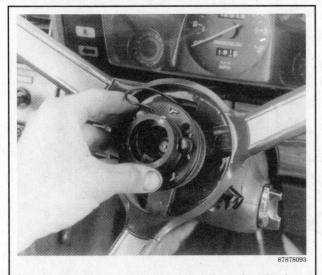

Fig. 85 Next remove the horn switch from the wheel

Fig. 86 Unscrew the wheel nut

Fig. 87 Mark the location of the wheel and shaft for installation

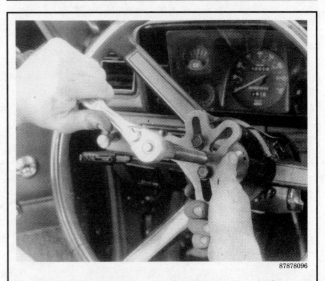

Fig. 88 Install a steering wheel puller on the shaft

Fig. 89 Pull the wheel off of the steering shaft

Fig. 90 Unscrew the column cover to access the switch

8. Install a new tie rod end in reverse of removal. Tighten the end nut to 50 ft. lbs. (68 Nm) and the locknut to 65 ft. lbs. (88 Nm).

9. Check the wheel alignment as soon as possible.

Power Steering Pump

REMOVAL & INSTALLATION

1. Disconnect the power steering hoses from the pump.
2. Remove the adjusting bolt and slip off the belt.
3. Support the pump, remove the mounting bolts and lift out the pump.
4. Installation is the reverse of removal. Tighten the hoses to 25 ft. lbs. (34 Nm), the belt adjusting bolt to 30 ft. lbs. (41 Nm), and the lower stud nut to 40 ft. lbs. (54 Nm). Adjust the belt to specifications.

Manual and Power Steering Gear

REMOVAL & INSTALLATION

➡An assistant will be needed to perform this procedure.

1. Loosen the wheel nuts. Raise the vehicle and support it securely by the body.
2. Detach the tie rod ends at the steering knuckles as described above.
3. Support the lower front suspension crossmember securely with a jack. Then, remove all four suspension crossmember attaching bolts. Lower the crossmember with the jack until it is possible to gain access to the steering gear and the lower steering column. Slide the gear off the steering column coupling.
4. Remove the splash shields and boot seal shields.
5. If the car has power steering, remove the fasteners from the hose locating bracket attachment points. Get a drain pan

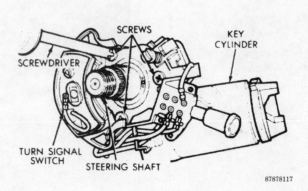

Fig. 91 Remove the three screws that hold the turn signal switch in place

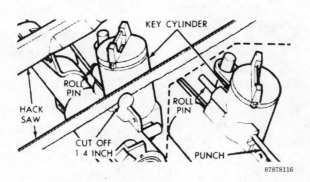

Fig. 92 Using a hacksaw blade, cut the upper ¼ in. (6mm) from the key cylinder retainer pin boot

Fig. 93 Loosen the nut on the end of the tie rod end to the steering arm

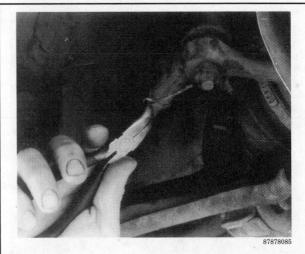

Fig. 95 Remove the cotter pin on the end of the tie rod end

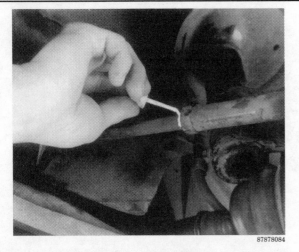

Fig. 94 Mark the position of the threads on the tie rod for installation

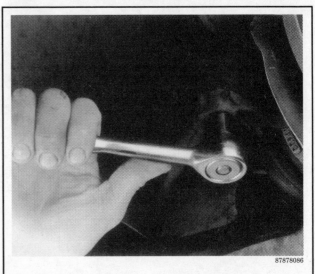

Fig. 96 Loosen the nut

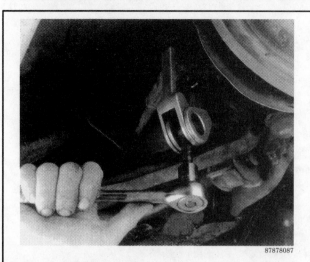

Fig. 97 Using a ball joint separator, remove the tie rod end from the knuckle

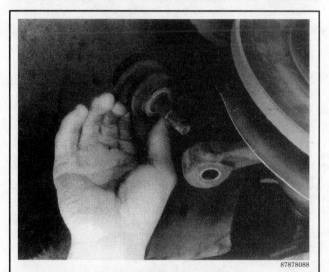

Fig. 98 Slip the tie rod end out of the knuckle

Fig. 99 Unscrew the end from the steering shaft

and disconnect both hoses at the opening nearest the steering gear and drain them into the pan. Discard the O-rings.

6. Remove the bolts attaching the power steering unit to the crossmember.

7. Remove the steering gear from the crossmember by pulling it off the steering column coupling and then removing it.

To install:

8. Position the steering gear on the crossmember. Tighten the fasteners to 250 inch lbs. (28 Nm).

9. Raise the crossmember into position with the jack, lining up the steering column coupling and the corresponding fitting on the end of the steering rack pinion shaft. Have an assistant inside the car help to position the column. If the car has manual steering, make sure the master serrations are lined up. Then, maneuver the crossmember/rack assembly so as to engage the column coupling and pinion shaft.

10. Position the crossmember so the bolt holes will line up. Install the bolts, but do not tighten them. Merely start the threads. Tighten the right rear bolt, which serves as a pilot bolt to properly located the crossmember. Then, tighten all four bolts to 90 ft. lbs. (122 Nm).

11. Reconnect the tie rod ends, as described above.

12. Wipe the ends of the power steering pump hoses and the ports in the steering gear. Install new O-rings on the hose tube ends and coat them with power steering fluid. Then, route the hose carefully in all clips and in such a way as to avoid kinks or close proximity to any exhaust system parts.

13. Make the hose connections and tighten them to 25 ft. lbs. (34 Nm). Refill the power steering pump with approved fluid.

14. Adjust toe in. Bleed the power steering system. Run the engine and check for leaks.

15. Have the wheel alignment checked as soon as possible.

Troubleshooting the Steering Column

Problem	Cause	Solution
Will not lock	• Lockbolt spring broken or defective	• Replace lock bolt spring
High effort (required to turn ignition key and lock cylinder)	• Lock cylinder defective • Ignition switch defective • Rack preload spring broken or deformed • Burr on lock sector, lock rack, housing, support or remote rod coupling • Bent sector shaft • Defective lock rack • Remote rod bent, deformed • Ignition switch mounting bracket bent • Distorted coupling slot in lock rack (tilt column)	• Replace lock cylinder • Replace ignition switch • Replace preload spring • Remove burr • Replace shaft • Replace lock rack • Replace rod • Straighten or replace • Replace lock rack
Will stick in "start"	• Remote rod deformed • Ignition switch mounting bracket bent	• Straighten or replace • Straighten or replace
Key cannot be removed in "off-lock"	• Ignition switch is not adjusted correctly • Defective lock cylinder	• Adjust switch • Replace lock cylinder
Lock cylinder can be removed without depressing retainer	• Lock cylinder with defective retainer • Burr over retainer slot in housing cover or on cylinder retainer	• Replace lock cylinder • Remove burr
High effort on lock cylinder between "off" and "off-lock"	• Distorted lock rack • Burr on tang of shift gate (automatic column) • Gearshift linkage not adjusted	• Replace lock rack • Remove burr • Adjust linkage
Noise in column	• One click when in "off-lock" position and the steering wheel is moved (all except automatic column) • Coupling bolts not tightened • Lack of grease on bearings or bearing surfaces • Upper shaft bearing worn or broken • Lower shaft bearing worn or broken • Column not correctly aligned • Coupling pulled apart • Broken coupling lower joint • Steering shaft snap ring not seated • Shroud loose on shift bowl. Housing loose on jacket—will be noticed with ignition in "off-lock" and when torque is applied to steering wheel.	• Normal—lock bolt is seating • Tighten pinch bolts • Lubricate with chassis grease • Replace bearing assembly • Replace bearing. Check shaft and replace if scored. • Align column • Replace coupling • Repair or replace joint and align column • Replace ring. Check for proper seating in groove. • Position shroud over lugs on shift bowl. Tighten mounting screws.
High steering shaft effort	• Column misaligned • Defective upper or lower bearing • Tight steering shaft universal joint • Flash on I.D. of shift tube at plastic joint (tilt column only) • Upper or lower bearing seized	• Align column • Replace as required • Repair or replace • Replace shift tube • Replace bearings
Lash in mounted column assembly	• Column mounting bracket bolts loose • Broken weld nuts on column jacket • Column capsule bracket sheared	• Tighten bolts • Replace column jacket • Replace bracket assembly

87878106

Troubleshooting the Steering Column (cont.)

Problem	Cause	Solution
Lash in mounted column assembly (cont.)	· Column bracket to column jacket mounting bolts loose	· Tighten to specified torque
	· Loose lock shoes in housing (tilt column only)	· Replace shoes
	· Loose pivot pins (tilt column only)	· Replace pivot pins and support
	· Loose lock shoe pin (tilt column only)	· Replace pin and housing
	· Loose support screws (tilt column only)	· Tighten screws
Housing loose (tilt column only)	· Excessive clearance between holes in support or housing and pivot pin diameters	· Replace pivot pins and support
	· Housing support-screws loose	· Tighten screws
Steering wheel loose—every other tilt position (tilt column only)	· Loose fit between lock shoe and lock shoe pivot pin	· Replace lock shoes and pivot pin
Steering column not locking in any tilt position (tilt column only)	· Lock shoe seized on pivot pin	· Replace lock shoes and pin
	· Lock shoe grooves have burrs or are filled with foreign material	· Clean or replace lock shoes
	· Lock shoe springs weak or broken	· Replace springs
Noise when tilting column (tilt column only)	· Upper tilt bumpers worn	· Replace tilt bumper
	· Tilt spring rubbing in housing	· Lubricate with chassis grease
One click when in "off-lock" position and the steering wheel is moved	· Seating of lock bolt	· None. Click is normal characteristic sound produced by lock bolt as it seats.
High shift effort (automatic and tilt column only)	· Column not correctly aligned	· Align column
	· Lower bearing not aligned correctly	· Assemble correctly
	· Lack of grease on seal or lower bearing areas	· Lubricate with chassis grease
Improper transmission shifting—automatic and tilt column only	· Sheared shift tube joint	· Replace shift tube
	· Improper transmission gearshift linkage adjustment	· Adjust linkage
	· Loose lower shift lever	· Replace shift tube

87878107

Troubleshooting the Ignition Switch

Problem	Cause	Solution
Ignition switch electrically inoperative	· Loose or defective switch connector	· Tighten or replace connector
	· Feed wire open (fusible link)	· Repair or replace
	· Defective ignition switch	· Replace ignition switch
Engine will not crank	· Ignition switch not adjusted properly	· Adjust switch
Ignition switch will not actuate mechanically	· Defective ignition switch	· Replace switch
	· Defective lock sector	· Replace lock sector
	· Defective remote rod	· Replace remote rod
Ignition switch cannot be adjusted correctly	· Remote rod deformed	· Repair, straighten or replace

87878108

Troubleshooting the Turn Signal Switch

Problem	Cause	Solution
Turn signal will not cancel	• Loose switch mounting screws • Switch or anchor bosses broken • Broken, missing or out of position detent, or cancelling spring	• Tighten screws • Replace switch • Reposition springs or replace switch as required
Turn signal difficult to operate	• Turn signal lever loose • Switch yoke broken or distorted • Loose or misplaced springs • Foreign parts and/or materials in switch • Switch mounted loosely	• Tighten mounting screws • Replace switch • Reposition springs or replace switch • Remove foreign parts and/or material • Tighten mounting screws
Turn signal will not indicate lane change	• Broken lane change pressure pad or spring hanger • Broken, missing or misplaced lane change spring • Jammed wires	• Replace switch • Replace or reposition as required • Loosen mounting screws, reposition wires and retighten screws
Turn signal will not stay in turn position	• Foreign material or loose parts impeding movement of switch yoke • Defective switch	• Remove material and/or parts • Replace switch
Hazard switch cannot be pulled out	• Foreign material between hazard support cancelling leg and yoke	• Remove foreign material. No foreign material impeding function of hazard switch—replace turn signal switch.
No turn signal lights	• Inoperative turn signal flasher • Defective or blown fuse • Loose chassis to column harness connector • Disconnect column to chassis connector. Connect new switch to chassis and operate switch by hand. If vehicle lights now operate normally, signal switch is inoperative • If vehicle lights do not operate, check chassis wiring for opens, grounds, etc.	• Replace turn signal flasher • Replace fuse • Connect securely • Replace signal switch • Repair chassis wiring as required
Instrument panel turn indicator lights on but not flashing	• Burned out or damaged front or rear turn signal bulb • If vehicle lights do not operate, check light sockets for high resistance connections, the chassis wiring for opens, grounds, etc. • Inoperative flasher • Loose chassis to column harness connection • Inoperative turn signal switch • To determine if turn signal switch is defective, substitute new switch into circuit and operate switch by hand. If the vehicle's lights operate normally, signal switch is inoperative.	• Replace bulb • Repair chassis wiring as required • Replace flasher • Connect securely • Replace turn signal switch • Replace turn signal switch
Stop light not on when turn indicated	• Loose column to chassis connection • Disconnect column to chassis connector. Connect new switch into system without removing old.	• Connect securely • Replace signal switch

Troubleshooting the Turn Signal Switch (cont.)

Problem	Cause	Solution
Stop light not on when turn indicated (cont.)	Operate switch by hand. If brake lights work with switch in the turn position, signal switch is defective.	
	· If brake lights do not work, check connector to stop light sockets for grounds, opens, etc.	· Repair connector to stop light circuits using service manual as guide
Turn indicator panel lights not flashing	· Burned out bulbs · High resistance to ground at bulb socket · Opens, ground in wiring harness from front turn signal bulb socket to indicator lights	· Replace bulbs · Replace socket · Locate and repair as required
Turn signal lights flash very slowly	· High resistance ground at light sockets · Incorrect capacity turn signal flasher or bulb · If flashing rate is still extremely slow, check chassis wiring harness from the connector to light sockets for high resistance · Loose chassis to column harness connection · Disconnect column to chassis connector. Connect new switch into system without removing old. Operate switch by hand. If flashing occurs at normal rate, the signal switch is defective.	· Repair high resistance grounds at light sockets · Replace turn signal flasher or bulb · Locate and repair as required · Connect securely · Replace turn signal switch
Hazard signal lights will not flash—turn signal functions normally	· Blow fuse · Inoperative hazard warning flasher · Loose chassis-to-column harness connection · Disconnect column to chassis connector. Connect new switch into system without removing old. Depress the hazard warning lights. If they now work normally, turn signal switch is defective. · If lights do not flash, check wiring harness "K" lead for open between hazard flasher and connector. If open, fuse block is defective	· Replace fuse · Replace hazard warning flasher in fuse panel · Conect securely · Replace turn signal switch · Repair or replace brown wire or connector as required

87878110

Troubleshooting the Manual Steering Gear

Problem	Cause	Solution
Hard or erratic steering	• Incorrect tire pressure	• Inflate tires to recommended pressures
	• Insufficient or incorrect lubrication	• Lubricate as required (refer to Maintenance Section)
	• Suspension, or steering linkage parts damaged or misaligned	• Repair or replace parts as necessary
	• Improper front wheel alignment	• Adjust incorrect wheel alignment angles
	• Incorrect steering gear adjustment	• Adjust steering gear
	• Sagging springs	• Replace springs
Play or looseness in steering	• Steering wheel loose	• Inspect shaft spines and repair as necessary. Tighten attaching nut and stake in place.
	• Steering linkage or attaching parts loose or worn	• Tighten, adjust, or replace faulty components
	• Pitman arm loose	• Inspect shaft splines and repair as necessary. Tighten attaching nut and stake in place
	• Steering gear attaching bolts loose	• Tighten bolts
	• Loose or worn wheel bearings	• Adjust or replace bearings
	• Steering gear adjustment incorrect or parts badly worn	• Adjust gear or replace defective parts
Wheel shimmy or tramp	• Improper tire pressure	• Inflate tires to recommended pressures
	• Wheels, tires, or brake rotors out-of-balance or out-of-round	• Inspect and replace or balance parts
	• Inoperative, worn, or loose shock absorbers or mounting parts	• Repair or replace shocks or mountings
	• Loose or worn steering or suspension parts	• Tighten or replace as necessary
	• Loose or worn wheel bearings	• Adjust or replace bearings
	• Incorrect steering gear adjustments	• Adjust steering gear
	• Incorrect front wheel alignment	• Correct front wheel alignment
Tire wear	• Improper tire pressure	• Inflate tires to recommended pressures
	• Failure to rotate tires	• Rotate tires
	• Brakes grabbing	• Adjust or repair brakes
	• Incorrect front wheel alignment	• Align incorrect angles
	• Broken or damaged steering and suspension parts	• Repair or replace defective parts
	• Wheel runout	• Replace faulty wheel
	• Excessive speed on turns	• Make driver aware of conditions
Vehicle leads to one side	• Improper tire pressures	• Inflate tires to recommended pressures
	• Front tires with uneven tread depth, wear pattern, or different cord design (i.e., one bias ply and one belted or radial tire on front wheels)	• Install tires of same cord construction and reasonably even tread depth, design, and wear pattern
	• Incorrect front wheel alignment	• Align incorrect angles
	• Brakes dragging	• Adjust or repair brakes
	• Pulling due to uneven tire construction	• Replace faulty tire

87878111

Troubleshooting the Power Steering Gear

Problem	Cause	Solution
Hissing noise in steering gear	· There is some noise in all power steering systems. One of the most common is a hissing sound most evident at standstill parking. There is no relationship between this noise and performance of the steering. Hiss may be expected when steering wheel is at end of travel or when slowly turning at standstill.	· Slight hiss is normal and in no way affects steering. Do not replace valve unless hiss is extremely objectionable. A replacement valve will also exhibit slight noise and is not always a cure. Investigate clearance around flexible coupling rivets. Be sure steering shaft and gear are aligned so flexible coupling rotates in a flat plane and is not distorted as shaft rotates. Any metal-to-metal contacts through flexible coupling will transmit valve hiss into passenger compartment through the steering column.
Rattle or chuckle noise in steering gear	· Gear loose on frame · Steering linkage looseness · Pressure hose touching other parts of car · Loose pitman shaft over center adjustment **NOTE:** A slight rattle may occur on turns because of increased clearance off the "high point." This is normal and clearance must not be reduced below specified limits to eliminate this slight rattle. · Loose pitman arm	· Check gear-to-frame mounting screws. Tighten screws to 88 N·m (65 foot pounds) torque. · Check linkage pivot points for wear. Replace if necessary. · Adjust hose position. Do not bend tubing by hand. · Adjust to specifications · Tighten pitman arm nut to specifications
Squawk noise in steering gear when turning or recovering from a turn	· Damper O-ring on valve spool cut	· Replace damper O-ring
Poor return of steering wheel to center	· Tires not properly inflated · Lack of lubrication in linkage and ball joints · Lower coupling flange rubbing against steering gear adjuster plug · Steering gear to column misalignment · Improper front wheel alignment · Steering linkage binding · Ball joints binding · Steering wheel rubbing against housing · Tight or frozen steering shaft bearings · Sticking or plugged valve spool · Steering gear adjustments over specifications · Kink in return hose	· Inflate to specified pressure · Lube linkage and ball joints · Loosen pinch bolt and assemble properly · Align steering column · Check and adjust as necessary · Replace pivots · Replace ball joints · Align housing · Replace bearings · Remove and clean or replace valve · Check adjustment with gear out of car. Adjust as required. · Replace hose
Car leads to one side or the other (keep in mind road condition and wind. Test car in both directions on flat road)	· Front end misaligned · Unbalanced steering gear valve **NOTE:** If this is cause, steering effort will be very light in direction of lead and normal or heavier in opposite direction	· Adjust to specifications · Replace valve

Troubleshooting the Power Steering Gear (cont.)

Problem	Cause	Solution
Momentary increase in effort when turning wheel fast to right or left	• Low oil level • Pump belt slipping • High internal leakage	• Add power steering fluid as required • Tighten or replace belt • Check pump pressure. (See pressure test)
Steering wheel surges or jerks when turning with engine running especially during parking	• Low oil level • Loose pump belt • Steering linkage hitting engine oil pan at full turn • Insufficient pump pressure • Pump flow control valve sticking	• Fill as required • Adjust tension to specification • Correct clearance • Check pump pressure. (See pressure test). Replace relief valve if defective. • Inspect for varnish or damage, replace if necessary
Excessive wheel kickback or loose steering	• Air in system • Steering gear loose on frame • Steering linkage joints worn enough to be loose • Worn poppet valve • Loose thrust bearing preload adjustment • Excessive overcenter lash	• Add oil to pump reservoir and bleed by operating steering. Check hose connectors for proper torque and adjust as required. • Tighten attaching screws to specified torque • Replace loose pivots • Replace poppet valve • Adjust to specification with gear out of vehicle • Adjust to specification with gear out of car
Hard steering or lack of assist	• Loose pump belt • Low oil level **NOTE:** Low oil level will also result in excessive pump noise • Steering gear to column misalignment • Lower coupling flange rubbing against steering gear adjuster plug • Tires not properly inflated	• Adjust belt tension to specification • Fill to proper level. If excessively low, check all lines and joints for evidence of external leakage. Tighten loose connectors. • Align steering column • Loosen pinch bolt and assemble properly • Inflate to recommended pressure
Foamy milky power steering fluid, low fluid level and possible low pressure	• Air in the fluid, and loss of fluid due to internal pump leakage causing overflow	• Check for leak and correct. Bleed system. Extremely cold temperatures will cause system aeration should the oil level be low. If oil level is correct and pump still foams, remove pump from vehicle and separate reservoir from housing. Check welsh plug and housing for cracks. If plug is loose or housing is cracked, replace housing.
Low pressure due to steering pump	• Flow control valve stuck or inoperative • Pressure plate not flat against cam ring	• Remove burrs or dirt or replace. Flush system. • Correct
Low pressure due to steering gear	• Pressure loss in cylinder due to worn piston ring or badly worn housing bore • Leakage at valve rings, valve body-to-worm seal	• Remove gear from car for disassembly and inspection of ring and housing bore • Remove gear from car for disassembly and replace seals

Troubleshooting the Power Steering Pump

Problem	Cause	Solution
Chirp noise in steering pump	• Loose belt	• Adjust belt tension to specification
Belt squeal (particularly noticeable at full wheel travel and stand still parking)	• Loose belt	• Adjust belt tension to specification
Growl noise in steering pump	• Excessive back pressure in hoses or steering gear caused by restriction	• Locate restriction and correct. Replace part if necessary.
Growl noise in steering pump (particularly noticeable at stand still parking)	• Scored pressure plates, thrust plate or rotor • Extreme wear of cam ring	• Replace parts and flush system • Replace parts
Groan noise in steering pump	• Low oil level • Air in the oil. Poor pressure hose connection.	• Fill reservoir to proper level • Tighten connector to specified torque. Bleed system by operating steering from right to left—full turn.
Rattle noise in steering pump	• Vanes not installed properly • Vanes sticking in rotor slots	• Install properly • Free up by removing burrs, varnish, or dirt
Swish noise in steering pump	• Defective flow control valve	• Replace part
Whine noise in steering pump	• Pump shaft bearing scored	• Replace housing and shaft. Flush system.
Hard steering or lack of assist	• Loose pump belt • Low oil level in reservoir **NOTE:** Low oil level will also result in excessive pump noise • Steering gear to column misalignment • Lower coupling flange rubbing against steering gear adjuster plug • Tires not properly inflated	• Adjust belt tension to specification • Fill to proper level. If excessively low, check all lines and joints for evidence of external leakage. Tighten loose connectors. • Align steering column • Loosen pinch bolt and assemble properly • Inflate to recommended pressure
Foaming milky power steering fluid, low fluid level and possible low pressure	• Air in the fluid, and loss of fluid due to internal pump leakage causing overflow	• Check for leaks and correct. Bleed system. Extremely cold temperatures will cause system aeriation should the oil level be low. If oil level is correct and pump still foams, remove pump from vehicle and separate reservoir from body. Check welsh plug and body for cracks. If plug is loose or body is cracked, replace body.
Low pump pressure	• Flow control valve stuck or inoperative • Pressure plate not flat against cam ring	• Remove burrs or dirt or replace. Flush system. • Correct
Momentary increase in effort when turning wheel fast to right or left	• Low oil level in pump • Pump belt slipping • High internal leakage	• Add power steering fluid as required • Tighten or replace belt • Check pump pressure. (See pressure test)
Steering wheel surges or jerks when turning with engine running especially during parking	• Low oil level • Loose pump belt • Steering linkage hitting engine oil pan at full turn • Insufficient pump pressure	• Fill as required • Adjust tension to specification • Correct clearance • Check pump pressure. (See pressure test). Replace flow control valve if defective.

Troubleshooting the Power Steering Pump (cont.)

Problem	Cause	Solution
Steering wheel surges or jerks when turning with engine running especially during parking (cont.)	· Sticking flow control valve	· Inspect for varnish or damage, replace if necessary
Excessive wheel kickback or loose steering	· Air in system	· Add oil to pump reservoir and bleed by operating steering. Check hose connectors for proper torque and adjust as required.
Low pump pressure	· Extreme wear of cam ring · Scored pressure plate, thrust plate, or rotor · Vanes not installed properly · Vanes sticking in rotor slots · Cracked or broken thrust or pressure plate	· Replace parts. Flush system. · Replace parts. Flush system. · Install properly · Freeup by removing burrs, varnish, or dirt · Replace part

87878115

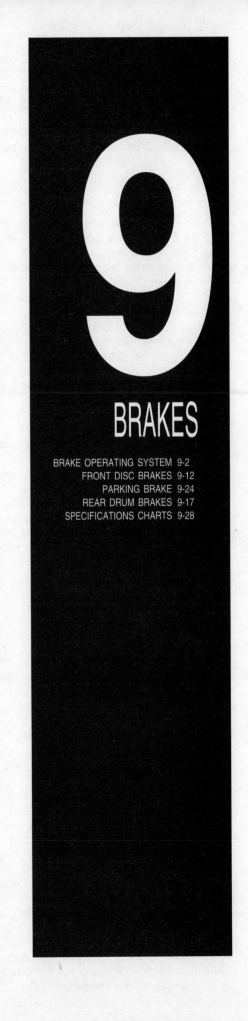

9

BRAKES

BRAKE OPERATING SYSTEM

Hydraulics

BASIC OPERATING PRINCIPLES

Hydraulic systems are used to actuate the brakes of all modern automobiles. The system transports the power required to force the frictional surfaces of the braking system together from the pedal to the individual brake units at each wheel. A hydraulic system is used for two reasons. First, fluid under pressure can be carried to all parts of an automobile by small hoses-some of which are flexible-without taking up a significant amount of room or posing routing problems. Second, a great mechanical advantage can be given to the brake pedal end of the system, and the foot pressure required to actuate the brakes can be reduced by making the surface area of the master cylinder pistons smaller than that of any of the pistons in the wheel cylinders or calipers.

The master cylinder consists of a fluid reservoir and either a single or double cylinder and piston assembly. Double type master cylinders are designed to separate the front and rear braking systems hydraulically in case of a leak.

Steel lines carry the brake fluid to a point on the vehicle's frame near each of the vehicle's wheels. The fluid is then carried to the wheel cylinders by flexible tubes in order to allow for suspension and steering movements.

Each wheel cylinder contains two pistons, one at either end, which push outward in opposite directions. In disc brake systems, the cylinders are part of the calipers. One or four cylinders are used to force the brake pads against the disc, but all cylinders contain one piston only. All pistons employ some type of seal, usually made of rubber, to minimize fluid leakage. A rubber dust boot seals the outer end of the cylinder against dust and dirt. The boot fits around the outer end of the piston on disc brake calipers, and around the brake actuating rod on wheel cylinders.

The hydraulic system operates as follows: When at rest, the entire system, from the piston(s) in the master cylinder to those in the wheel cylinders or calipers, is full of brake fluid. Upon application of the brake pedal, fluid trapped in front of the master cylinder piston(s) is forced through the lines to the wheel cylinders. Here, it forces the pistons outward, in the case of drum brakes, and inward toward the disc, in the case of disc brakes. The motion of the pistons is opposed by return springs mounted outside the cylinders in drum brakes, and by internal springs or spring seals, in disc brakes.

Upon release of the brake pedal, a spring located inside the master cylinder immediately returns the master cylinder pistons to the normal position. The pistons contain check valves and the master cylinder has compensating ports drilled in it. These are uncovered as the pistons reach their normal position. The piston check valves allow fluid to flow toward the wheel cylinders or calipers as the pistons withdraw. Then, as the return springs force the brake pads or shoes into the released position, the excess fluid reservoir through the compensating ports. It is during the time the pedal is in the released position that any fluid that has leaked out of the system will be replaced through the compensating ports.

Dual circuit master cylinders employ two pistons, located one behind the other, in the same cylinder. The primary piston is actuated directly by mechanical linkage from the brake pedal. The secondary piston is actuated by fluid trapped between the two pistons. If a leak develops in front of the secondary piston, it moves forward until it bottoms against the front of the master cylinder, and the fluid trapped between the pistons will operate the rear brakes. If the rear brakes develop a leak, the primary piston will move forward until direct contact with the secondary piston takes place, and it will force the secondary piston to actuate the front brakes. In either case, the brake pedal moves farther when the brakes are applied, and less braking power is available.

All dual-circuit systems use a switch to warn the driver when only half of the brake system is operational. This switch is located in a valve body which is mounted on the firewall or the frame below the master cylinder. A hydraulic piston receives pressure from both circuits, each circuit's pressure being applied to one end of the piston. When the pressures are in balance, the piston remains stationary. When one circuit has a leak, however, the greater pressure in that circuit during application of the brakes will push the piston to one side, closing the switch and activating the brake warning light.

In disc brake systems, this valve body also contains a metering valve and, in some cases, a proportioning valve. The metering valve keeps pressure from traveling to the disc brakes on the front wheels until the brake shoes on the rear wheels have contacted the drums, ensuring that the front brakes will never be used alone. The proportioning valve controls the pressure to the rear brakes to avoid rear wheel lock-up during very hard braking.

Warning lights may be tested by depressing the brake pedal and holding it while opening one of the wheel cylinder bleeder screws. If this does not cause the light to go on, substitute a new lamp, make continuity checks, and, finally, replace the switch as necessary.

The hydraulic system may be checked for leaks by applying pressure to the pedal gradually and steadily. If the pedal sinks very slowly to the floor, the system has a leak. This is not to be confused with a springy or spongy feel due to the compression of air within the lines. If the system leaks, there will be a gradual change in the position of the pedal with a constant pressure.

Check for leaks along all lines and at wheel cylinders. If no external leaks are apparent, the problem is inside the master cylinder.

Disc Brakes

BASIC OPERATING PRINCIPLES

Instead of the traditional expanding brakes that press outward against a circular drum, disc brake systems utilize a disc (rotor) with brake pads positioned on either side of it. Braking effect is achieved in a manner similar to the way you would squeeze a spinning phonograph record between your fingers. The disc (rotor) is a casting with cooling fins between the two braking surfaces. This enables air to circulate between the braking surfaces making them less sensitive to heat buildup and more resistant to fade. Dirt and water do not affect braking action since contaminants are thrown off by the centrifugal action of the rotor or scraped off the by the pads. Also, the equal clamping action of the two brake pads tends to ensure uniform, straight-line stops. Disc brakes are inherently self-adjusting.

There are three general types of disc brake:
• Fixed caliper
• Floating caliper
• Sliding caliper

The fixed caliper design uses two pistons mounted on either side of the rotor (in each side of the caliper). The caliper is mounted rigidly and does not move.

The sliding and floating designs are quite similar. In fact, these two types are often lumped together. In both designs, the pad on the inside of the rotor is moved into contact with the rotor by hydraulic force. The caliper, which is not held in a fixed position, moves slightly, bringing the outside pad into contact with the rotor. There are various methods of attaching floating calipers. Some pivot at the bottom or top, and some slide on mounting bolts. In any event, the end result is the same.

Drum Brakes

BASIC OPERATING PRINCIPLES

Drum brakes employ two brake shoes mounted on a stationary backing plate. These shoes are positioned inside a circular drum which rotates with the wheel assembly. The shoes are held in place by springs. This allows them to slide toward the drums (when they are applied) while keeping the linings and drums in alignment. The shoes are actuated by a wheel cylinder which is mounted at the top of the backing plate. When the brakes are applied, hydraulic pressure forces the wheel cylinder's actuating links outward. Since these links bear directly against the top of the brake shoes, the tops of the shoes are then forced against the inner side of the drum. This action forces the bottoms of the two shoes to contact the brake drum by rotating the entire assembly slightly (known as servo action). When pressure within the wheel cylinder is relaxed, return springs pull the shoes back away from the drum.

Most modern drum brakes are designed to self-adjust themselves during application when the vehicle is moving in reverse. This motion causes both shoes to rotate very slightly with the drum, rocking an adjusting lever, thereby causing rotation of the adjusting screw.

Power Boosters

BASIC OPERATING PRINCIPLES

Power brakes operate just as standard brake systems except in the actuation of the master cylinder pistons. A vacuum diaphragm is located on the front of the master cylinder and assists the driver in applying the brakes, reducing both the effort and travel he must put into moving the brake pedal.

The vacuum diaphragm housing is connected to the intake manifold by a vacuum hose. A check valve is placed at the point where the hose enters the diaphragm housing, so that during periods of low manifold vacuum brake assist vacuum will not be lost.

Depressing the brake pedal closes off the vacuum source and allows atmospheric pressure to enter on one side of the diaphragm. This causes the master cylinder pistons to move and apply the brakes. When the brake pedal is released, vacuum is applied to both sides of the diaphragm, and return springs return the diaphragm and master cylinder pistons to the released position. If the vacuum fails, the brake pedal rod will butt against the end of the master cylinder actuating rod, and direct mechanical application will occur as the pedal is depressed.

The hydraulic and mechanical problems that apply to conventional brake systems also apply to power brakes, and should be checked for if the tests below do not reveal the problem.

Test for a system vacuum leak as described below:
1. Operate the engine at idle without touching the brake pedal for at least one minute.
2. Turn **OFF** the engine, and wait one minute.
3. Test for the presence of assist vacuum by depressing the brake pedal and releasing it several times. Light application will produce less and less pedal travel, if vacuum was present. If there is no vacuum, air is leaking into the system somewhere.

Test for system operation as follows:
4. Pump the brake pedal with engine **OFF**, until the supply vacuum is entirely gone.
5. Put a light, steady pressure on the pedal.
6. Turn the engine **ON**, and operate it at idle. If the system is operating, the brake pedal should fall toward the floor if constant pressure is maintained on the pedal.

Power brake systems may be tested for hydraulic leaks just as ordinary systems are tested.

✳✳CAUTION

Brake linings may contain asbestos. Asbestos is a known cancer-causing agent. When working on brakes, remember that the dust which accumulates on the brake parts and/or in the drum contains asbestos. Always wear a protective face covering, such as a painter's mask, when working on the brakes. NEVER blow the dust from the brakes or drum! There are solvents made for the purpose of cleaning brake parts. Use them!

A conventional front disc/rear drum setup is used. The front discs are single piston caliper types; the rear drums are activated by a conventional top mounted wheel cylinder. Disc brakes require no adjustments, the drum brakes are self adjusting by means of the parking brake cable. The only variances in the system from those found on the majority of vehicles are that the system is diagonally balanced, that is, the front left and right rear are on one system and the front right and left rear on the other. No proportioning valve is used. Power brakes are optional.

Adjustment

DRUM BRAKES

▶ **See Figure 1**

All disc brakes are inherently self-adjusting. No adjustment is possible. Even though the drum brakes are self-adjusting in normal use, there are times when a manual adjustment is required, such as after installing new shoes or if it is required to back the shoes off the drum. A star wheel with screw type adjusters is provided for these occasions.

1. Remove the access slot plug from the backing plate.
2. Using a brake adjusting spoon pry downward (left side) or upward (right side) on the end of the tool (starwheel teeth moving up) to tighten the brakes. The opposite applies to loosen the brakes.

➡**It will be necessary to use a small screwdriver to hold the adjusting lever away from the starwheel. Be careful not to bend the adjusting lever.**

3. When the brakes are tight almost to the point of being locked, back off on the starwheel 10 clicks. The starwheel on each set of brakes (front or rear) must be backed off the same number of turns to prevent brake pull from side to side.
4. When all brakes are adjusted, check brake pedal travel and then make several stops, while backing the car up, to equalize all the wheels.

TESTING THE ADJUSTER

1. Raise the and safely support the vehicle.
2. Loosen the brakes by holding the adjuster lever away from the starwheel and backing off the starwheel approximately 30 notches.
3. Spin the wheel and brake drum in reverse and have an assistant apply the brakes. The movement of the secondary

87879011

Fig. 1 Brakes are adjusted using a brake spoon through the access slot in the rear of the drum

shoe should pull the adjuster lever up, and when the brakes are released the lever should snap down and turn the starwheel.

4. If the automatic adjuster doesn't work, the drum must be removed and the adjuster components inspected carefully for breakage, wear, or improper installation.

Master Cylinder

▶ **See Figure 2**

REMOVAL & INSTALLATION

With Power Brakes

▶ **See Figure 3**

1. Disconnect the primary and secondary brake lines from the master cylinder. Plug the openings.
2. Remove the nuts attaching the cylinder to the power brake booster.
3. Slide the master cylinder straight out, away from the booster.

To install:

4. Position the master cylinder over the studs on the booster, align the pushrod with the master cylinder piston and tighten the nuts to 16 ft. lbs. (22 Nm).
5. Connect the brake lines.
6. Bleed the brakes.

Without Power Brakes

▶ **See Figures 4 and 5**

1. Disconnect the primary and secondary brake lines and install plugs in the master cylinder openings.
2. Disconnect the stoplight switch mounting bracket from under the instrument panel.
3. Pull the brake pedal backward to disengage the pushrod from the master cylinder piston.

➡**This will destroy the grommet. Use a new one when installing the master cylinder.**

4. Remove the master cylinder-to-firewall nuts.
5. Slide the master cylinder out and away from the firewall. Be sure to remove all pieces of the broken grommet.

To install:

6. Install the boot on the pushrod.
7. Install a new grommet on the pushrod.
8. Apply a soap and water solution to the grommet and slide it firmly into position in the primary piston socket. Move the pushrod from side to side to make sure it's seated.
9. From the engine side, press the pushrod through the master cylinder mounting plate and align the mounting studs with the holes in the cylinder.
10. Install the nuts and tighten them to 16 ft. lbs. (22 Nm).
11. From under the instrument panel, place the pushrod on the pin on the pedal and install a new retaining clip.

➡**Be sure to lubricate the pin.**

12. Install the brake lines on the master cylinder.
13. Bleed the system.

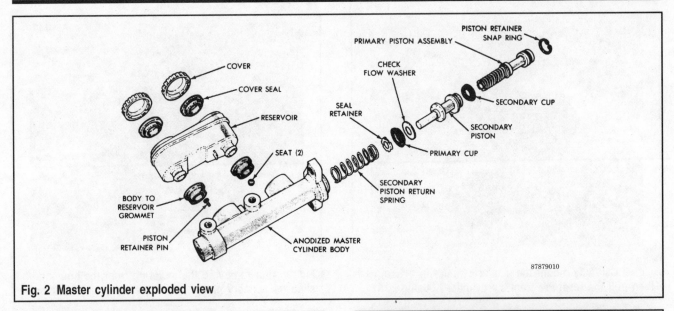

Fig. 2 Master cylinder exploded view

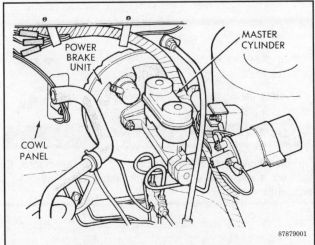

Fig. 3 On vehicles equipped with power brakes, the master cylinder is mounted to the booster

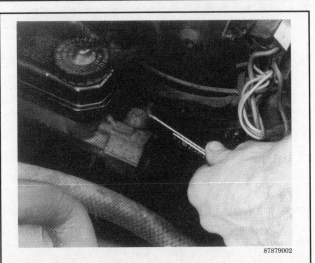

Fig. 4 Whenever possible, use a flare wrench to disconnect the master cylinder brake lines

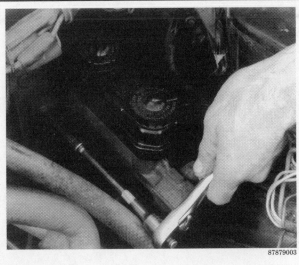

Fig. 5 Remove the master cylinder-to-firewall nuts

OVERHAUL

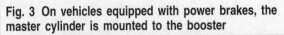 See Figures 6, 7, 8, 9, 10 and 11

✳✳CAUTION

Do not hone the master cylinder bore. Honing will remove the anodized finish.

1. Clean the housing and reservoir.
2. Remove the reservoir caps and empty the fluid.
3. Clamp the master cylinder in a soft-jawed vise.
4. Pull the reservoir from the master cylinder housing.
5. Remove the reservoir grommets.
6. Use needle-nosed pliers to remove the secondary piston pin from inside the housing.
7. Remove the snapring from the outer end of the housing.
8. Slide the primary piston out of the master cylinder bore.

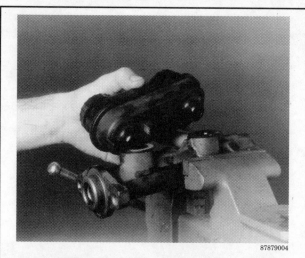

Fig. 6 Carefully mount the master cylinder in a vise, then pull the reservoir from the cylinder housing

Fig. 7 Remove the reservoir grommets

Fig. 8 Use needle-nosed pliers to remove the secondary piston pin from inside the housing

Fig. 9 After removing the snapring from the housing, slide the primary piston out of the master cylinder bore

9. Tap the open end of the cylinder on the bench to remove the secondary piston. If it sticks in the bore, it can be removed with light air pressure.

➡If air pressure is used to remove the piston, new cups must be installed.

10. Note the position of the rubber cups and remove all except the primary cup.

✳✳WARNING

Do not remove the primary cup from the primary piston. If the cup is worn, the entire primary piston assembly should be replaced.

11. If the brass tube seats are not reusable, replace them using a suitable tool.

12. Wash the entire housing in clean brake fluid and inspect for pitting or scratches. If any are found, replace the housing. If the pistons are corroded, they should be replaced. Discard all used rubber parts and replace piston caps and seals.

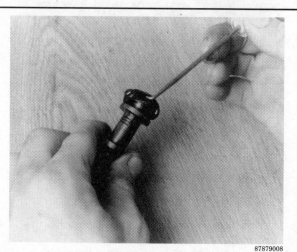

Fig. 10 Remove the rubber cups excluding the primary cup

13. Before assembly, dip all parts in clean brake fluid.

14. Install the check flow washer.

15. Install the secondary piston into the master cylinder bore. Be sure the cup lips enter the bore evenly. Keep well lubricated with brake fluid.

16. Center the primary piston spring retainer on the secondary piston and push the piston assemblies into the bore up to the primary piston cup.

17. Work the cup into the bore and push the piston in up to the secondary seal. Work the cup into the bore and push on the piston until fully seated.

18. Depress the piston and install the snapring.

19. Tap the secondary piston retainer pin into the housing.

20. Install new tube seats.

21. Install the reservoir grommets in the housing. Lubricate the area with clean brake fluid and install the reservoir. All the lettering should be properly read from the left side of the reservoir when it is properly installed. Make sure the bottom of the reservoir touches the top of the grommet.

Pressure Differential Valve and Warning Light Switch

OPERATION

The brake system is split diagonally. That means that the right rear and left front brakes are connected to the same reservoir. Both systems are routed through, but separated by, the pressure differential valve, which also contains the warning switch. The function of the valve is to activate the switch in the event of brake system malfunction. The warning light switch is the latching type. It will automatically recenter itself after the repair is made and brake pedal depressed.

The bulb can be checked each time the ignition switch is turned to the **ON** position or each time the parking brake is set.

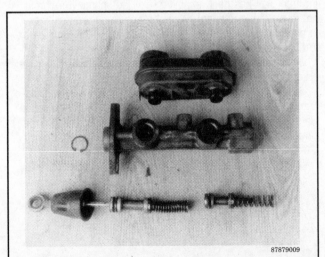

87879009

Fig. 11 Before assembly, dip all parts in clean brake fluid. Make sure you have all the parts!

Height Sensing Proportioning Valve

OPERATION

▶ **See Figure 12**

The Rampage and Scamp pickup models use a height sensing dual proportioning valve in addition to the regular differential warning switch. This valve is located under the bed just forward of the rear axle. It automatically provides optimum brake balance front-to-rear regardless of the vehicle load condition. The valve modulates the pressure to the rear brakes sensing the vehicle load condition through relative movement between the rear axle and the load floor.

➡ **It is important that aftermarket load leveling devices are NOT installed on this brake/suspension system. The installation of these devices will cause the rear brake height sensing proportioning valve to sense a light load condition that is actually a loaded condition being created by these add-on devices.**

TESTING

When a premature rear wheel slide is obtained on brake application, it could be an indication that the fluid pressure to the rear brakes is above the reduction ratio for the rear line pressure and that the proportioning valve is malfunctioning. To test the valve use the following procedures.

➡ **During the testing, leave the front brake lines connected to the valve.**

1. Disconnect the external spring at the valve end.

2. Install one gauge and the tee of tool set C-4007-A, or equivalent in the line from either master cylinder port and brake valve assembly.

3. Install the second gauge from tool set C-4007-A or equivalent to either rear brake line. Bleed the rear brake system.

4. Have an assistant exert pressure on the brake pedal (holding pressure) to get a reading on the valve inlet gauge and check the reading on the outlet gauge. The inlet pressure should read 1000 psi (6895 kPa) and the outlet pressure should read between 530-770 psi. (3654-5309 kPa). If either is not as specified, replace the valve.

INSTALLATION & ADJUSTMENT

▶ **See Figure 13**

➡ **After installing a new height sensing proportioning valve, both rear brakes should be bled.**

1. Raise the vehicle and support on jackstands so that the rear suspension is hanging free and the shock absorbers are fully extended. Leave the wheels and tires on the truck to help keep the suspension in the full rebound position.

2. Loosen the spring adjusting bracket nuts **A** and **B**.

3. Push the valve lever **C** rearward until it bottoms and hold it there.

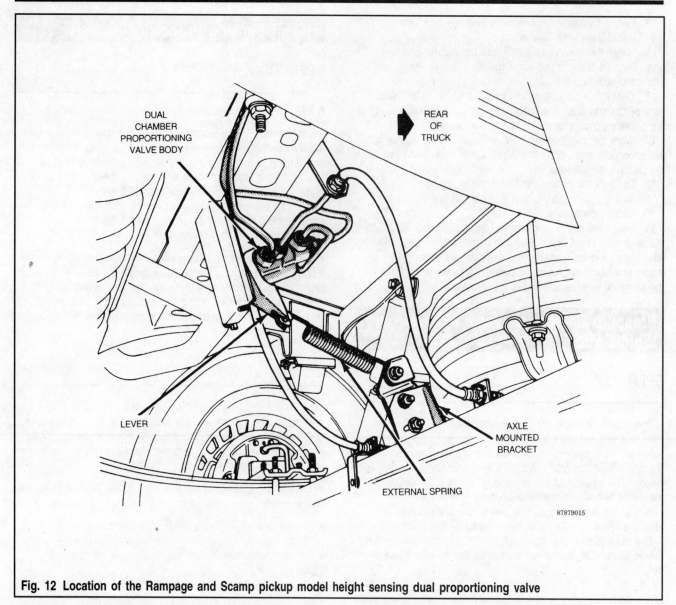

Fig. 12 Location of the Rampage and Scamp pickup model height sensing dual proportioning valve

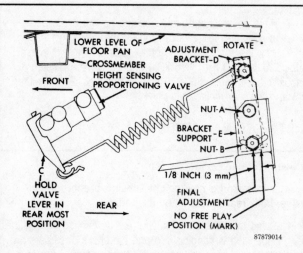

Fig. 13 Adjustment on the height sensing proportioning valve

4. Rotate the spring adjusting bracket **D** rearward until all the free play has been removed from the spring. (Be careful not to stretch the spring). While holding the adjusting bracket in position, release the valve lever. Tighten nut **B** temporarily, to hold the adjusting bracket in this position.

5. Mark the position of the adjusting bracket nut **B** on the bracket support **E**.

6. Loosen nut **B** and rotate the top of the adjusting bracket rearward so that nut **B** is 1/8 in. (3mm) forward of the no free play position. Tighten nut **B** to 21 ft. lbs. (28 Nm) while being careful not to move the bracket. Tighten nut **A** to 21 ft. lbs. (28 Nm).

Power Brake Booster

REMOVAL & INSTALLATION

1. Remove the master cylinder. It can be pulled far enough out of the way to allow booster removal without disconnecting the brake lines. Be careful not to damage the lines.
2. Disconnect the vacuum hose from the booster.
3. Under the instrument panel, pry the retainer clip center tang over the end of the brake pedal pin and pull the retainer clip from the pin. Discard the clip.
4. Remove the four booster attaching nuts.
5. Remove the booster from the vehicle.

To install:

6. Position the booster on the firewall.
7. Tighten the nuts to 20 ft. lbs. (27 Nm).
8. Carefully position the master cylinder on the booster.
9. Install the mounting nuts and tighten them to 18 ft. lbs. (26 Nm).
10. Connect the vacuum hose to the booster.
11. Coat the bearing surface of the pedal pin with chassis lube.
12. Connect the pushrod to the pedal pin and install a new clip.
13. Check the stoplight operation.

➡**Do not attempt to disassemble the power brake unit, since the booster is serviced as a complete assembly only.**

Bleeding the Brake System

▶ **See Figures 14, 15 and 16**

Any time a brake line has been disconnected the hydraulic system should be bled. The brakes should also be bled when the pedal travel becomes unusually long (soft pedal) or the car pulls to one side during braking. The proper bleeding sequence is: right rear wheel, left rear wheel, right front caliper, and left front caliper. You'll need a helper to pump the brake pedal while you open the bleeder valves.

➡**If the system has been drained, first refill it with fresh brake fluid. Following the above sequence, open each bleeder valve by ½ to ¾ of a turn and pump the brake pedal until fluid runs out of the valve. Proceed with the bleeding as outlined below.**

1. Remove the bleeder valve dust cover and install a rubber bleeder hose.
2. Insert the other end of the hose into a container about ⅓ full of brake fluid.
3. Have an assistant pump the brake pedal several times until the pedal pressure increases.
4. Hold the pedal under pressure and then start to open the bleeder valve about ½ to ¾ of a turn. At this point, have your assistant depress the pedal all the way and then quickly

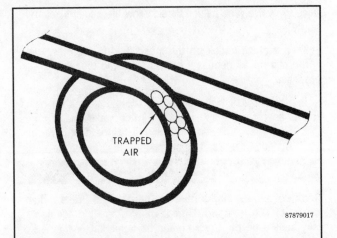

Fig. 14 ALWAYS thoroughly bleed the brake system after it has been opened; trapped air can cause a loss of braking ability

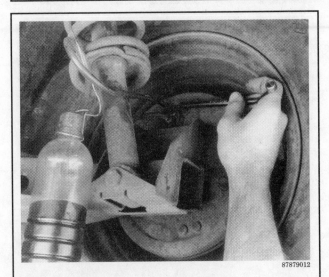

Fig. 15 Bleeding the brakes on the rear drum

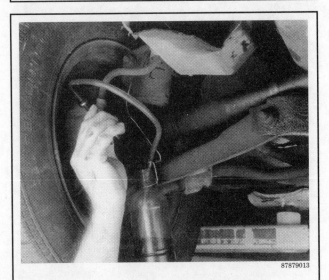

Fig. 16 Bleeding the brakes on the front caliper

close the valve. The helper should allow the pedal to return slowly.

➡ **Keep a close check on the brake fluid in the reservoir and top it up as necessary throughout the bleeding process.**

5. Keep repeating this procedure until no more air bubbles can be seen coming from the hose in the brake fluid.
6. Remove the bleeder hose and install the dust cover.
7. Continue the bleeding at each wheel in sequence.

✳✳WARNING

Don't splash any brake fluid on the paint as brake fluid will quickly soften and damage paint. Any fluid accidentally spilled on the body should be immediately flushed off with water.

Brake Hoses

It is important to use quality brake hose intended specifically for the application. Hose of less than the best quality, or hose not made to the specified length will tend to fatigue and may therefore create premature leakage and, consequently, a potential for brake failure. Note also that brake hose differs from one side of the car to the other and should therefore be ordered specifying the side on which it will be installed.

Make sure hose end mating surfaces are clean and free of nicks and burrs, which would prevent effective sealing. Use new copper seals on banjo fittings.

REMOVAL & INSTALLATION

▶ See Figures 17, 18 and 19

Front Brake Hose

1. Place a drain pan under the hose connections. First, disconnect the hose where it connects to the body bracket and steel tube.
2. Unbolt the hose bracket from the strut assembly.
3. Remove the bolt to disconnect the banjo connection at the caliper.
To install:
4. Position the new hose, noting that the body bracket and the body end of the hose are keyed to prevent installation of the hose in the wrong direction. First attach the hose to the banjo connector on the caliper.
5. Bolt the hose bracket located in the center of the hose to the strut, allowing the bracket to position the hose so it will not be twisted.
6. Attach the hose to the body bracket and steel brake tube.
7. Tighten the banjo fitting on the caliper to 19-29 ft. lbs. (26-39 Nm), the front hose to intermediate bracket to 75-115 inch lbs. (8-13 Nm), and the hose to brake tube to 115-170 inch lbs. (13-19 Nm).

Fig. 18 Remove the bolt to the banjo connection at the caliper

8. Bleed the system thoroughly.

Rear Brake Hose (Trailing Arm-to-Floor Pan)

1. Place a drain pan under the hose connections. Disconnect the double nut (using a primary wrench and a backup wrench) at the tube mounted on the floor pan. Then, disconnect the hose at the retaining clip.
2. Disconnect the hose at the trailing arm tube.
To install:
3. Install the new tube to the trailing arm connection first and tighten to 115-170 inch lbs. (13-19 Nm).
4. Then, making sure it is not twisted, connect it to the tube on the floor pan. Again, tighten the connection to 115-170 inch lbs. (13-19 Nm).
5. Bleed the system thoroughly.

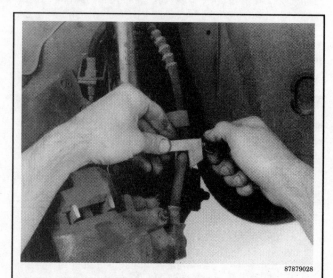

Fig. 17 Disconnect the hose bracket from the strut

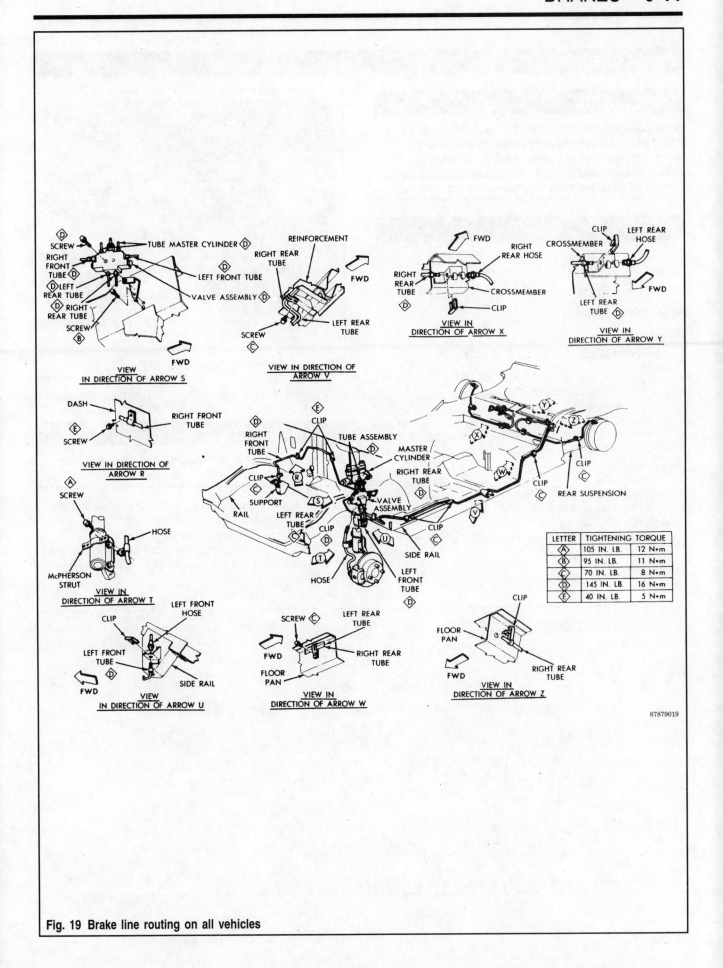

Fig. 19 Brake line routing on all vehicles

87879019

FRONT DISC BRAKES

⁕⁕CAUTION

Brake pads may contain asbestos, which has been determined to be a cancer causing agent. Never clean the brake surfaces with compressed air! Avoid inhaling any dust from any brake surface! When cleaning brake surfaces, use a commercially available brake cleaning fluid.

Brake Pads

REMOVAL & INSTALLATION

Kelsey Hayes Caliper

DOUBLE PIN

▶ See Figures 20, 21, 22, 23, 24, 25 and 26

1. Loosen the lug nuts on the front wheels.
2. Raise and support the vehicle.
3. Remove the wheels.
4. Take out the caliper guide pins.
5. Remove the caliper by slowly sliding the caliper off the brake disc. Hang the caliper by a piece of stiff wire. Do not allow it to hang by the brake line.
6. Remove the outboard brake pad from the adaptor.
7. Remove the disc from the studs.
8. Slide the inboard pad out of the adaptor.

To install:

9. Place the new pads in the adaptor.

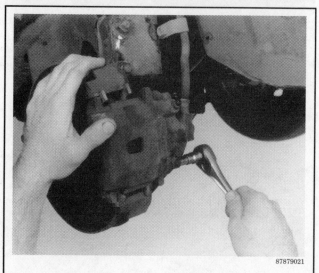

Fig. 21 Remove the caliper guide pins

10. Loosen the rear cap of the master cylinder reservoir and slowly push the caliper pistons back into the housing.

⁕⁕WARNING

Be sure the reservoir does not overflow, especially onto painted surfaces.

11. Hold the outboard lining in position and carefully slide the caliper into position on the adaptor.
12. Install the guide pins (lightly lubricated with silicone grease) and anti-rattle springs. The anti-rattle spring clips are installed with the closed loop toward the center of the car.
13. Bleed the brakes.
14. Install the wheels.

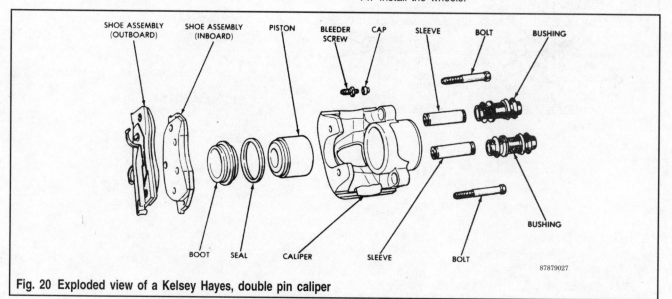

Fig. 20 Exploded view of a Kelsey Hayes, double pin caliper

Fig. 22 Remove the caliper . . .

Fig. 23 . . . then hang the caliper by a hook or piece of wire

Fig. 24 Remove the outboard brake pad from the adapter

Fig. 25 Remove the disc from the studs

Fig. 26 Next, slide the inboard pad from the caliper

15. Pump the pedal several times to remove clearance between pads and rotors.

➡ The pedal must give resistance at the normal position before attempting to drive the car. Drive the car at moderate speeds in an isolated area in order to apply the brakes several times to test the system and seat the new linings.

SINGLE PIN

1. Raise and support the front end on jackstands.
2. Remove the front wheels.
3. Remove the caliper guide pin by unscrewing it until it is free from the threads, then pull it out of the caliper adapter.
4. Using a small prybar, gently wedge the caliper away from the rotor, breaking the adhesive seals.
5. Slowly slide the caliper away from the rotor and off the caliper adapter. Support the caliper securely by hanging it from the body with wire (this is necessary to keep its weight from damaging the brake hose).
6. Slide the outboard pad off the caliper adapter. Then remove the disc by simply sliding it off the wheel studs.

7. Remove the inboard pad by sliding it off the caliper adapter.

8. If the caliper is to be removed, disconnect and cap the brake line. Then, remove it from the hanger and remove it.

To install:

9. Lubricate both bushing channels with silicone grease.

10. Remove the protective paper backing from the anti-squeal surfaces on both pads. Install the inboard pad on the adapter. Be careful to keep grease from the bushing channels from getting onto the pad as you do this.

11. Install the rotor onto the wheel studs of the steering knuckle. Install the outboard pad in the caliper and carefully slide it into place over the rotor.

12. If necessary, reconnect the brake line or remove the caliper from the hanger. Lower the caliper into position over the rotor and pads. Install the guide pin and tighten it to 35 ft. lbs. (47 Nm).

✳✳WARNING

It is easy to crossthread the guide pin. Start it carefully, turning it gently and allowing it to find its own angle.

13. Install the wheels and tighten the lugs to half the specified torque in a crisscross pattern. Then, tighten the lugs to full torque 95 ft. lbs. (129 Nm). If the brake line was disconnected, bleed the system thoroughly as described above. Pump the brake pedal several times to ensure that the brake pads seat against the rotor.

➡**The pedal must give resistance at the normal position before attempting to drive the car. Drive the car at moderate speeds in an isolated area in order to apply the brakes several times to test the system and seat the new linings.**

ATE Caliper

▶ **See Figures 27, 28 and 29**

1. Raise and safely support front the car.
2. Remove the front wheels.
3. Remove the hold-down spring from the caliper by pushing in at the middle of the spring and pushing it outwards.

4. Loosen, but do not remove the caliper guide pins until the caliper is free from the mount. removal of the guide pins is necessary only if the bushings or sleeves require replacement.

5. Lift the caliper out and away from the disc rotor. The inboard pad will remain in the caliper.

6. Support the caliper so that the strain is on the hose. Remove the inboard pad from the caliper. Lift the outboard pad from the adapter.

To install:

7. Push the piston back into the caliper bore. Install the inboard pad with the clamp locating it in the caliper piston.

8. Install the outboard pad in the adapter. Position the caliper over the rotor and secure with guide pins. Carefully tighten the guide pins to 18-22 ft. lbs. (24-30 Nm). Install the hold-down spring. Mount the front wheels and lower the vehicle.

9. Pump the brake pedal several times until a firm pedal is obtained. Check the master cylinder level and road test the vehicle.

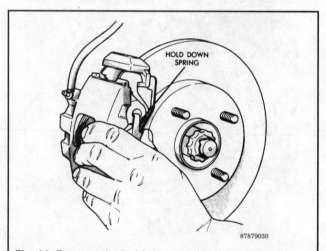

Fig. 28 Remove the hold-down spring from the caliper by pushing in at the middle of the spring and pushing it outwards

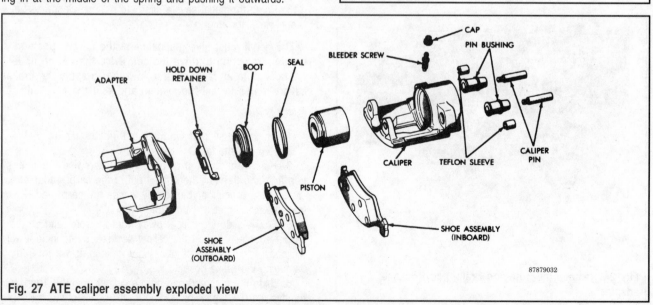

Fig. 27 ATE caliper assembly exploded view

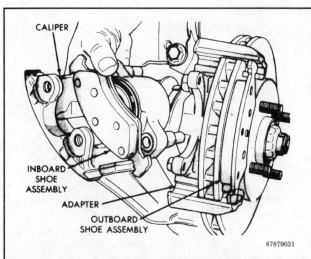

Fig. 29 Lift the caliper out and away from the disc rotor. The inboard pad will remain in the caliper.

INSPECTION

▶ See Figure 30

Disc pads (lining and shoe assemblies) should be replaced in axle sets (both wheels) when the thickness of the shoe and lining is less than $5/16$ in. (8mm).

➡️State inspection specifications take precedence over these general recommendations.

Note that disc pads in floating caliper type brakes may wear at an angle, and measurement should be made at the narrow end of the taper. Tapered linings should be replaced if the taper exceeds $1/8$ in. (3mm) from end-to-end (the difference between the thickest and thinnest points).

Always replace both sets on each wheel whenever one pad needs replacing.

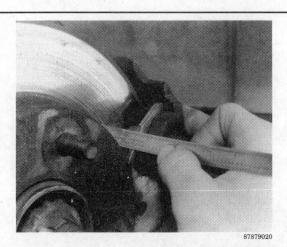

Fig. 30 Although an initial measurement may be taken with the pads installed, proper inspection requires removal of the pads to check for high spots or taper

Brake Caliper

REMOVAL & INSTALLATION

▶ See Figures 31 and 32

1. Raise and support the car.
2. Remove the wheels.
3. Take off the caliper guide pins and anti-rattle springs.
4. Remove the caliper by slowly sliding it off the adaptor.

➡️If the old pads are being reused, mark them so they can be installed in their original position.

5. If the caliper is being removed for overhaul, disconnect and plug the brake line.
   To install:
6. Attach the brake line if removed.

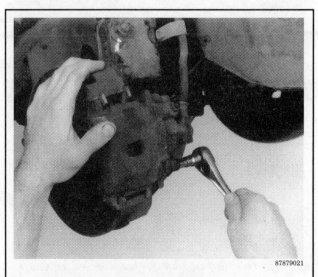

Fig. 31 Remove the caliper guide pins

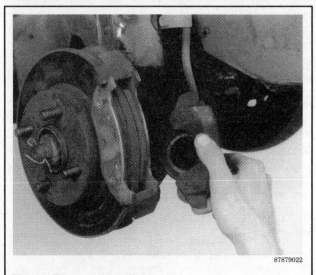

Fig. 32 Remove the caliper . . .

7. Loosen the rear master cylinder reservoir cap and slowly push the caliper pistons back into the housing.

❊❊WARNING

Be sure the reservoir does not overflow, especially onto painted surfaces.

8. Hold the outboard pad in position and slide the caliper onto the adaptor.
9. Install the guide pins and anti-rattle springs.
10. Bleed the brakes.
11. Install the wheels and lug nuts.
12. Lower the vehicle, then tighten the lug nuts.

OVERHAUL

1. Remove the caliper assembly from the car without disconnecting the hydraulic line.
2. Support the caliper assembly on the upper control arm and surround it with shop towels to absorb any brake fluid. Slowly depress the brake pedal until the piston is pushed out of its bore.

❊❊CAUTION

Do not use compressed air to force the piston from its bore; injury could result.

3. Disconnect the brake line from the caliper and plug it to prevent fluid loss.
4. Mount the caliper in a soft-jawed vise and clamp lightly. Do not tighten the vise too much or the caliper will become distorted.
5. Work the dust boot out with your fingers.
6. Use a small pointed wooden or plastic stick to work the piston seal out of the groove in the bore. Discard the seal.

❊❊WARNING

Using a screwdriver or other metal tool could scratch the piston bore.

7. Using the same wooden or plastic stick, press the bushings out of the housing.
8. Clean all parts in denatured alcohol or brake fluid. Blow out all bores and passages with compressed air.
9. Inspect the piston and bore for scoring or pitting. Replace the piston if necessary. Bores with light scratches or corrosion may be cleaned with crocus cloth. Bores with deep scratches may be honed if you do not increase the bore diameter more than 0.002 in. (0.05mm). Replace the housing if the bore must be enlarged beyond this.

➡**Black stains are caused by piston seals and are harmless.**

10. If the bore had to be honed, clean its grooves with a stiff, non-metallic rotary brush. Clean the bore twice by flushing it out with brake fluid and drying it with a soft, lint-free cloth.

To assemble:

11. Clamp the caliper in a soft-jawed vise; do not overtighten.
12. Dip a new piston seal in brake fluid or the lubricant supplied with the rebuilding kit. Position the new seal in one area of its groove and gently work it into place with clean fingers, so that it is correctly seated. Do not use an old seal.
13. Coat a new boot with brake fluid or lubricant (as above), leaving a generous amount inside.
14. Insert the boot in the caliper and work it into the groove, using your fingers only. The boot will snap into place once it is correctly positioned. Run your forefinger around the inside of the boot to make sure that it is correctly seated.
15. Install the bleed screw in its hole and plug the fluid inlet on the caliper.
16. Coat the piston with brake fluid or lubricant. Spread the boot with your fingers and work the piston into the boot.
17. Depress the piston, this will force the boot into its groove on the piston. Remove the plug and bottom the piston in the bore.
18. Compress the flanges of new guide pin bushings and work them into place by pressing in on the bushings with your fingertips, until they are seated. Make sure that the flanges cover the housing evenly on all sides.
19. Install the caliper on the car as previously outlined.

Brake Disc (Rotor)

REMOVAL & INSTALLATION

▶ **See Figures 33 and 34**

1. Raise and support the car.
2. Take off the wheels.
3. Remove the caliper, then suspend it from a wire.
4. Remove the brake disc from the drive flange studs.

To install:

5. Install the brake disc on the drive flange studs.
6. Install the caliper.
7. Seat the wheels, install the lug nuts.

87879022

Fig. 33 Remove the caliper . . .

Fig. 34 Remove the disc from the studs

8. Lower the vehicle, then tighten the lug nuts.

→The pedal must give resistance at the normal position before attempting to drive the car. Drive the car at moderate speeds in an isolated area in order to apply the brakes several times to test the system and seat the new linings.

REAR DRUM BRAKES

✳✳CAUTION

Brake shoes may contain asbestos, which has been determined to be a cancer causing agent. Never clean the brake surfaces with compressed air! Avoid inhaling any dust from any brake surface! When cleaning brake surfaces, use a commercially available brake cleaning fluid.

Brake Drums

REMOVAL & INSTALLATION

▶ See Figures 35, 36, 37, 38, 39, 40, 41, 42 and 43

1. Raise the car and support it safely.
2. Remove the plug from the brake shoe adjusting hole.
3. Using a brake spoon, release the brake shoes by moving the star wheel adjuster up (left side) or down (right side).
4. Remove the grease cap.
5. Remove the cotter pin. Never reuse the old cotter pin.
6. Remove the nut lock.
7. Loosen the nut, then remove the nut and washer.
8. Remove the locknut and washer.
9. Remove the brake drum and bearings.
To install:
10. Reposition the drum and install the bearings.
11. Adjust the wheel bearings.
12. Install the cotter pin, locknut and washer.
13. Install the grease cap.
14. Adjust the brakes.

INSPECTION

Light scoring is acceptable. Heavy scoring or warping will necessitate refinishing or replacement of the disc. The brake disc must be replaced if cracks or burned marks are evident.

Check the thickness of the disc. Measure the thickness at 12 equally spaced points 1 in. (25mm) from the edge of the disc. If thickness varies more than 0.001 in. (0.0125mm) the disc should be refinished, provided equal amounts are out from each side and the thickness does not fall below 0.4 in. (11mm).

Check the run-out of the disc. Total run-out of the disc installed on the car should not exceed 0.001 in. (0.0125mm). The disc can be resurfaced to correct minor variations as long as equal amounts are cut from each side and the thickness is at least 0.4 in. (11mm) after resurfacing.

Check the run-out of the hub (disc removed). It should not be more than 0.002 in. (0.05mm). If so, the hub should be replaced.

Fig. 35 Use the access slot at the rear of the drum to loosen the brake adjuster

15. Replug the adjusting hole.
16. Lower the car.

INSPECTION

▶ See Figures 44, 45, 46 and 47

Measure the drum run-out and diameter. If not according to specifications the drum should be replaced. The variation in diameter should not exceed 0.002 in. (0.06mm) in 30° or 0.003 in. (0.09mm) in 360°. All drums show markings of maximum diameter.

Fig. 36 Loosen and remove the grease cap.

Fig. 37 With pliers, remove the cotter pin, then throw it away. Never reuse a cotter pin

Fig. 38 With the cotter pin withdrawn, remove the castellated nut lock

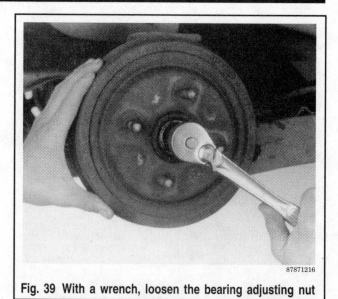

Fig. 39 With a wrench, loosen the bearing adjusting nut

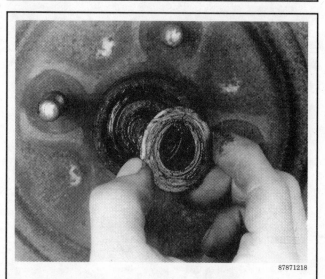

Fig. 40 With the nut removed you can access the washer

Fig. 41 Take the washer off the axle stub

Fig. 42 The bearing should come right out

Fig. 43 Remove the drum from the spindle

Once the drum is off, clean the shoes and springs with a stiff brush to remove the accumulated brake dust.

❄❄**CAUTION**

Avoid prolonged exposure to brake dust. The dust may contain asbestos which has been determined to cause cancer.

Grease on the shoes can be removed with alcohol or fine sandpaper.

After cleaning, examine the brake shoes for glazed, oily, loose, cracked or improperly worn linings. Light glazing is common and can be removed with fine sandpaper. Linings that are worn improperly or below 1/16 in. (2mm) above rivet heads or brake shoe should be replaced. The NHTSA advises states with inspection programs to fail vehicles with brake linings less than 1/32 in. (1mm). A good "eyeball" test is to replace the linings when the thickness is the same as or less than the thickness of the metal backing plate (shoe).

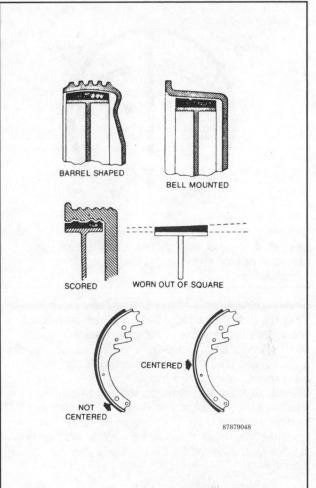

Fig. 44 Improperly worn linings are cause for concern only if braking is unstable and noise is objectionable. Compare the lining and drum wear pattern, the drum being more important, since the drum shapes the wear of the shoe

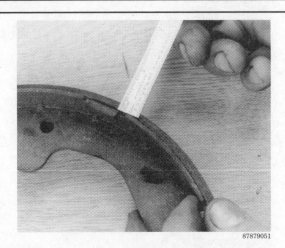

Fig. 45 Linings that are worn improperly or below 1/16 in. (2mm) above rivet heads or brake shoe should be replaced

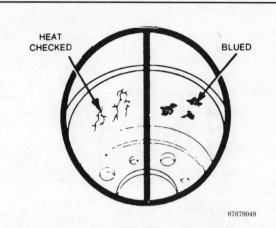

Fig. 46 A blued or severely heat cracked drum and blued or heavily glazed linings are the result of overheating

Wheel cylinders are a vital part of the brake system and should be inspected carefully. Gently pull back the rubber boots; if any fluid is visible, it's time to replace or rebuild the wheel cylinders. Boots that are distorted, cracked or otherwise damaged, also point to the need for service. Check the flexible brake lines for cracks, chafing or wear.

Check the brake shoe retracting and hold-down springs; they should not be worn or distorted. Be sure that the adjuster mechanism moves freely. The points on the backing plate where the shoes slide should be shiny and free of rust. Rust in these areas suggests that the brake shoes are not moving properly.

Brake Shoes

REMOVAL & INSTALLATION

▶ See Figures 48, 49, 50, 51, 52, 53, 54, 55, 56, 57 and 58

➡ If you are not thoroughly familiar with the procedures involved in brake replacement, disassemble and assemble one side at a time, leaving the other wheel intact, as a reference. Even experienced mechanics will usually leave one side intact, because you never know what small part's position you may forget.

1. Remove the brake drum. See the procedure earlier in this section.
2. Clean the area with a brake cleaning fluid.
3. Unhook the parking brake cable from the secondary (trailing) shoe.

Fig. 48 ALWAYS disassemble and assemble one side at a time, leaving the other wheel intact, as a reference

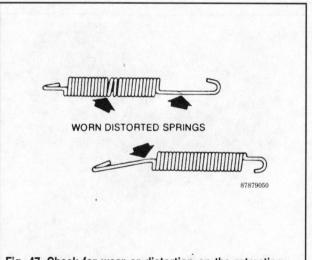

Fig. 47 Check for wear or distortion on the retracting and hold-down springs

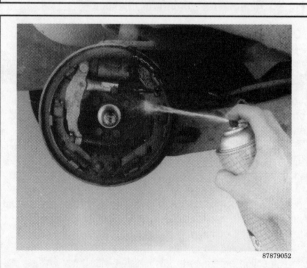

Fig. 49 Clean the area well with an evaporative spray brake cleaner

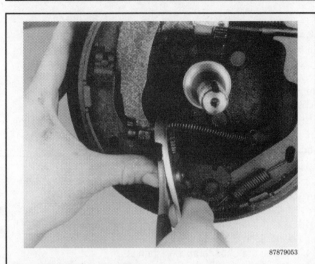

Fig. 50 Unhook the parking brake cable from the secondary (trailing) shoe

Fig. 52 Carefully remove the shoe-to-anchor springs (retracting springs)

4. Remove the shoe hold-down springs; compress them slightly and slide them off of the hold-down pins.

5. Remove the shoe-to-anchor springs (retracting springs). They can be gripped and unhooked with a pair of pliers.

6. Remove the adjuster screw assembly by spreading the shoes apart. The adjuster nut must be fully backed off.

7. Raise the primary (leading) shoe to release spring tension. Remove the shoe and disengage the spring end from the backing plate.

8. Raise the parking brake lever. Pull the secondary (trailing) shoe away from the backing plate so pull-back spring tension is released.

9. Remove the secondary (trailing) shoe and disengage the spring end from the backing plate.

To install:

10. Inspect the brakes (see procedures under Brake Drum Inspection).

11. Lubricate the six shoe contact areas on the brake backing plate and the web end of the brake shoe which contacts the anchor plate. Use a multi-purpose lubricant or a high temperature brake grease made for the purpose.

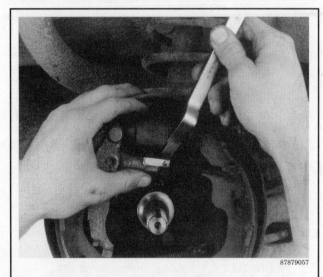

Fig. 53 Back off the adjuster nut fully

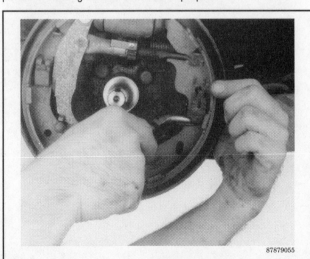

Fig. 51 Remove the shoe hold-down springs; compress them slightly and slide them off of the hold-down pins

Fig. 54 Remove the adjuster screw assembly by spreading the shoes apart

Fig. 55 Remove the primary (leading) from the backing plate

Fig. 56 Remove the secondary (trailing) shoe and disengage the spring end from the backing plate

Fig. 57 Lubricate the backing plate shoe contact areas using a multi-purpose lubricant or a high temperature brake grease made for that purpose

12. Chrysler recommends that the rear wheel bearings be cleaned and repacked whenever the brakes are renewed. Be sure to install a new bearing seal.

13. With the leading shoe return spring in position on the shoe, install the shoe at the same time as you engage the return spring in the end support.

14. Position the end of the shoe under the anchor.

15. With the trailing shoe return spring in position, install the shoe at the same time as you engage the spring in the support (backing plate).

16. Position the end of the shoe under the anchor.

17. Spread the shoes and install the adjuster screw assembly making sure that the forked end that enters the shoe is curved down.

18. Insert the shoe hold-down spring pins and install the hold-down springs.

19. Install the shoe-to-anchor springs.

20. Install the parking brake cable onto the parking brake lever.

21. Install the brake drum and tighten the nut to 240-300 inch lbs. (27-33 Nm) while rotating the wheel.

22. Back off the nut enough to release the bearing preload and position the locknut with one pair of slots aligned with the cotter pin hole.

23. Install the cotter pin. The end-play should be 0.003-0.001 in. (0.025-0.080mm).

24. Install the grease cap.

Wheel Cylinders

REMOVAL & INSTALLATION

▶ **See Figures 59, 60 and 61**

1. Raise and support the car.

2. Remove the brake drums.

3. Visually inspect the wheel cylinder boots for signs of excessive leakage. A slight amount of leakage is normal, but excessive leakage will necessitate boot replacement. Replace any boots that are torn or broken.

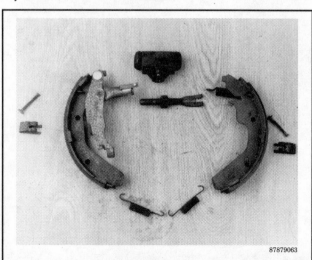

Fig. 58 When all of the brake parts have been removed, inspect them for wear and damage prior to replacement

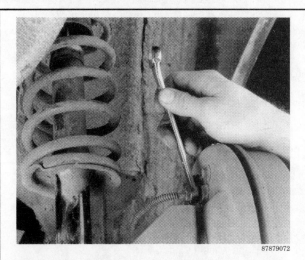

Fig. 59 Using a flare wrench, loosen the brake line fitting at the rear of the wheel cylinder

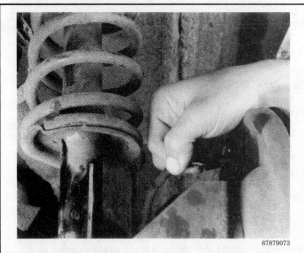

Fig. 60 Once the line is loosened, unthread it to free it from the cylinder

Fig. 61 Loosen and remove the wheel cylinder retaining bolt(s)

4. In case of a leak, also remove the brake shoes and check for contamination.

5. Disconnect and plug the brake line.

6. Unbolt and remove the wheel cylinder.

To install:

7. Reposition the wheel cylinder and bolt into place.

8. Reconnect the brake line.

9. Install the brake shoes and brake drum.

10. Bleed the brakes.

OVERHAUL

▸ **See Figures 62, 63, 64, 65 and 66**

1. Pry the boots away from the cylinder and remove the boots and piston as an assembly.

2. Disengage the boot from the piston.

3. Slide the piston into the cylinder bore and press inward to remove the other boot and piston. Also remove the spring with the cup expanders.

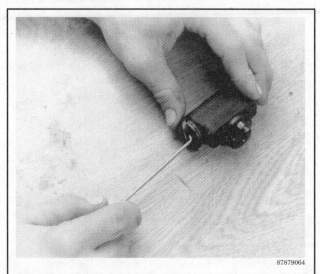

Fig. 62 Pry the boots away from the cylinder

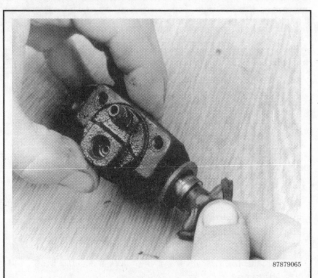

Fig. 63 Remove the piston and boot as an assembly

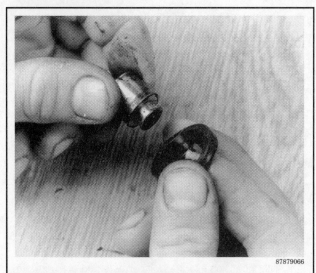

Fig. 64 Disengage the boot from the piston

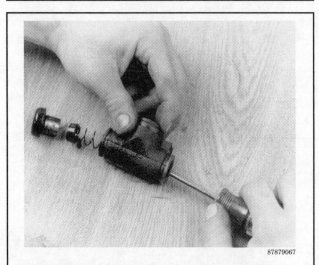

Fig. 65 Slide the piston into the cylinder bore and press inward to remove the other boot and piston

4. Wash all the parts (except rubber parts) in clean brake fluid and dry thoroughly. Do not use a rag; lint will adhere to the bore.

5. Inspect the cylinder bores. Light scoring can usually be cleaned up with crocus cloth. Black stains are caused by the piston cups and are no cause of concern. Bad scoring or pitting means that the wheel cylinder should be replaced.

6. Dip the pistons and new cups in clean brake fluid prior to assembly.

7. Coat the wheel cylinder bore with clean brake fluid.

8. Install the expansion spring with the cup expanders.

9. Install the cups in each end of the cylinder with the open ends facing each other.

10. Assemble new boots on the piston and slide them into the cylinder bore.

11. Press the boot over the wheel cylinder until seated.

12. Install the wheel cylinder.

Fig. 66 Wash all the parts (except rubber parts) in clean brake fluid and dry thoroughly. Do not use a rag; as lint will adhere to the bore

PARKING BRAKE

Front Brake Cable

REMOVAL & INSTALLATION

1. Raise and support the car.
2. Disconnect the brake cable from the connector.
3. Force the cable housing and attaching clip forward out of the body crossmember.
4. Fold back the left front edge of the floor covering and pry the rubber grommet out of the hole in the dash or from the floor pan.
5. Remove the cable-to-floor pan clip.
6. Engage the parking brake and work the cable out of the clevis linkage.

7. Force the upper end of the cable housing out of the pedal bracket.
8. Work the cable and housing assembly out of the floor pan.

To install:
9. Rework the cable and housing in the floor pan.
10. Install the cable to the pedal bracket.
11. Engage the parking brake and work the cable into the clevis linkage.
12. Install the cable-to-floor pan clip.
13. Install the rubber grommet in the hole in the dash or in the floor pan.
14. Connect the brake cable to the connector.
15. Adjust the parking and service brakes and test the operation of both.

Rear Brake Cable

REMOVAL & INSTALLATION

1. Raise and support the car.
2. Remove the rear wheels.
3. Disconnect the brake cable from the connector.
4. Remove the retaining clip from the rear cable bracket.
5. Take off the brake drum.
6. Remove the brake shoe return springs.
7. Take off the brake shoe retaining springs.
8. Remove the brake shoe strut and spring and disconnect the cable from the operating arm.
9. Compress the retainers on the end of the brake cable housing and remove the cable.
10. Installation is the reverse of removal. Adjust the service and parking brakes and test the operation of both.

ADJUSTMENT

▶ **See Figures 67, 68, 69, 70 and 71**

The cable operated parking brake is adjusted at the equalizer (connector) under the car.

1. Adjust the service brakes.
2. Release the parking brake lever and back off the parking brake cable until there is slack in the cable.
3. Clean and lubricate the adjuster threads.
4. Use a brake spoon to turn the starwheel adjuster until there is light shoe-to-drum contact. Back off the starwheel until the wheel rotates freely with no brake drag.
5. Tighten the parking brake adjustment until a slight drag is felt while rotating the wheels.
6. Loosen the cable adjusting nut until both rear wheels can be rotated freely, then back the cable adjuster nut off 2 full turns.
7. Apply the parking brake. The wheels should not turn. Relieve the parking brake. The rear wheels should rotate freely without dragging.

Fig. 67 Using a wire brush you can clean the adjuster threads on the parking cable

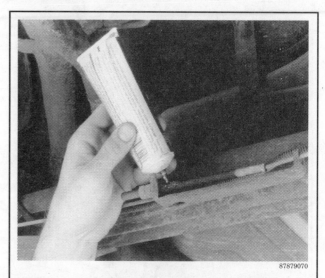

Fig. 68 Lubricate the threads to make adjustment easier

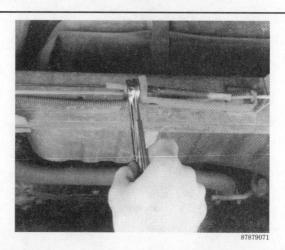

Fig. 69 Loosen the cable adjusting nut until both rear wheels can be rotated freely, then back the cable adjuster nut off 2 full turns

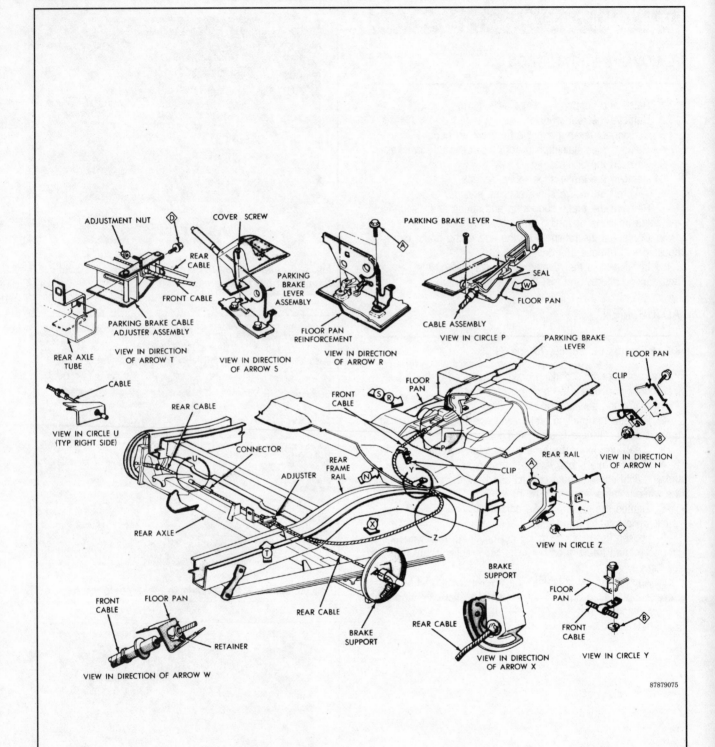

Fig. 70 Parking brake cable routing on the Rampage and Scamp models

87879075

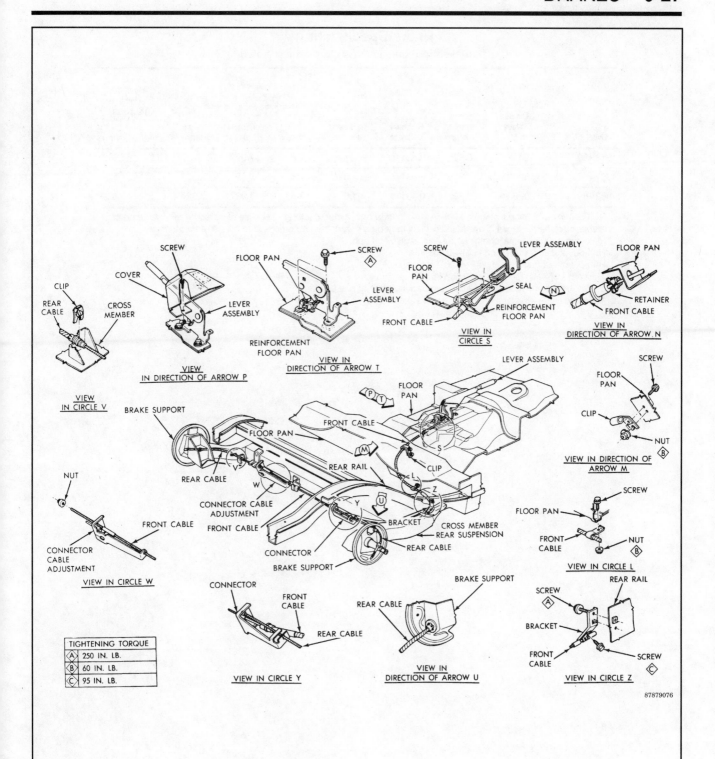

Fig. 71 Parking brake cable routing excluding the Rampage and Scamp models

87879076

Brake Specifications

All measurements given are (in.) unless noted

Model	Lug Nut Torque (ft./lb.)	Master Cylinder Bore	Brake Disc		Brake Drum			Minimum Lining Thickness	
			Minimum Thickness	Maximum Run-Out	Diameter	Max Machine O/S	Max Wear Limit	Front	Rear
1978–80	80–85	0.625	0.431 ②	①	7.87	7.927	7.927	③	⁵⁄₁₆
1981–82	80–85	0.875	0.431 ②	0.004	7.87	7.927	7.927	③	⁵⁄₁₆
1983–89	80–85 ④	0.827	0.431 ②	0.004	7.87	7.927	7.927	③	⁵⁄₁₆

NOTE: *Minimum lining thickness is as recommended by the manufacturer. Because of variations in state inspection regulations, the minimum allowable thickness may be different than recommended by the manufacturer.*

① Maximum 0.005 in. total combined run-out of disc and hub.
　Run-out of disc (installed on hub)—0.005 in.
　Run-out of hub (disc removed)—0.002 in.
② Thickness of new disc—0.490–0.505 in.
③ ⁵⁄₁₆ in.—minimum thickness of lining and backing plate at any point.
④ 1984 and later—95 ft. lbs.

87879080

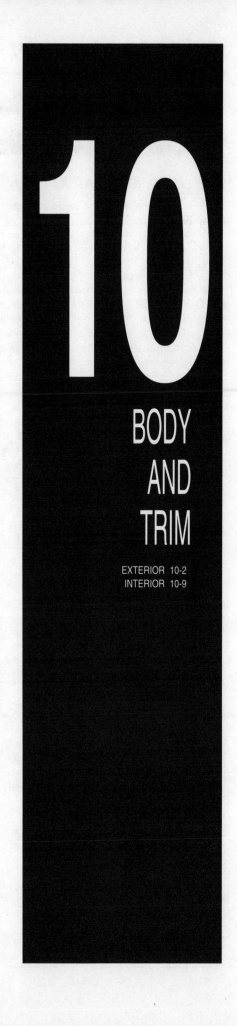

10

BODY AND TRIM

EXTERIOR

Doors

REMOVAL & INSTALLATION

▶ **See Figure 1**

1. Disconnect the door light wiring harness on models so equipped.

2. Remove the door opening check strap.

3. Support the door in the opened position. Use special tool C-4614 or C-4716 or equivalent, (depending on the size of the hinge pin) and remove the lower hinge pin. Insert special tool C-4741 or equivalent, in place of the pin.

4. Remove the upper hinge pin using the suitable special tool. Remove the lower alignment tool and remove the door.

5. Grind a chamfer on the hinge pins to make installation easier.

To install:

6. Install the door into the opening using alignment tools C-4741 or equivalent, in place of the hinge pins.

7. Use a small hammer and drive in the upper hinge pin from the bottom. Drive in the lower hinge pin from the top.

8. Install the door check strap, then reconnect the wiring harness on models so equipped.

ADJUSTMENT

▶ **See Figures 2 and 3**

The door hinges are welded to both the door panels and the door pillar. Fore and aft, up and down adjustments may be accomplished by bending the hinges using a special tool C-4736 or equivalent. Before bending the hinges, check for correct engagement of the door striker plate. Check hinge pin fit and condition and check for proper weatherstrip installation.

Bend the hinges as follows:

1. Examine the door fit to determine which direction is necessary to bend the hinge for correct alignment.

2. Place the adjusting tool C-4736 or equivalent, in position on the hinge to be corrected. The tool must be slipped completely over the hinge to prevent damage to the tool or the hinge.

3. Slowly apply pressure to bend the hinge. Check frequently until correct alignment is achieved.

The door latch should engage the striker squarely. The door should not rise up or down on the striker as it is closed. After the striker is adjusted the door should fit flush with the adjoining sheet metal. If necessary, adjust the striker as follows:

4. Mark the location of the striker for reference.

5. Loosen the striker attaching screws.

6. Move the striker to the desired location and tighten the mounting screws.

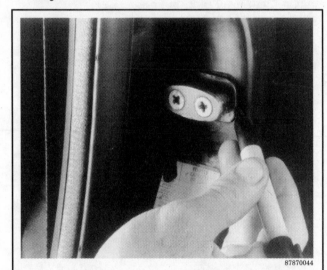

Fig. 2 Mark the location of the striker for reference

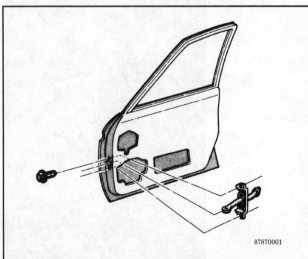

Fig. 1 The door opening check strap is usually secured by two bolts

Fig. 3 Use a screwdriver in good condition to prevent stripping the screw heads

7. Check alignment, readjust if necessary.

Door Latch

On late models, the outer latch can be replaced without removing the door trim panel.

The various links will hold the inner latch in position while the outer latch is removed. A thin punch can be used to align the inner latch while the outer latch is installed.

REMOVAL & INSTALLATION

◆ See Figure 4

1. Raise the door glass to the full up position.
2. Remove the door trim panel and plastic weathershield.
3. Remove the pushrod link, the remote control link, the outside handle link and the key cylinder link from the latch connectors.
4. Remove the latch attaching screws. Remove the outside and inside halves of the latch assembly.
5. Install in the reverse order.

ADJUSTMENT

◆ See Figure 5

➡Door panel removal may be necessary for access to provide full adjustment range.

1. Insert a ⁵/₃₂ in. Allen wrench through the access hole provided in the door face and loosen the Allen screw.
2. Move the Allen wrench and screw upwards in the slot to the position required. Tighten the Allen screw to 30 inch lbs.

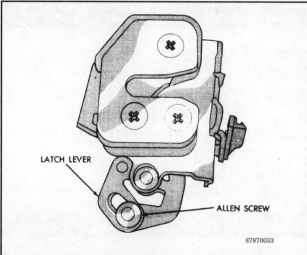

LATCH LEVER

ALLEN SCREW

87870033

Fig. 5 The Allen screw may be reached through the access hole provided in the door

3. Check the position of the outside door handle for flush appearance to the door panel. Check the operation of the latch. Readjust the latch as required.

Lock Cylinder

REMOVAL & INSTALLATION

◆ See Figure 6

1. Raise the window glass to the full up position.
2. Remove the door trim panel and plastic air shield.
3. Disconnect the remote link from the lock cylinder lever.
4. Remove the horseshoe retaining clip from the cylinder lock groove. Remove the retainer and the lock cylinder.
5. Install the lock cylinder in the reverse order of removal.

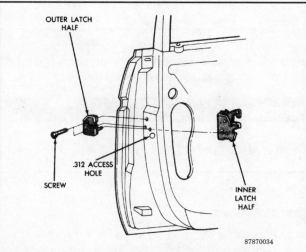

OUTER LATCH HALF

.312 ACCESS HOLE

SCREW

INNER LATCH HALF

87870034

Fig. 4 Exploded view of the inner and outer latch halves

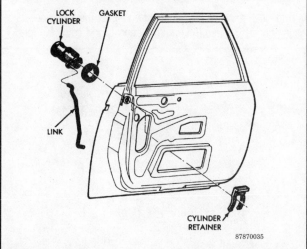

LOCK CYLINDER GASKET

LINK

CYLINDER RETAINER

87870035

Fig. 6 The lock cylinder is secured by a horseshoe-type retaining clip

Outside Door Handle

REMOVAL & INSTALLATION

▶ **See Figure 7**

1. Raise the door glass to the full up position.
2. Remove the door trim panel and plastic air shield.
3. Disconnect the handle link from the latch.
4. Remove the nuts that attach the handle to the door panel. Lift the handle and link from the door.
5. Install the door handle in the reverse order of removal.

Hood

REMOVAL & INSTALLATION

▶ **See Figures 8 and 9**

1. Mark the outline of the hinges on the hood.
2. Place a protective covering over the windshield area and both of the fenders.
3. Place a block of wood between the windshield and the hood in case of accidental rearward movement.
4. Remove the hinge bolts. With the aid of an assistant, remove the hood from the vehicle.

To install:

5. With the aid of an assistant, place the hood on the hinges and install the bolts loosely.
6. Align the scribed marks on the hood with the hinges, then tighten the bolts to 105 inch lbs. (12 Nm).
7. Remove the wood block and protective coverings.

ALIGNMENT

Prior to making any adjustments, inspect the clearance and alignment of the hood sides in relation to the cowl, fenders,

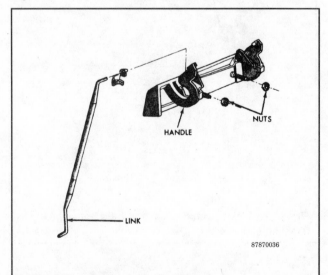

Fig. 7 The outside door handle is secured by two nuts

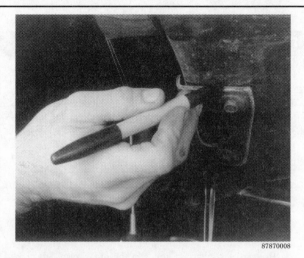

Fig. 8 Before loosening the bolts, mark the outline of the hinges on the hood

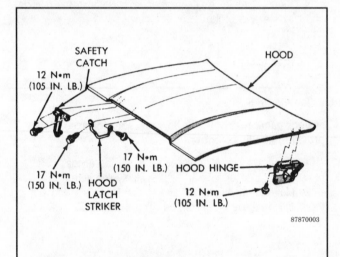

Fig. 9 Exploded view of the hood, latch and hinge assembly

and grille. The hood-to-cowl clearance adjustment should be made first. Elongated holes in the hinge permit the hood to be adjusted from side to side and fore and aft.

Hatchback

REMOVAL & INSTALLATION

▶ **See Figure 10**

Hatchback Assembly

1. Remove the hatchback in the full open position.
2. Mark the outline of the hinges on the hatchback.
3. Apply masking tape to the undersurface of the door and the rear edge of the roof to prevent damage during removal.
4. Remove the lift prop fasteners, then remove the lift props.

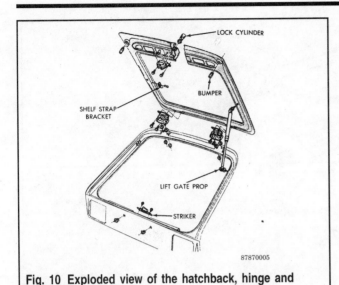

Fig. 10 Exploded view of the hatchback, hinge and latch assembly

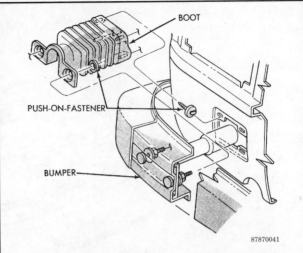

Fig. 11 It is necessary to remove the boot to access the bumper mounting bolts

5. With an assistant, take off the hinge-to-hatchback fasteners, then remove the hatchback.

6. Reverse the procedure to install. Use a rope type sealer to seal the hinges to the gate.

Hatchback Props

1. Support the hatchback on the side that is to be removed.

2. Remove the lift prop fasteners from the hatchback and body, then remove the prop.

To install:

3. Attach and tighten the lift prop to the body and hatchback lid.

4. Remove the support, check that it is secure, then lower the hatchback.

Bumpers

REMOVAL & INSTALLATION

Front

METAL BUMPERS

▶ See Figures 11 and 12

1. Remove the push-on fasteners securing the boot to the bumper fasteners.

2. Remove the nuts securing the bumper to the energy absorber unit.

3. Lower the bumper to the floor.

4. Installation is the reverse of removal. Tighten the mounting nuts to 20 ft. lbs. (28 Nm).

PLASTIC FACIA

▶ See Figure 13

1. Remove the two screws from the center of the upper fascia to the radiator yoke bracket.

2. Remove the four screws from the headlamp support braces.

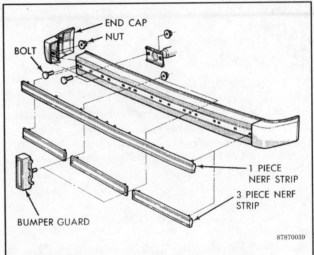

Fig. 12 Exploded view of the bumper mounting assembly

3. Disconnect the headlamp wire connectors.

4. Raise and support the front of the vehicle, then remove the 14 plastic rivets from the splash shields. Remove the shields.

5. Remove the 8 plastic rivets from the underside of the fascia to the fender mounting studs.

6. Grasp the fascia assembly at the upper louver and remove the fascia assembly.

➡️**It is recommended that the fascia be stored front side up to prevent permanent distortion.**

7. Installation is the reverse of removal.

Rear

RAMPAGE/SCAMP

1. Remove the push on fasteners securing the boot to the bumper fasteners.

2. Remove the nuts securing the bumper to the energy absorber unit.

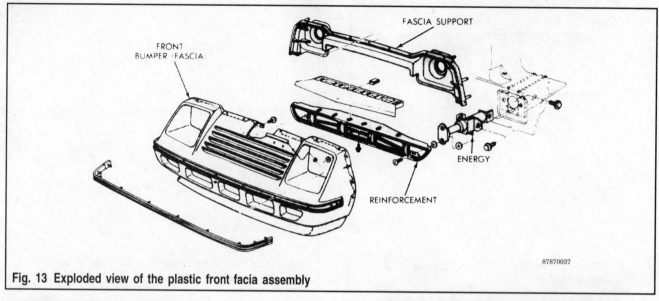

Fig. 13 Exploded view of the plastic front facia assembly

3. Lower the bumper to the floor.

4. Installation is the reverse of removal. Tighten the mounting nuts to 20 ft. lbs. (28 Nm).

TWO DOOR MODELS

1. Place a support under the bumper.
2. Remove the 10 fascia retainer nuts.
3. Remove the 6 energy absorber to bumper retaining nuts.
4. Lower the bumper to the floor.
5. Installation is the reverse of removal. Tighten the bumper mounting nuts to 20 ft. lbs. (28 Nm). Tighten the fascia to fender nuts to 5 ft. lbs. (7 Nm).

FOUR DOOR MODELS

1. Remove the push on fasteners securing the boot to the bumper fasteners.
2. Remove the nuts securing the bumper to the energy absorber unit.
3. Lower the bumper to the floor.
4. Installation is the reverse of removal. Tighten the mounting nuts to 20 ft. lbs. (28 Nm).

Grille

REMOVAL & INSTALLATION

▶ See Figures 14 and 15

The grille is mounted to the radiator yoke with plastic rivet type fasteners or screws. To remove the rivets, grasp the center portion with pliers and pull upward. The rivet may then be removed. After the fasteners are removed, the grille may removed from the vehicle. Installation is the reverse of removal.

Fig. 14 To remove the rivet, grasp the center portion of the rivet and pull upward. The rivet may then be removed

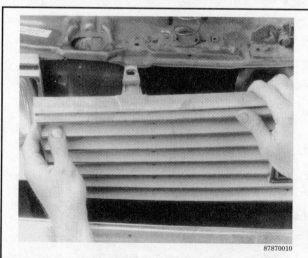

Fig. 15 After the fasteners are removed, pull the grille from the body of the vehicle

Outside Rear View Mirror

REMOVAL & INSTALLATION

▶ **See Figures 16 and 17**

1. Lower the glass to the full down position.
2. Remove the arm rest.
3. Remove the door trim panel and plastic air shield.
4. On remote control mirrors, remove the cable retaining nut. Remove the remote control cable from the retaining clips. Remove the plastic clip on the cable from the door.
5. Remove the mirror retaining nuts and remove the mirror from the outer door panel.
6. Installation is the reverse of removal.

Antenna

REMOVAL & INSTALLATION

▶ **See Figures 18 and 19**

1. Remove the radio from the vehicle.
2. Unplug the antenna lead from the radio.
3. Unscrew the antenna mast from the body of the vehicle.
4. Remove the cap nut, tool C-4816 or an equivalent may be used.
5. Remove the antenna adapter and gasket.
6. Unfasten the pins from the rear of the plastic fender well, then bend the shield out of the way.
7. From under the fender, remove the antenna lead and body assembly.
   To install:
8. Install the antenna body and cable from underneath the fender.

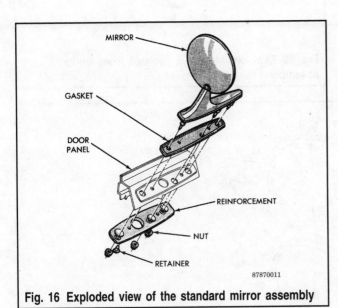

Fig. 16 Exploded view of the standard mirror assembly

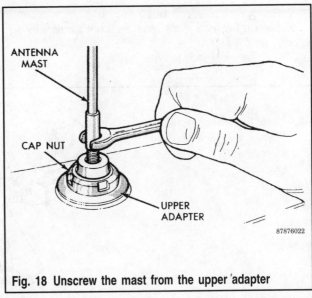

Fig. 18 Unscrew the mast from the upper adapter

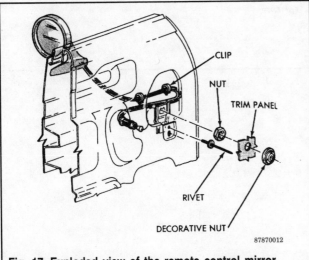

Fig. 17 Exploded view of the remote control mirror assembly

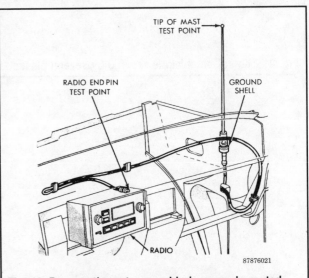

Fig. 19 Be sure the antenna cable is properly routed

9. Install the gasket, adapter and cap nut. Tighten the cap nut to 125 inch lbs. (14 Nm). You may need tool C-4816 or an equivalent.

10. Attach antenna mast to the body until the sleeve bottoms on thew antenna body.

11. Route the cable to the radio.

12. Install the radio.

Fenders

REMOVAL & INSTALLATION

▶ **See Figures 20 and 21**

1. Disconnect the park/turn signal wiring.

2. Detach the headlamp working.

3. Tape the forward edge of the door to avoid paint damage during fender removal.

4. Remove the plastic fasteners securing the splash shield to the fender.

5. Remove the headlamp bezel.

6. Support the hood in the open position if the right fender is being removed.

7. Remove the fender fasteners and lift the fender from the vehicle.

8. Reverse the procedure to install.

9. Align the fender to allow equal space between the cowl, door front edge and the door top edge.

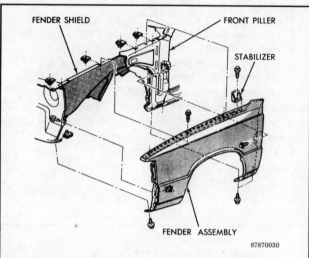

Fig. 20 Exploded view of a common front fender assembly

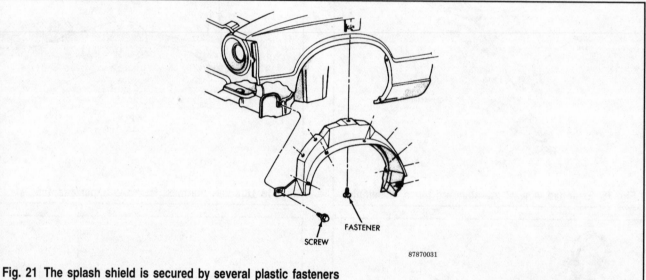

Fig. 21 The splash shield is secured by several plastic fasteners

INTERIOR

Door Panels

REMOVAL & INSTALLATION

▶ See Figures 22, 23, 24, 25 and 26

1. Remove the door lock knob.
2. Remove the inside door handle and bezel trim.
3. Remove the arm rest and window handle crank.
4. If equipped with a remote door mirror, remove the retaining trim nut.
5. Use a wide prying device and unclip the panel retainers from the door. Remove the panel, and plastic shield. If necessary, remove the screws securing the upper panel, then remove the panel.

Fig. 24 If equipped with a remote control mirror, remove the retaining nut

6. After the panel is removed there is a plastic shield covering all of the interior mechanisms. Remove this only if you need to access any inner parts.
7. Install the weather shield and door panel in the reverse order of removal.

Front Door Glass and Regulator

REMOVAL & INSTALLATION

▶ See Figure 27

1. To remove the window glass:
   a. Remove the door panel and weathershield.
   b. Remove the glass stops and stabilizers.
   c. Lower the window until the lift channel fasteners are visible. Remove the fasteners and disengage the glass from

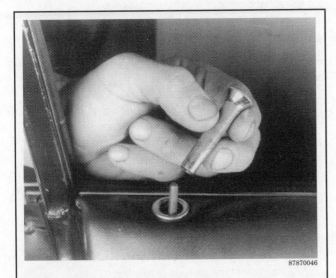

Fig. 22 Unscrew the door lock knob

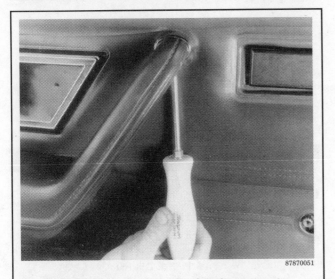

Fig. 23 Remove the screws securing the arm rest

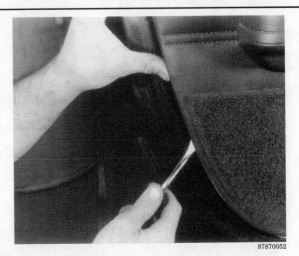

Fig. 25 Special tools are available for removing the door panel

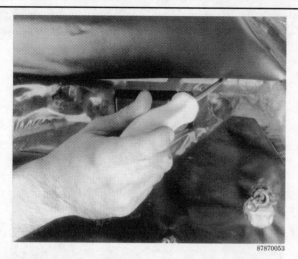

87870053

Fig. 26 If necessary, remove the screws securing the upper panel, then remove the panel

the lift channel. Remove the glass through the belt (upper) opening.

2. To remove the window regulator:

a. Remove the door panel and weathershield.

b. Secure the window in full up position.

c. Carefully drive out the center pin of the mounting rivets with a punch, then drill out the rivets with a suitable drill.

d. Disengage the regulator arm from the lift plate and remove the regulator through the access opening.

3. Install the regulator in the reverse order. Secure with suitable size bolts, lockwashers and nuts.

4. Install the window glass.

Rear Door Glass and Regulator

REMOVAL & INSTALLATION

▶ **See Figure 28**

1. To remove the glass:

a. Remove the door panel and weathershield.

b. Align the glass fasteners with the access hole and remove the fasteners. Lower the window glass after removing the lift fasteners.

c. Remove the lower division bar bracket screws and remove the bar bracket.

d. Disengage the division bar from the window glass and from the stationary glass and remove the bar through the main access hole.

e. Remove the stationary glass by applying a forward force to disengage the window seal from the door frame. Remove the door glass through the belt (upper) opening.

2. To remove the regulator:

a. Remove the door panel and weathershield.

b. Secure the window in full up position.

c. Carefully drive out the center pin of the mounting rivets with a punch, then drill out the rivets with a suitable drill.

d. Disengage the regulator arm from the lift plate and remove the regulator through the access opening.

3. Install the regulator in the reverse order. Secure with suitable size bolts, lockwashers and nuts.

4. Install the door glass.

Front Seat

REMOVAL & INSTALLATION

Seat Assembly

1. Remove the nuts/bolts securing the seat assembly to the floor.

2. Carefully lift the seat and remove it from the vehicle.

3. Installation is the reverse of removal. Tighten the fasteners until snug.

Seat Back

1. Remove the plastic cover from the recliner mechanism.

2. With the seat back in the upright position, remove the front seat back panel.

3. Remove enough plastic trim retainers from the outboard side to uncover the two screws which attach the seat back frame to the recliner unit.

4. Remove the seat back retaining bolts, then swing the seat forwards and remove the seat back.

5. To reassemble, reverse the above.

Recliner Mechanism

1. Remove the seat from the vehicle.

2. Remove the seat hinge cover.

3. Unscrew the seat back, and remove.

4. Remove the release cable bracket attaching screws from the recliner.

5. Remove enough hog rings to gain access to, and remove the recliner lower attaching screws.

6. Remove the recliner, then rotate it so to release the cable.

7. Reverse the procedure to install.

Release Cable

1. Unscrew and remove the seat hinge cover.

2. Remove the release cable bracket from the recliner.

3. Disconnect the release cable bracket from the release mechanism.

4. Rotate the release mechanism off the release cable.

5. Rotate the cable off of the recliner mechanism.

6. Remove the recliner cable.

7. Reverse the procedure to install.

Rear Seat

REMOVAL & INSTALLATION

Seat Back

1. Remove the right side seat belt retractor cover.

2. Remove the retaining clip from the seat back pivot.

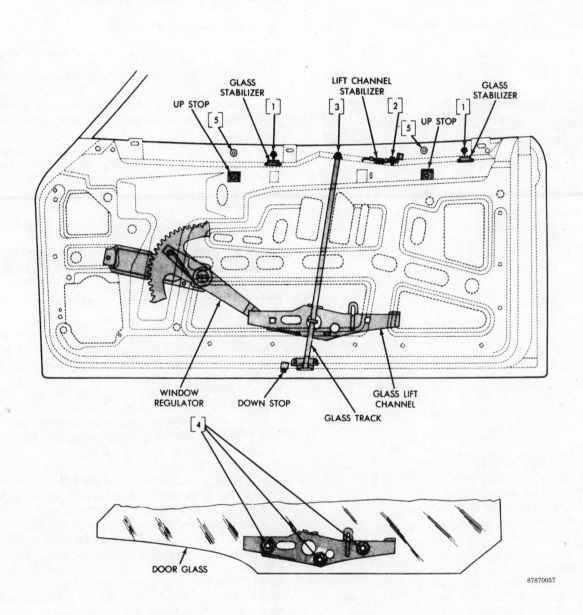

Fig. 27 A common front door glass and regulator used on the models covered by this manual

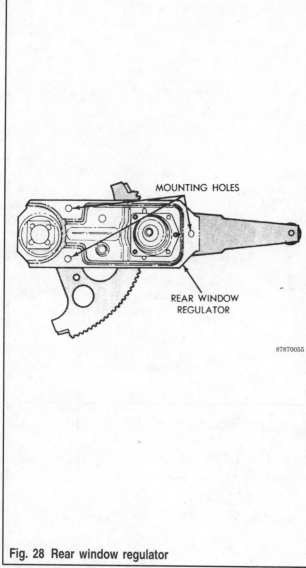

MOUNTING HOLES

REAR WINDOW REGULATOR

87870055

Fig. 28 Rear window regulator

3. Push the seat towards the left pivot bracket until the right pivot clears the bracket.
4. Remove the seat back from the vehicle.
5. Installation is the reverse of removal.

Seat Cushion

1. Remove the rear seat back.
2. Remove the cushion retaining screw.
3. Slide the cushion forward to disengage the front retainers and remove the seat from the vehicle.
4. Installation is the reverse of removal.

Inside Rear View Mirror

REMOVAL & INSTALLATION

1. Loosen the set screw and slide the mirror up and off of the button.

To install:
2. Slide the mirror over the button and tighten the set screw. Care should be exercised not to overtighten the screw.

Windshield

➡**The windshield is mounted with butyl tape, special tools and materials are required for installation.**

REMOVAL & INSTALLATION

1. Cover all areas around the windshield to prevent damage to the finish.
2. Remove the windshield wiper arm and blade assemblies. Remove the windshield mouldings that interfere with windshield replacement.
3. Use an electric knife (Miller Tool No. 4386, or the equivalent) and cut the existing butyl tape as close as possible to the mounting flange of the windshield frame. Remove the windshield.

To install:
4. Remove all remaining adhesive from the mounting flange with naphtha or comparable solvent.

✳✳CAUTION

Follow the warnings on the solvent can.

5. Apply butyl primer (Chrysler No. 3500883, or the equivalent) on the mounting flange and butyl tape remnants.
6. Start at either side of the windshield body opening and apply the butyl tape to the frame, with the tapered edge of the tape facing the reveal surface.
7. Cut off the excess tape and butt joint the ends. Apply sufficient pressure to ensure a good seal.
8. Clean the bonding surfaces of the windshield glass with clean cheesecloth moistened with Super-Kleen (Chrysler No. 4026030 or equivalent). Wipe off immediately with another piece of clean cheesecloth.
9. Apply butyl glass primer to the entire bonding surface of the windshield glass, both the inside surface and the edges. Allow the primer to dry for five minutes.
10. Locate the windshield in the center of the opening and make contact with the tape. Place spacers at the bottom of the glass between the glass edge and body opening. Locate one spacer on each side of the glass, over the site of the original spacer. Select spacers, or combination of spacers that will ensure a snug fit between the glass edge and frame while keeping the glass centered.
11. Use maximum hand pressure to push the glass down against the tape.
12. Inspect the bond. If the contact between the glass and tape is poor, repeat maximum hand pressure. The bond should be $1/4$ in. (6mm) wide or greater.
13. Check the spacers to make sure they are in the proper location.
14. Water test the seal. Repair any leaks with secondary sealer application.
15. Install any trim molding and the wiper arm and blade assemblies.

Hatchback Glass

REMOVAL & INSTALLATION

▶ **See Figure 29**

1. Remove the locking strip center cap and pull the locking strip from the groove.

2. Carefully push the glass out of the weatherstrip, starting at one corner and continuing around the glass until it is free from the weatherstrip. Remove the weatherstrip from the hatch frame.

To install:

3. Install the glass into the weatherstrip. Install cord between the glass and weatherstrip lip.

4. Place the glass into position in the frame opening. Apply pressure against the glass while an assistant pulls the cord through the window opening which will locate the weatherstripping lip over the frame.

5. Inspect for complete sealing of the weatherstrip around the frame.

6. Install the locking strip starting at the bottom center. Install the center locking cap.

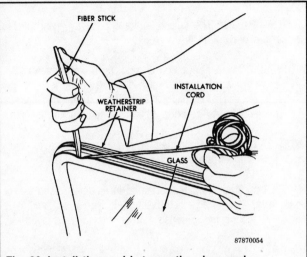

87870054

Fig. 29 Install the cord between the glass and weatherstrip lip

GLOSSARY

AIR/FUEL RATIO: The ratio of air-to-gasoline by weight in the fuel mixture drawn into the engine.

AIR INJECTION: One method of reducing harmful exhaust emissions by injecting air into each of the exhaust ports of an engine. The fresh air entering the hot exhaust manifold causes any remaining fuel to be burned before it can exit the tailpipe.

ALTERNATOR: A device used for converting mechanical energy into electrical energy.

AMMETER: An instrument, calibrated in amperes, used to measure the flow of an electrical current in a circuit. Ammeters are always connected in series with the circuit being tested.

AMPERE: The rate of flow of electrical current present when one volt of electrical pressure is applied against one ohm of electrical resistance.

ANALOG COMPUTER: Any microprocessor that uses similar (analogous) electrical signals to make its calculations.

ARMATURE: A laminated, soft iron core wrapped by a wire that converts electrical energy to mechanical energy as in a motor or relay. When rotated in a magnetic field, it changes mechanical energy into electrical energy as in a generator.

ATMOSPHERIC PRESSURE: The pressure on the Earth's surface caused by the weight of the air in the atmosphere. At sea level, this pressure is 14.7 psi at 32°F (101 kPa at 0°C).

ATOMIZATION: The breaking down of a liquid into a fine mist that can be suspended in air.

AXIAL PLAY: Movement parallel to a shaft or bearing bore.

BACKFIRE: The sudden combustion of gases in the intake or exhaust system that results in a loud explosion.

BACKLASH: The clearance or play between two parts, such as meshed gears.

BACKPRESSURE: Restrictions in the exhaust system that slow the exit of exhaust gases from the combustion chamber.

BAKELITE: A heat resistant, plastic insulator material commonly used in printed circuit boards and transistorized components.

BALL BEARING: A bearing made up of hardened inner and outer races between which hardened steel balls roll.

BALLAST RESISTOR: A resistor in the primary ignition circuit that lowers voltage after the engine is started to reduce wear on ignition components.

BEARING: A friction reducing, supportive device usually located between a stationary part and a moving part.

BIMETAL TEMPERATURE SENSOR: Any sensor or switch made of two dissimilar types of metal that bend when heated or cooled due to the different expansion rates of the alloys. These types of sensors usually function as an on/off switch.

BLOWBY: Combustion gases, composed of water vapor and unburned fuel, that leak past the piston rings into the crankcase during normal engine operation. These gases are removed by the PCV system to prevent the buildup of harmful acids in the crankcase.

BRAKE PAD: A brake shoe and lining assembly used with disc brakes.

BRAKE SHOE: The backing for the brake lining. The term is, however, usually applied to the assembly of the brake backing and lining.

BUSHING: A liner, usually removable, for a bearing; an anti-friction liner used in place of a bearing.

CALIPER: A hydraulically activated device in a disc brake system, which is mounted straddling the brake rotor (disc). The caliper contains at least one piston and two brake pads. Hydraulic pressure on the piston(s) forces the pads against the rotor.

CAMSHAFT: A shaft in the engine on which are the lobes (cams) which operate the valves. The camshaft is driven by the crankshaft, via a belt, chain or gears, at one half the crankshaft speed.

CAPACITOR: A device which stores an electrical charge.

CARBON MONOXIDE (CO): A colorless, odorless gas given off as a normal byproduct of combustion. It is poisonous and extremely dangerous in confined areas, building up slowly to toxic levels without warning if adequate ventilation is not available.

CARBURETOR: A device, usually mounted on the intake manifold of an engine, which mixes the air and fuel in the proper proportion to allow even combustion.

CATALYTIC CONVERTER: A device installed in the exhaust system, like a muffler, that converts harmful byproducts of combustion into carbon dioxide and water vapor by means of a heat-producing chemical reaction.

CENTRIFUGAL ADVANCE: A mechanical method of advancing the spark timing by using flyweights in the distributor that react to centrifugal force generated by the distributor shaft rotation.

CHECK VALVE: Any one-way valve installed to permit the flow of air, fuel or vacuum in one direction only.

CHOKE: A device, usually a moveable valve, placed in the intake path of a carburetor to restrict the flow of air.

CIRCUIT: Any unbroken path through which an electrical current can flow. Also used to describe fuel flow in some instances.

CIRCUIT BREAKER: A switch which protects an electrical circuit from overload by opening the circuit when the current flow exceeds a predetermined level. Some circuit breakers must be reset manually, while most reset automatically.

COIL (IGNITION): A transformer in the ignition circuit which steps up the voltage provided to the spark plugs.

COMBINATION MANIFOLD: An assembly which includes both the intake and exhaust manifolds in one casting.

COMBINATION VALVE: A device used in some fuel systems that routes fuel vapors to a charcoal storage canister instead of venting them into the atmosphere. The valve relieves fuel tank pressure and allows fresh air into the tank as the fuel level drops to prevent a vapor lock situation.

COMPRESSION RATIO: The comparison of the total volume of the cylinder and combustion chamber with the piston at BDC and the piston at TDC.

CONDENSER: 1. An electrical device which acts to store an electrical charge, preventing voltage surges. 2. A radiator-like device in the air conditioning system in which refrigerant gas condenses into a liquid, giving off heat.

CONDUCTOR: Any material through which an electrical current can be transmitted easily.

CONTINUITY: Continuous or complete circuit. Can be checked with an ohmmeter.

COUNTERSHAFT: An intermediate shaft which is rotated by a mainshaft and transmits, in turn, that rotation to a working part.

CRANKCASE: The lower part of an engine in which the crankshaft and related parts operate.

CRANKSHAFT: The main driving shaft of an engine which receives reciprocating motion from the pistons and converts it to rotary motion.

CYLINDER: In an engine, the round hole in the engine block in which the piston(s) ride.

CYLINDER BLOCK: The main structural member of an engine in which is found the cylinders, crankshaft and other principal parts.

CYLINDER HEAD: The detachable portion of the engine, usually fastened to the top of the cylinder block and containing all or most of the combustion chambers. On overhead valve engines, it contains the valves and their operating parts. On overhead cam engines, it contains the camshaft as well.

DEAD CENTER: The extreme top or bottom of the piston stroke.

DETONATION: An unwanted explosion of the air/fuel mixture in the combustion chamber caused by excess heat and compression, advanced timing, or an overly lean mixture. Also referred to as "ping".

DIAPHRAGM: A thin, flexible wall separating two cavities, such as in a vacuum advance unit.

DIESELING: A condition in which hot spots in the combustion chamber cause the engine to run on after the key is turned off.

DIFFERENTIAL: A geared assembly which allows the transmission of motion between drive axles, giving one axle the ability to turn faster than the other.

DIODE: An electrical device that will allow current to flow in one direction only.

DISC BRAKE: A hydraulic braking assembly consisting of a brake disc, or rotor, mounted on an axle, and a caliper assembly containing, usually two brake pads which are activated by hydraulic pressure. The pads are forced against the sides of the disc, creating friction which slows the vehicle.

DISTRIBUTOR: A mechanically driven device on an engine which is responsible for electrically firing the spark plug at a predetermined point of the piston stroke.

DOWEL PIN: A pin, inserted in mating holes in two different parts allowing those parts to maintain a fixed relationship.

DRUM BRAKE: A braking system which consists of two brake shoes and one or two wheel cylinders, mounted on a fixed backing plate, and a brake drum, mounted on an axle, which revolves around the assembly.

DWELL: The rate, measured in degrees of shaft rotation, at which an electrical circuit cycles on and off.

ELECTRONIC CONTROL UNIT (ECU): Ignition module, module, amplifier or igniter. See Module for definition.

ELECTRONIC IGNITION: A system in which the timing and firing of the spark plugs is controlled by an electronic control unit, usually called a module. These systems have no points or condenser.

END-PLAY: The measured amount of axial movement in a shaft.

ENGINE: A device that converts heat into mechanical energy.

EXHAUST MANIFOLD: A set of cast passages or pipes which conduct exhaust gases from the engine.

FEELER GAUGE: A blade, usually metal, of precisely predetermined thickness, used to measure the clearance between two parts.

FIRING ORDER: The order in which combustion occurs in the cylinders of an engine. Also the order in which spark is distributed to the plugs by the distributor.

FLOODING: The presence of too much fuel in the intake manifold and combustion chamber which prevents the air/fuel mixture from firing, thereby causing a no-start situation.

FLYWHEEL: A disc shaped part bolted to the rear end of the crankshaft. Around the outer perimeter is affixed the ring gear. The starter drive engages the ring gear, turning the flywheel, which rotates the crankshaft, imparting the initial starting motion to the engine.

FOOT POUND (ft. lbs. or sometimes, ft.lb.): The amount of energy or work needed to raise an item weighing one pound, a distance of one foot.

FUSE: A protective device in a circuit which prevents circuit overload by breaking the circuit when a specific amperage is present. The device is constructed around a strip or wire of a lower amperage rating than the circuit it is designed to protect. When an amperage higher than that stamped on the fuse is present in the circuit, the strip or wire melts, opening the circuit.

GEAR RATIO: The ratio between the number of teeth on meshing gears.

GENERATOR: A device which converts mechanical energy into electrical energy.

HEAT RANGE: The measure of a spark plug's ability to dissipate heat from its firing end. The higher the heat range, the hotter the plug fires.

HUB: The center part of a wheel or gear.

HYDROCARBON (HC): Any chemical compound made up of hydrogen and carbon. A major pollutant formed by the engine as a byproduct of combustion.

HYDROMETER: An instrument used to measure the specific gravity of a solution.

INCH POUND (inch lbs.; sometimes in.lb. or in. lbs.): One twelfth of a foot pound.

INDUCTION: A means of transferring electrical energy in the form of a magnetic field. Principle used in the ignition coil to increase voltage.

INJECTOR: A device which receives metered fuel under relatively low pressure and is activated to inject the fuel into the engine under relatively high pressure at a predetermined time.

INPUT SHAFT: The shaft to which torque is applied, usually carrying the driving gear or gears.

INTAKE MANIFOLD: A casting of passages or pipes used to conduct air or a fuel/air mixture to the cylinders.

JOURNAL: The bearing surface within which a shaft operates.

KEY: A small block usually fitted in a notch between a shaft and a hub to prevent slippage of the two parts.

MANIFOLD: A casting of passages or set of pipes which connect the cylinders to an inlet or outlet source.

MANIFOLD VACUUM: Low pressure in an engine intake manifold formed just below the throttle plates. Manifold vacuum is highest at idle and drops under acceleration.

MASTER CYLINDER: The primary fluid pressurizing device in a hydraulic system. In automotive use, it is found in brake and hydraulic clutch systems and is pedal activated, either directly or, in a power brake system, through the power booster.

MODULE: Electronic control unit, amplifier or igniter of solid state or integrated design which controls the current flow in the ignition primary circuit based on input from the pick-up coil. When the module opens the primary circuit, high secondary voltage is induced in the coil.

NEEDLE BEARING: A bearing which consists of a number (usually a large number) of long, thin rollers.

OHM:(Ω) The unit used to measure the resistance of conductor-to-electrical flow. One ohm is the amount of resistance that limits current flow to one ampere in a circuit with one volt of pressure.

OHMMETER: An instrument used for measuring the resistance, in ohms, in an electrical circuit.

OUTPUT SHAFT: The shaft which transmits torque from a device, such as a transmission.

OVERDRIVE: A gear assembly which produces more shaft revolutions than that transmitted to it.

OVERHEAD CAMSHAFT (OHC): An engine configuration in which the camshaft is mounted on top of the cylinder head and operates the valve either directly or by means of rocker arms.

OVERHEAD VALVE (OHV): An engine configuration in which all of the valves are located in the cylinder head and the camshaft is located in the cylinder block. The camshaft operates the valves via lifters and pushrods.

OXIDES OF NITROGEN (NOx): Chemical compounds of nitrogen produced as a byproduct of combustion. They combine with hydrocarbons to produce smog.

OXYGEN SENSOR: Used with the feedback system to sense the presence of oxygen in the exhaust gas and signal the computer which can reference the voltage signal to an air/fuel ratio.

PINION: The smaller of two meshing gears.

PISTON RING: An open-ended ring which fits into a groove on the outer diameter of the piston. Its chief function is to form a seal between the piston and cylinder wall. Most automotive pistons have three rings: two for compression sealing; one for oil sealing.

PRELOAD: A predetermined load placed on a bearing during assembly or by adjustment.

PRIMARY CIRCUIT: The low voltage side of the ignition system which consists of the ignition switch, ballast resistor or resistance wire, bypass, coil, electronic control unit and pick-up coil as well as the connecting wires and harnesses.

PRESS FIT: The mating of two parts under pressure, due to the inner diameter of one being smaller than the outer diameter of the other, or vice versa; an interference fit.

RACE: The surface on the inner or outer ring of a bearing on which the balls, needles or rollers move.

REGULATOR: A device which maintains the amperage and/or voltage levels of a circuit at predetermined values.

RELAY: A switch which automatically opens and/or closes a circuit.

RESISTANCE: The opposition to the flow of current through a circuit or electrical device, and is measured in ohms. Resistance is equal to the voltage divided by the amperage.

RESISTOR: A device, usually made of wire, which offers a preset amount of resistance in an electrical circuit.

RING GEAR: The name given to a ring-shaped gear attached to a differential case, or affixed to a flywheel or as part of a planetary gear set.

ROLLER BEARING: A bearing made up of hardened inner and outer races between which hardened steel rollers move.

ROTOR: 1. The disc-shaped part of a disc brake assembly, upon which the brake pads bear; also called, brake disc. 2. The device mounted atop the distributor shaft, which passes current to the distributor cap tower contacts.

SECONDARY CIRCUIT: The high voltage side of the ignition system, usually above 20,000 volts. The secondary includes the ignition coil, coil wire, distributor cap and rotor, spark plug wires and spark plugs.

SENDING UNIT: A mechanical, electrical, hydraulic or electromagnetic device which transmits information to a gauge.

SENSOR: Any device designed to measure engine operating conditions or ambient pressures and temperatures. Usually electronic in nature and designed to send a voltage signal to an on-board computer, some sensors may operate as a simple on/off switch or they may provide a variable voltage signal (like a potentiometer) as conditions or measured parameters change.

SHIM: Spacers of precise, predetermined thickness used between parts to establish a proper working relationship.

SLAVE CYLINDER: In automotive use, a device in the hydraulic clutch system which is activated by hydraulic force, disengaging the clutch.

SOLENOID: A coil used to produce a magnetic field, the effect of which is to produce work.

SPARK PLUG: A device screwed into the combustion chamber of a spark ignition engine. The basic construction is a conductive core inside of a ceramic insulator, mounted in an outer conductive base. An electrical charge from the spark plug wire travels along the conductive core and jumps a preset air gap to a grounding point or points at the end of the conductive base. The resultant spark ignites the fuel/air mixture in the combustion chamber.

SPLINES: Ridges machined or cast onto the outer diameter of a shaft or inner diameter of a bore to enable parts to mate without rotation.

TACHOMETER: A device used to measure the rotary speed of an engine, shaft, gear, etc., usually in rotations per minute.

THERMOSTAT: A valve, located in the cooling system of an engine, which is closed when cold and opens gradually in response to engine heating, controlling the temperature of the coolant and rate of coolant flow.

TOP DEAD CENTER (TDC): The point at which the piston reaches the top of its travel on the compression stroke.

TORQUE: The twisting force applied to an object.

TORQUE CONVERTER: A turbine used to transmit power from a driving member to a driven member via hydraulic action, providing changes in drive ratio and torque. In automotive use, it links the driveplate at the rear of the engine to the automatic transmission.

TRANSDUCER: A device used to change a force into an electrical signal.

TRANSISTOR: A semi-conductor component which can be actuated by a small voltage to perform an electrical switching function.

TUNE-UP: A regular maintenance function, usually associated with the replacement and adjustment of parts and components in the electrical and fuel systems of a vehicle for the purpose of attaining optimum performance.

TURBOCHARGER: An exhaust driven pump which compresses intake air and forces it into the combustion chambers at higher than atmospheric pressures. The increased air pressure allows more fuel to be burned and results in increased horsepower being produced.

VACUUM ADVANCE: A device which advances the ignition timing in response to increased engine vacuum.

VACUUM GAUGE: An instrument used to measure the presence of vacuum in a chamber.

VALVE: A device which control the pressure, direction of flow or rate of flow of a liquid or gas.

VALVE CLEARANCE: The measured gap between the end of the valve stem and the rocker arm, cam lobe or follower that activates the valve.

VISCOSITY: The rating of a liquid's internal resistance to flow.

VOLTMETER: An instrument used for measuring electrical force in units called volts. Voltmeters are always connected parallel with the circuit being tested.

WHEEL CYLINDER: Found in the automotive drum brake assembly, it is a device, actuated by hydraulic pressure, which, through internal pistons, pushes the brake shoes outward against the drums.

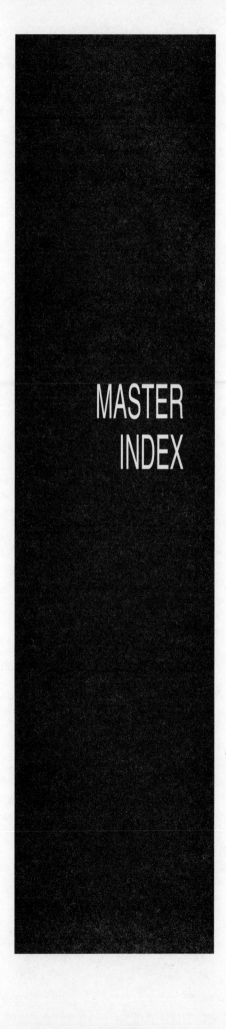

MASTER INDEX

Don't Miss These Other Important Titles
From NP/CHILTON'S®

——TOTAL CAR CARE MANUALS——
The ULTIMATE in automotive repair manuals

Features:
- Based on actual teardowns
- Each manual covers all makes and models (unless otherwise indicated)
- Expanded photography from vehicle teardowns
- Actual vacuum and wiring diagrams— not general representations
- Comprehensive coverage
- Maintenance interval schedules
- Electronic engine and emission controls

ACURA
Coupes and Sedans 1986-93
PART NO. 8426/10300

AMC
Coupes/Sedans/Wagons 1975-88
PART NO. 14300

BMW
Coupes and Sedans 1970-88
PART NO. 8789/18300
318/325/M3/525/535/M5 1989-93
PART NO. 8427/18400

CHRYSLER
Aspen/Volare 1976-80
PART NO. 20100
Caravan/Voyager/Town & Country 1984-95
PART NO. 8155/20300
Caravan/Voyager/Town & Country 1996-99
PART NO. 20302
Cirrus/Stratus/Sebring/Avenger 1995-98
PART NO. 20320
Colt/Challenger/Conquest/Vista 1971-89
PART NO. 20340
Colt/Vista 1990-93
PART NO. 8418/20342
Concorde/Intrepid/New Yorker/
LHS/Vision 1993-97
PART NO. 8817/20360
Front Wheel Drive Cars-4 Cyl 1981-95
PART NO. 8673/20382
Front Wheel Drive Cars-6 Cyl 1988-95
PART NO. 8672/20384
Full-Size Trucks 1967-88
PART NO. 8662/20400
Full-Size Trucks 1989-96
PART NO. 8166/20402
Full-Size Vans 1967-88
PART NO. 20420
Full-Size Vans 1989-98
PART NO. 8169/20422
Neon 1995-99
PART NO. 20600
Omni/Horizon/Rampage 1978-89
PART NO. 8787/20700
Ram 50/D50/Arrow 1979-93
PART NO. 20800

FORD
Aerostar 1986-96
PART NO. 8057/26100
Aspire 1994-97
PART NO. 26120
Contour/Mystique/Cougar 1995-99
PART NO. 26170
Crown Victoria/Grand Marquis 1989-94
PART NO. 8417/26180
Escort/Lynx 1981-90
PART NO. 8270/26240
Escort/Tracer 1991-99
PART NO. 26242
Fairmont/Zephyr 1978-83
PART NO. 26320
Ford/Mercury Full-Size Cars 1968-88
PART NO. 8665/26360
Full-Size Vans 1961-88
PART NO. 26400

Full-Size Vans 1989-96
PART NO. 8157/26402
Ford/Mercury Mid-Size Cars 1971-85
PART NO. 8667/26580
Mustang/Cougar 1964-73
PART NO. 26600
Mustang/Capri 1979-88
PART NO. 8580/26604
Mustang 1989-93
PART NO. 8253/26606
Mustang 1994-98
PART NO. 26608
Pick-Ups and Bronco 1976-86
PART NO. 8576/26662
Pick-Ups and Bronco 1987-96
PART NO. 8136/26664
Pick-Ups /Expedition/Navigator 1997-00
PART NO. 26666
Probe 1989-92
PART NO. 8266/26680
Probe 1993-97
PART NO. 8411/46802
Ranger/Bronco II 1983-90
PART NO. 8159/26686
Ranger/Explorer/Mountaineer 1991-97
PART NO. 26688
Taurus/Sable 1986-95
PART NO. 8251/26700
Taurus/Sable 1996-99
PART NO. 26702
Tempo/Topaz 1984-94
PART NO. 8271/26720
Thunderbird/Cougar 1983-96
PART NO. 8268/26760
Windstar 1995-98
PART NO.26840

GENERAL MOTORS
Astro/Safari 1985-96
PART NO. 8056/28100
Blazer/Jimmy 1969-82
PART NO. 28140
Blazer/Jimmy/Typhoon/Bravada 1983-93
PART NO. 8139/28160
Blazer/Jimmy/Bravada 1994-99
PART NO. 8845/28862
Bonneville/Eighty Eight/LeSabre 1986-99
PART NO. 8423/28200
Buick/Oldsmobile/Pontiac Full-Size
1975-90
PART NO. 8584/28240
Cadillac 1967-89
PART NO. 8587/28260
Camaro 1967-81
PART NO. 28280
Camaro 1982-92
PART NO. 8260/28282

Camaro/Firebird 1993-98
PART NO. 28284
Caprice 1990-93
PART NO. 8421/28300
Cavalier/Sunbird/Skyhawk/Firenza 1982-94
PART NO. 8269/28320
Cavalier/Sunfire 1995-00
PART NO. 28322
Celebrity/Century/Ciera/6000 1982-96
PART NO. 8252/28360
Chevette/1000 1976-88
PART NO. 28400
Chevy Full-Size Cars 1968-78
PART NO. 28420
Chevy Full-Size Cars 1979-89
PART NO. 8531/28422
Chevy Mid-Size Cars 1964-88
PART NO. 8594/28440
Citation/Omega/Phoenix/Skylark/XII
1980-85
PART NO. 28460
Corsica/Beretta 1988-96
PART NO. 8254/ 28480
Corvette 1963-82
PART NO. 28500
Corvette 1984-96
PART NO. 28502
Cutlass RWD 1970-87
PART NO. 8668/28520
DeVille/Fleetwood/Eldorado/Seville 1990-93
PART NO. 8420/ 28540
Electra/Park Avenue/Ninety-Eight 1990-93
PART NO. 8430/28560
Fiero 1984-88
PART NO. 28580
Firebird 1967-81
PART NO. 28600
Firebird 1982-92
PART NO. 8534/28602
Full-Size Trucks 1970-79
PART NO. 28620
Full-Size Trucks 1980-87
PART NO. 8577/28622
Full-Size Trucks 1988-98
PART NO. 8055/28624
Full-Size Vans 1967-86
PART NO. 28640
Full-Size Vans 1987-97
PART NO. 8040/28642
Grand Am/Achieva 1985-98
PART NO. 8257/28660
Lumina/Silhouette/Trans Sport/Venture 1990-99
PART NO. 8134/28680
Lumina/Monte Carlo/Grand Prix/Cutlass
Supreme/Regal 1988-96
PART NO. 8258/28682

Metro/Sprint 1985-99
PART NO. 8424/28700
Nova/Chevy II 1962-79
PART NO. 28720
Pontiac Mid-Size 1974-83
PART NO. 28740
Chevrolet Nova/GEO Prizm 1985-93
PART NO. 8422/28760
Regal/Century 1975-87
PART NO. 28780
Chevrolet Spectrum/GEO Storm 1985-93
PART NO. 8425/28800
S10/S15/Sonoma Pick-Ups 1982-93
PART NO. 8141/ 28860
S10/Sonoma/Blazer/Jimmy/Bravada
Hombre 1994-99
PART NO. 8845/28862

HONDA
Accord/Civic/Prelude 1973-83
PART NO. 8591/30100
Accord/Prelude 1984-95
PART NO. 8255/30150
Civic, CRX and del SOL 1984-95
PART NO. 8256/30200

HYUNDAI
Coupes/Sedans 1986-93
PART NO. 8412/32100
Coupes/Sedans 1994-98
PART NO. 32102

ISUZU
Amigo/Pick-Ups/Rodeo/Trooper 1981-96
PART NO. 8686/36100
Cars and Trucks 1981-91
PART NO. 8069/36150

JEEP
CJ 1945-70
PART NO. 40200
CJ/Scrambler 1971-86
PART NO. 8536/40202
Wagoneer/Commando/Cherokee 1957-83
PART NO. 40600
Wagoneer/Comanche/Cherokee 1984-98
PART NO. 8143/40602
Wrangler/YJ 1987-95
PART NO. 8535/40650

MAZDA
Trucks 1972-86
PART NO. 46600
Trucks 1987-93
PART NO. 8264/46602
Trucks 1994-98
PART NO. 46604
323/626/929/GLC/MX-6/RX-7 1978-89
PART NO. 8581/46800
323/Protege/MX-3/MX-6/626
Millenia/Ford Probe 1990-98
PART NO. 8411/46802

MERCEDES
Coupes/Sedans/Wagons 1974-84
PART NO. 48300

MITSUBISHI
Cars and Trucks 1983-89
PART NO. 7947/50200

3P1VerB

Total Car Care, continued

Eclipse 1990-98
PART NO. 8415/50400

Pick-Ups and Montero 1983-95
PART NO. 8666/50500

NISSAN
Datsun 210/1200 1973-81
PART NO. 52300

Datsun 200SX/510/610/710/
810/Maxima 1973-84
PART NO. 52302

Nissan Maxima 1985-92
PART NO. 8261/52450

Maxima 1993-98
PART NO. 52452

Pick-Ups and Pathfinder 1970-88
PART NO. 8585/52500

Pick-Ups and Pathfinder 1989-95
PART NO. 8145/52502

Sentra/Pulsar/NX 1982-96
PART NO. 8263/52700

Stanza/200SX/240SX 1982-92
PART NO. 8262/52750

240SX/Altima 1993-98
PART NO. 52752

Datsun/Nissan Z and ZX 1970-88
PART NO. 8846/52800

RENAULT
Coupes/Sedans/Wagons 1975-85
PART NO. 58300

SATURN
Coupes/Sedans/Wagons 1991-98
PART NO. 8419/62300

SUBARU
Coupes/Sedan/Wagons 1970-84
PART NO. 8790/64300

Coupes/Sedans/Wagons 1985-96
PART NO. 8259/64302

SUZUKI
Samurai/Sidekick/Tracker 1986-98
PART NO. 66500

TOYOTA
Camry 1983-96
PART NO. 8265/68200

Celica/Supra 1971-85
PART NO. 68250

Celica 1986-93
PART NO. 8413/68252

Celica 1994-98
PART NO. 68254

Corolla 1970-87
PART NO. 8586/68300

Corolla 1988-97
PART NO. 8414/68302

Cressida/Corona/Crown/MkII 1970-82
PART NO. 68350

Cressida/Van 1983-90
PART NO. 68352

Pick-ups/Land Cruiser/4Runner 1970-88
PART NO. 8578/68600

Pick-ups/Land Cruiser/4Runner 1989-98
PART NO. 8163/68602

Previa 1991-97
PART NO. 68640

Tercel 1984-94
PART NO. 8595/68700

VOLKSWAGEN
Air-Cooled 1949-69
PART NO. 70200

Air-Cooled 1970-81
PART NO. 70202

Front Wheel Drive 1974-89
PART NO. 8663/70400

Golf/Jetta/Cabriolet 1990-93
PART NO. 8429/70402

VOLVO
Coupes/Sedans/Wagons 1970-89
PART NO. 8786/72300

Coupes/Sedans/Wagons 1990-98
PART NO. 8428/72302

General Interest / Recreational Books

We offer specialty books on a variety of topics including Motorcycles, ATVs, Snowmobiles and automotive subjects like Detailing or Body Repair. Each book from our General Interest line offers a blend of our famous Do-It-Yourself procedures and photography with additional information on enjoying automotive, marine and recreational products. Learn more about the vehicles you use and enjoy while keeping them in top running shape.

ATV Handbook
PART NO. 9123

Auto Detailing
PART NO. 8394

Auto Body Repair
PART NO. 7898

Briggs & Stratton Vertical Crankshaft Engine
PART NO. 61-1-2

Briggs & Stratton Horizontal Crankshaft Engine
PART NO. 61-0-4

Briggs & Stratton Overhead Valve (OHV) Engine
PART NO. 61-2-0

Easy Car Care
PART NO. 8042

Motorcycle Handbook
PART NO. 9099

Snowmobile Handbook
PART NO. 9124

Small Engine Repair (Up to 20 Hp)
PART NO. 8325

Total Service Series

These innovative books offer repair, maintenance and service procedures for automotive related systems. They cover today's complex vehicles in a user-friendly format, which places even the most difficult automotive topic well within the reach of every Do-It-Yourselfer. Each title covers a specific subject from Brakes and Engine Rebuilding to Fuel Injection Systems, Automatic Transmissions and even Engine Trouble Codes.

Automatic Transmissions/Transaxles
Diagnosis and Repair
PART NO. 8944

Brake System Diagnosis and Repair
PART NO. 8945

Chevrolet Engine Overhaul Manual
PART NO. 8794

Engine Code Manual
PART NO. 8851

Ford Engine Overhaul Manual
PART NO. 8793

Fuel Injection Diagnosis and Repair
PART NO. 8946

Collector's Hard-Cover Manuals

Chilton's Collector's Editions are perfect for enthusiasts of vintage or rare cars. These hard-cover manuals contain repair and maintenance information for all major systems that might not be available elsewhere. Included are repair and overhaul procedures using thousands of illustrations. These manuals offer a range of coverage from as far back as 1940 and as recent as 1997, so you don't need an antique car or truck to be a collector.

Auto Repair Manual 1993-97
PART NO. 7919

Auto Repair Manual 1988-92
PART NO. 7906

Auto Repair Manual 1980-87
PART NO. 7670

Auto Repair Manual 1972-79
PART NO. 6914

Auto Repair Manual 1964-71
PART NO. 5974

Auto Repair Manual 1954-63
PART NO. 5652

Auto Repair Manual 1940-53
PART NO. 5631

Import Car Repair Manual 1993-97
PART NO. 7920

Import Car Repair Manual 1988-92
PART NO. 7907

Import Car Repair Manual 1980-87
PART NO. 7672

Truck and Van Repair Manual 1993-97
PART NO. 7921

Truck and Van Repair Manual 1991-95
PART NO. 7911

Truck and Van Repair Manual 1986-90
PART NO. 7902

Truck and Van Repair Manual 1979-86
PART NO. 7655

Truck and Van Repair Manual 1971-78
PART NO. 7012

"...and even more from CHILTON"

System-Specific Manuals

Guide to Air Conditioning Repair and Service 1982-85
PART NO. 7580

Guide to Automatic Transmission Repair 1984-89
PART NO. 8054

Guide to Automatic Transmission Repair 1984-89
Domestic cars and trucks
PART NO. 8053

Guide to Automatic Transmission Repair 1980-84
Domestic cars and trucks
PART NO. 7891

Guide to Automatic Transmission Repair 1974-80
Import cars and trucks
PART NO. 7645

Guide to Brakes, Steering, and Suspension 1980-87
PART NO. 7819

Guide to Fuel Injection and Electronic Engine Controls 1984-88
Domestic cars and trucks
PART NO.7766

Guide to Electronic Engine Controls 1978-85
PART NO. 7535

Guide to Engine Repair and Rebuilding
PART NO. 7643

Guide to Vacuum Diagrams 1980-86
Domestic cars and trucks
PART NO. 7821

Multi-Vehicle Spanish Repair Manuals

Auto Repair Manual 1992-96
PART NO. 8947

Import Repair Manual 1992-96
PART NO. 8948

Truck and Van Repair Manual 1992-96
PART NO. 8949

Auto Repair Manual 1987-91
PART NO. 8138

Auto Repair Manual 1980-87
PART NO. 7795

Auto Repair Manual 1976-83
PART NO. 7476

SELOC MARINE MANUALS

OUTBOARDS

Chrysler Outboards, All Engines 1962-84
PART NO. 018-7(1000)

Force Outboards, All Engines 1984-96
PART NO. 024-1(1100)

Honda Outboards, All Engines 1988-98
PART NO. 1200

Johnson/Evinrude Outboards, 1.5-40HP, 2-Stroke 1956-70
PART NO. 007-1(1300)

Johnson/Evinrude Outboards, 1.25-60HP, 2-Stroke 1971-89
PART NO. 008-X(1302)

Johnson/Evinrude Outboards, 1-50 HP, 2-Stroke 1990-95
PART NO. 026-8(1304)

Johnson/Evinrude Outboards, 50-125 HP, 2-Stroke 1958-72
PART NO. 009-8(1306)

Johnson/Evinrude Outboards, 60-235 HP, 2-Stroke 1973-91
PART NO. 010-1(1308)

Johnson/Evinrude Outboards, 80-300 HP, 2-Stroke 1992-96
PART NO. 040-3(1310)

Mariner Outboards, 2-60 HP, 2-Stroke 1977-89
PART NO. 015-2(1400)

Mariner Outboards, 45-220 HP, 2 Stroke 1977-89
PART NO. 016-0(1402)

Mercury Outboards, 2-40 HP, 2-Stroke 1965-91
PART NO. 012-8(1404)

Mercury Outboards, 40-115 HP, 2-Stroke 1965-92
PART NO. 013-6(1406)

Mercury Outboards, 90-300 HP, 2-Stroke 1965-91
PART NO. 014-4(1408)

Mercury/Mariner Outboards, 2.5-25 HP, 2-Stroke 1990-94
PART NO. 035-7(1410)

Mercury/Mariner Outboards, 40-125 HP, 2-Stroke 1990-94
PART NO. 036-5(1412)

Mercury/Mariner Outboards, 135-275 HP, 2-Stroke 1990-94
PART NO. 037-3(1414)

Mercury/Mariner Outboards, All Engines 1995-99
PART NO. 1416

Suzuki Outboards, All Engines 1985-99
PART NO. 1600

Yamaha Outboards, 2-25 HP, 2-Stroke and 9.9 HP, 4-Stroke 1984-91
PART NO. 021-7(1700)

Yamaha Outboards, 30-90 HP, 2-Stroke 1984-91
PART NO. 022-5(1702)

Yamaha Outboards, 115-225 HP, 2-Stroke 1984-91
PART NO. 023-3(1704)

Yamaha Outboards, All Engines 1992-98
PART NO. 1706

STERN DRIVES

Marine Jet Drive 1961-96
PART NO. 029-2(3000)

Mercruiser Stern Drive Type 1, Alpha, Bravo I, II, 1964-92
PART NO. 005-5(3200)

Mercruiser Stern Drive Alpha 1 Generation II 1992-96
PART NO. 039-X(3202)

Mercruiser Stern Drive Bravo I, II, III 1992-96
PART NO. 046-2(3204)

OMC Stern Drive 1964-86
PART NO. 004-7(3400)

OMC Cobra Stern Drive 1985-95
PART NO. 025-X(3402)

Volvo/Penta Stern Drives 1968-91
PART NO. 011-X(3600)

Volvo/Penta Stern Drives 1992-93
PART NO. 038-1(3602)

Volvo/Penta Stern Drives 1992-95
PART NO. 041-1(3604)

INBOARDS

Yanmar Inboard Diesels 1988-91
PART NO. 7400

PERSONAL WATERCRAFT

Kawasaki 1973-91
PART NO. 032-2(9200)

Kawasaki 1992-97
PART NO. 042-X(9202)

Polaris 1992-97
PART NO. 045-4(9400)

Sea Doo/Bombardier 1988-91
PART NO. 033-0(9000)

Sea Doo/Bombardier 1992-97
PART NO. 043-8(9002)

Yamaha 1987-91
PART NO. 034-9(9600)

Yamaha 1992-97
PART NO. 044-6(9602)

FOR THE TITLES LISTED, PLEASE VISIT YOUR LOCAL CHILTON RETAILER

For a FREE catalog of Chilton's complete line of Automotive Repair Manuals, or to order direct Call toll-free 877-4CHILTON

CHILTON'S. 1020 Andrew Drive, Suite 200 • West Chester, PA 19380-4291
www.chiltononline.com

3P3VerB